The Wiley Handbook of Developmental
Psychology in Practice

Wiley-Blackwell Handbooks of Developmental Psychology

This outstanding series of handbooks provides a cutting-edge overview of classic research, current research and future trends in developmental psychology.

- Each handbook draws together 25–30 newly commissioned chapters to provide a comprehensive overview of a subdiscipline of developmental psychology.
- The international team of contributors to each handbook has been specially chosen for its expertise and knowledge of each field.
- Each handbook is introduced and contextualized by leading figures in the field, lending coherence and authority to each volume.

The *Wiley-Blackwell Handbooks of Developmental Psychology* will provide an invaluable overview for advanced students of developmental psychology and for researchers as an authoritative definition of their chosen field.

Published

Blackwell Handbook of Adolescence
Edited by Gerald R. Adams and Michael D. Berzonsky

The Science of Reading: A Handbook
Edited by Margaret J. Snowling and Charles Hulme

Blackwell Handbook of Early Childhood Development
Edited by Kathleen McCartney and Deborah A. Phillips

Blackwell Handbook of Language Development
Edited by Erika Hoff and Marilyn Shatz

The Wiley-Blackwell Handbook of Childhood Cognitive Development, 2nd edition
Edited by Usha Goswami

The Wiley-Blackwell Handbook of Adulthood and Aging
Edited by Susan Krauss Whitbourne and Martin Sliwinski

The Wiley-Blackwell Handbook of Infant Development, 2nd Edition
Edited by Gavin Bremner and Theodore D. Wachs

The Wiley-Blackwell Handbook of Childhood Social Development
Edited by Peter K. Smith and Craig H. Hart

The Wiley Handbook of Developmental Psychology in Practice: Implementation and Impact
Edited by Kevin Durkin and H. Rudolph Schaffer

Forthcoming

The Handbook of Early Childhood Development Programs, Practices, and Policies
Edited by Elizabeth Votruba-Drzal and Eric Dearing

The Wiley Handbook of Developmental Psychology in Practice

Implementation and Impact

Edited by Kevin Durkin and H. Rudolph Schaffer

WILEY Blackwell

This edition first published 2016
© 2016 John Wiley & Sons, Ltd

Registered Office
John Wiley & Sons, Ltd, The Atrium, Southern Gate, Chichester, West Sussex, PO19 8SQ, UK

Editorial Offices
350 Main Street, Malden, MA 02148-5020, USA
9600 Garsington Road, Oxford, OX4 2DQ, UK
The Atrium, Southern Gate, Chichester, West Sussex, PO19 8SQ, UK

For details of our global editorial offices, for customer services, and for information about how
to apply for permission to reuse the copyright material in this book please see our website at
www.wiley.com/wiley-blackwell.

The right of Kevin Durkin and H. Rudolph Schaffer to be identified as the authors of the editorial
material in this work has been asserted in accordance with the UK Copyright, Designs and Patents
Act 1988.

Wiley also publishes its books in a variety of electronic formats. Some content that appears in
print may not be available in electronic books.

Designations used by companies to distinguish their products are often claimed as trademarks.
All brand names and product names used in this book are trade names, service marks, trademarks
or registered trademarks of their respective owners. The publisher is not associated with any
product or vendor mentioned in this book.

Limit of Liability/Disclaimer of Warranty: While the publisher and authors have used their
best efforts in preparing this book, they make no representations or warranties with respect to
the accuracy or completeness of the contents of this book and specifically disclaim any implied
warranties of merchantability or fitness for a particular purpose. It is sold on the understanding
that the publisher is not engaged in rendering professional services and neither the publisher
nor the author shall be liable for damages arising herefrom. If professional advice or other expert
assistance is required, the services of a competent professional should be sought.

Library of Congress Cataloging-in-Publication data applied for

Hardback – 9781405163361

A catalogue record for this book is available from the British Library.

Cover image: monkeybusinessimages/Getty

Set in 11/13.5pt Adobe Garamond by SPi Global, Pondicherry, India
Printed and bound in Malaysia by Vivar Printing Sdn Bhd

1 2016

Knowledge is the beginning of practice;
doing is the completion of knowing.
Wang Yang-Ming, Chinese philosopher,
1472–1529

Contents

Notes on Contributors

Jeanne Brooks-Gunn is Virginia and Leonard Marx Professor of Child Development and Education, Teachers College and College of Physicians and Surgeons, Columbia University; Co-director, National Center for Children and Families; Co-director, Columbia University Institute for Child and Family Policy. She has published extensively on child and family policy and programs, early childhood interventions, adolescent transitions, and the impact of poverty on development.

Rachel Calam is Professor of Psychology at the University of Manchester. Her research interests include parenting interventions, parenting in families with significant mental health difficulties, and computer-assisted interviewing techniques as a means of helping to give a voice to children.

Lindsey Cameron is a Lecturer in Psychology and Director of Graduate Studies at the University of Kent. Her research interests include: development of intergroup attitudes in children and the role of social norms, self-presentation, cognitive development and in-group identification in determining these attitudes; the development of school-based interventions to change children's intergroup attitudes; intergroup contact (direct and indirect) and novel interventions based on this approach; the experience of prejudice and discrimination, and its consequences for social development.

Dante Cicchetti is McKnight Presidential Chair, William Harris Professor of Child Development and Psychiatry, University of Minnesota. A specialist in developmental psychopathology, his research interests include child maltreatment, domestic violence, preventive interventions to inform developmental theory, and genetic and epigenetic moderation of intervention outcome. He is Editor of the journal *Development and Psychopathology*. Among many honors, he was awarded the Klaus J. Jacobs Research Prize from the Jacobs Foundation (2012).

Gina Conti-Ramsden is Professor of Child Language and Learning, University of Manchester and Director of the Manchester Language Study. Her research interests lie in language impairment (LI) and its longitudinal course from childhood to adolescence. She is also interested in the psycholinguistic development of children with LI, including: potential clinical markers for LI; the psychosocial outcomes of children with LI; the genetics/familiality of LI; the educational/life transitions of children and young people with LI; uses of new media and LI, and the overlap between Autism Spectrum Disorder (ASD) and SLI.

Janice Cooper is Country Representative for Health for the Carter Center in Liberia and project lead for the Mental Health Program. She oversees a national training, policy and support program to expand capacity for mental health services delivery. She is also responsible for interacting with national and international colleagues and partners of the program. A native Liberian and health services researcher specializing in children's mental health, Dr. Cooper has worked in the private, public, and nonprofit sectors in the United States and Liberia.

E. Mark Cummings is Professor and Notre Dame Chair in Psychology, University of Notre Dame. His research interests focus on family factors, especially socio-emotional processes, associated with normal development and the development of psychopathology in children, the influences of marital conflict and family processes on children's adjustment, the relations between political violence and child adjustment, parent-educational programs, and emotional security theory as a general model for children's development in families and communities. He is coauthor (with P.T. Davies) of *Marital conflict and children: An emotional security Perspective* (Guilford Press, 2010).

Thomas J. Dishion is Professor of Psychology at Arizona State University and Founding Director of the ASU REACH Institute. He conducts translational research on relationship dynamics associated with child, adolescent and young adult mental health and competence. His research focuses on peer, family and romantic relationship dynamics underlying the development of psychopathology and competence. His work uses various methods including longitudinal studies, observational and social neuroscience techniques such as high-density array EEG. His intervention research involves the design and testing of empirically supported interventions such as the Family Check-up, and identifying intervention strategies that are potentially iatrogenic to youth development.

Jean E. Dumas is Professor of Clinical Developmental Psychological at the University of Geneva, having worked previously in leading universities in Canada and the U.S. He has extensive clinical experience and conducts research and interventions in the field of psychopathology in children and adolescents. He has interests in the role of the family in the development and maintenance of behavioral disorders and anxiety disorders, as well the early prevention of these disorders. Among his several books are *Psychopathologie de l'enfant et de l'adolescent* (Brussels: De Boeck Supérieur, 2013) and, with Hervé Bénony and Christelle Bénony-Viodé, *Psychopathologie de la communication, des apprentissages et de l'hyperactivité chez l'enfant et l'adolescent* (Brussels: De Boeck Supérieur, 2012).

Kevin Durkin is Professor of Psychology at the University of Strathclyde. His research interests lie in the areas of social and communicative development. He has written a large number of journal articles and books, including the bestselling Blackwell title *Developmental Social Psychology*. He is editor of *First Language*. His current work is focused on young people and the media, language acquisition, and problem behaviour in adolescence.

Barbrina B. Ertle is an Assistant Professor at Adelphi University. Her research interests lie in the area of mathematics instruction, with a particular focus on instructional quality and measure development, the use of manipulatives in teaching mathematics, and teacher professional development.

W. Brad Faircloth is an Assistant Professor of Psychology at Montreat College. He is a research associate at the Family, Infant, and Preschool Program (FIPP) and investigator at the Center for Advanced Study of Early Childhood and Family Support Practices of the J. Iverson Riddle Developmental Center in Morganton, NC. His research interests include the effectiveness of Fatherhood support programs, ongoing testing of the Happy Couples Happy Kids program, and Early Head Start and Early Intervention program evaluation.

Rachel H. Farr is a Research Assistant Professor in the Department of Psychological and Brain Sciences at the University of Massachusetts at Amherst. She conducts research related to diverse family systems and issues of adoption through the lenses of Developmental and Community Psychology. She has particular interests in families headed by sexual minority parents and how issues of race (e.g., transracial adoption) and gender are relevant in adoptive families.

Herbert P. Ginsburg is Jacob H. Schiff Foundation Professor of Psychology & Education at Teachers College, Columbia University. He is a leading interpreter of children's understanding of mathematics, with research and teaching interests in intellectual development, mathematics education, and testing and assessment. He is a coauthor of the *Big Math for Little Kids* curriculum for prekindergarten and kindergarten.

Christina Hardway is an Assistant Professor in the Department of Psychology, Merrimack College. An applied developmental scientist, her research focus lies in understanding the role that family relationships play in the trajectory of a child's development and how these relationships are associated with psychological and achievement outcomes. She is interested ultimately in finding ways to better promote psychological well-being and academic achievement among children differing in individual qualities, across cultural boundaries.

Charles C. Helwig is Professor of Psychology at the University of Toronto. His research examines the development of moral and social judgments from the preschool years through adulthood, with a focus on the development of moral concepts related to societal issues and social institutions, such as freedoms, civil liberties, and democracy. He has investigated children's understandings of democratic decision making and rights not only in the context of society at large but in other social contexts, such as the family, the school, and the peer group, and in cross-cultural research conducted in China and Canada.

Rhona S. Johnston is Professor of Psychology at the University of Hull. Her research interests lie in the area of reading and memory. Her main focus of attention is on reading disorders, looking at word recognition and memory problems. One current focus of interest is the difficulties poor readers/dyslexics have in setting up phonological representations in long-term memory. Another area of current interest involves comparing the effects of different teaching techniques on learning to read. She is particularly interested in understanding why synthetic phonics accelerates the early learning of reading skills much faster than analytic phonics.

Jane Knitzer was Director of the National Center for Children in Poverty, and Clinical Professor of Population and Family Health in the Mailman School of Public Health at Columbia University. She was also a Clinical Professor of Population and Family Health at the Mailman School of Public Health at Columbia University. Her research was focused on improving public policies related to children's mental health, child welfare, and early childhood. Her work on mental health included the groundbreaking policy report, *Unclaimed Children: The Failure of Public Responsibility to Children and Adolescents in Need of Mental Health Services* (Children's Defense Fund, 1982). She died in 2009.

Penelope Leach is a Senior Research Fellow of the Institute for the Study of Children, Families and Social Issues, Birkbeck, University of London and of the Tavistock and Portman NHS Trust, as well as Visiting Professor at the University of Winchester. She is a prominent author of books and articles on child development and parenting issues, written for parents and grounded in developmental psychology. Her book *Your Baby and Child: From Birth to Age Five* (1977), has sold over two million copies to date and in 1998 won the British Medical Association award for "Best medical book for general audiences".

Jody Todd Manly is Clinical Director, Research Associate at the Mt. Hope Family Center, and Assistant Professor Department of Clinical and Social Sciences in Psychology, University of Rochester. Her research interests broadly include various aspects of developmental psychopathology, with a particular emphasis on treatment evaluation for intervention with maltreated children, definitions of child maltreatment, risk and protective factors relating to school adaptation, familial violence, early childhood development, and trauma in childhood.

Anne Martin is a Senior Research Scientist and the Coordinator at the National Center for Children and Families. Her research interests include both early childhood development and adolescent sexual behavior. Her work has focused on the effects of early intervention, infant health and development, the interplay between maternal and paternal supportive parenting, child care/classroom quality, adolescent sexual behavior, and young children's early self-regulation and cognition.

Kathleen McCartney is the President of Smith College, Massachusetts, and Professor Education, Emerita, Harvard University. Her research program concerns early experience and development, and she has published extensively on child care, early childhood education, and poverty. She is a member of the NICHD Early Child Care Research Network, and coedited *Experience and Development, The Blackwell Handbook of Early Childhood Development*, and *Best Practices in Developmental Research Methods*. In 2012, she was inducted as a member of the American Academy of Arts & Sciences, and in 2009 she received the Distinguished Contribution Award from the Society for Research in Child Development.

Kathleen P. McCoy is a Postdoctoral Fellow at the Family Studies Center, University of Notre Dame. Her research interests include family relations, interparental conflict and its sequelae, and suicidal ideation and behavior in youth in the juvenile justice system.

Angela D. Moreland is an Assistant Professor at the National Crime Victims Research and Treatment Center at the Medical University of South Carolina. Her research interests focus on prevention of child physical abuse and risk factors for maltreatment among parents of young children, the link between early victimization and high-risk behaviors, such as substance use and delinquency, among adolescents, and transforming victim services to better meet the needs of trauma victims and their families.

Wendy J. Nilsen is a Health Scientist Administrator at the NIH Office of Behavioral and Social Sciences Research (OBSSR). Her scientific focus is on the science of human behavior and behavior change, including: utilizing mobile technology to better understand and improve health, adherence, the mechanisms of behavior change and behavioral interventions in patients with multiple chronic conditions in primary care. She works in multiple trans-NIH initiatives in mobile and wireless health (mHealth), including leading the development of the NIH mHealth Public–Private Partnership.

Charlotte J. Patterson is a Professor in the UVA Department of Psychology and in the Center for Children, Families, and the Law, and is Director of UVA's interdisciplinary program, Women, Gender, and Sexuality (WGS). Her research focuses on the psychology of sexual orientation, with an emphasis on sexual orientation, human development, and family lives. In the context of her research, Patterson has worked with children, adolescents, couples, and families; she is best known for her studies of child development in the context of lesbian- and gay-parented families.

Adam Rutland is Professor of Social Developmental Psychology, Goldsmiths, University of London. His research interests cover: social-cognitive development, prejudice, intergroup relationships, social reasoning and morality; peer exclusion, rejection, group dynamics and victimization; cross-group friendships, intergroup attitudes, psychological well-being; interventions to reduce prejudice, intergroup contact; children's acculturation, ethnic and national identification. He is coauthor (with Melanie Killen) of *Children and Social exclusion: Morality, Prejudice and Group Identity* (Wiley-Blackwell, 2011).

Matthew R. Sanders is a Professor of Clinical Psychology and Director of the Parenting and Family Support Centre at the University of Queensland. He is founder of the Triple P-Positive Parenting Program. This internationally recognized program has twice won the National Violence Prevention Award from the Commonwealth Heads of Governments in Australia. Professor Sanders conducts research in the area of parenting, family psychology and the treatment and prevention of childhood psychopathology.

Patricia M. Schacht is an Associate Professor of Psychology at North Central College. Her research interests include the effects of parenting styles and parent–child relationships on children's social and emotional development. Currently, Dr. Schacht is studying the impact of parenting behaviors on children's coping skills and actions during peer conflict situations. She hopes to develop a prevention program aimed at helping parents and children stop the negative effects of bullying on children's outcomes.

H. Rudolph Schaffer (1926–2008) was Emeritus Professor of Psychology at the University of Strathclyde. An iconic figure in the field of developmental psychology, he wrote extensively on various aspects of child development, including *Introducing Child Psychology* (Wiley-Blackwell, 2003). He was a founding editor of the journal *Social Development*.

Alice C. Schermerhorn is an Assistant Professor at the Department of Psychology, University of Vermont and Director of the Socioemotional Neuroscience and Development Laboratory. Her research interests include: children's adaptation to family-related stressors, and temperament-related individual differences in adaptation to stress; mechanisms underlying associations between stress and psychological adjustment, including neurophysiological, adrenocortical, and emotional and cognitive processes; children's influence on family processes.

Peter K. Smith is Emeritus Professor of Psychology at Goldsmiths, University of London. His research interests are in social development, school bullying, play, and grandparenting. Among his many books are *Children and Play* (Wiley-Blackwell, 2010), the *Wiley-Blackwell Handbook of Childhood Social Development* (Wiley-Blackwell, 2nd edn. 2011), *Cyberbullying in the Global Playground: Research from International Perspectives* (Wiley-Blackwell, 2012), *Understanding School Bullying: Its Nature and Prevention Strategies* (Sage, 2014), and the 6th edition of his textbook *Understanding Children's Development* (Wiley-Blackwell, 2015).

James A. Thomson is Professor of Psychology at the School of Psychological Sciences and Health, University of Strathclyde, Glasgow, Scotland. His theoretical research interests in spatial orientation and the visual control of locomotion have given rise to a long-standing interest in the perceptual and cognitive factors underlying children's pedestrian behavior and vulnerability to injury in traffic. He has undertaken many intervention studies aimed at promoting the development of pedestrian competence in young children and has developed two training resources which have been adopted by the UK Department for Transport, one of which is discussed in this volume. He is currently investigating the relationship between executive functioning and pedestrian decision making.

Sheree L. Toth is Director of the Mt. Hope Family Center, Director of Clinical Training, and Professor of Psychology at the University of Rochester. Her research interests are broadly focused in the field of developmental psychopathology. She is especially interested in examining the effects of maltreatment and parental depression on child development, particularly in the domains of self-development and representational capacities, and the evaluation of preventive interventions for high risk populations. In addition to basic research, Dr Toth is committed to bridging research and clinical practice.

Joyce E. Watson was an Early Years teacher for a number of years. Her research interests lie in the teaching of reading with beginning readers. She completed her PhD on the effects of phonics teaching on children's progress in reading and spelling. She has collaborated with Rhona Johnston in numerous investigations of early reading, including the seven-year study into the effectiveness of synthetic phonics in Clackmannanshire, which showed dramatic results in reading achievement.

Shaogang Yang is a Professor of Psychology at Guangdong University of Foreign Studies and Director of Mental Health Education and the Institute of Mental Counselling in South China Business College, GDUFS. His research concerns the moral development of children and adolescents, especially comparisons of moral psychology, values, and culture between China and Western developed countries such as those in North America and Europe. In recent years he has examined the understanding of moral concepts such as rights, self-determination, democracy, and freedom in adolescents from rural and urban areas in China.

Miwa Yasui is an Assistant Professor at the University of Chicago's School of Social Service Administration. Her areas of interest include cultural influences on developmental and familial processes, such as ethnic identity development and ethnic–racial socialization, the examination of the culturally responsive assessments and interventions for ethnically diverse children and youth, intervention and prevention of problem behaviors among youth, and observational methodology. In particular, her research examines how multilevel cultural influences enhance or ameliorate the relationship between family processes and child psychopathology, especially among ethnic minority families.

In Memoriam

H. Rudolph Schaffer died during the early stages of preparing this Handbook. Rudolph was a leader of rigorous developmental psychological science and a passionate advocate of using that science for the benefit of children and their families. It was a privilege to work with him, and a great sadness that he is not among us to see this outcome. Many of his ideas and much of his role modelling are embedded here.

We also lost Jane Knitzer, another pre-eminent developmental scientist, a champion of the wellbeing of children, and a guiding exemplar of how to communicate the insights of research to policymakers. We are fortunate indeed that her work with Janice Cooper will continue to inspire and inform others through their chapter here. More on Jane's legacy can be found at: http://www.nccp.org/jk_directorship.html

And there were other personal losses, for the editors and authors. These are loved ones whose contributions, direct and indirect, underpinned much of what we offer in this volume, in more ways than we can record but will never forget. Rudolph would have known, and cared, that those of us who remain have learned much about attachment.

This volume is dedicated, with love, to their memories.

Kevin Durkin

PART I

Family Processes and
Child Rearing Practices

1

On Giving Away Developmental Psychology

Kevin Durkin and H. Rudolph Schaffer

The book you have just opened deals with thousands of billions of dollars – and much more.

If you are a taxpayer (or aspire to become a taxpayer), or a parent (or plan to become a parent), some of those dollars, euros or pounds will be yours. It costs a lot to raise children, to provide the care and services that they will need on the long journey to adulthood; these costs are met by families, public services, and charities. If you are a practitioner in a field related to human development and well-being, or a policymaker engaged in decisions about the distribution of resources across services, you will be aware that the costs borne by the broader community are enormous – so much so that we often do not have enough to address all needs.

And the costs multiply when things go wrong. Consider the economic costs:

- when children are exposed to abusive, discordant or inadequate family contexts (Cicchetti et al., Chapter 15; Cummings et al., Chapter 3; Dishion and Yasui, Chapter 17; Moreland and Dumas, Chapter 4; Sanders and Calam, Chapter 5);
- when millions of children receive poor child care (Hardway and McCartney, Chapter 7); or their parents encounter inadequate advice (Leach, Chapter 2);

The Wiley Handbook of Developmental Psychology in Practice: Implementation and Impact, First Edition.
Edited by Kevin Durkin and H. Rudolph Schaffer.
© 2016 John Wiley & Sons, Ltd. Published 2016 by John Wiley & Sons, Ltd.

- when educational services consign whole generations to methods of reading instruction that fly in the face of research evidence (Johnston and Watson, Chapter 9), fail to exploit the benefits of research-based innovations in mathematical education (Ginsburg and Ertle, Chapter 10) or fail to detect hidden disabilities that impact on learning yet are at least amenable to therapy (Conti-Ramsden and Durkin, Chapter 16);
- when children are victims of bullying (Smith, Chapter 12), avoidable accidents (Thomson, Chapter 13), or prejudice (Cameron & Rutland, Chapter 14, Patterson & Farr, Chapter 6);
- when societies fail to provide adequate help to children and young people with, or at risk of, mental health problems (Cooper and Knitzer, Chapter 18);
- when adolescents veer into antisocial behavior and high risk taking (Dishion and Yashui, Chapter 17);
- when teenagers become pregnant (Martin and Brooks-Gunn, Chapter 8);
- when young people enter society with poor understanding of their rights, responsibilities and opportunities as citizens (Helwig & Yang, Chapter 11).

As several of the contributors point out, the profoundly difficult topics with which they are dealing are associated with enormous, ongoing material costs to nations worldwide. The best available (most rigorously computed) estimates tend to be for the leading industrialized nations, but readers from other countries will be able to see the broad implications for their own economies. When things go wrong in child development, or in families, or as young people meet institutional or societal problems, or when children's potential is neglected or thwarted, there are immediate costs to the individuals and social structures involved, followed by financial repercussions that can extend over decades.

Importantly, the biggest costs are likely to be incurred when we do little or nothing to address the issues, problems and needs (Aboud & Yousafzai, 2015; Scott, Knapp, Henderson, & Maughan, 2001). The economics of intervention are complex and vary across contexts (including whether they are preventive or remedial) and time frames; this is not our primary concern here but it is relevant to bear in mind that interventions to support healthy development have been reported to show benefit-to-cost ratios ranging from 3:1 to 18:1 (Engle et al., 2011; Hardway & McCartney, Chapter 7, this volume; Heckman, 2006; Reynolds, Temple, White, Ou, & Robertson, 2011). Intervention does cost – but it also returns. Furthermore, provided that the benefits are demonstrable in high quality research, this is an equation that resonates with policymakers and the layperson (Moreland & Dumas, Chapter 4, this volume).

Readers will already have considered that, of course, in each of the above contexts there are other costs: the psychological costs of stress and suffering. It is sobering to reflect, as we progress through the authoritative reviews in the chapters ahead, that we are not surprised to learn that so many children face circumstances and events that are, literally, terrifying. Children suffer maltreatment and abuse at home. The caregivers that children depend upon may be in the throes of marital conflict that affects the whole household. In the playground or park, many children are victimized. Many face ethnic prejudice in their schools or communities. Some will enter gangs by their early teens, and some of these are soon on their way to prisons. Early sexual activities can lead to premature parenthood, with radical impact on individuals' circumstances and prospects. Still more tragically, the privations and cruelties that life can inflict are not distributed evenly; many young people are exposed to combinations or accumulations of these adversities. Our contributors speak to these concerns and, for many of the present authors, the alleviation of unhappiness and suffering is a key motivation for advancing applied developmental psychology.

Another dimension of costs, interrelated with the above, is the impact of developmental problems on the quality of society. As well as the economic liabilities of less-than-optimal literacy and numeracy education, these skills impact in countless ways on the conduct of everyday life. As well as the psychological detriment to direct victims of abuse or antisocial behavior, there are indirect costs to many more in terms of the ways we perceive and experience our communities. It is hard to quantify the economic costs of poor moral reasoning abilities or deficient civics education, but suppose a substantial sector of the population reaches adulthood with no conception of their own or others' rights. As Helwig and Yang (Chapter 11) draw to our attention, the consequences for society of shortcomings in moral understanding, grasp of the principles of justice, democratic processes, and the rights and duties of democratic citizenship are profound. Yet we still struggle with (or, in some societies, ignore completely) how this vital area of education can best be conducted. Their chapter demonstrates how applied developmental research has the potential to provide theoretically-based yet practical routes to stimulating advances in moral and civic education – but also that it is confronted by many real-world obstacles.

In the face of the diverse costs of the many potential problems besetting human development, it follows that we should be asking how developmental science can help us to address them. Answering this question is the central purpose of this Handbook. Accordingly, the volume sets out to describe and analyze what happens when researchers offer the fruits of their studies to potential recipients – be they professional workers in the field, local or national organizations, parents or the general public. Its aims are to examine the process of knowledge transfer and implementation, in order to investigate both the opportunities and obstacles involved and to consider the factors that lead to successes and disappointments. To this end we draw on the experience of a range of academics representing a variety of topics in developmental psychology with definite implications for practice, all of whom are willing to share the experiences they encountered when confronting the "giving away" process as part of their work.

Can we Give Away Developmental Psychology?

There is widespread awareness these days that developmental research is producing a considerable body of knowledge that is not only theoretically significant but is potentially useful in the real world. It follows that the outcomes of research studies ought, therefore, to be passed on to practitioners and policymakers, and many publications now include a section on the implications the findings obtained have for intervention. Nevertheless, the impact of research-based knowledge on practice has been patchy – notably successful in some areas, leading to significant advances in the well-being of children and their families, yet in other areas there is still a considerable gap between research and its application.

Clearly, the giving away process is not a straightforward one; in particular, one needs to question the still prevailing assumption among many people that it is a simple unidirectional matter of knowledgeable researchers communicating their findings to ignorant practitioners willing to abandon previous practices and adopt new ideas. Publicizing research results and pointing out their implications is only part of the story; their implementation is another; and it is the latter that is now in need of close attention.

Developmental psychologists are engaged in pursuing two aims. One is to add further to the body of knowledge we have accumulated so far about psychological development, in order to determine the processes responsible for change over age and formulate the theoretical principles which would help us to understand how and why development occurs. This is generally referred to as *basic* research, in that it is theory driven, is mostly conducted with traditional scientific methodology and constitutes understanding for the sake of understanding. The second aim is a practical one, namely to help children avoid or at least overcome the hazards of life, to make the most of their capacities and to attain optimal competence in social and cognitive spheres. Such *applied* research includes both prevention and intervention efforts; it takes place in real-life locations and sets out to solve society's problems as they impinge on children and their families.

These two aims – understanding and helping – have been somewhat uneasy bedfellows over the years. Various questions arise: Are the two compatible, in that both can be regarded as part of the same discipline? Moreover, can any one individual researcher effectively pursue both aims, even within the same investigation? Is one more "respectable" than the other? Do they require different skills and, therefore, different training courses? Can basic research benefit from the lessons learned by applied work, as much as vice versa? Developmental psychologists have taken different views as to how the tension between the two aims can be resolved, and there have indeed been "fashions" in the answer provided. Thus, even in the relatively short history of developmental psychology one can roughly distinguish three periods, in each of which a particular attitude prevailed.

Historical Shifts in Giving Away

The first period covers the beginnings of the scientific study of child development in the last two decades of the nineteenth century and the first four or five decades of the next century, when the simultaneous pursuit of both aims was not regarded as in any way problematic and, indeed, the initial motivation to learn about children arose from applied concerns. As Sears put it, "Child development was formed by external pressures broadly based on desires to better the health, the rearing, the education, and the legal and occupational treatment of children…The field grew out of relevance" (Sears, 1975, p. 4). When the first formal research center in North America was set up in 1919 it was named the Iowa Child Welfare Station, and given the brief of conducting research directed at all problems of children's development and welfare. And, for that matter, the early fathers and mothers of child psychology almost without exception conducted research motivated by a mixture of basic and applied goals. G. Stanley Hall, for example, was convinced that child psychology research is capable of providing crucial guidance to those engaged in educational practice; John B. Watson applied his behavioristic principles to the rearing of children and publicized his ideas in the form of popular articles and books addressed to parents; and Gesell, a student of Hall, intended his charts of psychological norms not just to add to our scientific knowledge of children's development but also to act as a guide to parents in avoiding unrealistic expectations as well as helping pediatricians to distinguish normality from pathology. The spirit of the times was well summarized by Charlotte Bühler (1935), when at the very beginning of the Introduction to her textbook *From Birth to Maturity*, she stated:

> The development of modern child psychology in the last 10 to 20 years, through its scientific study of the child in all its life situations, enables us today not only to present a very complete scientific picture of mental development but also to solve many of the practical problems which children present. Psychology can now give us information and advice in regard to those practical problems that confront parents and teachers in the understanding, upbringing and education of children. It can in addition assist us in meeting such community problems as the care, placement and treatment of orphans, children of the poor, feeble-minded, delinquent, adopted and foster children.

Overoptimistic, perhaps, yet the view expressed in this quotation reflects the predominant belief in those early decades in the history of child psychology, that there is no incompatibility between the motives to understand and to help, either for the discipline as a whole which can, indeed should, pursue both, or for individual academics who need not align themselves with one or the other approach. A general assumption prevailed that scientific knowledge is bound to lead to practical advances, and accordingly psychologists saw it as their task to employ their knowledge for social reform. What was not recognized at that time, however, was that merely publicizing that knowledge was not in itself sufficient to bring about change; the intricate connections between research and practice that now preoccupy many developmental psychologists were not yet recognized.

In the 1940s and 1950s a very different view began to emerge. Psychology, it was concluded, had to demonstrate that it was a "real" science, and pursuing applied research can only compromise its aspirations to respectability. As a result, primarily under the influence of learning theory, the use of controlled experimentation, generally under laboratory conditions away from the messiness of the real world, became the primary way of building up the body of theoretical principals required to account for the nature of child behavior. Motivation for research was generally provided by theory-inspired questions rather than by applied concerns, for it was not considered part of the job descriptions of academics to solve the problems of society. Take the views of Wayne Dennis, as reported by Milton Senn (1975) in the course of a discussion with him:

> There is certainly nothing of the reformer in me at all, except that I hope the truth has some good effects. I am more interested in finding out what a child is actually like. I am not trying to change them. I hope that whatever child psychology as a scientific study discovers will be useful, but that is to be determined later and not before you start your investigation. (Senn, 1975, p. 64)

In fact, Dennis's studies of institutionalized infants, carried out in the 1940s and 1950s and summarized in his book *Children of the Crèche* (Dennis, 1973), were extremely influential in improving the conditions of orphanages and in preventing or at least reversing the ill-effects of deprivation. However, to bring about such changes was not Dennis's motive in setting out on his investigations, and it was left to others with a more applied orientation to make practical use of the data he had supplied. A sharp divide thus appeared between basic and applied interests, in that the two were widely regarded as quite separate enterprises. Professional advancement in universities depended largely on contributing to basic research, and little attempt was made by academics to build bridges with practitioners and learn about their concerns, let alone to provide solutions. The introduction of rigorous methodology and pursuit of theoretically motivated questions was, of course, of great importance, but the price paid was a view of psychology among practitioners and the general public as an arid subject that only incidentally had anything to offer them in their struggles with everyday life.

Fortunately this phase did not last long, and from the 1960s and 1970s onwards the pendulum began to swing back once more to a view of child psychology as an enterprise that could be used for practical as well as theoretical purposes. The event that heralded this change is generally considered to be George Miller's presidential address to the American Psychological Association in 1969, in which he made a passionate plea to the members of his profession to "give psychology away". Rarely can a three-word phrase have had as much impact and been quoted so often since. A few more words of Miller's also repay careful attention:

> I can imagine nothing we could do that would be more relevant to human welfare, and nothing that could pose a greater challenge to the next generation of psychologists, than to discover how best to give psychology away...Psychological facts should be passed out freely to all who need and can use them...[Thus] our scientific results will have to be instilled in the public consciousness in a practical and usable form so that what we know can be applied to ordinary people. (Miller, 1969, p. 1074)

And yet, as Miller wisely warned:

> I am keenly aware that giving psychology will be no simple task. In our society there are depths of resistance to psychological innovations that have to be experienced to be believed...Many who have tried to introduce sound psychological practice into school, clinics, hospitals, prisons or industries have been forced to retreat in dismay. They complain, and with good reason, that they have been unable to buck the "System", and often their reactions are more violent than sensible. The System, they say, refuses to change even when it does not work. (Miller, 1969, p. 1071)

Why the change back to a belief in the legitimacy of psychology as a science with applied interests? Two sets of influences can be singled out, one arising from within psychology itself and marked by the demise of learning theory. The reductionist philosophy on which the theory was based had served its somewhat limited purpose and was increasingly seen as arid; conceptualizing psychological phenomena in mental as well as in behavioral terms became increasingly acceptable once more; and the emerging attention paid to the context in which human beings functioned as a determinant meant that researchers began to abandon the laboratory as the only setting for their studies and once again collected their data in the hurly burly of the real world. The other set of influences came from changes taking place in society. In the latter part of the twentieth century in particular, the conditions under which many children were being brought up began to arouse increasing concern. Phenomena such as the rise in the rate of divorce and single parenthood, the realization that even in the wealthiest countries a large number of children are living in poverty, the growing disquiet felt about child abuse, the prevalence of addiction, antisocial behavior and mental ill-health among the young, and the worry that technological innovations such as television and computers may have adverse as well as beneficial effects – all these resulted in society turning once more to psychologists and bringing pressure on them to come up with explanations and solutions.

The psychological profession has by and large responded positively to this challenge. There were, it is true, some initial misgivings as to the effects that becoming increasingly involved in applied issues would have on the scientific status of the discipline (Morrison, Lord, & Keating, 1984), but as Cairns has pointed out, this has not occurred – "on the contrary, carefully evaluated social applications have helped create a more robust, verifiable and relevant science" (Cairns, 1998, p. 92). The result is that Applied Developmental Psychology (or Applied Developmental Science, as it has come to be known in order to include the contributions of other sciences such as biology, education, economics and sociology) is now a respected and rapidly growing field, especially in the United States, with its own journals, associations and training courses, "that seeks to significantly advance the integration of developmental science with actions that address … pressing human problems" (Lerner, Fisher, & Weinberg, 2000, p. 11).

In short, we have reached the position where, as Lerner (2012) argues persuasively, the notion of a separation of "pure" and "applied" is anachronistic within developmental science. In the course of a single research study or program it is possible both to contribute to basic theory and to help in solving applied problems (Schwebel, Plumert, & Pick, 2000). Furthermore, if we are to generate and test meaningful theories, our work has to be "embedded in the actual ecology of human development in order to have generalizability to the lived experiences of individuals and as such … constitute intervention (applied) research and, *at the same time*, research testing basic explanatory processes of human development" (Lerner, 2012, p. 32, emphasis added). In a similar spirit, Cicchetti et al. (Chapter 15, this volume) point out that: "The ultimate goal of science is to benefit from the generation of a knowledge base."

Our knowledge of our participants, their progress and problems, would be truly impoverished (and nonscientific) if we did not take account of where they live, what they do, and how they respond to their experiences. Offering numerous examples of Lerner's "both at the same time" maxim, every chapter in this collection draws on basic research and every chapter reviews findings that speak to the theories, models and interests of basic researchers, while locating their enquiries very much in the realities of people's lives. The work assembled here aspires towards the goal Lerner recommends for the future of our discipline, namely that the emphasis is on "rigorous, theory-predicated research about the mutually influential relations among individual and ecological processes, about the embodiment of human development within the rich and complex ecology of human life, [that] will continue to be at the forefront of developmental science" (Lerner, 2012, p. 33).

Implications and Implementation

There is no doubt that the gap between theory and application is becoming less wide than it was at one time. This is seen, for example, in the forging of a working relationship in many areas between psychological science and public policy, thanks largely to the inspiring example set by certain individuals, such as Edward Zigler (Aber, Bishop-Josef, Jones, McLearn, & Phillips, 2007). It is also found in the establishment of training courses for the application of developmental research, open not only to developmental scientists but also to those from a policy and practice background, thus providing an opportunity to learn a common language, share problems and acquire similar sets of methodological tools to tackle these problems (Lerner, Jacobs, & Wertlieb, 2005). And it is also seen in the many reports of basic research that now have a concluding section on the implications of their findings for practice.

Highlighting the practical implications of a scientific study is a valuable, indeed essential aspect of the research-to-action process, but it is by no means the end of the story. Implication needs to be followed by implementation, that is, ensuring that potentially useful findings are in fact used. To disseminate research results among the relevant policy and practitioner groups, even if the right outlets and the appropriate language are used, does not in itself guarantee action. There are still academics who assume that if one can demonstrate by means of objective research that A is better than B at a statistically significant level of 0.05 or better, the power of such evidence will by itself persuade everyone concerned to drop course B and adopt A instead. That, alas, is a naive attitude; there are many reasons for taking or not taking decisions other than knowledge alone.

Let us emphasize that by no means everything that psychological research has to offer encounters such problems. As Phillip Zimbardo (2004) in his presidential address to the American Psychological Association – 35 years after that given by Miller – pointed out, there are many research findings which have been readily accepted by the public and are now so pervasive that they are generally taken for granted: work on psychological testing, positive reinforcement, prejudice and discrimination, psychological stress and many other topics has widely been recognized as of great potential value in fostering human welfare. At the same time, and often at a personal as well as an official level, numerous creative working relationships have been established between academics on the one hand and policymakers and practitioners on the other, ensuring that evidence based findings result in interventions to the benefit of clients in need. And yet, as the contributors to this volume make clear, there are numerous other areas where this does not apply, where certain factors operate in creating obstacles to spanning the research–practice gap. Clearly these factors need to be identified and, given the move from a unidirectional to a bidirectional view, respected in the transmission process. This is perhaps the most important task now confronting anyone working on the giving away of psychology.

About this Book

While every aspect covered by developmental psychology has the potential to be exploited for its use in applied settings, in some such exploitation has gone much further. It is from these that we have chosen certain topics, the choice depending, in part, on just how active the effort has been in transferring research findings to practitioners and, in part, on the wish to cover a wide diversity of areas in order to examine the extent to which they share both the problems confronting anyone engaged in knowledge transfer and the conclusions to be drawn from efforts to solve them. There are no doubt many other topics we could have selected, but those included here do serve as examples of the efforts that have been made on the part of a growing number of workers in applying a research orientation to real-world problems. Inevitably, many chapters address themselves to aspects of dysfunction and atypical development, but it is in these areas that there is the greatest need for informed policy and action and that have consequently attracted most attention from applied psychologists.

The chapters chosen are grouped in three sections, entitled Family Processes and Child Rearing Practices, Educational Aspects, and Clinical Aspects. These groupings are not rigid or impermeable and readers will encounter many areas of overlap across sections and chapters.

The authors are all eminent researchers whose studies have definite implications for practice and who have confronted the giving away process as part of their work. We asked contributors, where appropriate, to follow a particular structure when writing their chapters. In each case, there is a conventional component, namely setting out the scene by presenting a succinct overview of the relevant research. Then, we asked authors to reflect on how they had experienced the giving away process, what they had learned from it and what they would wish to share with potential future researchers and practitioners in their field of expertise. This could include accounts of the actual implementation of the research and its reception by the relevant individuals and institutions in the field, and the myriad factors bearing on the course of their programs, including interactions with policymakers and other external influences.

With respect to their own areas of specialism, each chapter tells its own story. Rather than reiterate their thoughtful expositions here, we will attempt instead to preview some of the recurrent and generic themes concerning the giving away process. Some of these are obvious areas that researchers will have to grapple with if they work in the real world, and some may be less obvious; yet, crucially, most of them receive far less attention in the scientific literature than they warrant. They bear very directly on our work and the processes of implementing and translating research – but they are not often taught, and many researchers learn about them the hard way. They concern working with policy makers, working with external institutions and agencies, working with the media, and reflections on the history of research programs.

Working with policymakers

When research is addressed to questions concerning how children should be raised, how families can be supported, how we can help those with difficulties, how educational systems can be improved, it is very likely to intersect with the interests of policymakers. Many of the chapters in this collection report aspects of such intersections.

As Hardway and McCartney discuss, in most areas of human development some kind of policy is inevitable and some kind of research is likely: it would be good to bring them together but, for reasons they elaborate, this is often not achieved. Cooper and Knitzer, addressing related issues, remind us that public policy is a blunt tool, fashioned in contexts that meet some needs and fail to tackle others. Furthermore, policy can change (and sometimes for the better) as research gathers momentum and publicity. Smith, for example, describes how bullying was once an area of policy vacuum yet, in a relatively short space of time, became the focus of mandatory policy that affected every school in his country.

Several of the chapters ahead also describe encountering indifference, resistance and political pressures. While many of the contributors can point to areas where public policies have been helpful, none is able to enter a "Completely satisfactory" report. This is not because policymakers are bad people: they work in very different systems with very different agendas. An important part of the giving away process is learning to communicate in ways that are meaningful to them.

Other institutions: Schools, child care centers, community agencies and the legal system

As has become increasingly apparent, and as will be amplified in several chapters here, giving away research is not a unidirectional process (McCall & Groark, 2000), where knowledgeable researchers hand over their conclusions to ignorant practitioners and grateful policymakers only too willing to adopt the new ideas. Any potential consumer of research is not a tabula rasa, but is influenced by many considerations other than knowledge alone, such as political and ideological factors, financial constraints, perceived threat to professional role, emotional resistance, sheer inertia and a range of other obstacles to change.

Much applied developmental research has implications for the institutions in which children spend much of their time, such as schools and child care centers, or other community-based agencies that deliver services to families and children (Cooper and Knitzer). Often, and especially in the wake of broader economic crises, these bodies are working in the context of financial stringencies that bear on how adequately they can meet their primary purposes (Cicchetti et al.). To gain access to these institutions to run research programs and interventions, and to collaborate with the staff, usually entails seeking approval from educational authorities, directors, principals, and head teachers. This may involve careful and sometimes protracted negotiations with senior administrators who may have many other calls on their time and resources. Cicchetti, Ginsberg and Ertle, and Moreland and Dumas, in their respective chapters, describe important practical issues that can arise when working with the directors of child care centers and agencies, even when the directors are very enthusiastic about the project.

The staff in these workplaces (including teachers, assistants, educational psychologists, and other therapists) are generally highly motivated, skilled and experienced professionals who are very committed to the well-being and advancement of the children in their care. They are also extremely busy and, in most educational systems, subject to a lot of pressure from policymakers, their own management, parents, and other sources. Their work is highly accountable and they are required to tick (literally) a lot of boxes, often on a daily basis. Thus, when it comes to implementing and testing the fruits of rigorous developmental research in the classroom, what seems like a good plan from the perspective of a research institution may be confronted with the rude reality that teachers sometimes have competing priorities and, occasionally, strong reasons not to want to do what the researcher believes would be a good thing to do. Even incontrovertibly desirable activities, such as teachers providing a series of practical training sessions to instruct 5–7-year-olds how to manage traffic hazards in the street, may be too much to add to teachers' already high workloads (Thomson). Ginsburg and Ertle provide a frank and very revealing description of the issues facing teachers – and, hence, their own applied developmental work with them – in the process of giving away a rich and creative, research-based mathematics curriculum for 4- and 5-year old children, in predominantly low-income schools and childcare centers in New York City and New Jersey. This project also enjoyed the full support of district level officials.

Any project with a longitudinal dimension will face challenges in recruiting and retaining participants; these challenges are likely to be still greater when the sample of interest has high levels of social disadvantage or stress. Moreland and Dumas offer very practical guidance on how to address these challenges.

The legal system is another important environment in which applied developmental psychology interacts with the structures, assumptions and processes of the larger society. Child and adolescent offenders have been a longstanding focus of applied developmental research (Dishion and Yasui). Indeed, children's involvement with the law – as the subjects of custody decisions, as victims and witnesses – has been one of the most active areas of applied developmental research and implementation over the last few decades (Cashmore & Bussey, 1996; Ceci, Markle, & Chae, 2005; Patterson & Farr, Chapter 6, this volume; Saywitz, 1989; Zajac, O'Neill, & Hayne, 2012).

The legal system has to make decisions about the well-being of young people, often in very complex and fraught circumstances (Schaffer, 1998). Frequently, the system is ready, even keen, to draw on the evidence base provided by developmental researchers (Cicchetti et al., Patterson and Farr). As Patterson and Farr illustrate, there are direct ways in which developmental psychology enters into and influences legal decision making (including formal citation of research findings and consultation of expert witnesses), as well as indirect ways, such as the dissemination of ideas through the mass media, which in turn may form part of the backdrop of assumptions of lawyers and judges. These authors show, in an account of the evolving of the American legal system in relation to parenting by gay and lesbian people, that the impact of developmental research can be difficult to predict. Successful legal actions, such as litigation by victims of bullying (Smith), can impact greatly on policymakers' sensitivity to issues.

Delivery of any successful service in any human workplace depends on the quality, skills and motivation of the relevant staff and their managers. This is very much the case in respect of the kinds of projects undertaken by applied developmentalists. Training staff appropriately and thoroughly is essential and several chapters discuss the practicalities involved in their particular sphere of interest (for example, Cicchetti et al. on the selection and training of staff in family centers). As Cummings et al. report, one further constraint – very salient to most researchers – that bears on the training of research and intervention personnel is that sources of funding are usually fluctuating, subject to gaps or disappearance. This is not unique to our employment sector but, as in others, it can mean that investment in the right people can be put under pressure as they are compelled for their own economic security to seek more stable sources of income. Interestingly, in some contexts, volunteers can be recruited to, and trained for, applied research projects with positive results (see Thomson on volunteer trainers working to improve child pedestrian safety).

Sensitivity is needed when offering practitioners new ways of doing things. As authors report, whether it be promoting child pedestrian safety (Thomson) or teaching mathematics (Ginsburg and Ertle), some will be alert to the possibility of implied criticism of their current practices, and this has the potential to create a barrier to the researcher's message. Indeed, professional self-preservation in the face of divergent and sometimes conflicting advice can lead to teachers sometimes adopting eclectic approaches to pre-empt possible criticism of oversight or neglect (Johnson and Watson).

The media

The media are relatively neglected in developmental research (Durkin & Blades, 2009). Even research into the most popular topic in this area, effects of media violence, is more often conducted by social psychologists than developmentalists. Yet most applied developmentalists will come into contact with the media at some stage – reactively and/or proactively – and it is striking how often the topic comes up (unprompted!) in the chapters that follow.

The topics on which we work relate to the well-being of developing people, equity and support. Specific research projects or findings will attract the attention of journalists. In many cases, this can be an innocuous process (e.g., the press report the launch of a newly funded project, perhaps basing the story very closely on the research institution's press release) or even beneficial (e.g., media publicity helps with participant recruitment or access to other organizations). Smith discusses how media coverage raised public awareness of the problems of school bullying, leading to action from policymakers, more funding for research and more investment in effective school procedures. Cameron and Rutland describe how very strong working relationships with practitioners were triggered by researchers' appearances in the media. Sometimes, experienced researchers will initiate such coverage deliberately and often media outlets are willing to assist because they see the human interest of the research.

Several chapters report on uses of media may as part of the research and/or intervention process (for example, Smith, on the provision of help packs and telephone helplines to address school bullying). In some cases, information relayed via media may be the most readily available, or even the only, option for reaching families which are unable or unwilling to participate in face-to-face, on-site sessions (for example, Cummings et al., Sanders and Calam).

Media may be exploited also for translational purposes, to communicate with, inform and coordinate key stakeholders (Thomson). Conti-Ramsden and Durkin describe the ways in which researchers and practitioners are using the Internet to promote public and professional awareness of an often hidden childhood disability (language impairment) and to make research findings accessible to affected individuals, their families and others. Hardway and McCartney emphasize the need for researchers to work effectively with the media to communicate our messages to policymakers. Researchers and policymakers, they point out, have much to learn from each other but operate within very different constraints, a reality that makes communication much more difficult that it might at first appear.

Sanders and Calam provide an extensive account of the potential role of media in teaching parenting skills, particularly in connection with the Triple P Program. They offer a conceptual framework for how the media can be used and, drawing on their own considerable experience, discuss the many concerns that researchers and practitioners may have about working with and via media. Again, their strategies and findings will be of benefit to colleagues in other areas of applied developmental psychology who are planning to include media components in intervention or translational work.

Working with the media can be precarious. Well-being is, by definition, desirable but many people do not have it. To achieve it may require changes to the status quo (for example, changes in the distribution of resources or the provision of new services); changes (or proposed changes) to the status quo are contentious, so there is potential for adverse reactions within the media. These may take the form of direct criticism of the project (e.g., a hostile column or editorial) or an active search for opposition. For example, one of us once held a research grant to investigate aspects of children's understanding of gender role stereotypes in television. His university issued a short press release to summarize the background and purposes of the work, which included an interest in testing children's reactions to counterstereotyped portrayals (male nurses, female plumbers, etc.). A local newspaper responded with a column headed 'Boys will be boys', in which the journalist explained that gender roles and behavior were given by nature and he urged that public monies should not be wasted on academic projects that did not recognize the irreversibility of evolution's achievements. It was scarcely a devastating critique, and debate and challenge are to be welcomed (furthermore, the paper accepted a rebuttal). But media objections do have the potential to foster a climate in which a research venture is inconvenienced (for example, inducing reluctance in schools to grant access to potential participants, or attracting further critiques from politicians who may not be sympathetic to change). Media interventions are often attempted in contexts where there are strong countervailing sociocultural assumptions and it cannot be guaranteed that the messages delivered will be effective; some critics will object that even covering the issue will furnish a climate of complicity – see, for example, Martin and Brooks-Gunn on reactions to television programs intended to help deter teenage pregnancy. Another pernicious example (potentially harmful to good teaching practice) can be seen in media reactions to research on the effectiveness of synthetic phonics in reading (Johnston and Watson).

A common journalistic strategy is to seek contrary opinions to engender controversy. In a democratic society, this is a reasonable process but it does mean that the terms of debate can shift radically outside those that might be assumed within academic contexts (which is not to attribute to the latter environment a complete absence of emotions, biases, and competing interests!). So, for example, a major research project, such as might be headed by many of the contributors to this volume, can be pitted on national radio against a vocal critic representing a pressure group that subscribes to opposing goals and values. In some cases, the critic may have legitimate credentials (professional expertise in the domain of interest) and in some cases she or he may not.

This is not to assume that we (researchers) are right and the media (or the opposing lobby group, politicians, or individuals) are wrong. Nor should we expect that media outlets be staffed exclusively by professionals who see things much as we do and wait only for news from us that they can translate into empathetic articles. The more important point is that research which engages with the real world is likely to find itself dealing with the real world, and this can be a delicate process in which it behoves researchers to anticipate, where possible, and to deal with, where necessary, ramifications of their work that go beyond the parameters taken for granted in academic discourse. For better or worse, this makes for a different context from running E-prime experiments testing undergraduates' reactions to transient visual stimuli – and, as shown in the work of many contributors to this volume, it calls for a different mixture of skills.

Penelope Leach is well versed in dealing with the mass media. As a leading practitioner in writing books and articles and presenting television programs for parents, she has reached very large audiences to present parenting advice based on psychological research. In Chapter 2, she provides a rich historical overview of the ways in which the developing science of developmental psychology has both responded to prevailing sociopolitical and cultural assumptions and impacted upon them.

Reflections on the history of programs

We also encouraged authors, where appropriate, to reflect on historical developments related to the subjects of their chapter. This was not for the traditional reason of documenting the development of the background literature. As above, historical perspectives help us to see how ideas emerge (and fade) and invariably remind us of how closely scientific developments are tied to the sociocultural and ideological climates in which they unfold (Arnett & Cravens, 2006; Leach, Chapter 2, this volume; Lerner, Fisher & Weinberg, 2000; Mülberger, 2014; Oppenheimer & Barrett, 2011). This is of particular interest to the present collection in terms of what it reveals about the conditions under which developmentalists attempt to give the fruits of their specialisms away and the ways in which they are received.

Smith, in summarizing the recent history of research and practice relating to bullying, makes the thought-provoking observation that only a few decades ago there was scant interest in bullying as a research topic. A similar point could be made about research into parenting by gay and lesbian people (Patterson and Farr). In the case of bullying, the prevailing assumption seems to have been that it was part of life; in the case of gay parenting, perhaps the assumption was that it was *not* part of life – in both cases, these assumptions are now consigned to the dustbin of history and applied developmental research has played an important role in responding to and facilitating changes in societal perspectives. Cicchetti et al. describe how, through collaboration with researchers and over the course of a decade, service providers came to shift an initially resistant stance to the notion of random assignment of participants in the course of evaluation. Thomson shows how research helped practitioners come to terms with the fact that there is much more to child pedestrian safety than telling children to be careful when crossing the road.

In other contexts, historical perspectives reveal telling contrasts between the refinement of intellectual activity in a given field and the resistance of practice to any change at all. Consider, for example, the exciting developments in moral development theory over the last 30 or so years versus what is observable in moral and civics education in many classrooms (Helwig & Yang, Chapter 11, this volume). And history can highlight the consequences of undirected eclecticism: Johnson and Watson offer fascinating observations about the "archeology" of the last few decades of teaching practice in reading in UK schools, in which prevailing methods retain fossilized strands of earlier, sometimes intuitive, approaches, now juxtaposed with – and, unfortunately, potentially undermining – more recent evidence-based techniques.

There is another sense in which the history of research programs is revealing. Good researchers are good learners, and good learners profit from their errors and other feedback. Thwarted plans, disappointments, serendipity, and obstacles tell us a lot, not only about what works and does not work at the practical level but also about where our theories and methods are in need of improvement. Several contributors describe in valuable detail how their progress and practices were reshaped in the light of discoveries made in implementation in the "actual ecology of human development." These accounts, in turn, provide invaluable guidelines to future applied researchers, as well as what Dishion and Yasui show, in a very positive sense, is the reassuring "comfort of failure" and the rewards of resilience.

Conclusions

In sum, our contributors show that giving away developmental psychology involves much more than is captured in the traditional sections of a scientific report. Whether it be negotiating with policymakers, collaborating with practitioners from very different professional backgrounds, or communicating with or via the mass media, there are many variables at play. These are not background "noise" to the scientific project but the inevitable settings – part of the ecology – in which research is applied and implemented. Unless you are very fortunate, you do not get taught this stuff in graduate school!

We hope, then, that this Handbook will be more than a fascinating compilation of cutting edge research, eloquently summarized by leading exponents. We hope that it will be *useful*. Distinctively, it assembles the wisdom, experiences, self-reflections and, occasionally, warnings of a wide range of experts who have grappled with the many challenges – and rewards – of giving developmental psychology away. Future researchers, drawn to these and other areas of developmental implementations, will profit from careful attention to the authoritative reports here of what happens when developmental research is put in action.

References

Aber, J. L., Bishop-Josef, S. J., Jones, S. M., McLearn, K. T., & Phillips, D. A. (Eds.) (2007). *Child development and social policy: Knowledge for action*. Washington, DC: Amercian Psychological Association.

Aboud, F. E., & Yousafzai, A. K. (2015). Global health and development in early childhood. *Annual Review of Psychology, 66*, 433–457.

Arnett, J. J., & Cravens, H. (2006). G. Stanley Hall's Adolescence: A centennial reappraisal: Introduction. *History of Psychology, 9*, 165–171.

Bühler, C. (1935). *From birth to maturity*. London: Routledge Kegan Paul.

Cairns, R. B. (1998). The making of developmental psychology. In W. Damon (General Editor), *Handbook of child psychology, 5th ed. Vol. 1: Theoretical models of human development* (Ed. R. M. Lerner) (pp. 25–105). New York: John Wiley & Sons, Inc.

Cashmore, J., & Bussey, K. (1996). Judicial perceptions of child witness competence. *Law and Human Behavior, 20*, 313–334.

Ceci, S. J., Markle, F., & Chae, J. (2005). Children's understanding of the law and legal processes (pp. 105–133). In M. Barrett and E. Buchanan-Barrow (Eds.), *Children's understanding of society*. Hove, UK and New York, NY: Psychology Press.

Dennis, W. (1973). *Children of the crèche*. New York: Appleton-Century-Crofts.

Durkin, K., & Blades, M. (2009). Young people and the media: Special Issue. *British Journal of Developmental Psychology, 27*, 1–12.

Engle, P. L., Fernald, L. C., Alderman, H., Behrman, J., O'Gara, C., Yousafzai, A., & Iltus, S. (2011). Strategies for reducing inequalities and improving developmental outcomes for young children in low-income and middle-income countries. *The Lancet, 378*(9799), 1339–1353.

Heckman, J. J. (2006). Skill formation and the economics of investing in disadvantaged children. *Science, 312*(5782), 1900–1902.

Lerner, R. M. (2012). Developmental science: Past, present, and future. *International Journal of Developmental Science, 6*, 29–36.

Lerner, R. M., Fisher, C. B., & Weinberg, R. A. (2000). Toward a science for and of the people: promoting civil society through the application of developmental science. *Child Development, 71*, 11–20.

Lerner, R. M., Jacobs, F., & Wertlieb, D. (Eds.) (2005). *Applied developmental science: An advanced textbook.* Thousand Oaks, CA: Sage.

McCall, R. B., & Groark, C. J. (2000). The future of child developmental research and public policy. *Child Development, 71*, 187–204.

Miller, G. (1969). Psychology as a means of promoting human welfare. *American Psychologist, 24*, 1063–1075.

Morrison, F. J., Lord, C., & Keating, D. P. (Eds.) (1984). *Applied developmental psychology.* Orlando, FL: Academic Press.

Mülberger, A. (2014). The need for contextual approaches to the history of mental testing. *History of Psychology, 17*, 177–186.

Oppenheimer, L., & Barrett, M. (Eds.) (2011). National identity and ingroup-outgroup attitudes in children: The role of socio-historical settings. Special Issue of *The European Journal of Developmental Psychology, 8*(1).

Reynolds, A. J., Temple, J. A., White, B. A., Ou, S. R., & Robertson, D. L. (2011). Age 26 cost–benefit analysis of the Child-Parent Center Early Education Program. *Child Development, 82*, 379–404.

Saywitz, K. J. (1989). Children's conceptions of the legal system: "Court is a place to play basketball." In S. J. Ceci, D. F. Ross, & M. P. Toglia (Eds.), *Perspectives on children's testimony* (pp. 131–157). New York: Springer Verlag.

Schaffer, H. R. (1998). *Making decisions about children: Psychological questions and answers* (2nd ed.). Oxford: Blackwell Publishing.

Schwebel, D. C., Plumert, J. M., & Pick, H. L. (2000). Integrating basic and applied developmental research: a new model for the twenty-first century. *Child Development, 71*, 222–230.

Scott, S., Knapp, M., Henderson, J., & Maughan, B. (2001). Financial cost of social exclusion: follow up study of antisocial children into adulthood. *British Medical Journal, 323*(7306), 191.

Sears, R. R. (1975). Your ancients revisited: A history of child development. In E. M. Hetherington (Ed.), *Review of child development research*, vol.5, (pp.1–73). Chicago, IL: University of Chicago Press.

Senn, M. J. E. (1975). Insights on the child development movement in the United States. *Monograph of the Society for Research in Child Development, 40,* Serial no. 161.

Zajac, R., O'Neill, S., & Hayne, H. (2012). Disorder in the courtroom? Child witnesses under cross-examination. *Developmental Review, 32*, 181–204.

Zimbardo, P. (2004). Does psychology make a significant difference to our lives? *American Psychologist, 59*, 339–351.

2

The Role of Popular Literature in Influencing Parents' Behavior

Penelope Leach

Specialists in child development communicate with parents in many different ways, and parents use different routes to reach them for ideas or advice. One of the most enduring and, over time, potentially most wide reaching is via print. Considering that it is part of a Handbook of developmental psychology, this chapter might appear to have rather little psychology in it. The chapter focuses on popular literature as an influence on parental behavior and, of course, such literature existed for centuries before psychology was recognized as a science or anything was written specifically for the purpose of influencing parents. "Emile" (Rousseau, 1762), often referred to as the founding text of child-centered upbringing and education, is a novel. In revolutionary America authors such as Daniel Defoe (1722, 1724), Laurance Sterne (1760/1765) and Samuel Richardson (1740, 1748) produced best selling novels that often centered on parents' child rearing practices and children's relationships with them. And who can doubt the impact on parents of Laura Ingalls Wilder, whose novel *Farmer Boy* (Ingalls Wilder, 1933), describing her husband's childhood in the 1860s, might have been describing the background of America's first childcare expert, L. Emmett Holt, and whose *Little House on the Prairie* is still

The Wiley Handbook of Developmental Psychology in Practice: Implementation and Impact, First Edition.
Edited by Kevin Durkin and H. Rudolph Schaffer.
© 2016 John Wiley & Sons, Ltd. Published 2016 by John Wiley & Sons, Ltd.

part of children's literature? It is impossible to measure precisely the effects of particular representations of childhood or child rearing, whether in novels or non-fiction, but we do know that much popular literature on these topics reaches immense audiences and is discussed, interpreted and sometimes acted upon.

This chapter confines itself to consideration of popular literature that was written for the purpose of influencing parental behavior, especially the genre known as "baby books" or "parenting manuals", but even among those works many predate the science of child development or child psychology by a century or more. Furthermore, even in the twentieth century and currently, only a few books for parents are directly based on the psychological research of their day and some contradict aspects of it. Nevertheless, the topic of the chapter is very relevant to this Handbook because some of this popular literature has served as gift wrapping for aspects of developmental psychology, and it is possible that in the modern world of mass communication more use could be made of this conduit of information. Information filtered and disseminated through popular advisory texts becomes part of the lay psychology of parenting. Its contributions and influences are not extensively investigated and part of the purpose of the present chapter is to argue that it warrants closer attention if we are to understand the processes and context of "giving away" developmental psychology.

Baby books have the potential to influence many parents because of their very large readership, which is constantly renewed. Most women, including many who do not buy or read books under other circumstances, buy and read at least one such book around the time of a child's birth and during his or her infancy, and many men do, too. A substantial minority of parents buy and read "everything that's out there"; some subsequently complaining of being confused (Grant, 1998). However, if the potential audience for such books is large, their reach is often limited. Parents tend to buy books that directly address their own immediate concerns in caring for a baby and toddler, and it is relatively rare for them to move on to subsequent books by a particular writer. Even the author of the world's best-selling baby book, Benjamin Spock (1946), did not attract comparable sales to his books about older children or wider issues of parenting (Spock, 1970, 1984); the same has been true for other authors. Including more years and aspects of development in one book and using that book as a platform from which to reach out to parents of older children in other media (Leach, 1979, 1992) has sometimes been more successful than producing age-sequenced books.

However it is done, though, using baby or childcare books to take developmental psychology to parents is a high risk strategy, very different from offering more specific and focused expertise to policy makers or to relatively small and specialized groups of professionals who are usually able to maintain some distance between themselves and their work (Hardway and McCartney, Chapter 7, this volume).

Writing for parents about their own current parenting means asking them to accept the writer's expertise as a "gift", even though it is being applied to *their* child. Such gifts easily appear to patronize parents or fail to resonate with personal feelings or to fit comfortably with their own upbringing. And since everyone was once a child, everyone, parent or not, has some personal interest in parenting and many will have strong opinions on the process; so bringing up children is a public issue and a "hot" one. The issue is becoming increasingly public, and discussion increasingly heated, as mass media spread and become more interactive and audience-controlled (e.g., through blogs, online parental discussion forums). The influence of mass media themselves on parental behavior is beyond the scope of this chapter but their effect on the role and relevance of popular literature cannot be ignored.

Literature for Parents, Origins and Evolution

Literature touching on the development of children goes back to ancient times, most famously to the works of Plato, whose sentiments, in a good translation, seamlessly segue into current thinking. Babies should be held and rocked, he tells us, "living as if always rocking at sea", and children up to three should play freely in open air: "Thus does the use of exercise and motion in the earliest years of life greatly contribute to create a part of virtue in the soul" (Clendon-Lodge & Frank, 2000, p. 26).

However, work specifically intended to influence individual parents' behavior towards their own children was scarcely seen before the eighteenth century. Medieval Europe had children, of course, and parents and nurses who doted on them, but it did not yet have a concept of conjugal family that shared a home with and was responsible for only its biological offspring, rather than for widespread and often impersonal lineage. It was the sixteenth century before that sense of family began to emerge (Corbichon, 1556) and it was not until the seventeenth century that children past infancy began to be recognized as qualitatively different from adults. At that time, children were perceived as fragile creatures of God, requiring both reformation (from original sin) and protection from current temptation and bad example, through the imposition of disciplined and rational manners. Loving parents, such as Mme de Sevigne (1672, trans. 1982) were accused by moralists and pedagogues of "coddling" or "spoiling" their children. As M. d'Argonne (1690, trans. 1962, p. 172) put it, "Too many parents value their children only in so far as they derive pleasure from… their caresses… and antics". This conviction that parents overindulge children, and treat them, inappropriately, as "charming toys", certainly contributed to the eventual widespread acceptance of the need for "experts" in child rearing, and was a recurring theme until the middle of the twentieth century, as we shall see. In the meantime, seventeenth century parents were not even considered worthy recipients of philosophers' and educationalists' thinking about children. It was not to parents that John Locke (1660) addressed his "Thoughts concerning education", but to educational theorists in the universities.

The immediate forerunners of popular books for parents were neither treatises on children's education nor addressed to parents. They were manuals of etiquette addressed to anyone and everyone of any age who might not know "the manners and customs approved by people of honour and virtue" (Della Casa, 1609, trans. 1986, pp. 162–168). Della Casa's *Galatee* was so widely adopted by the Jesuits that it was printed and translated from the Latin into French, German and Spanish. It has minutely detailed descriptions of acceptable personal hygiene, table manners and avoiding offence to other people by "… not grinding ones teeth, whistling, gurgling or rubbing stones (sic) together…". Gradually, though, the "voice" of these manuals changed. In 1671, *La Civilite Nouvelle* (cited by Philippe Aries, 1962) addressed parents specifically, telling them what they should do to bring up well-behaved children, what manners to insist upon at table (no scratching or spitting), how to punish children and for what, when to start teaching them their letters and how to ensure their modesty. By the end of the seventeenth century, practical treatises on children's education were appearing that were presented as direct advice to parents and, eventually, informed more by intuitive notions of child psychology than by social etiquette. Parents were now urged to model good behavior for their children, to be aware of their playmates and to be sensitive to each child's current progress and difficulties: "Adjust yourselves as far as you can to their weakness, stammering with them, so to speak, in order to help them learn their little lessons…" (Varet, 1680, p. 28).

Some Influential Books Published Before 1920

Once there were any childcare manuals there were soon many – and there have been ever since (Grant, 1998). However, until mass publication and a mass reader-ship were established, very few influenced sufficient numbers of parents lastingly enough to leave a trail. Do these influential few share identifiable characteristics?

An early convincing "success" predates Rousseau and comes out of England rather than France where we began, or America, where we shall end up. Described by Levene (2006, pp. 30–36), the title of William Cadogan's 1748 paper, *An Essay Upon Nursing and the Management of Children from their Birth to Three years of age*, sounds ordinary to modern readers but was extraordinary in the mid-eighteenth century when not everyone thought of any part of childhood (except babyhood) as having special requirements, and few considered one particular span of years as having distinctive developmental features. The term "age group" is a modern one. The book sought to change then-current nursery practices towards simpler and more child-friendly regimes. Cadogan also sought to achieve more influence for fathers, albeit by stressing the scientific basis of medical men's skill and the ignorance of women:

"This business (of childrearing) has been too long fatally left to the Management of Women, who cannot be supposed to have proper Knowledge to fit them for such a Task notwithstanding they look upon it to be their own Province." (Levene, 2006, p. 32)

However, it was Cadogan's specific recommendations that were most influential, in the sense of altering the practices of the day. He argued persuasively for an end to swaddling (and to stays for little girls), insisting that even new infants should wear loose light clothing that left their limbs free. Although there is no way of knowing how many midwives and mothers and grandmothers immediately accepted this advice, swaddling does not appear to have been recommended by any subsequent authority in Europe.

This little book was widely read by medical men and parents alike, translated into several languages and an inspiration for a host of similar manuals. Why? It seems clear that, like several subsequently successful manuals described later, the book appeared in the right place and at the right political time. In mid-eighteenth century England, well-to-do people, including especially those associated with London's Foundling hospital, were becoming increasingly concerned by a level of infant mortality that took almost one-third of under one year olds born in the city. This was not only beginning to be recognized as a waste of human life but also as a threat to the supply of healthy young adults to serve England's growing empire and trading interests. It was to those well-to-do – and influential – people that the book was addressed.

Victorian England produced paeans of praise for Motherhood but no individual writers who were lastingly influential among parents. Popular literature's most notable successes in impacting on the behavior of parents started more than a century later, and in America. Again, the time and the place were both important. With the Victorian era over, agrarian America was becoming urbanized so rapidly that around half the population would be living in cities by 1920. Macrochanges in society went, as always, with direct and indirect, broad and detailed changes in the nature, organization and operation of families. "Family economy" was gradually giving way to waged employment of adult males outside their homes, supporting dependent wives, and decreasing numbers of children, many of whom spent their adolescence in High School rather than working the land as their fathers had done. For professionals and the educated elite it was the Age of Enlightenment; medicine and psychology were moving out of quackery into science; and the specialty of Pediatrics, first recognized in 1880, was gaining credence. For the less privileged majority of parents, though, it was a time of confusion and concern. Victorian child upbringing had relied on parents serving as models for children at home and this no longer seemed appropriate in an urban, wage-earning world. Indeed, many parents felt overwhelmed by the need to rear children for a future that had nothing to do with the life they had been prepared for by their own parents; a future that they themselves could not even imagine. Furthermore, with one in six American children dying before they reached the age of five, tragedy and despair threatened every family. As in England a century earlier, this death rate focused the attention of well-to-do and benevolent individuals on child health. The scene was set for the first professionalization of child rearing.

In 1897, a National Congress of Mothers was held at which its chair, the Swedish feminist reformer Ellen Key launched an "entirely new conception of the vocation of motherhood" and promised that with sufficient effort, enlightenment concerning child rearing would be forthcoming "from the laboratory" within a generation (Key, 1909, pp. 1–9). "Let mothers, fathers, nurses, educators, ministers, legislators, and, mightiest of all in its swift, far-reaching influence, the press, make the child the watchword and ward of the day and hour", Key urged, "Let all else be secondary, and those of us who live to see the year 1925 will behold a new world and a new people".

Key's book was published under the title *The Century of the Child*. That title was soon applied to the era itself. Key observed "at present a lax hesitation between all kinds of pedagogical methods and psychological opinions, in which the child is thrown about here and there like a ball, in the hands of grown people" (Key, 1909, p. 21). The similarity with complaints made by Erikson fifty years later at the time of the White House Conference on Children and Youth is notable (Witmer & Kontinsky, 1952). But whereas in the nineteen hundreds Key was one of many confidently calling on science to rescue children from inept parenting, by 1950 "Scientific parenting", as it was then understood, had been tried and found wanting and Benjamin Spock was calling on parents to rescue themselves and their children from science (Richards, 1951).

In the meantime, with the relevance of traditional parental authority being openly questioned by grandparents, parents and offspring and by lay and professional people alike, a new authority came forward, arguably the first "child rearing expert". This was not Ellen Key, as might have been expected, but Dr Emmett Holt. Holt was an eminent pediatrician who was President of the American Pediatrics Association from 1898 and whose name came to be synonymous with "scientific motherhood". It was not only Holt's original book, *The Care and Feeding of Children: A Catechism for the Use of Mothers and Children's Nurses* (Holt, 1894), that influenced the behavior of parents but also the Infant Care bulletins based on it; these were issued by the Federal Children's Bureau between 1914 and 1921 and relied upon by millions of mothers. Holt made a trail that cannot be missed: his arguments for the need for radical changes in child rearing echo down the years to the present day on both sides of the Atlantic. Only differences in actual language and the absence of mention of television, social media or obesity separate Holt's thoughts from those of Plato already quoted, or of today's social commentators, for example:

> "…our American life is every year becoming more complex… The conditions which kept child life simple and natural fifty years ago have largely changed since that time; on every side there is more to stimulate the nervous system and less opportunity for muscular development… One of the most important reasons for this is the far greater proportion of children now than formerly who are reared in cities and large towns." (Holt, 1894, p. 230)

Unlike some of today's commentators who look back to the "good old days" through rose-tinted spectacles, Holt had an optimistic vision of the future and clear-cut proposals for achieving it, and this may be one reason for his success in influencing parents. His vision was of a society increasingly constructed along professional and managerial lines; his solution to the difficulties families were experiencing was for middle class motherhood to become a vocation featuring professional management as well as maternal nurture. Mothers must concentrate their time and energy on equipping children – girls as well as boys – "to grapple successfully with the complex conditions and varied responsibilities which will be their lot". This "Scientific antidote to sentimentalism", as Ann Hulbert termed it in her *tour de force, Raising America* (Hulbert, 2003), was immediately appealing to middle class women, many of whom were searching for a worth-while role.

Holt – and the experts who followed him – said remarkably little about fathers. But because they were fathers themselves, and held in almost awe-struck regard by mothers, they ushered a degree of masculinity into the world of child care which, despite Cadogan's eighteenth century efforts, had been exclusively the preserve of women in the Victorian age. However, by making motherhood into an intellectu-ally demanding vocation they reduced newly-absent wage-earning fathers to amateur status, as parents or "assistant mothers". Perhaps this contributed to the gender-imbalance in parenting that dominated the twentieth century and is still detectable today (Katz-Wise, Priess, & Hyde, 2010).

It is not immediately obvious why this particular book was taken up not just for a middle class readership but for mass distribution and became so spectacularly successful in influencing parents, especially as it reads like a training manual for nursery nurses and did indeed start out as a manual for women working in the New York Foundling Hospital (of which Holt became Director in 1899) where the infant mortality rate was as high as 25%. However, it may be that the schoolmasterly tone and high demands that might have been expected to put mothers off were part of what attracted them. Under his influence, "scientific mothers" were to stem the terrifying tide of infant and child deaths, especially from diarrhea, that bedeviled every American home. Unless they were breastfeeding (and Holt reckoned that only a quarter of the well-to-do mothers who were his patients did so), they were to learn how to make up exceedingly complicated formulae for bottle feeding; measure and record their children's food intake, daily weight gain and bowel movements; map their sleep, limit stimulating play and observe their moods with cool affection. Holt seemed to offer a solution to a previously intractable problem that loomed as large in national as in family life, and he made mothers – many somewhat under occupied or under stretched by urban domestic life – his instrument. The more he asked of them, the more they did and the prouder they were to do it. By the early 1920s, infant mortality was down by one-third and while Holt's work was certainly not responsible for this drop he was given at least some credit for it.

The advice and instruction Holt wrote for mothers was very much wider than his expertise as a pediatrician and specialist in infant nutrition. His scientific motherhood was scientific only in its stress on the importance of hygiene and careful measurement in infant feeding. All the rest of his information and advice, on children's development, behavior and desirable discipline, came from observation of his patients and his five children, and from their devoted mother, his wife, Linda. However, Holt had produced a syllabus for being a good mother and the award of a good degree at the end was a living child.

It was that syllabus that influenced Watson (1928) to add the role of childcare expert to his profession of experimental psychologist. This was the type of combination Keys had in mind when she promised parents that child rearing solutions would come out the laboratory, but Watson's refinement and extension of Holt's ideas were not based on evidence or orderly observation and brought him far less lasting fame among the general public. It is as the "father of Behaviorism" that Watson is remembered, not as a child rearing expert. A comparison between the outstanding success of Holt and relatively lesser success of Watson in "giving away" their knowledge and ideas and, thereby, influencing parents, may illuminate the whole topic. Both men addressed themselves primarily to an audience of urban, middle class American women but in very different ways. Watson's attacking tone may have compared unfavorably with Holt's collegial (even paternal) approach to the mothers he sought to influence. Where Holt saw women's relative freedom from agrarian labor and many children as a chance for them to use their education to do better at the vital job of mothering, Watson wrote bluntly, "Wives haven't enough to do today. Scientific mass production has made their tasks so easy that they are overburdened with time. They utilize this time in destroying the happiness of their children" (Watson, 1928, p. 162). Where both recommended rational, scientific child rearing and a cool, objective relationship with children, with minimal petting, Watson went to extremes, "Never hug and kiss them, never let them sit on your lap… Try it out. In a week's time you will find how easy it is to be perfectly objective with your child and at the same time kindly. You will be utterly ashamed of the mawkish, sentimental way you have been handling it" (Watson, 1928, pp. 81–82). Watson even suggested that children would be better fitted for modern (entrepreneurial, capitalist) life – more independent, productive, skillful – if they were not raised in individual families at all: "The only danger there is, is the danger of too strong fixation by the child upon the father or mother" (Watson, 1928, p. 163).

Many women were proud to be scientific mothers for their children's sakes, but few wanted to hear that being a loving mother was shameful and that their children might be better off without them. Furthermore, mothers may well have been less motivated by the entrepreneurial children Watson promised to mothers who followed his way than they had been by Holt's promises of infant survival.

Some Influential Books Published Between 1925 and the Present Day

By the mid 1920s, the "new world and new people" predicted by Key in 1898 were evident but not the successful application of science to child rearing that she had expected. Indeed, speakers at the Conference on Modern Parenthood, held in 1925, were eager to disassociate themselves from turn of the century scientific motherhood, acknowledging only Holt (whose work formed the basis of pamphlets still being distributed by Government) as a respectable predecessor. Hulbert (2003, p. 99) quotes one speaker: "The literature of child psychology is so muddled and contains so much twaddle that the average American mother should be warned against it".

A new field termed "child development" was attracting funding from philanthropic foundations (including the embryonic Rockefeller Foundation) and dozens of new experts were carrying out different types of clinical and experimental work, behaviorist, psychoanalytic, Gestalt, developmental and a combined approach that was termed the "mental hygiene movement". This might have been the moment when developmental psychology began to flow to parents. However, although these interwar professionals had better equipped laboratories, grander theories and more regard to "evidence" than Key's pre-First World War generation, they were just as incapable of consensus. Debate raged about the laws that governed a child's nature and should, therefore, direct his or her upbringing. The only judgment common to all was one which clearly echoed the conference of 1897: mothers were incompetent, often frivolous and always inconsistent; parenting was in crisis and. children were out of control.

The next notably successful "parent expert" – and the first with a real claim to basing his recommendations to parents on scientific findings – was Arnold Gesell. Gesell had taken an active part in the 1925 conference, and had furthered the called-for move to a more psychological approach to child study by coining the term "personality" to replace "nature", but he neither criticized nor exhorted parents. Gesell did not set out to influence the behavior of parents, but to understand and record the behavior and development of children through large-scale quantitative studies. He was, of course, the first to publish evidence of regularities and sequences in cognitive development comparable to those recognized in physical development, and to build schedules from which the Gesell Development Quotient, or DQ (widely employed as a measure of infant intelligence but now rarely used), could be derived.

Although many of his books (Gesell & Ilg, 1940, 1949; Gesell, Ilg, and Ames, 1956) were intended as scientific records rather than childcare advice, they were very widely read by parents. Just as the sales of Holt's pamphlets and the numbers of follow-up questions they evoked suggest that he had considerable influence on parents, so the extensive sales of Gesell's books and. high levels of attendance at his lectures are evidence of his immediate influence. However whereas Holt's work remains interesting only as part of the history of childcare advice, Gesell's continues to resonate with mainstream approaches to charting reliable sequences in child development (Horowitz, 2014).

Two factors seem to have ensured that Gesell's research work reached a wide spectrum of parents and impacted on them. Firstly, from 1926 onwards most of his observations of children (about 12 000 of them) were filmed with a still-novel motion picture camera. These visual records, amazing to audiences innocent of television or documentary film, were shown in lectures to parents: the first time that parenting was the subject of any other media than visual arts or the printed or spoken word. Secondly – and just as crucially – instead of extolling the virtues of cool aloofness from children, as his predecessors had done, Gesell's observations encouraged – and demonstrated – close, sensitive and sometimes participant observation of every detail of children's behavior and abilities, feelings and moods. To women who wanted to feel that their mothering was modern, thoughtful, and scientific, but who also wanted to be closely and warmly involved with each child, Gesell must have appeared the ideal expert. However, although Gesell made some important recommendations to parents, including being a successful protagonist for "rooming in" in maternity hospitals, it was not his advice that assured his vast audience and influence but his norms for children's accomplishment and behavior at successive age stages. His books set out schedules of development – milestones – which parents could, and did, apply, anxiously or proudly, but always with considerable time and effort, to their own children. Hulbert quotes Gesell's daughter-in-law, Peggy, returning charts completed for her newborn daughter:

> You will note a wide variation here and there in her feeding schedule. That is not due to Self Demand but to my incapacity to catch up with Father Time and my housework or sleep… frankly, science is nothing to me when compared to a few minutes more sleep. (Hulbert, 2003, p. 183)

Keeping Gesell's records was a considerable undertaking for parents and the developmental patterns that emerged were often the source of boundless anxiety – and eventually, perhaps, played some part in the development of a phenomenon that has come to be known as the "pushy parent". Gesell, like Watson, contributed more to the infant science of child development than to parents' understanding of it and, like Watson, left parents anxious. Professionals still had a poor opinion of parents, especially mothers, while parents regarded all doctors as authority figures and were especially in awe of pediatricians. The American government and popular press blamed the low caliber of recruits to the Second World War on poor parenting and when postwar America needed men to fight in the Korean war, anxious government attention was focused on how the health and moral stamina of youth could be improved.

Looking back from our twenty-first century vantage point, politicians' belief that health professionals could bring about a substantial improvement within a few years seems entirely unrealistic. However, a generation earlier, at the Conference on Modern Parenthood, held in 1925, professionals had promised that a comprehensive description of children together with predictions about their development would soon come out of their laboratories, and those promises seem to have been believed. Reports of the day, especially from the New York Times, suggest that President Truman, politicians and scientists all looked to the 1950 mid-century White House Conference on Children and Youth, whose topic was "The healthy personality", to "make its greatest contribution by bringing together, systematizing and integrating the accumulated knowledge of the behavior of children and young people and by seeing how social institutions and individuals concerned with children were making use of this knowledge" (Richards, 1951, p. 16).

All were to be disappointed, however. The professionals who came together to prepare for the conference found themselves trying to consolidate – and above all trying to corroborate – many disparate theories, methodologies and collections of data, including the legacy of Freud, whose academic and public influence had soared in the wake of his death in 1939. A multidisciplinary fact finding committee, including Erik Erikson, Margaret Mead and Benjamin Spock, could arrive at no consensus, discovering instead "Great chasms of ignorance… our nation at mid-century has within it many unknowns – processes and patterns – operating beyond our control or in undetermined ways… the best now known is still known so tentatively" (Senn, 1950, p. 72). Erikson, star of the conference, called his first talk "On 'The Expert'", using those inverted commas to stress that advice and instructions delivered to parents as scientific fact in 1925 had reversed themselves by 1950 "… the publicists of expertness ride on a wave of sensationalism which quickly withdraws, only to return as something brand-new with the next wave or the wave after next…" (Witmer & Kotinsky, 1952, p. 6).

It was into this concern and confusion that Spock had launched *The Common Sense Book of Baby and Child Care* (Spock, 1946). It was only four years after its publication that the previously little-known pediatrician and psychoanalyst was made vice-chair of the conference.

Born at the beginning of the twentieth century and almost seeing it out (1903–1998), Spock was the only practicing physician of his time with that dual qualification and a conviction that much of the prevailing "parenting expertise" was unhelpful, even damaging. Spock startled both parents and his colleagues by assuring them that mothers and fathers were the true experts on their own children and that lavishing affection on them would not "spoil" children but make them happier and more secure. Instead of one-size-fits-all rules and self-conscious restraint, Spock recommended that parents be flexible, individualizing their care of each child and striving positively to enjoy life as parents.

It is not difficult to understand why parents welcomed publication of Spock's 25 Cent Pocket Book nor why not all his colleagues were entirely accepting of his populist approach and popular success. However, as Erikson made publicly clear, academic research had failed to provide the guidance politicians and policymakers required or the reassurance and empowerment bewildered parents sought. Spock's most famous message, "You know more than you think you do" (Spock, 1946, p. 1), was the best available. The book went through seven editions and sold more than 50 million copies in 39 languages. Only the Bible has yet sold more. Spock's ideas have become so embedded in Western culture that it is easy to forget that they were revolutionary, and difficult to keep them separate from those which followed.

Spock made advice on child rearing parent- (and child-) friendly but he did not make it more scientific. In fact, it can be argued that he diverted the trend towards using research findings to inform child care, as Gesell was doing. Spock was a clinician, not a researcher, and he had strong social and moral convictions rather than a hunger for information. He relied on his own highly trained and experienced observations rather than on quantitative data and saw no reason to separate his parenting advice from his personal views. Indeed, after twenty years of working feverishly on behalf of children and parents and against the Vietnam war, Spock had become a household name and even ran for President on a third-party ticket in 1972. Spock was a passionate peace campaigner and paid a heavy price in popularity but it did not silence him. Sharing a platform in Boston (the only time they appeared in public together), Spock, Berry T. Brazelton (Brazelton, 1989; Brazelton & Sparrow, 2002) and the present author became so immersed in conversation backstage that the organizer, serving as go-between for a large audience of parents wanting to ask about potty training, weaning and play, begged "couldn't you be a little less political?" Spock answered for all of us: "I really doubt it", he said.

Some commentators regard the 1970s and 1980s as the heyday of popular literature's influence on parents. For example, Hulbert says, "In the late 1970s Ben Spock's successor Dr T Berry Brazelton, joined by the British psychologist Penelope Leach, introduced the Spock-marked generation to the learning-by-loving-and-listening child rearing ethos of the cognitive era" (Hulbert, 2003, p. 13). Spock's enormous popularity and public support certainly helped the latter two to be heard. And although they communicated with parents from different backgrounds – one a male pediatrician in the United States, the other a female research psychologist from the United Kingdom – both were attempting to base advice to parents on the findings of child development research. The similarities of their approaches probably helped them both. Other media of the time also increasingly supported the influence of their popular books for parents. Although Spock was moving towards retirement, all three were in demand as speakers by the then-flourishing parents' organization in the United States, sometimes drawing audiences in four figures. All three made regular TV appearances, and Lifetime cable-TV ran a long Brazelton series for parents and then a 72-part TV series with Leach and a live participant parent audience that was given the same title as her book (Leach, 1992).

However, as the twentieth century moved towards its end, the audience for child-care advice and the processes by which it was disseminated were both changing. As "baby boomers" embarked on parenthood, more and more advice-books for parents were published, five times as many in 1997 as in 1975. But although a lot of new titles seemed to follow Spock's lead, parents increasingly chose books of a different kind: specialized, instructional rather than informational, and sometimes tick-box volumes, often dealing with the management of specific problems, such as toilet training or toddler tantrums, rather than with developing children. Various explanations for this gradual shift have been put forward. Some commentators – again led by the *New York Times* – suggested that feminism had made mothers feel that loyalty to a particular expert, or the need for a guru, were old fashioned; others thought that increasingly time-starved wage-earning mothers were selecting only advice they immediately needed, packaged in the smallest possible number of words. Both may have been true.

Certainly, pressures on many mothers were growing and America – and Americanized European countries – seemed less and less family-friendly. As Hulbert (2003, p. 14) put it: "With Brazelton and Leach in the lead… the 'child-centered' contingent graduated from manuals to manifestos denouncing an impersonal and competitive society as, in Leach's words, 'inimical to children' (Leach, 1994)." Sales figures suggest that such works had far less influence on parents (as opposed, perhaps, to policymakers) than the earlier manuals. Wide-ranging works considering all aspects of parenting, family relationships and children's development were going out of fashion. New authors were selling programmatic visions of child rearing and problem solving and these were increasingly promoted by other media: "From 'affirmative parenting' to 'attachment parenting', trademarked approaches got multimedia promotion. Even Dr Brazelton had become plugged in, signed up with Procter & Gamble as chairman of their Web Site…" (Hulbert, 2003, p. 15).

The topic that seemed most in demand, or perhaps the one that best fitted the demand for highly specific advice to parents within a programmatic approach to child rearing (and assured media interest), was "discipline". Brazelton (1989) addressed the topic in a developmentally-based book but the concept and techniques of disciplining children became a vehicle not for psychological understanding but for the conservative family values campaign, epitomized by James Dobson. Dobson was a psychologist but he was also self-styled champion of Judeo–Christian values, founder of Focus on the Family, a rightwing Christian radio 'ministry" with a following in the millions, and author of the popular *Dare to Discipline* (Dobson, 1986). Dobson was joined by other "disciples of discipline", notably John Rosemond (1989), a proponent of affirmative parenting and an open critic of Spock and the "nouveau parenting" experts and their complicated psychological ideas. Rosemond declared for a return to "the voice of granma". However, in his "Managerial Parent Skillshop" and in the more recent "John Rosemond's Traditional Parenting" (www.rosemond.com), it is not traditional common sense that is heard but the voice of the Christian Right. Popular literature was certainly being used to influence parents but towards articles of faith rather than research findings (Gershoff, 2013, provides a research-based critique of the advocacy of spanking).

As advice on parenting spread to the Web, was promoted through multimedia, and focused on behavioral problems rather than development, the tone in which parents were addressed by popular authors seemed to become less individual and intimate. None of the hundreds of writers whose books filled ever-growing child care sections in bookshops became widely known individuals, even if their techniques, such as *Toilet Training in Less than a Day* (Azrin & Foxx, 1976/1989), were eagerly followed. None of the disciples of discipline had large personal followings outside middle America and neither does the last writer, selected as an example of success in influencing parents' behavior.

Gina Ford's books have considerable influence over parents in the United Kingdom. But, although she is widely written about in the press and on the Web and is sometimes mentioned on TV, she seems to receive (and certainly offers in print) little personal warmth, even amongst parents who act upon her every instruction. It seems to be less the person on whom parents rely for guidance than her program, on which they rely for exact instruction. One mother put it to the author like this, "Nobody cares what she really thinks; all we care about is what she says we're to do". Ford (2002) offers her own methods of infant management based on rigid and highly detailed routines, and the promise that any parent following them exactly will have a controllable, predictable infant within a few weeks of the birth. The approach might seem to have a basis in developmental theory, as it owes much to the concept of "sleep training" and the delayed-response method first formulated by Ferber (1985) a generation ago. However, Ford does not share but rather distorts Ferber's research base, by generalizing Ferberesque arguments and techniques, including "controlled crying", from solving sleeping problems in the middle of an infant's first year to managing all the difficulties and conflicts that may arise in caring for an infant from birth onwards. Once a parent has decided to adopt such a scheme, the burden of judgement and decision making is lifted because following each day's routine is mindless – though far from effortless.

For the first months, these routines effectively dominate the caregiver's waking hours. Nevertheless, there are many mothers who find them worthwhile. One plausible explanation comes from recent surveys (Wicks & Asato, 2002; Institute for Public Policy Research [IPPR], 2003), which have directly asked large samples of parents whether children make them happy, and have collected ambivalent replies. It seems that, as well as finding the transition to parenthood demanding and difficult, many women are finding the ongoing actuality of mothering disappointing and its lasting effects on previous adult-only lifestyles and careers unexpectedly distressing (Biehle & Mickelson, 2012; Harwood, McLean, & Durkin, 2007). In that social context it is understandable that a set of strategies that promise to empower women to control infants' behavior and limit their demands might be attractive. Perhaps Ford's influence today has a parallel with Holt's a century ago. Holt's infant feeding regime was almost as difficult and time consuming for mothers as Ford's routines. It was attractive to women because they felt it empowered them in the face of a high possibility of their babies dying.

Reflections on the Contemporary Scene

Influence

During the long period in which popular literature aimed at influencing the behavior of parents has been produced, its volume and its influence grew to a peak around 1990, but its scientific content did not. Early literature, of course, pre-dated developmental psychology as well as being constrained by scarce resources for printing, production and distribution, and the limited literacy that meant limited popularity. Through the nineteenth and twentieth centuries, though, more and more was written and read and while it is difficult to define the notion of a book's influence, the words and ideas of a few bestselling authors – Holt, for example, and Spock – can clearly be seen to have reached large numbers of individual parents and changed the behavior of at least some of them, and to have played a part in changing attitudes towards children, and even some of the family policies of whole generations. It was Holt's life-saving infant feeding regimes that first made the importance of hygienic preparation widely known to rural and poor families as well as to the urban middle classes, and, if Holt's work was not responsible for the falling perinatal mortality rate, it seems churlish to deny it any influence. Certainly, it was the government's realization of the importance of ensuring the widest possible reach for Holt's work that first made the circulation of childcare information a public health commitment in the United States. As for Spock, while it is more difficult to catalogue the changes he may have brought about in the actual behavior of parents, there is no doubt that he changed attitudes. Spock presented infants and young children to literally millions of parents worldwide as potentially reasonable human beings needing not only care but also love and affection, from fathers as well as from mothers. That message has never been entirely lost, indeed it is difficult for today's young people to realize that it has not always been accepted: that it was new and revolutionary thinking after the Second World War.

Spock's message was not based in science, though, and it could have been. With Gesell's observational research to build on and Spock's own psychoanalytic background to inform his years of experience in communicating with parents and perhaps laying some of the ghosts in their nurseries, his attitude to children and their relationship with parents could have gift-wrapped many aspects of developmental psychology, including attachment theory, and sent them around the world. However, Spock himself was not interested in scientific research outside pediatric medicine; he had an unrivalled following as a "parenting expert" but not as an expert in child development or child psychology. Instead of meshing more closely together as they had seemed likely to do after the Second World War, those two strands became more separate in Spock's era, and by the time others with interests in both strands were on the scene, popular literature for parents was becoming fragmented and the influence of individual authors diluted.

From a few professionals to many interested individuals

Perhaps the most notable feature of the modern world is that more people communicate in more ways about more issues than in any previous time. Fragmentation and dilution of professional advice, in every field, is one direct result. Anyone can hold forth about anything, from personal minutiae to public issues, and confidently expect to be heard and responded to. No qualifications or currently unusual skills are needed to blog, tweet, participate in an online forum, e-mail or text, and amongst a plethora of Web topics, parenting is a popular one (Plantin & Daneback, 2009).

So, instead of a relatively small number of recognized or aspiring "experts" writing for the largest achievable audience of parents, there are unrecorded and uncountable numbers of individuals offering advice and opinion, comment and criticism, stories and tips, to anyone who happens to be logged on. Such easy, informal communication between parents (and children), blurring boundaries of age and gender, geography and culture, may be valuable in many ways, but because it also blurs the boundaries between information and opinion, objective fact and subjective fantasy, let alone cause and effect and correlation, it increases the difficulty of giving developmental psychology to parents. Andrew Keen sees, the Web 2.0 complex of sites and blogs and podcasts as the "cult of the amateur (that) is killing our culture" (Manzoor, 2007), while the statutory television and radio regulator in the United Kingdom, Ofcom, is said to be aware that it will soon be difficult for audiences to tell the difference between regulated (television) and nonregulated (Web) content because increasingly both will be accessed on the same devices. There are many parenting sites that offer apparently authoritative advice columns and Questions and Answers. For example, the online forum *mumsnet* offers "The Answers to Everything" on perennial topics concerned with pregnancy, and with babies and toddlers. Yet, in most of these contexts, only the occasional live guest or named contributor is a recognizably qualified or experienced professional with a transparent background and consistent standpoints. It is easy to find space for research findings on the Web (there is room for everything) but extraordinarily difficult to make their meaning clear and protect their veracity. A blog or an Amazon "review" from someone with no basis for judgement saying "I don't believe a word of this" can be as damning on line as outright refusal by a peer-reviewed journal in academia. Not surprisingly, when parents themselves participate in online discussions about parenting matters (e.g., via question boards or forums), they often express confusion, uncertainty and sometimes distress about the conflicting advice that they can easily find within the multitude of internet sources (Appleton, Fowler, & Brown, 2014; Porter and Ispa, 2013).

From information and informed opinions to hands-on techniques in books and other media

With the cult of the parenting expert waning in the face of popular participation, the large number of contemporary books published, together with other popular media, seem to influence parents more by putting out instructions and recommending particular child rearing programs and techniques than by advancing arguments or theories, explanations or evidence. If individuals who give advice become well known to parents it is less likely to be because they are professionals in child development or clinicians than because they are proponents of popular techniques, probably techniques concerned with discipline or "behavior problems". Two examples are Ford (2002) and television's transatlantic "Supernanny" Jo Frost (2006), neither of whom has any formal child development qualifications or substantial professional training. Ford's controlled-crying-based routines and Frost's time-out and reward chart techniques spawn many books and ensure their huge sales and, according to surveyed parents themselves, considerable influence over many parents' behavior. In a survey of almost four thousands adults carried out by MORI for the National Family and Parenting Institute (NFPI, 2006), 83% of the 795 parent television viewers with children under sixteen reported that specific techniques shown were "personally helpful". While more than half of these endorsed "praising good behavior", specific behavior management techniques such as time-out, sticker charts and the "naughty step" were each endorsed by one third.

The influence of television has not only grown but its nature has also changed. In the last twenty years of the twentieth century, television exposure assisted in the building of "expert" public profiles and, therefore, helped to sell the books that parents read. Now neither expert nor nonexpert advice on child rearing is disseminated primarily via print. Television influences parents directly, with many learning about children and child rearing largely by watching other, often more troubled, families on their TV screens, and books follow. About three quarters of all UK parents with a child under the age of sixteen have watched at least one such program and more than a third regard them as the next most useful source of parenting advice after family and friends., more useful than books, magazines or the internet

(NFPI, 2006). Given such a large potential for passing developmental psychology to parents, it is regrettable that most such television programs fail to follow research or ethical guidelines and that some contradict both.

Television may even be increasing parents' swing away from academically qualified proponents of developmental psychology. A majority of "fact-based" or "documentary" programs now have a fly-on-the-wall and/or interactive format, with maximum participation by selected "ordinary people" and minimal contributions by what used to be known as "talking heads". There are powerful arguments for this trend – not least the fact that it draws many viewers to topics they might otherwise ignore – but there are powerful arguments against it, too. Involvement in popular television programs may present opportunities to communicate with a wide and interested audience but it can also raise serious professional concerns. Some people in health, the helping professions and social research are reluctant to take part in programs, such as "Baby Borrowers", "House of Tiny Tearaways", "Brat Camp" or "Bringing up Baby", that use the selectively edited problems of volunteer parents and their volunteered children to provide entertainment, feeling that such programs are ethically dubious. Not everyone of good will refuses to participate, of course. It is tempting to believe that professional influence can be exercised from inside popular television, especially when a production company, anxious to add an academic researcher to the team, gives flattering assurances. Most soon learn, however, that their desire to present a balanced picture of current knowledge and ongoing research cannot be indulged in the clear-cut, fast-moving world of popular television. There is no time, no space, for the ifs and buts, for "it appears" and "it seems", for "on the one hand... and on the other". So, having learned, some of the professionals who have the most information and experience concerning currently controversial topics, such as the effects of nursery or center care on babies and young toddlers, refuse all invitations, sometimes even telephone calls, from television production companies. They know that their off-screen advice may well be disregarded and that any on-screen contribution is likely to be cut to a carefully chosen and selectively edited minute or two. Selective editing has become an increasing problem since digitization made it possible for interviews given, and probably recorded, in good faith, to be edited for extra excitement, or controversy, or the "clarity" of rendering black and white judgments of issues that are every shade of grey. As a former Commissioning Editor for Channel Four put it "...most television is like an impatient child – noisy, easily bored and desperately seeking attention. This need to be noticed is driven by a desire for ratings which prompts program makers to do everything and anything to lure viewers to stay tuned" (Butterworth, 2007). The separation between "parenting" and developmental psychology which Spock permitted in the popular literature of the 1950s may be even deeper in today's multimedia.

Can – and Should – the Balance of Influence be Shifted from Mixed Media Back Towards Popular Literature?

Popular books have more lasting influence than TV programs, which are seen by millions but quickly forgotten, so popular literature can be more valuable. In discussing what might rebuild the influence of popular writing for parents, though, it is important not to take the desirability of doing so for granted. Books can also be more lastingly harmful than other media; the difficulty is agreeing which types of book are having which types of consequence. We all know that parents' behavior is open to influence and we would all prefer it to be influenced in directions we personally approve – even the most objective researcher would rather parents chose options that have been shown to lead to good rather than poor child outcomes. However, of the thousands of popular books marketed to parents, many contradict each other, the views of a range of psychologists and the findings of child development research. There are popular books on discipline that recommend corporal punishment with implements from the first year of life and Internet sites where American entrepreneurs market paddles made for the purpose. There are books for and about adolescents that recommend abstinence as the principal plank of sex education and only form of contraception; books that recommend three years of breast feeding for every child and books that recommend toilet training energetically and early, or laissez faire and late.

Irrespective of their specific content, though, books may seek to influence parents' behavior in different ways and, judging by the past, some seem more likely than others to be relatively successful. One writer may put forward a particular and unusual position and seek to encourage and steer parental behavior towards it. Another may identify and seek to discourage and redirect what is regarded as bad parenting, while a third may seek to inform parents of many options and consequences, leaving it open to them to make their own decisions and choices. The explorations of this chapter suggest that positive exhortation is usually more readily accepted than negative, and that balanced information is better received than it is acted upon.

The ease and extent of any book's influence is also affected by the context of the advice being given, especially its position relative to current parenting ideas and practices. Parents are, of course, most ready to accept and act on information that they want to believe. It was because parents desperately wanted to believe that they could do something to prevent their children dying in infancy that they followed Holt's demanding regime. And it seems likely that, after two generations of patronage and exhortation from other experts, it was Spock's respect for parents as important and powerful people in their children's lives that first predisposed them to pay attention to him. Parents may also accept literature that does not tell them what they want to hear but at least does not cut across their existing beliefs and sensitivities. The phenomenal sales of the *What to Expect* series of manuals (Eisenberg, Murkoff, & Hathaway, 1990, 2002) may be partly due to a format that is heavy on information and light on values, informing everyone while offending no one. However, parents overwhelming desire to do the best they can for their children makes even difficult messages acceptable if the facts presented are clearly important to children's safety and well-being, believable, and reiterated often enough that a critical mass of parents becomes aware of them. Examples abound in the field of physical safety and accident prevention where popular literature has influenced parents into behavioral changes that are highly conflictual or inconvenient for them. It is the very rare twenty-first century Western parent who puts a baby to sleep prone, despite the long-established parent lore that says that babies are more comfortable, settle better and are less likely to choke in that position than on their backs. Likewise, few parents dip a dummy in syrup despite the eagerness with which a restless infant will suck on it.

Acceptance is more difficult – though not impossible – to achieve when new, or newly presented, information deals with other aspects of child welfare that are less generally recognized than physical safety and is in an area of marked parental sensitivity. Topical examples include the physical and emotional benefits to infants of breastfeeding, and the importance to all children of continuing relationships with both parents after separation or divorce. There seems to be little argument about these propositions in the literature; academic papers that deal with these topics at all, such as those noted here, report findings that support both breastfeeding and the importance of children remaining close to both parents after separation (Brennan, 2005; Friesen, Gilbert, Katz-Leavy Osher, & Pullman, 2003; Hopkinson, 2003; Moore, 2001; Smyth, 2012). Some resistance from parents to both these messages is to be expected as both impinge heavily not only on parenting but also on the adult lifestyles of parents. However, most parents are aware that breastfeeding and postdivorce arrangements are important issues in children's well-being, so it is unlikely that adult-centric concerns explain why so few infants in the English speaking world are breast fed for more than a few weeks and so many children are the butt of access disputes. It seems likely that in these and similar instances it is not that popular literature fails to influence parents to behave as psychological research suggests would be best for their children, but that popular literature does not accurately convey these research findings or their implications. Popular writers – or writers seeking to be popular – are often reluctant to deliver messages that will upset their readers, or lead to criticism or misrepresentation in the media, so the messages they convey to parents on sensitive subjects are far from unequivocal. The accepted "line" on infant feeding, for example, in all media, seems to be to pay lip service to "breast is best" but to present breastfeeding and formula feeding as a mother's individual choice between the two options, each of which has pros and cons. Writers usually maintain that they do this to protect mothers who do not, or cannot, breastfeed from feelings of failure. Few researchers are likely to see this as a valid reason for withholding or distorting information. The following quotation from a popular book, *Secrets of a Baby Whisperer*, is typical of the end-points of such discussions.

> The proverbial bottom line is that while it *is* good for a baby to have some breast milk, especially in the first month, if that's not the mother's choice or if for some reason the mother *can't* breast feed, formula feeding is a perfectly acceptable alternative – for some the preferable alternative. (Hogg, 2001, pp. 97–98)

An unintended but insidious effect of presenting breast feeding in this way may be to reduce the extent to which it is taken for granted as the ordinary way for babies to be fed, and, therefore, ironically, to increases in the number of mothers who feel that they "cannot" breast feed or who "try and fail".

Child development information is, of course, most difficult to give away to parents when it is actually contradicted by the teaching of powerful lobby groups; contrariwise it is easiest to give away when the information "offered" is in line with the teaching of influential proselytizing bodies. In the last decade or so, for example, the Christian Right in the United States and campaigns by organizations such as Families for Discipline (now Families First) (www.families-first.org.uk) in the United Kingdom have made it difficult to reach parents and policymakers with the accumulating evidence against negative discipline, especially physical punishment. However, during the same period in the United Kingdom, research findings concerning the importance of stimulation and "educational play" to the development of even the youngest infants have been readily accepted and assimilated by most parents, partly at least because New Labour's agenda for children, made very public through documents such as *Every Child Matters: Change for Children* (Department for Education and Science [DfES], 2002) and *The Birth to Three Matters Framework* (DfES, 2003), prioritized early educational achievement and backed it with the only free child care nationally available: the right to part-time nursery education for three and four year olds.

It is perhaps regrettable that contemporary governments are not much concerned with popular literature for parents. In the twentieth century heyday of such books, the views and attitudes of a few highly regarded experts were relatively widely listened to by media, politicians and policymakers as well as by parents. In the United States, for example, as we have seen, those experts contributed to a major national conference on child development and parenting in each of five generations. From the first three – the National Congress of mothers in 1899, the Conference on Modern Parenthood in 1925 and the Mid-century White House Conference on Children and Youth in 1950 – politicians from Presidents downwards confidently (though somewhat unwisely) anticipated practical assistance with urgent national problems and the press flocked to cover the proceedings. The two gatherings that bracketed the last period, President Carter's White House Conference on Families in 1980 and the Clintons' White House Conference on Early Childhood Development and Learning in 1997 (known as the "conference on the brain") were more exclusively academic and both political and popular interest was lower key. Almost two decades later it is unlikely that a conference on child development would be funded by government or top the agenda of Heads of State or the national news.

The difficulties in "giving away" developmental psychology do not stem only from the potential recipients. Some are implicit in the "information" itself and its modes of transmission. Information should only be presented as "factual" if it reflects consensus or near consensus within the professions concerned with child development, or at least stands well explored and uncontradicted. It takes time and considerable preliminary work and debate for that position to be reached on a particular topic, and even then a new generation and fresh research (often using new technology) may reverse it. The largest and most important current case in point is the growing understanding of early brain development. Popular literature clearly cannot hope – and perhaps should not try – to bring parents practical advice, as opposed to information, based on findings from research frontiers such as this. Professional specialists sometimes address theoretical books to a wide audience including both other professionals and "educated parents", but while the temptation to get important ideas – and usually opinions and conclusions based on them – "out there" is very great, parents' behavior is unlikely to be influenced by a book that gives them little guidance on applying what they read to the care of their own children. If a book does prematurely promote practical application by parents of early research-in-progress (Sunderland, 2006) it risks not only overstating a case that is not yet completely made but also delaying the time when media and parents will take it seriously. Even at this early stage, though, manifesto-type literature addressed to a wide audience (Gerhardt, 2004) may make a powerful contribution to the intellectual context in which research findings come to be understood and parents can eventually be directly addressed.

Even when information that is interesting and relevant to parents is generally agreed, though, even the most straightforwardly factual may be far more difficult to promulgate than it seems. For example, most accidents requiring hospital treatment take place in children's homes, and the nature and number of such accidents is known (Sengoelge, Hasselberg, & Laflamme, 2011). This is information that is of considerable importance to researchers and policymakers, and enormous concern to parents can be of little use in the home itself because such statistics tell parents nothing about the probability or the seriousness of any particular risk to their individual child and, therefore, provide no practical guidance. What they do provide is grist for the media mill where such "facts" are often prominently featured and may do more to provoke risk aversity than to keep children safe. In the early 1990s, balloons were suddenly frowned upon at preschool parties because deflated balloons might be a choking hazard. Right now there are childcare settings where no finger foods – no squares of bread and butter, no slices of apple – are served to babies for fear of choking and consequent litigation. And there are many homes in which children must reach secondary school age before they are allowed to make a cup of tea. The risks are real. Which professional would risk publicly condemning such cautious care because those risks are infinitesimal?

Just as modern communications and attitudes have ended the exclusivity and privilege of professionals' communication with parents, so the sophistication of modern research methods, data analysis and presentation has made its findings difficult for nonspecialists to understand or specialists to explain. Contemporary developmental psychology could be more widely and usefully gifted to parents and others concerned with children if the donors (health professionals as well as researchers), the intermediaries (such as journalists and broadcasters), and the recipients shared some understanding of basic statistical concepts and methods, such as the analysis and presentation of risks and probabilities, the importance of outcome studies and blind trials, the concept of statistical significance and the presentation of different levels, and the vital difference between correlation and causation. There are powerful arguments for the more general teaching of statistics in schools (and that means also in teacher training, of course), but even if "interpreting statistics" came to the forefront of the IT curriculum a filtering process would still be required between research data and popular literature for parents. If the resulting information is to be readily accepted, some of the filtering needs to be through influential groups and proselytizers, perhaps led by government and public services.

The widespread and rapid acceptance amongst UK parents of the importance of providing for children's learning from infancy, already referred to, demonstrates how powerful a juxtaposition of information from developmental psychology and government policy can be. However, as long as such effects depend on the chance sharing of interests, they will be rare. More often, political and socioeconomic considerations make it difficult for governments to bring particular findings from developmental psychology clearly to parents. A topical example is the accumulating data on the quality of nonfamilial child care. The importance of relatively high ratios of caregiving adults to children, especially infants, is stressed in many studies and denied in none. However, there is no group of childcare stakeholders for whom these findings are welcome. With almost all child care in the English speaking world paid for by demand-side funding, ameliorated only by a tangle of tax arrangements, the balance between what childcare businesses and local authorities need to charge and what parents can pay is precarious. More staff inevitably means higher charges. More expensive child care means a reduction in the numbers and/or hours of employed parents and, thus, increases the burden on the exchequer and/or the likelihood of children spending time in unregulated care. It is as unsurprising as it is unfortunate that policy statements and popular reporting of the issue are confused and contradictory. Yet the evidence is persuasive that investment in child care pays, for the child, the family, and the broader society (Havnes & Mogstad, 2011).

Political and socioeconomic considerations can also come to bear on the reception of information and advice. Authors of books written for the lay market need to be aware that opposition will be voiced. This is often appropriate, reflecting the complexity of evidence and the plurality of opinions about child development. However, sometimes the criticism reflects entrenched opinions that are closed or irrelevant to the contents, as the present author found when a recent text on Family Breakdown (Leach, 2014) was greeted with objections in the media before it had even been published – or read. Some of these objections attributed positions – even words – to the author that she had not advocated or pronounced. The processes of giving away can be contentious!

Conclusion

Ever since there has been popular literature aimed at influencing parents, some books have clearly influenced some parents, and some policymakers, judging by changes in established practices, such as swaddling in the eighteenth century, and by government pamphlets and the numbers of readers and their feedback questions in the early twentieth century. However, the use of childcare books as vehicles to carry developmental psychology to parents can be seen as a missed opportunity.

The opportunity was missed largely because of professionals' attitudes to parents. From the very beginning of popular literature of any genre in the seventeenth century, right up until the mid-twentieth century, professionals who wrote about the upbringing of children addressed themselves to their peers, other clinicians or educators, and either ignored or heaped scorn on parents. Perhaps these attitudes to parents are not surprising in the earlier period, when the modern concept of conjugal families and parental rights and responsibilities was only gradually developing, and literacy still separated a mini-minority of educated individuals from everyone else. However, as we have seen, similarly dismissive or antiparent sentiments continued and can be tracked through nineteenth and early twentieth century America via quotes from speakers at the three national conferences held there, one per generation, in 1898, 1925 and 1950. Whatever was wrong with youth, especially the poor caliber of ill-nourished and ill-educated recruits to successive armies, parents were to blame. Less privileged parents were seen as feckless; the most privileged, especially urban middle class mothers, as overindulgent. All this has changed but there are still echoes of these attitudes to be heard in discussions of out of control adolescents, curfews in the United States, ASBOS (antisocial behavior orders) in the United Kingdom and debate on both sides of the Atlantic about the advisability of fining parents for their children's bad behavior.

The late nineteenth and early twentieth century saw parents, on both sides of the Atlantic, beset by their own fertility and their children's mortality and blamed for both by the professional classes. When American experts began to suggest that science could be brought to bear on problems of child health and upbringing, and Holt addressed himself to parents as to nurses, it seems that many parents were eager to listen and to do as he said, even though what he told them to do was difficult. The stakes – infant survival – were high and Holt empowered women to do at least something to make them more favorable. Hundreds of thousands of Holtian leaflets when out to women even in still-rural parts of America and, judging by the thousands of questions that came back, their influence on parents' behavior was real.

Holt passed the best that science then had to offer to as many parents as the media of the day could reach. And Gesell brought child development research to parents, as collaborators as well as audience. But the trend did not continue. Between the wars the experts, as Erikson was scornfully to refer to them in 1950, had contradicted themselves and each other on almost every topic except the poor quality of parenting. Although there was exciting developmental research taking place it was widely dissipated and narrowly known. This was a watershed for popular literature as transport for developmental psychology to parents. Had the next parents' guru been a researcher, or even a clinician whose own practice was firmly research-based, the relationship might have grown alongside research findings. But the next parents' guru was Spock, who was not only apparently uninterested in research himself, but also eager to help parents, vilified for so long, feel able to rely on themselves and their own feelings rather than on information from outside experts.

Spock, of course, became the outside expert; a new father-figure for parents and at last a kindly and understanding one. His success in this role was such that, like any good father, he worked himself out of a job and parents into relative autonomy. By the end of the twentieth century it was clear that most parents no longer needed – or wanted – a guru to guide their child rearing, whether it was a soothing paternalistic voice or information from research professionals. There was, therefore, far less scope for passing on developmental psychology. Indeed, since parenting impacts not only on children but also on parents' own self-image and adult relationships, attempts to influence and change peoples' parenting were often perceived – and sometimes resented – as attempts to change them. The contemporary equivalent of "love me, love my child" is "criticize my child rearing, criticize me". Parents sought practical help with problems they themselves identified, and would accept it from anybody in any medium, but more readily from each other than from outside professionals.

Parental self-confidence, the ending of the cult of the child rearing expert and a lessening of the chasm between those who do their best and those who know best have a twofold price. Firstly, when parenting information and advice from professionals, qualified and self-styled, commentators and parents are all given equal media exposure and parental weight, it is extraordinarily difficult to differentiate information that is based on research or clinical experience from the rest. Secondly, without the controls of professional ethics and peer review there is no control over the content or quality of information or advice given to parents. Some of what is being put out on "reality television" contradicts contemporary developmental psychology and may influence the behavior of some parents in ways that will be damaging to infants (Hird, 2007).

However, if most people no longer want advice to parents to be the exclusive privilege of professionals, almost all parents are as anxious to do the best for their children as they have ever been and are, therefore, still open to convincing information concerning children's well-being, and to practical suggestions as to how they can improve it. If contemporary writers concentrated on providing only that information and those suggestions to parents, popular literature could still play a major role in gifting developmental psychology to them. Such literature would need to expand the horizons of what parents recognize as children's well-being – from physical to emotional care, for example, from the behavior of children and parents to their feelings, and from the development of the rest of children's bodies to the development of their brains. The information such literature provided to parents would need to be more focused than generic baby books, as well as being less ephemeral than other media. Perhaps most importantly of all, information should be factual, in the sense of research-based, and interpretations of it should be clearly distinguishable from opinions. Such literature would be regarded as trustworthy not only by parents but by representatives of other media, politicians and policymakers with all of whom two-way relationships as colleagues and as communicators could be established. Such literature, while "popular" in the sense of being intended as resources for all parents, should not be expected to compete with mass media primarily intended as entertainment but to help it towards accuracy and be helped by its reach.

These are long-term goals. Perhaps the most immediately important role for those who wish to see developmental psychology gifted to parents is to serve as a filter of research findings, and a conduit of information from them, to all who teach the teachers of parents, to those who advise government and policymakers and to sections of the media that can be encouraged to concern their programming more with real life than with reality shows. Some of the best advice for parents ever printed was given by Anna Freud in the last of the Harvard Lectures, "Prohibitions and Permissiveness". My favorite section is on the drives. "Each drive should be looked at and treated on its merits… Is there really a need for the child to repress his oral desires fully? Well, there is not. There is so much opportunity in later life to satisfy these desires in a sublimated form, in a displaced form… It is quite different with the anal drives. There is very little room if any for the anal drives in adult life so they demand… a different attitude from the parents to lead the child's ego to modify them" (Freud, 1952, p. 131). This is not "popular literature for parents" but literature that has been valuable for more than half a century to all who teach or write for parents and, although its source may not always be recognized or acknowledged, is still invaluable today. Once information from developmental psychologists reaches groups of people to whom parents listen, it scarcely matters who writes the final popularization that they read. It was not Holt's original book which carried his influence all over a decade and a continent, but hundreds of thousands of government pamphlets based on it (Holt, 1894). On the other hand John Bowlby, of course, took both the roles of academic researcher and popular communicator himself, with equal success (Bowlby, 1951, 1953) and enduring influence in the lay community (Holmes, 2012).

References

Appleton, J., Fowler, C., & Brown, N. (2014). Friend or foe? An exploratory study of Australian parents' use of asynchronous discussion boards in childhood obesity. *Collegian*, *21*, 151–158.

d'Argonne, M. (1690). L'Education de Monsieur Monncade. Cited in P. Aries (1962) *Centuries of childhood* (trans. R. Baldick), London: Jonathan Cape Ltd.

Azrin, N., & Foxx, R. (1976/1989). *Toilet training in less than a day*. New York: Pocket Books, Simon & Schuster.

Biehle, S. N., & Mickelson, K. D. (2012). First-time parents' expectations about the division of childcare and play. *Journal of Family Psychology, 26*, 36–45.

Bowlby, J. (1951). *Maternal care and mental health*. Geneva: World Health Organization.

Bowlby, J. (1953). *Childcare and the growth of love*. London: Penguin.

Brazelton, B. T. (1989). *Toddlers and parents: A declaration of independence*. Boston, MA: Dell Trade Paperback.

Brazelton, B. T., & Sparrow, J. D. (2002). *Touchpoints: Birth to three: Your child's emotional and behavioral development*. Boston, MA: da Capo Press.

Brennan, D. (2005). Children and families: Forty years of analysis and commentary in the Australian Journal of Social Issues. *Australian Journal of Social Issues, 40*, 73–90.

Butterworth, S. (2007). The press's difficulty in playing by the rules it has created. *The Guardian,* 16 July, 8.

Cadogan, W. (1748). An essay upon nursing and the management of children from their birth to three years of age. In A. Levene (2006) Reasonable creatures: A common sense guide to childcare, *History Today, 56*(12), 30–36.

Clendon-Lodge, R., & Frank, S. (2000). *Plato's theory of education.* London: Routledge Library of Ancient Philosophy.

Corbichon, J. (1556). *Le grand proprietaire de toutes choses* (compiled in Latin by B. de Glanville). Cited in P. Aries (1962) *Centuries of childhood* (trans. R. Baldick), London: Jonathan Cape Ltd.

Defoe, D. (1722). *Moll Flanders* (Ed. A. J. Rivero, 2004). New York: Norton.

Defoe, D. (1724). *Roxanna; The fortunate mistress* (Ed. J. Jack, 1969). Oxford: Oxford University Press.

Della Casa, G. (1609). *Galatee, Manual of etiquette* (French translation) (pp. 162–168). France: Encyclopedia Universalis.

DfES (2002). *Every child matters: Change for children.* London: Department for Education & Science.

DfES (2003). *The birth to three matters framework.* London: Department for Education & Science.

Dobson, J. (1986). *Dare to discipline.* Wheaton, IL: Tyndale.

Eisenberg, A., Murkoff, H. E., & Hathaway, S. E. (1990). *What to expect when you're expecting.* New York: Workman Publishing.

Eisenberg, A., Murkoff, H. E., & Hathaway, S. E. (2002). *What to expect the first year.* New York: Workman Publishing.

Ferber, R. (1985). *Solve your child's sleep problems.* London: Dorling Kindersley.

Ford, G. (2002). *The new contented little baby book.* London: Vermilion.

Freud, A. (1952). Prohibitions and permissiveness. In J. Sandler (Ed.) (1992), *The Harvard Lectures* (pp. 119–133). Institute of Psycho Analysis, London: Karnac Books.

Friesen, B., Gilbert, M., Katz-Leavy J., Osher, T., & Pullman M. (2003). Research in the service of policy change: The "Custody Problem". *Journal of Emotional and Behavioral Disorders, 11,* 39–47.

Frost, J. (2006). *Ask Supernanny: What every parent wants to know.* London: Hodder & Stoughton.

Gerhardt, S. (2004). *Why love matters: How affection shapes a baby's brain.* Hove: Brunner-Routledge.

Gershoff, E. T. (2013). Spanking and child development: We know enough now to stop hitting our children. *Child Development Perspectives, 7,* 133–137.

Gesell, A., & Ilg, F. (1940). *Infant and child in the culture of today.* New York: Harper & Bros.

Gesell, A., & Ilg, F. (1949). *The child from five to ten.* New York: Harper & Bros.

Gesell, A., Ilg, F., & Ames, L. B. (1956). *Youth: The years from ten to sixteen.* New York: Harper & Bros.

Grant, J. (1998). *Raising baby by the book: The education of American mothers.* New Haven, CT: Yale University Press.

Harwood, K., McLean, N., & Durkin, K. (2007). First-time mothers' expectations of parenthood: What happens when optimistic expectations are not matched by later experiences? *Developmental Psychology, 43,* 1–12.

Havnes, T., & Mogstad, M. (2011). No child left behind: subsidized child care and children's long-run outcomes. *American Economic Journal: Economic Policy, 3,* 97–129.

Hird, C. (2007). Small screen. *Prospect, 135,* 77.

Hogg, T. (2001). *Secrets of the baby whisperer.* London: Vermilion.

Holmes, J. (2012). *John Bowlby and attachment theory.* London: Routledge.

Holt, L. E. (1894). *The care and feeding of children: A catechism for the use of mothers and children's nurses.* New York: D. Appleton and Co.

Hopkinson, J. (2003). Advantages ofbreastfeeding: Scientific basis for breastfeeding. In: P. Berens., E. Brun., R. Edwards., S. Ellis., J. Hopkinson., & H. Sullivan (Eds.), *Principals of lactation management* (pp. 2–10). Austin, TX: Department of State Health Services.

Horowitz, F. D. (2014). *Exploring developmental theories: Toward a structural/behavioral model of development.* London: Psychology Press.

Hulbert, A. (2003). *Raising America; experts, parents and a century of advice about children.* New York: A. A. Knopf.

Ingalls Wilder, L. (1933). *Farmer boy.* New York: Harper.

IPPR (2003). *The Lever Faberge family report.* London: Institute for Public Policy Research.

Katz-Wise, S. L., Priess, H. A., & Hyde, J. S. (2010). Gender-role attitudes and behavior across the transition to parenthood. *Developmental Psychology, 46,* 18–28.

Key, E. (1909, reprint 1997). *The century of the child.* New York: Arno.

Leach, P. (1979). *Your baby and child.* London/New York: Penguin Books/A. A.Knopf.

Leach, P. (1992). *Your baby and child with Penelope Leach.* Lifetime Television (1992–1995).

Leach, P. (1994). *Children first, what society must do – and is not doing – for children today.* London/New York: Penguin Books/A.A.Knopf.

Leach, P. (2014). *Family breakdown.* London: Random House.

Levene, A. (2006). Reasonable creatures: A common sense guide to childcare, *History Today, 56*(12), 30–36.

Locke, J. (1660). Thoughts concerning education. In P. Nidditch (Ed.) (1975), *The works of John Locke.* Oxford: Clarendon.

Manzoor, S. (2007). The end of mystique. *The Guardian,* 17 July, 29.

Moore, M. (2001). Current research continues to support breastfeeding benefits. *Journal of Perinatal Education, 10*(3) 38–41.

NFPI (2006). *The power of parenting TV programmes: Help or hazard for today's families.* London: National Family and Parenting Institute.

Plantin, L., & Daneback, K. (2009). Parenthood, information and support on the internet. A literature review of research on parents and professionals online. *BMC Family Practice, 10*(1), 34.

Porter, N., & Ispa, J.M. (2013). Mothers' online message board questions about parenting infants and toddlers. *Journal of Advanced Nursing, 69,* 559–568.

Richards, E. A. (Ed.) (1951). *Proceedings of the mdcentury Whitehouse conference on children and youth: Report of the Conference sessions Dec 3–7 1950* (p. 16). Raleigh, NC: Health Publications Institute.

Richardson, S. (1740). *Pamela; or, virtue rewarded.* London: Rivington & Osborn.

Richardson, S. (1748). *Clarissa, or the history of a young lady.* London: Rivington & Osborn.

Rosemond, J. (1989). *John Rosemond's six-Point Plan for Raising Happy, Healthy Children.* Kansas City, MO: Andrews.

Rousseau, J. J. (1762). *Emile* (A. Bloom (Ed.), 1979). New York: Basic Books.

Sengoelge, M., Hasselberg, M., & Laflamme, L. (2011). Child home injury mortality in Europe: a 16-country analysis. *The European Journal of Public Health, 21,* 166–170.

Senn, M. J. E. (Ed.) (1950). *Symposium on the healthy personality: Transactions of special meetings of the conference on infancy, and childhood, June 8–9 & July 3–4 1950.* New York: Josiah Macy Jr. Foundation.

de Sevigne, Mme (1672). *Lettres* (trans. & Ed. L. Tancock, 1982). *Harmondsworth,* London: Penguin Classics.

Smyth, L. (2012). The social politics of breastfeeding: Norms, situations and policy implications. *Ethics and Social Welfare, 6,* 182–194.

Spock, B. (1946). *The common sense book of baby and child care.* New York: Pocket Books.

Spock, B. (1970). *A teenagers guide to life and love.* New York: Simon & Schuster.

Spock, B. (1988). *Spock on parenting.* New York: Simon & Schuster.

Sterne, L. (1760–1765). *Tristram Shandy,* Vols 1–8. The Columbia Encyclopedia, 6th ed. (2001–2007), New York, NY: Columbia University Press.

Sunderland, M. (2006). *The science of parenting.* London: Dorling Kindersley.

Varet, M. (1680). De L'Education chretienne des enfants. Cited in P. Aries (1962) *Centuries of childhood* (trans. R. Baldick), London: Jonathan Cape Ltd.

Watson, J. B. (1928). *Psychological care of the infant and child.* New York: Norton.

Wicks, R., & Asato, J. (2002). *The family report.* London: The Social Market Foundation.

Witmer, H. L., & Kotinsky, R. (1952). *Personality in the making: The fact-finding report of the midcentury Whitehouse conference on children and youth.* New York: Harper.

3

Opportunities and Obstacles in Giving Away Research on Marital Conflict and Children

E. Mark Cummings, W. Brad Faircloth, Patricia M. Schacht, Kathleen P. McCoy, and Alice C. Schermerhorn

The purpose of this chapter is to consider some of the issues and obstacles for making research on children and marital conflict available in a manner than can directly and effectively benefit the well-being of children and families. Highlighting the significance of this goal, a considerable body of research has accumulated over the past two decades to indicate that marital conflict can threaten the well-being and healthy development of children (Cummings & Davies, 2010; Cummings & Schatz, 2012). Moreover, evidence has also emerged to indicate how parents should or should not express marital disagreements for the sake of the children. Furthermore, great strides have been made in the development of theory concerning how and why marital conflict affects children, potentially providing a further guide for parents on how to handle their disagreements for the sake of the children. Thus, there is a solid research-based foundation for helping parents improve their conduct of everyday disagreements and conflicts for the sake of the children. At the same time, it is clear that it is not enough simply to publish or even publicize research results and indicate implications for parents, children and families to optimally benefit. More concrete steps must be taken to make these findings available and useable for families.

The Wiley Handbook of Developmental Psychology in Practice: Implementation and Impact, First Edition.
Edited by Kevin Durkin and H. Rudolph Schaffer.
© 2016 John Wiley & Sons, Ltd. Published 2016 by John Wiley & Sons, Ltd.

These issues are pertinent to the notion of translational research as a strategy for more effectively giving away the lessons learned from research on marital conflict and children. Translational research is the process by which practitioners and researchers link together their expertise to reduce societal problems, such as divorce and marital dissatisfaction, which ultimately lead to child adjustment problems. Yet, although many prevention and intervention programs are well intentioned, they often lack critical components to being able to create a truly effective program. Therefore, there are both obstacles and opportunities for the future in examining what are the critical components for effective prevention and intervention programs and how they can be implemented successfully.

The gap addressed by translational research merits brief discussion. Just as it is not enough to generate research and theory in the hope that parents will eventually benefit from the availability of this information in the scientific literature, it is not enough simply to develop programs that have good intentions for helping children and families. Programs need to be informed by the available research, on the one hand, and evaluated with regard to their efficacy, on the other. Although many well-meaning policies and programs are designed to ameliorate problems for children and families, there are frequently disconnects between the characteristics of applied programs on the one hand and the relevant scholarly research base on the other. That is, the elements of applied programs may be no more than loosely-based on actual evidence, even when the term "evidence based" is ascribed to these programs. Moreover, many applied programs are rarely, if ever, subjected to rigorous evaluation, which limits both confidence in the effectiveness of these programs and opportunities to improve the programs over time.

Translational research is concerned with addressing the gaps between scholarly wisdom and evidence-based practice. Optimal programs seek to cull key findings, principles and concepts from scholarly and academic directions and then translate these elements into applied programs that are applicable and effective "in the real world". Steps in the development of optimal translational research programs include (i) translating evidence from basic research into evidence-based, consumer-friendly programs, and (ii) rigorously evaluating the efficacy of the applied intervention programs.

This chapter is concerned with the efforts that have been made towards accomplishing these goals over the past several years for the clinically-relevant problem of children and marital conflict. Specifically, it is concerned with describing the bases for developing a program on marital conflict and children and the programmatic steps that we have undertaken over the past several years to advance a program that achieves the aim of preventing marital discord for the sake of children in community samples. We present brief descriptions of the two prevention trials that have been published in this line of work (Cummings, Faircloth, Mitchell,

Cummings, & Schermerhorn, 2008; Faircloth & Cummings, 2008) and then close with a discussion of potential contributions, including potential for the actual implementation of the research, and outline future directions for further advancing this line of research.

Culling Key Findings, Principles and Concepts from Scholarly and Academic Directions

A critical aspect of evidence-based research is that the program be closely based on an empirical foundation. Our experience is that this term may be used rather loosely. Our commitment is to truly evidence-based work that serves to "give away" research in the context of programs accessible and appealing to community families. Moreover, we have been committed over time to the generation of research findings that would support prevention for marital conflict for the sake of the children. To clarify this aspect of our program, lines of research and evidence that support the elements of our prevention programs are now briefly reviewed. We feel attention to this aspect of program development is critical; one cannot "give away" research if one does attend first to whether programs adequately reflect latest advances in the relevant research.

What are the bases for advocating prevention of marital conflict for children's sake?

Marital conflict is linked with a wide range of adjustment problems, including depression, alcohol problems, and divorce in adults, and behavioral, emotional and academic problems in children (Cummings & Davies, 2002, 2010). Moreover, marital conflict affects children directly through exposure, and indirectly by affecting parenting and parent–child relationships (Davies & Cummings, 2006). For example, parental conflicts about money (Papp, Cummings, & Goeke-Morey, 2009) may bear on subsequent decisions about the material circumstances and activities of their offspring. Furthermore, children are often quite well aware of interparental conflicts, even if they are not physically present in the same room as the conflicts are expressed (Cummings & Davies, 2010). Crucially, the effects of parental conflict are not limited to the proximal period of the child's life; interparental conflict when children are around kindergarten age has ramifications for the children's adjustment in middle childhood and adolescence (Cummings, George, McCoy, & Davies, 2012; Kouros, Cummings, & Davies, 2010).

What is the gain from preventing marital conflict in community families?

In addition to adding to risk for family with clinically significant problems (e.g., parental depression) (Cummings & Davies, 1994), interparental conflict serves as a risk factor for a broad spectrum of community families (Amato & Booth, 2001; Grych & Fincham, 1990), including families without clinically significant problems (Cowan, Cowan, & Schulz, 1996; Liberman, van Horn, & Ippen, 2005). That is, the risk for future problems with marital conflict is present for virtually all families (Cowan, Cowan, & Schultz, 1996; Cowan and Cowan, 2002; Liberman, van Horn, & Ippen, 2005).

Moreover, despite this evidence, there is a scarcity of programs to systematically educate parents about the effects of marital conflict on children. The advisability of teaching couples better ways to handle their conflicts before serious marital problems develop supports prevention approaches (Cummings & Davies, 2002). Couples in distressed marriages are faced with myriad factors hindering benefiting from prevention at this point in the relationship, including sensitization, with accompanying behavioral and emotional over-reactivity in conflict situations (Davies, Sturge-Apple, Winter, Cummings, & Farrel, 2006). Among other factors undermining the possibility for reversing conflict process once it has escalated, couples in distressed marriages evidence negative tracking of partner behavior and communications and negative cognitive distortions about the partner's motives and behaviors (Cummings & Davies, 1994). Thus, after a certain point of marital distress, there is little "right" a spouse can do from the perspective of the partner, and thus reduced possibilities for improving the marital relationship. In sum, these problems are far easier to reverse before they become chronic, escalated, and highly negative.

That is, it is likely cheaper and easier to intervene early in trajectories of risk processes than to wait until problems become full-blown and stable, and therefore resistant to amelioration (Cummings, Davies, & Campbell, 2000). Given the well-established links between negative marital conflict strategies and children's adjustment problems, prevention efforts aimed at changing parents' conflict tactics before they become severe hold promise for altering family dynamics and risk and protective processes in the family.

What are the key findings, principles and concepts?

An initial step was to discern the key messages from research concerning marital conflict and children, including the themes and issues that might serve as bases for a prevention program. The first element we decided to include was information about how specifically parents can handle conflicts for the sake of the children. This element of the program was relatively straightforward for us to decide to incorporate, as a core direction in our research over the past two decades has been to conduct research that has implications for parents on the distinctions between constructive and destructive conflict for the sake of the children (Cummings & Davies, 1994). Moreover, prevention research is little informed by research on marital conflict and children. Despite the claims sometimes made, truly "evidence-based" programs have not been developed or tested that are closely based on the now extensive literature on children and marital conflict (Cummings & Davies, 2002; Davies & Cummings, 2006). Accordingly, this direction was the primary and focal element in our initial one-visit program (Faircloth & Cummings, 2008). We also incorporated some of the effective programmatic elements from past couple therapy research, specifically, communication training directions from empirically-supported couple conflict programs.

Encouraged by promising initial evidence to support this direction (Faircloth & Cummings, 2008), we decided that it would be possible and desirable for community parents to participate in a somewhat longer program extended over four visits. Accordingly, we also felt we had the time and resource to incorporate more material. Notably, we also added an explicit theoretical foundation, both to more coherently guide the elements of the program (Borkowski, Smith, & Aka, 2007) and also to provide an integrative theme for parents to understanding the concepts underlying our program. We next briefly consider, in turn, the scientific and scholarly bases for including each of these elements of our program.

Empirical bases: What are constructive and destructive conflict for children?

There is consensus in the literature that it is not whether, but how, couples handle conflicts that matters for children (Cummings & Davies, 1994; Grych & Fincham, 1990). Also, there is agreement that couple conflicts, even daily disagreements, cannot truly be avoided. Thus, better-managed conflicts are the appropriate aim of prevention or intervention (Gottman, 1994). Identifying the characteristics of constructive and destructive conflict thus is pertinent to teaching parents how to more effectively handle interparental conflicts for the sake of the children.

Some forms of marital conflict tactics, strategies and communications have been indicated as risk factors, that is, they increase children's risk probabilistically for adjustment problems and negative reactivity. Interspousal aggression, verbal aggression, stonewalling (silent treatment, sulking, withdrawal), and child-related conflict have each been linked with children's adjustment problems. Moreover, children's immediate stress responses support interspousal aggression, verbal aggression, stonewalling, and child-related conflict as risk factors (Cummings & Davies, 1994).

Until recently, less was known about possibly compensatory marital conflict behaviors *during* conflict or behaviors that promote children's positive responding as opposed to simply reducing negative reactivity. Moreover, another gap was scant demonstration of the impact of exposure *in the home*, leaving questions about generalizability and ecologically validity of findings.

Towards addressing these questions, recent work has advanced the theoretical and empirical bases or criteria for distinguishing between constructive and destructive conflict. Children are not simply affected by the frequency or physical characteristics of parental conflict behaviors; children's perceptions of the meaning of conflicts for themselves and their families are critical to the impact of conflict. Moreover, this meaning of conflict for children is most informatively discerned from their responding. Accordingly, it follows that children's responding is the best indicator of distinctions between behaviors and categories of constructive versus destructive conflicts.

According to emotional security theory (EST), the meaning of marital conflict is related to children's assessment of the emotional security implications of conflict, which can be discerned from children's emotional, behavioral, and cognitive reactions. For example, following EST, Goeke-Morey, Cummings, Harold, and Shelton (2003) classified behaviors eliciting significantly more negative than positive emotions as "destructive", based on the notion that exposure reduced children's sense of emotional security based on the induced negative reactivity. By contrast, behaviors resulting in more positive than negative behaviors were categorized as "constructive", based on the principle that increased positivity reflects increased well-being in the face of conflict.

Applying these criteria, support, problemsolving, and affection were identified as constructive behaviors occurring *during* conflict. Moreover, these same criteria indicated that conflict resolution *at the end* of conflicts is constructive (Cummings & Davies, 1994; Goeke-Morey, Cummings, and Papp, 2007). Applying the criteria for classifying behaviors as destructive, threat to the intactness of the marriage, physical aggression towards the spouse or with objects, marital pursue and withdrawal, nonverbal anger, verbal hostility were classified as destructive.

Addressing issues of the external validity, children's reactions to forms of parental expressions of conflict behaviors in the home were also examined. Affection, support, calm discussion, and resolution emerged as constructive behaviors whereas threat, personal insult, verbal hostility, defensiveness, nonverbal hostility, withdrawal, and personal distress qualified as destructive behaviors (Cummings, Goeke-Morey, & Papp, 2003, 2004; Goeke-Morey et al., 2007). Cummings, Goeke-Morey, Papp, and Dukewich (2002) reported that parents' positive emotionality during marital conflicts in the home were constructive from the children's perspective whereas their negative emotionality, including mad, sad, and scared responses, was destructive. Moreover, Goeke-Morey, Papp, and Cummings (2013) found that, with 8–19-year-olds followed over a three-year period, increases in exposure to hostile marital conflict were associated with *increases* in children's negative emotionality, threat, self-blame, and skepticism about resolution.

Theoretical bases: EST

Optimal intervention programs are informed by, and developed through, empirical research and guided by a theoretical framework (Borkowski, Smith, & Aka, 2007; Nation et al., 2003). Emotional security theory guides the present proposal and provides a well-established theoretical basis for accounting for the effects of discord on adolescents' adjustment (Davies & Cummings, 1994).

A useful analogy is to think about emotional security as a bridge between the child and the world. When the marital relationship is functioning well, it serves as a secure base, a structurally sound bridge, supporting the child's exploration and relationships with others. When destructive marital conflict erodes the bridge, children may become hesitant to move forward and lack confidence, or may move forward in a dysregulated way, unable to find appropriate footing within themselves or in interaction with others.

EST proposes that interparental conflict is harmful to children because it decreases children's confidence in the stability, safety and emotional availability of the family. Destructive conflict undermines children's emotional security, reflected in children's intense negative emotional reactions to conflict, behavioral strategies to reduce the threat of conflict, and cognitive representations of the family as unstable and conflicts as unresolvable. Over time, these reactions may contribute to chronic anxiety or depression, tendencies to act out aggressively, and impairments in social and academic functioning. Consistent with the theme that all elements be empirically based, EST is supported by several recent and rigorous longitudinal tests of its theoretical propositions (Cummings, Schermerhorn, Davies, Goeke-Morey, & Cummings, 2006; Davies, Harold, Cummings, & Goeke-Morey, 2002; Davies, Sturge-Apple, Bascoe, & Cummings, 2014; Winter, Davies, & Cummings, 2010).

Accordingly, principles of EST were also added to the program as a second major program element. That is, towards fostering parents' understanding of the principles and concepts underlying parental educational components, the significance of maintaining emotional security, even during conflicts, was stressed in our program, including the importance of secure interparental attachment, parent–child attachment, and children's emotional security about the interparental relationship. Thus, parents are encouraged to keep foremost in mind the value these relationships, even when faced with threatening or intense conflict situations.

Benefiting from past work on ameliorating couple conflicts

Elements of the program for parents also build upon approaches derived from couples therapy and research, especially the communication training. That is, although our work addressed a unique gap towards improving marital conflict for the sake of the children based on translating this research literature into prevention materials, we also sought to benefit from successful elements from adult marital conflict interventions. There is support for relations between marital communication training approaches towards improving couple communication and conflict management (Gottman & Gottman, 1999; Gottman, Katz, & Hooven, 2013; Markman & Floyd, 1980). Thus, communication training is another element of the program, building upon intervention techniques receiving empirical support in the literature on interventions for marital conflict. These elements of the program also provided parents with an opportunity for active training in handling marital conflict for parents, adding to the diversity of the program materials, which is another characteristic of successful prevention programs (Borkowski, Smith, & Aka, 2007).

Translating Basic Research into Applied Programs

The development of applied programs at the level of the "nuts and bolts" concerns largely unfamiliar matters for investigators trained in scholarly research traditions. At the same time, individuals comfortable in applied contexts may have limited understanding of scholarly traditions for evaluating evidence, including research design issues essential to advancing the scientific bases for applied programs and the sophisticated approaches to coding observational data and statistical analyses that may be needed. These facts present significant and fundamental challenges and obstacles to achieving the goal of translating basic research into applied programs.

Strengths of a psychoeducational approach for giving away research

An initial decision was to base on the program on a psychoeducational approach. This decision was consistent with the form of information that we wished to convey (i.e., research-based knowledge about marital conflict and children) and that the program was intended as prevention not therapy for community families. There is considerable basis for holding that community families can benefit from the presentation of information about family functioning (Webster, 1994; Sanders & Calam, Chapter 5, this volume). Teaching parents "to understand and identify which aspects of their behavior are detrimental to child adjustment can be a powerful intervention in itself" (Turner & Dadds, 2001, p. 403). Educational programs may increase knowledge, leading to improvements in behavior and capabilities in handling future problems (Morgan, Nu'Man-Shepard, & Allin, 1990). Important for prevention efforts, such programs may be less daunting and more appealing to more individuals than intensive interventions (Pehrson & Robinson, 1990). Group methods of dissemination are more also cost effective than individual methods (Johnson, 1994), which is another consideration if relatively large groups of community families are the intended audience. At the same time, if the focus of the program is information, it is essential that the information be sound and likely to benefit parents and families. Carefully ensuring that information is firmly based on the latest research is one way to meet that goal.

The inherent challenge of translating research findings into a prevention program

The development of effective program materials is as much art as science, and there is a limited template with regard to the characteristics of the best programs (Borkowski, Smith, & Aka, 2007). Thus, the development of program materials that translate research materials into an effective program constitute a significant challenge, minimally, and can be a significant obstacle. Moreover, some of these demands may vary depending on the goals of the program. For example, a common wisdom is that prevention efforts should be comprehensive but at the same time it is important to determine the "right amount of treatment" (Borkowski, Smith, & Aka, 2007).

Thus, it is not the case that "more is necessarily better" when providing programs for community families that are concerned with "giving away" research findings. Investigators must be careful to not provide too little or too much treatment, such that participants are left needing more or, alternatively, are overwhelmed with the amount of visits that they must partake in. When too much is asked of participants (e.g., too many visits, too much time required for the treatment), programs may experience high attrition levels, which ultimately influences that researcher's ability to evaluate the effectiveness of the program. In our most recently completed program (Cummings & Schatz, 2012) we endeavored to provide a balance by asking participants to partake in four visits that lasted on average two and a half hours. This level of participation proved manageable for many community families, as indicated by low attrition levels during the course of the four week program.

Using varied teaching methods

In addition to the art of attempting to present the appropriate amount of treatment, preventative approaches are advised to employ multiple teaching methods, so that the information being conveyed is interesting and engaging (Borkowski, Smith, & Aka, 2007). Presenting the material by utilizing several different modes of instruction helps to keep the participants' attention as well as make the material memorable. For example, we decided that simply lecturing adults would not have made the information optimally memorable or interesting and, therefore, would have decreased the effectiveness of the program. Keeping the presentation of information lively helps to lower attrition rates and keep individuals committed to programs. Thus, the information was conveyed through multiple different mechanisms, including PowerPoint, games, one-on-one training, and small-group discussions (Cummings & Schatz, 2012). For elements of the program designed for children, as another example, puppets, stories and games were among the mechanisms used to teach the children about the program. A multimethod presentation advanced keeping the visits lively, interesting and fun for the participants.

Evaluating participant satisfaction

Related to these points, another important goal is to assess how much families found the program enjoyable, which ultimately relates to the potential of the program to reach as many families as possible. With regard to this goal, we administered a consumer satisfaction questionnaire at the end of the program to ask for the participants' opinions about the administration of our program, and to ensure the information was conveyed in ways that were appealing to participants. The results, which indicated high levels of participant satisfaction with the program (Cummings & Schatz, 2012), reassured us that participants were satisfied with the way the visits were conducted and, in fact, enjoyed them. Thus, we concluded that the characteristics of our program, including using a mix of teaching materials, supported an appealing program, and thus contributed to the potential of the program to optimally give away the lacunae of research about marital conflict and children.

Well trained staff and positive relationships with participants

Other recommendations made in the literature for optimal prevention programs include fostering positive relationships with participants and training the staff well (Borkoswki, Smith, & Aka, 2007; Nation et al., 2003). We have found that maintaining well trained and enthusiastic staff is essential to delivering and presenting the program materials. Staff must receive extensive training to ensure that the treatment is being administered appropriately and consistently. It is also vital that experimenters create a warm relationship with participants to make the environment one in which everyone is comfortable. Having a warm environment invites participants to ask questions whenever they please and to feel at ease, which is fundamental to an optimal learning environment for a parent education program. Quality checks on staff interactions with participants, as well as formally assessing participant satisfaction, help to ensure that a warm, comfortable environment is created for each family. These elements are vital to reducing attrition and successfully recruiting all family members when this is required, including mothers, fathers and children.

Manualized programs and fidelity checks

Manualizing program materials contributes to the uniform and consistent presentation of the program, and also fosters the replicability of the program by other investigators. That is, having protocols manualized minimizes discrepancies and differences among those who administer programs. In Cummings and Schatz (2012), all members of the research team followed a manualized protocol that outlined all elements and features of the program, with a separate manual developed for each visit. The protocols not only outlined the procedures, but also exactly what the experimenters were expected to say. Additionally, each visit was recorded and quality checks were performed randomly throughout the project to ensure that the protocol was being followed; that is, trained observers watched the visits to score treatment fidelity and ensure that standards for meeting criteria for adequate treatment fidelity were met.

Significant obstacles: Maintaining sufficient size, stability and quality of staff

Prevention research makes great demands on staffing. For example, the procedures described in Cummings and Schatz (2012) require that 6–8 staff participate in every visit for each family. Given the multimethod forms of the programs, the inclusion of program elements for children in some cases and the need often to offer care for siblings in many cases, the requirements for videotaping and other data collection and storage, and many other elements, the demands on staffing are high. More requirements for staff follow from the relatively long-term nature of data collection and program implementation, and the need for staff stability and staff with advanced degrees to accomplish many of the goals. Moreover, advancing an optimal program for giving away research in this area requires a programmatic series of studies, which puts further demands on staff size, stability and quality.

Accordingly, given that the most expensive aspect of behavioral research is personnel cost, prevention and intervention research is likely to be expensive. In this context, obtaining and maintaining sufficient funding is a significant obstacle for research. Prevention, as opposed to clinical intervention, may also be less favorably viewed by federal agencies funding behavioral research. Moreover, funding is highly competitive, and it is very challenging to maintain funding between projects. Thus, there are obstacles to ensuring that key staff can remain. In the fortunate event of the receipt of major funding, it may be necessary to start over and recruit and train a relatively large staff, including the most advanced members of the research team. One cannot expect key personnel to stay on projects as one awaits the outcomes of lengthly and uncertain review processes for external funding, with even further delays between likely between notice of upcoming awards and the funding being received on-campus. We have been fortunate to obtain major funding for projects in this area. Nonetheless, the optimal solution is a standing commitment, at least to key staff committed to translational research, by the pertinent University or other supporting institution, in order to minimize the negative impact of staff uncertainty and staff attrition between awards of external funding for the conduct of translational research projects.

Research Design Considerations and Evaluation of Applied Programs

Another critical element for optimal translational research is appropriate research design and evaluation to demonstrate the efficacy of the program. This element is either missing or may be inadequate in many applied research projects. Discussion of some of the requirements, opportunities and obstacles for adequately conducting this phase of translational research is provided here.

Randomized control trials

Critical to the interpretability of findings is that participants are randomly assigned to conditions, including treatment and control conditions. Otherwise, it is not possible to determine whether any results are to the treatment condition or preexisting differences between the groups.

Randomized control trials (RCTs) are increasingly required for publication in top refereed journals and have become the gold standard for prevention trials. Related to this, decisions about control conditions are critical, including whether to use a no-treatment control (e.g., wait-listed control group) (Faircloth & Cummings, 2008) or a control group that carries more demanding tests for treatment efficacy. For Cummings and Schatz (2012), the comparison group was a self-study control given text-based resources that presented findings in text form on marital conflict, parenting and children comparable to the treatment conditions. Thus, similar information was made available to both groups, with the control group based on a self-help model (Wolchik et al., 2000). This approach reduced the likelihood of treatment outcomes due to placebo effects, but also advanced the possibility that both treatment and control groups would evidence gains, thereby reducing the likelihood of treatment effects.

Pretesting, short-term and long-term follow-up tests

Pretesting is essential to further controlling for the possibility of pre-existing differences contributing to treatment effects. Another major concern is to show that treatment effects are more than short term, for example, evident only at testing at the end of treatment. Thus, follow-up testing (e.g., 6 month and 1 year follow-ups) is needed to more completely demonstrate the value of prevention programs. Long-term follow-up tests may be especially important for prevention trials, as benefits may only emerge over time when participants are at-risk but do not yet demonstrate problems. In the case of prevention for marital conflict, benefits for children may be expected to be found from improved marital conflict behavior, but these effects are not necessarily immediately apparent. That is, changes in marital conflict may need to be in place for some time for one to reasonably expect that child adjustment will be beneficially affected. Thus, Cummings and Schatz (2012) found that child adjustment improved in parental treatment conditions, but only over time and as a function of improvements in marital conflict behavior.

Multimethod assessments

Given the focus of prevention trials on administering programs, there is a temptation, and to some extent a need, to minimize the demands of assessment. Assessment packages are necessarily limited in relation to research that focuses on developmental process. However, it can be a mistake for goals of providing cogent evidence for the value of prevention trials to neglect advancing appropriate assessment.

Thus, use of only questionnaire measures of intended outcomes may limit the interpretability of outcomes in some cases, since such measures are prone to social desirability effects. Questionnaires may also be relatively imprecise in documenting program effects. For example, extant marital conflict instruments make relatively few distinctions among marital conflict behaviors.

For this reason, one direction for assessment should be to develop measures that document whether the most specific outcomes targeted by the program are affected. For example, in our studies we developed a brief questionnaire to test parents' knowledge of the best ways to handle marital conflicts, based on the material presented in the psychoeducational program (Cummings & Schatz, 2012; Faircloth & Cummings, 2008).

One can also code much more detail about any changes in marital conflict behaviors based on observational records of marital conflict behaviors in the laboratory, and such coding provides more objective record of any changes. We found that observational records provided valuable indices of positive changes in marital conflict behaviors associated with participation in the program (Cummings & Schatz, 2012).

Finally, one may want to document that any changes that occur are seen in the home as well as the laboratory. Thus, it may also be worth considering the use of records of changes in marital conflict behaviors in the home. For example, use of diary recording procedures can increase the ecological validity of program effects (Cummings, Goeke-Morey, & Papp, 2003). This direction in coding marital conflict in the home based on parents' diary records is being pursued in an ongoing prevention project for parents and adolescents.

The CONSORT method

There are increasing demands with regard to the conduct and reporting of prevention and intervention trials. The CONSORT (consolidated standards of reporting trials) method provides uniform standards, fostering high quality reports of the results of RCTs. Biased treatment effects are associated with poorly designed and reported RCTs (Altman et al., 2001). Poorly designed interventions reporting inadequate information pose a serious threat to the validity and application of evidence-based practices.

With regard to the history of the CONSORT method, in 1996 the Asilomar Working Group on Recommendations for Reporting of Clinical Trials in the Biomedical Literature, along with 30 other experts comprised of medical journal editors, clinical trial experts, epidemiologists, and methodologists, met to produce a single coherent recommendation for presenting the results of RCTs. This meeting resulted in the publication of the Consolidated Standards of Reporting Trials (CONSORT) Statement in the *Journal of American Medical Association* (*JAMA*).

In 2001, the revised CONSORT statement (www.consort-statement.org) was concurrently published in three separate medical journals (Moher, Schulz, & Altman, 2001a, 2001b, 2001c, 2012). The CONSORT statement was originally prepared for researchers conducting medical research. However, it was soon shown that the CONSORT items are applicable to psychosocial trials (Stinson, McGrath, & Yamada, 2003). Over 300 journals have endorsed the CONSORT statement to date, with many supporting journals requiring the use and report of the CONSORT flow diagram. Meeting the requirements of the CONSORT method is thus an important requirement, and possible obstacle, for advancing the likelihood of positive evaluation of these directions.

The CONSORT statement includes a Checklist, consisting of 22 items identi-fied as essential for judging the reliability of findings (e.g., "How participants were allocated to interventions" and "Interpretation of the results"), and a Flow Diagram that visually depicts the flow of participants taking part in a RCT (i.e., the number of participants who were enrolled, given the intervention, followed-up with, and included in the primary data analysis). The majority of items on the checklist address key threats to internal validity (i.e., randomization, blinding, attrition, etc.), with one item vaguely asking for information on generalizability (Glasgow, McKay, Piette, & Reynolds, 2001). Future iterations of the CONSORT statement will likely focus more on reporting of external validity issues such as the represen-tativeness of the setting and the sustainability of the intervention from the point of view of the provider and the participant (Glasgow et al., 2006).

The main purpose of the CONSORT statement is to allow researchers to accu-rately and transparently report the conduct of RCTs. Additionally, the CONSORT statement can be utilized by prevention researchers at various stages of RCT conception, design, and implementation. For instance, researchers may wish to rely on the checklist as a tool for planning and developing study methodology, as a tracking tool during the recruitment period, and as a guide for analyses. Presentation of the CONSORT flow chart in RCT reports allows readers/other researchers to evaluate the merits of an RCT, the extent to which attrition or recruitment prob-lems serve as confounds to the study findings, and whether "intent to treat" (ITT) or "per protocol" analyses have been conducted.

Evaluating treatment effects by ITT requires the inclusion of all randomized participants in the analyses regardless of whether they actually comply with entry criteria, receive the treatment they were assigned to, or withdraw from the study. In contrast, evaluation of treatment effects following the "per protocol" approach requires the inclusion of only those participants who meet criteria for inclusion and adhere to the project protocol (Lewis & Machin, 1993). Each of these approaches to evaluating RCT's has its proponents and critics. For instance, it has been argued that omitting any participant from evaluation, for any reason, biases tests of treatment effects because it no longer compares the groups as randomized (Peto et al., 1976). Alternatively, by retaining participants in the evaluation who either did not meet inclusion criteria, received a treatment different from that which they were randomly assigned, or withdrew from the study pose threats to the external validity and generalization of findings. These two approaches are commonly contrasted, and when the results of both approaches yield similar results the strength of any conclusions drawn are strengthened (Lewis & Machin, 1993).

Findings from Initial Marital Conflict Focused Prevention Trials

Reviewed next are the two translational prevention studies that we have published to date on marital conflict focused psychoeducational programs, including the implications of the findings for practice and policy.

The one-visit program

Faircloth and Cummings (2008) tested the effectiveness of a one-session prevention program for improving marital conflict resolution skills, as well as parents' knowledge about marital conflict, based on questionnaire-based evaluations. Fifty-five couples with an oldest child no more than six years of age were randomly assigned to either an immediate treatment (n = 41) or a six-month wait-listed control (n = 14) group, with assessments at pretest, posttest, and six month and one year follow-ups.

The goal was to educate couples about the research findings regarding the behavioral and emotive characteristics of constructive and destructive forms of conflict, as identified by children's responses to witnessing conflict between their parents (Goeke-Morey, Cummings, Harold, & Shelton, 2003). A unique feature of the intervention was that *the implications of marital conflict for the children* were central in the presentation of all program materials, based on extensive empirical and theoretical work on children and marital conflict (Cummings & Davies, 1994, 2002). The second portion of the program taught couples specific principles, skills and techniques they could use to identify, understand, and replace destructive behaviors with constructive behaviors. These techniques were adapted from active listening techniques widely used in empirically informed couples therapy and premarital counseling programs (Rogers, 1965). Notably, a 19-item questionnaire was developed for this study; it assessed couples' knowledge of the effects of marital conflict on children and the family, to provide a targeted assessment of the effectiveness of the psychoeducational program (also used later in Cummings & Schatz, 2012).

Results indicated program effectiveness in improving parents' knowledge regarding marital conflict across all assessment periods (but without comparisons to the control group) and in increasing parents' knowledge relative to a wait-list control group at the posttest. Relative to preprogram assessments, couples in the treatment group displayed less hostility in front of their children six months after the program, and improved in conflict tactics at both follow-ups.

Thus, as expected, parents participating in this evidence-based parental education about marital conflict showed greater knowledge about constructive versus destructive conflict tactics and resolution strategies in comparison to a wait-list control group in this randomized trials research design. Other findings supported a positive relationship between parents' knowledge about more optimal marital conflict strategies and reported actual behaviors during marital conflicts.

The results of this study thus support the promise of parental educational approaches emphasizing the protective and beneficial effects of positive and constructive conflict behaviors and tactics and the proposition that parents' knowledge about marital conflict issues can be an "active ingredient" in prevention programs for improving parents' conflict behavior in the family. Initial support was thus found for the effectiveness of this direction in programs for helping parents, marriages and children, by reducing destructive marital conflict during everyday marital conflicts. The findings also add to the case for preventive work concerning the application of basic research findings for targeting known precursors to maladaptive development (Cicchetti & Cohen, 1995).

In summary, suggesting the promise of a short-term interventions, Faircloth and Cummings (2008) reported improvements in multiple dimensions of marital conflict in couples with children six years of age or younger from a single psycho-educational session. However, although the findings were intriguing, small sample sizes, limited posttest comparisons between treatment and control conditions, the possibility of placebo effects with a wait-list control, and the reliance on self-report about marital conflict limited interpretation of this program. Moreover, the presentation of the evidence-based information about marital conflict was constrained in a single session and, thus, there may well be the potential to foster greater gains with the presentation of more extensive prevention programs.

The four-visit program

Cummings and Schatz (2012) tested a more elaborate program, including much more extensive parent education about marital conflict, also testing a child psycho-educational program. Specifically, a four-session psychoeducational program about marital conflict for community families was developed. Couples with children between four and eight years of age were randomly blocked into one of three groups: (i) a parent-only group (PO, n = 24); (ii) a parent–child group (PC, n = 33); or (iii) a self-study control group (SS, n = 33). Both fathers and mothers participated in parent programs. Assessments were conducted during pretest and posttest, and at six month and one year follow-ups.

Compared to Faircloth and Cummings (2008), this program included a more extensive psychoeducational program, comparisons between treatment and control conditions pretest and posttest, and at six month and one year follow-ups, a self-study control group to reduce placebo effects, and observational assessments of marital conflict. The approach represents a balance between either very short (Faircloth & Cummings, 2008) or lengthy (i.e., clinical treatments) programs. The focus was on improving parents' ways of expressing disagreement, rather than necessarily decreasing the frequency of conflict, although better conflict resolution skills may reduce rates of conflict. The program was also more explicitly guided by EST, emphasizing the significance of maintaining the quality of emotional bonds among all family members during marital conflict. Moreover, it was expected that improving marital conflict would eventually result in positive changes in family-wide functioning (Cowan & Cowan, 2002; Cummings & Davies, 2002). Parents in the self-study condition were given relevant materials to read, including books on marital conflict and children, parenting, and an extensive supplemental reading list. The child component was concerned with teaching children about emotional and social coping with marital conflict and family stress.

The focus in analyses was on whether (i) participation in a psychoeducational program for parents improved marital conflict, especially based on observational assessments of marital conflict, and (ii) changes in marital conflict subsequently improved marital satisfaction, parenting and child adjustment. Given the absence of hypotheses about expected differences between these groups on marital conflict (e.g., the parent program was the same for PO and PC groups), the treatment groups were combined for the purposes of examining effects on marital conflict.

Greater constructive and less destructive marital conflict was observed at all assessments for treatment groups. Most evident were changes in conflict behaviors, indicating that parents changed their basic orientation with their partners in conflict situations, towards an approach of being more respectful of their emotional relationship with each other, and fostering the security of family relationships. Thus, following participation in the psychoeducational program, parents were more supportive of their partner, more emotionally positive during interactions, more likely to advance towards the resolution of arguments, and more constructive during conflict discussions, consistent with the message of the program that preserving and advancing the quality of emotional relationships in the family is more important than dominating the outcomes of arguments.

These changes were also linked with improvements in other family processes. That is, changes in marital conflict in the treatment group were linked with positive changes over time in marital satisfaction, parenting, and child adjustment. Changes in knowledge over time were linked with changes in conflict behaviors, suggesting that knowledge may be an active agent in improvements found in the treatment group. Additionally, it is encouraging that, over time, positive changes in marital conflict were linked with positive changes in marital satisfaction, parenting, and child adjustment. The program did not target these broader family processes, so such changes were expected to be contingent on improvements in marital conflict.

The possibilities for implementation of the findings in community samples were further advanced by the high consumer satisfaction with the program. The results thus supported the hypothesis that improvements in marital conflict in community samples can be accomplished in the context of a relatively brief program and that these changes may be sustained in relation to a control group for at least one year. The findings thus further supported the promise of brief, psychoeducational programs for marital conflict for community samples.

Directions for Future Work

Given that the results of the first studies in this line of work have not been publicly available for long, it is too early to comment extensively on experiences, reflections and conclusions regarding the implementation of these programs in community settings, or on the reception by relevant individuals and institutions in the field with regard to the actual use of these programs. We have been pleased with the positive responses from funding agencies and the highly constructive reviews our manuscripts have received from journals in the review process. We feel that our programs are potentially valuable for use in community settings for community families, especially given the evidence supporting efficacy, the relatively limited requirements for participation (i.e., four visits), which is likely to be a better for community families than more lengthly programs, and the high satisfaction reported by participants in our studies (see also Shifflett & Cummings, 1999). We do have some further thoughts, directed towards future research, and we will close with the consideration of these directions.

Program administration

Another aspect of program administration for prevention programs for community families that merits consideration is utilizing the lowest dose possible, while maintaining reasonable levels of efficacy. The reality of modern life is that families are already overscheduled, and participating in a psychoeducational program may be impractical for many families if the challenges for participation are great. Thus, identifying the lowest dosage needed for successful outcomes (fewest sessions, shortest duration) is a critical consideration for researchers in this area. In addition, program information needs to be presented in a way that is accessible to a wide range of families, in order to facilitate maximal benefit from participation. For example, in our own work, as we have noted, we combine verbal and PowerPoint presentation of program information, along with engaging activities, in order to appeal to a variety of learning styles. Another approach to consider is qualitative research methodologies, such as clinical interviews to assess marital functioning. Qualitative research facilitates in-depth study of a phenomenon of interest, offering opportunities to advance understanding of family functioning at a more close-up level.

Complexity of families

Families are highly complex systems. They are hierarchically organized, with individuals nested within dyads and triads, which are nested within families (Schermerhorn & Cummings, 2008). Recognition of the complexity of the study of families presents theoretical and practical challenges. Currently, much of the literature on families reflects a narrow conceptualization of families, focusing on only one or a couple of family members. Thus, statistical models based on such conceptualizations are likely to be misspecified, if important processes are omitted. The narrow focus also presents problems for clinicians, possibly endorsing therapies that may poorly fit the needs of real families because of failure to consider important dimensions of family life and family functioning. Thus, one important direction for research on families is to examine multiple dimensions of family life and family functioning. For example, this work needs to assess multiple aspects of family members' functioning, multiple domains of family relationships, and multiple family members.

A child component

A child component may potentially add to the benefits of the parent program, either by helping children cope more effectively with marital conflict, or by increasing the child's own ability to cope with their own conflicts. Because of the promise of a combined parent and child program possibly being more beneficial than a parent program alone, in our four-visit program we tested whether the PC program held greater benefits for children than the PO program. Consistent with other reports on programs designed primarily for improving the parents' relationships (i.e., divorce) (Wolchik et al., 2000), we have found to date limited evidence for the efficacy of the prevention program. A challenge for programs designed to help children cope is that marital conflict is truly a threat to the well-being of children and families. Thus, children are to some extent realistic in being concerned about marital conflict, even though it is important to encourage children not to take responsibility for these conflicts.

In an ongoing study with adolescents we are examining whether an adolescent program for handling conflicts may be more effective than a program for coping with marital conflict. We hope to not only teach adolescents about the possible consequences of conflict on their development, but to also improve the communication between parents and their adolescents. It is hypothesized that adolescents who are better able to communicate with their parents will be more likely to avoid the negative consequences that may result from frequent and destructive conflict in the home. Also, the overall well-being of the family may improve by educating both parents and adolescents about the stage salient issues that are taking place at this time during children's development. By teaching parents and children to better understand one another, we hope to improve their relationships and communication.

Other formats

Another direction is to explore other formats for "giving away" developmental psychology by means of translational approaches. Didactic material in the traditional of translational research can be provided in take-home formats or through interactive web sites. For example, evidence-based information about children and marital conflict might be disseminated through self-paced take-home programs, with some support for the value of such approaches (Halford, Moore, Wilson, Farrugia, & Dyer, 2004). While much more research is needed, including unexplored questions about whether there are any long-term benefits, these approaches hold promise at least for helping families not capable or willing to attend group workshops. Another strong point, to be amplified by Sanders and Calam (Chapter 5), is that content can be delivered in compact, easily accessible formats, such as web-based streaming video, DVDs, and the iPod (i.e., podcasting). Translational research programs can also be tailored for use with practitioners and community groups, such as schools and local mental health centers.

Conclusions

The themes and goals of this Handbook are very timely. In the area of marital conflict and children, as in many other areas of developmental research, a tremendous body of knowledge has accumulated that is highly relevant to the well-being and mental health of children and other family members. Thus, there is thus an urgent need to more effectively make this information available to practitioners and the public. As we have contended in this chapter, the themes and directions of translational research offer encouraging possibilities for advancing these aims beyond what can be accomplished by traditional means of publication in respected journals and by publicizing research (e.g., writing for or speaking in the media).

At the same time, endorsing a premise in the letter of invitation for this book, we have found that the process of "giving away" developmental research has many obstacles and is not a straight forward matter. In fact, we have frequently remarked amongst ourselves about how difficult this work is to accomplish, how long these projects take to develop, and how little the payoff seems to be in terms of publications or related outputs in relation to the amount of work, time, creativity, and effort required. Notably, some of us have remarked on occasion that we are grateful for our "day jobs" of traditional developmental research in the context of developing translational research projects. Yet, directions towards translating research findings into useful applications are urgently needed and we are enthusiastic about the possibilities (Cummings & Schatz, 2012; Cummings & Valentino, 2015).

References

Altman, D. G., Schulz, K. F., Moher, D., Egger, M., Davidoff, F., & Elbourne, D. et al. (2001). The revised CONSORT statement for reporting randomized trials: Explanation and elaboration. *Annals of Internal Medicine, 134,* 663–694.

Amato, P. R., & Booth, A. (2001). The legacy of parents' marital discord: Consequences for children's marital quality. *Journal of Personality and Social Psychology, 81,* 627–638.

Borkowski, J. G., Smith, L. E., & Akai, C. E. (2007). Designing effective prevention programs: How good science makes good art. *Infants and Young Children: An Interdisciplinary Journal of Special Care Practices, 20,* 229–241.

Cicchetti, D., & Cohen, D. J. (1995). Perspectives on developmental psychopathology. In D. J. Cohen & D. Cicchetti (Eds.) *Developmental psychopathology, Vol. 1,: Theory and methods* (pp. 3–20). Oxford, UK: John Wiley & Sons, Ltd.

Cowan, P. A., & Cowan, C. P. (2002). What an intervention design reveals about how parents affect their children's academic achievement and behavior problems. In J. G. Borkowski, S. L. Ramey, & M. Bristol-Power (Eds.). *Parenting and the child's world: Influences on academic, intellectual, and social-emotional development.* (pp. 75–97). Mahwah, NJ: Lawrence Erlbaum Associates, Inc.

Cowan, P. A., Cowan, C. P., & Schulz, M. S. (1996). Thinking about risk and resilience in families. In E. M. Hetherington & E. A. Blechman (Eds.), *Stress, coping, and resiliency in children and families* (pp. 1–38). Hillsdale, NJ: Lawrence Erlbaum Associates, Inc.

Cummings, E.M., & Davies, P.T. (1994). *Children and marital conflict: The impact of family dispute and resolution.* New York, NY: Guilford Press.

Cummings, E. M., & Davies, P. T. (2002). Effects of marital conflict on children: Recent advances and emerging themes in process-oriented research. *Journal of Child Psychology and Psychiatry and Allied Disciplines, 43,* 31–63.

Cummings, E. M., & Davies, P. T. (2010). *Marital conflict and children: An emotional security perspective.* New York, NY: Guilford Press.

Cummings, E. M., Davies, P. T., & Campbell, S. B. (2000). *Developmental psychopathology and family process: Theory, research, and clinical implications.* New York, NY: Guilford Press.

Cummings, E. M., Faircloth, B. F., Mitchell, P. M., Cummings, J. S., & Schermerhorn, A. C. (2008). Evaluating a brief prevention program for improving marital conflict in community families. *Journal of Family Psychology, 22,* 193–202.

Cummings, E. M., George, M. R., McCoy, K. P., & Davies, P. T. (2012). Interparental conflict in kindergarten and adolescent adjustment: prospective investigation of emotional security as an explanatory mechanism. *Child Development, 83,* 1703–1715.

Cummings, E. M., Goeke-Morey, M. C., & Papp, L. M. (2003). Children's responses to everyday marital conflict tactics in the home. *Child Development, 74,* 1918–1929.

Cummings, E. M., Goeke-Morey, M. C., & Papp, L. M. (2004). Everyday marital conflict and child aggression. *Journal of Abnormal Child Psychology, 32,* 191–202.

Cummings, E. M., Goeke-Morey, M. C., Papp, L. M., & Dukewich, T. L. (2002). Children's responses to mothers and fathers' emotionality and conflict tactics during marital conflict in the home. *Journal of Family Psychology, 16,* 478–492.

Cummings, E. M., & Schatz, J. N. (2012). Family conflict, emotional security, and child development: Translating research findings into a prevention program for community families. *Clinical Child and Family Psychology Review, 15*(1), 14–27.

Cummings, E. M., Schermerhorn, A. C., Davies, P. T., Goeke-Morey, M. C., & Cummings, J. S. (2006). Interpersonal discord and child adjustment: Prospective investigations of emotional security as an explanatory mechanism. *Child Development, 77,* 132–152.

Cummings, E. M., & Valentino, K. (2015). Developmental Psychopathology. In W. F. Overton & P. C. M. Molenaar (Eds.). *Theory and Method.* Volume 1 of the *Handbook of child psychology and developmental science* (7th ed.) (pp. 566–606), Editor-in-Chief: Richard M. Lerner. Hoboken, NJ: John Wiley & Sons, Inc.

Davies, P. T., & Cummings, E. M. (1994). Marital conflict and child adjustment: An emotional security hypothesis. *Psychological Bulletin, 116,* 387–411.

Davies, P. T., & Cummings, E. M. (2006). Interparental discord, family process, and developmental psychopathology. In D. J. Cohen & D. Cicchetti (Eds.). *Developmental psychopathology, Vol. 3: Risk, disorder, and adaptation* (2nd ed.) (pp. 86–128). Hoboken, NJ: John Wiley & Sons, Inc.

Davies, P. T., Harold, G. T., Goeke-Morey, M. C., & Cummings, E. M. (2002). Child emotional security and interparental conflict. *Monographs of the Society for Research in Child Development, 67*(3).

Davies, P. T., Sturge-Apple, M., Bascoe, S. M., & Cummings, E. M. (2014). The legacy of early insecurity histories in shaping adolescent adaptation to interparental conflict. *Child Development, 85*(1), 338–354.

Davies, P. T., Sturge-Apple, M. L., Winter, M. A., Cummings, E. M., & Ferrell, D. (2006). Child adaptational development in contexts of interparental conflict over time. *Child Development, 77,* 218–233.

Faircloth, W. B., & Cummings, E. M. (2008). Evaluating a parent education program for preventing the negative effects of marital conflict. *Journal of Applied Developmental Psychology, 29,* 141–156.

Glasgow, R. E., Green, L. W., Klesges, L. M., Abrams, D. B., Fisher, E. B., Goldstein, M. G., et al. (2006). External Validity: We need to do more. *Annals of Behavioral Medicine, 31*(2), 105–108.

Glasgow, R. E., McKay, H. G., Piette, J. D., & Reynolds, K. D. (2001). The RE-AIM framework for evaluating interventions: What can it tell us about approaches to chronic illness management? *Patient Education and Counseling, 44,* 119–127.

Goeke-Morey, M. C., Cummings, E. M., Harold, G. T., & Shelton, K. H. (2003). Categories and continua of destructive and constructive marital conflict tactics from the perspective of Welsh and US children. *Journal of Family Psychology, 17,* 327–338.

Goeke-Morey, M. C., Cummings, E. M., & Papp, L. M. (2007). Children and marital conflict resolution: Implications for emotional security and adjustment. *Journal of Family Psychology, 21*(4), 744–753.

Goeke-Morey, M. C., Papp, L. M., & Cummings, E. M. (2013). Changes in marital conflict and youths' responses across childhood and adolescence: A test of sensitization. *Development and Psychopathology, 25,* 241–251.

Gottman, J. M. (1994). *What predicts divorce? The relationship between marital processes and marital outcomes.* Hillsdale, NJ: Lawrence Erlbaum Associates, Inc.

Gottman, J.M., & Gottman, J.S. (1999). The marriage survival kit: A research-based marital therapy. In R. Berger & M. T. Hannah (Eds.), *Preventive approaches in couples therapy.* (pp. 304–330). Philadelphia, PA: Brunner/Mazel, Inc.

Gottman, J. M., Katz, L. F., & Hooven, C. (2013). *Meta-emotion: How families communicate emotionally.* London: Routledge.

Grych, J. H., & Fincham, F. D. (1990). Marital conflict and children's adjustment: A cognitive-contextual framework. *Psychological Bulletin, 108,* 267–290.

Halford, K.W., Moore, E., Wilson, K. L., Farrugia, C., & Dyer, C. (2004). Benefits of flexible delivery relationship education: An evaluation of the couple CARE program. *Family Relations, 53*(5), 469–476.

Johnson, J. R. (1994). High-conflict divorce. *Future of Children, 4*(1), 165–182.

Kouros, C. D., Cummings, E. M., & Davies, P. T. (2010). Early trajectories of interparental conflict and externalizing problems as predictors of social competence in preadolescence. *Development and Psychopathology, 22,* 527–538.

Lewis, J. A., & Machin, D. (1993). Intention to treat – who should use ITT? *British Journal of Cancer, 68,* 647–650.

Liberman, A.F., Van Horn, P., & Ippen, C.G. (2005). Toward evidence-based treatment: Child-parent psychotherapy with preschoolers exposed to marital violence. *Journal of the American Academy of Child and Adolescent Psychiatry, 44,* 1241–1248.

Markman, H. J., & Floyd, F. (1980). Possibilities for the prevention of marital discord: A behavioral perspective. *American Journal of Family Therapy, 8(2),* 29–48.

Moher, D., Schulz, K. F., & Altman, D. G. (2001a). The CONSORT statement: Revised recommendations for improving the quality of reports of parallel group randomized trials. *Annals of Internal Medicine, 134,* 657–662.

Moher, D., Schulz, K. F., & Altman, D. G. (2001b). The CONSORT statement: Revised recommendations for improving the quality of reports of parallel group randomized trials. *Journal of American Medical Association, 285,* 1987–1991.

Moher, D., Schulz, K. F., & Altman, D. G. (2001c). The CONSORT statement: Revised recommendations for improving the quality of reports parallel group randomized trials. *Lancet, 357*(9263):1191–1194.

Moher, D., Hopewell, S., Schulz, K. F., Montori, V., Gøtzsche, P. C., Devereaux, P. J., & Altman, D. G. (2012). CONSORT 2010 explanation and elaboration: updated guidelines for reporting parallel group randomised trials. *International Journal of Surgery, 10,* 28–55.

Morgan, J. R., Nu'Man, S. J., & Allin, D. W. (1990). Prevention through parent training: Three preventive parent education programs. *Journal of Primary Prevention, 10,* 321–332.

Nation, M., Crusto, C., Wanderman, A., Kumofer, K. L., Sevbolt, D., Morrissey, K. E., et al., (2003). What works in prevention? Principles of effective prevention programs. *American Psychologist, 58,* 229–456.

Papp, L. M., Cummings, E. M., & Goeke-Morey, M. C. (2009). For richer, for poorer: Money as a topic of marital conflict in the home. *Family Relations, 58,* 91–103.

Pehrson, K. L., & Robinson, C. C. (1990). Parent education: Does it make a difference? *Child Study Journal, 20,* 221–236.

Peto, R., Pike, M. C., Armitage, P., Breslow, N. E., Cox, D. R., Howard, S. V., et al., (1976). Design and analysis of randomized clinical trials requiring prolonged observation of each patient. I. Introduction and design. *British Journal Cancer, 34,* 585–612.

Rogers, C. R. (1965). A humanistic conception of man. In R.E. Farson (Ed.) *Science and human affairs* (pp. 18–31). Palo Alto, CA: Science and Behavior Books, Inc.

Schermerhorn, A. C., & Cummings, E. M. (2008). Transactional family dynamics: A new framework for conceptualizing family influence processes. In R. V. Kail (Ed.), *Advances in Child Development and Behavior, Volume 36,* (pp. 187–250). San Diego, CA: Elsevier Academic Press.

Shifflett, K., & Cummings, E. M. (1999). A program for educating parents about the effect of divorce and conflict on children: An initial evaluation. *Family Relations, 48,* 79–89.

Stinson, J. M., McGrath, P. J., & Yamada, J. T. (2003). Clinical trials in the Journal of Pediatric Psychology: Applying the CONSORT statement. *Journal of Pediatric Psychology, 28,* 159–167.

Turner, C. M., & Dadds, M. R. (2001). Clinical prevention and remediation of child adjustment problems. In F. D. Fincham & J. H. Grych (Eds.), *Interparental conflict and child development: Theory, research, and applications* (pp. 387–416). New York, NY: Cambridge University Press.

Webster, S. C. (1994). Advancing videotape parent training: A comparison study. *Journal of Consulting and Clinical Psychology, 62,* 583–593.

Winter, M. A., Davies, P. T., & Cummings, E. M. (2010). Children's security in the context of family instability and maternal communications. *Merrill-Palmer Quarterly, 56,* 131.

Wolchik, S. A., West, S. G. Sandler, I. N., Tein, J.-Y., Coatsworth, D., & Lengua, L., et al. (2000). An experimental evaluation of theory-based mother and mother-child programs for children of divorce. *Journal of Consulting and Clinical Psychology, 68,* 843–856.

4

Implementing a Preventive Parenting Program with Families of Young Children: Challenges and Solutions

Angela D. Moreland and Jean E. Dumas

Child disruptive behavior, including aggressive, oppositional, and defiant behavior, is a prominent problem that often begins in the preschool years (Dishion & Patterson, 2006; Dishion and Yasui, Chapter 17, this volume; Shaw, Dishion, Supplee, Gardner, & Arnds, 2006). Among children who display disruptive behavior in early years, approximately 4–6% continue to exhibit these behaviors into school age (Briggs-Gowan, Carter, Skuban, & Horwitz, 2001; Fanti & Henrich, 2010; Raver & Knitze, 2002), which often continues into adolescence and adulthood (Bub, McCartney, & Willett, 2007; Campbell, 2002).

Psychosocial interventions for young children who present significant behavioral or emotional challenges have long focused as much on parents in their role of key socialization agents as on the children themselves. Over time, programs designed to train parents to manage their young children's problematic behaviors have emerged as the interventions of choice in this area, largely because they benefit from strong empirical evidence. Known generically as *parent training*, this form of intervention has rapidly gained in popularity for several reasons: (i) it offers practical solutions

The Wiley Handbook of Developmental Psychology in Practice: Implementation and Impact, First Edition.
Edited by Kevin Durkin and H. Rudolph Schaffer.
© 2016 John Wiley & Sons, Ltd. Published 2016 by John Wiley & Sons, Ltd.

to problematic behaviors that significantly interfere with family life and child adjustment; (ii) it is relatively inexpensive and can be implemented by trained para-professionals; (iii) it yields results more rapidly than traditional forms of psycho-therapy; and (iv) it is effective. Reviews show that parenting programs are particularly effective in reducing child oppositional and antisocial behavior at home and school, and in improving parental personal adjustment; and that their results often persist when children and families are followed up for extended periods of time (Eyberg, Nelson, & Boggs, 2008; Kazdin, 2005; Sandler, Schoenfelder, Wolchik, & MacKinnon, 2011).

While parent training has frequently been used to treat existing disruptive behavior problems (Barkley et al., 2000; Sanders, Markie-Dadds, Tully, & Bor, 2000), recent efforts have been made to *prevent* such problems by "nipping early risk factors in the bud" (Sanders, 2008; Zubrick et al., 2005). Most prevention efforts to date have relied in part or exclusively on a parenting approach, largely because that approach has been shown to be effective in reducing child opposi-tional and antisocial behavior and because ineffective parenting, parental stress and disturbed family relationships are major risk factors in this area (Dumas, Lemay, & Dauwalder, 2001; Lunkenheimer, Kemp, & Albrecht, 2013; Pearl, French, Dumas, Moreland, & Prinz, 2014; Soltis, Davidson, Moreland, Felton, & Dumas, 2013). Contrary to the widespread belief that antisocial behavior is difficult to prevent, there is strong evidence that preventive interventions are often successful. Specifically, meta-analyses have shown that, although there is considerable heterogeneity in the nature of the interventions reviewed, many programs significantly (i) reduced anti-social and related problems, and (i) increased coping competence across social, affective, and achievement domains (Sandler et al., 2011).

This chapter presents a group-based intervention aimed at preventing child disruptive behavior by working with parents of preschool children. Specifically, PACE – *Parenting Our Children to Excellence* – is a preventive parenting program designed to increase coping competence and to reduce the risk of antisocial behavior in the preschool years. The intervention's contents and conceptual framework are first described, prior to focusing on the challenges encountered in delivery and solutions implemented to address them.

PACE – Program Description and Conceptual Framework

PACE is a manualized parent training program delivered in groups. It is designed to promote parenting effectiveness and child coping competence, and to reduce the risk of child disruptive behavior. As evidence indicates, focus on preschool children reflects the fact that caregivers play a critical role in fostering effective coping skills in their children from an early age. The theoretical model of child coping competence states that all young children face daily social, affective, and achievement challenges in their environments, with which they must learn to cope in prosocial ways if they are to develop positive, healthy relationships with adults and peers (Moreland & Dumas, 2007). More specifically, it is widely recognized that effective coping in the early years: (i) helps insure that children grow up to become competent, prosocial adolescents and young adults, and (ii) is key to the prevention of behavioral and emotional problems in later childhood and beyond – especially delinquency, substance abuse, and school failure (Compas, Conner-Smith, Saltzman, Thomsen, & Wadsworth, 2001; Dumas, 2005; Moreland & Dumas, 2007).

Program description

PACE is delivered over eight two-hour modules, conducted in groups of 10–15 parents by a trained group leader (GL) (Box 4.1). In each session, the GL introduces the topic, asks participants' opinions and experiences, presents short videotaped vignettes of effective and ineffective parenting to prompt group discussion, and suggests practical home activities designed to promote practice of the approaches (with simple handouts). Though structured, sessions leave time for participants to discuss important parenting issues and concerns, and to share and support each other. GL's are trained to solicit parental input, to manage lively exchanges, and to encourage participants' offers of help and support.

Conceptual framework

Child coping competence, which is at the heart of PACE, hinges on three key elements: challenges, ways of coping, and effective communication (Dumas, Prinz, Smith, & Laughlin, 1999).

Challenges. Every day, each child faces challenges that require or prompt different coping responses. Challenges are features of the environment – such as unavoidable demands and difficulties, as well as developmental tasks and major life events – for which the child does not have an immediate, well-practiced response. Consequently, they tax or are beyond the child's coping capacity, evoke strong emotions, and are often experienced as stressful. Challenges fall into three overlapping domains: *social challenges* stem from interpersonal and social situations and demands; *affective challenges* require solutions to emotional difficulties; and *achievement challenges* pertain to goal-directed activities, such as self-care tasks, and school

Box 4.1   The PACE Modules

Module 1: *Introduction to the program and bringing out the best in our children*

Purpose: To introduce participants to the program; to explore the importance of praise, rewards, and positive activities in parenting, and to help participants recognize and focus on their children's strengths to build them further. This module discusses various forms of praise and rewards, differences between praise and criticism and rewards and bribery, and activities that encourage positive parent–child interactions to bring out the best in children.

Module 2: *Setting clear limits for our children*

Purpose: To explore ways to encourage positive child behavior, and to reduce child misbehavior and parental stress. This module concentrates on setting clear limits and rules at home, on giving effective commands, and on using natural and logical consequences to teach children to be responsible for their actions.

Module 3: *Helping our children behave well at home and beyond*

Purpose: To explore nonaggressive means of teaching children to obey requests. Discussion and group activities focus on ignoring unacceptable behaviors and on establishing effective time-outs by explaining the procedure and addressing difficult situations – all in order to help children behave well at home and beyond.

Module 4: *Making sure our children get enough sleep*

Purpose: To help children go to bed without fussing and get a good night's sleep. Discussions and group activities concentrate on establishing a regular bedtime routine for families in which putting a child to bed is a challenge. This routine is only one example of the types of routines children need to feel safe and learn (a point to be covered in later modules).

Module 5: *Encouraging our children's early thinking skills*

Purpose: To explore the importance of reading and playing with young children to encourage early thinking skills that are critical to school success. This module discusses practical reading and play activities that participants can do daily with their children, as ways of giving them positive attention that will help them to think and to behave well. The module also discusses and encourages family routines and traditions that help children feel safe.

Module 6: *Developing our children's self-esteem*

Purpose: To help participants devise practical ways to build their children's self-esteem, through play, positive feedback, and shared positive routines. Through group discussions and activities, this module stresses the importance of appreciating and respecting children's individual needs and preferences as a means of developing their self-esteem.

Module 7: *Helping our children do well at school*

Purpose: To explore ways in which participants can help their children do well at school, from getting ready on time in the morning to developing a positive relationship with teachers. Through discussions and practical activities, this module returns to the importance of working actively to help children do well in all settings – at home, at school, and in the community.

Module 8: *Anticipating challenges and seeking support*

Purpose: To help participants recognize the importance of parenting as a life-long task that requires the ability to manage different sources of stress. Discussions and group activities help participants learn to reduce/control their stress by: obtaining nurturing support from other adults within and beyond the family, using relaxation techniques, and controlling negative self-talk. This module concludes with a group party that brings the program to an end.

and work-related demands and responsibilities (Moreland & Dumas, 2007). Hence, the overarching goal of PACE, namely to help parents foster social, affective, and achievement competence in their young children to prevent the development of behavioral and emotional problems.

Ways of coping. Like adults, children can cope with challenges in three ways. When coping *prosocially*, they respond by resolving, or attempting to resolve, the challenge in a constructive manner, focusing not only on their own feelings and preferences but taking the constraints of the situation into account; or they enlist the help of adults or peers to find a prosocial solution. When coping *antisocially*, children attempt to resolve the challenge in an aggressive, destructive, or deceitful manner, or deny any responsibility in solving the challenge, often hurting others and themselves in the process. And when coping *asocially*, children respond by withdrawing from the situation and from others, or by hurting themselves, in an attempt to minimize or dismiss the stressful impact of the challenge (e.g., they cry excessively or give up in the face of difficulties). The coping competence model recognizes that all young children exhibit antisocial and asocial ways of coping that serve an important role in survival and development. For example, crying signals the infant's need for affection, food, and protection. Avoidance of unfamiliar persons and situations prevents the toddler from getting into danger by straying far from adults. And impatient demands and angry outbursts are early expressions of assertiveness and affect that adults use to teach the child to express emotions in more suitable fashion. In most cases, with repeated exposure to countless challenges coupled with consistent support, guidance, and limits, older children and adults acquire predominantly prosocial ways of coping, even though they rely occasionally on antisocial and asocial strategies (Moreland & Dumas, 2007).

Effective communication. The coping competence model assumes that the acquisition of prosocial ways of coping takes much of childhood and adolescence, and is closely linked to the mastery of effective communication skills (Dumas, Prinz, Smith, & Laughlin, 1999). Effective communication – at home and, later, at school and in other social settings – consists of three interrelated processes in which language is central. In successful *information exchange*, individuals use words and actions to disclose their feelings, thoughts, and experiences, and watch and listen to each other attentively and nonjudgmentally to understand each other's perspectives and needs. With practice, this teaches children to give and receive relevant and truthful information about challenges, and to think and regulate their own behavior through self-instructions. In families, children experiencing difficulties at school, for example, must learn to express their feelings and describe their frustrating experiences, and to formulate potential coping strategies. If family members listen carefully and convey acceptance and support of the child, problems are reduced or dissipate, often without overt behavior influence or problem solving.

In successful *behavior influence*, individuals use words to prompt each other to act when faced with a challenge. Behavior influence can be present-oriented (e.g., "I have finished my homework, can I watch my show?") or future-oriented (e.g., "If you help me with my math homework tonight, I will make your lunch for tomorrow."). Through behavior influence, children learn to exercise control over others in prosocial fashion and, over time, to control their own actions. Finally, in successful *problem solving*, individuals use words to recognize and devise mutually acceptable, often long-term, solutions to challenges that require all persons involved to change and monitor their own behavior. As such, problem solving necessitates repeated use of effective information exchange and behavior influence. The incentive for problem solving does not lie in any immediate reward but in its impact on the enduring quality of the relationships people share or on long-term personal goals (e.g., school success).

To summarize, the coping competence model assumes that the preschool years are essential in the development of effective communication with others and self. Specifically, effective communication is the means by which prosocial coping comes to supplant antisocial and asocial coping in the course of development, providing competent youth and adults with the tools to influence others and themselves in a positive manner. As children learn to understand and use language, they become able to modify their behavior, first in response to immediate adult instructions and later through self-verbalizations and internalization of these instructions. With maturation, repeated practice, and authoritative guidance from trusted adults, children become increasingly capable of self-initiated planning and monitoring, and show greater flexibility in their control strategies of others and self as a function of changing situational demands. Thus, with growing competence, self-regulation encompasses complex abilities much beyond compliance with immediate instructions, including "delay of gratification, control of impulses and affect, modulation of motor and linguistic activities, and the ability to act in accordance with social norms in the absence of external monitors" (Kopp, 1991, p. 38).

PACE – Implementation Challenges and Solutions

PACE began in 2000 in Indianapolis, IN, USA with the enthusiastic participation of 50 childcare centers located throughout this large, Midwestern city. Versions have subsequently been developed in French and Spanish (Dumas, Arriaga, Begle, & Longoria, 2011; Lucia & Dumas, 2013). Program implementation challenges and solutions are discussed here under the following headings: childcare center recruitment and advisory boards; staff recruitment, training, and supervision; recruitment, interviewing, and retention of families; adherence to protocol (fidelity monitoring); and methods to reduce barriers to engagement.

Childcare center recruitment and advisory boards

Center recruitment. All participants were recruited through childcare centers, making the choice of appropriate centers a major step in program implementation. The conceptual framework and funding requirements made centers eligible to participate if: (i) they served a minimum of 35 families with children between the ages of three and six years, and (ii) the majority of families they served had financial needs (i.e., over 50% of families whose children attended the center qualified for subsidized child care). To identify centers who could host the PACE program, the research team relied on a childcare provider training and licensing agency that had been associated with the project since its inception; a variety of childcare registries (e.g., State of Indiana registry, church-affiliated listings); the telephone directory; and recommendations from directors whose centers already participated in PACE.

   Once potential centers had been identified, the project manager contacted their director by mail to provide a brief description of the program and request an appointment. Most center directors agreed to the appointment and attended in person, or delegated the responsibility to a member of their staff. The only refusals came from centers already offering a parenting program and from centers affiliated with a nationwide provider of childcare services (apparently because their head office did not accept services that were not provided directly by their corporation). When meeting with center directors, the project manager explained the program in detail and stressed that PACE was offered free of charge and that centers were only expected to make their facilities available at no cost. When directors were interested, but before they enrolled their center in the program, the manager inquired about where the PACE sessions would be held, as a minimum of two rooms were needed, one for the parents and the other for their children (as PACE offered free child care during each program session).

Not surprisingly, gaining support from directors or their designees was crucial, as they were usually the main contact for parents at the center and many parents based their decision to participate on the opinion and attitude of center staff. More specifically, too little or too much support were both problematic. Some directors expressed what appeared to be genuine interest in the program but later were unwilling or unable to follow through. For example, directors may have failed to attend planning meetings that were necessary to recruit families and run the program, or they may not have communicated adequately with staff, who may have, in turn, been unsupportive of the program (because they had not been properly informed and engaged, or because of personal animosities).

Overinvolvement by center directors and staff could be just as problematic. For example, one of the first directors who enrolled her center in PACE was enthusiastically supportive and took it upon herself to talk personally to every parent to encourage them to enroll – so much so that several parents did, not out of interest, but because they felt coerced. As most of them did not attend any group session, our data showed a much higher level of attrition for that center compared to others. This and similar situations where actual or potential pressure may have been put on parents to enroll led us to spend considerable time discussing and reviewing the research protocol with *all* center directors and staff. In some cases, this amounted to educating our community partners about research and ethical requirements, without dampening their genuine interest in PACE and their desire to see parents participate. Practically, we emphasized that all forms of coercion, not matter how "gentle," could not be cautioned, as it was a violation of the ethical standards all project staff must have respected and contradicted the research requirement that all participants must have been recruited in the same manner.

Advisory boards. To encourage involvement of centers in the promotion and delivery of PACE, an advisory board was set up at each center prior to any research or program activity. Each 5–6-member board consisted of the director or designee and of volunteer parents and teachers. Boards met biweekly throughout the six-week recruitment period and the eight-week program. Board members were paid $15 for each board meeting they attended. Most boards proved very helpful at facilitating the recruitment process at each center and, once recruited, at encouraging parents to attend sessions regularly (e.g., by calling parents weekly to remind them). Board members also helped address various concerns raised by parents prior or during the program (e.g., about confidentiality, transportation).

Once the program had ended, the project manager kept in regular contact with the director and staff for several reasons. First, this greatly facilitated the process of data collection for the one-year follow-up, as many parents chose to complete the data collection interviews at the childcare center. Second, this helped maintain a positive community image of PACE and facilitated the recruitment of new centers. Directors often recommended additional childcare centers to recruit for the program; and interested directors of new centers at times talked with their counterparts who had already hosted the program before making a commitment to PACE.

Staff recruitment, training, and supervision

Successful implementation of a large prevention program necessitates the recruitment, training, and supervision of an adequate number of reliable staff (Cummings et al., Chapter 3, this volume; Nation et al., 2003).

Project manager and research assistants. The project manager was a university-trained professional with prior research and service delivery experience in community settings *and* excellent effective communication skills. This last point is essential and probably more important than the manager's specific training and experience. Responsible for the daily implementation of all facets of the project – including recruiting childcare centers, hiring, supervising, and scheduling several members of staff, tracking parents, and overseeing data collection – the manager must be a skillful negotiator, an excellent organizer, a good listener, and an attentive and assertive supervisor. The PACE program also relied on numerous research assistants, who were responsible for a number of research-related tasks, including data collection and tracking of participants; consent procedures and forms; management of databases; adherence to protocol; coding of fidelity data; and data entry.

Group leaders. GLs delivered the PACE program at each participating center. Consequently, they played a major role in the success and overall reputation of the program. They were recruited with the help of the childcare provider training and licensing agency already mentioned, and by placing announcements on various community bulletin boards. Minimum qualifications were: (i) a bachelor's degree in a family- or child-related field or equivalent experience, and (ii) successful completion of a standardized training program. This eight-hour, manualized program provided a practical introduction to PACE, its conceptual framework, and its intervention components. Following this training program, each GL observed or acted as an assistant for one or more ongoing PACE group sessions, before being assigned his/her own PACE group. All GLs were consistently supervised and given frequent feedback regarding their performance – both in terms of their adherence to program contents (i.e., coverage of all topics relevant to each session) and process (i.e., reliance on effective communication skills). The procedures followed to demonstrate adherence to protocol are described in detail below.

Should parents and group leaders be "matched" on key variables? Prevention and clinical wisdom suggest that matching parents and GLs on variables such as ethnicity, socioeconomic status, and parenting beliefs may be central to program success, as it increases intervention relevance and maximizes comfort and trust (Reis & Brown, 1999). A meta-analysis found that ethnic match predicted higher rates of attendance and lower rates of dropout in minority clients (Maramba & Hall, 2002). Effect sizes were small, however, and the authors concluded that match was not a strong predictor of attendance or dropout beyond the initial sessions. We reached a similar conclusion in a study based on PACE data, in which we assessed social, ethnic, and belief similarities between parents and group leaders (Dumas, Moreland, Gitter, Pearl, & Nordstrom, 2006). The amounts of variance accounted for by those similarities were significant but relatively modest. This suggests that matching may be a less salient issue in preventive parenting interventions than is commonly assumed.

As the PACE program served a diverse population, attempts were always made to match the majority of parents in a group and their GL on ethnicity (socioeconomic matching was generally impossible given the educational qualifications required of group leaders). However, practical considerations (e.g., scheduling or transportation conflicts) did not always permit it. It was our observation that this was not an issue, as long as GLs listened genuinely to all participants and were effective, respectful communicators. A more important issue in the eyes of some center directors, advisory board members, and parents was whether the GL had children and could, therefore, talk with authority about parenting issues. Some GLs had extensive experience working with children and families but no children of their own. They were instructed to address the issue at the beginning of the first session, immediately after the introduction to the program, and found that this diffused the situation before it might have become problematic.

Recruiters/interviewers. Competent and professional recruiters/interviewers (R/Is) are crucial to the success of any research project involving longitudinal data collection (Nation et al., 2003). R/Is were recruited by placing announcements on various community bulletin boards. Candidates were interviewed by the project manager who, following Prinz et al.'s (2002) recommendations, looked for people who exhibited effective communication skills, were comfortable approaching and interacting with parents from diverse backgrounds, maintained a nonjudgmental approach, and were organized and attentive to detail. In line with the same recommendations, preference was given to R/Is who lived in the communities from which parents were recruited and who had flexible schedules, as many parents could only be reached in the evening or on weekends.

Once hired, R/Is were required to complete an intensive, standardized training program, which included background information on the PACE program, recruitment and interviewing rules and timeline, and safety guidelines. Particular emphasis was put on effective and ethical ways of approaching parents to explain the program and encourage participation, and on interviewing conduct and procedures. Before they were assigned to a daycare center, R/Is were required to become thoroughly familiar with each survey they would administer, by reading them aloud on several occasions, and administering each of them to the program manager in the course of a mock interview. The program manager acted then as a naïve parent, asking questions or making statements that would test the R/I's interviewing skills and mastery of ethical and research requirements. This training reflects Prinz et al.'s (2002) recommendation that R/Is be "overtrained" through intensive practice in order to be able to recruit and interview effectively, while maintaining ethical conduct and adhering to the research protocol.

For supervision purposes, the program manager conducted quality and validity checks of all scheduled recruitment sessions and completed interviews. Specifically, the manager contacted the daycare center director on a frequent basis and occasionally "dropped by" each center unannounced during a recruitment session, to ensure that R/Is were working and following all program guidelines. In addition, each R/I provided a list of all interviews he/she had completed to the manager on a weekly basis. The manager then randomly selected and called 25% of participants to verify that the interview was conducted and that information was obtained from the right respondent, to check that the information collected was accurate, and to ensure that the R/I was punctual and courteous. Falsification of data or failure to follow the PACE protocol was never tolerated and was cause for immediate dismissal. Throughout our program's implementation, two R/Is had to be dismissed for such reasons.

R/Is could only be hired as part-time employees, as PACE recruiting and data collection took place in "waves" (i.e., before the beginning of a group, at the end, and at a one-year follow-up). This contributed to high turnover in spite of staff efforts to retain the most competent and reliable R/Is. Turnover was also affected by the fact that the project mostly attracted R/Is who had multiple and often conflicting commitments, such as university students. We found that most students were competent and motivated, although they regularly requested time off during examination periods and holidays, something that cannot always be accommodated into a data collection schedule. To address this issue, we sought to have a large number of trained R/Is available at all times. However, that number could not be too large (around eight persons for PACE). Otherwise, there was not sufficient work for all of them, which contributed to the turnover problem because R/Is sought other sources of employment to supplement their income.

Recruitment, interviewing, and retention of families

Recruiting families. Once the start date of the PACE program at a particular center had been set, two R/Is were assigned to the center, where they were in charge of recruitment and data collection. Recruitment began six weeks prior to the first program session. At that time, handouts were sent to each family with a 3–6-year-old child at the center. The handout briefly described the PACE program and provided practical information – that is, start date and time, location, incentives, and person to contact to register or obtain additional information. PACE offered the following incentives to all participants: free meal held at the childcare center prior to each session and open to parents and all of their children; free child care; and reimbursement for transportation costs ($3 paid in cash at the end of the session). (We initially considered using vans and buses belonging to the centers for transportation. This option was abandoned after consultation with center directors, because of cost and liability issues.) In addition to the handouts sent home, two colored posters that contained the same information as the handout were displayed prominently in each center to advertise the program.

Throughout the recruitment period, R/Is visited their assigned center once per week for two hours to host a recruitment table to advertise the program, answer questions, and enroll interested parents. To ensure that a maximum number of parents could be reached, the recruitment table was held on different days each week from 4 to 6 p.m., a time when parents typically came to collect their children. R/Is were instructed to approach each parent entering or leaving the childcare center and to offer to explain the program and answer questions. They also offered program handouts, magnets, and pens with PACE contact information. Questions parents typically asked revolved around the parenting strategies the program promotes and the incentives PACE offered. In line with evidence showing that recruitment strategies are most effective when they are personalized (Schlernitzauer, Bierhals, & Geary, 1998), numerous parents who have enrolled in PACE have commented that they appreciated the personal contact and information the R/Is provided about aspects of the program that could not be found in the handouts or posters. We believe that this is particularly important in prevention efforts, as the population targeted is rarely seeking services. The majority of parents who attended PACE were not reporting significant parenting challenges when we approached them, even though such challenges regularly emerged later in the course of group discussions. R/Is must be sensitive to this issue and trained to present the program in a preventive perspective: it is not designed to remedy parental deficiencies or shortcomings, or to treat children with behavior problems, but rather to enhance parental competencies as participants discuss common childrearing issues that *all* parents are confronted with.

Interviewing families. Parents who enrolled in the PACE program provided R/Is with their telephone number(s) and address, along with information on one or two alternate contacts that could be reached if the parent was unavailable. Prior to the start of the program, an R/I contacted each parent to schedule a time to conduct a Parent Survey, a structured interview in which information was collected about child adjustment, parenting practices, and family sociodemographic characteristics. The interview took place at the childcare center or at the parent's home. At the end of the PACE program and at a one-year follow up, the R/I contacted again each parent who enrolled in the program, regardless of attendance, to complete the same survey. Procedures were in place to ensure that each parent was contacted in the same manner. Specifically, prior to each survey, the R/I attempted to contact the parent via telephone on five occasions. If the parent could not be reached, the R/I proceeded in the following order: (i) phoned an alternate contact on five occasions, (ii) sent a letter to the parent's last known address, (iii) consulted with the childcare center director in an attempt to reach the parent through the center, (iv) went to the parent's home (last known address) in order to complete the interview without an appointment. If the parent was not home, the R/I left a "Sorry I Missed You" note on the door, which contained the R/I's name and telephone number. Each R/I kept a log of all contact attempts that included dates, times, modes of attempted contact, and results.

Retaining families. Once parents enrolled in PACE, they were regularly tracked to preserve the integrity of the research sample. As the program reached parents who were often disadvantaged and lived in precarious conditions, many PACE families moved and/or changed telephone numbers frequently. Staff attempted to address this challenge to retention in different ways. First, all target children received birthday cards with complete PACE contact information. These cards served to: (i) recognize children on this important day; (ii) remind parents to contact the PACE office if a move or change in telephone number has occurred or was planned; and (iii) notify PACE staff of a move if the birthday card was returned by the postal service. Second, PACE staff contacted parents once every three months in order to update the family's contact information and, if applicable, to remind them of their upcoming one-year follow-up interview. All parents were contacted for tracking purposes in the same manner as they were to schedule the Parent Survey interviews. In spite of concerted efforts, tracking remained a major challenge for PACE staff. Specifically, 79% of parents completed the one-year follow up interview. These parents were successfully contacted by telephone (18%), by sending a letter or birthday card to either the child's home or daycare center (6%), by phoning an alternate contact (<1%), or through a combination of these methods (55%). Of the remaining 21% of parents, 4% declined to participate in the follow-up interview and 17% could not be contacted because they had disconnected phone numbers, had provided inaccurate or incomplete contact information, and/or had moved without leaving a forwarding address.

Adherence to protocol (fidelity monitoring)

Adherence to protocol is an essential element of sound research and service delivery (Dumas, Lynch, Laughlin, Smith, & Prinz, 2001). In other words, in a program such as PACE, it is imperative that researchers demonstrate that intervention content (the delivery of services) and process (the manner of delivery) are comparable across groups and faithful to the program manual (Moncher & Prinz, 1991). To monitor content and process fidelity, all group sessions were audiotaped. Group leaders wore a lapel microphone connected to a small recording device they carried on their belt or in a pocket. The microphone captured their voice but not that of the participants, thus ensuring the latter that we did not obtain a permanent record of their contributions to the group. Each tape was then coded by trained fidelity coders. Coders were trained and supervised by a senior graduate student, who also served as reliability checker. Coder training took place over a four-week period and required approximately 15–20 hours of both group and individual meetings. It was based on a detailed coding manual developed for that purpose, as well as on specific coding situations that had proved to be particularly challenging in the past. Throughout training, coders were required to complete set assignments until they met a satisfactory level of reliability. They were then assigned tapes to code weekly and, if necessary, were retrained when their level of reliability dropped.

Two types of fidelity were assessed. *Content fidelity* reflected the extent to which the intervention components were actually delivered. Coders listened to each audiotape in its entirety to assess content fidelity. They did so with purpose-made coding sheets that listed each session component in the order in which the session was designed to unfold, and provided space to check whether the GL covered the component or failed to do so. *Process fidelity* reflected the manner in which the session was conducted (i.e., the extent to which the GL used effective communication skills). Coders listened to a randomly-selected 30-minute segment of each tape and recorded critical incidents of ineffective communication if they occurred, before rating the GL's overall performance on each of ten critical skills (e.g., listens attentively; allows parents to present their thoughts/ideas; presents materials in a clear, correct, and simple manner).

Fidelity data reported here are based on 324 coded sessions. PACE strived to maintain average fidelity statistics above 80%. However, individual session ratings often varied, either because events beyond the GL's control challenged the leader's ability to adhere to the program, or because the leader deviated from the program. In the latter case, deviations from protocol were discussed in weekly supervision with the GL and steps were taken to remedy the situation. For example, fidelity coding may have shown that a GL gave examples and shared opinions about child discipline with the group that varied from the parenting strategies taught in the manualized program. When this occurred, the project manager conducted an individual training session with the GL focusing on the importance of adhering to the empirically supported strategies.

Data showed that, on average, GLs demonstrated high levels of content (92%) and process (94%) fidelity, but that they regularly struggled to follow the time guidelines associated with each session activity. Specifically, they only conducted 47% of the activities within their prescribed time limits, in part because these limits applied to average groups of 10–12 participants but were more difficult to follow with smaller or larger groups. Finally, coder reliability was assessed weekly on approximately 25% of tapes coded. Overall percentage agreement was satisfactory for both content (84%) and process fidelity (73%).

Methods to address barriers to engagement

While preventive interventions have been shown to be effective in reducing negative parent and child outcomes, the validity and large-scale dissemination of empirically-based programs are often threatened by limited parental engagement (Spoth & Redmond, 2000). Specifically, studies of prevention trials have indicated that 35–50% of participants do not attend the first appointment/session, and that 50% of participants do not complete the intervention (Miller & Prinz, 2003). Research studying this lack of engagement in prevention programs has highlighted several contributing factors (Cunningham et al., 2000), with limited time availability and conflict and cost associated with engagement serving as the most prominent factors. To address these common barriers to engagement, the PACE program utilized several strategies specifically targeting these factors.

Logistical barriers. To address time and scheduling demands for parents enrolled in PACE, the program took place at the child's daycare center at times that were convenient to parents. Typically, the program took place immediately after school, so the parents could pick up their children at their usual time and then remain at the school for the duration of the program. In addition, PACE offered transportation, child care, and dinner to the families attending the program, in an attempt to remove cost and inconvenience for parents.

Monetary incentives. To increase engagement, some prevention programs provide monetary incentives to improve attendance at sessions (Guyll, Spoth, & Redmond, 2003; Heinrichs, 2006). To evaluate the impact of this strategy on engagement in the PACE program, daycare centers were randomized into incentive (PACE-I) and non-incentive (PACE-NI) conditions. In PACE-I, parents received $3 per session for the first two sessions they attended, $6 for the next two sessions, $10 for the two sessions after that, and $15 for the last two sessions. Comparisons of the two conditions showed that parents did not enroll in greater numbers, attend more sessions, or participate more actively in PACE-I than in PACE-NI (Dumas, Begle, French, & Pearl, 2010). In other words, our data suggest that monetary incentives may not be an effective strategy for improving engagement in preventive parenting programs.

Cultural sensitivity

Although we have focused here on the original American program, we note that adaptations of an intervention, such as PACE for use with families from minority backgrounds and/or in other nations, do, of course, call for sensitivity to cross-linguistic issues and to the parenting styles, needs and values specific to those cultural settings (Vesely, Ewaida, & Anderson, 2014; Dishion and Yasui, Chapter 17, this volume). Achieving the optimal balance between these considerations and the strategies and goals of the original program incurs additional challenges, and calls for extensive consultation with local experts and parents. Fuller accounts of how this was addressed in adapting PACE for implementation with Latino families in the United States and French-speaking families in Switzerland are available elsewhere (Dumas, Arriaga, Begle, & Longoria, 2010; Dumas & Lucia, 2012).

Conclusions

There is considerable agreement among researchers, interventionists, and policy-makers that serious and often chronic disorders, such as disruptive behavior disorders, are best prevented, rather than cured. If prevention makes sense – humanely, socially, and economically – systematic efforts informed by sound research are still in their early development and the field has much to gain from sharing the lessons learned so far in individual projects. The aim of this chapter was to share the lessons learned through the PACE program and to describe the manner in which practical challenges in its implementation were met.

Beyond the challenges addressed here, we are constantly reminded as we set up new PACE groups that most of the parents we are attempting to reach are *not* seeking parenting advice or behavioral help for their young children. Rather, they state that they are interested in participating in order to discuss common challenges that all parents face to some extent with preschool children, and to give and receive social support in the process.

More generally, we believe that the PACE program can be helpful at a time when most parents are able to exercise adequate and positive authority over their children – and can thus prevent behavioral and emotional difficulties before they arise. Our major challenge is to convince parents that the program can be beneficial, even though they are not specifically looking for help. This is the challenge faced by all who seek to prevent any harmful effect – to convince, without coercing, that a small investment of time and effort now may pay large dividends months or years later.

Most importantly, empirical evidence has shown that higher engagement in the PACE program was effective in reducing negative parent and child outcomes at pre- and postintervention, and one-year follow-up (Begle & Dumas, 2011). Specifically, results indicated that higher attendance in the program predicted reduced child abuse potential ($d = 0.15$) and parenting stress ($d = 0.17$), and increased child coping competence ($d = 0.23$) and parental satisfaction ($d = 0.24$). Statistics reported in effect sizes (d), where the larger the effect size (d), the greater the strength of the relationship between two variables. According to Cohen (1992), an effect size (d) of 0.2 is considered small, 0.48 is considered medium, and 0.8 is considered large. Thus, these results demonstrate that small-to-medium improvements in child and parent outcomes were seen immediately following program completion and maintained (or improved) in the following year. Further, parent participation was equivalent to or higher than comparable programs in the field (Barkley et al., 2000; Conduct Problems Prevention Research Group, 2000). A detailed description of the results can be found elsewhere (Begle & Dumas, 2011).

Although most laypersons are unlikely to be convinced of the potential benefit of a preventive parenting program on the basis of research evidence alone, many may accept the argument that a relatively small investment of time and effort now may pay large dividends months or years later – especially when this argument appears to be supported by research. However, we recognize that it is a difficult argument to make to parents with young children, who have a busy schedule and many conflicting and often stressful demands on their time and energy. But this is the only argument we have – one that, we hope, will become easier to make as more and more projects such as ours show that it is worth preventing oppositional and conduct disorders, and that children are the main beneficiaries.

Acknowledgments

Preparation of this manuscript was supported by grant R49/CCR 522339 from the Centers for Disease Control and Prevention (CDC) to the second author. We thank our CDC collaborators for their invaluable advice and support, especially Linda Anne Valle and Michele Hoover. We also thank our PACE collaborators, especially Amanda Mosby, Sharon Hampton, and Stephanie Wynder, for their genuine efforts on behalf of the project. In addition, we would like to thank Megan Buckley and Corey Connelly for assistance in final preparation of the manuscript. Finally, and most importantly, we thank the many parents, teachers, and center directors and staff without whom PACE would not exist.

References

Barkley, R. A., Shelton, T. L., Crosswait, C., Moorehouse, M., Fletcher, K., Barrett, S., et al. (2000). Multi-method psycho-educational intervention for preschool children with disruptive behavior: Preliminary results at post-treatment. *Journal of Child Psychology and Psychiatry, 41,* 319–332.

Begle, A. M., & Dumas, J. E. (2011). Child and parental outcomes following engagement in the preventive parenting program: Efficacy of the PACE Program. *Journal of Primary Prevention, 32*(2), 67.

Briggs-Gowan, M. J., Carter, A. S., Skuban, E. M., & Horwitz, S. M. (2001). Prevalence of social-emotional and behavioral problems in a community sample of 1- and 2-year-old children. *Journal of the American Academy of Child & Adolescent Psychiatry, 40,*(7), 811–819.

Bub, K. L., McCartney, K., & Willett, J. B. (2007). Behavior problem trajectories and first-grade cognitive ability and achievement skills: A latent growth curve analysis. *Journal of Educational Psychology, 3,* 653–670.

Campbell, S. B. (2002). *Behavior problems in preschool children: Clinical and developmental issues.* New York: Guilford Press.

Cohen, J. (1992). A power primer. *Psychological Bulletin, 112*(1), 155–159.

Compas, B., Conner-Smith, J., Saltzman, H., Thomsen, A., & Wadsworth, M. (2001). Coping with stress during childhood and adolescence: Problems, progress, and potential in theory and research. *Psychological Bulletin, 127,* 87–127.

Conduct Problems Prevention Research Group. (2000). Merging universal and indicated prevention problems: The Fast Track model. *Addictive Behaviors, 25,* 913–927.

Cunningham, C. E., Boyle, M., Offord, D., Racine, Y., Hundert, J., Secord, M., et al. (2000). Tri-ministry study: Correlates of school-based parenting course utilization. *Journal of Consulting and Clinical Psychology, 68,* 928–933.

Dishion, T. J., & Patterson, G. R. (2006). The development and ecology of antisocial behavior in children and adolescents. In D. Cicchetti & D. J. Cohen (Eds.), *Developmental psychopathology, Vol. 3: Risk, disorder, and adaptation* (2nd ed.) (pp. 503 – 541). Hoboken, NJ: John Wiley & Sons, Inc.

Dumas, J. E. (2005). The dynamics of positive parenting: Psychological, social and cultural contexts. In H. Grietens, W. Lahaye, W. Hellinckx, & L. Vandemeulebroecke (Eds.), *In the best interests of children and youth. International perspectives* (pp. 27–46). Leuven, Belgium: Leuven University Press.

Dumas, J. E., Arriaga, X., Begle, A. M., & Longoria, Z. (2010). "When will your program be available in Spanish?" Adapting an early parenting intervention for Latino families. *Cognitive and Behavioral Practice, 17*(2), 176–187.

Dumas, J. E., Arriaga, X. B., Begle, A. M., & Longoria, Z. N. (2011). Child and parental outcomes of a group parenting intervention for Latino families: A pilot study of the CANNE program. *Cultural Diversity and Ethnic Minority Psychology, 17*(1), 107–115.

Dumas, J. E., Begle, A. M., French, B., & Pearl, A. (2010). Effects of monetary incentives on engagement in the PACE parenting program. *JCCAP, 39,* 302–313.

Dumas, J. E., & Lucia, S. (2012). Promoting coping competence in young children. *Swiss Journal of Psychology, 71*(2), 67–72.

Dumas, J. E., Lemay, P., & Dauwalder, J.-P. (2001). Dynamic analyses of mother-child interactions in functional and dysfunctional dyads: A synergetic approach. *Journal of Abnormal Child Psychology, 29,* 317–329.

Dumas, J. E., Lynch, A. M., Laughlin, J. E., Smith, E. P., & Prinz, R. J. (2001). Promoting intervention fidelity: Conceptual issues, methods, and preliminary results from the EARLY ALLIANCE prevention trial. *American Journal of Preventive Medicine, 20,* 38–47.

Dumas, J. E., Moreland, A., Gitter, A., Pearl, A., & Nordstrom, A. (2006). Engaging parents in preventive parenting groups: Do ethnic, socioeconomic, and belief match between parents and group leaders matter? *Health Education and Behavior.*

Dumas, J. E., Prinz, R. J., Smith, E. P., & Laughlin, J. (1999). The EARLY ALLIANCE prevention trial: An integrated set of interventions to promote competence and reduce risk for conduct disorder, substance abuse, and school failure. *Clinical Child and Family Psychology Review, 2,* 37–53.

Eyberg, S.M., Nelson, M.M., & Boggs, S.R. (2008). Evidence-based psychosocial treatments for children and adolescents with disruptive behavior. *Journal of Consulting and Clinical Psychology, 37*(1), 215–237.

Fanti, K. A., & Henrich, C. C. (2010). Trajectories of pure and co-occurring internalizing and externalizing problems from age 2 to age 12: findings from the National Institute of Child Health and Human Development Study of Early Child Care. *Developmental Psychology, 46*(5), 1159–1175.

Guyll, M., Spoth, R., & Redmond, C. (2003). The effects of incentives and research requirements on participation rates for a community-based preventive intervention research study. *Journal of Primary Prevention, 24,* 25–41.

Heinrichs N. (2006). The effects of two different incentives on recruitment rates of families into a prevention program. *Journal of Primary Prevention, (27),* 345–365.

Kazdin, A. E. (2005). *Parent management training.* New York: Oxford University Press.

Kopp, C. B. (1991). Young children's progression to self-regulation. In M. Bullock (Ed.), *The development of intentional action: Cognitive, motivational, and interactive processes* (pp. 38–54). Basel, Switzerland: Karger.

Lucia, S., & Dumas, J. E. (2013). Entre-parents: Initial outcome evaluation of a preventive-parenting program for French-speaking parents. *Journal of Primary Prevention, 34,* 135–146.

Lunkenheimer, E. S., Kemp, C. J., & Albrecht, E. C. (2013). Contingencies in mother–child teaching interactions and behavioral regulation and dysregulation in early childhood. *Social Development, 22,* 319–339.

Maramba, G. G., & Hall, G. C. N. (2002). Meta-analyses of ethnic match as a predictor of dropout, utilization, and level of functioning. *Cultural Diversity and Ethnic Minority Psychology, 8,* 290–297.

Miller, G. E., & Prinz, R. J. (2003) Engagement of families in treatment for childhood conduct problems. *Behavioral Therapy, 34*(4), 517–534.

Moncher, F., & Prinz, R. J. (1991). Treatment fidelity in outcome studies. *C Psy R, 11,* 247–266.

Moreland, A. D., & Dumas, J. E. (2007). Evaluating child coping competence: Theory and measurement. *Journal of Child and Family Studies, 17,* 437–454.

Nation, M., Crusto, C., Wandersman, A., Kumpfer, K. L., Seybolt, D., Morrissey-Kane, E., & Davino, K. (2003). What works in prevention principles of effective prevention programs. *American Psychologist, 58*(6/7), 449–456.

Pearl, A. M., French, B. F., Dumas, J. E., Moreland, A. D., & Prinz, R. (2014). Bidirectional effects of parenting quality and child externalizing behavior in predominantly single parent, under-resourced African American families. *Journal of Child and Family Studies, 23*(2), 177–188.

Prinz, R., Smith, E., Dumas, J., Laughlin, J., White, D., & Barron, R. (2002). Recruitment and retention of participants in prevention trials involving family based interventions. *American Journal of Preventive Medicine, 20,* 31–37.

Raver, C. C., & Knitze, J. (2002). *Ready to Enter: What Research Tells Policymakers About Strategies to Promote Social and Emotional School Readiness Among Three- and Four-Year-Olds.* Promoting the Emotional Well-Being of Children and Families, Policy Paper No. 3. New York: National Center for Children in Poverty, Columbia University.

Reis, B. F., & Brown, L. G. (1999). Reducing psychotherapy dropouts: Maximizing perspective convergence in the psychotherapy dyad. *Psychotherapy: Theory, Research, Practice, Training, 36,* 123–136.

Sanders, M. (2008). Triple P-Positive Parenting Program as a public health approach to strengthening parenting. *Journal of Family Psychology, 22,* 506–517.

Sandler, I. N., Schoenfelder, E. N., Wolchik, S. A., & MacKinnon, D. P. (2011). Long-term impact of prevention programs to promote effective parenting: Lasting effects but uncertain processes. *Annual Review of Psychology, 62,* 299–329.

Schlernitzauer, M., Bierhals, A., & Geary, M. (1998). Recruitment methods for intervention research in bereavement-related depression: Five years' experience. *American Journal of Geriatric Psychiatry, 6,* 67–74.

Shaw, D. S., Dishion, T. J., Supplee, L., Gardner, F., & Arnds, K. (2006). Randomized trial of a family-centered approach to the prevention of early conduct problems: 2-year effects of the family check-up in early childhood. *Journal of Consulting and Clinical Psychology, 74*(1), 1–9.

Soltis, K., Davidson, T. M., Moreland, A., Felton, J., & Dumas, J. E. (2013). Associations among parental stress, child competence, and school-readiness: Findings from the PACE study. *Journal of Child and Family Studies, 24*(3), 649–657.

Spoth, R., & Redmond, C. (2000). Research on family engagement in preventive interventions: Toward improved use of scientific findings in primary prevention practice. *Journal of Primary Prevention, (21)*, 267–284.

Vesely, C. K., Ewaida, M., & Anderson, E. A. (2014). Cultural competence of parenting education programs used by Latino families: A review. *Hispanic Journal of Behavioral Sciences, 36*(1), 27–47.

Zubrick, S. R., Northey, K., Silburn, S. R., Williams, A. W., Blair, E., Robertson, D., et al. (2005). Prevention of child behavior problems via universal implementation of a group behavioral family intervention. *Prevention Science, 6*, 287–304.

5

Parenting Information and Advice and the Mass Media

Matthew R. Sanders and Rachel Calam

Modern parents are raising their children in an age of technology where access to parenting advice has never been so great. In addition to the many portrayals of family life in the media, the hundreds of parenting books, web sites and now reality television shows, such as "Super Nanny" and "Nanny 911", which focus on how to raise children and deal with parenting problems have placed the provision of parenting advice within the popular culture. The mass media, including television, radio, the World Wide Web, and print media (e.g., newspapers, newsletters) has a potentially important role to play in the provision of parenting advice as part of a comprehensive, population-based strategy to improve the confidence, skills and knowledge of parents in the task of raising children. As Leach shows (Chapter 2, this volume), philosophers, developmental scientists and a range of others have been well aware of this potential over the last few centuries; recent advances in mass communications have expanded greatly the contents and reach of media that can provide perspectives on caregiving.

In parallel, as parents are becoming increasingly sophisticated consumers of parenting information, and as access to the Internet increases, more parents turn

The Wiley Handbook of Developmental Psychology in Practice: Implementation and Impact, First Edition.
Edited by Kevin Durkin and H. Rudolph Schaffer.
© 2016 John Wiley & Sons, Ltd. Published 2016 by John Wiley & Sons, Ltd.

to technology for advice to complement more traditional ways of accessing parenting wisdom and advice, such as through the extended family and/or group and individual parenting programs run by service providers. This generation of parents is not frightened by technology; it expects high standards and is hard to impress. However, the proliferation of online content also predisposes parents to consume conflicting and/or unhelpful advice when it is needed most. For example, a Google search of "positive parenting" yields 1,180,000 sites; yet only a tiny proportion of these sites are derived through an evidence-based lens. Accordingly, while these technological developments have the potential to facilitate new ways of engaging parents in positive practices, they require the establishment of new approaches to delivery and to research evaluating outcomes. They also present new ethical challenges. This chapter explores the potential role of the mass media in promoting improved parenting and as a result better developmental outcomes in children.

Why the Mass Media is Important as a Parenting Intervention

The mass media has the potential to offer a more efficient and affordable format for providing quality information about parenting to families than do traditional approaches to parenting interventions. The media form part of a larger system of support available to families, complementing more intensive support and extending the reach of parenting programs to those who might not otherwise be reached. This includes both resource-based and psychological barriers to program reach. Some families may live in areas where there are low levels of access to services available, perhaps for geographical reasons. In some areas, service resources may be very stretched and parents who seek help may experience long waiting times. Other families may have ready access to high quality services locally, but opt not to partake in these options, for a wide range of reasons. Alternatively, others may simply not be aware of the potential help that would be available. The mass media has the possibility to overcome many of these barriers, both by providing information about parenting and by demonstrating the power of parenting interventions to bring about positive change.

The range and type of mass media have grown substantially, with new formats and broadcast possibilities emerging at a rapid pace due largely to the influence of the Internet. However, television remains a primary source and continues to exert a considerable influence over attitudes, beliefs, awareness, and behavior, making it potentially one of the most powerful educators (Zimmerman, 1996; Viswanath & Finnegan, 2002; Wakefield, Loken, & Hornik, 2010).

Limited impact of traditional parenting programs

There is substantial evidence showing that parenting interventions can reduce a range of childhood problems including conduct problems, ADHD, and internalizing problems (Cummings et al., Chapter 3, this volume; Sanders, 2012). However, relatively few parents actually participate in group or individually administered parenting programs. For example, one study demonstrated that only a minority (14%) of parents of 4–7 year old children had participated in any form of parenting program (Sanders, Ralph, et al., 2008). Many families who could benefit from parenting programs receive no services at all. The potential of parenting programs to reduce the prevalence of problematic outcomes for children in the entire population is diminished, and the value of proven programs remains limited (Biglan & Metzler, 1998). Hence, alternative forms of reaching parents with empirically supported parenting information are needed (Sanders & Turner, 2002).

The relatively low level of penetration of parenting programs into the community led to the development of the Triple P-Positive Parenting Program (Sanders, 2012). Triple P is a multilevel system of parenting interventions which seeks to increase the confidence and skills of parents to bring about reductions in social, emotional and behavioral problems in children and adolescents. The multilevel system includes a dedicated media and communications strategy that is designed to increase access of the program to parents and to reduce the stigma associated with seeking parenting support. Some of the key features of the Triple P system are outlined here.

Providing flexible options for parents

Parents differ in terms of how they prefer to obtain parenting information and support. Attendance at a parenting group, a common medium for the delivery of parenting advice, is only one of a number of possibilities (albeit a strongly evidence-based one). One survey of how parents wished to receive parenting advice showed that television was the third most preferred means of receiving parenting advice (Centre for Community Child Health, 2004). A web survey of working parents in the United Kingdom indicated that approximately 15% of parents said they wished to receive a workplace parenting program as a self-help program and 25% as a web-delivered program (Sanders, Haslam, Calam, Southwell, & Stallman, 2011). The corresponding figures for individual and group programs were 29 and 27%, respectively. No single modality accounted for more than 30% of parents.

Improving the reach of parenting programs. A primary advantage of a mass media-based strategy over traditional parent education methods is its capacity to increase the reach of parenting programs without relying on attendance at a parenting group or individual sessions. Parents themselves express clear preferences for delivery of parenting via formats such as television, online programs, and written materials over formats such as home visits, therapists, and multiweek parenting groups (Metzler, Sanders, Rusby, & Crowley, 2012). The mass media has a pervasive impact on people's lives (Brown & Walsh-Childers, 2002). Virtually all households with children have at least one television. The average number of TV sets in households around the world ranges from 1.23 in developing countries such as Tanzania up to three in the United States (Tekcarta, 2015). The average American watches 4.5 hours of television per day (EurodataTV, 2005). The amount of total media use by American youngsters is now estimated at 7 hours 38 minutes per day (Rideout, Foehr, & Roberts, 2010). Increasingly, people are turning to television for both information and entertainment. This "infotainment" genre has become increasingly popular in recent years. Recent data indicate that traditional reality shows (e.g., "Big Brother") are declining in popularity and being replaced by "coach" shows, in which experts help individuals improve their health, well-being, and daily functioning (EurodataTV, 2005). The popularity of shows such as Supernanny and Nanny 911 in the United States and "Driving Mum and Dad Mad" and "Little Angels" in the United Kingdom have demonstrated that parenting coach shows have tremendous audience pulling power; audiences appear eager for information and entertainment about the ways in which other people handle problems and challenges (McAlister & Fernandez, 2002). Supernanny and Nanny 911 averaged approximately 8–9.5 million viewers per episode in their first seasons in the United States (Worrell, 2005). The six-week infotainment series Driving Mum and Dad Mad was broadcast in early 2005 during prime time on the largest commercial television network in the United Kingdom (ITV) and attracted a peak audience of 5.9 million viewers and an average weekly audience of over 4.23 million viewers (market share of approximately 25%).

Capacity to reach the target audience. Television programs on parenting that feature parents of children with conduct problems are an effective vehicle for reaching the target age demographic (i.e., adults 25–40 years old who are parents). Nanny 911 frequently prevailed in its time slot among adults and women 18–34 and 25–34, and was ranked in the top 20 shows for 12–34 year olds. Similarly, Supernanny was ranked in the top 20 shows for 18–49 year olds (Media Life, 2005). This increased capacity to reach the target audience with messages about effective parenting can contribute to greater awareness regarding the importance of children's well-being, effective parenting techniques, and ways that parents can access additional support if needed. The mass media also has the potential to reach families who may not otherwise access any parenting support at all. For instance, Sanders, Ralph, et al. (2008) found that only 17% of parents of children with conduct problems in their community sample had accessed services for their children's behavioral problems.

Learning through modeling. There is considerable research evidence derived from Bandura's cognitive social learning theory (Bandura, 1977, 1986, 2011) that has established the efficacy of modeling in promoting behavior change (Harwood & Weissberg, 1987). Video modeling has been used successfully to teach a variety of complex skills across many psychological and educational applications (Harwood & Weissberg, 1987), and provides demonstration of skills not possible in written self-help material (Flay, 1987). In addition, the notion of self-efficacy, a central feature of a self-regulation approach, also underpins the effectiveness of video-based modeling. Individuals witnessing a model who successfully enacts a behavior tend to improve their own self-efficacy (Bandura, 1977, 1986). Witnesses are more likely to act on intentions to change their behavior to the extent that they have high self-efficacy, or believe that they are competent to enact the intended behavior. Furthermore, behavioral changes achieved with the aid of video-based messages are more likely to be attributed to one's own efforts (Flay, 1987), which can empower people and increase their sense of competence.

Providing normative information about children's development. Mass media interventions have the potential to provide useful information to parents about child development. Parents' beliefs about child development serve as the foundation of their teaching and behavior management practices (McGillicuddy-De Lisi, 2009; McGillicuddy-De Lisi & Sigel, 1995). Television can help parents recognize early warning signs of children's behavioral and emotional problems (Sanders & Markie-Dadds, 1996), encourage parents to seek professional help early when interventions are more likely to be effective, and provide information on available services (Sanders, Turner, & Markie-Dadds, 1996).

Normalizing help seeking for parenting. Media-based strategies about parenting also have the potential to normalize parenting assistance in a nonstigmatizing context. Positive messages about parenting assistance may enable parents to conveniently access useful information, advice, and support. These messages also compete with other more alarmist, sensationalized, and sometimes accusatory parent- or child-blaming messages concerning child and family issues that can appear in some sectors of the media. By framing media messages about parenting with a universal premise that positive parenting methods are for all caregivers, and by making programs readily accessible to parents (e.g., via public media as well as primary care settings and schools), the delivery context for parenting interventions can be broadened to be more universal and therefore more inclusive.

Principle of sufficiency. A key concept in a public health approach to prevention is to provide the minimally sufficient level of intervention that parents need to be successful in undertaking parenting tasks. The advantages of adhering to this principle in terms of cost efficiency are obvious, but there are other benefits as well. Too often, interventions are structured using a format that imposes the maximum-available intensity of intervention on all participants. This "overkill" approach has drawbacks. Sometimes it is more than parents want or need, and it can promote dependence rather than fostering parents' self-sufficiency and personal efficacy (Sanders, 1999). By its nature, a mass media-based approach is forced to adopt a minimally sufficient requirement for practical reasons, which also lends itself to flexible utilization by parents.

Use of a self-regulatory framework. A distinctive feature of the Triple P-Positive Parenting Program system is its emphasis on self-regulation. This occurs at several levels: (i) parents learn to promote self-regulation in children; (ii) parents learn to apply self-regulatory principles in their positive parenting methods and with regard to their own coping skills; and (iii) practitioners use delivery methods that promote self-regulation in parents by mastering program content. The media-approach builds on this principle via self-administration of the program and by promoting self-regulatory concepts in the program content itself. The importance and roles of self-regulatory processes in child development and parent–child relations are well established (Bronson, 2000; Drake, Belsky, & Fearon, 2013; Wahler & Smith, 1999).

Influence on community norms and awareness. Television programs on parenting may contribute to redefining social norms and cultural attitudes about parenting by promoting community awareness of the importance of positive parenting skills and of positive family relationships (Abt & Seesholtz, 1994; Bandura, 2002). This is a potentially powerful means of promoting change at a societal level.

Engaging content and formats. No matter how empirically supported the principles and methods of a parenting program are, the program can fail if the participants do not find the program content interesting and engaging. This principle is consistent with key facets of social learning theory, such as modeling and reinforcement (Bandura, 1986), as well as with educational tenets of effective instruction (Engelmann & Carnine, 1982) and information processing (Parrott, 1995). In the media strategies linked to Triple P, therefore, programming on parenting is designed to be presented in an engaging, interesting, and concise manner.

Mass Media and the Public Health Approach to Parenting Support

A key assumption of population-based approach is that parenting intervention strategies should be widely accessible in the community. In addition, a public health approach to behavior change assumes that the mass media plays an important role in reaching individuals to affect their knowledge, attitudes, and behaviors;

in changing public norms; and in affecting institutional policies (Hornik, 2002; Wakefield et al., 2010).

Observational documentaries and "coach" shows, in which experts help individuals improve their health, well-being, and daily functioning have become a popular genre. Shows like Supernanny and Little Angels have put dialogue about raising children into the popular culture and have demonstrated that parenting shows have tremendous audience appeal. Audiences appear receptive to information and entertainment about the ways in which other people handle problems and challenges (McAlister & Fernandez, 2002). However, few of these popular programs have been subjected to empirical evaluation to determine their effects on parents or children.

Given the potential for substantial public health impact, research is needed that examines the effects the mass media has for teaching parenting skills (Biglan & Metzler, 1998; Sanders, Montgomery, & Blechman-Toussaint, 2000). Little is known about the impact of reality television programs on parenting. It is unclear what types of families benefit or are adversely affected by media interventions, how media messages are received by parents, or how media messages can be designed to maximize the likelihood of producing change in parents' parenting practices. A few studies document the beneficial effects of parenting television programmes (Sanders, Montgomery, & Brechman-Toussaint, 2000).

Investigating the application of Triple P as a media intervention

Sanders et al. (2000) evaluated the effects of a primetime television series on parenting, "Families", shown in New Zealand. Each of the 12 episodes included brief examples of causes of child behavior problems from a social learning perspective, provided guidance on monitoring behavior, and modeled parenting strategies to encourage desirable behavior, prevent problems and manage difficult behavior. Strategies were integrated into plans for dealing with common problems, promoting children's development, and managing developmental issues. Parents watching the series showed a significantly greater reduction in the percentage of children scoring in the clinically elevated range (46% to 14%) following intervention. Mothers also reported increased sense of competence and satisfaction in their parenting abilities.

A Conceptual Framework for the Use of the Media

The media can play an important role in raising parents' awareness and willingness to attend a parenting program. Specifically, the media strategy is used to: (i) promote the use of positive parenting practices in the community (increase parental self-sufficiency);

(ii) increase the receptivity of parents towards participating in parenting programs and family/child interventions; (iii) Destigmatize and normalize the process of seeking help for children with behavioral and emotional problems; (iv) increase the visibility and reach of various interventions; and (v) counter alarmist, sensational or parent-blaming messages in the media.

Different media messages can be used to demystify what is involved in a parenting program by providing relevant, meaningful and accurate information for parents. Media messages can provide parent testimonials and depict the parent's experiences of receiving professional support. Some message content can change parents' negative attributions for their child's misbehavior by providing alternative explanations (e.g., tantrums maintained by parental attention and food rewards). Radio, print and television media provide models of positive parenting skills and effective discipline strategies with the view of creating positive expectancies for change and enhancing parental self-efficacy.

The conceptual framework for the development of media strategies is outlined in Figure 5.1. The aim is to use the media to move nonparticipating parents from a precontemplative stage (i.e., the parent has not considered doing a parenting program), to contemplating becoming involved at whatever level meets the parent's needs and minimizes their cost of being involved (e.g., watching a television current affairs story on Triple P, attending a Triple P seminar, calling a telephone counselling service such as Parentline). The media strategy aims to increase social support for the parenting role and, thereby, increase parental self-efficacy to implement depicted parenting information and maintain changes in parenting practices.

Rather than having a time limited media campaign that relies on any specific media outlet, it is possible to develop a longer term, cumulative strategy based on building positive relationships with local media. The Every Family study, described

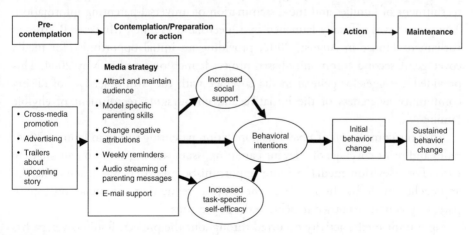

Figure 5.1   Conceptual model for media-based parenting interventions.

in the next section, gives an example of this. A blend of responding to media-initiated news-driven requests for comment or information and planned, project-initiated activities – such as press releases, provision of newspaper columns and advertising – was used in this particular context and provides an example of the development of a comprehensive, long term media strategy.

Case Examples of Media Strategies in Action

In this section, three examples are given of studies that have utilized media-based delivery of Triple P, and which have been systematically evaluated. These studies, based in Australia, New Zealand and the United Kingdom, indicate the potential for successful engagement with the media in promoting change in parenting.

Every Family

Every Family (Sanders, Ralph, et al., 2008) funded by *beyondblue:* The National Depression Initiative was a large scale population level parenting intervention targeting 12,000 parents of children in the 4–7 age group who were transitioning to school. The five-level Triple P-Positive Parenting Program system was implemented over a three-year period and provides an example of a study incorporating a strong media strategy. The focus of the media strategy in the initial stages was primarily on developing awareness of the parenting project and promoting interest from families. Media activities then progressively focused on continued engagement and recruitment of families and the dissemination of universal parenting information. The project was officially launched by Queensland Premier, Mr Peter Beattie, at Parliament House in August, 2002, providing an initial opportunity for media coverage. A second community-based project launch occurred in May 2004. This provided a trigger for general media coverage with the twin objectives of raising community awareness of the initiative and encouraging recruitment of eligible families.

After the completion of a baseline population parenting survey in January 2004, radio and print coverage of relevant parenting issues was organized on an ongoing basis. For television media, a more opportunistic approach was taken, whereby approaches made by the media to the project, requesting comments on topical parenting issues, were used to achieve the above aims.

Significant media activity occurred throughout the project. Radio coverage has included Community Service Announcements (CSAs) on several local radio stations (e.g., 4KQ, 97.3, 4BC), fortnightly Radio National talk-back segments and numerous interviews on a range of parenting topics. Print media included stories and editorials published in newspapers (e.g., local Quest newspapers, *Courier Mail, Sunday Mail, The Australian*); magazines (e.g., *Take 5* and *Better Homes and Gardens*); professional publications (e.g., *Education Views*), and specific publications aimed at parents (e.g., *Parents and Schools, Woman and Child*).

Television media included several current affairs-style programs (e.g., Channel 9: *Extra* and *A Current Affair*; Channel 7: *Today Tonight*; ABC: *7.30 Report*) and a recent feature on the *Catalyst* science-based program on ABC. An innovative series of Community Service Announcements was produced by Channel 7, introduced by local television news presenters. These CSAs featured several young children aged 4–8, delivering positive parenting messages.

Other promotional and media-related strategies implemented as part of *Every Family* included the development of an *Every Family* web site, parenting newsletters sent home monthly to all parents of children in target schools (preschool, Years 1–3), and a range of promotional materials designed to advertise seminars, groups and other events.

As part of the media and information campaign, an *Every Family* web site was developed by the Parenting and Family Support Centre (PFSC) at The University of Queensland, with the aim of promoting positive parenting and healthy family relationships and increasing community awareness of *Every Family*. This web site was designed as a comprehensive Internet-based resource for parents, trained Triple P practitioners and the general public with three specific objectives: (i) to facilitate the dissemination of information about *Every Family*, including the project aims, media strategy and project partners; (ii) to provide a mechanism through which both parents and practitioners receive support and feedback; and (iii) to increase awareness of the project at a community, state, national and international level.

The *Every Family* web site aimed to support parents by providing tools and resources including: quality parenting information through online Triple P tips, *Every Family* Parent Newsletters and media features, including parenting columns and radio clips; an online form for the submission of parenting questions to a Triple P accredited psychologist; information about accessing Triple P strategies and resources and a schedule of upcoming Triple P seminars and group programs in local areas; and an online submission form for enquiries and enrolments.

The web site was another vehicle of support for *Every Family* trained Triple P practitioners and provided: research and practice updates, including information about upcoming events for practitioners; information about Triple P interventions and how to become a trained Triple P practitioner; a catalogue of *Every Family* newsletters and an online form for submitting practitioner enquiries or clinical questions to accredited Triple P training personnel.

The project web site has been particularly useful as a tool for promoting parental awareness of the project and engaging parents. Since its launch, approximately 80 parents have used online forms to enquire about or register interest in attending Triple P seminars or group programs or submit parenting questions. Moreover, the web site has facilitated the engagement of local parents in Triple P Seminar Series or group programs who indicated they had not heard about the programs from any other source. Web site usage does not appear to be as common among *Every Family* trained practitioners as with parents in the local community. Finally, numerous community personnel engaged in work with children, parents or families have used an online e-mail enquiry form to express interest in accessing Triple P services or resources or becoming involved with the project. As such, the web site has been valuable in promoting awareness of *Every Family* and facilitating the dissemination of relevant information about the initiative.

As an index of the impact of the media strategy, 82% of parents in the target intervention community were aware of Triple P and only 43% in the care as usual communities. There were no significant differences in program awareness for any other parenting program, including a completely fictitious program know as the Brick and Mortar Parenting Program.

Families television series

This New Zealand-based study established the feasibility of using a television series on parenting to promote positive family outcomes (Sanders et al., 2000). Sanders et al. (2000) evaluated a media campaign on parenting based around a television series, Families, shown during primetime on commercial television. This series provided empirically validated parenting information in an interesting and entertaining format. It was also designed to provide parents with specific information and an accurate model that would enable them to put suggested strategies into practice. It aimed to normalize the challenge of being a parent and to raise parents' expectations that positive change in child behavior could be achieved. In addition, the program aimed to raise community awareness of the significant role positive family relationships play in the health and well-being of young people across the life span.

The 12, 30-minute episode series was an infotainment-style program to ensure the widest reach possible for Triple P. Using an entertaining format to provide practical information and advice to parents on a variety of common behavioral and developmental problems in children, the main segments were: (i) a feature story presenting brief discussions on a number of family issues (e.g., school involvement, role of fathers); (ii) a celebrity family discussing issues about their family; (iii) family health care tips; (iv) animal care and integrating pets into family life; (v) interesting facts about the current state of families in society; and (vi) a Triple P segment. The 5–7 minute Triple P segment each week enabled parents to complete a 12-session Triple P intervention at home. The Triple P segments provided brief examples of the causes of child behavior problems from a social learning perspective; provided guidance on how to monitor child behavior; and presented clear guidelines and modelled a range of parenting strategies to encourage desirable behavior in children, prevent problems from occurring, and manage difficult behavior. These strategies were integrated into plans for dealing with common problems (e.g., whining, disobedience, aggression), for promoting children's development (e.g., encouraging creativity and involvement in physical activities, helping with homework), and for managing developmental issues (e.g., cooperative play; sleeping and eating difficulties). A cross-promotion strategy using newspapers, posters, and magazines was used to encourage parents to watch the program and to contact a Triple P telephone line for more information. The Families tip sheets (engaging written materials that provided a back-up self-help strategy based on the information in the Triple P segment) were also available by writing to a Triple P center, calling the Triple P information line, or through a retail chain store.

To evaluate whether the television series alone had a significant impact on family functioning, Sanders et al. (2000) randomly assigned 56 mothers with 2–8-year-old children either to the media intervention or a wait-list control group. Intervention mothers were given the television series in the form of videos and tip sheets. They watched two episodes of the series per week, in their own homes and at a time convenient to them, and read the relevant tip sheets. Control group mothers received no intervention for six weeks. As predicted, mothers in the media intervention group reported significant reductions in the number of child behavior problems posttreatment in comparison to the control group (Cohen's $d = 0.68$). The percentage of control children scoring in the clinical range for problem behavior did not change from pre- to postintervention, yet there was a significant decrease in the percentage of media-intervention children who scored in the clinical range – from 46% prior to intervention to 14% remaining in the clinical range following the intervention. Mothers in the media condition also reported an increased sense of competence and satisfaction in their parenting abilities relative to mothers in the control group ($d = 0.59$).

Driving Mum and Dad Mad Reality Parenting Series

This UK-based study examined the effects of Triple P presented as a reality series on British television. Triple P was the subject of a six-episode, 30-minute observational documentary television series known as Driving Mum and Dad Mad.

This series depicted the experiences and emotional journey of five families with severe conduct-problem children as they participated in Group Triple P (an eight-session intensive group program). The effects of the series on viewers were evaluated in a randomized trial, the Great Parenting Experiment, involving 500 families via a web-based assessment prior to and following the broadcast of the series (Sanders, Calam, Durand, Liversidge, & Carmon, 2008). The study compared the effects of two viewing conditions (standard versus enhanced). Families in the standard condition watched the six-episode series and had access to written information in the form of tip sheets on the ITV web site. This practice of supplementing a program with informational fact sheets is a standard practice on most networks. Families in the enhanced condition also received individually tailored support through a 10-session self-paced workbook and access to a specially designed web site, which included downloadable tip sheets corresponding to each episode, e-mail reminders to watch the show, key message prompts to implement program tips, audio-streamed positive parenting messages, video-streamed segments from the Triple P video *Every Parent's Survival Guide* providing more detailed demonstrations and explanations of the parenting techniques, and, finally, and e-mail support from trained Triple P providers.

All five participating on-air families made significant gains on all key indices of outcome, including reduced conduct problems, parental distress, coercive parenting, and marital conflict over parenting, and improved self-efficacy. In addition the study showed that although parents in both the standard and the enhanced media viewing conditions reported significant improvement in child behavior, the enhanced program provided additional benefits on measures of dysfunctional parenting, parental anger about child behavior, and parental disagreements about discipline. This study demonstrated the audience potential of a parenting series based on the actual experiences of real families undergoing the Triple P group intervention. As one study participant said:

> "I have just finished watching your final program and it has been wonderful to watch. Just to know that you are not alone and there are many families out there that have children with similar behavioral problems".

The results found that both groups showed significant improvements in parenting skills, child behavior and parental adjustment, with the enhanced group showing additional effects of reduced couple conflict and higher consumer satisfaction. A second study (Calam, Sanders, Miller, Sadhnami, & Carmont, 2008), using data from both the screening of the first series and the second series, examined potential predictors of program outcomes and continued participation in the project. Contrary to predictions, families showing high vulnerability (i.e., those with more severe problems on a range of indices of sociodemographic and psychological variables) had better outcomes, were more likely to watch all episodes and to complete postintervention and follow-up assessments. These findings challenge the notion that only families with mild-to-moderate levels of difficulty would watch and benefit from the intervention. Indeed, families with quite serious problems who were not accessing any services participated, suggesting that traditional means of delivering services had not been successful with these families. Feedback from one participant exemplified the benefits of this form of intervention, compared to the barriers to accessing face to face support:

> "I think the idea of a TV program and workbook together is great. I work and could not take advantage of a local parenting class run at my health center... Your TV programs were helpful but combined with the workbook made a difference and were therefore much more helpful than any book or TV program I had seen before. The workbook helped me to apply what I had seen in the programs to my specific situation. I am now much more aware of how much my behavior/mood influences the children's behavior which doesn't mean I have solved the problem but I am better at recognizing when I have to try harder to keep calm... It was also nice to know I could e-mail someone with a query as getting in touch with a health visitor to ask for advice on dealing with average behavior issues seemed a bit silly and as I am at work my access to them is limited".

As well as accessing families who are not in contact with professionals, interventions of this kind can help build parental confidence in seeking solutions to difficulties in collaboration with their existing services. An example of this from the same participant is:

> For the first time I don't feel so despondent about the call from school as I have more strategies and easily accessible ideas available to me than ever before. We'll continue to push for more professional help at school and from our healthcare providers until we finally get the help in school she needs for her attention deficit problems but for now we've watched her closely as you suggested for the last few weeks and are drawing up plans and strategies with her and the school to get back on track.

Strenthening the Impact of Media-Based Parenting Programs

A successful media strategy requires media outlets that are willing to broadcast material. This, in turn, requires interventionists to become better informed about the requirements, interests, and priorities of the media. Many professionals are apprehensive about working with the media because of concerns ranging from being personally misrepresented to concerns about exposing clients to exploitation by the media.

Effective working relationships must be based on a mutuality of respect and good communication and relationships between interventionists and the media. Interventionists need to understand how the media operates. Mass media outlets are often approached by organizations trying to get coverage for what they believe are "worthwhile" causes. Positive parenting is only one of many potential social issues to which the media could devote time. A variety of factors may influence the media's level of interest in covering a parenting issue or initiative, including how "worthy" they see the issue being and whether there is a news angle. The media will also be concerned to consider how it fits with their particular intended public image, and how the media outlet be acknowledged.

Many practitioners are anxious and distrustful of the media. The media usually want to interview an "expert" about the issue who has access to real families who can be interviewed. Many practitioners are reluctant to get involved. They may have specific concerns about their own ability to provide concise, helpful messages in media-friendly formats. Consequently, a parenting initiative may need to provide coaching and support to professionals in their work with the media, and to become comfortable with the notion of the "sound bite". This can include learning skills such as speaking briefly, the avoidance of jargon and technical language, the use of examples to illustrate points being made, and translating complex findings into everyday language. Practitioners may also be concerned over the risk of negative consequences for themselves if their work is not well represented by the media. Careful negotiation and clear communication are essential in minimizing this risk.

Practitioners will also be appropriately concerned to safeguard the interests of families for whom they have responsibility, and may have concerns for the way that families may be required to interact with the media. Careful negotiation with the media on these issues is essential. Where the media interest is appropriate and respectful of these issues, however, the real-life accounts of families who have experienced positive outcomes can be significant in helping other families towards positive change.

Generally speaking, the media will not give any editorial control to others, so that decisions about what to include or leave out from the actual story are in the hands of someone else. Consequently, it is important to convey to producers, directors and reporters any concerns about the use of self-fulfilling prophecies. An example would be:

> Meet Stefan, a 5-year-old boy with some very big problems. This kid is on a course to becoming a delinquent unless something is done about it.

Messages that make specific negative predictions about individual children can potentially be damaging to the children involved. Engaging producers with the notion that a positive message has the potential to bring about population benefits is worthy. A more compelling and immediate argument for producers, however, may be that a positive message will help attract viewers to watch so that they can see how to bring about change in their own families.

Implications

As the mass media becomes more heavily involved in social issues such as parenting, families will present to service providers after have prior exposure to parenting techniques and strategies through either self-help or media-based programs. In the past, when parents received advice on how to discipline children or promote positive behaviors, they were receiving the advice in some instances for the first time. Practitioners now have to work with families who will be well versed in the notion of the "naughty step" or "star charts", although they may have misconceptions about appropriate use of these concepts and approaches. Professionals may easily conclude that media approaches do not work. However, they are likely to be seeing parents who are "nonresponders" (a subsample of the population of parents who have been exposed) through the media to the program. It is hard to estimate how many parents do not need to refer to other services because of successful exposure to helpful ideas gained through the media.

Other professionals may be concerned that psychologists who are "giving away" the discipline via the media are at risk of losing control over delivery and implementation, with the possible outcome that this will harm the discipline. These concerns, while understandable, have more to do with protecting the discipline than benefiting children; genies, good and bad, are already out of their bottles. We contend that the realistic depiction of what parents are likely to be required to commit to in an evidence-based parenting program leads parents to have more realistic expectations about what is involved. The media can help demystify and destigmatize the parenthood preparation process.

To improve the quality of media programs targeting parenting, programs would benefit greatly from the infusion of concepts from social, developmental, communication and learning theory. For example, the likelihood of parents identifying with parental role models would be increased by having parents who are perceived to be similar or in similar situations to the viewer. Parents' implementation of depicted solutions might be enhanced by viewing the material with other parents and by discussing how they intend to use the advice and facing parenting concerns. Media material can be developed to enhance a parent's expectation that a favorable outcome can be achieved and that change is possible. The stories and experiences of families overcoming complex or difficult personal situations can be inspiring for parents who may feel overwhelmed or defeated by their children.

There is always a danger that individual children could be adversely affected by being depicted in the media. Steps need to be taken to ensure that consenting families who participate in stories are supported prior to and following the screening of material that involves the disclosure of personal material.

Differences in Professional Opinion and the Mass Media

The rise of reality parenting programs has led to a mixture of public condemnation of programs such as Supernanny from some parenting experts and praise from others for the heroic efforts in turning around difficult children. Although these public debates between professionals show parents that professionals cannot agree amongst themselves and that there is no single right way to parent, it also leads parents to become more informed consumers and, over time, this will create pressure on service providers to be explicit and articulate what they advocate and do in their parenting programs. There is also the potential to develop approaches to enhance the critical awareness of parents, so that they can identify messages that are likely to be based on sound psychological principles.

Challenges and Future Directions

There is much to learn about the impact of media-based parenting interventions. There have only been a small number of randomized controlled trials assessing the impact of these programs. Although studies to date have been encouraging most research has focused on the effects of television programs. There is little research examining the effects of web-based delivery of programs and almost no research examining whether the proliferation of Internet sites designed for parent use are effective in changing parenting practices.

A new generation of studies is needed that experimentally manipulate variables thought to enhance the impact of media messages. Such research can include analogue studies in the first instance, as it is difficult to randomize individual parents to watching or not watching broadcast media. Grasping these issues has tremendous potential to offer parents constructive guidance at exactly the moment that they need it. The technological developments that allow viewers to access TV programs and the Internet at their own convenience provides the potential for parents to have expert exemplars on tap just when they are needed, day or night, and however remote the family's location.

A cautionary note

The ease with which web pages can be established and changed means there is likely to be further proliferation of information on parenting. Numerous commercial sites have been developed, some with exaggerated claims for efficacy of the advice. Some of the available sites provide generally high quality information while others are poorly informed by evidence. The sheer volume of information available can be confusing and, at times, overwhelming for busy parents (Leach, Chapter 2, this volume). A small number of sites providing limited but high quality information may be much more effective than sites that aim for comprehensiveness but end up having little substance.

An inadvertent negative side effect of media-based parenting advice is that parents may become dependent or overly reliant on "Google" for parenting solutions and not trust their own judgement and common sense. From a self-regulation perspective, perhaps the goal should be to encourage parents to use external sources of information, including the web and television programs, to provide the "minimally sufficient" level of support that will enable the parent to become an independent problem solver.

Summary

This chapter has made a case for the judicious use of mass media strategies to enhance the impact of parenting programs. The primary benefits are greater population reach and the cost efficacy of the interventions. We argue that there is much to learn about the effects of media programs and much more theoretically informed research is needed to identify program elements that optimize parents learning and engagement in media-based programs. Various professional concerns about working with the media have been outlined, including concern about this means of giving away developmental psychology and adverse effects on children and parents.

References

Abt, V., & Seesholtz, M. (1994). The shameless world of Phil, Sally, and Oprah: Television talk shows and the deconstructing of society. *Journal of Popular Culture, 28*(1), 171–191.

Bandura, A. (1977). *Social learning theory.* Englewood Cliffs, NJ: Prentice-Hall.

Bandura, A. (1986). *Social foundations of thought and action: A social cognitive theory.* Englewood Cliffs, NJ: Prentice-Hall.

Bandura, A. (2002). Social cognitive theory of mass communication. In J. Bryant & D. Zillmann (Eds.) *Media Effects: Advances in Theory and Research* (pp. 121–154). Mahwah, NJ: Lawrence Erlbaum Associates.

Bandura, A. (2011). Social cognitive theory and media production. In *Using the media to achieve reproductive health and gender equity* (pp. 30–38). Shelburne, VT: Population Media Center. Retrieved on July 9, 2015 from http://www.populationmedia.org/wp-content/uploads/2012/02/UNFPA_Best_practices_ENG.pdf#page=36

Biglan, A., & Metzler, C. W. (1998). A public health perspective for research on family-focused interventions. In R. S. Ashery, E. B. Robertson, & K. L. Kumpfer (Eds.), *Drug abuse prevention through family interventions.* NIDA Research Monograph 177, NIH Publication NO. 994135 (pp. 430–458). Washington, DC: National Institute on Drug Abuse.

Bronson, M. B. (2000). Overview of theoretical perspectives on self-regulation. In M. B. Bronson (Ed.), *Self-regulation in early childhood* (pp. 11–30). New York: Guilford.

Brown, J. D., & Walsh-Childers, K. (2002). Effects of media on personal and public health. In J. Bryant & D. Zillmann (Eds.) *Media effects: Advances in theory and research* (pp. 453–488). Mahwah, NJ: Lawrence Erlbaum Associates.

Calam, R., Sanders, M. R., Miller, C., Sadhnami, V., & Carmont, S. A. (2008). Can technology and the media help reduce dysfunctional parenting and increase engagement with preventative parenting interventions? *Child Maltreatment, 13*(4), 347–361.

Centre for Community Child Health (2004). *Parenting Information Project.* Department of Family and Community Services, Australian Government. Retrieved on July 21, 2015 fromhttp://www.parentingrc.org.au/index.php/sharing-knowledge/project-archive/213-parenting-information-project

Drake, K., Belsky, J., & Fearon, R. M. (2013). From early attachment to engagement with learning in school: The role of self-regulation and persistence. *Developmental Psychology, 50*(5) 1350–1361. doi: 10.1037/a0032779

Engelmann, S., & Carnine, D. (1982). *Theory of instruction.* New York: Irvington.

EurodataTV. (2005). Cited in Dale, D. (2005). The tribal mind. *Sydney Morning Herald.* Retrieved on May 18, 2015 from http://www.smh.com.au/news/TV--Radio/The-Tribal-Mind/2005/05/16/1116095903140.html?oneclick=true

Flay, B. R. (1987). Mass media and smoking cessation: A critical review. *American Journal of Public Health, 77*(2), 153–160.

Harwood, R. L., & Weissberg, R. P. (1987). The potential of video in the promotion of social competence in children and adolescents. *Journal of Early Adolescence, 7*(3), 345–363.

Hornik, R. C. (2002). *Public health communication. Evidence for behavior change*. Mahwah, NJ: Lawrence Erlbaum Associates.

McAlister, A. L., & Fernandez, M. (2002). "Behavioral journalism" accelerates diffusion of healthy innovations. In R. C. Hornik (Ed.), *Public health communication. Evidence for behavior change* (pp. 315–326). Mahwah, NJ: Lawrence Erlbaum Associates.

McGillicuddy-DeLisi, A. V. (2009). Parental beliefs about developmental processes. *Human Development, 25*, 192–200.

McGillicuddy-De Lisi, A. V., & Sigel, I. E. (1995). Parental beliefs. In M. H. Bornstein (Ed.), *Handbook of parentings: Vol. 3. Status and social conditions of parenting* (pp. 333–358). Mahwah, NJ: Lawrence Erlbaum Associates.

Media Life. (2005). Fox's suddenly very hot "Nanny 911." *Media Life Magazine, March 22*, 2005.

Metzler, C. W., Sanders, M. R., Rusby, J. C., & Crowley, R. N. (2012). Using consumer preference information to increase the reach and impact of media-based parenting interventions in a public health approach to parenting support. *Behavior Therapy, 43*, 257–270.

Parrott, R. L. (1995). Motivation to attend to health messages: Presentation of content and linguistic considerations. In E. Maibach & R. L. Parrott (Eds.) *Designing health messages: Approaches from theory and public health practice* (pp. 7–23). Thousand Oaks, CA: Sage.

Rideout, V. J., Foehr, U. G., & Roberts, D. F. (2010). *Generation M ^{2}: Media in the lives of 8-to 18-year-olds*. Menlo Park, CA: Henry J. Kaiser Family Foundation.

Sanders, M. R. (1999). Triple P-Positive Parenting Program: Towards an empirically validated multilevel parenting and family support strategy for the prevention of behavior and emotional problems in children. *Clinical Child and Family Psychology Review, 2*(2), 71–90.

Sanders, M. R. (2012). Development, evaluation, and multinational dissemination of the Triple P-Positive Parenting Program. *Annual Review of Clinical Psychology, 8*, 345–379. doi: 10.1146/annurev-clinpsy-032511-143104

Sanders, M. R., Calam, R. M., Durand, M., Liversidge, T. & Carmont, S. A. (2008). Does self-directed and web-based support for parents enhance the effects of viewing a reality television series based on the Triple P-Positive Parenting Programme? *Journal of Child Psychology and Psychiatry, 49*(9), 924–932.

Sanders, M. R., Haslam, D. M., Calam, R., Southwell, C., & Stallman, H. (2011). Designing effective interventions for working parnets: a web-based survey of parents in the UK workforce. *Journal of Children's Services, 6*(3), 186–200.

Sanders, M. R., & Markie-Dadds, C. (1996). Triple P: A multilevel family intervention program for children with disruptive behaviour disorders. In P. Cotton & H. Jackson (Eds.), *Early intervention and prevention in mental health* (pp. 59–85). Melbourne, Australia: Australian Psychological Society Ltd.

Sanders, M. R., Montgomery, D., & Brechman-Toussaint, M. (2000). The mass media and the prevention of child behavior problems: The evaluation of a television series to promote positive outcomes for parents and their children. *Journal of Child Psychology and Psychiatry, 41*(7), 939–948.

Sanders, M. R., Ralph, A., Sofronoff, K., Gardiner, P., Thompson, R., Dwyer, S., & Bidwell, K. (2008). Every Family: A population approach to reducing behavioural and emotional problems in children making the transition to school. *Journal of Primary Prevention, 29,* 197–222.

Sanders, M. R., & Turner, K. M. (2002). The role of the media and primary care in the dissemination of evidence-based parenting and family support interventions. *Behavior Therapist, 25*(9), 156–166.

Sanders, M. R., Turner, K. M., & Markie-Dadds, C. (1996). Paediatric psychology and the treatment of childhood disorders. In P. R. Martin & J. S. Birnbrauer (Eds.), *Clinical psychology: Profession and practice in Australia* (pp. 287–314). Melbourne, Australia: Macmillan Education.

Tekcarta (2015). TV Sets: Average Number of TV Sets per TV Household (68 countries). Retrieved on July 16, 2015 from http://www.generatorresearch.com/tekcarta/databank/tv-sets-average-number-of-tv-sets-per-tv-household/

Viswanath, K., & Finnegan, J. R., Jr. (2002). Reflections on community health campaigns: Secular trends and the capacity to effect change. In R. C. Hornik (Ed.), *Public health communication. Evidence for behavior change* (pp. 289–312). Mahwah, NJ: Lawrence Erlbaum, Associates.

Wahler, R. G., & Smith, G. D. (1999). Effective parenting as the integration of lessons and dialogue. *Journal of Child and Family Studies, 8*(2), 135–149.

Wakefield, M. A., Loken, B., & Hornik, R. C. (2010). CSU 169/2011: Use of mass media campaigns to change health behaviour. *The Lancet, 376*(9748), 1261–1271.

Worrell, N. (2005). The Ratings Wizard. *Television Week, May 9, 2005.*

Zimmerman, J. D. (1996). A prosocial media strategy: "Youth against violence: Choose to de-fuse." *American Journal of Orthopsychiatry, 66,* 354–361.

6

Children of Lesbian and Gay Parents: Reflections on the Research–Policy Interface

Charlotte J. Patterson and Rachel H. Farr

Around the world today, the extent to which legal recognition should be provided for relationships among lesbian and gay parents and their children is a subject of active debate. For many years, the family relationships of lesbian and gay parents and their children were not legally recognized in most parts of the United States, or in most countries of the world. However, in many places, the situation is currently in transition. Same-sex relationships are recognized in some countries, not in others, and the matter is under active debate in still others. With regard to the social and legal status of lesbian and gay relationships, we are living in a time of tremendous social change.

In the context of rapidly changing environments, social science research can play a role in legal and policy debates. In this chapter, we hope to describe some of the ways in which this can take place, and to discuss contributions that social science data can make to public discussion of these issues. We have five main aims. First, we describe some of the diverse family arrangements that have been created by lesbian and gay adults. Next, we summarize the current status of legal and policy issues relevant to lesbian and gay parents and their children in the United States

The Wiley Handbook of Developmental Psychology in Practice: Implementation and Impact, First Edition.
Edited by Kevin Durkin and H. Rudolph Schaffer.

and around the world today. Third, we provide an overview of research evidence about lesbian- and gay-parented families, with special emphasis on the development of children living within them. Fourth, we describe some of the ways in which research findings have been brought to bear on legal and policy debates. Finally, we offer some reflections on the interface of research and policy, as this is relevant to sexual orientation and family lives.

Pathways to Parenthood for Lesbians and Gay Men

Lesbians and gay men become parents in many different ways (Goldberg, 2010, 2012; Patterson, 2007, 2013). Lesbian and gay adults may have children within the context of a prior heterosexual relationship or within the context of a nonhetero-sexual identity. Lesbian and gay adults may become parents through donor insemination, surrogacy, foster parenting or adoption.

Some lesbian and gay parents had children within a previous heterosexual relationship. Some may continue to parent within an ongoing heterosexual relationship, while other lesbian and gay parents divorce their heterosexual partners and live in separate households (Tornello & Patterson, 2012). For both parents and children in these homes, family relationships may involve a complex network of both other-gender and same-gender past and present relationships, and a series of family changes that may include parental separation, divorce, and repartnership (Goldberg, 2010).

In recent years, many lesbian and bisexual women have had children in the context of nonheterosexual identities. These families have variously been called *families of the lesbian baby boom, planned lesbian mother families* (Bos, van Balen & van den Boom, 2003, 2004; Golombok, Murray, & Tasker, 1997; Patterson, 2000) or *de novo families* (Hayman, Wilkes, Jackson, & Halcomb, 2013; Perlesz, Brown, McNair, Lindsay, Pitts, & de Vaus, 2006). Many of the children in these families were conceived by lesbian mothers using donor insemination at a clinic, or via self-insemination, using donor sperm. Various family arrangements with sperm donors have been reported. Some donors remain anonymous, while others are known to the family; known donors may become involved in family life to a greater or lesser extent (Goldberg, 2010; Patterson, 2000, 2013; Power et al., 2010, 2012).

Gay men have become fathers in a number of different ways (Golombok & Tasker, 2010; Pawelski et al., 2006). Some create coparenting arrangements with lesbian mothers. Some gay fathers have become known sperm donors for lesbian mothers, while others have no genetic connection with children they coparent. Surrogacy agreements have also enabled some gay men to become fathers (Bergman,

Rubio, Green, & Padron, 2010). Both traditional surrogacy (in which the surrogate mother is genetically related to the baby) and gestational surrogacy (in which the baby is carried in pregnancy by a surrogate, but is genetically related to another woman who has donated the egg) have been used by gay men in order to become fathers. Arrangements may be made through an agency, or they may be made privately, in the context of family or friendship networks. Gay fathers may choose surrogacy over adoption because they want a biological connection with their child, because they want to rear a child from birth, because surrogacy is less complicated legally than adoption in their locality, or because they would prefer that their child be spared potential emotional difficulties due to having been placed for adoption (Downing, Richardson, Kinkler, & Goldberg, 2009; Lev, 2006).

Gay men and lesbians also have become parents by serving as adoptive or foster parents (Gates, 2011). At least in the United States, there are many opportunities for prospective lesbian and gay adoptive parents. A national survey of adoption agencies found that 60% of responding adoption and child welfare organizations indicated that they accepted applications from lesbians and gay men, and approximately 40% of agencies reported that they had actually placed a child with a lesbian or gay parent (Brodzinsky & Staff of the Evan B. Donaldson Adoption Institute, 2003). In this survey, agencies that provide foster care described themselves as being more open to lesbian or gay prospective parents than did adoption agencies. Despite greater openness, lesbians and gay men who have applied to become foster or adoptive parents still do, however, report sporadic suspicion and rejection on the part of agencies, social workers, and families of origin (Downs & James, 2006; Goldberg, Moyer, Kinkler, & Richardson, 2012; Matthews & Cramer, 2006; Riggs, 2006).

Some parenting arrangements for children of lesbian or gay parents involve two parents, with a lesbian or a gay couple living together and parenting together. Other arrangements involve two parents living apart, or single parenting by a lesbian mother or a gay father. Some are multiparental, composed of two couples or a same-sex couple and a third person who do not live together. Like other families, the families of lesbians and gay men take many forms (Patterson, & Riskind, 2010; Tasker & Patterson, 2007).

Diversity arises not only in terms of the influence of nonheterosexual identities on family lives, but also as these issues intersect with those based on other identities, such as cultural and religious commitments. Little research has addressed how cultural variations influence the context of family life for lesbian mother or gay father families. A few personal accounts have explored the impact of disability on lesbian motherhood (D'Aoust, 1995; Drucker, 1998). Bowen (1995) discusses identity and choice in relation to her own experiences of motherhood as a black lesbian feminist. Increasingly, empirical studies have focused on African American as well as other lesbian mothers (Hill, 1987; Moore, 2008, 2011), but much remains to be learned in this area.

Socioeconomic status, occupational grouping, race, and ability/disability contextualize family lives. Variation in age, cohort, and community climate may also be important (Oswald, Cuthbertson, Lazarevic, & Goldberg, 2010). It is reasonable to think that the lives of lesbian and gay parents and their children could be markedly different in rural versus urban or suburban settings. Indeed, evidence has emerged to show that contextual factors, such as the percentage of other lesbian, gay, bisexual, transgender (LGBT) people in the area, can be associated with well-being among lesbian and gay parents and their offspring (Lick et al., 2012).

Legal Status of Lesbian and Gay Parents and Their Children

Consideration of the legal status of lesbian and gay parents and their children involves at least three interrelated areas of law. The first involves legal recognition of same-sex couple relationships, which may take the form of marriage, civil union, or domestic partnership. The second involves the status of parental sexual orientation in disputes about custody of and visitation with minor children. The third involves the role of parental sexual orientation in adoption and foster care proceedings. The legal situation of lesbian and gay parents in different jurisdictions reveals a patchwork of varied arrangements that are changing rapidly in many parts of the world.

Legal recognition of same-sex couples

Legal recognition of same-sex couples varies widely throughout the world (Patterson, Riskind & Tornello, 2013; Patterson & Tornello, 2010). In many countries, particularly in Africa, the Middle East and Southeast Asia, homosexuality remains illegal. Same-sex couples in these countries do not receive legal recognition or protection, and are vulnerable to prosecution under the law. Many countries in the world do, however, offer some degree of legal recognition. At the time of this writing, same-sex marriage is legal in Argentina, Belgium, Canada, Denmark, France, Iceland, Luxembourg, The Netherlands, New Zealand, Norway, Portugal, South Africa, Spain, Sweden, the United Kingdom, and Uruguay. Legally obtained marriages are recognized in Israel, in Mexico, and by the federal government of the United States. Civil unions or registered partnerships are legal for same-sex couples in many other nations.

In the United States, the rights to marry, to procreate, and to rear children as one sees fit are regarded as inalienable. These rights have long been held by the United

States Supreme Court to be fundamental and, as such, have been seen as guaranteed by the Constitution. Despite being taken for granted by the majority of Americans, these rights have often been denied to lesbian and gay Americans.

At the time of writing, the status of marriage equality in the United States is changing rapidly. Massachusetts provided legal recognition for the marriages of same-sex couples in 2004 and many states have followed this lead. At the time of writing, marriage equality has become law in 35 of the 50 states in the United States. There are legal cases pending in all of the other states. Variations among the decisions of appellate courts suggest that the United States Supreme Court will soon take up the issue. Thus, in many jurisdictions in the United States and in many other parts of the world, the legal situation for same-sex couples is in rapid flux (Patterson, 2013; Patterson et al., 2013).

Child custody and visitation involving lesbian mothers and gay fathers

While families headed by lesbian and gay adults are not legally recognized nor protected in countries where homosexuality remains a crime, a growing number of nations have laws regarding child custody and visitation that are favorable to lesbian and gay parents. For example, in a growing number of European countries, lesbian and gay adults are permitted to adopt the biological children of their same-sex partner.

In the United States, the extent to which a parent's sexual identity is considered relevant in deciding a child's best interest, for purposes of child custody and visitation, varies from state to state. In many states, parental sexual orientation is considered relevant to custody and visitation disputes only if a parent's nonheterosexual identity can be shown to have an adverse impact on the child. In order to use this argument in these states, a connection, or *nexus*, must be demonstrated between a person's sexual orientation, on the one hand, and a negative outcome for the child, on the other. Such a connection can be difficult or impossible to establish (Wald, 2006). For instance, in a Maryland visitation case, the court refused to limit children's visitation with their gay father in the presence of his same-sex partner because there was no evidence of harm to the children from such visitation (*Boswell v. Boswell*, 1998).

At the other end of the spectrum, some states have presumptions against lesbian or gay parents. Even though these may not any longer rise to the level of a *per se* rule against parental fitness among lesbian and gay adults, they may nevertheless remain influential. In the *Bottoms v. Bottoms* (1995) case, for example, the Virginia Supreme Court included the mother's sexual orientation among factors considered to make her an undesirable parent (*Bottoms v. Bottoms*, 1995, p. 108).

The legal standards for custody in a number of states fall somewhere between these two extremes. In one case (*Burgess v. Burgess*, 1999), the Indiana Supreme Court rejected a gay father's request for review of a lower court's decision that denied him custody of his son. Indiana law does not allow parental sexual orientation to be considered as a determinative factor in placement of a child, but the court noted in its decision that the father's sexual orientation "raises the specter of an aberrant lifestyle" (*Burgess v. Burgess*, 1999). In another case, a gay father in North Carolina was denied custody of his two sons because of the court's concern about his long-term relationship with a male partner, who was helping to care for the boys (*Pulliam v. Smith*, 1998). Thus, in some jurisdictions, child custody and visitation for lesbian and gay parents after the break-up of heterosexual marriages continue to be adjudicated in an atmosphere of antigay prejudice.

Adoption and foster care

Around the world, the right to foster or adopt children is granted to lesbian and gay adults to varying degrees by different countries. In nations that continue to ban homosexuality, there are no legal protections for lesbian and gay parents and their children. However, at the time of writing, in Argentina, Belgium, Brazil. Canada, Denmark, France, Iceland, Luxembourg, Malta, the Netherlands, New Zealand, Norway, South Africa, Spain, Sweden, the United Kingdom, and Uruguay, lesbian and gay adults can adopt children as individuals or with a same-sex partner.

Legal adoptions of minor children by lesbian and gay adults can be seen as falling into one of two types (Patterson, 1995). When biological parents are unable or unwilling to care for a child, and an adoptive parent who is unrelated to the biological parents offers to provide that child with a home, the result is called a *stranger adoption*. In such cases, the courts dissolve existing legal bonds and create a new legal relationship between the child and the adoptive parent. *Second parent adoptions* are pursued by lesbian and gay couples who rear a child together, although only one member of the couple – the biological parent or legal adoptive parent – is viewed as a parent in law. These couples seek legal recognition of the relationship between the other parent and the child. In recent years, both types of adoptions have been completed by openly lesbian and gay individuals in the United States.

Like laws on custody and visitation, those governing adoption vary considerably across the United States. At the time of this writing, adoption of minor children by lesbian or gay individuals or couples is permissible in most states. Second-parent adoptions are, however, available in a smaller number of states. This situation is changing rapidly in the face of changing marriage laws.

In summary, the legal and policy landscape in the United States for lesbian and gay parents and their children is remarkably varied. At one end of the spectrum, in a state such as Massachusetts – in which same-sex marriage is permitted, in which parental sexual orientation is considered irrelevant to child custody and visitation proceedings, and in which the state's highest court has affirmed the legality of second parent adoptions – the legal climate for lesbian and gay parents and their children is generally positive. At the other end of the spectrum, in a state such as Montana – in which same-sex marriage is not yet legal, in which lesbian and gay parents may be disadvantaged in custody and visitation proceedings by negative presumptions about their parental fitness, and in which second parent adoptions have not yet been reported – the legal atmosphere for lesbian and gay parents and their children is less desirable. Although the pace of change may vary from jurisdiction to jurisdiction, the direction of movement over time is clearly toward provision of greater legal recognition of the many different family types formed by lesbian and gay adults.

Social Science Research on Children of Lesbian and Gay Parents

Within the framework of law and policy surrounding lesbian and gay parents and their children, social science research has often been seen as important. Research can assist in the evaluation of common assumptions about child development, mental health, and family functioning. Results of research can reveal important information about barriers and supports for the efforts of lesbian and gay parents and their children to live healthy, satisfying lives. Given the antigay character of some judicial decision making over the past years, it is perhaps not surprising that much research has been devoted to evaluation of concerns about the development of children with lesbian and gay parents.

Before turning to research on children, it is worthwhile to note that research on lesbian and gay parents themselves has found that, overall, they tend to display many of the same characteristics that other parents do (Patterson, 2013). For example, same-sex couples who have adopted children do not differ from heterosexual couples who have adopted children in terms of their perspectives and practices with respect to the child's contact with her or his birth parents (Farr & Goldberg, 2015). Same-sex parent couples do, however, report more egalitarian sharing of household duties than do heterosexual couples (Farr & Patterson, 2013). Results of research suggest that, in general, lesbian and gay parents take much the same, or even more positive, approaches to childrearing as do heterosexual parents (Golombok et al., 2014).

Three major types of concerns about the development of children with lesbian and gay parents have, nevertheless, guided a great deal of research. Each one compares children of lesbian and gay parents with those of heterosexual parents, and suggests that those with nonheterosexual parents will be disadvantaged. The first is that development of sexual identity will be impaired among children of lesbian and gay parents. A second category of concerns is that other aspects of children's personal development, such as conduct and self-esteem, may be impaired among children of nonheterosexual parents. A third category of concerns is that children of lesbian and gay parents may experience difficulty in social relationships within the family, with other adults, or with peers. None of these concerns is supported by the results of empirical research (Perrin, & the Committee on Psychosocial Aspects of Child and Family Health, 2002).

Sexual identity

Research has considered three aspects of sexual identity: *gender identity*, which concerns a person's self-identification as male or female; *gender-role behavior*, which concerns the extent to which a person's activities and occupations are regarded by the culture as masculine, feminine, or both; and *sexual orientation*, which refers to a person's attractions, behaviors, and relationships with persons of the same or different sex. Research relevant to each of these three major areas of concern is summarized here.

Gender identity. In studies of children and adolescents, results of projective testing and related interview procedures have revealed that development of gender identity among children of lesbian mothers follows the expected pattern (Kirkpatrick, Smith, & Roy, 1981). More direct assessment techniques to assess gender identity have been used by Golombok, Spencer, and Rutter (1983) with the same result; all children in this study reported that they were comfortable with their gender, and that they had no wish to be a member of the opposite sex. No evidence has been reported in studies using the Preschool Activities Inventory (PSAI; Golombok & Rust, 1993), a maternal report questionnaire designed to identify "masculine" and "feminine" behavior among children, to suggest problems in gender identity among children of lesbian or gay parents as compared with children with heterosexual parents (Farr, Forssell, & Patterson, 2010; Goldberg, Kashy, & Smith, 2012; Golombok & Tasker, 2010; Patterson, 2013).

Bos and Sandfort (2010) studied 8–12-year-old Dutch children with lesbian or heterosexual parents. These investigators studied gender contentedness (i.e., the degree to which children felt content with their gender identity) and gender typicality (i.e., the sense that one is a "typical girl" or a "typical boy"), as well as peer pressure to conform to gender stereotypes. They reported no significant differences as a function of parental sexual orientation for any of these variables. Children of lesbian mothers did, however, report feeling less pressure from their parents to conform to gender stereotypes and more inclination to question their own heterosexual attractions than did children of heterosexual parents.

Gender-role behavior. A number of studies have reported that gender-role behavior among children of lesbian mothers falls within typical limits for conventional sex roles (Brewaeys, Ponjaert, Van Hall, & Golombok, 1997; Golombok et al., 1983; Hoeffer, 1981; Kirkpatrick et al., 1981; Kweskin & Cook, 1982; Patterson, 1994, 2006). For instance, Kirkpatrick and her colleagues (1981) found no differences between children of lesbian versus those of heterosexual mothers in toy preferences, activities, interests, or occupational choices. Brewaeys and her colleagues (1997) assessed gender-role behavior among children who had been conceived via donor insemination by lesbian couples, and compared it to that of children who had been conceived via donor insemination and "natural means" by heterosexual couples. The researchers found no differences between children of lesbian and children of heterosexual parents in preferences for gendered toys, games, and activities (Brewaeys et al., 1997). Similar findings have been reported among samples of children adopted by lesbian, gay, and heterosexual parents (Farr et al., 2010).

Gender-role behavior of children was assessed by Green and his colleagues (1986). In interviews, no differences between children of divorced lesbian and children of divorced heterosexual mothers were found with respect to children's favorite television programs, favorite television characters, or favorite games or toys. There was some indication in interviews with children that the offspring of lesbian mothers had less sex-typed preferences for activities at school and in their neighborhoods than did children of heterosexual mothers. Consistent with this result, lesbian mothers were more likely than heterosexual mothers to report that their daughters often participated in rough-and-tumble play or occasionally played with masculine toys such as trucks or guns, but they reported no differences in these areas for sons. Lesbian mothers were no more and no less likely than heterosexual mothers to report that their children often played with feminine toys such as dolls.

In a more recent study by MacCallum and Golombok (2004), the Children's Sex Role Inventory was used to study gender role development among young adolescent offspring of lesbian and heterosexual mothers. These researchers found that boys with lesbian mothers reported more feminine (but not less masculine) gender role preferences compared to boys with heterosexual mothers. They reported no differences as a function of parental sexual orientation among girls. Thus, while one earlier study reported some differences among girls but not among boys, this one found some differences among boys, but not among girls.

Studies by Fulcher, Sutfin and Patterson (2008) and by Sutfin, Fulcher, Bowles, and Patterson (2008) both examined gender development among 4–6-year-old children. Using the Sex Role Learning Index and also a Gender Transgression Questionnaire, they reported that parental sexual orientation was unrelated to children's knowledge of sex role stereotypes, and also unrelated to children's preferences among current activities or future adult occupations. On the other hand, these authors also found that lesbian mothers had more liberal attitudes about gendered behavior and provided more egalitarian models of division of labor in their households than did heterosexual mothers. Lesbian mothers were even described as decorating their children's bedrooms in less gender stereotypic ways than did heterosexual mothers. For these reasons, it was not surprising that children of lesbian mothers reported feeling less pressured to conform to conventional gender roles than did children of heterosexual mothers (Fulcher et al., 2008; Sutfin et al., 2008). Similar findings regarding the greater likelihood of gender neutral behaviors and preferences among young adopted children with lesbian mothers as compared to those with heterosexual parents have been reported by other researchers (Goldberg et al., 2012).

Considered together, findings of research in this area suggest that, although children with lesbian and gay parents may receive different input (such as parental decoration of their homes), and hence they may develop more liberal attitudes about gender, their gender-relevant behavior is nevertheless very similar to that of children with heterosexual parents. There is more information about younger than about older children, and more on those with lesbian mothers than on those with gay fathers. Overall, however, the research suggests that while gender-related attitudes may be more liberal among children of lesbian and gay parents than among children of heterosexual parents, actual gender-role behavior is very similar in the two groups.

Sexual orientation. A number of investigators have also studied a third component of sexual identity – sexual orientation (Bailey, Bobrow, Wolfe, & Mickach, 1995; Golombok & Tasker, 1996; Tasker & Golombok, 1997). In all studies, the great majority of offspring of both lesbian mothers and gay fathers described themselves as heterosexual. For instance, Huggins (1989) interviewed adolescents, half of whom had lesbian mothers and half of whom had heterosexual mothers. No children of lesbian mothers identified themselves as lesbian or gay, but one child of a heterosexual mother did; this difference was not statistically significant. Bailey and his colleagues (1995) asked gay fathers whether their adult sons were heterosexual, bisexual, or gay and found that the large majority were heterosexual with only 9% considered as gay or bisexual.

Golombok and Tasker (1996; Tasker & Golombok, 1997) studied young adults reared by divorced lesbian mothers and young adults reared by divorced heterosexual mothers. They reported that offspring of lesbian mothers were no more likely than those of heterosexual mothers to describe themselves as feeling attracted to same-sex sexual partners. If they were attracted in this way, however, young adults with lesbian mothers were more likely to report that they would consider entering into a same-sex sexual relationship and they were more likely to have actually participated in such a relationship. They were not, however, more likely to identify themselves as nonheterosexual (i.e., as lesbian, gay, or bisexual). These results were based on a small sample, and should be interpreted with caution. At the same time, the study is the first to follow children of divorced lesbian mothers into adulthood, and it offers a detailed and careful examination of important issues.

More recently, Gartrell and her colleagues studied reports about sexual behavior of 17-year-olds with lesbian mothers and compared it to reports about sexual behavior among a nationally representative sample of 17-year-olds who partici-pated in the (United States) National Survey of Family Growth. An early report from this group (Gartrell, Bos, & Goldberg, 2011) seemed to indicate some differ-ences between the two groups, but these were minimized when better matched data from a more recent wave of data collection became available (Gartrell, Bos, & Goldberg, 2012). With comparisons based on the best matched sample, neither girls nor boys differed from those in the national sample on reports of engaging in same-sex sexual behavior. Girls with lesbian mothers reported being older at first sexual encounters with boys, and boys with lesbian mothers reported that they were less likely to have had sex with girls than did those in the nationally representative sample. None of the findings suggested any differences in sexual orientation as a function of parental sexual orientation. In summary, there is no reliable evidence of associations between sexual orientation of parents and children.

Social development

Research on peer relations among children of lesbian mothers has been reported by Golombok and her colleagues (1983, 1997), by Green and his colleagues (1978, 1986), and by Patterson and her colleagues (Patterson, 1994; Wainright & Patterson, 2008). Reports by both parents and their offspring suggest normal development of peer relationships. For example, as would be expected, most school-aged children reported same-sex best friends and predominantly same-sex peer groups (Golombok et al., 1983; Green, 1978; Patterson, 1994). The quality of children's and adolescents' peer relations was described, on average, in positive terms by researchers (Golombok et al., 1983; Wainright & Patterson, 2008) as well as by mothers and their children (Green et al., 1986; Golombok et al., 1997;

Wainright & Patterson, 2008). Adolescent and young adult offspring of divorced lesbian mothers did not recall being the targets of any more childhood teasing or victimization than did the offspring of divorced heterosexual mothers (Tasker & Golombok, 1995, 1997; Wainright & Patterson, 2006). The number and quality of adolescents' and young adults' romantic relationships has also been found to be unrelated to maternal sexual orientation (Tasker & Golombok, 1997; Wainright, Russell, & Patterson, 2004).

Studies of relationships with adults among the children of lesbian and gay parents have also resulted in a generally positive picture (Brewaeys et al., 1997; Golombok et al., 1983; Wainright et al., 2004). For example, adolescent relationships with their parents have been described as equally warm and caring, regardless of whether parents have same- or opposite-sex partners (Wainright et al., 2004). Golombok and her colleagues (1983) found that children of divorced lesbian mothers were more likely to have had recent contact with their fathers than were children of divorced heterosexual mothers. Another study, however, found no differences in this regard (Kirkpatrick et al., 1981). Harris and Turner (1985/1986) studied the children of gay fathers as well as those of lesbian mothers, and reported that parent–child relationships were described in positive terms. One significant difference was that young adult offspring of divorced lesbian mothers described themselves as communicating more openly with their mothers and with their mothers' current partners than did adult children of divorced heterosexual parents (Tasker & Golombok, 1997).

Research has also focused on children's contacts with members of the extended family, especially grandparents. Parents are often facilitators and gatekeepers of contact between generations in families (Orel & Fruhauf, 2006). Because grandparents are generally seen as supportive of their grandchildren, any strains in parents' relationships with grandparents might have adverse effects on the frequency of children's contacts with grandparents, and hence also have a negative impact on grandchildren's development. Patterson and her colleagues have evaluated these possibilities in two separate studies (Fulcher, Chan, Raboy, & Patterson, 2002; Patterson, Hurt, & Mason, 1998). Their findings revealed that most children of lesbian mothers were described as being in regular contact with grandparents (Patterson et al., 1998). In one study, based on a systematic sampling frame and in which lesbian and heterosexual parent families were well-matched on demographic characteristics, there were no differences in the frequency of contact with grandparents as a function of parental sexual orientation (Fulcher et al., 2002). Gartrell and her colleagues (2000) have also reported that grandparents were very likely to acknowledge the children of lesbian daughters as grandchildren. Thus, available evidence suggests that, contrary to popular concerns, intergenerational relationships in lesbian mother families are satisfactory.

Other aspects of personal development

Studies of other aspects of personal development among children of lesbian and gay parents have assessed a broad array of characteristics. Among these have been separation-individuation, psychiatric evaluations, behavior problems, personality, self-concept, locus of control, moral judgment, school adjustment, and intelligence (Patterson, 2000, 2007, 2013). Research suggests that concerns about difficulties in these areas among children of lesbian or gay parents are unwarranted (Farr & Patterson, 2013; Golombok et al., 2014; Patterson, 2013). As was the case for sexual identity, studies of these aspects of personal development have revealed no major differences between children of lesbian and gay versus heterosexual parents.

Summary of the research evidence

Overall, the evidence from social science research is exceptionally clear in pointing to generally healthy development among children of lesbian and gay parents. This reading of the research literature is reflected in the American Psychological Association *Resolution on Sexual Orientation, Parents, and Children* (2004), which states, in part, that: "results of research suggest that lesbian and gay parents are as likely as heterosexual parents to provide supportive and healthy environments for their children". Other professional associations in the United States, including the American Academy of Pediatrics, the American Academy of Family Physicians, and the American Medical Association, have come to similar conclusions and have endorsed statements advocating equal rights for nonheterosexual partners and their children (Pawelski et al., 2006; Perrin et al., 2013). In short, there is general consensus on the conclusions justified by research in this area.

This body of research has been used as evidence supporting the advancement of legal recognition for lesbian- and gay-headed families. For instance, Pawelski and colleagues (2006) argued that granting same-sex couples access to civil marriage would promote healthy families by conferring a whole host of benefits, protections, and rights. Civil marriage can "help foster financial and legal security, psychosocial stability, and an augmented sense of societal acceptance and support," and can improve the ability of parenting couples to care for their children and each other (Pawelski et al., 2006).

Contributions of Research to Legal and Policy Debates

How should results of social science research be used in debates on legal and policy questions? Research findings might find their way into legal and policy debates through a number of different routes. Results of empirical research may be introduced into legal and policy debates by expert witnesses and by *amicus curiae* ("friend of the court") briefs from interested parties. Empirical findings may also reach the public through media sources (e.g., press releases about published journal articles) and/or through the efforts of advocacy groups. The ways in which these sources disseminate information may shape the reception of and attitudes toward results of social science research.

In reflecting on this issue, we can begin with the fact that some of the claims in such debates are empirical ones. For instance, in his ruling on a child custody case, one judge wrote that if he were to award custody of a girl to the girl's gay father, "social condemnation… will inevitably afflict her relationships with peers" (*Roe v. Roe*, 1985, p. 694). This is an empirical claim – that children's relationships with peers are negatively affected by parental nonheterosexuality – which empirical research has since established as likely to be false (see, for example, Wainright & Patterson, 2008). Establishment of public policies that are based on false assumptions would not normally be viewed as desirable. Evaluation of such empirical arguments is thus an important contribution that can be made by social science research on children of lesbian and gay parents.

The findings of scientific research are, however, only one factor in policy debates and in legal decision making (Huston, 2008). Many characteristics of scientific findings themselves are relevant to decisions about their utility in policy discussions. For instance, consistent findings from a series of high-quality research studies should receive more weight in policy debates than inconsistent results from low-quality studies. Even in cases where scientific findings are exceptionally clear and robust, however, they cannot in themselves be determinative with regard to policy. Values will always be significant in policy debates. It is, nevertheless, clear that information generated by social science research can also have an important place in policy discussions about lesbian and gay parents and their children.

In the United States, there are several pathways through which research findings may be brought to bear on legal and policy debates relevant to sexual orientation and parenting. Some of the pathways are direct, as when results of research are introduced into court records or specifically cited during legislative debates. Other pathways are more indirect, as when results of research are reported in professional journals and in the media, and exert influence on some aspect of public opinion. In what follows, we discuss both direct and indirect uses of results from scientific research, using examples from a specific case, *Howard v. Arkansas* (2006).

The case known as *Howard v. Arkansas* (2006) began in 1999, when the Arkansas Child Welfare Agency Review Board established a policy that "no person may serve as a foster parent if any adult member of that person's household is a homosexual…" Matthew Howard, a teacher and father of two children, living in Arkansas, had hoped to become a foster parent. As an openly gay man, and living with his longtime same-sex partner, however, Howard was not eligible to become a foster parent after the 1999 policy went into effect. Together with other complainants, Howard challenged the validity of the policy. Following a number of pretrial hearings, the case eventually came to trial at the end of 2004.

During the trial, expert witnesses testified about psychological research evidence relevant to lesbian and gay parents and their children. For example, Michael Lamb, a professor of psychology and child development at the University of Cambridge, was qualified as an expert in developmental psychology and specifically in parenting and children's adjustment. Basing his testimony upon the findings of social science research, Lamb stated that there is no child welfare basis on which to categorically exclude gay or lesbian people from being foster parents, and that such categorical exclusion could be harmful to children because it would exclude a pool of effective foster parents. He testified that there is no factual basis for the view that being reared by lesbian or gay parents has a negative impact on children's adjustment. He further testified that research has established that being reared by lesbian or gay parents does not increase the risk of psychological problems, the risk of problems in adjustment, or the risk of academic or behavioral problems among children. He indicated that research findings do not support the idea that children would be harmed by placement in foster homes with lesbian or gay foster parents. Since Lamb was serving as an expert witness, these results were introduced directly into court proceedings. The judge subsequently included them among his findings of fact and ruled that the policy excluding lesbian and gay adults from becoming foster parents was not valid under Arkansas law.

On appeal to the Supreme Court of Arkansas, research findings were introduced into the case again, this time via an *amicus* brief from the American Psychological Association. Based on the 2004 American Psychological Association Policy on "Sexual Orientation, Parents, and Children", the *amicus* brief summarized much of the same research and made many of the same points that had been made in the lower court by Professor Lamb (American Psychological Association, 2005). For instance, the brief stated that psychological research had found parental sexual orientation to be unrelated to parenting ability and unrelated to children's adjustment. It further noted that lesbian and gay parents are as likely as other parents to provide supportive and healthy environments for their children (American Psychological Association, 2005). Relying in part upon this information, the Supreme Court of Arkansas upheld the lower court ruling, making it legal again for lesbian and gay adults to serve as foster parents in that state (*Howard v. Arkansas*, 2006).

Thus, findings from psychological research were brought to bear directly on the *Howard* case at two different points in the judicial process. In one instance, research was introduced through expert testimony and, in another, policy statements from professional organizations formed the basis for *amicus* briefs that were introduced into legal proceedings. Both expert testimony and *amicus* briefs became part of the court record, and were incorporated into the court's decisions.

Research may also affect policy debates through less direct pathways, but these are usually more difficult to document. For example, when research is reported not only in professional social science journals, but also in law reviews, it may influence legal opinion. When research is reported in the popular press, it may influence public opinion. Members of the judicial and legislative branches of government are, of course, also members of the public, and their opinions may be influenced by their exposure to issues covered by the popular media. Another indirect route through which research may reach the public is the dissemination of research findings by relevant organizations, such as the Child Welfare League of America. Such organizations may collaborate with researchers in making research results more accessible to the public by condensing information and putting it into formats that are easily distributed (e.g., downloaded from the organization's web site). Thus, research findings may enter into policy and legal debates in any of a number of different ways.

Reflections on the Interface of Research, Law and Policy

What can be said about the influence of social science research upon law and policy relevant to lesbian and gay parents and their children? The clearest observation is that its impact has been difficult to predict. In some cases, clear and consistent evidence from research has been heeded, and has had an impact; the *Howard* case seems to be one such example (*Howard v. Arkansas*, 2006). In other cases, however, research findings have had less influence.

Variability in the impact of the same or very similar research findings is nowhere clearer than in the outcomes of same-sex marriage cases. A major argument against legalizing same-sex marriage has been that children would be harmed if reared by same-sex couples. Very similar *amicus* briefs have been filed by American Psychological Association in a number of different state courts, as well as in the U.S. Supreme Court, summarizing results of research and suggesting that this argument is factually incorrect.

It is interesting to note that, after studying these briefs, judges in different jurisdictions have come to quite varied conclusions. In Massachusetts, for example, the court wrote: "Protecting the welfare of children is a paramount State policy. Restricting marriage to opposite-sex couples, however, cannot plausibly further this policy" (*Goodridge v. Department of Public Health*, 2003, p. 25). This reasoning led the Massachusetts court to rule in favor of legal recognition for same-sex marriage (*Goodridge v. Department of Public Health*, 2003). Soon thereafter, however, in

New York, the justices of the state's highest court were offered essentially the same information but ruled on other grounds, deciding against legalization of same-sex marriage (*Hernandez v. Robles*, 2006). Later, the New York State Legislature passed a Marriage Equality Act, which took effect in June of 2011; but the role of social science research in the legislative process is difficult or impossible to ascertain. In any case, exposure to the clear and consistent results of social science research brought divergent results in these and other court cases.

Because it is difficult to predict the impact of research on law and policy, and because its impact may sometimes be negligible, the place of the researcher in the policy process can also be difficult to gauge. When research is influential on the outcome of a legislative debate or legal case, as it apparently was in *Howard v. Arkansas* (2006), researchers may feel that their work is useful and has contributed in important ways. On the other hand, when decisions fly in the face of accepted findings, researchers may well feel marginalized or powerless in the policy process. Legal and policy debates unfold over time, and issues may be considered and reconsidered as circumstances change; as this happens, researchers' reactions may also fluctuate.

As the policy process unfolds over time, whether in legislative or judicial contexts, varied strategies and reactions may be warranted. In a 1996 same-sex marriage case in Hawaii, one of us (Patterson) was among the expert witnesses to testify in a hearing of the case (*Baehr v. Miike*, 1996). The judge wrote a decision that relied heavily upon expert testimony about research evidence in justifying his decision that legal marriages should be available to same-sex couples. In 1998, however, while this decision was on review before the Hawaii Supreme Court, voters in Hawaii approved a constitutional amendment allowing the legislature to limit marriage to other-sex couples. In view of the amendment, the Hawaii Supreme Court ultimately dismissed the litigation as moot (*Baehr v. Miike*, 1999). In this case, although research findings initially appeared to have been influential, in the end, they were relegated to the dustbin as political realities took precedence over other considerations.

Thus, important characteristics for researchers and others who hope to influence public policy include patience, persistence, and probably also longevity. Even the most constructive changes in law and policy often occur in ways that appear to be both slow and uneven to those awaiting justice. Two steps forward may often be followed by at least one step backward. Only those who are willing and able to persist in their efforts over long periods of time are likely to have much impact.

Another important lesson is the researcher's need for allies (Huston, 2008). If the results of research are to have any impact on public policy or law, they must not only be published in professional journals but also taken up by others. For this to occur, the research must be noticed and reviewed by social scientists and by legal scholars, as well as digested and made available to the public by members of the media. Research findings must be put forward in public arenas, where they can be explained, where they can be defended against inevitable criticism, and where their relevance can be established. The results of research must be presented to courts and legislatures in ways that are appropriate to these contexts. These are often size-able undertakings that require the skills of many different kinds of people.

In the end, do the results of social science research on lesbian and gay parents and their children affect law or policy? The answer to this question depends, of course, upon the public reception of research, and upon prevailing evaluations of its importance. The impact of research findings is difficult to predict and may change over time. Thus, answers to questions about impact may change over time and circumstances, and are rarely final. Like programs of research themselves, the influences of research findings on law and policy are continually in flux.

References

American Psychological Association (2004). *Resolution on sexual orientation, parents, and children*. Washington, DC: American Psychological Association.

American Psychological Association (2005). *Amicus brief in Howard v. Arkansas*. Washington, DC: American Psychological Association.

Baehr v. Miike (1996). WL 694235 (Haw. Cir. Ct. Dec. 3, 1996).

Baehr v. Miike (1999). 994 P. 2d 566 (Haw. 1999).

Bailey, J. M., Bobrow, D., Wolfe, M., & Mikach, S. (1995). Sexual orientation of adult sons of gay fathers. *Developmental Psychology, 31*, 124–129.

Bergman, K., Rubio, R., Green, R.-J., & Padron, E. (2010). Gay men who become fathers via surrogacy: The transition to parenthood. *Journal of GLBT Family Studies, 6*, 111–141.

Bos, H., & Sandfort, T. G. (2010). Children's gender identity in lesbian and heterosexual two-parent families. *Sex Roles, 62*, 114–126.

Bos, H., van Balen, F. & van den Boom, D. C. (2003). Planned lesbian families: Their desire and motivation to have children. *Human Reproduction, 18*, 2216–2224.

Bos, H.., van Balen, F., & van den Boom, D. C. (2004). Experience of parenthood, couple relationship, social support, and child-rearing goals in planned lesbian mother families. *Journal of Child Psychology and Psychiatry, 45*, 755–764.

Boswell v. Boswell (1998). 352 Md. 204; 721 A.2d 662.

Bottoms v. Bottoms (1995). No. 941166 (Va. 1995).

Bowen, A. (1995). Another view of lesbians choosing children. In K. A. Arnup (Ed.), *Lesbian parenting: Living with pride and prejudice* (pp. 253–264). Charlottetown, PEI: Gynergy Books.

Brewaeys, A., Ponjaert, I., Van Hall, E. V., & Golombok, S. (1997). Donor insemination: Child development and family functioning in lesbian mother families. *Human Reproduction, 12*, 1349–1359.

Brodzinsky, D. M., & Staff of the Evan B. Donaldson Adoption Institute (2003). *Adoptions by lesbians and gays: A national survey of adoption agency policies, practices and attitudes*. Final project report. New York: Evan B. Donaldson Adoption Institute (www.adoptioninstitute.org).

Burgess v. Burgess (1999). 708 N. E. 2d 930; 1999 Ind. App. LEXIS 300.

D'Aoust, V. (1995). Non-existent & struggling for identity. In K. A. Arnup (Ed.), *Lesbian parenting: Living with pride and prejudice* (pp. 276–296). Charlottetown, PEI: Gynergy Books.

Downs, A. C., & James, S. E. (2006). Gay, lesbian, and bisexual foster parents: Strengths and challenges for the child welfare system. *Child Welfare Journal, 85*, 281–298.

Downing, J., Richardson, H., Kinkler, L., & Goldberg, A. (2009). Making the decision: Factors influencing gay men's choice of an adoption path. *Adoption Quarterly, 12*(3–4), 247–271.

Drucker, J. L. (1998). *Lesbian and gay families speak out: Understanding the joys and challenges of diverse family life*. Cambridge, MA: Perseus Publishing.

Farr, R. H., Forssell, S. L., & Patterson, C. J. (2010). Parenting and child development in adoptive families: Does parental sexual orientation matter? *Applied Developmental Science, 14*, 164–178.

Farr, R. H., & Goldberg, A. E. (2015). Contact between birth and adoptive families during the first year post-placement: Perspectives of lesbian, gay, and heterosexual parents. *Adoption Quarterly, 18*, 1–24.

Farr, R. H., & Patterson, C. J. (2013). Coparenting among lesbian, gay, and heterosexual couples: Associations with adopted children's outcomes. *Child Development, 84*, 1226–1240.

Fulcher, M., Chan, R. W., Raboy, B., & Patterson, C. J. (2002). Contact with grandparents among children conceived via donor insemination by lesbian and heterosexual mothers. *Parenting: Science and Practice, 2*, 61–76.

Fulcher, M., Sutfin, E., & Patterson, C. J. (2008). Individual differences in gender development: Associations with parental sexual orientation. *Sex Roles, 58*, 330–341.

Gartrell, N., Banks, A., Reed, N., Gross, H., Hamilton, J., Rodas, C., & Deck, A. (2000). The National Lesbian Family Study: 3. Interviews with mothers of five-year-olds. *American Journal of Orthopsychiatry, 70*, 542–548.

Gartrell, N., Bos, H., & Goldberg, N. (2011). Adolescents of the U.S. National Longitudinal Lesbian Family Study: Sexual orientation, sexual behavior, and sexual risk exposure. *Archives of Sexual Behavior, 40*, 1199–1209.

Gartrell, N., Bos, H., & Goldberg, N. (2012). New trends in same-sex sexual contact for American adolescents. *Archives of Sexual Behavior, 41*, 5–7.

Gates, G. J. (2011). Family formation and same-sex couples raising children. *National Council of Family Relations Family Focus on LGBT Families Newsletter, FF51*, 1–4.

Goldberg, A. E. (2010). *Lesbian and gay parents and their children: Research on the family life cycle*. Washington, DC: American Psychological Association.

Goldberg, A. E. (2012). *Gay dads: Transitions to adoptive fatherhood*. New York: New York University Press.

Goldberg, A. E., Kashy, D. A., & Smith, J. Z. (2012). Gender-typed play behavior in early childhood: Adopted children with lesbian, gay, and heterosexual parents. *Sex Roles, 67*(9–10), 503–515.

Goldberg, A. E., Moyer, A. M., Kinkler, L. A., & Richardson, H. B. (2012). "When you're sitting on the fence, hope's the hardest part": Challenges and experiences of heterosexual and same-sex couples adopting through the child welfare system. *Adoption Quarterly, 15*(4), 288–315.

Golombok, S., Mellish, L., Jennings, S., Casey, P., Tasker, F., & Lamb, M. E. (2014). Adoptive gay father families: Parent–child relationships and children's psychological adjustment. *Child Development, 85,* 456–468.

Golombok, S., Murray, C., & Tasker, F. (1997). Children raised in fatherless families from infancy: Family relationships and the socioemotional development of children of lesbian and single heterosexual mothers. *Journal of Child Psychology & Psychiatry, 38,* 783–791.

Golombok, S., & Rust, J. (1993). The Preschool Activity Inventory: A standardized assessment of gender role in children. *Psychological Assessment, 5,* 131–136.

Golombok, S., Spencer, A., & Rutter, M. (1983). Children in lesbian and single-parent households: Psychosexual and psychiatric appraisal. *Journal of Child Psychology and Psychiatry, 24,* 551–572.

Golombok, S., & Tasker, F. (1996). Do parents influence the sexual orientation of their children? Findings from a longitudinal study of lesbian families. *Developmental Psychology, 32,* 3–11.

Golombok, S., & Tasker, F. (2010). Gay fathers. In M. E. Lamb (Ed.), *The role of the father in child development.* Hoboken, NJ: John Wiley & Sons, Inc.

Goodridge v. Department of Public Health (2003). SJC-08860 (Mass., 2003).

Green, R. (1978). Sexual identity of 37 children raised by homosexual or transsexual parents. *American Journal of Psychiatry, 135,* 692–697.

Green, R., Mandel, J. B., Hotvedt, M. E., Gray, J., & Smith, L. (1986). Lesbian mothers and their children: A comparison with solo parent heterosexual mothers and their children. *Archives of Sexual Behavior, 7,* 175–181.

Harris, M. B., & Turner, P. H. (1985/1986). Gay and lesbian parents. *Journal of Homosexuality, 12,* 101–113.

Hayman, B., Wilkes, L., Jackson, D., & Halcomb, E. (2013). De novo lesbian families: Legitimizing the other mother. *Journal of GLBT Family Studies, 9*(3), 273–287.

Hernandez v. Robles (2006). 855 N.E. 2d 1 (N.Y. 2006).

Hill, M. (1987). Child rearing attitudes of Black lesbian mothers. In Boston Lesbian Psychologies Collective (Ed.), *Lesbian psychologies: Explanations and challenges* (pp. 215–226). Urbana, IL: University of Illinois Press.

Hoeffer, B. (1981). Children's acquisition of sex-role behavior in lesbian-mother families. *American Journal of Orthopsychiatry, 5,* 536–544.

Howard v. Child Welfare Agency Review Board (2004). WL 3200916 (Ark. Cir. Ct. 2004).

Huggins, S. L. (1989). A comparative study of self-esteem of adolescent children of divorced lesbian mothers and divorced heterosexual mothers. In F. W. Bozett (Ed.), *Homosexuality and the family* (pp. 123–135). New York: Harrington Park Press.

Huston, A. C. (2008). From research to policy and back. *Child Development, 79,* 1–12.

Kirkpatrick, M., Smith, C., & Roy, R. (1981). Lesbian mothers and their children: A comparative survey. *American Journal of Orthopsychiatry, 51,* 545–551.

Kweskin, S. L., & Cook, A. S. (1982). Heterosexual and homosexual mothers' self-described sex-role behavior and ideal sex-role behavior in children. *Sex Roles, 8,* 967–975.

Lev, A. I. (2006) Gay dads: Choosing surrogacy. *Lesbian and Gay Psychology Review, 7,* 73–77.

Lick, D. J., Tornello, S. L., Riskind, R. G., Schmidt, K. M., & Patterson, C. J. (2012). Social climate for sexual minorities predicts well-being among heterosexual offspring of lesbian and gay parents. *Sexuality Research and Social Policy, 9,* 99–112.

MacCallum, F., & Golombok, S. (2004). Children raised in fatherless families from infancy: A follow-up of children of lesbian and single heterosexual mothers at early adolescence. *Journal of Child Psychology and Psychiatry, 45,* 1407–1419.

Matthews, J. D., & Cramer, E. P. (2006). Envisaging the adoption process to strengthen gay- and lesbian-headed families: Recommendations for adoption professionals. *Child Welfare Journal, 85,* 317–340.

Moore, M. R. (2008). Gendered power relations among women: A study of household decision making in Black, lesbian stepfamilies. *American Sociological Review, 73*(2), 335–356.

Moore, M. (2011). *Invisible families: Gay identities, relationships, and motherhood among Black women.* Berkeley, CA: University of California Press.

Orel, N. A., & Fruhauf, C. A. (2006). Lesbian and bisexual grandmothers' perceptions of the grandparent-grandchild relationship. *Journal of GLBT Family Studies, 2,* 43–70.

Oswald, R, Cuthbertson, C., Lazarevic, V., & Goldberg, A. (2010). New developments in the field: Measuring community climate. *Journal of GLBT Family Studies, 6,* 214 – 228.

Patterson, C. J. (1994). Lesbian and gay families. *Current Directions in Psychological Science, 3,* 62–64.

Patterson, C. J. (1995). Adoption of minor children by lesbian and gay adults: A social science perspective. *Duke Journal of Gender Law and Policy, 2,* 191–205.

Patterson, C. J. (2000). Sexual orientation and family life: A decade review. *Journal of Marriage and the Family, 62,* 1052–1069.

Patterson, C. J. (2006). Children of lesbian and gay parents. *Current Directions in Psychological Science, 15,* 241–244.

Patterson, C. J. (2007). Lesbian and gay family issues in the context of changing legal and social policy environments. In K. J. Bieschke, R. M. Perez, & K. A. DeBord & (Eds.), *Handbook of counseling and psychotherapy with lesbian, gay, bisexual and transgender Clients* (2nd ed.). Washington, D.C.: American Psychological Association.

Patterson, C. J. (2013). Family lives of lesbian and gay adults. In G. W. Peterson & K. R. Bush (Eds.), *Handbook of marriage and the family.* New York: Springer Science.

Patterson, C. J., Hurt, S., & Mason, C. D. (1998). Families of the lesbian baby boom: Children's contacts with grandparents and other adults. *American Journal of Orthopsychiatry, 68,* 390–399.

Patterson, C. J., & Riskind, R. G. (2010). To be a parent: Issues in family formation among gay and lesbian adults. *Journal of GLBT Family Studies, 6,* 326–340.

Patterson, C. J., Riskind, R. G., & Tornello, S. L. (2013). Sexual orientation, marriage and parenthood. In A. Abela & J. Walker (Eds.), *Contemporary issues in family studies: Global perspectives on partnerships, parenting and support in a changing world* (pp. 189–202). New York: John Wiley & Sons, Inc.

Patterson, C. J., & Tornello, S. L. (2010). Gay fathers' pathways to parenthood: International perspectives. *Zeitschrift fur Familienforschung (Journal of Family Psychology), Sonderheft,* 5, 103–116.

Pawelski, J. G. et al. (2006). The effects of marriage, civil union, and domestic partnership laws on the health and well-being of children. *Pediatrics, 118,* 349–364.

Perlesz, A., Brown, R., Lindsay, J., McNair, R., de Vaus, D. & Pitts, M. (2006). Families in transition: parents, children and grandparents in lesbian families give meaning to 'doing family'. *Journal of Family Therapy, 28,* 175–199.

Perrin, E. C., & the Committee on Psychosocial Aspects of Child and Family Health (2002). Technical Report: Coparent or second-parent adoption by same-sex parents. *Pediatrics, 109,* 341–344.

Perrin, E. C. et al. (2013). Promoting the well-being of children whose parents are gay or lesbian. *Pediatrics, 131*(4), e1374–e1383.

Power, J. et al. (2010). Diversity, tradition and family: Australian same-sex attracted parents and their families. *Gay and Lesbian Issues and Psychology Review, 6,* 66–81.

Power, J. et al. (2012). Bisexual parents and family diversity: Findings from the Work, Love, Play study. *Journal of Bisexuality, 12,* 519–538.

Pulliam v. Smith (1998). 348 N. C. 616; 501 S. E. 2d 898.

Riggs, D.W. (2006). Developmentalism and the rhetoric of "best interest of the child": Challenging heteronormative constructions of families and parenting in foster care. *Journal of GLBT Family Studies, 2,* 57–73.

Roe v. Roe (1985). 324 S.E. 2d 691, 228 Va. 722.

Sutfin, E., Fulcher, M., Bowles, R., & Patterson, C. J. (2008). How lesbian and hetero-sexual parents convey attitudes about gender to their children: The role of gendered environments. *Sex Roles, 58,* 501–513.

Tasker F. & Golombok S. (1995). Adults raised as children in lesbian families. *American Journal of Orthopsychiatry, 65,* 203–215.

Tasker, F., & Golombok, S. (1997). *Growing up in a lesbian family.* New York: Guilford Press.

Tasker, F., & Patterson, C. J. (2007). Research on gay and lesbian parenting: Retrospect and prospect. *Journal of GLBT Family Issues, 3,* 9–34.

Tornello, S. L., & Patterson, C. J. (2012). Gay fathers in mixed-orientation relationships: Experiences of those who stay in their marriages and of those who leave. *Journal of GLBT Family Studies, 8,* 85–98.

Wainright, J. L., & Patterson, C. J. (2006). Delinquency, victimization, and substance use among adolescents with female same-sex parents. *Journal of Family Psychology, 20,* 526–530.

Wainright, J. L., & Patterson, C. J. (2008). Peer relations among adolescents with female same-sex parents. *Developmental Psychology, 44,* 117–126.

Wainright, J. L., Russell, S. T., & Patterson, C. J. (2004). Psychosocial adjustment and school outcomes of adolescents with same-sex parents. *Child Development, 75,* 1886–1898.

Wald, M. S. (2006). Adults' sexual orientation and state determinations regarding placement of children. *Family Law Quarterly, 40,* 381–434.

7

Child Care at the Nexus of Practice, Policy, and Research

Christina Hardway and Kathleen McCartney

Internationally, there is an increasingly supportive policy environment for early child-care and education. The cumulative and ever-growing body of research documenting the long-term benefits of attending high-quality early childcare and education (ECCE) has, in part, precipitated these important changes. Equally important, a strong network of grassroots advocates working to build opportunities for children has also played a role in this increasing support for ECCE. Despite improvements, most children in the world still do not have access to high-quality ECCE (UNESCO, 2007). It is, therefore, a good time to reflect on what has made some of these collaborations between researchers, practitioners, and policymakers successful so that we may understand our past achievements and build upon these foundations for the future.

Enrollment Patterns for Early Child Care

Worldwide, access to preprimary education is on the rise. Almost 124 million children (about 37% of children between the ages of three and primary-school aged) were enrolled in preprimary education, representing a 10.7% increase between1999

The Wiley Handbook of Developmental Psychology in Practice: Implementation and Impact, First Edition.
Edited by Kevin Durkin and H. Rudolph Schaffer.
© 2016 John Wiley & Sons, Ltd. Published 2016 by John Wiley & Sons, Ltd.

and 2004. About 32% of children in developing countries and about 77% of children in developed countries attend preprimary education. Comparatively, countries have fewer programs aimed at serving children under the age of three; in the countries UNESCO surveyed for its Global Monitoring Report, only 53% reported having at least one formal ECCE program for infants and toddlers (UNESCO, 2007).

Enrollment rates vary across children's country of residence. Some of the highest rates of access are found in Western European countries like Norway, in which 94.5% of 3–5-year-olds and 51.3% of children under the age of three are enrolled in formal care. In other parts of the world, fewer children are typically enrolled in such services. For example, in Chile, 9.8% of 0–3-year-olds are enrolled in formal services and 62.6% of children aged 3–5 participate in such services (OECD, 2012). Perhaps not surprisingly, children in sub-Saharan African and Arab states are less likely to attend preprimary education programs than children in other parts of the world (UNESCO, 2007).

In the United States, 31.4% of children aged 0–3 and 55.7% of children aged 3–5 are enrolled in formal care; opportunities to attend quality child care vary greatly across states (OECD, 2012). Many children in the United States are in nonregulated care including family-based and unregulated center-based care. Within the United States, enrollment patterns vary based on children's ages. According to the National Household Education Survey of parents sampled across the United States (NCES, 2015), 42% of children less than a year of age were in nonparental care, 53% of children aged 1–2 were in nonparental care, and 73% of children aged 3–5 were in such care at least once a week. Enrollment in center-based care was higher for children aged 3–5 (78%) than it was for children in the first year (28%). Many parents rely on a network of family, friends, and neighbors to care for children, particularly infants and toddlers. These kinds of arrangements account for about 46% of nonfamily care in the United States for children from birth through the age of two (Kreader & Lawrence, 2006).

Quality of Child Care

Researchers have worked to delineate the specific dimensions of childcare quality that are associated with child outcomes. More specifically, what constitutes a high-quality versus a low-quality early childcare program and which aspects of quality make a difference in the lives of children? Assessments of child care quality generally fall under two broad categories: those that assess structural features of child care (e.g., educational level of the teacher, group size, teacher:child ratio, staff wages) and those that assess classroom processes (e.g., teacher behaviors and practices, child behaviors, and the interactions between teachers and children) (Klein & Knitzer, 2006; Lamb & Ahnert, 2006; Vandell & Wolfe, 2000). More extensive reviews of child care effects can be found elsewhere (Allhusen, Clark-Stewart, & Miner, 2006; Barnett, 1995; Burchinal, Lowe Vandell, & Belsky, 2014; Lamb & Ahnert, 2006; NICHD ECCRN, 2005a; Phillips, McCartney, & Sussman, 2005; Shonkoff & Phillips, 2000).

It has been difficult to disentangle the specific effects of these two strains of quality because structural and process features typically covary (Lamb & Ahnert; 2006; Vandell & Wolfe, 2000). Furthermore, associations between structural aspects of quality and child outcomes are likely mediated through effects on processes between teachers and children (NICHD ECCRN, 2002; Vandell & Wolfe, 2000). An additional challenge in studying the specific impact of child care on child outcomes is that the quality of child care to which children have access is almost always confounded with their socioeconomic status and other family-related variables (McCartney, 1984; NICHD ECCRN, 2005a).

Children may benefit differentially from various aspects of quality in child care depending on the ages of the children or the outcomes assessed (Melhuish & Petrogiannis, 2006; Vandell & Wolfe, 2000). In a review of the impact on child care quality and child outcomes, Vandell and Wolfe (2000) suggest that structural features of the classroom, including group size and group ratios, may be more important than other measures to process quality in infant and toddler care settings, whereas teacher education may be a better predictor of process quality in settings with preschool-aged children. Different dimensions of quality may also be more or less associated with specific child outcomes. Findings from an international study on the association between indicators of preschool quality and child outcomes suggest that level of teacher education is related to children's language performance at age seven, whereas the variety of learning materials available in the preschool setting is associated with other measures of children's cognitive performance at age seven (Montie, Xiang, Schweinhart, 2006).

Researchers believe that the attributes and behaviors of the child care staff are the most important predictor of the overall quality of child care. A review of the association between caregivers' educational credentials and the quality of the classroom environments they provide indicates a modest association between caregivers' educational attainment and classroom quality (Tout, Zaslow, & Berry, 2005). Both within the United States and internationally, there is evidence of a link between caregiver education and children's language abilities, in particular (Burchinal, Cryer, Clifford, & Howes, 2002; Melhuish, 2006; Montie et al., 2006). Generally, however, the associations between the academic credentials of caregivers and child-related outcomes are small (Klein & Knitzer, 2006), and many studies have revealed no consistent association between higher levels of caregiver education and preschool classroom quality or child cognitive skills (Early et al., 2007).

In the end, the quality of care children receive depends on the relationships they are able to form with their caregivers (Shonkoff & Phillips, 2000). One hallmark of this association is the longevity of children's relationships with their teachers. When children experience many changes in their nonparental care, their abilities to form secure relationships may suffer (Ahnert, Pinquart, & Lamb, 2006; Lamb & Ahnert, 2006; NICHD ECCRN, 1997). Children explore their environments more when they are with regular caregivers who have been caring for them a long period of time (Lamb & Ahnert, 2006). When upset, toddlers are more likely to seek out comforting contact and are more easily quieted by stable caregivers. They also show more preference toward stable caregivers when they are not upset (Barnas & Cummings, 1994; Lamb & Ahnert, 2006). The security of children's attachment to their caregivers is not simply an outgrowth of a secure relationship with parents but is also determined by the relationship that they build with their childcare providers (Goossens & Van IJzendoorn, 1990; Lamb & Ahnert, 2006). Those children who have more intense and sensitive interactions with their caregivers and simply spend more time with their caregivers are more likely to be securely attached to them (Goossens & Van IJzendoorn, 1990; Ritchie & Howes, 2003).

Taken together, these findings suggest that children benefit most from child care opportunities that allow them to build secure, ongoing relationships with sensitive and professional caregivers (Lamb & Ahnert, 2006; Shonkoff & Phillips, 2000). There is mounting evidence that increasing the educational levels of early childcare teachers alone will not be a sufficient measure to increase the quality of care or actualize children's academic potentials (Early et al., 2007), perhaps because professional training and development programs do not consistently incorporate research-based best practices in the field (Pianta, Barnett, Burchinal, & Thornburg, 2009). Securing structural (and perhaps more easily regulable) aspects of the caregiving environment that will allow teachers to provide a responsive and stimulating environment for the *groups* of children in their care may have a more immediate impact on the quality of care (Ahnert & Lamb, 2000; Lamb & Ahnert, 2006; Ahnert et al., 2006). More optimum structural features facilitate better teacher child interactions, which are more likely to lead to positive child outcomes (NICHD ECCRN, 2002).

A significant threat to children's ability to develop ongoing relationships with their nonparental caregivers is the high rates of staff turnover. Over the course of a 20-month study of both nationally accredited and nonaccredited centers, staff turnover was about 50% and sometimes exceeded that level (Whitebook, Sakai, & Howes, 1997). Those centers that were able to retain more of their skilled teachers were more likely to be rated as higher in quality whether or not they were accredited by a national association (Whitebook et al., 1997). Staff turnover tends to be lower in centers with higher teacher wages (Whitebook, Sakai, & Howes, 2004).

Unfortunately, preschool teachers in the United States have salaries that are less than half of those paid to kindergarten teachers. Preschool teachers are also paid less than janitors, secretaries, and other professions requiring a high school diploma. Assistant teachers earn even less, with the average full-time wages for this group insufficient to support a family of three above the threshold for poverty (Barnett, 2003).

The size of groups and the adult:child ratios are other regulable aspects of care that are associated with the quality of the interactions between children and their caregivers (Frede, 1995; Hwang, 2006; NICHD ECCRN, 2002). Programs in which teachers have more close physical contact with children, respond to children's vocalizations more often, ask children questions, praise children, and generally talk to children in positive ways are higher in quality (NICHD ECCRN, 2001). Teachers are able to provide this more sensitive and responsive care in programs with lower adult:child ratios, and the children in their care have better cognitive and social outcomes (NICHD ECCRN, 2002).

Additionally, ongoing opportunities for caregivers to reflect on their teaching practices with the proper support from others are likely to improve their performance. On-site mentoring programs give teachers immediate feedback on their teaching practices, which helps them consider the implications of their actions within the context of their daily interactions with children in their care (Frede, 1995; Klein & Knitzer, 2006). Pianta and colleagues (Pianta, Mashburn, Downer, Hamre, & Justice, 2008) examined the impact of a web-based professional development program aimed at helping preschool teachers improve the quality of their interactions with children. In a randomized control study of the program, one group of teachers received access to web-based videos of high quality interactions between teachers and children. A second group of teachers received access to these videos and also received consultation with targeted feedback on uploaded videos of the teachers' own interactions with the children for whom they cared. Those teachers who received individual feedback showed a greater increase in the quality of their caregiving, compared with those who received only access to exemplar video clips. Practices aimed at reducing the level of staff turnover and increasing the responsivity and sensitivity of caregivers as they interact with the children in their care may have the most direct impact on the quality of care they provide.

Child Care and Child Development

Studies by researchers examining the associations between time in child care and child outcomes have generally fallen under two categories: those that investigate the impact of general child care experiences on development and those that investigate whether there are specific benefits of attending early childhood education programs for children from disadvantaged backgrounds (Barnett, 1995; Shonkoff & Phillips, 2000). Much like the larger public, researchers working in both of these areas are concerned with the endurance of early child care effects, both positive and negative (Barnett, 1995; Belsky et al., 2007).

Child care and the mother–child relationship

Much of the earliest research on the general effects of child care focused on possible detriments to the mother–child relationship as a function of extensive infant child care (Barnett, 1995; Shonkoff & Phillips, 2000). In 1991, a longitudinal study designed to assess the long-term impact of time in child care on the mother–child relationship was launched. This longitudinal study, funded by the National Institute of Child Health and Human Development Study of Early Childcare and Youth Development (NICHD SECCYD) was conducted by a consortium of researchers, the NICHD Early Childcare Research Network (NICHD ECCRN) (NICHD ECCRN, 2005a). It studied 1,364 U.S. children born in 1991 to examine the effects of child care on child outcomes. Results from the NICHD SECCYD, which examined the moderating impact of family and school quality, indicated no main effect for children's attendance in child care and their attachment to mothers at fifteen months of age. Specifically, quality of care, hours in care, and early entry into child care did not increase the likelihood that children were insecurely attached to mothers (NICHD ECCRN, 1997). For children whose mothers were insensitive or unresponsive, there was, however, a slight increased risk of insecure attachment to the mother when the children also experienced extensive, unstable, or poor quality child care. In these cases, the interaction between poor mothering and extensive poor quality care resulted in a decreased likelihood of being securely attached to one's mother (NICHD ECCRN, 1997).

Child care and social development

There is a robust literature linking hours in child care with externalizing behavior (Belsky, 2001). Time spent in center-based child care, in particular, is associated with behavior problems (Belsky et al., 2007; Lamb & Ahnert, 2006; NICHD ECCRN, 2005a, 2005b). In primary school, time spent in center-based care is associated with more externalizing problems, teacher–child conflict as rated by teachers, and higher levels of mother–child conflict as rated by mothers (NICHD ECCRN, 2005b), and, in sixth grade, time spent in center-based care continues to predict higher levels of problem behaviors (Belsky et al., 2007). The question remains whether the association is a selection effect, a child effect, and/or moderated by the child care experience. Two recent papers shed light on this issue, which is of great concern to parents, practitioners, and policymakers alike. Using the NICHD data set, McCartney et al. (2010) tested a series of causal propositions relating time in child care to children's externalizing problems. They described the evidence linking child care hours with externalizing behavior as "equivocal," because it was not robust across model specifications. For the most part, the association disappeared in more rigorous models, for example fixed-effects analyses. In addition, they could find no evidence of a child effect, that is, children with more behavior problems are not placed in child care for more hours. The most important finding was that the association was moderated by childcare quality; the effect of child care hours was smaller under higher quality conditions and larger under lower quality conditions. Thus, childcare quality protects children to some extent from any adverse effect of child care hours. They also identified family factors that predicted externalized problems, positively and negatively. Sensibly, the authors conclude that externalizing problems is the result of "a constellation of variables from multiple contexts" (McCartney et al., 2010, p. 14), a point made persuasively by Newcombe (2003).

When examining the relation between time spent in child care and later problem behaviors in countries with higher levels of support for early childcare services, a somewhat different picture emerges. For example, analyses of a longitudinal sample in Norway indicate the effects sizes for the association between quantity of child care and externalizing behaviors were small. Additionally, these researchers employed careful analytic techniques to address possible selection effects. In addition to accounting for missing data by performing a list-wise deletion, they conducted the analyses using a somewhat newer approach to managing missing data – multiple imputation. While the effect sizes for the association between quantity of child care and externalizing behaviors were small using list-wise deletion, they were reduced further with the multiple imputation analyses. Moreover, when these researchers employed sibling and individual fixed-effects models to examine the association between quantity of child care and externalizing behaviors, effect sizes were reduced further and close to zero in most cases (Zachrisson, Dearing, Lekhal, & Toppelberg, 2013). Even in the United States, the impact of time spent in child care was moderated by the quality of care the child received, and the association has been found to be smaller for children who received higher quality care (McCartney et al., 2010). These overall cross-national differences may be attributable to the general quality of care provided in cultural contexts more generally and financially supportive of early child care. While the United States only meets three of the ten benchmarks UNICEF has proposed for assessing whether countries provide adequate supports for early child care and education, Norway meets eight of these, and Sweden meets all ten (UNICEF Innocenti Research Center, 2008; Zachrisson et al., 2013).

Child care and cognitive development

Experiences in child care are linked to children's cognitive skills as well (Belsky et al., 2007; NICHD ECCRN, 2005b). Children who experience higher quality care perform better on general tests of cognitive performance (like the memory for sentences subtest of the Woodcock-Johnson), mathematics tests, and language-related tests (like the Picture Vocabulary subtest) (NICHD ECCRN, 2005b) than children experiencing lower quality care. Early childcare quality continues to predict academic functioning into adolescence. Fifteen-year-olds who attended child care in the moderate-to-high-quality range performed better cognitively and academically than children who attended lower quality care. The effects of early childcare quality endure into adolescence, in part but not entirely, through their effects on children earlier in elementary school (Vandell et al., 2010). International studies of children's performance in primary grades also find that experiences in preschool predict cognitive and language performance, with dimensions of quality predicting these skills in primary school (Montie et al., 2006).

Child care and the development of low-income children

In the United States, the gap between achievement levels of children from high and low income families has widened over the past four decades. At the same time, the correlation between family income and educational achievement has strengthened over the years. This achievement gap is evident at the beginning of kindergarten; children from the upper 10% of the income distribution score over a standard deviation higher than children from the lowest 10% of the income distribution when they enter school (Reardon, Valentino, & Shore, 2012). Particularly for children from these low-income families, attending a high-quality early childhood education program is associated with positive outcomes in childhood and adulthood. In a review of decades of research on the impact of early childhood programs on cognitive and school outcomes, Barnett (1995) concludes that ECCE can produce large short-term IQ gains during early childhood. More importantly, these programs can have a persistent impact on the long-term academic functioning of attendees, including increased likelihood to graduate from high school. The strongest effects of these programs are on the decreased likelihood for attendees to be referred to special education classes or retained in a grade for a second year

(Barnett, 1995). Furthermore, attending high-quality ECCE programs is associated with a wide range of positive adult outcomes, including lower levels of crime, lower rates of teenage pregnancy, higher incomes, higher levels of educational attainment (Schweinhart et al., 2005) and lower levels of depression in adulthood (McLaughlin, Campbell, Pungello, & Skinner, 2007).

The benefits of attending high-quality early child care and education extend not only through the lifetime of the attendee but also to the larger society (Heckman, 2000; Lynch, 2004). Resources invested in children at a very young age have a profound impact on learning and socialization skills; they produce higher returns than the same investments made at older ages (Heckman, 2000). The cognitive skills of children from low-income families seem to benefit both directly from their experiences in high-quality child care but also indirectly through the impact that these higher quality child care experiences have on the children's home environments. Low-income children who attend higher quality care perform better in various measures of cognitive skills than low-income children who attend lower quality care and those who have no formal childcare arrangements (McCartney, Dearing, Taylor, & Bub, 2007). These cognitive benefits extend into middle childhood, in part, because those children who attended higher quality care enter school with better school-readiness skills. These early school-readiness skills mediate the association between early childcare opportunities and their math and reading skills in middle childhood (Dearing, McCartney, & Taylor, 2009).

A second pathway by which the quality of child care is associated with children's cognitive skills is indirect and operates through improved home environments. Measurements of the quality of the home environment at 36 months, but not at six months, is predicted by the interaction between the income-to-needs ratio of the child's family and higher quality child care, even after controlling for home quality at six-months of age (McCartney et al., 2007). Not only is there evidence that the poorest children benefit from such high quality ECCE opportunities, analyses indicate that children living close to 200% above the poverty line performed better on tests of school achievement after spending more time in higher quality care ECCE (Dearing et al., 2009).

Research to Policy

National early childhood education policy

There exists some legislation regarding early child care and education in at least 80 countries. Some of these developments are quite recent; 20 of the 30 countries that have at least one year of mandated preprimary education have implemented these policy changes since 1990 (UNESCO, 2007). Strong policies for young children confer long-lasting financial benefits to an individual child as well as to the society in which he or she resides (Heckman, 2000; Lynch, 2004). By some estimates, every dollar invested in children through the provision of high quality early childhood development programs generates three or more dollars in return (Lynch, 2004). A cost–benefit analysis of the High/Scope Perry Preschool Program, an intervention study in which low income children were randomly assigned to either receive high-quality preschool education or continue with their usual care, suggests that the monetary return on such investments can be much higher. Analyses of the public returns for investments into this childcare program have indicated that for every dollar invested, the public has received $12.90 in return, and the participants themselves have received an additional benefit of $3.24 by the time they had reached the age of 40 (Schweinhart et al., 2005). Providing children with such opportunities would reduce the burden on the criminal justice system, the welfare system, and needs for remedial educational services as well as increase the tax income generated by recipients (Lynch, 2004; Schweinhart et al., 2005).

Several barriers limit the development of such policies across both industrialized and underdeveloped countries. In addition to resource-related barriers in the avail-ability of financial and human capital, these barriers consist of cultural ones, like ambivalence about the extent to which governments should be involved in the lives of families, as well as logistical barriers including a lack of public awareness regarding the potential benefits of early child care and education (UNESCO, 2007). For researchers to help their communities overcome these impediments, they must become better informed about the cultures of those groups that engage in direct practice and policy development (Shonkoff, 2000).

Countries differ in the extent to which child care is regarded as the private responsibility of the family or the responsibility of the community as a whole and thus a public concern (Education International, 2010; Melhuish & Petrogiannis, 2006; Waldfogel, 2006). In Scandinavian countries, like Sweden, the provision of publicly supported child care reflects an ongoing cultural practice of supporting families through domestic policies including public child care as well as generous parental leave policies (Hwang, 2006; Waldfogel, 2006). Because of public sub-sidization, parents in Sweden pay about 8–10% of the real costs of center-based and family day care. In its guidelines for child care, Sweden includes mandates to provide opportunities for children to develop both their social and cognitive potentials (Hwang, 2006).

The United States represents an extreme in its regard for early child care as a private concern, and thereby the responsibility of parents (Melhuish & Petrogiannis, 2006; Waldfogel, 2006). Even so, the United States has made progress in the last 30 years in providing opportunities for parents to access regulated child care.

Between 1979 and 2002, there was, approximately, a 500% increase in the number of licensed child care centers and a 200% increase in the number of regulated family childcare homes, but opportunities for child care are unevenly dispersed across income groups (Muenchow & Marsland, 2007). The federal and state governments have worked to increase the availability of quality child care for children within the United States. Reflecting long-held belief that these matters are better placed under the guidelines of locally-based institutions, the U.S. government has provided its funding in the form of block grants to states to support local efforts (OCC, 2012).

There is some indication that the United States federal government may become more active in facilitating children's access to high quality child care. In his 2013 State of the Union address, President Barack Obama stated, "In states that make it a priority to educate our youngest children… studies show students grow up more likely to read and do math at grade level, graduate high school, hold a job, form more stable families of their own. We know this works. So let's do what works and make sure none of our children start the race of life already behind" (The White House, Office of the Press Secretary, 2013). Part of this proposed initiative to increase low and moderate American children's access to quality child care includes plans to develop federal–state cost-sharing partnerships to reach children living at or below 200% of the poverty line, with proposed guidelines suggesting a require-ment for early education to meet benchmarks associated with better child outcomes, promoting assessment, employing qualified teachers in all preschool classrooms, and encouraging overall state-level standard for quality in care (The White House, Office of the Press Secretary, 2013).

Regional child care policy

Many U.S. state programs aimed at improving the quality of child care reflect research-based concepts of what constitutes the best practices. Some are expansions of earlier state-based programs that proved successful in promoting the expansion of quality child care across an entire region, like the North Carolina "Smart Start" initiative. As part of an evaluation of this program, Bryant, Maxwell, and Burchinal (1999) collected data from 180 childcare centers in 12 North Carolina counties and found that this community-based initiative increased quality of child care between 1994 and 1996, as measured using the Early Childhood Environment Raring Scale (ECERS) (Harms & Clifford, 1980).

Two programs implemented in this initiative, T.E.A.C.H. and WAGE$, address the problems with educational qualifications and the low pay common among childcare personnel. The T.E.A.C.H. program (Teacher Education and Compensation

Helps) makes funding available for childcare professionals to obtain college or university credit in the field of early childhood education. The number of states participating in these quality improvement initiatives has grown. In 2011, early childhood educators in 22 states received T.E.A.C.H. scholarships to support their efforts to pursue courses in higher education (CCSA, 2011). WAGE$ provides supplements to childcare teachers and administrators in order to reduce teacher turnover and encourage additional training and education (Taylor & Bryant, 2002). In North Carolina, the turnover rate of childcare staff in counties that participated in the WAGE$ program was 12% in 2010, whereas the turnover rate for counties not participating was 31%, indicating that programs like these hold promise (Smart Start, 2010).

Unfortunately, in this time of fiscal austerity, even programs with evidence-based support of their effectiveness, such as Smart Start, are in peril. In 2011, as North Carolina faced budget shortfalls, the legislature voted to cut support of early childhood education in that state by 20%. Some argue, however, that this state-funded support would have been cut even further if the original architects of the program, Governor Jim Hunt and his staff, had not "cemented" the program into local community structures. By giving stakeholders in local communities programmatic decision making powers about such programs, Governor Hunt provided some enduring protection for early childhood education (Gormley, 2012).

Despite these economic setbacks, many states have developed early learning guidelines for preschoolers, and several states have chosen to develop guidelines for infants and toddlers as well. Perhaps the most comprehensive way by which states are improving the quality of ECCE is through the implementation of Quality Rating Systems, a research-based system developed in the late 1990s to provide accountability for ECCE that also helped communicate to parents and community members the quality of the programs available (Mitchell, 2005; Zellman & Fiene, 2012). In 2010, these Quality Rating Systems had been implemented or were being developed and piloted in more than 25 states or local districts (Tout et al., 2010) and more states are in the process of developing these programs, now referred to as Quality Rating and Improvement Systems (QRIS) (NACCRRA, 2011).

Many of these rating systems have several features in common, including the presence of standards for child care, accountability, financial incentives for meeting standards for quality, support for practitioners, and efforts to educate and inform parents about childcare quality (Tout et al., 2010). Among these criteria are structural qualities such as staff qualifications, compensation, professional development activities, group sizes, and adult:child ratios. Financial incentives for achieving higher ratings include tiered reimbursement systems, whereby the state reimburses licensed and higher quality programs at a higher rate when qualifying low income families attend (Mitchell, 2005). Often these quality rating systems include accreditation with an organization like the National Association for the Education of

Young Children (NAEYC) as part of their guidelines (Mitchell, 2005; Tout et al., 2010). Research suggests that states with more stringent childcare regulations have higher numbers of childcare programs in the process of NAEYC accreditation (Apple, 2006). Offering higher reimbursement rates to accredited centers compared to nonaccredited centers also seems to have a positive impact on rates of accreditation within a state, but only when the differential reimbursement is high (over 15%) (Gormley & Lucas, 2000).

Accreditation and improving childcare quality

Both center-based and family childcare providers have the opportunity to become accredited with a national organization that recognizes programs which meet a detailed set of standards for quality. To achieve accreditation, organizations must engage in a voluntary process through which they demonstrate adherence to a set of guidelines and standards for the environment they provide to the children in their care. Family childcare providers can become accredited through the National Association for Family Childcare (NAFCC). Childcare centers can receive accreditation through the National Early Childhood Program Accreditation (NECPA) or the National Association for the Education of Young Children (NAEYC) (Tout et al., 2010). The NAEYC is a childcare advocacy group founded in 1926 (NAEYC, 2012a).

There were previously criticisms of the NAEYC accreditation, suggesting that even those programs that achieve accreditation may be inadequate (scoring below 5 on the ECERS; Whitebook et al., 1997). Even those programs with acceptable overall ECERS scores (which include a range of dimensions) may have scored in the inadequate range on one or more of those items related to delivering high quality curriculum to their students (Zan, 2005). In 2006, NAEYC revamped its accreditation standards and placed a stronger focus on children's development and learning, aligning their guidelines with evidence-based best practices in the area of ECCE (NAEYC, 2012b). These newly adopted guidelines include criteria for both structural and process-oriented aspects of care and detail benchmarks in the areas of teaching, curriculum, and assessment of child progress. Programs must meet other criteria for accreditation as well, including standards for administration practices and qualifications for adequate teaching staff (NAEYC, 2012c). For example, Standard 1 of the ten standards focuses exclusively on relationships, and includes in its guidelines that "Teaching staff function as secure bases for children. They respond promptly in developmentally appropriate ways to children's positive initiations, negative emotions, and feelings of hurt and fear by providing comfort, support, and assistance" (NAEYC, 2012d).

Improving the quality of family child care

Many children in nonparental care, particularly infants and toddlers, receive child care from in-home family providers. Family childcare providers face unique challenges, and efforts to help these providers improve their practices are a necessary component of addressing the overall quality of child care. Unlike center-based teachers, family childcare providers are small business owners who work with siblings in mixed-aged groups. These family childcare providers need additional training in setting up their home-based childcare facilities, best business practices, and nutrition. Yet, many of the training opportunities in the field are focused on center-based childcare providers (Hamm, Gault, & Jones-DeWeever, 2005).

Both regulable (like caregiver education and caregiver:child ratios) and nonregulable aspects of family child care (like the child-centered beliefs of the caregivers) are associated with the quality of care caregivers deliver. Children who attend family child care with more educated and trained caregivers have higher cognitive and language scores (Clarke-Stewart, Lowe Vandell, Burchinal, O'Brien, & McCartney, 2002). Reviewing mostly unpublished papers, Norris (2001) reports that training programs are associated with higher quality family child care, but there have been stronger improvements from those programs that have incorporated home visiting or mentoring components. Using a case study approach, Buell, Pfister, and Gamel-McCormick (2002) provide some insight into the process by which on-site mentoring relationships might help improve the quality of care. Through interviews, Buell et al. found that these mentoring relationships increased sense of support and professionalism among family childcare providers.

The Institute for Women's Policy Research (IWPR) gathered experts in the field who suggested that the most effective kinds of professional development programs for family childcare providers would include both group courses that involved opportunities for discussion with peers and colleagues as well as on-site mentoring with professionals. In the home, mentors have the opportunity to discuss specific needs of the family childcare provider as well as help the caregiver apply concepts learned in the classroom (like the need for caregiver sensitivity) in the context in which it is delivered (Hamm et al., 2005). Other research has identified specific benefits for the global quality of care provided by family childcare professionals who receive a video-feedback intervention. A randomized control trial indicated that providing in-home caregivers with discussions of quality, based on videotaped structured play sessions, improved both the global ratings of quality as well as care-givers' attitudes toward sensitive caregiving, though there was no direct impact on observed sensitive caregiving subsequent to the intervention (Groeneveld, Vermeer, van IJzendoorn, & Linting, 2011). States and local organizations have recognized the importance of family child care in the system of early childcare opportunities. Many states and local areas that have implemented a Quality Rating System have included licensed family childcare homes in their structures (Tout et al., 2010). According to the NAEYC, the majority of states that provide higher reimbursement for accredited programs include family-based child care in their reimbursement system (NAEYC, 2012e).

Head Start

In the United States, the Head Start and the Early Head Start initiatives represent one of the longest ongoing collaborations between researchers, policymakers, and practitioners in the realm of child care and childcare policy. For over forty years, researchers have worked with practitioners and policymakers in their efforts to understand the impact that early child care opportunities can have on low-income children and their families (Golden, 2007; Phillips & Styfco, 2007). Head Start addresses the intellectual and social needs of children aged 3–5, and Early Head Start addresses the needs of children from birth to three. Assessments of Head Start indicate that children make significant gains in literacy skills and behavioral skills, particularly when they enter the program at age three. While children who enter Head Start at age four make literacy gains, they show no comparative improvement in the social and emotional skills. Evaluations of Early Head Start using a control group research design indicate that those children attending Early Head Start programs have better vocabulary skills, lower rates of behavior problems, and better interactions with their parents. Within the context of Head Start research, child outcomes have been linked to teacher salaries, comprehensive curriculum, and the length of the school day (Love, Tarullo, Raikes, & Chazan-Cohen, 2006).

Children who attend Head Start experience some initial benefits from the intervention and begin elementary school with relatively higher test scores. These effects, however, tend to diminish by the time children reach middle and high school. Just as is the case with the long-term effects of attending model programs like the Perry Preschool project, however, there are substantial benefits of attending a Head Start preschool in adulthood. Based on a composite score of six adult outcomes, including high school graduation, college attendance, and teen parenthood, Head Start attendance reduced the gap in adult well-being between those raised in families whose incomes were at the median level and those that were in the bottom quartile. This is particularly encouraging given that the Head Start programs cost about 60% of model programs like the Perry Preschool but yield about 80% of the benefits (Deming, 2009).

Research to Public Awareness

Parents are interested in quality child care but often lack information about what constitutes program quality. Ways to educate the public include brochures, web sites, posters, certificates, decals, pins and other items of display (particularly in the centers themselves). In Tennessee, television stations run a feature announcing the results of the child care on the quality of programs that are rated each week (Mitchell, 2005). Many states participating in the Quality Rating System have implemented some form of outreach to parents, including web sites, billboards, brochures, and radio and television advertising. Outreach efforts also involve information provided to the general public and the providers themselves, most often in the form of web site-based materials. When funds are set aside to support these outreach efforts, the amounts typically range from less than 1% to less than 10% of the overall Quality Rating System budget (Tout et al., 2010).

Over 40 states have implemented or are developing communication systems to supply parents and providers with information through web-based materials, directories, and searchable databases (Mitchell, 2012). North Carolina's marketing campaign provides a model for high impact campaigns with relatively low costs. This state uses web sites to inform both parents and providers; it has developed web-based tools with searchable databases that provide parents with the opportunity to search for child care by ratings; it has distributed posters and other materials in both English and Spanish; and it has provided monthly newsletters to legislators listing programs that had earned high-quality ratings (ACF, 2013). Other states, such as Idaho, maintain Facebook pages as part of their outreach efforts and these provide details about state QRIS policies and efforts.

Reflections from Seven Developmentalists on Working at the Nexus

There was a time when developmentalists believed that there needed to be a sharp divide between research and policy in order to assure that science remained pure, that is unbiased. Two separate movements changed this context and ushered in the field of applied developmental science. First, postmodern thinking challenged the notion of an unbiased scientist within any discipline, a widely accepted notion today. Second, the U.S. federal government called on developmentalists to join them in a War on Poverty. Leading scholars, such as Julius Richmond, Edward Zigler, and Sheldon White, devoted their careers to improving the life chances of children in poverty through research and policy work. Soon thereafter, the Bush Foundation set up four Centers to promote child development and social policy doctoral training – at Yale University, University of Michigan, University of North Carolina, and University of California, Los Angeles (Phillips & Styfco, 2007). Then, the Society for Research in Child Development opened an office in Washington, DC, to facilitate collaboration between developmentalists and policymakers. As Edward Zigler often reminded colleagues in our field, "They are going to make policy with or without our input; it seems clear that policy should be informed by science".

The next generation of developmentalists was better trained to work at the nexus of research, practice, and policy. It is important to begin with a caveat, namely that academics are typically not rewarded within the academy for dissemination and outreach activities with practitioners and policymakers. Instead, academics are rewarded for research productivity in the form of articles, chapters, and books. What then motivates academics to provide testimony, to serve on state task force or a panel for a national association, or to write a government report? Although some of these activities are arguably prestigious, the main motivation for academics to work with practitioners and policymakers can only be an intrinsic motivation for one's work to have impact. One of us (McCartney) was surprised to learn that two members of the NICHD Early Childcare Research Network, of which she is a member, refused an invitation to summarize the network's findings for the National Council of State Legislators in July 2002. McCartney accepted the invitation because childcare legislation is made at the state level; nevertheless, in accepting the invitation she recognized that it would take about three days of work to prepare the talk, travel, and present the findings. In the Spring of 2007, we surveyed six other researchers who work to apply sound developmental science to policymaking on child care: William Gormley (Professor of Government and Public Policy, Georgetown Public Policy), Jack Shonkoff (Julius B. Richmond FAMRI Professor of Child Health and Development and Director, Center on the Developing Child at Harvard University), Deborah Vandell (Chair of the Department of Education at the University of California, Irvine), Lynn Vernon-Feagans (William C. Friday Distinguished Professor of Early Childhood, Families and Literacy and Professor of Psychology at the University of North Carolina-Chapel Hill School of Education), Jane Waldfogel (Professor of Social Work and Public Affairs, Columbia University School of Social Work), and Hirokazu Yoshikawa (Professor of Education at the Harvard Graduate School of Education). Their reflections, as well as our own, highlight the opportunities and obstacles to bridging the gap between what we know as scientists and what we do as citizens to promote childcare practice and policy.

There is surely a disconnect between research and policy on child care, as one of us has previously argued, because research and policy on child care have developed along parallel tracks (Phillips & McCartney, 2005). Further, the rules of science and the rules of policymaking could not be more different. Science begins with the scientific method, shared guidelines for best practices in research. In contrast, all's fair in policymaking, which involves "bargaining, obfuscation, and compromise" (White & Phillips, 2001, p. 83). Consider Shonkoff's observation that the "culture of science is rooted in skepticism" on two counts. First, research begins with the assumption that the null hypothesis is true, and second, researchers seldom agree about the interpretation of studies. Policymaking is often based in an implicit theory that transcends available data, about a given policy leading to a desired change. Despite their differences, both science and policy are concerned with effective investments in the lives of children, and this shared goal unites the two enterprises. Increasingly, Congress is using science to support argument.

Does childcare research inform public policy in any real sense? Gormley argues that research utilization is fairly common in the real world if you define it in the right way. Gormley has relied on Whiteman's (1985) work on how policy analysis is used in congressional decision making. As Whiteman explains "the institution once envisioned to be tied most closely to the common sense of the common man, is now being confronted with increasingly complex problems that appear to require considerable specialized knowledge" (Whiteman, 1985, p. 294). Whiteman outlines three ways in which research influences decision making. The first is *substantive*, defined as the use of policy research "in the absence of a strong commitment to a specific solution" (Whiteman, 1985, p. 298). Or as Gormley explains, the research is so compelling that a legislative body like Congress decides to act in accordance with it. This is probably relatively rare, despite the wishes of researchers. The second is *elaborative*, defined as "the use of analytic information in extending and refining, within the boundaries established by a commitment to a specific approach, the components of a position" (Whiteman, 1985, p. 298). In this case, research helps policymakers adjust their course of action. The third kind is *strategic*, defined as "the process of advocating or reconfirming the merit of this position" (Whiteman, 1985, p. 298). Again, Gormley's parsing is informative – with strategic utilization, research supports what a policymaker wants to do anyway.

The childcare researchers we surveyed provided examples of all three kinds of impact. Gormley's example provides an illustration of substantive impact. He conducted research on Vermont's differential monitoring system for childcare centers. As the number of centers increased, it became more difficult for inspectors to monitor centers effectively, given time constraints. As a result, Vermont switched from annual inspections to a differential monitoring system, whereby centers with code violations were observed more often than other centers. Gormley's research yielded good news and bad news: no worsening of conditions for centers with more code violations that were observed more often, but a worsening of conditions for centers that initially had fewer violations and as a result were subsequently observed less often. Vermont decided to return to annual assessments for all centers. This is a great example of substantive impact, because the legislature acted on the basis of a single study. In general, single studies are unlikely to have impact. This study's effectiveness is perhaps due to the fact that the research was focused on a problem of interest, defined by the state, and to the fact that the findings were conclusive.

Waldfogel's work in the United Kingdom provides evidence of strategic and elaborative impact. In the United Kingdom, policymakers have relied heavily on research evidence to guide investments of resources. In 2001, the United Kingdom held a conference at the Treasury on persistent poverty and lifetime inequality. The research provided evidence in support of several government early childhood initiatives, including universal part-time preschool and community-based home visiting for children at risk from the poorest neighborhoods. Later, Waldfogel was asked to make recommendations to extend efforts to improve social mobility. She offered four concrete steps: extending paid parental leave to 12 months; offering a more flexible package of supports to families with children under age two or three; providing high-quality center-based care for two-year olds, beginning with children from economically disadvantaged families; and providing a more integrated system of high-quality care and education for 3–5 year olds. These recommendations were adopted by the government and included in its Ten Year Childcare Strategy, and accompanying budget, released in December 2004. Research on government initiatives demonstrated strategic impact, while Waldfogel's recommendations on next steps provided evidence of elaborative impact. In both cases, the collaboration between policymakers and researchers is a model for countries who desire to invest in evidence-based programs.

It is far more common for researchers to bring a body of literature to bear on a policy question rather than a single study. As Vandell noted, practice and policy typically reflect "*robust, accumulated findings.*" Vandell and Wolfe (2000) summarized the literature on childcare quality for the U.S. Department of Health and Human Services in an influential paper entitled, *Childcare quality: Does it matter and does it need to be improved?* The paper yields about 92,700 results in a Google search, many in papers by policymakers and practitioners both in the United States and in other countries. Shonkoff agrees that individual studies rarely have impact in and of themselves, because most have methodological limitations; this is not the case with a careful synthesis of a literature. In his 2000 edited volume with Phillips, *From Neurons to Neighborhoods: The Science of Early Childhood Development*, a National Research Council volume, Shonkoff and others helped policymakers understand that early experiences shape brain circuitry or architecture, leading policymakers throughout the globe to invest in early childhood programs (Shonkoff & Phillips, 2000). Bringing together a large body of research helps developmentalists get beyond "the battle of dueling statistics." Shonkoff argues that one of the best ways to influence policy is through novel understandable concepts, like brain architecture, that influence public will. Strategic communication helps researchers translate findings to the public in a way that is understandable as well as compelling.

Vernon-Feagans had trouble explaining her findings to other academics who were serving on the Clinical Practice Guideline Panel for the Agency for Health Care Policy. Most of the people on the panel were medical doctors, specifically otolaryngologists, pediatricians, and surgeons. There were three nonphysicians: an audiologist, a speech pathologist, and Vernon-Feagans, a developmentalist. Their charge was to develop guidelines for physicians in the "prevention, diagnosis, treatment, and management" of otitis media (ear infections) with effusion (fluid in the middle ear that causes hearing loss in most children). Vernon-Feagans' research revealed a statistical interaction between chronic otitis media and quality of child care, such that the risk from otitis media is restricted to children attending poorer-quality centers (Vernon-Feagans, Emanuel, & Blood, 1997). Members of the panel could not understand how one could fail to detect a main effect of otitis media yet detect an interaction. Because children in child care have a 3–4 times increased risk of otitis media compared with other children, Vernon-Feagans focused the group on detection in child care settings without consideration of quality. The guidelines have been adopted by the National Academy of Pediatrics and are shared with family physicians and pediatricians throughout the United States.

It is not just legislators who are consumers of research. Advocates are eager to apply research that supports their point of view. Yoshikawa, along with Weisner and Lowe, edited a book, entitled *Making it Work*, on the Milwaukee New Hope program, an experimental evaluation of an antipoverty program that provided health and child care subsidies, wage supplements, and other services to full-time low-wage workers (Yoshikawa, Weisner, & Lowe, 2006). Advocacy groups such as the National Partnership for Women and Families are already using the findings in their work, for example high levels of job cycling were detrimental to children's development. It is important to note that Yoshikawa and his colleagues have devised an outreach plan to disseminate the key findings to practitioners and policymakers. With a grant from the W. T. Grant Foundation, they have been able to share copies of their book.

Strategies for Success

Conversations among practitioners, policymakers, and researchers as they confront this and other challenges is often impaired by discipline-specific differences in language and expectations (Shonkoff, 2000). In the realm of translating research regarding trajectories of child development as it is related to child care, Shonkoff, Vandell, and

Waldfogel agree that it is essential to give precedence to the cumulative body of knowledge accrued by developmentalists over the many years of accumulated work. Taken together, the findings from decades of research on child care is that quality of care has an impact on child outcomes. Moreover, there is a growing body of research delineating what constitutes quality and ways in which it can be fostered (Golden, 2007; Huston, Bobbitt, & Bentley, 2015).

Based on our review of the literature; our discussions with researchers who have successfully bridged the gap between what we know (research) and what we do (practice and policy); and our own experiences, it is clear that researchers must become better communicators of knowledge. One model for effectively conveying these messages is to work directly with journalists or communications professionals, who can guide researchers in their efforts to frame their findings in a way that is accessible to the larger public (Gruendel & Aber, 2007; personal communication with Shonkoff, 2007). As researchers engaged in the scientific project, we typically invite ambiguity, offer alternative interpretations for findings, and we spend a great deal of time discussing the many limitations to any particular study (Gruendel & Aber, 2007; Shonkoff, 2007). Policymakers and practitioners do not have these luxuries; instead, they must work each day to directly improve the lives of children or make the resources available for others to do so. They must be able to rely better on researchers to help convey the most important and most reliable points derived from the many years of developmental research available to them so that they can target scarce resources most effectively.

The National Scientific Council on the Developing Child is a model program for researchers wishing to bridge the gap between research and policy. A collaborative and multidisciplinary effort, the National Science Council is working to synthesize, analyze, and disseminate decades of research on early child development for use by those involved with public policy. The National Science Council's goal is to provide the public with the necessary information about the benefits to public investment during the early childhood years (Center on the Developing Child, 2008) and can serve as a model for researchers who would like to communicate more clearly and effectively with policymakers and practitioners. Working at the nexus of research, policy, and practice provides the most powerful way to improve early child care and education. As researchers, it is critical for us to engage in outreach efforts to share usable knowledge with practitioners and policymakers.

References

ACF (Administration for Children and Families) (2013). *Public Awareness. Quality Rating and Improvement System: Resource Guide*. Retrieved on May 7, 2013 from http://www.acf.hhs.gov/programs/occ/qris/resource/wwwroot/index.cfm?do=question&sid=8&qid=350

Ahnert, L., & Lamb, M. (2000). Infant-care provider attachments in contrasting childcare settings: II. Individual-oriented care before German reunification. *Infant Behavior & Development, 23*, 211–222.

Ahnert, L., Pinquart, M., & Lamb, M. (2006). Security of children's relationships with nonparental care providers: A meta-analysis. *Child Development, 77*, 664–679.

Allhusen, V. D., Clarke-Stewart, K. A., & Miner, J. L. (2006). Childcare in the United States: Characteristics and consequences. In E. Melhuish & K. Petrogiannis (Eds.), *Early childhood care and education: International Perspectives* (pp. 7–26). New York: Routledge Taylor & Francis Group.

Apple, P. (2006). A developmental approach to early childhood program quality improvement: The relation between state regulation and NAEYC accreditation. *Early Education and Development, 17*, 535–552.

Barnas, M., & Cummings, E. (1994). Caregiver stability and toddlers' attachment-related behavior towards caregivers in day care. *Infant Behavior & Development, 17*, 141–147.

Barnett, W. S. (1995). Long-term effects of early childhood programs on cognitive and school outcomes. *The Future of Children, 5*, 25–50.

Barnett, W. S. (2003). Low wages=low quality: Solving the real preschool teacher crisis. *Preschool Quality Matters, 3*. Retrieved on July 31, 2007 from http://nieer.org/resources/policybriefs/3.pdf

Belsky, J. (2001). Emanuel Miller lecture: Developmental risks (still) associated with early childcare. *Journal Of Child Psychology And Psychiatry, 42*, 845–859.

Belsky, J., Vandell, D. L., Burchinal, M., Clarke-Stewart, K., McCartney, K., & Owen, M. T. et al. (2007). Are there long-term effects of early childcare? *Child Development, 78*, 681–701.

Bryant, D., Maxwell, K., & Burchinal, M. (1999). Effects of a community initiative on the quality of childcare. *Early Childhood Research Quarterly, 14*, 449–464.

Buell, M., Pfister, I., & Gamel-McCormick, M. (2002). Caring for the caregiver: Early Head Start/family childcare partnerships. *Infant Mental Health Journal, 23*, 213–230.

Burchinal, M., Cryer, D., Clifford, R., & Howes, C. (2002). Caregiver training and classroom quality in childcare centers. *Applied Developmental Science, 6*, 2–11.

Burchinal, M. R., Lowe Vandell, D., & Belsky, J. (2014). Is the prediction of adolescent outcomes from early child care moderated by later maternal sensitivity? Results from the NICHD study of early child care and youth development. *Developmental Psychology, 50*, 542–553.

CCSA (Child Care Services Association) (2011). Pathways and opportunities: Opening doors to higher education for the early childhood workforce: T.E.A.C.H Early Childhood and Childcare WAGE$. National Annual Report, 2011 Retrieved on September 28, 2012 from http://www.childcareservices.org/_downloads/TEACH_AnnualReport_2011.pdf

Center on the Developing Child (2008). *National Scientific Council on the Developing Child*. Retrieved on March 20, 2008 from http://www.developingchild.harvard.edu/content/council.html

Clarke-Stewart, K., Lowe Vandell, D., Burchinal, M., O'Brien, M., & McCartney, K. (2002). Do regulable features of child-care homes affect children's development? *Early Childhood Research Quarterly, 17*, 52–86.

Deming, D. (2009). Early childhood intervention and life-cycle skill development: Evidence from Head Start. *American Economic Journal: Applied Economic, 1*, 111–134.

Dearing, E., McCartney, K., & Taylor, B. A. (2009). Does higher quality early childcare promote low-income children's math and reading achievement in middle childhood? *Child Development, 80*, 1329–1349.

Education International (2010). *Early childhood education: A global scenario: A study conducted by the Education International ECE Task Force*. Retrieved on July 16, 2015 from http://download.ei-ie.org/Docs/WebDepot/ECE_A_global_scenario_EN.PDF

Early, D., Maxwell, K., Burchinal, M., Bender, R., Ebanks, C., Henry, G., et al. (2007). Teachers' education, classroom quality, and young children's academic skills: Results from seven studies of preschool programs. *Child Development, 78*, 558–580.

Frede, E. C. (1995). The role of program quality in producing early childhood program benefits. *The Future of Children, 5*, 115–132.

Golden, O. (2007). Policy looking to research. In J. L. Aber, S. J. Bishop-Josef, S. M. Jones, K. T. McLearn, & D. A. Phillips (Eds.). *Child development and social policy: Knowledge for action* (pp. 29–42). Washington, DC: American Psychological Association.

Goossens, F., & Van IJzendoorn, M. (1990). Quality of infants' attachments to professional caregivers: Relation to infant-parent attachment and day-care characteristics. *Child Development, 61*, 832–837.

Gormley, W. T. (2012). *Voices for Children: Rhetoric and public policy*. Washington, DC: Brookings Institution Press.

Gormley, W., & Lucas, J. (2000). *Money, accreditation, and childcare center quality*. Working paper series, New York: Foundation for Child Development.

Groeneveld, M. G., Vermeer, H. J., van IJzendoorn, M. H., & Linting, M. (2011). Enhancing home-based childcare quality through video-feedback intervention: A randomized controlled trial. *Journal of Family Psychology, 25*, 86–96.

Gruendel, J., & Aber, J. L. (2007). Bridging the gap between research and child policy change: The role of strategic communications in policy advocacy. In J. L. Aber, S. J. Bishop-Josef, S. M. Jones, K. T. McLearn, & D. A. Phillips (Eds). *Child development and social policy: Knowledge for action* (pp. 43–59). Washington, DC: American Psychological Association.

Hamm, K., Gault, B., & Jones-DeWeever, A. (2005). *In our own backyards: Local and state strategies to improve the quality of family childcare*. Institute for Women's Policy Research. Retrieved on July 11, 2015, from http://www.iwpr.org/publications/pubs/in-our-own-backyards-local-and-state-strategies-to-improve-the-quality-of-family-child-care

Harms, T., & Clifford, R. M. (1980). *Early childhood environment rating scale*. New York: Teachers College Press.

Heckman, J. J. (2000). *The real question is how to use the available funds wisely. The best evidence supports the policy prescription: Invest in the very young*. Chicago: Ounce of Prevention Fund and the University of Chicago Harris School of Public Policy Studies. Retrieved on July 11, 2015 from www.theounce.org/pubs/HeckmanInvestInVeryYoung.pdf?v=1

Huston, A. C., Bobbitt, K. C., & Bentley, A. (2015). Time spent in child care: How and why does it affect social development? *Developmental Psychology, 51*, 621–634.

Hwang, C. P. (2006). Policy and research on childcare in Sweden. In E. Melhuish & K. Petrogiannis (Eds.), *Early childhood care and education: International perspectives.* (pp. 77–94). New York: Routledge Taylor & Francis Group.

Klein, L., & Knitzer, J. (2006). *Pathways to Success: Issue Brief No. 2: Effective Preschool Curricula and Teaching Strategies.* New York: National Center for Children in Poverty, Columbia University, Mailman School of Public Policy. Retrieved on July 19, 2007 from http://www.nccp.org/publications/pdf/text_668.pdf

Kreader, J. L., & Lawrence, S. (2006). *Toward a national strategy to improve family, friend, and neighbor childcare: Report of a symposium.* New York: National Center for Children in Poverty, Columbia University, Mailman School of Public Policy. Retrieved on December 19, 2007 from http://www.nccp.org/publications/pdf/text_676.pdf

Lamb, M., & Ahnert, L. (2006). Nonparental childcare: Context, concepts, correlates, and consequences. In K. A. Renninger, I. E Sigel, W. Damon, & R. M Lerner (Eds.), *Handbook of child psychology: child psychology in practice* (6th ed.) (Vol 4, pp. 950–1016). Hoboken, NJ: John Wiley & Sons, Inc.

Love, J., Tarullo, L., Raikes, H., & Chazan-Cohen, R. (2006). Head Start: What do we know about its effectiveness? What do we need to know? In K. McCartney & D. Phillips (Eds.), *Blackwell Handbook of Early Childhood Development* (pp. 550–575). Malden, MA: Blackwell Publishing.

Lynch, R. G. (2004). *Exceptional Returns: Economic, Fiscal, and Social Benefits of Investment in Early Childhood Development.* Washington, DC: Economic Policy Institute. Retrieved on March 24, 2013 from https://docs.google.com/viewer?url=http://www.epi.org/page/-/old/books/exceptional/exceptional_returns_(full).pdf&hl=en_US&chrome=true

McCartney, K. (1984). Effect of quality of day care environment on children's language development. *Developmental Psychology, 20*, 244–260.

McCartney, K., Burchinal, M., Clarke-Stewart, K. A., Bub, K. L., Owen, M. T., & Belsky, J. (2010). Testing a series of causal propositions relating time in childcare to children's externalizing behavior. *Developmental Psychology, 46*, 1–17.

McCartney, K., Dearing, E., Taylor, B., & Bub, K. (2007). Quality childcare supports the achievement of low-income children: Direct and indirect pathways through caregiving and the home environment. *Journal of Applied Developmental Psychology, 28*, 411–426.

McLauglin, A. E., Campbell, F. A., Pungello, E. P., & Skinner. M. (2007). Depressive symptoms in young adults: The influences of the early home environment and early educational childcare. *Child Development, 78*, 746–756.

Melhuish, E. (2006). Policy and research on preschool care and education in the UK. In E. Melhuish & K. Petrogiannis (Eds.), *Early childhood care and education: International perspectives* (pp. 43–65). New York: Routledge Taylor & Francis Group.

Melhuish, E., & Petrogiannis, K. (2006). An international overview of early childhood care and education. In E. Melhuish & K. Petrogiannis (Eds.), *Early childhood care and education: International perspectives* (pp. 167–177). New York: Routledge Taylor & Francis Group.

Mitchell, A.W. (2005). *Stair steps to quality: A guide for states and communities developing quality rating systems for early care and education.* Alexandria, VA: United Way: Success by Six. Retrieved on September 28, 2012 from http://www.earlychildhoodfinance.org/downloads/2005/MitchStairSteps_2005.pdf

Mitchell, A. W. (2012). *Quality Rating and Improvement Systems: A State by State Listing of QRIS Websites.* QRIS National Learning Network. Retrieved on May 7, 2013 from http://www.qrisnetwork.org/sites/all/files/resources/gscobb/2012-05-28%2008:04/WebsitesforQRIS.pdf

Montie, J., Xiang, Z., & Schweinhart, L. (2006). Preschool experience in 10 countries: Cognitive and language performance at age 7. *Early Childhood Research Quarterly, 21,* 313–331.

Muenchow, S., & Marsland, K. W. (2007). Beyond baby steps: Promoting the growth and development of U.S. childcare policy. In J. L. Aber, S. J. Bishop-Josef, S. M. Jones, K. T. McLearn, & D. A. Phillips (Eds). *Child development and social policy: Knowledge for action* (pp. 97–112). Washington, DC: American Psychological Association.

NACCRRA (National Association of Childcare Resource & Referral Agencies) (2011). *Brief background: Quality Rating Improvement System (QRIS).* Retrieved on May 7, 2013 from http://www.naccrra.org/sites/default/files/default_site_pages/2012/qris_one_pager_pdf.pdf

NAEYC (National Association for the Education of Young Children) (2012a). *About NAEYC.* Retrieved on September 28, 2012 from http://www.naeyc.org/content/about-naeyc

NAEYC (National Association for the Education of Young Children) (2012b). *Introduction to the NAEYC accreditation standards and criteria.* Retrieved on September 28, 2012 from http://www.naeyc.org/academy/primary/standardsintro

NAEYC (National Association for the Education of Young Children) (2012c). *Overview of the NAEYC early childhood program standards.* Retrieved on September 28, 2012 from http://www.naeyc.org/files/academy/file/OverviewStandards.pdf

NAEYC (National Association for the Education of Young Children) (2012d). *NAEYC: All criteria document.* Retrieved on September 28, 2012 from http://www.naeyc.org/files/academy/file/AllCriteriaDocument.pdf

NAEYC (National Association for the Education of Young Children) (2012e). *NAEYC Chart: States with tiered reimbursement programs.* Retrieved on September 28, 2012 from http://www.naeyc.org/policy/tieredprograms

NCES (National Center for Education Statistics) (2015). Digest of Education Statistics, 2013. U. S. Department of Education, Institute of Education Sciences.

Newcombe, N. S. (2003). Some controls control too much. *Child Development, 74,* 1050–1052.

NICHD ECCRN (1997). The effects of infant childcare on infant-mother attachment security. *Child Development, 68,* 860–879.

NICHD ECCRN (2001). A new guide for evaluating childcare quality. *Zero to Three, 21,* 40–47.

NICHD ECCRN (2002). Child-care structure→process→outcome: Direct and indirect effects of child-care quality on young children's development. *Psychological Science, 13,* 199–206.

NICHD ECCRN (2005a). *Childcare and child development.* New York: Guilford Press.

NICHD ECCRN (2005b). Early childcare and children's development in the primary grades: Follow-up results from the NICHD study of early childcare. *American Educational Research Journal, 42,* 537–570.

Norris, D. (2001). Quality of care offered by providers with differential patterns of workshop participation. *Child & Youth Care Forum, 30,* 111–121.

OCC (Office of Childcare) (2012). *FY 2011 CCDF final allocations (including reallocated funds).* Retrieved on September 28, 2012 from http://www.acf.hhs.gov/sites/default/files/occ/final_allocations_2011.pdf

OECD (Organisation for Economic Co-operation and Development) (2012). OECD Family Database, OECD, Paris (www.oecd.org/social/family/database) Retrieved on July 16, 2015 from http://www.oecd.org/els/family/database.htm

Phillips, D., & McCartney, K. (2005). *The disconnect between research and policy on childcare.* New York: Cambridge University Press.

Phillips, D., McCartney, K., & Sussman, A. (2006). Childcare and early development. In K. McCartney & D. Phillips (Eds.) *Blackwell handbook of early childhood development* (pp. 471–489). Malden, MA: Blackwell Publishing.

Phillips, D. A. & Styfco, S. J. (2007). Child development research and public policy: triumphs and setbacks on the way to maturity. In J. L. Aber, S. J. Bishop-Josef, S. M. Jones, K. T. McLearn, & D. A. Phillips (Eds), *Child development and social policy: Knowledge for action* (pp. 11–29). Washington, DC: American Psychological Association.

Pianta, R. C., Barnett, W., Burchinal, M., & Thornburg, K. R. (2009). The effects of preschool education: What we know, how public policy is or is not aligned with the evidence base, and what we need to know. *Psychological Science In The Public Interest, 10*(2), 49–88. doi:10.1177/1529100610381908

Pianta, R. C., Mashburn, A. J., Downer, J. T., Hamre, B. K., & Justice, L. (2008). Effects of web-mediated professional development resources on teacher-child interactions in pre-kindergarten classrooms. *Early Childhood Research Quarterly, 23*(4), 431–451. doi:10.1016/j.ecresq.2008.02.001

Reardon, S. F., Valentino, R. A., & Shores, K. A. (2012). Literacy challenges for the twenty-first Century. *The Future of Children, 22,* 17–37

Ritchie, S., & Howes, C. (2003). Program practices, caregiver stability, and child-caregiver relationships. *Journal of Applied Developmental Psychology, 24,* 497–516.

Schweinhart, L. J., Montie, J., Xiang, Z., Barnett, W. S., Belfield, C. R., & Nores, M. (2005). The High/Scope Perry preschool study through age 40: Summary, conclusions, and frequently asked questions. High/Scope Educational Research Foundation. Ypsilanti, MI. Retrieved on March 22, 2013 from http://www.highscope.org/file/Research/PerryProject/specialsummary_rev2011_02_2.pdf

Shonkoff, J. (2000). Science, policy, and practice: Three cultures in search of a shared mission. *Child Development, 71,* 181–187.

Shonkoff, J. P., & Phillips, D. A. (2000). *From neurons to neighborhoods: The science of early childhood development.* Washington DC: National Academy Press.

Smart Start (2010). Studies point to importance of education for NC's early childhood teachers. Retrieved on September, 28, 2012 from http://www.smartstart.org/tag/wages

Taylor, K., & Bryant, D. (2002). *Demonstrating effective childcare quality improvement. A report by the FPG Smart Start evaluation team at UNC-CH*. Retrieved on September 28, 2012 from http://fpg.unc.edu/resources/demonstrating-effective-child-care-quality-improvement

Tout, K., Zaslow, M., & Berry, D. (2005). Quality and qualifications: Links between professional development and quality in early care and education settings. In M. Zaslow & I. Martinez-Beck (Eds.), *Critical issues in early childhood professional development* (pp. 77–110). Baltimore, MD: Paul H. Brookes Publishing Co.

Tout, K., Starr, R., Soli, M., Moodie, S., Kirby, G., & Boller, K. (2010). The Childcare Quality Rating System (QRS) assessment: Compendium of Quality Rating Systems and Evaluation, OPRE Report. Washington, DC: Office of Planning, Research and Evaluation, Administration for Children and Families, US Department of Health and Human Services. Retrieved on July 16,, 2015 from http://archive.acf.hhs.gov/programs/opre/cc/childcare_quality/compendium_qrs/

UNESCO (2007). *Strong foundations: Early childhood care and education*. EFA Global Monitoring Report 2007. Retrieved on September 16, 2007 from http://unesdoc.unesco.org/images/0014/001477/147794E.pdf

UNICEF Innocenti Research Center. (2008). *The child care transition*. Florence, Italy: The United Nations Children's Fund. Retrieved on May 5, 2013 from http://www.unicef-irc.org/publications/pdf/rc8_eng.pdf

Vandell, D., Belsky, J., Burchinal, M., Steinberg, L., Vandergrift, N., & NICHD Early Childcare Research Network (2010). Do effects of early childcare extend to age 15 years? Results from the NICHD study of early childcare and youth development. *Child Development, 81,* 737–756.

Vandell, D., & Wolfe, B. (2000). *Childcare quality: Does it matter and does it need to be improved?* Retrieved on July, 31, 2007 from http://www.aspe.hhs.gov/hsp/ccquality00/ccqual.htm

Vernon-Feagans, L., Emanuel, D. C., & Blood, I. (1997). The effect of otitis media and quality of daycare on children's language development. *Journal of Applied Developmental Psychology, 18*(3), 395–409.

Waldfogel, J. (2006). Early childhood policy: A comparative perspective. In K. McCartney & D. Phillips (Eds.), *Blackwell handbook of early childhood development* (pp. 576–594). Malden, MA: Blackwell Publishing.

White, S. H., & Phillips, D. A. (2001). Designing Head Start: Roles played by developmental psychologists. In D. L. Featherman and M. Vinofskis (Eds), *Social science and policy making* (pp. 83–118). Ann Arbor, MI: University of Michigan Press.

The White House, Office of the Press Secretary (2013). Fact Sheet President Obama's Plan for Early Education for all Americans [Press Release]. Retrieved on March 23, 2013 from http://www.whitehouse.gov/the-press-office/2013/02/13/fact-sheet-president-obama-s-plan-early-education-all-americans

Whitebook, M., Sakai, L., & Howes, C. (1997). *NAEYC accreditation as a strategy for improving childcare quality: An assessment. Final report*. Washington, DC: Center for the Childcare Workforce.

Whitebook, M., Sakai, L., & Howes, C. (2004). Improving and sustaining center quality: The role of NAEYC accreditation and staff stability. *Early Education and Development, 15*, 305–325.

Whiteman, D. (1985). The fate of policy analysis in congressional decision making: three types of use in committees. *The Western Political Quarterly, 38*, 294–311.

Yoshikawa, H., Weisner, T. S., & Lowe, E. D. (2006). *Making it work: Low-wage employment, family life, and child development.* New York, NY: Russell Sage Foundation.

Zachrisson, H. D., Dearing, E., Lekhal, R., & Toppelberg, C. O. (2013). Little evidence that time in child care causes externalizing problems during early childhood in Norway. *Child Development, 84*(4), 1152–1170.

Zan, B. (2005). NAEYC accreditation and high quality preschool curriculum. *Early Education and Development, 16*, 85–102.

Zellman, G. L., & Fiene, R. (2012). *Validation of quality rating and improvement systems for early care and education and school-age care.* Research-to-Policy, Research-to-Practice Brief OPRE, 2012-29. Washington, DC: Office of Planning, Research and Evaluation, Administration for Children and Families, US Department of Health and Human Services. Retrieved on March 25, 2013 from http://www.acf.hhs.gov/sites/default/files/opre/val_qual_early.pdf

8

Teenage Childbearing in the United States: Do Our Programs and Policies Reflect Our Knowledge Base?

Anne Martin and Jeanne Brooks-Gunn

The birth rate among teenagers in the United States has been on the decline since 1991 (Ventura, Hamilton, & Mathews, 2014), but policymakers, practitioners, and the general public still consider teenage childbearing a compelling social problem. First, a greater proportion of teenagers' births than older women's births are unintended (Mosher, Jones, & Abma, 2012). Second, a greater proportion occur outside the context of marriage (Martin, Hamilton, Ventura, Osterman, & Mathews, 2013), which is troubling because the children of married parents tend to fare better than those of single parents (Waldfogel, Craigie, & Brooks-Gunn, 2010). Third, teenage mothers, particularly the youngest among them, are less likely than older mothers to obtain prenatal care (Menacker, Martin, MacDorman, & Ventura, 2004; Osterman, Martin, Mathews, & Hamilton, 2011). Fourth, the cost of the medical and social services associated with teenage childbearing and parenting is often borne by taxpayers because teenage mothers are typically unable to pay (Hoffman, 2006). Fifth, childbearing during adolescence is associated with lower

The Wiley Handbook of Developmental Psychology in Practice: Implementation and Impact, First Edition.
Edited by Kevin Durkin and H. Rudolph Schaffer.
© 2016 John Wiley & Sons, Ltd. Published 2016 by John Wiley & Sons, Ltd.

socioeconomic status later in life, as well as poorer developmental outcomes for children (as discussed later in detail).

Substantial variability in teenagers' birth rates according to demographic characteristics suggests that teenage childbearing is a function of social inequality more than preference. Although the overall rate of teenage (aged 15–19) child-bearing in 2012 was 29.4 per 1,000, the rate was for much higher for minorities (43.9 for African Americans and 46.3 for Hispanics) than for non-Hispanic whites (20.5) (Ventura et al., 2014). Teenagers whose families are poor, who live in single-parent households, whose mothers have had less education, whose families earn less income, who have received welfare and who reside in socioeconomically depressed neighborhoods are all more likely than teenagers without those characteristics to become mothers before reaching their adult years (Ellis et al., 2003; Hardy, Astone, Brooks-Gunn, Shapiro, & Miller, 1998; Jaffee, 2002; South & Baumer, 2000).

This chapter discusses the key program (privately or publicly funded interventions) and policy (legislation on the federal, state or local level) issues surrounding teenage childbearing in the United States. These issues include the implications of child-bearing for teenagers and their children, the factors that minimize unwanted outcomes, and the programs and policies designed to assist teenage mothers. We pay particular attention to the extent to which our policies and programs align with our knowledge base. Finally, we conclude with current efforts to prevent teenage child-bearing, again emphasizing potential mismatches between our body of knowledge and current policies and practices.

Teenage Mothers' Parenting Skills

There is reason for concern about teenage mothers' ability to parent, given their immaturity. Additional concern is warranted in light of the strong association between mothers' mental health and their parenting behaviors (Goodman & Gotlib, 1999; Hodgkinson, Beers, Southammakosane, & Lewin, 2014; Lovejoy, Graczyk, O'Hare, & Neuman, 2000). Adolescents are more emotionally labile (Rosenblum & Lewis, 2003) and impulsive (Steinberg et al., 2008) than adults, and adolescent girls are at particularly high risk for depression (Martel, 2013; Mollborn & Morningstar, 2009; Nolen-Hoeksema & Girgus, 1994). Teenage mothers are also at higher risk of postpartum depression (Kleiber & Dimidjian, 2014).

The literature on teenage mothers' parenting is mixed but the preponderance of evidence suggests that they demonstrate a lower quality of parenting than older mothers. Observational data show that compared to older mothers, teenage mothers stimulate their infants less (Garcia-Coll, Hoffman, & Oh, 1987; Wasserman, Brunelli, Rauh, & Alverado, 1994), are more likely to sit silently or engage in parallel play while their child plays (Teberg, Howell, & Wingert, 1983), and are less verbal with their child (Culp, Appelbaum, Osofsky, & Levy, 1988; Osofsky, Hann, & Peebles, 1993). They are also more intrusive, punitive and restrictive than older mothers (Berlin, Brady-Smith, & Brooks-Gunn, 2002; Lee, 2009; Lewin, Mitchell, & Ronzio, 2013; Osofsky et al., 1993), are less knowledgeable about developmental milestones (Bornstein, Cote, Laynes, Hahn, & Park, 2010; Osofsky et al., 1993) and have less complex beliefs about parenting (Benasich & Brooks-Gunn, 1996).

However, some teenage mothers have better parenting skills than others. Research shows that among teenage mothers, maturity and self-esteem (Hess, Papas, & Black, 2002), egocentrism (Flanagan, McGrath, Meyer, & Garcia Coll, 1995), cognitive readiness to parent (Lounds, Borkowski, Whitman, Maxwell, & Weed, 2005), beliefs about parenting (Chen & Luster, 1999) and level of reflectivity (Brophy-Herb & Honig, 1999) are all associated with the quality of parenting skills.

Teenage Mothers' Educational Attainment

Scholars have concluded that raw differences among adult women according to whether they were teens at first birth are in part driven by selection effects. Specifically, girls who become teenage mothers differ from other girls on a number of dimensions, many of which are known to predict educational attainment. First, teenage mothers are more likely to come from more socioeconomically disadvantaged families than other teenage women (Kirby, Lepore, & Ryan, 2005). Second, they score lower than other teenage women on measures of academic performance, even as early as age four (Hardy et al., 1998; Hotz, McElroy, & Sanders, 2005; Jaffee, 2002). Nevertheless, studies designed to isolate the causal impact of teenage childbearing conclude that there is a negative effect on educational attainment and income, even controlling for such pre-existing differences.

Specifically, several studies show that women who become mothers in their teenage years are less likely to graduate from high school or obtain postsecondary education than women who delay childbearing until adulthood (Ashcraft, Fernandez-Val, & Lang, 2013; Fletcher & Wolfe, 2009; Hofferth, Reid, & Mott, 2001; Levine & Painter, 2003). Given the link between education and future earnings, it is not surprising that teenage childbearing is also associated with income later in adulthood (Corcoran & Kunz, 1997; Hotz et al., 2005).

Factors That Influence Teenage Mothers' Well-being

Relationship with their own mothers

Teenage mothers who have higher quality relationships with (Hess et al., 2002; Lewin et al., 2013; Sellers, Black, Boris, Oberlander, & Myers, 2011) or receive more social support from (Bunting & McAuley, 2004; Uno, Florsheim, Uchino, 1998) their own mothers demonstrate higher quality parenting skills. Paradoxically, however, teenage mothers who live with a parent or older adult tend to have poorer parenting skills (Black & Nitz, 1996; Chase-Lansdale, Brooks-Gunn, & Zamsky, 1994; Cooley & Unger, 1991; Field, Widmayer, Adler, & de Cubas, 1990; Spieker & Bensley, 1994).

Approximately three-quarters of unmarried teenage mothers live with their own mother (the child's grandmother) (Gordon, 1999). It appears that coresident grandmothers provide child care and financial assistance to teenage mothers (Gordon, 1999), resulting in mothers' increased involvement in school and work, and by their late 20s, greater educational attainment (Mollborn, 2007). But coresidence with the grandmother is also associated with decreased involvement in parenting (East & Felice, 1996). It has been suggested that a teenage mother's coresidence with the grandmother may support her more in her role as daughter than as mother (Black et al., 2002). In addition, one study found greater mother–grandmother conflict among dyads that coresided (East & Felice, 1996). The strain caused by this conflict may negatively impact the mother's parenting (Wakschlag, Chase-Lansdale, & Brooks-Gunn, 1996). One study of urban, African American adolescent mothers found that at multiple points during the first two years following childbirth, up to 75% reported conflict with their mother (Buckingham-Howes, Oberlander, Hurley, Fitzmaurice, & Black, 2011). Two small samples of urban adolescent mothers found that those who displayed greater individuation from their mother demonstrated higher quality parenting skills (Pittman, Wakschlag, Chase-Lansdale, & Brooks-Gunn, 2012; Sellers et al., 2011).

In 1996, the Personal Responsibility and Work Opportunity Reconciliation Act revised the eligibility criteria for teenage mothers seeking cash assistance (Temporary Assistance to Needy Families, or TANF) by requiring that they live at home with a parent or adult guardian and they attend school or an approved training program once their infant turns 12 weeks old. Critics have voiced concern that these rules might result in the denial of benefits to needy families (Acs & Koball, 2003; Collins, Stevens, & Lane, 2000). Interestingly, a national comparison of teenage mothers before and after the requirement was enacted found no significant changes in the percentage who lived with their mother, attended school or a General Educational

Development (GED) program, or graduated from such a program (Acs & Koball, 2003), perhaps because rates of all three were already high.

Relationship with the baby's father

Teenage mothers who maintain a relationship with the baby's biological father (Gee & Rhodes, 2003) and consider him more involved in caregiving (Kalil, Ziol-Guest, & Coley, 2005) have lower parenting stress and depression than other teenage mothers. The baby's biological father is more likely to stay involved in his child's life if he remains romantically involved with the baby's mother (Herzog, Umana-Taylor, Madden-Derdich, & Leonard, 2007), but the relationship is not likely to last beyond the baby's first few years of life (Gee & Rhodes, 2003; Larson, Hussey, Gilmore, & Gilchrist, 1996). It should be noted that one study found that what predicted lower maternal depression was not greater father involvement *per se* but greater maternal satisfaction with the degree of involvement (Fagan & Lee, 2010).

Little research has addressed the effects of teenage mothers' coresidence with the biological father. There are no national estimates of the frequency of this arrangement, but three samples yield a range of 11% to 49% at child age 1 (Howard, Lefever, Borkowski, & Whitman, 2006; Hubbs-Tait, Osofsky, Hann, & Culp, 1994; Martin, Brazil, & Brooks-Gunn, 2013). In a national study of urban births, 20% of teenage mothers coresided with the baby's father (and the baby) consistently for the first three years of the child's life (A. Martin et al., 2013). Compared to the other teenage mothers, these mothers were more likely to have a secure attachment with their child. However, it does not stand to reason that teenage mothers should be encouraged to live with their baby's father. It may be that in A. Martin et al. (2013), the fathers who coresided stably in the first three years of life were exceptionally conscientious or devoted to family. The literature on older couples shows that paternal coresidence increases household income, lowers maternal stress, and increases paternal involvement in caregiving (Carlson & Corcoran, 2001; Cooper, McLanahan, Meadows, & Brooks-Gunn, 2009; Lamb, 2010). However, the men who father children with teenage mothers have less education and employment and a greater likelihood of committing abuse, being incarcerated, and using illicit drugs than other fathers (Lopoo, 2005; Tan & Quinlivan, 2006). Sixty-five percent are, in fact, 20 years or older (Landry & Forrest, 1995). Similarly, there is no evidence to suggest that encouraging teenage mothers to marry the father of their baby is advantageous. Mollborn (2007) found that married teenage mothers had lower educational attainment than other teenage mothers, perhaps because they were burdened by caregiving duties.

Emotional and material support

All mothers benefit from social support, which can be emotional or material in nature (Crnic, Greenberg, & Slough, 1986; Leahy-Warren, McCarthy, & Corcoran, 2012; Simons, Beaman, Conger, & Chao, 1993). However, teenage mothers are in critical need of assistance because they are more disadvantaged than other teenagers, even before the birth of their baby. For example, teenage mothers are more likely than other teenage women to come from single parent and poor families (Kirby, Lepore, & Ryan, 2005). Therefore, compared to older mothers, they may have fewer material resources on which to draw in their family of origin. It is ironic, then, that teenage mothers are more likely than older mothers to seek support from their families, as opposed to peers (Schilmoeller & Baranowski, 1985). However, they are also more likely than older mothers to benefit from social and material support. Adolescent mothers' perceived support from friends, mentors, and relatives is associated with their emotional well-being and parenting quality (Hurd & Zimmerman, 2010; Nitz, Ketterlinus, & Brandt, 1995; Voight, Hans, & Bernstein, 1996), and their perceived level of family support more closely corresponds to their parenting quality than among older mothers (LeTourneau, Stewart, & Barnfather, 2004).

Rapid repeat birth

Approximately one-quarter of teenage mothers have a second birth within 24 months of their first, and one-third have a second birth while still in their teenage years (Manlove, Mariner, & Papillo, 2000). Based on a nationally representative sample of teenage mothers, Manlove and colleagues (2000) found that living with a boyfriend (instead of with a parent or by oneself) and failing to obtain a high school diploma or GED increased the risk of a second teenage birth. Other longitudinal studies have found low educational aspirations (Furstenberg, Brooks-Gunn, & Morgan, 1987), low parental education (Kalmuss & Namerow, 1994) and aggressive behavior (Crittenden, Boris, Rice, Taylor, & Olds, 2009; Gillmore, Lewis, Lohr, Spencer, & White, 1997) predict rapid repeat childbearing.

The most perilous consequence of a rapid second birth is the impediment it poses to continued education. One of the key findings of the Baltimore Study was that the spacing between the adolescents' first and second births predicted their economic well-being 17 years later through its association with education and employment (Furstenberg et al., 1987). Teens who had two or more additional children in the five years following their first birth were nearly four times more likely to be on welfare than other teens (Furstenberg et al., 1987). In addition to stalling educational and job advancement, a rapid second birth increases the chances of rapid third and higher-order births, which in turn reduce the likelihood of high school or GED completion (Furstenberg et al., 1987; Seitz & Apfel, 1993).

Child care

The type of child care a teenage mother relies on affects both her likelihood of a repeat second birth and her educational attainment. A recent national study found that teenage mothers who were full-time caregivers for their child had poorer outcomes when the child was age four than teenage mothers who used child care (Mollborn & Blalock, 2012). Specifically, compared to teenage mothers who were full-time caregivers, those using a family member to provide free care got slightly more education, those using center-based child care were less likely to have another birth, and those either using center care or paying for home-based care had higher household incomes. Interestingly, the children of teenage mothers benefited more cognitively and behaviorally than the children of older mothers from the use of nonparental care. However, teenage mothers who were the exclusive caregivers came from more disadvantaged families than those who used nonparental care, suggesting that affordability may have been a primary consideration behind their care arrangement. As discussed below, many programs for teenage mothers provide case management, which can help secure child care. However, if the arrangements are not affordable they may be impossible to take advantage of.

Contraceptive coverage and health insurance

Many hospitals counsel teenage mothers at the time of their birth about contraception, and some provide it as well. Not surprisingly, the use of more versus less effective contraceptive methods affects a teenage mother's risk of rapid repeat pregnancy (as well as her risk of a sexually transmitted infection) (Cox, Buman, Woods, Famakinwa, & Harris, 2012; Stevens-Simon, Kelly, & Kulick, 2001). However, over the child's first year, low-income mothers tend to lose access to contraceptive services because the Medicaid coverage that covered them prenatally and post-partum ends. One intervention designed to prevent rapid repeat pregnancy found greater effects when mothers were continuously covered by health insurance (Barnet et al., 2009). It has been suggested that pediatricians are well-suited to assess teenage mothers' contraceptive needs, given that they are the healthcare professionals likely to have the greatest contact with teenage mothers, particularly in the first two years of the child's life when well-child visits should ideally occur with frequency (Wilson, Samandari, Koo, & Tucker, 2011).

Interventions for Teenage Mothers

Professional support services for teenage mothers have taken many forms. Some focus on a single domain, such as advancing education, improving parenting skills, or preventing a rapid repeat birth. Evaluations of such programs show that they can be quite effective. For example, a meta-analysis of 16 interventions designed to delay second births found that, on average, they halved the risk of a closely-spaced second birth, but home-based programs were excluded from consideration (Corcoran & Pillai, 2007). Meta-analyses of teenage parenting programs have concluded that such programs are often, but not consistently, successful at improving the quality of participants' parenting (Barlow et al., 2012; Coren, Barlow, & Stewart-Brown, 2003); however, these analyses excluded home visiting programs from consideration. Many programs cover multiple domains at once, such as high school completion, parenting, and social support (LeTourneau et al., 2004), and these too have been found to be effective. There are three settings where interventions for teenage mothers take place: at school, at home, or in the community (typically hospital- or clinic-based). Examples of programs in each setting are briefly described here. These are selected not to represent all programs of their type but rather to call attention to the diversity of program models.

School-based programs

An example of a school-based program is an intervention for pregnant and parenting teens at a high school in South Carolina. It features case management provided by a social worker who has a master's degree and is culturally matched to participants. Located at the school, the social worker provides coaching, referrals to service agencies, and follow-up on referrals. She also facilitates weekly group meetings. A female pediatrician specializing in adolescent medicine sees participants and their children at a nearby ambulatory care center. Participants have access to her pager 24 hours a day. The social worker provides occasional home visits, attends medical visits, and meets with the pediatrician weekly to discuss each participant. An evaluation of this program found that repeat births within two years among program participants occurred at half the rate of matched controls (Key, Gebregziabher, Marsh, & O'Rourke, 2008). The mean number of case management sessions over a two-year period was six, and the mean number of medical visits was five. Interestingly, teenagers who were pregnant at enrollment were more likely to attend a minimum of six case management sessions than were teenagers who were already parenting at enrollment, whereas parenting teens were more likely to attend a minimum of

17 group meetings. The evaluators believed that the cross-disciplinary nature of services was the key to the program's success.

A demonstration program in the 1990s comparing several models of school-based programs for pregnant and parenting teens in Arizona also suggested the importance of support services (Warrick, Christianson, Walruff, & Cook, 1993). The first model evaluated was a program folded into a typical high school, so that participants could take all regularly offered classes, along with parenting classes, child care, case management, counseling and on-site primary health care for mothers and infants. The other program models included a separate classroom that offered child care and health care, a separate school that offered child care and health care, a separate school that did not offer these services, and a regular school attended by pregnant and parenting teens. A four-year evaluation found that the first model was the most successful at reducing drop-out.

Home-based programs

Parents Too Soon is a home visiting program that serves high-risk mothers, including teenagers, in Illinois. The Ounce of Prevention Fund, a private organization, provides funds and technical assistance to community-based agencies (http://www.theounce. org/). Agencies may choose from three home-visiting service models with demonstrated efficacy (Healthy Families, Parents as Teachers, and Nurse Family Partnership) to fit local needs. Most agencies provide parent support groups and community education in addition to home visiting two times a month. Program goals include: strengthening the parent–child relationship; lowering rates of child abuse/neglect; improving mothers' contraceptive use; increasing referrals for domestic violence, substance abuse and mental health services; raising rates of children's immunizations and developmental screenings; and securing a regular medical care provider for both mothers and babies. Services last for two years.

A similar home visiting program, the Early Intervention Program (EIP), is provided by a county health department in Southern California but is targeted at primiparous teenage mothers (Koniak-Griffin, Anderson, Verzemnieks, & Brecht, 2000). The EIP aims to improve outcomes in five domains: health, sexuality and family planning, maternal role, life skills, and social support. The program is delivered by public health nurses using case management beginning in pregnancy and lasting one year postpartum. The protocol calls for approximately 17 home visits, as well as classes during the third trimester covering topics such as the transition to motherhood and parent–child communication. Home visit activities include discussion, videotape instruction and feedback, completion of problem-solving worksheets and referrals for mental health counseling, family planning and child care.

Research shows that home visiting programs can improve teenage mothers' outcomes even when they do not target mothers based solely on their age (Culp, Culp, Blankemeyer, & Passmark, 1998; Hammond-Ratzlaff & Fulton, 2001; Olds, Henderson, Chamberlin, & Tatelbaum, 1986). One of the most successful perinatal home visiting programs to date, the Nurse Family Partnership (NFP), is designed to serve at-risk mothers more broadly – not just teenagers. The program model calls for home visiting during pregnancy and two years postpartum. In one evaluation of the NFP based on a sample of disadvantaged women, including teenagers, in a semirural county in upstate New York, poor teenage mothers in the treatment group had more months of employment four years postpartum than their peers who had been randomly assigned to the control group (Olds, Henderson, Tatelbaum, & Chamberlin, 1988). This was driven by a lower rate of rapid subsequent pregnancies (Olds et al., 1988). Also, in the first two years postpartum, teenagers in the treatment group were less like likely to have abused their children (Olds et al., 1986).

Community-based programs

An example of a community-based program is the Teen Alliance for Prepared Parenting (TAPP) program, which was designed to prevent rapid repeat childbearing among teenage mothers in Washington, DC (Patchen, LeTourneau, & Berggren, 2013). This is a hospital-based program that enrolls pregnant teens and serves them during the delivery and for the following 24 months. It subscribes to a positive youth development model, which promotes resilience and competence in a variety of contexts. Staff represent multiple disciplines. Social workers provide case management and promote life skills, focusing on educational attainment and job training. Physicians provide medical care, while a nurse health educator provides childbirth classes, contraceptive counseling, and breastfeeding support to individuals and groups. A service plan is updated every three months in a meeting among medical personnel, a social worker, and either a youth development specialist or a health educator. An evaluation found that it halved the risk of a rapid subsequent birth (Patchen et al., 2013). The researchers noted that a high proportion of participants used long-acting reversable contraception.

Another program designed to provide "one-stop shopping" for teenage mothers is located in an urban children's hospital and serves children and even fathers as well as the mothers. Raising Adolescent Families Together aims to provide comprehensive medical care and case management, avert rapid repeat childbearing, and improve life skills (Cox et al., 2012). Pregnant teenagers receive prenatal care at an adjacent hospital, and program staff meet monthly with obstetrical staff to plan for postnatal care. This includes well-child visits and urgent and sick care. There are evening hours, and late arrivals are allowed. At each medical visit, participants receive contraceptive counseling and services, and an assessment of their family's social service and childcare needs. Social workers are available five days a week for emergencies. There are Spanish-speaking staff and adolescent parents serve on an advisory board.

Another community-based program is the Adolescent Parenting Program (APP), a free case management program provided by local social service agencies to pregnant and first-time parenting adolescents in 30 counties in North Carolina. Participants are eligible for the program as long as they stay in school and do not have a second birth (Sangalang, Barth, & Painter, 2006). Case managers meet with participants 3–4 times a month, individually or in a group. The program links participants to reproductive health services, parenting education and employment services, and tries to establish a supportive family network for the teen and her child.

Obstacles Faced by Programs Serving Teenage Mothers

Program setting and focus

One important consideration for practitioners and funders is the optimal setting for interventions to assist teenage mothers. Advantages and disadvantages exist within each type. School-based programs developed in response to Title IX of the 1972 Education Amendments, which prohibits federally funded schools from discriminating against students on the basis of their sex or parenting status. It mandates that pregnant students have access to all the same classes and extracurricular programs that other students do, both during pregnancy and after delivery. Since then, school districts have devised ways of serving pregnant and parenting teens within regular schools or, less frequently, in special programs or schools.

Advantages of school-based programs are their accessibility, regularity of provider–participant contact, and provision of peer support. Another advantage is that schools are often able to provide child care, which not only discourages absenteeism and drop-out but can also model parenting skills and directly benefit children. A disadvantage of school-based programs is that they cannot serve teenage mothers who have dropped out of school (Sadler et al., 2007). Also, it is unclear whether teenage mothers should be mainstreamed or whether they should attend special schools or programs within schools. Programs designed for pregnant and parenting teens can offer greater flexibility in schedules, encourage breastfeeding, and provide child care, but they typically do not include the advanced and diverse classes available in mainstream schools and may limit teenage mothers' interactions with peers who are not pregnant or parenting (Amin, Browne, Ahmed, & Sato, 2006; Marcy, 2003; Stephens, Wolf, & Batten, 1999). Further, it is unclear how mainstream schools should treat absences following childbirth. In 2008, a group of teenage mothers in Denver, CO, was denied four weeks of "leave" following childbirth. Treating this period as unexcused may impede graduation (Grome, 2011).

Home visiting programs can reach all teenage mothers (and are typically directed at disadvantaged mothers more generally). They can provide individualized treatment plans and circumvent problems with appointments due to the teenager's lack of transportation. A great advantage of both home visiting and community-based programs is that they typically also directly serve children. However, given the chaotic lifestyle of many teenage mothers, such programs may find it particularly difficult to sustain participation (discussed in greater detail below). In the coming years, there is likely to be an influx of data on how home visiting programs can best serve teenagers. In 2010, the federal Patient Protection and Affordable Care Act established the Maternal, Infant, and Early Childhood Home Visiting (MIECHV) program, which authorized $1.5 billion to fund home visiting programs in at-risk communities for five years. Most of these funds must be spent on programs with demonstrated effectiveness. States receive the funds and then determine which programs to support (although three states declined) (Michalopoulos et al., 2013). A thorough evaluation of funded programs is ongoing.

An experience common to programs in all three service settings has been the expansion of the service menu to address issues that interfere with participants' success. For example, teenage mothers may use drugs (Gillmore, Gilchrist, Lee, & Oxford, 2006), get arrested (Black et al., 2006) or be depressed (Brown, Harris, Woods, Buman, & Cox, 2012; Cox et al., 2012; Deal & Holt, 1998; Hodgkinson et al., 2014; Sadler et al., 2007). Teenage mothers who are in the foster care system often need new placements following the birth of their child and also require coordination of benefits across multiple social service systems (Levin-Epstein & Schwartz, 2005; Stockman & Budd, 1997). One school-based program for teenage mothers found that 39% had experienced housing instability over the past year (Sadler et al., 2007). Teenage mothers in school may struggle with poor performance (Ispa & Sharp, 2002). Programs have had to address the needs impinging on teenage mothers' daily lives in order to meet their intervention goals.

Program participation

Home- and community-based programs consistently face the problem of sustaining participation over time in light of the competing needs detailed above (Hodgkinson et al., 2014; Stockman & Budd, 1997). One review of parenting programs suggested that the ingredients for success included, among other elements, duration of at least one year (LeTourneau et al., 2004). However, one-year programs chronically report difficulties keeping participants engaged, and even shorter programs do, too. For example, during an eight-session home visiting program in Ontario, Canada aimed at increasing adolescent mothers' sensitivity to their infants, 20% of visits had be to rescheduled because the mother was not home at the pre-arranged time, despite confirmation by phone within the last 24 hours (Moran, Pederson, & Krupka, 2005). In a survey of agencies serving teenage mothers in foster care in Illinois, providers reported that barriers to program attendance were logistical (e.g., lack of transportation), emotional (e.g., mothers' low self-esteem) and familial (e.g., contradictory messages sent by family members) in nature (Stockman & Budd, 1997).

Some teenage mothers may not receive enough services for the program to be effective. Black and colleagues (2006) reported on a program consisting of 19 home visits conducted by unmarried, African American, college-educated women in their 20s who presented themselves as "big sisters" to their clients. A randomized trial of this program found that it had a dose-response effect on repeat births, such that the more visits received by participants, the lower their risk of repeat birth. In fact, none of the participants who received eight or more visits had a repeat birth. However, only 40% of the treatment group met this criterion due to the cancellation of visits.

Thus it is critical that impediments to participation be weighed when implementing programs derived from theories of developmental psychology. The strategies programs report using to boost attendance included serving food at sessions, providing transportation, providing financial incentives, and awarding certificates of participation (Brindis & Philliber, 1998; Stockman & Budd, 1997). One hospital-based program encouraged sustained participation after the child's first year of life by providing a free play space for toddlers (Rothenberg & Weissman, 2002). Another approach may be to involve members of teenage mothers' support network (LeTourneau et al., 2004). In the TAPP program described previously, coresident biological fathers participate in the case management plan, in part because project leaders believe that boyfriends discourage participants from attending school because they are jealous of interactions with other young men (Warrick, Christianson, Walruff, & Cook, 1993). Rothenberg and Weissman (2002) stressed the importance of providing a consistently nonjudgmental and supportive environment for participants who experience undesired outcomes like a rapid repeat pregnancy or school failure. Seitz and Apfel (1999) suggested that a supportive professional may be particularly influential around two months postpartum, since that is when the teenager may be willing to resume sexual activity and issues surrounding contraception become salient. This may also be the time when regular routines begin to be established, and once-enthusiastic friends and family members are less available for support (Gee & Rhodes, 1999; Seitz & Apfel, 1999).

The teenage mother population

Some of the hurdles programs serving teenage mothers face are intrinsic to the age of their participants. For one, parenting educators have noted that the egocentrism typical of adolescence makes it particularly difficult for teenage mothers to be responsive to their infants (Osofsky & Thompson, 2000). Also, because they rely on others so much for help, teenage mothers may find it difficult to practice the skills taught by parenting programs without reinforcement from family and friends (Nitz et al., 1995; Voight et al., 1996).

Another problem parenting programs confront is the lack of parenting role models for many teenage mothers (Hulsey, Wood, & Rangarajan, 2005; SmithBattle, 2000). Some authors have speculated that teenagers become mothers to compensate for the lack of affection they feel from their family of origin (Crump et al., 1999; Kaplan, 1997). In addition, teenage mothers' own mothers are especially likely to have themselves been teenage mothers (Jaffee, Caspi, Moffitt, Belsky, & Silva, 2001; Hardy et al., 1997), and are often struggling with financial insecurity and insufficient social support.

Teenage mothers are often embroiled in unsupportive relationships with the father of their baby (Roye & Balk, 1996), and these relationships are predominantly unstable (Larson et al., 1996). For example, a study of a school for pregnant and parenting adolescents in a midwestern city found that only 17% of participants had the same boyfriend at the two study waves, which were one year apart (Gee & Rhodes, 1999). Break-ups generally decrease the likelihood of sustained father involvement in caregiving (Herzog et al., 2007). Indeed, past research with teenage mothers shows that fathers' involvement steadily decreases over the child's first few years of life. One study of urban teenage fathers found that by 18 months postpartum, only 37% had daily contact with their children (Rivara, Sweeney, & Henderson, 1986). Teenage mothers may also be preoccupied with the vicissitudes of a new romantic relationship. One evaluation of a support program for teenage mothers in Baltimore found that half were in a new romantic relationship within two years of childbirth (Black et al., 2006).

Primary Prevention of Teenage Pregnancy and Childbearing

Until this point, we have discussed the service needs of teenage mothers and the policies and programs that may help or hinder their progress. Another set of policies and programs relevant to teenage mothers are those that might prevent pregnancies from occurring in the first place. We now turn to the primary prevention of teenage pregnancy and childbearing, considering how the policies and programs in place align with our knowledge base.

A substantial literature shows that the antecedents of teenage pregnancy and childbearing include diverse individual and family characteristics (e.g., poor cognitive functioning, antisocial behavior, having a single parent, being poor), some of which emerge as early as the preschool years (Kirby et al., 2005). However, as common sense would suggest, the most proximate determinant of pregnancy risk is sexual behavior – namely whether a teen has intercourse and, if so, how contraception is used (the effectiveness of the selected method, if any, and the consistency with which it is used) (Bruckner, Martin, & Bearman, 2004). Thus, the favored primary prevention strategy from a public health perspective has always been school-based sexuality education ("sex education").

Like other educational matters in the United States, sex education falls under the purview of state and local governments. States have discretion as to whether to mandate that sex education be part of the public school curriculum, and local school districts are usually responsible for formulating the sex education curriculum. Therefore, at both the state and local policy levels, sex education curricula have been the subject of intense political debate among youth advocates, religious leaders, public health professionals and parents.

Some involved in this debate favor "abstinence-only" sex education curricula, which teach that abstinence (in most cases, until marriage) is the only recommended method of pregnancy and sexual infection prevention. Proponents argue that presenting information about contraception tacitly encourages sexual activity. Therefore, these curricula either do not mention contraception or portray it as ineffective. The opposing view champions "comprehensive" sex education curricula, which portray both abstinence and contraception as effective methods of pregnancy and sexual infection prevention. Local school boards may choose their sex education curriculum depending on their philosophy, but the availability of federal funds to support sex education may also play a role. To date, federal funding of sex education has not always prioritized evidence of curriculum effectiveness over philosophical orientation.

Specifically, the 1996 federal welfare law authorized funds aimed at reducing adolescent childbearing by supporting abstinence-only sex education, which could include information on contraception but not advocate its use. Notably, at the time, the evidence suggested that unlike several comprehensive curricula, no abstinence-only curricula reduced risky sexual behavior (Kirby, 1997). A decade later, using a randomized design, Trenholm et al. (2007) found that participants in abstinence-only programs and control groups had the same age at onset of intercourse, number of partners, and likelihood of condom use. Stanger-Hall and Hall (2011), in a correlational study of 48 states, reported that the higher the level of abstinence-only emphasis in a state's educational policies, the higher the level of teen pregnancies and births. In 2010, a new Presidential administration created generous funding streams to allow states to support both comprehensive and abstinence-only sex education programs; the bulk of funds is restricted to programs that have been proven effective. As of this writing, there is pending legislation to abolish the abstinence-only funding stream when it expires.

As of 2014, 22 states mandated sex education, 19 of which required that it stress the importance of engaging in sexual activity only when married (Guttmacher Institute, 2014). Eighteen states and the District of Columbia required that information on contraception be provided, and 13 states required that sex and HIV education be medically accurate (Guttmacher Institute, 2014). In 2006, 65% of American high schools required health education courses that covered condom efficacy, and 38% taught students how to use a condom (Centers for Disease Control, 2006). Only 3% of school districts had a policy that made condoms available to middle or high school students (Centers for Disease Control, 2012). Thus substantial portions of teenagers lack access to the kind of sex education that is most likely to result in effective contraceptive use.

Given the challenges of directly addressing sexual risk-taking among adolescents, it is profitable to think creatively about alternative programs that may achieve similar goals in the longer term. For example, early childhood programs have been shown to be effective at boosting academic achievement (Phillips & Lowenstein, 2011), and greater achievement is associated with lower risk for teenage childbearing (Kirby et al., 2005). Similarly, several interventions are known to reduce antisocial behavior during middle childhood (Durlak, Fuhrman, & Lampman, 1991; Kazdin & Weisz, 1998), another risk factor for teenage childbearing (Kirby et al., 2005). Research is needed to determine whether existing programs aimed at influencing early and middle childhood outcomes have the desirable but perhaps unintended consequence of reducing the risk of childbearing during adolescence. It is entirely possible that in the future, there will be a new instantiation of teenage childbearing prevention programs that targets neither teenagers nor sexual behavior, but intervenes earlier in the life course with the aim of setting children on healthy developmental trajectories that will serve them in good stead during adolescence.

Practical Reflections: What Helps and Where Next?

Having reviewed what is known about the antecedents and consequences of teenage childbearing as well as the efficacy of programs to reduce it, we conclude with personal reflections on obstacles, opportunities and successes in "giving away" developmental psychology in this fraught area of (some) adolescents' lives. Both of us have conducted research as well as designed or evaluated programs targeting girls at risk of early pregnancy or girls who have become mothers. Our involvement spans over two decades. How much has changed during this period in what is known about adolescent parenthood, and what might be done to lessen its impact on young mothers and their children? We consider experiences with the Baltimore Study of Teenage Motherhood, several early childhood education programs (most notably, Early Head Start) and a proposed program for multigenerational households with a teenage mother. Issues addressed include the consequences of teenage motherhood and the efficacy of programs to reduce the impact of early parenting upon family members.

It is remarkable that most of the major findings from the Baltimore Study of Teenage Motherhood (Furstenberg et al., 1987) hold up today. This small cohort of pregnant girls from an inner-city hospital in Baltimore during the early 1970s was followed for almost 20 years. The experiences that led to more successful adult lives (with respect to work, education and relationships) included education, multigenerational living arrangements right after the birth of the child, delayed marriage and delay of the second birth.

Of particular interest is the importance of completing high school, a goal that was facilitated by attendance at a special school for pregnant girls (the Poe School). Findings such as these were cited as reasons that the 1996 welfare reform law included provisions mandating that pregnant and parenting teenagers remain in school. However, special schools for pregnant teenagers have all but vanished, as young women today typically continue in their current high schools. Whether high school education would be enhanced by more special schools today is not known. Given the popularity among teens for staying with their friends in their existing schools, it is unlikely that we will see a resurgence of special schools.

An outcome in the Baltimore Study that surprised us in the 1980s was how many of the mothers returned to school for some sort of postsecondary education as their own children entered the preschool and elementary school years. Given the need to balance child care, dating, work, and relationships with female relatives, teenage mothers are unlikely to progress directly to college. The various pathways they take, and the delays they experience, have not been addressed by current policies or programs. However, there is growing recognition that college students increasingly include unmarried parents (Goldrick-Rab & Sorensen, 2010).

Another surprise in the Baltimore Study was that the young mothers' living situations were more fluid than were expected. Most of the girls stayed with their mothers (or in some cases, their grandmothers) when their child was young, and such arrangements were linked to later adult success. Early marriages were not likely to last, and mothers who entered them were likely to drop out of high school.

Today, almost no teenage mothers get married around the time of the child's birth, unlike a quarter of a century ago, when the Baltimore Study participants were adolescents. Given the fragility of the marriages we witnessed, the decision today not to marry at such young ages seems reasonable. At the same time, we found that continued residence with the mother or grandmother for more than the first four years of the child's life was detrimental to later outcomes. It is not clear whether the important factor is the age of the child or the age of the young mother (since we found more competent parenting in teenage mothers who lived with their own mothers in cases where the teenager was 17 years of age or younger but not for older teenage mothers) (Chase-Lansdale et al., 1994; Wakschlag, Chase-Lansdale, & Brooks-Gunn, 1996). It remains to be seen whether the cash aid requirement that teenage mothers coreside with the baby's grandmother will hurt or help the mothers, the children, and the grandmothers, some of whom might consider unexpected childrearing duties later in life an imposition.

We found in the Baltimore Study that later success was linked to the timing of a second birth; young women who delayed additional childbearing were more likely to do well later in life. Many programs serving teenage mothers seek to postpone further childbearing. A large part of this effort involves counseling mothers about, and providing them with, contraception. The importance of providing adequate contraceptive services to teenage mothers cannot be overstated. Research suggests that the decline in teenage childbearing rates over the last two decades is primarily attributable to better usage of contraception, not higher rates of sexual abstinence (Boonstra, 2014; Santelli, Lindberg, Finer, & Singh, 2007). Better use of contraception includes consistent use, use of multiple methods, and use of more effective methods. It is particularly important to enable access to long-acting reversible contraceptives (IUDs and hormonal implants) because they do not depend on adolescents' careful and consistent use during every sexual encounter (American College of Obstetricians and Gynecologists, 2012). Programs serving teenage mothers have observed that many of their clients do not use contraception consistently or at all, despite their intention to avoid pregnancy, because they do not expect to have sex, are dissatisfied with their current method, lack information about options, or have no reliable source of care (Barnet et al., 2009; Wilson et al., 2011). More experimentation with program and policy models, as well as elaboration and testing of theories of adolescent decision-making and behavior change, are needed to meet this challenge.

Another possible programmatic response to teenage parenthood has to do with the provision of early childhood education for their children. While few educationally-oriented programs focus solely on the offspring of teenage mothers, those children constitute a relatively high proportion of their population (at least among the programs that have been evaluated). For example, the national evaluation of

Early Head Start examined the impact of the program (services for pregnant woman and mothers with children up to age three) on teenage mothers; findings indicate that program impacts were comparable for teenage versus older mothers (Love et al., 2002). In the Infant Health and Development Program, which provided services from birth to age three to families with low birth weight prematurely born children, treatment effects were similar for younger and older mothers (Brooks-Gunn, Klebanov, Liaw, & Spiker, 1993; Infant Health and Development Program, 1990). These programs did not offer special services to teenage mothers and did not offer contraceptive information to them, so perhaps it is not surprising that impacts did not differ for younger and older mothers and their children.

At the same time, most home visiting programs and even early childhood education programs do focus on enhancing parenting competencies. Theoretically, such programs might influence younger mothers more than older mothers, since the former are more likely to exhibit high rates of detached or hostile parenting behavior (Berlin et al., 2002), even when controlling for income and education, and across ethnic groups. Perhaps larger impacts are not seen for teenage mothers in these programs *because of* their focus on parenting.

It is our impression that teenage childbearing no longer receives the public and professional attention it did in the 1980s, which is perhaps not surprising, given the downward trend in incidence. Additionally, much of the concern about teenage mothers in the 1980s reflected concern about motherhood outside marriage, but nonmarital childbearing has increased since then among women of all ages. In 1980, 18% of all births occurred outside marriage, compared to 41% in 2011 (Martin, Hamilton et al., 2013). Whereas teenagers constituted half the nonmarital births in 1970, they constituted 23% in 2007, while women in their 20s, constituted another 60% (Ventura, 2009). The last decade has seen a proliferation of research on the consequences of nonmarital childbearing for mothers of all ages.

The rise in nonmarital childbearing among women in their 20s suggests that programs that once targeted teenage mothers might expand to serve slightly older mothers, but this has not occurred. One reason might be that teenage mothers are uniquely at-risk because of their emotional and cognitive immaturity (Moore & Brooks-Gunn, 2002). For example, conflicts with their own mothers over caregiving for the child may be expected, given that adolescence is a period for establishing autonomy and individuality from parents. Teenage mothers may also find it difficult to parent when they themselves still need parenting (Pittman et al., 2012). They are also likely to imitate dysfunctional interactive behaviors demonstrated by their own mothers. To the extent that women in their 20s are increasingly likely to have children outside marriage, further research is needed to understand just how the life courses of unwed teenage mothers (and their children's) differ from those of their slightly older (20–24-year-old) unwed counterparts.

Despite declining attention to teenage childbearing, controversy emerged in 2009–2010 when MTV created several serials documenting the lives of pregnant and parenting teens ("16 and Pregnant," "Teen Mom," "Teen Mom 2," and "Teen Mom 3"). Although the stated intention of MTV was to deter teenage childbearing, critics argued that it normalized and even glamorized it (Henson, 2011). In point of fact, a study found that the geographic areas in which the shows first aired experienced earlier declines in teenage childbearing (Kearney & Levine, 2014). Critics remain skeptical (Dockterman, 2014). A public debate about these programs has unfolded along much the same lines that debates about sex education have in the past. Teenage sexuality evokes deeply-held moral belief systems that may not be changed by empirical data.

Conclusion

In closing, we note that it behooves us to continually monitor how knowledge garnered through research is translated into policies and programs aimed at preventing teenage childbearing and minimizing its consequences. Future efforts to translate knowledge into practice may spur us to create innovative service delivery strategies, such as preventing teenage childbearing by promoting cognitive development in early childhood, or improving teenage mothers' parenting without directly focusing on it. Ideally, research and practice will continue to inform each other, such that the knowledge gained in one arena is introduced into the other. This cycle should give rise to the kind of policies and programs that have the capacity to positively transform the lives of adolescent mothers and their children.

References

Acs, G., & Koball, H. (2003). *TANF and the status of teen mothers under age 18*. New Federalism: Issues and Options for States Series A, No. A-62. Washington, DC: The Urban Institute.

American College of Obstetricians and Gynecologists (2012). Adolescents and long-acting reversible contraception: Implants and intrauterine devices. Committee Opinion, No. 539. *Obstetrics & Gynecology, 120*, 983–988.

Amin, R., Browne, D. C., Ahmed, J., & Sato, T. (2006). A study of an alternative school for pregnant and/or parenting teens: Quantitative and qualitative evidence. *Child and Adolescent Social Work, 23*, 172–195.

Ashcraft, A., Fernandez-Val, I., & Lang, K. (2013). The consequences of teenage childbearing: Consistent estimates when abortion makes miscarriage non-random. *The Economic Journal, 123*, 875–905.

Barlow, J., Smailagic, N., Bennett, C., Huband, N., Jones, H., & Coren, E. (2012). *Individual and group based parenting programmes for improving psychosocial outcomes for teenage parents and their children (Review)*. John Wiley & Sons, Inc.: The Cochrane Collaboration.

Barnet, B., Liu, J., DeVoe, M., Duggan, A. K., Gold, M. A., & Pecukonis, E. (2009). Motivational intervention to reduce rapid subsequent births to adolescent mothers: A community-based randomized trial. *Annals of Family Medicine, 7*, 436–445.

Benasich, A. A., & Brooks-Gunn, J. (1996). Maternal attitudes and knowledge of child-rearing: Associations with family and child outcomes. *Child Development, 64*, 815–829.

Berlin, L. J., Brady-Smith, C., & Brooks-Gunn, J. (2002). Links between childbearing age and observed maternal behaviors with 14-month-olds in the Early Head Start Research and Evaluation Project. *Infant Mental Health Journal, 23*, 104–129.

Black, M. M., Bentley, M. E., Papas, M. A., Oberlander, S., Teti, L. O., McNary, S., et al. (2006). Delaying second births among adolescent mothers: A randomized, controlled trial of a home-based mentoring program. *Pediatrics, 118*, 1087–1099.

Black, M. M., & Nitz, K. (1996). Grandmother co-residence, parenting, and child development among low income, urban teen mothers. *Journal of Adolescent Health, 18*, 218–226.

Black, M. M., Papas, M. A., Hussey, J. M., Hunger, W., Dubowitz, H., Kotch, J.B., et al. (2002). Behavior and development of preschool children born to adolescent mothers: Risk and 3-generation households. *Pediatrics, 109*, 573–580.

Boonstra, H. (2014). What is behind the declines in teen pregnancy rates? *Guttmacher Policy Review, 17*, 15–21.

Bornstein, M. H., Cote, L. R., Haynes, O. M., Hahn, C. S., & Park, Y. (2010). Parenting knowledge: experiential and sociodemographic factors in European American mothers of young children. *Developmental Psychology, 46*, 1677–1693.

Brindis, C., & Philliber, S. (1998). Room to grow: Improving services for pregnant and parenting teenagers in school settings. *Education and Urban Society, 30*, 242–260.

Brooks-Gunn, J., Klebanov, P. K., Liaw, F., & Spiker, D. (1993). Enhancing the development of low birth weight, premature infants: Changes in cognition and behavior over the first three years. *Child Development, 64*, 736–753.

Brophy-Herb, H. E., & Honig, A. S. (1999). Reflectivity: Key ingredient in positive adolescent parenting. *Journal of Primary Prevention, 19*, 241–250.

Brown, J. D., Harris, S. K., Woods, E. R., Buman, M. P., & Cox, J. E. (2012). Longitudinal study of depressive symptoms and social support in adolescent mothers. *Maternal and Child Health Journal, 16*, 894–901.

Bruckner, H., Martin, A., & Bearman, P. S. (2004). Ambivalence and pregnancy: Adolescents' attitudes, contraceptive use and pregnancy. *Perspectives on Sexual and Reproductive Health, 36*, 248–257.

Buckingham-Howes, S., Oberlander, S. E., Hurley, K. M., Fitzmaurice, S., & Black, M. M. (2011). Trajectories of adolescent mother-grandmother psychological conflict during early parenting and children's problem behaviors at age 7. *Journal of Clinical Child & Adolescent Psychology, 40*, 445–455.

Bunting, L., & McAuley, C. (2004). Research review: Teenage pregnancy and parenthood: The role of fathers. *Child & Family Social Work, 9*, 295–303.

Carlson, M. J., & Corcoran, M. E. (2001). Family structure and children's behavioral and cognitive outcomes. *Journal of Marriage and Family, 63*, 779–792.

Centers for Disease Control and Prevention (2006). *SHPPS 2006. School Health Policies and Programs Study: Pregnancy Prevention.* Retrieved November 19, 2014 from http://www.cdc.gov/healthyyouth/shpps/2006/factsheets/pdf/FS_PregnancyPrevention_SHPPS2006.pdf

Centers for Disease Control and Prevention (2012). *SHPPS 2012. School Health Policies and Programs Study: Pregnancy Prevention.* Retrieved November 19, 2014 from http://www.cdc.gov/healthyyouth/shpps/2012/factsheets/pdf/FS_PregnancyPrevention_SHPPS2012.pdf

Chase-Lansdale, P. L., Brooks-Gunn, J., & Zamsky, E. S. (1994). Young African American multigenerational families in poverty: Quality of mothering and grandmothering. *Child Development, 65*, 373–393.

Chen, F. M., & Luster, T. (1999). Factors related to parenting behavior in a sample of adolescent mothers with two-year-old children. *Early Child Development and Care, 153*, 103–119.

Collins, M. E., Stevens, J. W., & Lane, T. S. (2000). Teenage parents and welfare reform: Findings from a survey of teenagers affected by living requirements. *Social Work, 45*(4), 327–338.

Cooley, M. L., & Unger, D. G. (1991). The role of family support in determining developmental outcomes in children of teenage mothers. *Child Psychiatry and Human Development, 21*, 217–234.

Cooper, C. E., McLanahan, S. S., Meadows, S. O., & Brooks-Gunn, J. (2009). Family structure transitions and maternal parenting stress. *Journal of Marriage and Family, 71*, 558–574.

Corcoran, M. E., & Kunz, J. P. (1997). Do unmarried births among African-American teens lead to adult poverty? *Social Service Review, 71*, 274–287.

Corcoran, J., & Pillai, V. K. (2007). Effectiveness of secondary pregnancy prevention programs: A meta-analysis. *Research on Social Work Practice, 16*, 5–18.

Coren, E., Barlow, J., & Stewart-Brown, S. (2003). The effectiveness of individual and group-based parenting programmes in improving outcomes for teenage mothers and their children: A systematic review. *Journal of Adolescence, 26*, 79–103.

Cox, J. E., Bumin, M. P., Woods, E. R., Famakinwa, O., & Harris, S. K. (2012). Evaluation of raising adolescent families together program: A medical home for adolescent mothers and their children. *American Journal of Public Health, 102*, 1879–1885.

Crittenden, C. P., Boris, N. W., Rice, J. C., Taylor, C. A., & Olds, D. L. (2009). The role of mental health factors, behavioral factors, and past experiences in the prediction of rapid repeat pregnancy in adolescence. *Journal of Adolescent Health, 44*, 25–32.

Crnic, K. A., Greenberg, M. R., & Slough, N. M. (1986). Early stress and social support influences on mothers' and high-risk infants' functioning in late infancy. *Infant Mental Health Journal, 7*, 19–33.

Crump, A. D., Haynie, D. L., Aarons, S. J., Adair, E., Woodward, K., & Simons-Morton, B. G. (1999). Pregnancy among urban African-American teens: Ambivalence about prevention. *American Journal of Health Behavior, 1*, 32–42.

Culp, R. E., Appelbaum, M. I., Osofsky, J. D., & Levy, J. A. (1988). Adolescent and older mothers: Comparison between prenatal maternal variables and newborn interaction measures. *Infant Behavior & Development, 11*, 353–362.

Culp, A. M., Culp, R. E., Blankemeyer, M., & Passmark, L. (1998). Parent education home visitation program: Adolescent and nonadolescent mother comparison after six months of intervention. *Infant Mental Health Journal, 19*, 111–123.

Deal, L. W., & Holt, V. L. (1998). Young maternal age and depressive symptoms: Results from the 1998 National Maternal and Infant Health Survey. *American Journal of Public Health, 88*, 266–270.

Dockterman, E. (2014). Does *16 and Pregnant* prevent or promote teen pregnancy? *Time*. Retrieved November 17, 2014 from http://time.com/825/does-16-and-pregnant-prevent-or-promote-teen-pregnancy/.

Durlak, J. A., Fuhrman, T., & Lampman, C. (1991). Effectiveness of cognitive-behavioral therapy for maladapting children: A meta-analysis. *Psychological Bulletin, 110*, 204–214.

East, P., & Felice, M. (1996). *Adolescent pregnancy and parenting*. Hillsdale, NJ: Lawrence Erlbaum Associates.

Ellis, B. J., Bates, J. E., Dodge, K. A., Fergusson, D. M., Horwood, L. J., Pettit, G. S., et al. (2003). Does father absence place daughters at special risk for early sexual activity and teenage pregnancy? *Child Development, 74*, 801–821.

Fagan, J., & Lee, Y. (2010). Perceptions and satisfaction with father involvement and adolescent mothers' postpartum depressive symptoms. *Journal of Youth and Adolescence, 39*, 1109–1121.

Field, T., Widmayer, S., Adler, S., & De Cubas, M. (1990). Teenage parenting in different cultures, family constellations, and caregiving environments: Effects on infant development. *Infant Mental Health Journal, 11*, 158–174.

Flanagan, P. J., McGrath, M. M., Meyer, E. C., & Garcia Coll, C. T. (1995). Adolescent development and transitions to motherhood. *Pediatrics, 96*, 273–277.

Fletcher, J. M., & Wolfe, B. L. (2009). Education and labor market consequences of teenage childbearing: Evidence using the timing of pregnancy outcomes and community fixed effects. *Journal of Human Resources, 44*, 303–325.

Furstenberg, F. F., Brooks-Gunn, J., & Morgan, P. S. (1987). *Adolescent mothers in later life*. New York: Cambridge University Press.

Garcia-Coll, C. T., Hoffman, J., & Oh, W. (1987). The social ecology and early parenting of Caucasian adolescent mothers. *Child Development, 58*, 955–963.

Gee, C. B., & Rhodes, J. E. (1999). Postpartum transitions in adolescent mothers' romantic and maternal relationships. *Merrill-Palmer Quarterly, 45*, 512–532.

Gee, C. B., & Rhodes, J. E. (2003). Adolescent mothers' relationship with their children's biological fathers: Social support, social strain and relationship continuity. *Journal of Family Psychology, 17*, 370–383.

Gillmore, M. R., Gilchrist, L., Lee, J., & Oxford, M. L. (2006). Women who gave birth as unmarried adolescents: Trends in substance use from adolescence to adulthood. *Journal of Adolescent Health, 39*, 237–243.

Gillmore, M. R., Lewis, S. M., Lohr, M. J., Spencer, M. S., & White, R. D. (1997). Repeat pregnancies among adolescent mothers. *Journal of Marriage and the Family, 59*, 536–550.

Goldrick-Rab, S., & Sorensen, K. (2010). Unmarried parents in college. *The Future of Children, 20*, 179–203.

Goodman, S. H., & Gotlib, I. H. (1999). Risk for psychopathology in the children of depressed mothers: A developmental model for understanding mechanisms of transmission. *Psychology Review, 106*, 458–490.

Gordon, R. A. (1999). Multigenerational coresidence and welfare policy. *Journal of Community Psychology, 27*, 525–549.

Grome, B. L. (2011). The four-week challenge: Student mothers, maternity leaves, and pregnancy-based sex discrimination. *Albany Government Law Review, 4*, 538–561.

Guttmacher Institute (2014). *Sex and HIV Education.* State Policies in Brief (November 1, 2014). New York: Guttmacher Institute.

Hammond-Ratzlaff, A., & Fulton, A. (2001). Knowledge gained by mothers enrolled in a home visitation program. *Adolescence, 36*, 435–442.

Hardy, J. B., Astone, N. M., Brooks-Gunn, J., Shapiro, S., & Miller, T. L. (1998). Like mother, like child: Intergenerational patterns of age at first birth and associations with childhood and adolescent characteristics and adult outcomes in the second generation. *Developmental Psychology, 34*, 1220–1232.

Hardy, J. B., Shapiro, S., Astone, N. M., Miller, T. L., Brooks-Gunn, J., & Hilton, S. C. (1997). Adolescent childbearing revisited: The age of inner-city mothers at delivery is a determinant of their children's self-sufficiency at age 27 to 33. *Pediatrics, 100*, 802–809.

Henson, M. (2011, May 4). MTV's 'Teen Mom' glamorizes getting pregnant. *CNN Opinion.* Retrieved on November 17, 2014 from http://www.cnn.com/2011/OPINION/05/04/henson.teen.mom.show/

Herzog, M. J., Umana-Taylor, A. J., Madden-Derdich, D. A., & Leonard, S. (2007). Adolescent mothers' perceptions of fathers' parental involvement: Satisfaction and desire for involvement. *Family Relations, 56*, 244–257.

Hess, C. R., Papas, M. A., & Black, M. M. (2002). Resilience among African American adolescent mothers: Predictors of positive parenting in early infancy. *Journal of Pediatric Psychology, 27*, 619–629.

Hodgkinson, S., Beers, L., Southammakosane, C., & Lewin, A. (2014). Addressing the mental health needs of pregnant and parenting adolescents. *Pediatrics, 133*, 114–122.

Hofferth, S. L., Reid, L., & Mott, L. (2001). The effects of early childbearing on schooling over time. *Family Planning Perspectives, 33*, 259–267.

Hoffman, S. D. (2006). *By the numbers: The public costs of teen childbearing.* Washington, DC: The National Campaign to Prevent Teen Pregnancy.

Hotz, V. J., McElroy, S. W., & Sanders, S. G. (2005). Teenage childbearing and its life cycle consequences: Exploiting a natural experiment. *Journal of Human Resources, 40*, 683–715.

Howard, K. S., Lefever, J. E. B., Borkowski, J. G., & Whitman, T. L. (2006). Fathers' influence in the lives of children with adolescent mothers. *Journal of Family Psychology, 20*, 468–476.

Hubbs-Tait, L., Osofsky, J. D., Hann, D. M., & Culp, A. M. (1994). Predicting behavior problems and social competence in children of adolescent mothers. *Family Relations, 43*, 439–446.

Hulsey, L. K., Wood, R. G., & Rangarajan, A. (2005). *The implementation of maternity group home programs: Serving pregnant and parenting teens in a residential setting*. Princeton, NJ: Mathematica Policy Research. Retrieved April 27, 2007 from http://aspe.hhs.gov/hsp/grouphomes04/imp05/

Hurd, N. M., & Zimmerman, M. A. (2010). Natural mentoring relationships among adolescent mothers: A study of resilience. *Journal of Research on Adolescence, 20*, 789–809.

Infant Health and Development Program (1990). Enhancing the outcomes of low birth weight, premature infants: A multi-site randomized trial. *Journal of the American Medical Association, 263*, 3035–3042.

Ispa, J. M., & Sharp, E. A. (2002). Andreya earns her high school degree: The role of Early Head Start. In: The Early Head Start Research Consortium, *Making a difference in the lives of infants and toddlers and their families: The impacts of Early Head Start. Vol. III: Local contributions to understanding the programs and their impacts* (pp. 55–68). Washington, DC: US Department of Health and Human Services.

Jaffee, S. R. (2002). Pathways to adversity in young adulthood among early childbearers. *Journal of Family Psychology, 16*, 38–49.

Jaffee, S., Caspi, A., Moffitt, T. E., Belsky, J., & Silva, P. (2001). Why are children born to teen mothers at risk for adverse outcomes in young adulthood? Results from a 20-year longitudinal study. *Development and Psychopathology, 13*, 377–397.

Kalil, A., Ziol-Guest, K. M., & Coley, R. L. (2005). Perceptions of father involvement patterns in teenage-mother families: Predictors and links to mothers' psychological adjustment. *Family Relations, 54*, 197–211.

Kalmuss, D. S., & Namerow, P. B. (1994). Subsequent childbearing among teenage mothers: The determinants of a closely spaced second birth. *Family Planning Perspectives, 26*, 149–153, 159.

Kaplan, E. B. (1997). *Not our kind of girl*. Berkeley, CA: University of California Press.

Kazdin, A., & Weisz, J. R. (1998). Identifying and developing empirically supported child and adolescent treatments. *Journal of Consulting and Clinical Psychology, 66*, 19–36.

Kearney, M. S., & Levine, P. B. (2014). Media influences on social outcomes: The impact of MTV's *16 and Pregnant* on teen childbearing. NBER Working Paper No. 19795. Retrieved on November 17, 2014 from http://www.nber.org/papers/w19795

Key, J. D., Gebregziabher, M. G., Marsh, L. D., & O'Rourke, K. M. (2008). Effectiveness of an intensive, school-based intervention for teen mothers. *Journal of Adolescent Health, 42*, 394–400.

Kirby, D. (1997). *No easy answers: Research findings on programs to reduce teen pregnancy*. Washington, DC: National Campaign to Prevent Teen Pregnancy.

Kirby, D., Lepore, G., & Ryan, J. (2005). *Sexual risk and protective factors*. Washington, DC: ETR Associates.

Kleiber, B. V., & Dimidjian, S. (2014). Postpartum depression among adolescent mothers: A comprehensive review of prevalence, course, correlates, consequences, and interventions. *Clinical Psychology: Science and Practice, 21*, 48–66.

Koniak-Griffin, D., Anderson, N. L., Verzemnieks, I., & Brecht, M.-L. (2000). A public health nursing early intervention program for adolescent mothers: Outcomes from pregnancy through six weeks postpartum. *Nursing Research, 49*, 130–138.

Lamb, M. (2010). How do fathers influence children's development? Let me count the ways. In M. Lamb (Ed.), *The role of the father in child development* (pp. 1–26), 5th ed.. Hoboken, NJ: John Wiley & Sons, Inc.

Landry, D. J., & Forrest, J. D. (1995). How old are US fathers? *Family Planning Perspectives, 27*, 159–161 + 165.

Larson, N. C., Hussey, J. M., Gilmore, M. R., & Gilchrist, L. D. (1996). What about Dad? Fathers of children born to school-age mothers. *Families in Society, 77*, 279–289.

Lee, Y. (2009). Early motherhood and harsh parenting: The role of human, social, and cultural capital. *Child Abuse & Neglect, 33*, 625–637.

Leahy-Warren, P., McCarthy, G., & Corcoran, P. (2012). First-time mothers: Social support, maternal parental self-efficacy and postnatal depression. *Journal of Clinical Nursing, 21*, 388–397.

LeTourneau, N. L., Stewart, M. J., & Barnfather, A. K. (2004). Adolescent mothers: Support needs, resources, and support-education interventions. *Journal of Adolescent Health, 35*, 509–525.

Levin-Epstein, J., & Schwartz, A. (2005). *Improving TANF for Teens*. Pub no. 05-39. Washington, DC: Center for Law and Social Policy. Retrieved July 12, 2015 from http://www.clasp.org/resources-and-publications/files/0236.pdf

Levine, I. D., & Painter, G. (2003). The schooling costs of teenage out-of-wedlock childbearing: Analysis with a within-school propensity score matching estimator. *Review of Economics and Statistics, 85*, 884–900.

Lewin, A., Mitchell, S. J., & Ronzio, C. R. (2013). Developmental differences in parenting behavior: Comparing adolescent, emerging adult, and adult mothers. *Merrill-Palmer Quarterly, 59*, 23–49.

Lopoo, L. (2005, June). *A profile of the men who father children with unwed, teenage women*. Working Paper No. 05-21-FF. Princeton, NJ: Center for Research on Child Wellbeing, Princeton University.

Lounds, J. J., Borkowski, J. G., Whitman, T. L., Maxwell, S. E., & Weed, K. (2005). Adolescent parenting and attachment during infancy and early childhood. *Parenting: Science and Practice, 5*, 91–118.

Love, J. M., Kisker, E. E., Ross, C. M., Schochet, P. Z., Brooks-Gunn, J., Paulsell, D., et al. (2002). *Making a difference in the lives of children and families: The impacts of Early Head Start programs on infants and todlers and their families*. Washington, DC: U.S. Department of Health and Human Services.

Lovejoy, M. C., Graczyk, P. A., O'Hare, E., & Neuman, G. (2000). Maternal depression and parenting behavior: A meta-analytic review. *Clinical Psychology Review, 20*, 561–592.

Manlove, J., Mariner, C., & Papillo, A. R. (2000). Subsequent fertility among teen mothers: Longitudinal analyses of recent national data. *Journal of Marriage and the Family, 62*, 430–448.

Marcy, H. M. (July, 2003). *Prepped for success? Supporting pregnant and parenting teens in Chicago schools*. Chicago, IL: Center for Impact Research.

Martel, M. M. (2013). Sexual selection and sex differences in the prevalence of childhood externalizing and adolescent internalizing disorders. *Psychological Bulletin, 139*, 1221–1259.

Martin, A., Brazil, A., & Brooks-Gunn, J. (2013). The socioemotional outcomes of young children of teenage mothers by paternal coresidence. *Journal of Family Issues, 34*, 1217–1237.

Martin, J. A., Hamilton, B. E., Ventura, S. J., Osterman, J. K., & Mathews, T. J. (2013). *Final Data for 2011*. National Vital Statistics Reports (Vol. 62, No. 1). Hyattsville, MD: National Center for Health Statistics.

Menacker, F., Martin, J. A., MacDorman, M. F., & Ventura, S. J. (2004). *Births to 10–14 Year-Old Mothers, 1990–2002: Trends and Health Outcomes*. (National Vital Statistics Report, Vol. 53, No. 7). Hyattsville, MD: National Center for Health Statistics.

Michalopoulos, C., Duggan, A., Knox, V., Filene, J. H., Lee, H., Snell, E. K., & Ingels, J.B. (2013). *Revised design for the mother and infant home visiting program evaluation*. OPRE Report 2013-18. Washington, DC: U.S. Department of Health and Human Services.

Mollborn, S. (2007). Making the best of a bad situation: Material resources and teenage parenthood. *Journal of Marriage and Family, 69*, 92–104.

Mollborn, S., & Blalock, C. (2012). Consequences of teen parents' child-care arrangements for mothers and children. *Journal of Marriage and Family, 74*, 846–865.

Mollborn, S., & Morningstar, E. (2009). Investigating the relationship between teenage childbearing and psychological distress using longitudinal evidence. *Journal of Health and Social Behavior, 50*, 310–326.

Moore, M. R., & Brooks-Gunn, J. (2002). Adolescent parenthood. In M. H. Bornstein (Ed.), *Handbook of parenting* (Vol. 3, pp. 173–214). Mahway, NJ: Lawrence Erlbaum Associates.

Moran, G., Pederson, D. R., & Krupka, A. (2005). Maternal unresolved attachment status impedes the effectiveness of interventions with adolescent mothers. *Infant Mental Health Journal, 26*, 231–249.

Mosher, W. D., Jones, J., & Abma, J. C. (2012). *Intended and unintended births in the United States: 1982–2010*. National Health Statistics Report (No. 55). Hyattsville, MD: National Center for Health Statistics.

Nitz, K., Ketterlinus, R. D., & Brandt, L. J. (1995). The role of stress, social support, and family environment in adolescent mothers' parenting. *Journal of Adolescent Research, 10*, 358–382.

Nolen-Hoeksema, S., & Girgus, J. S. (1994). The emergence of gender differences in depression during adolescence. *Psychological Bulletin, 115*, 424–443.

Olds, D. L., Henderson, C. R., Chamberlin, R., & Tatelbaum, R. (1986). Preventing child abuse and neglect: A randomized trial of nurse home visitation. *Pediatrics, 78*, 65–78.

Olds, D. L. Henderson, C. R., Tatelbaum, R., & Chamberlin, R. (1988). Improving the life-course development of socially disadvantaged mothers: A randomized trial of nurse home visitation. *American Journal of Public Health, 78*, 1436–1445.

Osofsky, J. D., & Thompson, M. D. (2000). Adaptive and maladaptive parenting: Perspectives on risk and protective factors. In J. P. Shonkoff & S. J. Meisels (Eds.), *Handbook of early childhood intervention* (pp. 54–75). 2nd ed. Cambridge, UK: Cambridge University Press.

Osofsky, J. D., Hann, D. M., & Peebles, C. (1993). Adolescent parenthood: Risks and opportunities for parents and infants. In C. H. Zeanah (Ed.), *Handbook of infant mental health* (pp. 106–119). New York: Guilford Press.

Osterman, M. J. K., Martin, J. A., Mathews, T. J., & Hamilton, B. E. (2011). *Expanded data from the new birth certificate, 2008*. National Vital Statistics Reports (Vol. 59, No. 7). Hyattsville, MD: National Center for Health Statistics.

Patchen, L., LeTourneau, K., & Berggren, E. (2013). Evaluation of an integrated services program to prevent subsequent pregnancy and birth among urban teenage mothers. *Social Work in Health Care, 52*, 642–6255.

Phillips, D. A., & Lowenstein, A. E. (2011). Early care, education, and child development. *Annual Review of Psychology, 62*, 483–500.

Pittman, L., Wakschlag, S. L., Chase-Lansdale, P. L., & Brooks-Gunn, J. (2012). "Mama, I'm a person, too!" Individuation and young African-American mothers' parenting competence. In P. Kerig, M. S. Schulz, & S. T. Houser (Eds.), *Adolescence and beyond: Family processes and development* (pp. 177–199). Mahwah, NJ: Lawrence Erlbaum Associates.

Rivara, F. P., Sweeney, P. J., & Henderson, B. F. (1986). Black teenage fathers: What happens when the child is born? *Pediatrics, 78*, 151–158.

Rosenblum, G. D., & Lewis, M. (2003). Emotional development in adolescence. In G. R. Adams & M. D. Berzonsky (Eds.), *Blackwell handbook of adolescence* (pp. 269–289). Malden, MA: Blackwell Publishing Ltd.

Rothenberg, A., & Weissman, A. (2002). The development of programs for pregnant and parenting teens. *Social Work in Health Care, 35*, 65–83.

Roye, C. F., & Balk, S. J. (1996). The relationship of partner support to outcomes for teenage mothers and their children: A review. *Journal of Adolescent Health, 19*, 86–93.

Sadler, L. S., Swartz, M. K., Ryan-Krause, P., Seitz, V., Meadows-Oliver, M., Grey, M., et al. (2007). Promising outcomes in teen mothers enrolled in a school-based parent support program and child care center. *Journal of School Health, 77*, 121–130.

Sangalang, B. B., Barth, R. P., & Painter, J. S. (2006). First-birth outcomes and timing of second births: A statewide case management program for adolescent mothers. *Health & Social Work, 31*, 54–63.

Santelli, J. S., Lindberg, L. D., Finer, L. B., & Singh, S. (2007). Explaining recent declines in adolescent pregnancy in the United States: The contribution of abstinence and improved contraceptive use. *American Journal of Public Health, 97*, 150–156.

Schilmoeller, G., & Baranowski, M. (1985). Childrearing of firstborns by adolescent and older mothers. *Adolescence, 20*, 805–822.

Seitz, V., & Apfel, N. H. (1993). Adolescent mothers and repeated childbearing: Effects of a school-based intervention program. *American Journal of Orthopsychiatry, 63*, 572–581.

Seitz, V., & Apfel, N. H. (1999). Effective interventions for adolescent mothers. *Clinical Psychology: Science and Practice, 6*, 50–66.

Sellers, K., Black, M. M., Boris, N. W., Oberlander, S. E., & Myers, L. (2011). Adolescent mothers' relationships with their own mothers: Impact on parenting outcomes. *Journal of Family Psychology, 25*, 117–126,

Simons, R. L., Beaman, J., Conger, R., & Chao, W. (1993). Stress, support, and antisocial behavior trait as determinants of emotional well-being and parenting practices among single mothers. *Journal of Marriage and the Family, 55*, 385–398.

SmithBattle, L. (2000). Developing a caregiving tradition in opposition to one's past: Lessons from a longitudinal study of teenage mothers. *Public Health Nursing, 17*, 85–93.

South, S. J., & Baumer, E. P. (2000). Deciphering community and race effects on adolescent premarital childbearing. *Social Forces, 78*, 1379–1408.

Spieker, S. J., & Bensley, L. (1994). Roles of living arrangements and grandmother social support in adolescent mothering and infant attachment. *Developmental Psychology, 30*, 102–111.

Stanger-Hall, K. F., & Hall, D. W. (2011). Abstinence-only education and teen pregnancy rates: why we need comprehensive sex education in the U.S. *PloS One, 6*(10), e24658.

Steinberg, L., Albert, D., Cauffman, E., Banich, M., Graham, S., & Woolard, J. (2008). Age differences in sensation seeking and impulsivity as indexed by behavior and self-report: Evidence for a dual systems model. *Developmental Psychology, 44*, 1764–1778.

Stephens, S. A., Wolf, W. C., & Batten, S. T. (1999). *Improving outcomes for teen parents and their young children by strengthening school-based programs.* Center for Assessment and Policy Development. Retrieved March 21, 2007 from http://www.capd.org/pubfiles/pub-1999-04-01.pdf

Stevens-Simon, C., Kelly, L., & Kulick, R. (2001). A village would be nice but… It takes a long-acting contraceptive to prevent repeat adolescent pregnancies. *American Journal of Preventive Medicine, 21*, 60–65.

Stockman, K. D., & Budd, K. S. (1997). Directions for intervention with adolescent mothers in substitute care. *Families in Society, 78*, 617–623.

Tan, L. H., & Quinlivan, J. A. (2006). Domestic violence, single parenthood, and fathers in the setting of teenage pregnancy. *Journal of Adolescent Health, 38*, 201–207.

Teberg, A. J., Howell, V. V., & Wingert, W. A. (1983). Attachment interaction behavior between young teenage mothers and their infants. *Journal of Adolescent Health, 4*, 61–66.

Trenholm, C., Devaney, B., Fortson, K., Quay, L., Wheeler, J., & Clark, M. (2007). *Impacts of Four Title V, Section 510 Abstinence Education Programs.* Washington, DC: Mathematica Policy Research, Inc.

Uno, D., Florsheim, P., & Uchino, B. N. (1998). Psychosocial mechanisms underlying quality of parenting among Mexican-American and white adolescent mothers. *Journal of Youth and Adolescence, 27*, 585–605.

Ventura, S. J. (2009). *Changing patterns of nonmarital childbearing in the United States.* NCHS Data Brief, No. 18. Hyattsville, MD: National Center for Health Statistics.

Ventura, S. J., Hamilton, B. E., & Mathews, T. J. (2014). *National and state patterns of teen births in the United States, 1940–2013.* (National Vital Statistics Report, Vol. 63, No. 4). Hyattsville, MD: National Center for Health Statistics.

Voight, J. D., Hans, S. L., & Bernstein, V. J. (1996). Support networks of adolescent mothers: Effects on parenting experience and behavior. *Infant Mental Health Journal, 17,* 58–73.

Wakschlag, L. S., Chase-Lansdale, P. L., & Brooks-Gunn, J. (1996). Not just "ghosts in the nursery": Contemporaneous intergenerational relationships and parenting in young African-American families. *Child Development, 67,* 2131–2147.

Waldfogel, J., Craigie, T., & Brooks-Gunn, J. (2010). Fragile families and child wellbeing. *Future of Children, 20,* 87–112.

Warrick, L., Christianson, J., Walruff, J., & Cook, P. (1993). Educational outcomes in teenage pregnancy and parenting programs: Results from a demonstration. *Family Planning Perspectives, 25,* 148–155.

Wasserman, G. A., Brunelli, S. A., Rauh, V. A., & Alvarado, L. E. (1994). The cultural context of adolescent childrearing in three groups of urban minority mothers. In G. Lamberty, C. T. Garcia-Coll (Eds.), *Puerto Rican women and childbearing: Issues in health, growth, and development* (pp. 137–160). New York: Plenum.

Wilson, E. K., Samandari, G., Koo, H. P., & Tucker, C. (2011). Adolescent mothers' postpartum contraceptive use: a qualitative study. *Perspectives on Sexual and Reproductive Health, 43,* 230–237.

PART II

Educational Aspects

9

The Trials and Tribulations of Changing How Reading is Taught in Schools: Synthetic Phonics and The Educational Backlash

Rhona S. Johnston and Joyce E. Watson

In this chapter, we will briefly look at our research into the effectiveness of synthetic phonics teaching for developing the reading and spelling abilities of new school entrants. We will also outline the long-term effectiveness of synthetic phonics teaching. This teaching method has now been introduced as the recommended method for teaching phonics in England. However, there is has been great deal of resistance to the introduction of this method, and the latter part of this chapter will address these issues.

Summary of Research into the Effectiveness of Synthetic Phonics Teaching

In 1992, we started to examine the effects of phonics teaching on children's reading and spelling skills. Our approach at first was to examine how phonics was being taught in schools in Scotland, where the phonics was of the analytic type. What we

The Wiley Handbook of Developmental Psychology in Practice: Implementation and Impact, First Edition.
Edited by Kevin Durkin and H. Rudolph Schaffer.
© 2016 John Wiley & Sons, Ltd. Published 2016 by John Wiley & Sons, Ltd.

found, in a three-year longitudinal study of around 300 children in 12 schools, was that although phonics was still being taught (unlike in many schools in England), the pace of the phonics teaching had been greatly slowed down. The education authority's Guidelines provided a gradual analytic phonics program for the first three years of schooling. We found that two terms in the first year of school were typically taken up with the teaching of letter sounds; these were taught at the pace of one a week, in the initial position of words. At the start of the third term, children learnt about letters in the final position of words, and then in the middle position. At this point, children might be taught to sound and blend simple consonant–vowel–consonant (CVC) words, for example, c-a-t -> "cat". In the second year of school, children learnt about consonant digraphs, consonant blends and vowel digraphs. Children were shown word families with similar spelling patterns, that is: consonant digraphs, for example, "chin", "chop", "chill"; initial consonant blends, for example, "sting", "stand", "stop"; final consonant blends, for example "mast", "lost", "fist"; vowel digraphs, for example "coat", "boat", "float". Split vowel digraphs, for example "cake", "bake", "make" were often taught in the third year of school.

We found, therefore, that in a typical analytic phonics program children initially learnt to read largely via sight–word recognition for two terms, aided by letter–sound knowledge applied only at the beginning of words. We found that few had any independent reading skill at the end of the second term of school (Watson, 1998). However, just over two months later, having been taught about the importance of letter sounds in all positions of words, the children's mean reading age had increased by over six months. In one particular class, the teacher taught overt sounding and blending before the end of the second term. At this point, these children were found to be reading at a higher level than the children in the other classes.

This led us to carry out a training study to see what effect a synthetic phonics approach had on children's word reading skills. The key characteristic of synthetic phonics is that at the start of reading tuition children learn a few letter sounds, say three consonants and a vowel, then the letters are arranged to form unfamiliar words, and the children sound the letters and blend them to find out what the words are. Next, a new letter sound is taught, new words are shown using this and the previously learnt letters, and the children sound and blend them. The vowels introduced at this stage are simple ones, for example, "pat", and words with adjacent consonants are introduced early on, for example, "pats". Once all the single letter sounds, consonants, and vowels have been taught in this way, the children are introduced to consonant and vowel digraphs (e.g., "ch" as in chip, "oa" as in coat), and they sound and blend words containing these elements. They are not taught to recognize word families, as in analytic phonics.

In our first training study we took three groups of new school entrants (total n = 92) for extra teaching sessions outside the classroom, giving all of the groups exposure to the same new print vocabulary (Johnston & Watson, 2004, Experiment 2). One group learnt about the words with a whole-word look–say approach (the no letter group); another group (the accelerated analytic phonics group) learnt about letter sounds in the initial position of the words; the final group (the synthetic phonics group) learnt to sound and blend letters, and did some segmentation of spoken words for spelling, using these words. The latter two groups learnt letter sounds at the pace of two a week. All of the children continued to learn by the classroom analytic phonics approach. After a 10-week training program, consisting of two 15-minute sessions a week, the children were tested on their word reading ability. The group learning by the synthetic phonics approach read significantly better than the two other groups. Interestingly, they also had better letter–sound knowledge than the others, even though the analytic phonics group had learnt the letter sounds at the same speed. We also examined the children's performance at the start of the second year at school, two terms after the training had ended. The children we had taught by the synthetic phonics approach were still reading and spelling significantly ahead of the other two groups, even though by this time all of the children had learnt about the role of letter sounds in all positions of words. It was clear that learning to sound and blend early on, the key characteristic of the synthetic phonics approach, was much more effective than learning that letter sounds play a role all through words after a largely sight–word approach to reading has been established.

We also found that the synthetic phonics method had been the most effective in developing the children's phoneme awareness, that is, being able to say that a spoken word like "zoo" consists of the sounds /z/ /oo/. This led us to our second study, which was carried out in Clackmannanshire in Scotland with around 300 children (Johnston & Watson, 2004, Experiment 1). In this study, we again had an analytic phonics condition that was implemented according to the method we had observed in our three-year longitudinal study, with letter sounds being taught in the initial position of words at the pace of one letter a week. However, in our second condition, although half of the session was devoted to analytic phonics teaching, in the other half the children had a phonological awareness training program that was mostly devoted to developing phonemic awareness. This was to examine whether learning how to blend and segment the phonemes in spoken words aided the development of the children's word reading and spelling skills, as a number of authors have argued that it is beneficial for children to be trained in phonological awareness skills before learning to read (Goswami, 1999). In the third condition, similar phoneme blending and segmenting activities were carried out, but this time using letters and print; that is, the children received a synthetic phonics program plus a segmenting for spelling program. In this condition, letter sounds were necessarily introduced at a faster rate, that is, six letter sounds were taught every eight days. In each condition, the training lasted for 20 minutes a day, and all of the programs ran for 16 weeks, commencing a few weeks after the children started school at an average age of five.

The findings were very clear-cut. The children taught by the synthetic phonics program read on average a significant seven months ahead of the two analytic phonics groups, and their spelling was 8–9 months ahead. The group that had had an analytic phonics program supplemented by phonological awareness training was found to have better awareness of phonemes in spoken words than the other analytic phonics group, but did not have better word reading or spelling. Furthermore, their phoneme awareness performance was significantly below that of the synthetic-phonics taught group. We know that these gains for the synthetic phonics group were not merely due to accelerated letter learning, as we had found gains with synthetic phonics teaching even when speed of letter sound learning was controlled for (Johnston & Watson, 2004, Experiment 2). The two analytic-phonics taught groups then learnt to read by the synthetic phonics program, completing this by the end of the year. As soon as the data from the first year of the study were available, Clackmannanshire Council decided to introduce this method of teaching reading into all of its primary schools.

In most training studies, the gains are lost a few years after the end of the program (NICHD, 2000). This was not found to be the case in Experiment 1, as word reading and spelling skills increased cumulatively year after year. Our final testing of the children took place at the end of the seventh year of school. At this stage, word reading was 42 months ahead of chronological age, spelling was 20 months ahead, and reading comprehension was 3.5 months ahead, all comparisons with chronological age being statistically significant. There were very low levels of underachievement at the end of the study, despite the fact that around 40% of the children came from areas of deprivation; only 5.6% of children were more than two years behind chronological age in word reading, 10.1% were behind in spelling, and 14% were behind in reading comprehension.

An unexpected finding was that at the end of the third year of the study, the boys pulled ahead of the girls in word reading; in many studies they are found to perform less well than girls (Mullis, Martin, Gonzalez, & Kennedy, 2003). The boys stayed ahead of the girls right through to the end of the study, where we found that they had a significant 11-month advantage. By this stage, they were also a significant eight months ahead of the girls in spelling. The boys and girls did not differ in reading comprehension.

Another unexpected finding was that, for most of their time in primary school, the children from less advantaged homes did not perform below the level of those from better off homes; they only started to show signs of poorer performance at the end of the seventh year at school. Studies have shown that children from lower socioeconomic status (SES) homes generally fall behind children from better off homes in reading right from the start of schooling (Duncan & Seymour, 2000; Stuart, Dixon, Masterson, &Quinlan, 1998). More recently, lower attainment in children from areas of deprivation has been reported by England's Office for Standards in Education (Ofsted, 2007). However, even when the lower SES children in our study had started to fall behind, they were still reading around 38 months ahead of what was expected for their age, and spelling 16 months ahead, with reading comprehension being age-appropriate. Reading comprehension received less of a boost; however, comprehending text at age level would not be expected in low-SES children. SES background has a much greater impact on reading comprehension than on word recognition and spelling, as it relies more heavily on factors such as general language skills and knowledge of the world.

Experiences in Implementing Synthetic Phonics Studies

Our experiences in implementing the synthetic phonics program in Clackmannanshire were very positive. We had the full support of Clackmannanshire Council, and indeed a development officer was appointed at the start of the study, part of her remit being to oversee the implementation of the programs. The teachers carried out the programs with enthusiasm and commitment, regardless of the training condition in which they were working. The feedback about the effectiveness of the synthetic phonics program from the head teachers of the schools included in the study was very positive indeed, all of them commenting that reading, spelling and writing skills had been accelerated. They also reported that the children were very moti-vated, enjoyed the program and had improved confidence in their literacy skills. The teachers now had higher expectations of their pupils, and in terms of detecting children needing learning support, they were able to do this much earlier than before (Johnston & Watson, 2007, Chapter 9).

However, our more recent experiences in implementing synthetic phonics programs in other areas have by no means been so positive. In one region, despite an agreement that a study could be carried out using our synthetic phonics program, the region's literacy advisers briefed teachers against implementing our program while the study was running.

We have also found that it is very difficult to eradicate previous teaching practices. For example, in 1999 the National Literacy Strategy in England produced a phonics program which was largely of the analytic type, but it also had whole language characteristics, as it encouraged children to guess unknown words from context (*Progression in Phonics*, DfEE, 1999). Furthermore, the phonics approach had a heavy emphasis on segmenting the spoken word for spelling, which was seen as a way of teaching phoneme awareness. It included some sounding and blending for reading, but this element was introduced at the end of the first year or at the start of the second year of school. Where sounding and blending was done, the children were told what the word was beforehand, which meant that they did not have to blend to read the word. Many teachers using the program also trained the children in sight–word reading using flashcards. However, given the great opposition to phonics teaching methods at the time, it is very likely that there was an element of compromise in the production of the *Progression in Phonics* (PiPs) program. There is now a wide acceptance in England of the need for phonics teaching, but we find that even when we introduce teachers to our synthetic phonics program (Watson & Johnston, 2010), some still get children to guess words from context, and train them in sight–word reading using flashcards. It is not well understood that synthetic phonics is an approach that is designed to develop sight–word reading; sounding and blending is only used to decode *unfamiliar* words. Many children will only need to decode an unfamiliar word a few times by sounding and blending, and will then develop sight–word recognition of that word. However, it will be a sight–word approach well underpinned by spelling information, whereas sight–word reading developed via the use of flashcards will not.

There is also a view that different children need different ways of learning to read. This probably reflects the idea that some children, especially those with special needs, can only learn to read by a sight–word approach. However, we have found that special needs children do very well with the synthetic phonic method, and we have documented this at length in a case study (Johnston & Watson, 2005, 2007 [Chapter 8], 2011). Special needs children sometimes have to spend a lot of time learning how to sound and blend, frequently revisiting the method. However, although it is effortful, there is no reason not do this. If special needs children are taught by a purely sight–word method, this will ultimately retard their reading development. They will only be able to read words to which they have had a great deal of exposure, with a skilled reader on hand to tell them what the words are. When they have grasped how to sound and blend, however, they will have developed an effective self-teaching approach. The crux of the matter is that teaching to these children's relative strengths, and not helping them with their weaknesses, is a short-term fix that will not stand them in good stead later on. Certainly, the very low level of underachievement we have found with a synthetic phonics approach does not support the idea that some children do not benefit from learning by this method. Indeed, in our study in Clackmannanshire, we had no nonreaders (Johnston and Watson, 2005).

We have found that when a new program is introduced, it tends to overlie rather than replace the previous program. In schools in England, we see a palimpsest of look–say, guessing from context, and segmenting for spelling approaches, with sounding and blending for reading often being a poor relation. This is like an archaeological record of the last 30 years of teaching practice in reading, except that the lowest substratum, traditional phonics teaching, has disappeared. This mixed approach is not an unconscious process, as there is a view that the more different approaches that are used, the more balanced and effective the program will be. Certainly, if a teacher uses multiple approaches, it is a useful hedge against criticism when asked if a particular approach is being included. However, teaching children to read words by sight, or encouraging them to guess words using context, actively undermines the effectiveness of the synthetic phonics method.

Reactions to the Introduction of Synthetic Phonics Teaching by Educationalists

It is very clear from our studies that a form of phonics teaching that uses sounding and blending right from the start of schooling is very much more effective in developing reading than introducing this approach towards the end of the first year at school. This is an important distinction with respect to curriculum changes in England, because the National Literacy Strategy (NLS) program *Progression in Phonics* (*PiPs*) (DfEE, 1999) has been described as a synthetic phonics program (NLS, 2003). However, *PiPs* only introduced sounding and blending towards the end of the first year at school, after a long period of teaching letter sounds in the initial position of words, and a lot of largely sight word learning. At this point, the emphasis turned to segmenting for spelling rather than sounding and blending for reading; the child would hear a spoken word, segment it into phonemes, select the appropriate letters to represent the phonemes, and then sound and blend the word. However, Lloyd (2003, p. 25), the author of a synthetic phonics program, has explained that the method used in *PiPs* is not synthetic phonics because it starts with whole printed words, rather than letter sounds, and has the teacher saying the word out loud first. Although Brooks (2002) correctly described the synthetic phonics approach as being where the child discovers the pronunciation of an unfamiliar word by sounding and blending the letters in the word, he supported the view that *PiPs* was a synthetic phonics approach. He said that if Lloyd "meant to suggest that only this entirely bottom-up variety of phonics merits the name 'synthetic', this seems to me too extreme. I can envisage a 'whole-word synthetic phonics' which would begin with whole words but which, unlike analytic phonics, did use grapheme–phoneme translation and blending" (Brooks, 2003). However, this "whole word synthetic phonics method" is a good description of the traditional analytic phonics method used in Scotland (Watson, 1998).

Brooks (2003) concluded that the NLS had the approach right, but needed to speed up the introduction of vowels, as Progression Phonics introduced children to six consonant phonemes and 14 consonant graphemes before teaching any vowels.

The NLS subsequently introduced a new program called *Playing with Sounds* (DfES, 2004), which was a speeded up version of *PiPs*, having the same heavy emphasis on segmenting for spelling, less emphasis on sounding and blending for reading, and the late introduction of vowels. In 2007, Tymms and Merrell found that the NLS had had a limited impact on reading standards, although 500 million pounds had been spent on costly literacy schemes in England since the inception of the NLS in 1998.

In 2005, a UK House of Commons Select Committee considered evidence on effective approaches to teaching reading. It recommended that the Department for Education and Skills (DfES) should consider carrying out in England a similar study to our Scottish ones, to see how the existing program compared in effectiveness with the synthetic phonics approach. However, instead of doing this, the DfES instituted the Early Reading Development Pilot; this was a speeded up version of *Playing with Sounds* (DfES, 2004). It still did not resemble the synthetic phonics program that we used, as there was far more segmenting for spelling than blending for reading. Furthermore, there was no control group, and no use of standardized reading tests before and after the program, so that the outcome could not be compared with scientific studies of synthetic phonics.

At the same time, the Rose Review (Rose, 2006) was set up to examine the effective teaching of reading. This review concluded that children should be taught to read by a systematic synthetic phonics program starting by the age of five. The DfES has now brought out a fully-fledged synthetic phonics program called *Letters and Sounds* (DFES, 2007), where sounding and blending for reading receives due emphasis and is appropriately balanced with segmenting for spelling.

There is evidence that primary schools that have effectively implemented synthetic phonics teaching have very good results in reading at Key Stage 1 (at the end of the third year at school). The Office for Standards in Education looked at a sample of 12 very effective schools in England, and found that all schools had a program of rigorous systematic synthetic phonics work as the prime approach to decoding print (Ofsted, 2010). All of the schools were judged to be outstanding in their last inspection, and they had above-average results in the government reading tests. However, a lot of schools have not fully embraced the synthetic phonics method, and to ensure that they do the DfE has introduced a check of phonics skills at the end of Year 1 (the end of the second year at school). This test contains not only single words in isolation, but also nonwords, which can only be read by using a phonic approach. Pilot testing was carried out in around 300 schools in England. This showed that only 32% of six-year-olds who took the screening check reached what the Schools Minister Nick Gibb called the "appropriately challenging" expected level, which was set by about 50 teachers whose schools were involved in the pilot (DfE, 2011). Schools and teachers' unions have argued that they are already doing phonics, but the results of this pilot test demonstrate that a little bit of phonics is not enough, it has to be carried out very rigorously and systematically to get the gains we showed in our studies.

Teachers do feel rather jaundiced about these continual changes in the curriculum they are supposed to implement. There has been a backlash in England against the introduction of the synthetic phonics approach to teaching reading – not only from teachers' unions but also, as we will see, from educationalists in universities.

Reactions by Educationalists in Universities

Lefstein (2008) argues that literacy crises come and go, and quotes the Bible as saying "what has been is what will be… there is nothing new under the sun " (Ecclesiastes). This implies that he thinks that research into effective methods of teaching reading is unlikely to bring about any improvements. Thus, rather than addressing reading research as such, he carries out an ethnographic analysis of the debate about the introduction of synthetic phonics schools in England, as looked at by the BBC current affairs program "Newsnight". He concludes that television is very limited in representing educational issues, and suggests that the May and June 2005 Newsnight programs on synthetic phonics used many aspects of the genre of entertainment makeover programs. These programs showed Ruth Miskin intro-ducing her synthetic phonics program to a school in a very deprived area, where there was significant underachievement in reading; children's word reading increased greatly in a period of 16 weeks. Here Lefstein (2008) discerns the structure of a fairytale – the school (a damsel in distress) is rescued by the brave heroine (Ruth Miskin) who wields a magic weapon (synthetic phonics). These analogies, amusing as they are, are meant to trivialize the benefits of synthetic phonics teaching.

Lefstein (2008) employs a number of rhetorical devices that reinforce the impres-sion that the author has an antiscientific approach to educational research. He proposes that the recent movement towards a scientific approach in educational research is motivated by the belief that policymakers will take notice of and fund such research; the word "scientific" appears in inverted commas in this context, as do the words "evidence-based" policy and "research evidence" elsewhere in the article. Indeed, Lefstein argues that the academics interviewed on the Newsnight programs varied in their communicative effectiveness according to whether or not they took a scientific /academic approach (all of the academics interviewed were antisynthetic phonics). Wyse is portrayed as having an ineffective approach because he based his arguments on scientific evidence, whereas Dombey is portrayed as being more effective because she used a more concrete approach. However, both academics made serious errors in what they said, regardless of the approach they took. Wyse said that the Clackmannanshire Study had not been published in a peer-reviewed journal, whereas it had been in print for a year. Dombey said there was no evidence that the children enjoyed or understood what they read, and that the analytic phonics control condition was set up to fail. She also said that Clackmannanshire Council had had a lot of other interventions going on at the same time, which could have accounted for the gains made by the synthetic-phonics taught children.

The claim that there were other interventions in Clackmannanshire concurrent with our own study comes from a newspaper article by Ellis (2005), published in the Scottish edition of the Times Educational Supplement. Lefstein (2008) would probably like this article, as it uses a cake making analogy throughout. A number of claims are made that are attributed to conversations Ellis had with teachers in Clackmannanshire. Ellis states that the schools introduced other interventions at the same time as synthetic phonics, that is, nursery nurses in Primary 1, story bags, home link teachers, homework clubs and nurture groups. In fact, the only interventions that were current at the time of our study were a "books for babies" scheme, and the appointment of four home-school link workers. However, the home-school link workers were not allowed to support parents with literacy or to help in the classroom during the research intervention. If there are any remaining doubts, two of these home-school link workers were in schools in the synthetic phonics condition, and two were in schools in the analytic phonics plus phoneme awareness condition. The children in the latter condition performed significantly less well than the children in the synthetic phonics condition, so it is clear that the gains were due to the synthetic phonics program. We have explained to Ellis that she is referring to schemes that were not in place at the time of the study, but despite this she has repeated these claims in another article (Ellis, 2007, p. 288). She also implies that we have conceded that these other initiatives had been concurrent with the phonics study (Ellis, 2007, p. 291)!

In this same article, Ellis also presents Primary 7 data from the Scottish 5–14 national testing for the schools in the Clackmannanshire intervention study. However, as she explains, these are unstandardized tests that are administered by class teachers at any time in the year when they feel that a child or group of children has attained a 5–14 level. Ellis (2007) concludes that such testing should not be seen as a direct challenge to the standardized tests we used. Clearly, the use of such test results is problematical, as Ellis herself realizes. It should certainly be of concern that at the point in our longitudinal study where children from more advantaged homes performed significantly better than those from disadvantaged homes, the national test results showed that some of the classes from schools in disadvantaged areas were outperforming those from more advantaged areas. There is evidence that the standardized test we used is a good predictor of the English national test scores for reading (where the same test was given to the children all at the same time). Moreover, we should also point out that 22% of the pupils in these schools in Primary 7 were not in our intervention, so these overall figures for classes are not comparable with our own data.

As to the other points made by Dombey, we have found that children in Clackmannanshire have as positive an attitude to reading as they do in England (Johnston, Watson, & Logan, 2009). We have also found (Johnston, McGeown, & Watson, 2012) that at the age of 10, the children in the Clackmannanshire Study comprehended what they read significantly better than children in England taught by *Progression in Phonics* (DfEE, 1999). Dombey has also suggested that we set up our analytic phonics condition to fail. However, as we explained before, we observed analytic phonics teaching for three years before implementing the approach in our studies, and this approach closely resembled the method used in *Progression in Phonics* (DfEE, 1999). As previously stated, there is absolutely no doubt that the Clackmannanshire teachers carried out the programs to the very best of their ability, regardless of the training condition in which they were working.

Wyse's viewpoint is more fully fleshed out in an article in a published in the teachers' magazine *Literacy*. Here, Wyse and Styles (2007) criticise the Rose Review's (Rose, 2006) recommendation that all children should learn by a systematic synthetic phonics approach by the age of five. They argue that this conclusion in favor of synthetic phonics contradicts research published over the last 30 years. This suggests the existence of a large body of research on this topic, but in fact there has been very little research over that period of time that has compared the effectiveness of analytic and synthetic phonics programs within the same tightly-controlled study.

Wyse and Styles (2007) attempt to review our research comparing the effectiveness of synthetic and analytic phonics approaches (Johnston & Watson, 2004), and it is interesting that, in doing so, they feel the need to use rhetorical devices to try to undermine it. For example, they claim that Experiment 2 in our study was carried out to "correct the mistakes" made in Experiment 1, where the synthetic-phonics taught children learnt letters at a faster rate than those in the analytic phonics conditions. An experienced researcher would not assume that studies are reported in chronological order; in fact, as shown earlier, Experiment 2 was carried out first.

Wyse and Styles (2007) do not seem to understand the purpose of Experiment 1. They may not be aware that there is a strongly held view that children learn to read better if they are firstly taught to segment and blend sounds in spoken words, that is, receive phonological awareness training (see *Letters and Sounds* (DfES, 2007), Phase 1, Aspect 7). Experiment 1 is clearly described in our article as an examination of whether phonological awareness training has any benefits for children's reading. The condition in which blending and segmenting is carried out with letters and print, the synthetic phonics condition, necessarily involves teaching more letter sounds than the condition where this training is carried out without letters. It was very evident that the children made better progress in reading when letters and print were used whilst blending and segmenting.

Experiment 2 examined whether synthetic phonics was more effective than analytic phonics and, therefore, we controlled for speed of letter sound knowledge between these two conditions. As we reported before, we found that synthetic phonics was indeed more effective than analytic phonics in developing word reading and spelling. Thus, we can conclude that the large gains in reading for the synthetic phonics group in the Clackmannanshire Study were due to the synthetic phonics method, not to the accelerated letter learning.

Wyse and Styles (2007) also claim that the comprehension findings in Experiment 1 are unclear. They comment on the fact that we reported that at the second posttest there was no significant difference between the groups in reading comprehension. It is possible that they have not realized that by this time all of the groups had carried out the synthetic phonics program. What was being examined at the end of the second year of school was the effect of early versus late synthetic phonics teaching on reading comprehension, word reading, and spelling (Johnston & Watson, 2004, Tables 3 and 4, p. 340). We found that those who did synthetic phonics early on had better spelling, even when compared with the group that had carried out a phonological awareness training program. Subsequent analyses have also shown that the girls read words better when they learnt by the synthetic phonics method early on (Johnston & Watson, 2005).

One of the problems that Wyse and Styles (2007) have with synthetic phonics is that they believe that reading books are introduced too late in such schemes; indeed this may be the major difficulty that they have with the synthetic phonics approach. They cite the evidence we gave to the Select Committee (House of Commons Education and Skills Committee, 2005, EV 61), where we said that "with this approach, before children are introduced books, they are taught letter sounds", and also claim that throughout our program the children were denied reading books. Perhaps if we had said "taught *some* letter sounds", they might not have got hold of the wrong end of the stick. However, we made it very clear in our research article (Johnston & Watson, 2004, p. 333) that reading books were introduced six weeks after the phonics program started (which was the normal time for introducing reading books for the schools in the study). Wyse and Styles (2007) also mention the Jolly Phonics scheme (Lloyd, 1998), where the handbook says that children are not expected to read books during the first 8–9 weeks of the program. However, it is common practice, with this and other phonics programs, to read books aloud to the children in this period of time.

When we first studied analytic phonics, we became concerned that this was a form of word study that did not connect well with the reading of books. With analytic phonics in the United Kingdom, children may have to spend two to three terms reading books without any means of deciphering unfamiliar words for themselves. One of our reasons for examining whether synthetic phonics is more effective than analytic phonics was to see whether it allows an earlier link with book reading, and it is now very clear that it does. If children are expected to read words before they have learnt about the role of letter sounds in decoding unfamiliar words, some of them may develop a primitive form of sight–word reading that actually retards their reading development. It is better, therefore, to wait for a little while before introducing children to books, until they have learnt some letter sounds and how to sound and blend them. However, if decodable books are available, children can be reading these within days of starting a synthetic phonics program. We certainly support the view that phonics teaching should be integrated with reading comprehension – as soon as children have an understanding of how to decipher unknown words.

It seems that Wyse and Styles (2007) support an ideological position whereby children should have reading books before they can recognize printed words, or when at best they have a primitive recognition of words, based on logographic information and picture cues rather than grapheme–phoneme conversion skills. Such an opinion needs to be supported by empirical evidence to show that it is beneficial for children's reading, but Wyse and Styles (2007) do not cite any such evidence. Instead, Wyse and Styles (2007) spend much of their article trying to argue that our studies are flawed. Thus, the approach they take is to put up a smokescreen by attacking synthetic phonics studies, to obscure the fact that they have no evidence to support their own preferred teaching methods.

There are many reasons why the magazine *Literacy* should not have published this article, as it contains so many errors. Indeed, so does the editorial for that issue (Dombey, 2007), where it is claimed that the Clackmannanshire Study had not yet appeared in a peer review journal. However, *Literacy* received a high number of searches on the Wyse and Styles (2007) article on the publisher's web page, so it must have been saying what people want to hear. Our own experience of this magazine is very revealing. We sent in an article some years ago where we showed that boys read significantly better than girls with synthetic phonics teaching in the

Clackmannanshire Study. We were told that because the study was carried out in Scotland, it lacked relevance to England. We wrote to the editor pointing out that the magazine was published by the *United Kingdom* Reading Association (now the UK Literacy Association), but we got no reply!

A Meta-Analysis of Studies Comparing the Effectiveness of Synthetic and Analytic Phonics Teaching

Wyse and Styles (2007) also raise the issue of the meta-analysis by C. Torgerson, Brooks, and Hall (2006), in which it is concluded that there is no clear evidence favoring the greater effectiveness of either synthetic or analytic phonics. It is interesting that Wyse and Styles (2007) place so much weight on this article as it has not been peer reviewed, yet that is the criticism they make of our longitudinal study in Clackmannanshire (Johnston & Watson, 2005). This review, funded by the DfES, limited itself to an examination of a subset of the small amount of literature available, because it chose to include only randomised controlled trial studies. This means that C. Torgerson et al. (2006) excluded the controlled trial Clackmannanshire Study, which they erroneously claimed suffered from regression to the mean effects. Regression to the mean is a statistical artefact whereby lower performing participants gain higher scores (closer to the mean) on retest, whereas higher performing participants get a lower score on retest. C. The argument of C. Torgerson et al. (2006) is that as the children in the synthetic phonics group came from more deprived backgrounds, they had started out with much lower scores than the children in the other two groups and so their gains on retest were much greater. They conclude that the synthetic phonics group's greater progress was probably illusory. However, a proper reading of our study would have shown that the synthetic phonics group did not perform below the level of the other groups at pre-test (Johnston & Watson, 2004, Table 1, p. 334). Indeed, most of the children in the study were nonreaders on the test at this stage, so regression to the mean cannot have occurred as it only operates on *actual* scores. Furthermore, it is well known that children from deprived backgrounds do not learn to read as well as children from more advantaged homes, right from the start of reading tuition (Duncan & Seymour, 2000; Stuart et al., 1998). Therefore the gains made by the synthetic phonics group in the Clackmannanshire Study, who were from the most deprived areas, are all the more remarkable.

Having limited their analysis to randomized controlled trial studies, C. Torgerson et al. (2006) made many errors that greatly affected the conclusions they drew. First of all, it is very important to select the correct scores to enter into such analyses;

it is not appropriate to enter posttest data on the children's reading of trained words, as the gains may not transfer to untrained words, and so would be of little utility. Secondly, care should be taken to ensure that posttest scores are taken after there has been a significant amount of training. Thirdly, care needs to be taken if an unpublished study is to be included in the analysis; the National Reading Panel meta-analysis (Ehri, Nunes, Stahl, & Willows, 2001) scrupulously excluded all work that had not been subjected to peer review.

The C. Torgerson et al (2006) meta-analysis makes all of these errors. One study they included is only available in manuscript form, having been delivered at a conference (Skailand, 1971); it has not subsequently been published. C. Torgerson et al. (2006) argue that such studies should be included because it is well known that studies which produce nonsignificant results are much less likely to be published. However, this argument does not hold as this study did report a significant effect; the fact that it has not been published suggests doubts about its quality, as we will see later. Furthermore, C. Torgerson et al. (2006) take posttest data from the children's reading of the trained words (where a significant difference between conditions was reported). However, the children were also posttested on untrained words (where there was no significant difference between the conditions), but these data were not entered into the analysis. For the study they include by J. Torgesen et al. (1999), C. Torgerson et al. (2006) take posttest scores from one-fifth of the way into the intervention, at a point where one group (the embedded phonics group) had done early word recognition work, but the synthetic phonics group had a spent a lot of time on preliminary phonological awareness training tasks. They conclude from this analysis that the condition that resembled analytic phonics (actually it was embedded phonics) was more effective than the synthetic phonics condition. This outcome would surely be very surprising to J. Torgesen et al. (1999), as they concluded, on the basis of their final posttest data, that the synthetic phonics approach was the most effective for developing the word recognition skills of children at risk of reading failure. The third study included is one carried out by ourselves (Johnston & Watson, 2004, Experiment 2), where there was a large effect favoring synthetic phonics. Pooling the estimates of the effect sizes for these three studies, C. Torgerson et al. (2006) find a nonsignificant effect that does not favor either analytic or synthetic phonics.

We have recalculated the effect size for the J. Torgesen et al. (1999) study by taking scores from the end of the intervention, and have pooled this with the effect size from our own study (Johnston & Watson, 2004, Experiment 2). We have left out the Skailand (1971) study, as it had an invalid implementation of the synthetic phonics method. (Fifty percent of the items the kindergarten children were trained on were silent "e" words, such as "tape"; children at this stage will not be able to use the sounding and blending procedure on such items, and so may pronounce them as "tapee"). Our calculations show a pooled estimate of effect size of 0.77, $p < 0.0001$. An effect size of 0.2 is seen as small, an effect size of 0.5 is seen as medium, and an effect size of 0.8 is seen as large. The very clear conclusion from this is that both normal school entrants (Johnston & Watson, 2004, Experiment 2) and children at risk of reading failure (J. Torgesen et al., 1999) learn to read better if taught by a good synthetic phonics program.

Conclusion

Our foray into research that has educational applications has certainly been a very interesting one for us. We have been accustomed to academic debates about research but these arguments have always been based on data. It has been a matter of great surprise to us to discover how debates take place in some areas of education. Here ideology seems to be at the forefront, and some academics apparently feel no need to produce data to support their arguments. Lacking any evidence to support their views, some of these academics go on the attack to try to argue that a research study that does not have the "right" outcome is flawed. In doing so, we have shown that they often exhibit a lack of understanding of the theoretical issues that the studies address. There are also a number of fabrications circulating about the Clackmannanshire Study, and we probably have not heard of all of them. Recently, a researcher for a documentary told us that they had been informed that the children in the Clackmannanshire Study were not doing well in secondary school. However, no testing has been carried out on the children's reading in secondary school. Indeed, our own attempts to chart the children's progress in secondary school have foundered, as we were turned down twice for funding to examine how well they were doing. Meanwhile, some educational researchers are doing very well out of attacking synthetic phonics, swelling their publication lists and getting numerous TV appearances! In all this, we see little evidence of any desire to make sure that children get the best possible reading tuition in school.

Summary

In this chapter, we have outlined our studies on the effects of synthetic phonics teaching on children's reading. We found that this method led very early on to accelerated reading and spelling skills. In our study in Clackmannanshire, these gains were not only maintained but increased year after year. At the end of primary schooling, the children were reading words 42 months ahead of age level, spelling was 20 months ahead, and reading comprehension was 3.5 months ahead, significantly so in all cases. Given that many of the children in the study came from areas of deprivation, even the reading comprehension scores were a very good outcome. Indeed, we found that the children from areas of deprivation only started to fall behind the children from better off areas at the end of primary schooling. Unexpectedly, the boys pulled ahead of the girls in word reading at the end of the third year at school, and at the end of schooling they were a significant 11 months ahead. The boys' spelling was also a significant eight months ahead at this stage. Their reading comprehension was also as good as that of the girls, although surveys in many countries typically shown that boys fall significantly behind girls in this skill.

The synthetic phonics approach has now been recommended for introduction in to all schools in England, and the Primary National Strategy devised its own synthetic phonics program, *Letters and Sounds* (DfES, 2007). However, there is considerable opposition to the introduction of the method by teachers' unions and by educational academics. The latter have been particularly vociferous. Lacking any data of their own to show that their own preferred method is equally or more effective, they have attacked the Clackmannanshire Study. One approach has been to argue that other interventions were being carried out at the same time (although they were not). Another approach has been to argue that there were flaws in the experimental design (although there were not). More surprising has been the findings of a meta-analysis (C. Torgerson et al., 2006), paid for by England's Department for Education and Skills. This argues that when our study and others looking at synthetic phonics were combined, there was no overall significant effect size favoring synthetic phonics. However, many rudimentary errors were made, taking data from inappropriate test points, and including an inappropriate study. Our recalculations show that there is, in fact, a large and significant effect size favoring synthetic phonics across relevant randomized controlled trial studies.

References

Brooks, G. (2002). Phonemic awareness is a key factor in learning to be literate: How best should it be taught. In M. Cook (Ed.), *Perspectives on the teaching and learning of phonics*. Royston, UK: UKRA.

Brooks, G. (2003). *Sound sense: the phonic element of the National Literacy Strategy*. Retrieved on July 21, 2015 from http://dera.ioe.ac.uk/4938/5/nls_phonics0303gbrooks.pdf

DfE (2011). A third of children reach expected level in the pilot of phonics check. Retrieved March 9, 2012 from http://www.education.gov.uk/inthenews/inthenews/a00200672/a-third-of-children-reach-expected-level-in-pilot-of-phonics-check

DfEE (1999). *Progression in Phonics*. London: DfEE. Retrieved March 8, 2012 from http://www.eric.ed.gov/ERICWebPortal/search/detailmini.jsp?_nfpb=true&_&ERICExtSearch_SearchValue_0=ED472282&ERICExtSearch_SearchType_0=no&accno=ED472282

DfES (2004). *Playing with sounds: A supplement to progression phonics*. London: DfES. Retrieved March 8, 2012 from http://dera.ioe.ac.uk/4902/2/nls_phonics028004intro.pdf

DfES (2007). *Letters and Sounds*. London:DfES. Retrieved February 27, 2012 from https://www.education.gov.uk/publications/standard/publicationdetail/Page1/DFES-00281-2007

Dombey, H. (2007). Editorial. *Literacy, 41*(1), 1–2.

Duncan, L. G., & Seymour, P. H. K. (2000). Socio-economic differences in foundation level literacy. *British Journal of Psychology, 91*, 145–166.

Ehri, L., Nunes, S., Stahl, S., & Willows, D. (2001). Systematic phonics instruction helps students learn to read: Evidence from the National Reading Panel's meta-analysis. *Review of Educational Research, 71*, 393–447.

Ellis, S. (2005). Phonics is just the icing on the cake. *TES Scotland*, September 23.

Ellis, S. (2007). Policy and research: Lessons from the Clackmannanshire Synthetic Phonics Initiative. *Journal of Early Childhood Literacy, 7*, 281–297.

Goswami, U. (1999). Causal connections in beginning reading: the importance of rhyme. *Journal of Research in Reading, 22*, 217–240.

House of Commons Education and Skills Committee (2005). *Teaching children to read*. Eighth Report of Session 2004–05. The Stationery Office, Ltd: London. Retrieved March 8, 2012 from http://image.guardian.co.uk/sys-files/Education/documents/2005/04/06/reading.pdf

Johnston, R. S., & Watson, J. (2004). Accelerating the development of reading, spelling and phonemic awareness. *Reading and Writing, 17*(4), 327–357.

Johnston, R. S., & Watson, J. (2005). *The effects of synthetic phonics teaching on reading and spelling attainment, a seven year longitudinal study*. Published by the Scottish Executive Education Department. Retrieved July 12, 2015 from http://www.scotland.gov.uk/Publications/2005/02/20688/52449

Johnston, R. S., & Watson, J. (2007). *Teaching Synthetic Phonics*. Exeter, UK: Learning Matters.

Johnston, R. S, McGeown, S., & Watson, J. (2012). Long-term effects of synthetic versus analytic phonics teaching on the reading and spelling ability of 10 year old boys and girls. *Reading and Writing, 25*, 1365–1384.

Johnston, R. S., Watson, J. E., & Logan, S. (2009). Enhancing word reading, spelling and reading comprehension skills with synthetic phonics teaching: studies in Scotland and England. In C. Wood & V. Connelly, *Reading and Writing: Issues and Debates*: Elsevier.

Johnston, R. S., & Watson, J. (2011). The right blend. *SEN Magazine, 53*, 57.

Lefstein, A. (2008). Literacy makeover: Educational research and the public interest on prime time. *Teachers College Record, 110*, 3.

Lloyd, S. (1998). *The phonics handbook*, 3rd ed. Chigwell, UK: Jolly Learning Ltd.

Lloyd, S. (2003). 'Synthetic phonics – what is it?' *Reading Reform Foundation Newsletter, 50*(Spring), 25–27.

Mullis, I. V. S., Martin, M. O., Gonzalez, E. J., & Kennedy, A. M. (2003). *PIRLS 2001 International Report: IEA's study of reading literacy achievement in primary schools*, Chestnut Hill, MA: Boston College.

NLS (National Literacy Strategy) (2003). *Teaching phonics in the National Literacy Strategy.* Retrieved on July 21, 2015 from http://dera.ioe.ac.uk/4938/8/nls_phonics0303nls.pdf

NICHD (2000). *Report of the National Reading Panel: Teaching children to read.* Washington, DC: National Institute of Child Health and Human Development.

Ofsted (2007). The Annual Report of Her Majesty's Chief Inspector 2006/07. Retrieved on July 21, 2015 from https://www.gov.uk/government/uploads/system/uploads/attachment_data/file/250518/1002.pdf

Ofsted (2010). Reading by six: How the best schools do it. Retrieved March 9, 2012 from http://www.ofsted.gov.uk/resources/reading-six-how-best-schools-do-it

Rose, J. (2006). *Independent review of the early teaching of reading.* Retrieved on July 21, 2015 from http://dera.ioe.ac.uk/5551/2/report.pdf

Skailand, D. B. (1971). A year comparison of four language units in teaching beginning reading. Paper presented at annual meetings of the American Educational Research Association, New York, February 7, 1971.

Stuart, M., Dixon, M, Masterson, J., & Quinlan, P. (1998). Learning to read at home and at school. *British Journal of Educational Psychology, 68,* 3–14.

Torgerson, C. J., Brooks, G., & Hall, J. (2006). *A systematic review of the research literature and use of phonics in the teaching of reading and spelling.* DfES, research reports RR711. Retrieved March 9, 2012 from http://www.education.gov.uk/rsgateway/DB/RRP/u014389/index.shtml

Torgesen, J. K., Wagner, R. K., Rose, E., Lindamood, P., Conway, T., & Garvan, C. (1999). Preventing reading failure in children with phonological processing disabilities: group and individual responses to instruction. *Journal of Educational Psychology, 91,* 579–593.

Tymms, P., & Merrell, C. (2007). *Standards and quality in English primary schools over time: The national evidence* (Primary Review Research Survey 4/1). Cambridge, UK: University of Cambridge Faculty of Education.

Watson, J. E. (1998). *An investigation of the effects of phonics teaching on children's progress in reading and spelling.* PhD Thesis, University of St Andrews.

Watson, J. E., & Johnston, R. S. (2010). *Phonics Bug.* Harlow, UK: Pearson.

Wyse, D., & Styles, M. (2007). Synthetic phonics and the teaching of reading: the debate surrounding England's Rose Report. *Literacy, 41,* 35–42.

10

Giving Away Early Mathematics: Big Math for Little Kids *Encounters the Complex World of Early Education*

Herbert P. Ginsburg and Barbrina B. Ertle

We begin this chapter with a section summarizing the theoretical background and pedagogical goals of a research based mathematics curriculum for 4- and 5-year-old children, namely *Big Math for Little Kids* (BMLK) (Ginsburg, Greenes, & Balfanz, 2003). In this section, we first show how a large body of research in cognitive developmental psychology and related areas has changed our views of young children's mathematical competence: what they know and can learn is far from trivial or simple. Second, we describe the goals of mathematics education for young children: just as children's everyday mathematical knowledge is broad and deep, so must early mathematics education encompass challenging mathematics of several types, ranging from number to pattern. Third, we describe the different ways in which adults can promote young children's mathematics learning, with special attention to the idea of a planned curriculum. We conclude this section by describing BMLK itself.

In the next section, we relate our experiences in giving away BMLK. First, we describe classroom observations showing that young children want to learn

The Wiley Handbook of Developmental Psychology in Practice: Implementation and Impact, First Edition.
Edited by Kevin Durkin and H. Rudolph Schaffer.

mathematics and can enjoy being taught mathematics in school. Second, we describe the social context that has stimulated efforts to implement early mathematics programs, as well as various barriers that stand in the way of effective implementation. Third, we focus on the teachers: sometimes they are obstacles to progress and sometimes they are wonderful resources. Fourth, we examine the process of teaching early mathematics: it is more complex than usually assumed and involves many of the same challenges faced by mathematics teachers at all age levels. Fifth, we discuss the results of an evaluation of the effectiveness of BMLK and what it teaches us about giving away mathematics. We conclude by discussing the implications of our work, particularly for the training of teachers, which is the central problem of early mathematics education, and indeed of mathematics education at all levels.

Research and the Creation of BMLK

BMLK was inspired by and derived from many years of research on children's mathematical thinking.

Young children's mathematical thinking is surprisingly competent (as well as limited)

The top line (just above) is our bottom line. Over the past 35 years or so, researchers in a variety of fields (particularly cognitive developmental psychology, educational psychology, and mathematics education) have shown that starting even in infancy young children demonstrate more advanced mathematical thinking than was earlier supposed. Because the literature is comprehensive and has been summarized in many extensive reviews (Baroody, Lai, & Mix, 2006; Clements & Sarama, 2007; Ginsburg, Cannon, Eisenband, & Pappas, 2006), we present only a brief summary of what we take as the main conclusions.

Spontaneous interest

From birth to age five (and beyond), young children develop an *everyday mathematics* – informal mathematical ideas and skills about numbers, shapes, space, patterns, and other mathematical topics. Naturalistic research has shown that young children spontaneously engage in a variety of everyday mathematical activities. Young children spontaneously count out loud (Saxe, Guberman, & Gearhart, 1987; Walkerdine, 1988), and children as young as three sometimes even say numbers as high as "ten" (Durkin, Shire, Riem, Crowther, & Rutter,

1986). Court (1920) reported that her five-year-old child was interested in learning to count by fives. Indeed, children at this age enjoy counting up to relatively large numbers, like 100 (Irwin & Burgham, 1992). Moreover, counting ability in the preschool years predicts mathematics performance in first grade (Manfra, Dinehart, & Sembiante, 2014).

Preschoolers are interested in adding too. Anderson (1993) reports that at three years of age her daughter was spontaneously interested in the composition of numbers. She wanted to know "What's another way [apart from holding up one hand] to make five [fingers]?" (Anderson, 1993, p. 28). She then attempted to hold up four fingers and one more, as well as other combinations. At age five, Anderson's daughter created addition problems, asking, "Two and three, how many's that?" (Anderson, 1993, p. 28). Court (1920) also reported that her son displayed interest in creating addition problems. He brought his mother three blocks, asked whether she wanted four, and then brought her another block.

Our own research (Ginsburg, Pappas, & Seo, 2001) shows that during free play, young children frequently get involved in exploring shapes and patterns (as when they decide to make squares out of the triangular shaped blocks), are concerned with "relative magnitude" (as in "My tower is bigger than yours"), and deal with number (as when they say, "I think I need three more blocks").

Everyday mathematics is inevitable. How can children or anyone else get around in life without knowing about more and less, and over and under, and many and few, and the shapes that make one thing a ball and another a box? Indeed, everyday mathematics is so fundamental and pervasive a feature of a child's cognition that it is hard to see how children could function without it. It is key to the transition from informal to formal mathematics (Ginsburg, Duch, Ertle, & Noble, 2012; Purpura, Baroody, & Lonigan, 2013).

Concrete and abstract

Young children's minds are not necessarily "concrete," as a misinterpretation of Piaget sometimes suggests. From an early age, they are concerned to know what is the "largest number" (Gelman, 1980), clearly a very abstract, mathematical issue. Even at age three, children know that "adding makes more" (Brush, 1978). By age four, they can spontaneously develop, without adult help (Groen & Resnick, 1977), various general methods or "strategies" for solving addition problems, like counting on from the larger number (Baroody & Wilkins, 1999). Young children can easily do addition problems involving concrete objects placed right in front of them, but they can also solve similar mental problems involving imaginary apples.

Yet young children's everyday mathematics suffers from some limitations, as when attention to the superficial appearance of things dominates their thinking. Young children are sometimes "concrete," as when they have difficulty understanding that a set of seven objects spread out in a long line is the same number as a set of seven objects arranged in a shorter line. Even when children count each group and determine that there are seven in both cases, they argue that one line of objects has more because it is longer than the other (Piaget, 1952). Another example involves shapes. They will easily say that a figure with three equal straight sides is a triangle. But shown an extremely elongated, non-right-angle "skinny" shape with three sides (a scalene triangle), children often refuse to believe that it is a triangle (Clements, 1999). To complicate matters further, they can easily see that the long skinny three-sided shape is obviously not a square or a circle or a rectangle. Their thinking is not simple. It is at the same time concrete and abstract, competent and limited. They are sometimes overly influenced by the appearance of things but can understand abstract ideas.

The role of language

Language plays a surprising role in mathematical thinking. Mathematical vocabulary is established quite early. The words *more* and *another* are among the first that toddlers learn (Bloom, 1970). Indeed young children's early language comprises many words that refer to quantity, shape, location, and the like, such as *one, only one, the most, round, straight, in front of, behind, underneath, big, bigger,* and *biggest.* At the same time, children and adults often use these everyday words in imprecise ways, as when the child says that one object is "bigger" than another, when in fact he is referring to the objects' height, or when the adult refers to a block as the "square": the *face* is a square, but the object is a *cube.* Also, children may interpret mathematical language in unusual ways, as when one child we interviewed stood up on a chair when we asked him to count "as high as you can." Although children acquire many everyday mathematical words, these are often used imprecisely and do not map perfectly onto the corresponding *formal* mathematical terms. Everyday mathematical words sometimes serve the useful function of pointing to mathematical concepts but may at the same time be a source of misunderstanding.

An even more important function of language is to express and justify mathematical thinking. Children need to learn to say things like, "I think this is a circle because it is round. This one is not a circle because the sides are straight." This kind of language is not simply a list of vocabulary words, although they are certainly needed. It is instead a way to express reasoning and to justify mathematical arguments (and other kinds too). Mathematical language of this type – the language of thought and rationality – begins to develop in children as young as four or five years of age (Pappas, Ginsburg, & Jiang, 2003).

Low-income children's abilities

As in many other areas, low-income preschool children generally perform more poorly on simple mathematical tasks than do their more privileged peers (Denton & West, 2002). Yet the test scores that are the gold standard of conventional educational research are crude and may fail to reveal children's competence. A closer look at low-income children's mathematical abilities reveals a complex and interesting situation. First, cognitive developmental research shows that although low-income children's *performance* on informal addition and subtraction problems usually lags behind middle-income children's, the two groups often employ similar *strategies* to solve problems (Ginsburg & Pappas, 2004; Ginsburg & Russell, 1981). Further, in response to some (game-based) interventions to promote strategies, low-income children gain at least as much in number understanding as do children from middle-income backgrounds (Ramani & Siegler, 2011). Second, although low-income children exhibit difficulty with *verbal* addition and subtraction problems, they perform roughly as well as middle-income children on *nonverbal* forms of these tasks (Jordan, Huttenlocher, & Levine, 1994). Third, naturalistic observation shows that lower and middle-income children exhibit few if any differences in the everyday mathematics they spontaneously employ in free play (Ginsburg et al., 2001). The low-income children traffic in pattern and shape, quantity differences, and number in the same ways and as frequently as do middle-income children. Fourth, cross-cultural research reveals unsuspected mathematical skill among uneducated children (Nunes, Schliemann, & Carraher, 1993) and adults (Petitto & Ginsburg, 1982). Many aspects of mathematical thinking appear to be universal (Klein & Starkey, 1988).

In brief, the test scores are real and tell us something important, namely that the low-income children's school achievement is not what it should be. At the same time, cognitive research shows that, despite limitations, they do not lack for basic competence, even though conventional tests may not reveal it.

The Nature of Early Mathematics Education

Children's mathematical thinking is broad and can be deep (and it can be limited as well). Hence, early childhood mathematics education (ECME) is far more complex than usually assumed.

Big ideas

Drawing on cognitive research like that described above, the leading professional organizations in the field recommend that early mathematics instruction cover the "big ideas" of mathematics in such areas as number and operations, geometry (shape and space), measurement, and "algebra" (particularly pattern) (National Association for the Education of Young Children & National Council of Teachers of Mathematics, 2002). The research-based expectation is that ECME should involve ideas and concepts and should be more challenging than usually assumed.

For example, consider some big ideas connected with "enumeration" – the apparently simple activity of determining how many objects are in a set. One is that any kind of elements in a set can be counted. You can count nickels and cats, big things and small things. You can count one group of apples and another group of oranges. You can count a group containing both apples and oranges. You can even count fantastical ideas like red unicorns existing only in the mind. Counting is an enormously powerful tool that can be applied to any discrete real or imagined object.

A second big idea involves one–one correspondence: each number word, "one, two…" must be associated once and only once with each of the objects in the set, and you are not allowed to skip any object in the set. If shown a haphazard arrangement of objects, including a red block, a small stuffed dog, and a penny, you point at the red block and say "one", the dog and say "two", and the penny and say "three". You cannot say both "one" and "two" referring to the red block, even though you describe it with two words, "red" and "block". You cannot skip the dog, even if you do not like dogs.

A third idea is that the final number in any sequence does not refer to the last object alone. In the above example, "three" does not refer to the penny alone. You first pointed to the block and said "one." It is true: there is one block. Then you pointed to the dog and said "two." But it's not true that there are two dogs. The two indicates that you have already counted two items, not that the second item, the dog, is itself two. Similarly, even though you say "three" while pointing to the penny, the number word describes not that individual object but instead the whole group of objects – how many there are all together. You could have started your count with the penny, in which case it would have been "one," not "three." Indeed, *any* of the objects in the group could have been "one," "two," or "three," but the group as a whole has three objects whatever the order in which they are counted. The individual counting words are transitory; only the final count word indicates the number of objects in the set as a whole – the total quantity, the cardinal value.

Notice that enumeration entails a very strange and distinctive use of language. In ordinary speech, we call an object a block or a dog or a penny because that is its name. You cannot legitimately call a penny a red block. But when we enumerate, the number name we assign to the object does not refer to the individual object but to a very abstract property of the set as a whole. When, finishing the enumeration, we point to the penny and say "three," we do not mean that "three" is the name for the penny but that it is a property of all the things we have enumerated as a collection.

And that is just the beginning of the depth of the idea of cardinality. Suppose now you also count the idea of Homer, a mental image of a pink unicorn, and an apartment building. Again there are three altogether, and that three is the same three as the number of the set comprised of the red block, small stuffed dog, and penny. Three is three regardless of who or what belongs to the club.

Given this knowledge, you can also use written symbols in a meaningful way to designate cardinal value. You associate the written numeral "3" (as well as the word "three") with the abstract idea of three as defined above.

The purpose of focusing on big ideas is of course *not* to impose on young children the (often dull) activities designed for higher grades. The proposal is *not* to give young children textbooks, worksheets, and all the deadly drills that too often characterize (unsuccessful) elementary mathematics education. The goal is rather to engage children in the kind of conceptual activity that is at the heart of mathematics and that, unfortunately, bears little resemblance to the overly simple mathematics that early childhood teachers usually teach.

Mathematics as thinking

Mathematics involves not only the content – the big ideas – but also ways of *thinking*. Take again the example of number. Thinking about it involves reasoning (if 2 and 3 is five, then 3 and 2 must be the same number) (Baroody, 1985), making inferences (if we add something other than 0 to 3, the sum must be bigger than 3) (Baroody, 1992), developing a mental number line (100 is much further away from 2 than is 20) (Case & Okamoto, 1996), and inducing patterns from examples (what comes after 11, 13, 15, ?) (Jordan, Kaplan, Olah, & Locuniak, 2006). Children spontaneously engage in thinking of this type. ECME should help them do it better and more deeply.

Children also need to *mathematize* – to conceive of problems in explicitly mathematical terms (Ginsburg, Jamalian, & Creighan, 2013; Kaartinen & Kumpulainen, 2012). They need to understand that the action of combining one bear with two others can be meaningfully interpreted in terms of the mathematical *principles* of addition and the *symbolism* 1 + 2. One of the functions of mathematics education is to help children to advance *beyond* their informal, intuitive mathematics – what Vygotsky (1986) called "everyday knowledge." In Vygotsky's view, the goal is to help children develop, over a period of years, a meaningful, powerful, symbolic and organized "scientific" knowledge – in this case the formal concepts, procedures, and symbolism of mathematics.

Methods for Promoting Mathematics Learning

ECME involves several different approaches to helping children learn mathematics.

The environment

The preschool classroom or childcare center should contain a rich variety of objects and materials – such as blocks, water table and puzzles – that can set the stage for mathematics learning. Some of these materials have proven themselves over the course of many years. In the 1850s, Froebel introduced a system of guided instruction centered on various "gifts," including blocks, variations of which have since then been widely used all around the world to help young children learn basic mathematics, especially geometry (Brosterman, 1997). Modern electronic toys and computers can be useful too, but the classroom should also contain simple objects like beads, blocks, puzzles, and books and more books.

Of course, providing a stimulating physical environment is only the first step. The crucial factor is not what the environment makes possible, but what children *do* in it.

Play

The second important component is *play*, which of course has many benefits for young and old alike (Ginsburg, 2006; Ginsburg et al., 2013; Wager, 2013; Weisberg, Hirsh-Pasek, & Golinkoff, 2013). Children have a good time when they play; it can help them to learn to interact with others and to develop self-regulation; it stimulates cognitive development; *and* we know that children do indeed learn a good deal of everyday mathematics on their own in the course of free play (Seo & Ginsburg, 2004).

What is there not to like about play in an enriched environment? It provides children with valuable opportunities to explore and to undertake activities that can be surprisingly sophisticated from a mathematical point of view and can at the same time involve fun, social learning, and other kinds of learning. But play *alone* is not enough. It does not by itself prepare children for school and usually does not help children to mathematize – to interpret their experiences in explicitly mathematical form and understand the relations between the two.

The teachable moment

The third component is the *teachable moment*, a form of adult guidance that enjoys widespread acceptance in the preschool world. The teachable moment involves the teacher's careful observation of children's play and other activities in order to identify the spontaneously emerging behavior that can be exploited to promote learning. The *Creative Curriculum* program (Dodge, Colker, & Heroman, 2002), extremely popular in the United States, relies heavily on use of the teachable moment.

The teachable moment, accurately perceived and suitably addressed, can provide a superb learning experience for the child (Copley, Jones, & Dighe, 2007; Palmér, Henriksson, & Hussein, 2015). For example, if a teacher sees children building symmetrical structures in the block area, he/she could seize on the opportunity to explore and expand upon the concept of symmetry. But exploiting the teachable moment is by no means simple. First, the teacher must take the time to carefully observe what the child is doing. Given the responsibility of managing a classroom full of children, teachers often lack the time and opportunity for careful, concentrated observation. Second, the teacher must recognize and understand the mathematics underlying the behavior – in this case, symmetry. Unfortunately many early childhood teachers lack deep mathematical understanding. Finally, the teacher must be able to design an activity – on the fly – that can further the child's learning. But creating good activities is difficult, even for curriculum designers, and it is unfair to expect teachers to do it well. In brief, it is simply not possible for teachers to notice, understand or exploit all the teachable moments that may arise. The teachable moment is not a proactive strategy for promoting learning; it is reactive to events that happen to be noticed (often by teachers not well trained in noticing them). By itself, the teachable moment, although valuable, cannot be expected to accomplish the major goals of ECME and must, therefore, be supplemented by other methods.

Projects

A fourth component involves *projects* (Edwards, Gandini, & Forman, 1993; Helm & Katz, 2000). These are extensive teacher initiated and guided explorations of complex topics related to the everyday world. For example, the teacher can engage the children in figuring out how to create a map of the classroom. On the first day, the teacher might start out by showing the children different aspects of the room, like the water table in the corner and the blocks near the rectangular table. A discussion of the location and position of major objects in the room can present an interesting challenge. The teacher can ask the children to describe in words where the puzzles are stored and where the bathroom is located. After this kind of background experience, the teacher can introduce use of a map to "tell" where an object is hidden. Now the teacher puts a large piece of paper on the floor and asks the children to imagine that it is their classroom. Suppose the door is over here and the windows there. Where would the table be located? This kind of activity, which of course extends over a period of days, can very challenging for children because it involves ideas of representation, perspective, scale, approximation and projection of three dimensions onto two.

Although projects can be enormously effective and motivating, the danger is that they may turn into a "… a grab bag of any mathematics-related experiences that seem to relate to a theme…" (National Association for the Education of Young Children & National Council of Teachers of Mathematics, 2002, p. 10). Projects need to be guided by a larger plan (Helm & Beneke, 2003), namely a *curriculum*, which is the fifth component of ECME.

Curriculum

A curriculum can be characterized as "…a written instructional blueprint and set of materials for guiding students' acquisition of certain culturally valued concepts, procedures, intellectual dispositions, and ways of reasoning…" (Clements, 2007, p. 36). A curriculum offers a carefully planned sequence of activities for the teaching of mathematics. The sequence should be based, at least in part, on knowledge of children's "learning trajectories" (Clements, Sarama, & DiBiase, 2004), that is, the progression in which they normally learn mathematical concepts. Note that a curriculum is not necessarily a textbook. It very well may be a textbook for older children but not for the younger children with whom we are concerned. A curriculum is a comprehensive, planned program of activities deliberately *taught* to young children.

Big Math for Little Kids

Big Math for Little Kids (BMLK)(Ginsburg et al., 2003) is a curriculum involving a sequence of mathematical topics, arranged in six units, to be covered over the course of the year. For example, the first unit, *Number*, involves such topics as the *counting words* (ones and tens); *enumeration* (finding out how many in a collection); *comparing sets* (more, less, and same); *reading, writing and representing* numbers; and *ordinal numbers* (first, second, third…). The next five units cover *Shape* (two- and three-dimensional, and symmetry); *Pattern and Logic* (identifying, creating, and extending patterns and using deductive logic); *Measurement* (using nonstandard and standard units to compare and order dimensions like length or weight); *Operations on Number* (comparing, adding, subtracting, and representing numbers and operations). The last and fairly short unit is *Space*, which involves *positions and locations* (such as right and left, forward and backward): *directions* (for example, using a verbal statement to find a hidden object); and *maps* (reading them).

The content of the curriculum is extensive and arranged in a planned sequence. The order of the large topics – Number, Shape, Pattern and the rest – to some extent derives from mathematical considerations. For example, you have to do the basics of number before you can do operations on number. But within a unit – a large mathematical topic – the dominating principle of organization is the sequence in which children normally learn the various concepts – the "developmental trajectory." Thus, BMLK introduces enumeration – figuring out how many – before concrete addition. And it introduces recognizing shapes before analyzing them.

The curriculum not only specifies the order of major units; it also lays out a planning chart for the various activities within a unit. Indeed the planning chart (one is shown in Figure 10.1) is the operational definition of a curriculum. The planning chart designates that a counting words activity called *Count, Clap and Stomp* is to take place during the first three weeks of instruction. *Show Me*, which introduces cardinal number, is also scheduled for week 1 and *My Number Book*, in which children represent numbers, is scheduled for week 5. The grey area of the chart, extending from week 8 to the end of year indicates that these activities are to be practiced for the rest of the year – not necessarily every day, but frequently. Thus, *Numbers with Pizzazz* is essentially a counting word activity in which children may learn to count to 100 by the end of the year. Practice makes perfect.

Each activity has several features, illustrated by Activity 3 in Figures 10.2 and 10.3. The first thing to note is that this material is intended for the teacher. The children never see a textbook. The teacher's guide indicates the overall purpose of the activity, describes a time line for doing it, and suggests an optimal group size for different "tasks" (subactivities). In this case, the activity involves a storybook and various materials that the teacher should prepare beforehand. The description of each task is clear and provides general guidelines for the activity. Sometimes there is a "script" (indicated in bold font). It is intended only as suggested wording; field testing showed that teachers wanted it. But the description of each task makes clear that the teacher has a good deal of freedom in how to implement it. The program does not promote robot-like teaching.

Each activity has been designed to help children engage with it in a thoughtful way that promotes both skills and concepts. For example, early in the number unit, a cardinality activity called *Bag It* is introduced. In the first task of *Bag It*, individual

Planning Chart

The planning chart will help you organize and schedule the activities in this unit. It shows a recommended sequence of activities. The chart also shows a recommended time frame of nine weeks for the entire unit and how the unit fits into a 32-week Big Math curriculum. To follow the schedule, plan to dedicate at least 30 minutes a day to working on math. Suggested pacing, included with each activity, will further describe the duration and the repetition of an activity. You may adapt this time frame and sequence to suit your school calendar and the needs of the children in your class.

For each activity, an X indicates the week in which the activity is introduced. Additional Xs indicate that the activity should be continued in those weeks. Shading to the right of an X indicates that the activity is linked to Continuing Assessment and should be repeated regularly throughout the school year.

What Are Numbers?

No.	Activity	Pg.	1	2	3	4	5	6	7	8	9	10	11	12	13	14	15	16	17	18	19	20	21	22	23	24	25	26	27	28	29	30	31	32
1	Count, Clap, and Stomp	1	X	X	X	X	X																											
2	Show Me	2	X																															
3	Henrietta Sees Numbers	4	X	X																														
4	Bag It!	6		X	X	X																												
5	Did I Make a Mistake?	8			X	X																												
6	Find the Match	9				X	X																											
7	My Number Book	11					X																											
8	What Comes Next?	13				X	X																											
9	Number Match	15					X	X																										
10	Numbers With Pizzazz!	20					X	X																										
11	Let's Line Up!	22						X																										
12	If You're Happy and You Know It	24						X																										
13	Animal Parade	26								X	X																							
14	Tell a Story	28						X																										
15	A Fishy Game	29								X	X																							

Key

The Unit Storybook is introduced.

The Take-Home Game may be sent home after completing this activity.

This activity may be used for Focused Assessment.

What Are Numbers?   ix

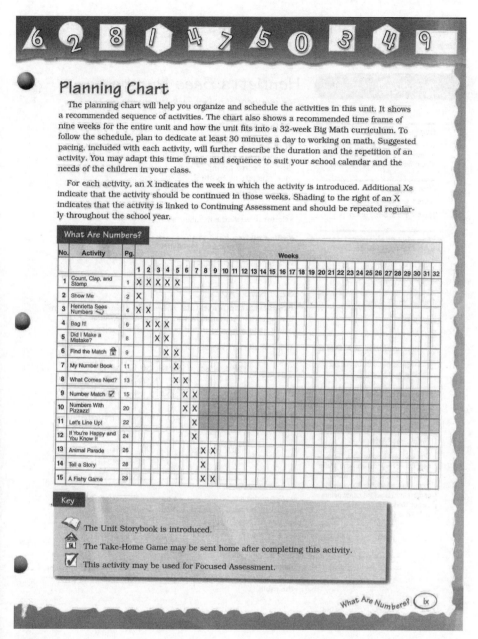

Figure 10.1 Teacher's planning chart.

children are given clear plastic bags, each labeled with a numeral, and also several small objects. The children's task is to select the number of objects indicated by the numeral on each bag, to place the correct number of objects in the appropriate

---

Activity 3	**Henrietta Sees Numbers**

See numbers of objects without counting

ABOUT THE ACTIVITY

In Brief

Shown pictures of small sets of objects, children learn first to "see" the correct number without counting and then to check their answers by counting.

Activity Goals

• Recognize one to five objects in a set without counting.

• Count to verify the number "seen."

Skills Children Need at the Start

• Count one to five objects.

• Count from 1 to 5 aloud.

GETTING READY

Preparing the Materials Make three different sets of number cards for the numbers 1 to 5. Make the cards as shown below using stickers, cutout pictures, or drawings.

• Set of different object cards

• Set of same-but-different cards (showing objects that differ from one another only by color or size)

• Set of dot cards

Setting Up For Tasks 2 and 3, seat a small group of three or four children at a table. Place the three sets of number cards on the table.

Suggested Pacing

Over a two-week period, allow several days to complete this activity and repeat Tasks 1–3 as time permits.

Group Size

Tasks 1 and 4: Whole class

Tasks 2 and 3: Small group

Language of Mathematics

count from 1 to 5

count to tell how many

1, 2, 3, 4, 5

Things You'll Need

☐ Crayons

☐ Stickers (optional)

☐ 4-by-6-inch index cards, 15 in all

☐ Classroom storybook *Henrietta Sees Numbers*

☐ Take-Home Storybooks of the same title, one for each child

Field-Test Note

One field-test teacher said, "To connect the activity to the theme of the month in our classroom, I used theme-related stickers to make the cards. I laminated the cards before putting them in my math center for children to use on their own."

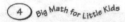
4 Big Math for Little Kids

Figure 10.2 Example number activity (subitizing).

bags, and, finally, to put each bag in a bin labeled with the same numeral. Thus, the child sees a bag with the numeral 3 on it; selects 3 objects to place in the bag; and then puts that bag into a bin also labeled 3. This activity provides children with the

LET'S GO!

Task 1 Read the classroom storybook *Henrietta Sees Numbers* to the whole class. Point out the importance of counting to verify the number of objects "seen."

Task 2 Show the card with three objects from the different object card set to the group of children. Say, **When I look at this card, I see three objects. I can see three objects quickly, without counting them.** Explain that it is important to learn to "see" how many objects there are in a group and that counting can always be used to check the number. Children take turns "seeing," as quickly as possible, the number of objects on all the sets of cards that show the numbers 1 to 3. After deciding on the number "seen," each child checks the answer by carefully pointing to and counting the objects or dots on the card.

Task 3 Repeat Task 2 but increase the number to 5. Introduce cards with one to five objects or dots in random order and frequently ask children to check their answers by pointing to and counting the pictured objects.

Task 4 After children have heard the story *Henrietta Sees Numbers* several times, distribute the Take-Home Storybooks. Read the story with the children once again and have them fill in the blanks in the incomplete sentences on pages 12–14. Then have children color their storybooks. Children can take their completed storybooks home to share with their families.

MORE TO DO

Distribute five index cards and crayons or stickers to each child. Have the children paste stickers or draw objects, from one to five, on the fronts of the cards and record the numerals on the backs. Give children templates for forming the numbers or you may record the numbers yourself. Pairs of children can then play "See the Number." One child holds up a card and a friend tries to see the number of objects as quickly as possible. The friend checks by counting and then reads the number on the back of the card.

What Are Numbers? (5)

Figure 10.3 Example number activity (importance of counting).

opportunity to relate a specific numeral to a specific quantity of items and is intended to help them to learn the concept of cardinality. Sometimes the three objects are all the same, sometimes they may be different in size, color, shape, and so on. Any objects, with any attributes can form a set of a given number. Identical red blocks can make three and so can a ball, book, and beast. When these items are tumbled around in the bags, children learn that the physical arrangement makes no difference to number. Then, in later tasks, children compare bags taken from different bins to gain an understanding of *more* and *less*.

Giving Away BMLK

Next we describe what happened when we tried to implement BMLK. Over some five years or so, we took field notes of what we saw in local preschools and child care centers, almost all of them serving lower income children, as teachers attempted to implement the program. The "we" here refers not only to the authors but also to teams of dedicated Teachers College students and others[1] who had a deep interest in the project and who devoted considerable time and energy to producing an accurate record of what occurred. We all learned to take field notes together. We reviewed each other's notes. We compared notes taken by two observers in the same classroom; and we observed videotaped lessons and commented on them. As time went by we developed a format to help observers focus on key classroom phenomena and to organize notes for ease of future reference. The format included sections on administrative details, description of the classroom environment, classroom activities, discussions with the teacher, and personal reflections. We organize the field notes in terms of several major themes, beginning with the children themselves.

Children learning math in school

It is one thing to observe children at home or in everyday play. It is another to see how young children respond to mathematics *instruction* deliberately introduced into the preschool classroom.

> On the first day of school, 4-year-old Anita announces, "Teach me something!" When the startled teacher asked her what she wanted to learn, Anita replied that she was the teacher and should know.

Young children generally begin schooling with positive motivation and self-confidence. They eagerly ask parents to purchase school supplies and look

[1] We acknowledge the excellent observational and writing skills of Joanna Cannon, Maria Cordero, Tracy Curran, Janet Eisenband, Michelle Galanter, Ashley Lewis, Leslie Manlapig, Mary Elizabeth Miller, Melissa Morgenlander, Ayla Tektas, and Angelika Yiassemides.

forward with great eagerness (and some anxiety as well) to going to nursery school or kindergarten. Of course, they may be frightened when they first have to leave a parent at the class room door, but they see going to school as part of growing up and are at first excited to be students. Even preschool children ask teachers for homework, because that is what they have seen big children do. They are not yet afraid of learning mathematics. It is unfortunate that students' motivation often decreases within the first few years of school, most likely because of educational factors like boring and inappropriate teaching (Arnold & Doctoroff, 2003, p. 521). But at the outset, young children are thrilled about going to school.

For this reason, children can have a wonderful time working with BMLK, even though the teacher has determined the topic and "imposes" the activity on them. For example, four-year-old children were engaged in a pattern activity in which they were asked to copy a particular pattern involving different types of pasta.

> *Once a child had made the same pattern on the string, Ms. Sally would tie it off, have the child put it on as a necklace, and send them off to play in another area. The children LOVED it! And the other children in the room were now paying attention, so as soon as one child left, another would take her place.*

In another example, kindergarten children had just finished one of the BMLK activities.

> *As they got into line at the door, Ms. Mary started helping one child, and the other children started asking me questions. So I started asking them questions, too. "What's your favorite number? How high can you count?" Gianni claimed she could count to 100. So I asked if I could hear her. All of the children joined in. They clapped as they counted. When they got to 19, they paused a moment before Gianni said "20". Then they all chimed back in with 21. When they got to 29, they paused, but instead of saying 30, Gianni said, "100". Ms. Mary corrected her, saying, "30". So they counted 30 to 39. Again, they paused, and again, Gianni said, "100". This time Ms. Mary let it go.*

So children can enjoy mathematics in school as well as at home. We have written (Ginsburg, 2006) about another example in which a group of low-income kindergarten children decided during free play to count a large collection of beads until they reached 100. In the same classroom, two girls invented a game in which they counted by 2s until they were beyond 30. In other words, children may freely play with formal mathematics, just as they play with blocks. They also like to play teacher, giving each other various tasks and even assessing the learning outcome.

Children's enjoyment of instruction and mathematical activities extends beyond number. We have seen children exhibit great excitement as they engage in activities like using information on a map to search for hidden objects or, without looking, reaching in a bag to find the shape that is a triangle or hexagon.

Of course, young children do not always love to learn mathematics in school. Sometimes they are bored; sometimes the tasks or materials they are given are boring; and sometimes the teacher is boring. A domineering teacher can frighten them. We have seen many bad mathematics lessons involving teachers trying to implement BMLK. Our point is that it need not be so. There is nothing necessarily painful or pressured about early mathematics instruction. Children look forward to schooling and can enjoy skillful mathematics instruction. So the children are ready for school. Are the schools and teachers ready for them?

The Social and Political Context

We attempted to give away BMLK to teachers who must operate within a larger social and political context – the world of governmental requirements and social inequalities within the United States.

Pressure to implement ECME

The United States suffers from a major and unacceptable educational problem: low-SES children, a group comprised of a disproportionate number of African Americans and Latinos (National Center for Children in Poverty, 1996), show lower average levels of academic achievement than do their middle and upper SES peers (Arnold & Doctoroff, 2003; Denton & West, 2002) and also suffer more than do others from deficient and deplorable schooling (Lee & Burkham, 2002). Some years ago, the federal government passed the "No child left behind" legislation (NCLB, 2001), the laudable purpose of which was to improve academic achievement, especially among the poor. Several states, including Texas and New Jersey, have mandated ECME for low-income children. Head Start is considering expansion of its limited mathematics curriculum.

Various prestigious reports advocated implementation of ECME as one step towards remedying an unacceptable situation. A committee of the National Research Council (Bowman, Donovan, & Burns, 2001) proposed that children are "eager to learn" and that organized preschool instruction should help them to do so. Soon thereafter, the two leading early childhood professional organizations issued a joint position statement providing guidelines for mathematics teaching and curriculum appropriate for this age group (National Association for the

Education of Young Children & National Council of Teachers of Mathematics, 2002).[2] The National Research Council issued a report proposing extensive ECME (Cross, Woods, & Schweingruber, 2009). The National Science Foundation and the Institute for Educational Sciences have funded the development of new mathematics curricula for young children (including BMLK). And the recent Common Core initiative (National Governors Association Center for Best Practices & Council of Chief State School Officers, 2010) has again stressed the importance of teaching basic mathematics concepts to young children.

This was the larger political and intellectual context in which our work took place. The result was that states and local governments felt strong pressure to implement ECME. Another way of putting it was that the impetus for ECME came from the top down: states and school districts *mandated* ECME to many schools thaat did not implement it at all or in what we would consider a serious and extensive form.

In our experience, parents' reaction to these developments was largely related to social class. We have seen two major points of view. Curiously, both upper income and lower income parents favored rigorous ECME, whereas middle income parents tended to favor a laissez faire approach.

Upper income parents were concerned about their children's chances of eventually being admitted to very prestigious colleges.

The mothers at [wealthy preschool A] are worried about whether their kids will be admitted into Harvard or Columbia.

These parents were very much in favor of anything that could increase their children's chances of admission to prestigious private schools and eventually colleges. They were willing and financially able to provide their children with tutors and therapists. For example, after the senior author gave a talk arguing that they should not exert too much pressure on their children, several upper income parents offered to hire him as a mathematics tutor. For these parents, ECME was another promising method for promoting their children's success.

Low-income parents also supported ECME, but for another reason.

The parents at [low-income center B] are worried about whether their kids will be placed in special education.

These parents knew that school failure was common for low-income children and saw special education as a pit from which their children would never emerge.

---

[2] We are not neutral with respect to these reports. The senior author served on all of these committees.

Most low-income parents we encountered cared deeply about their children and wanted them to receive a good education, beginning with "learning their numbers." Low-income parents – like their upper income counterparts, living in another world – supported any efforts made to prepare their children for school. One of the observers captured the key differences between the two social class groups as follows:

> *The Center A mothers are concerned about getting the best for their kids; the mothers at Center B are concerned about avoiding the worst. From the earliest days of preschool the social class disparities are blatant and shocking.*

We did not work a great deal with middle class parents but found that they seemed to take a laissez faire approach. They certainly cared about their children and wanted them to succeed in school, but were also concerned about placing too much pressure on them. Many parents had every reason to believe that their children would do well in elementary school and, hence, did not feel the need for ECME, which they may have seen as a potentially unpleasant academic (in the pejorative sense) intrusion into their children's natural and happy development.

In any event, in the United States, not only do the federal and state education authorities wish to promote ECME; many parents do as well. The result is pressure to implement ECME, particularly for low-income children.

Introducing the program from the top down

Our attempts to implement BMLK took place mostly in low-income schools and childcare centers in New York City and New Jersey. In these places, district level officials – not the teachers – made the decision to implement BMLK. We will describe teacher reactions in more detail later, but for now we can say that generally neither they or the center directors or building principals were eager to implement *any* mathematics program. Our experience reflected what we think is a general situation in education: many of the intended recipients of a particular innovation did not ask for or want the wonderful thing others created. In the United States, the push for ECME came from the top and has largely been imposed on unwilling teachers.

We have felt ambivalent about this situation. We believe that imposing a solution on the unwilling is morally unappealing and perhaps ineffective as well. It would be preferable to have the masses of teachers yearning for effective ECME. But because that is simply not the case, our judgment is that the need to promote children's education should trump the teachers' and administrators' sensibilities. We hope that eventually teachers and other educators can be helped to understand the necessity for ECME and to realize that it can be enjoyable and developmentally appropriate as well.

In any event, having made the decision to implement ECME, the higher educational authorities have an obligation to execute it with care and efficiency. The way in which a new program is introduced can be crucial for its future success. But we were struck over and over with how dysfunctional education systems can be, at least in the poor areas (of some major cities!) in which we worked. In one district, we learned that the BMLK curriculum materials intended for a particular school seemed to have disappeared. Only after a period of weeks did we learn that someone had placed them in a closet, not in the appropriate classroom.

In another school, the center director agreed to implement the curriculum, but failed to communicate her intention to the teachers or other relevant staff. This led to some embarrassment for a member of our team who was in the classroom to help the teacher implement BMLK.

The math teacher, Ms. Silver, was in the room with a bucket of plastic shapes. Ms. Wilson, the center director, introduced me to her. I attempted to explain who I am, and why I am in the room that she is supposed to teach math in. This was an awkward moment: no one had informed the math teacher that we or at least the curriculum exists!

In a large urban district, the administration decided to implement BMLK, but failed to tell the teachers to stop using the curriculum already in their classrooms. Some of the teachers tried to do both, which led to considerable confusion.

This lengthy anecdote reports some obstacles that an outsider may find hard to believe. Certainly, the observer was incredulous about what occurred.

First stop: Mrs. Baker's kindergarten class. I was informed beforehand that at 9 a.m. the class had their scheduled Math time. This seemed too convenient to be true. Indeed, upon arrival I was told that the children were still elsewhere having breakfast. Then I was surprised to find two surprised teachers (Mrs. Baker and her aide). I soon realized that they had no idea about me coming today. In addition I was informed that Tuesday is the day that they have "prep time" at 9 a.m., during which another teacher takes over the class for math.

I explained that we would have to figure out a good time that I would be able to come in and observe her implementing the curriculum. We all went downstairs to the teachers' room where we made desperate attempts to figure out a good time for all. The following scene lasted about an hour: They ran me through their morning schedule during which every single day is packed with specified activities and topics, as well as meetings with a purpose unknown to an outsider. At this point another teacher showed up, sat down and would not stop talking: she demanded to know who I am, where I am from, why I am there, had I taught before and where, and proceeded to tell me her life story which consisted mostly of information on the topic "Why I hate teaching kindergarten."

After this, I met another administrator, Ms. Green, who offered to help me. But she had no idea which classrooms we were supposed to visit, in what order, and where they were located. Another administrator, Ms. Anderson, gave us the math schedule, which happens to be the same for every single one of the Pre-Ks. How was I to be present at all three at the same time was beyond me.

Clearly, those who decide to impose a new program need to take careful and extensive measures to introduce it effectively and to provide appropriate supports. At the very least, administration, principals or directors, and teachers all need to agree that the program will be implemented and that the materials for it will be available. Although the need for communication among these groups seems obvious, our experience was that they hardly spoke with one another. Dysfunctional school systems are a major obstacle to successful introduction of any new program.

But even if dysfunction is ameliorated, other real obstacles remain.

Five major challenges

1. *Competing initiatives*. One challenge we faced was to introduce a new mathematics curriculum at the same time that teachers were just beginning to implement new "literacy" curricula. In the United States, federal authorities have exerted considerable pressure on educators to improve literacy and indeed introduced this mandate before they stressed the importance of mathematics. Consequently, teachers who are just beginning to come to grips with the challenge to introduce literacy activities – a subject they regard with less apprehension than they do mathematics – must now also take on the (to them) less attractive task of learning to teach mathematics. The teachers are on overload.

2. *The accountability constraint*. Early childhood teachers in the United States also face a second challenge, namely preparing children for high stakes testing and preparing for their own "testing" in the form of outside evaluations, all of which are intended to hold teachers, centers, and administrations accountable.

Sadie explained to me that tomorrow a lot of people from the Board of Ed. will be coming over to evaluate her classroom. She had gone through great pains to label everything in both English and Spanish, for example.

Isabelle removed from the wall all of the letters she had placed there because she was about to receive an outside evaluation and did not want to be caught in an unauthorized practice (the district felt that letters were inappropriate for children).

In another instance, we were told to suspend implementation of BMLK because teachers had to prepare their children to take the Terra Nova, a standard achievement test. Although perhaps necessary, standardized testing and outside evaluations can occupy a good deal of teachers' time and promote anxiety as well. Although many advocate that teachers and schools not "teach to the test", it is still widely done, which seems to indicate recognition that current teaching practices are insufficient for academic preparation.

3. *Finding and training good teachers*. A third challenge is staffing. In some cases, the classrooms lack sufficient personnel to effectively manage the children, let alone teach mathematics effectively. In other cases, the classrooms lack teachers who are qualified or able to teach the mathematics – examples of this are discussed in the next section.

4. *Money*, *money*, *and money*. A fourth challenge is the lack of financial resources – in the affluent United States! – for schools, for training teachers, and for parents. Many districts lack money to buy materials, to provide meaningful professional development, to provide sufficient, qualified staff to implement a mathematics curriculum effectively, and indeed to pay teachers a decent salary. Traditionally, early childhood teachers are paid at even a lower level than are elementary school teachers. Clearly low pay does not attract the most talented and able teachers and is insufficient reward for attempting the difficult task of implementing a new program.

Some individuals who could be good teachers cannot afford to go to college. At a New York City public school in which we worked:

> *A young man served as a volunteer teacher. He was wonderful with the children, who clearly could benefit from a good male role model. But more importantly, he showed talent as a teacher, helping children to do some pretty complex activities. I asked him whether he was planning to become a teacher. He said that he had to drop out of Community College [a two year college] and would not be able to get his teaching degree because college is too expensive.*

Many parents lack funds to provide meaningful material support for children's learning at home. For example:

> *After a workshop on computers in which the kindergarten children helped parents to learn what to do with computers and how to run various programs, a child asked his mother if she could get him a computer. Looking sad and defeated, the mother told her child, "No, baby, I can't get you one."*

5. *Researcher–teacher communications*. A fifth challenge is the gulf between the university and the teachers, particularly when they are from minority groups. At an initial meeting with teachers the observer was attempting to explain the need for the BMLK program and to induce them to participate in the program:

> *I suggested that they already do some interesting math activities but that they could do them better and that we could help. I sensed that they were uncomfortable. I said that we were not "picking on them," that in general the early childhood area does not support teachers much in doing educational work with young children. Then Tonia said she was*

wondering if we were working just with their school. I said that we were also going to work with [higher SES] schools and that everyone needs help in dealing with young children and that we were going to try to help teachers in other places too.

I think the somewhat unspoken issue is this from Tonia's point of view: "Why are you mostly white academics from Columbia working with us? Do you think that we are such bad teachers? You have been nice to us and we get something out of it, but are you saying that we don't know what we are doing?"

She seemed reassured that we intend to work with schools at different income levels. We need to stress that everyone at the preschool level needs help in dealing with the education of young kids, both [high and low SES], and both white and black. We have been approaching the issue by saying that we believe that the [low SES] black and Latino kids are competent, and that we are in effect advocates for them. But the issue for the teachers is not that at all: it is instead whether we think they are competent.

How hard it is to communicate with them, even though we have been there for several years, and even though they trust us to a certain degree! The barrier between the teachers and their director is large, and between us and them is even larger. We waltz in several days a week but are not really there. We are of different backgrounds. It is hard for university people to work with teachers in general, but in this case, the focus on early childhood, and the racial and SES issues magnify the difficulty tremendously.

The teachers

American teachers, particularly those teaching the poor, work under very difficult conditions, and deserve both admiration and support. Yet they can be impediments to implementing a mathematics curriculum. Or they can be heroes that make the dream come true. In our work, we encountered both types.

To begin with, many early childhood teachers simply do not want to teach mathematics. One of the senior author's students very honestly said, "My previous history as a poor math student makes me fear teaching math to young children in the future, that being partially my reason for choosing early childhood education." Another early childhood education student reported, "Many teachers do not like to teach math. In my last student teaching placement, my supervising teacher told me to take over the math lessons for the class." These students' sentiments and experiences are typical, we think, of the general population of early childhood educators.

We observed that some teachers lacked interest in or commitment to implementing the BMLK curriculum.

In one center, we watched as one teacher turned the complete responsibility of teaching the curriculum over to her assistant. Although she continued to attend the monthly workshops, she took no part in the instruction. The assistant, though, was not attending the monthly workshops. She was holding down the fort on those days, allowing the head teacher to attend.

Some teachers simply did not take the time to prepare the activities, or found excuses not to teach it.

Jenny was not prepared to do a Big Math lesson at all, but sort of attempted to introduce the Shape unit, without having read the curriculum. She admitted that she hadn't had time to read the curriculum at all.

Other teachers openly resisted implementing BMLK, claiming that it is not "developmentally appropriate" to teach mathematics to preschoolers. We have heard this unfortunate phrase bandied about more times than even we can count. Many early childhood practitioners are in a time warp. They hold to an outmoded view asserting that young children are incapable of learning something as abstract as mathematics and that intentional teaching and curriculum must be harmful to them. Those who hold this view, and hold it with ferocious passion, have admirable motives – they want children to blossom and not to suffer from a deadly educational system. They believe so deeply in what they consider to be a developmentally appropriate approach that they ignore their professional association's latest advice on the matter: that teaching can be developmentally appropriate (Bredekamp & Copple, 1997), that curriculum is necessary (National Association for the Education of Young Children & National Council of Teachers of Mathematics, 2002), and that early education should place heavy emphasis on mathematics (Cross, Woods, & Schweingruber, 2009). This is unfortunate; perhaps in-service professional development can help these teachers to rethink what is essentially a rigidly held article of faith.

Some teachers resisted teaching BMLK because they claimed they were already teaching a good deal of mathematics. Our observations showed that this was not true: what they considered to be teaching mathematics involved doing a few scattered and trivial counting or shape activities. These teachers did not understand what teaching mathematics – especially teaching the big ideas – is all about. They did not see why they have to change the way they are teaching mathematics, or why the mathematics they are teaching already is not good enough. They may not even understand the difference between the mathematics they are already teaching and the mathematics presented in BMLK.

Other obstacles arise when the teachers' personal beliefs regarding teaching are not in alignment with the philosophy with which the curriculum was designed. For example, BMLK was designed to give children – and teachers – an opportunity to engage in mathematical activities in an enjoyable way. However, some teachers believed that mathematics instruction is not fun, and should not be fun.

> *Sandra struggled to keep the kids' attention. She told them that she knew it was a beautiful day outside, and that they would get to go outside later. But first they had to do this. The way she said it, didn't make it sound like it was a fun activity, but a necessary drudgery. She also told them a few times, "We're almost done, I promise!" Which wasn't true. She started saying that 10 minutes into the hour-long activity.*

Other troublesome philosophies involve the methods and overall purposes for teaching mathematics activities. For example, after observing two different teachers teach *Bag It*, the cardinality activity described earlier, one observer wrote:

> *[Making a contrast between Catherine's teaching of the activity and Nora's…] if anyone were to ask me who I would want teaching my preschooler, I would say Catherine. Catherine had this relaxed attitude teaching the children. She let the children try to figure things out. She then had them explain and show what they did. I felt like she was really trying to see what the children understood.*
>
> *Nora had the bins, bags, and got through the task but she didn't seem so interested in seeing what the children understood. Her brisk "let's-get-through-with-this-activity-and-then-you-can- do-something-else" manner (shown by her immediate "Venus fly trap" closing of the bag once the appropriate number of items were in) made me feel like she was more interested in getting the activity done than really figuring out what her children really knew.*

Finally, some teachers disrespect their students.

> *The most shocking observation of my first day was the manner in which the teachers interacted with the children. There seems to be a widespread attitude, which I can best characterize as "teacher-centered." Teachers at this school seem to ignore the fact that these children are thinking beings with emotions, and that they too can understand comments made about them. Teachers would repeatedly make comments on the children's "inappropriate" behavior, or inability to perform a certain task in their presence, as if the children were not present! For example, one of the Room 2 teachers explained to me how one of the children is incapable of eating by himself since his mother "does everything for him" and has not allowed him to eat alone. And all these comments were made in a condescending tone, while holding the child's hand in an attempt to show him how to eat with the spoon. In Room 3, after a child had failed to answer a question, the head teacher explained to me in front of the child that the child to whom the question was addressed is not all that bright.*

To this point, we have accentuated the negative. But some teachers demonstrate a great deal of commitment (although commitment in itself is not sufficient to guarantee success).

I do have to note how my feelings of Bonnie changed today. Yes, her class is still as chaotic, and her manners are frequently still harsh and abrupt and indicate her lack of patience and control. She's always been fairly friendly, but never anything that impressed me to say that she enjoyed our presence in her classroom. But today, with the end-of-the-year interview, Bonnie really opened up to me. She is extremely grateful for what she's learned in the workshops and using the curriculum. She recognizes her personal struggles as a teacher – or at least, some struggles – and is deeply concerned and troubled with her own need to do better. During our conversation, her deep feelings toward the children, and her role as their "caretaker" each day, became quite evident. She had some very deep remarks regarding teaching, its importance, and its difficulties that truly surprised – and impressed – me. It made me realize that she's a teacher that probably has little natural talent for teaching, or few characteristics of which I consider valuable within a classroom (particularly early childhood). However, she has a desire and a deep commitment…

We have also seen teachers with a strong desire to learn the mathematics and improve their teaching. For example, after observing Christa teach *Bag It* to a small group of children, the observer noted the following discussion:

As soon as all of the children had been sent off to play, Christa turned to us and said she had a question. She quickly rearranged the bins to take them out of numerical sequence, and asked, "Should I do this?"

… I was impressed with our discussion. Her question regarding the arrangement of the bins reflected a depth of thinking that took me by surprise. She was really thinking about the impact that such presentation would have on the activity. And she was so enthusiastic and eager to talk to us and share with us.

Another example describes a vital flexibility and humility on the part of the teacher. Without these qualities, it is difficult to be open to learning something as demanding as a new curriculum.

Tracy quickly adapted her teaching to improve her work with pattern. For example, she figured out a way to help the children to better focus on the task of creating patterns. Her facilitation with each individual child, though far from perfect, adapted to each situation. I was quite impressed to see her struggle and adapt in doing this task. …Tracy seems to truly want to learn and improve. Her enthusiasm and humility are wonderful! And even though she demonstrated some limitation to her understanding of pattern (by asking "what comes next" before showing the children a whole pattern), her flexibility in looking at patterns from either end – whether intentional on her part, or not – shows great promise. So many people are so set in their thinking and their ways that they are not able to adapt or even learn. They can't get their minds out of the "little boxes" they've placed them in. But Tracy seems so flexible, so adaptable, and like she really wants to understand. I don't think she's placed such constraints on her potential.

And finally, we reiterate that many early childhood teachers are very good at what they do. Many learned to implement BMLK with skill and enjoyment. In fact, at our end-of-the-year debriefings, many teachers are enthusiastic about participation in the program and want to continue.

Teaching

Next, we discuss the teacher's use of intentional instruction. One thing we have learned is that teaching at this age level is far more complex than we had supposed. In fact, quality mathematics teaching for young children is just as complex as for older ones (Ginsburg & Amit, 2008). In a way, this should come as no surprise (although it surprised us): if young children's mathematical knowledge can be abstract and the mathematics we attempt to teach them is both deep and broad, then why should teaching such material to younger children be essentially different from teaching mathematics to elementary or even older children?

We have chosen to highlight three key aspects of teaching: knowledge of subject matter; understanding the child's mind; and productive use of materials.

Knowledge of subject matter

Teaching mathematics requires deep knowledge of the content itself. Teachers need to understand: the basic mathematical ideas; the ideas prerequisite to them (that is, what makes them possible); and how these ideas lead to further learning and concepts (that is, what comes next). The teacher also needs to know how to represent the mathematical ideas effectively for children and to recognize how a child's ideas relate to those being taught. As Dewey put it, "Really to interpret the child's present crude impulses in counting, measuring, and arranging things in rhythmic series, involves mathematical scholarship – a knowledge of the mathematical formulae and relations which have, in the history of the race, grown out of such crude beginnings" (Dewey, 1976, p. 282).

Consider what is involved, for example, in teaching pattern. The teacher must first understand what a pattern is. Most important is the idea that a pattern is a manifestation of an underlying general rule. The underlying rule may be, for example, alternation; the manifestation of it is the child's creation of a line of blocks following the sequence red (R), yellow (Y), R, Y (and so on). The "and so on" is important: the rule is general, so that the pattern can continue indefinitely. The rule enables its user not only to continue a pattern, but also to determine the color to be found if one element is hidden (as in R, Y, R, Y, _, Y...) and even to determine what color goes in the nth place (R if the number is odd and Y if it is even).

Some of the teachers we observed were able to draw upon their knowledge of pattern as they taught a lesson. For example, the next observation was made during a pattern activity that followed the reading of one of six books included with the BMLK curriculum, entitled *The Table of Phinneas Fable*. The book describes a baker making patterns out of pasta shapes – triangle, circle, square, and the like. After the book was read, four-year-old Joseph engaged in an activity that involved using different sizes (not shapes) of pasta to create pattern necklaces.

> *Joseph came to the table and had started putting a "pattern" together. Big, big, medium, medium, small, small, medium... and the child was reaching for another piece of pasta when Karen asked him to name his pattern. The child points to the left and starts naming, "triangle, square, circle..." Karen asks if these are really those shapes, and the child says "no". She asks him if he's pretending to be Phinneas, and the boy shakes his head "yes". She then asks him to continue, and name the pieces. The boy started over again, but this time pointed to the right end, and started naming right to left. Karen said, "you can start from that side if you want," but after it became clear that he wasn't really making a pattern, Karen reminded him that a pattern is something that goes over and over again. She suggested that he stop with the first two – medium, small – and had him repeat it.*

In brief, because Karen understood that a pattern must be based on an underlying rule and that it need not go in a particular direction, she was able to help Joseph begin to grapple with the idea of pattern.

Understanding of the mathematics also enables the teacher to focus children's attention on salient features of an activity to facilitate understanding. Donna demonstrates this ability during her teaching of *Bag It* to a group of four-year-olds.

> *Donna pointed to the "two" bag she had just been working on with the children. She asked, "How many buttons do you see?" The children responded, "one." She then pointed to the number on the bag, "What number do you see?" "2." She then talked them through adding another button, then had them count the buttons again, identify the number on the bag, and asked whether they matched. She then repeated this process for a "one" bag, then went to the "three" bag. For each bag, when she would ask how many buttons there were in the bag, she would cover the numeral with her hand so they weren't looking at it.*

Donna knew the difference between the cardinal number of objects in the bag and the numeral representing the number. She knew that the children needed to link these two ideas, and that a strategy was needed to guide the children's selection of the objects that determine the cardinal number demanded by the numeral. Knowing these things, she was able to direct children's attention, as appropriate, to the objects' cardinal number and its representation.

Unfortunately, not all teachers we observed had mathematical knowledge as sound as Karen's or Donna's. For example, we have seen many early childhood teachers showing children two objects, like R, Y, and then asking the children, "What comes next?" The correct answer is, of course, that it is impossible to tell because sufficient evidence is not yet available. Also, some teachers insist that a pattern can only be examined from left to right.

> Jackie told her [a four-year-old child] to name her pattern. The little girl pointed to the wheel on the right side of her mat and began pointing and naming, right to left. Jackie stopped her, though, and said, "No, start from the other side."

Unfortunately, research has shown that elementary teachers often lack a deep understanding of the mathematics they teach (Ball, 1993; Ma, 1999). It is perhaps not surprising that many early childhood teachers – who typically have less education than do elementary school teachers – would also lack understanding of the (nontrivial) mathematics they are now expected to teach (often for the first time). But there is no way around it. A teacher must know what he/she is to teach if he/she is to help the students learn it deeply.

Understanding the child's mind

A second key aspect of teaching mathematics is being able to understand the child's mind (Ginsburg, 2009). (Karen did this when she inferred from Joseph's use of the shape names that he was trying to imitate Phinneas.) Knowledge of children's understanding is necessary for planning appropriate instruction. Acquiring such knowledge enables a teacher to recognize that a child may know the underlying concept even when she gets a *wrong* answer, and that another child may not understand the concept even when he gets a *correct* answer. That is, the child who seems to know something does not and the child who seems not to know something does. The first step in being able to understand the child is having an explicit intent to do so.

To illustrate what is involved in understanding the child's thinking, we describe a "challenge question" activity we have given to our BMLK (and other) teachers.

Figure 10.4 Challenge question.

The challenge involves asking teachers to interpret various children's correct or incorrect responses to the cardinality activity *Bag It*, as shown in Figure 10.4.

Consider the child's response to the bag labeled 2. He clearly placed the wrong number of objects into the bag, so that the teacher who considers only right and wrong answers will conclude that the child does not understand the number 2. But in this case, the child may have interpreted the task as requiring the placement of pairs of objects – that is, two of the same kind– in the bag. The child certainly knows what two objects are in the context of pairs, although from this response it is not clear if he knows about 2 in other contexts.

Or consider the response to the 4 bag. Many teachers say that the wrong response could have been a result of simple miscounting of objects and does not *necessarily* indicate lack of knowledge of 4. Another teacher raised another possibility: conceivably, the child may have placed in the bag 4 different *types* of objects, fruit, doll, block, and vehicle. This is unlikely, although possible. But whether or not the interpretation is correct, it does involve an admirable attempt to take the child's perspective and to arrive at an understanding of his thinking.

Another example is the 3 bag. Here are two different teacher responses.

> *The child understood the concept. The child put the correct amount of objects in the bag. I appreciated the child putting the same objects in the bag.*

Note that this answer – which is entirely plausible – simply focuses on correct response. But here is another, more sophisticated interpretation.

> *Yes, the child could understand about quantity, but also not understand about differences of objects. He might believe that every object has to be the same in order to match the number.*

The second teacher of course notes the child's correct answer and appreciates that it might indicate understanding. But she goes beyond the child's response to contemplate other ways in which the child might understand the problem. In a sense, the first teacher takes a "behaviorist" approach, and the second a "cognitive" approach. The example does not provide sufficient information to eliminate either teacher's hypothesis, but the exercise reveals key aspects of the teachers' approaches, each of which clearly leads to different teaching strategies.

Here is an example of a teacher who takes the behaviorist approach in her classroom.

> *Nora gave each child a bag with 0, 1, 2, and 3. Then she gave each child another bag with 6 items inside. She told the children to dump the items from this bag out onto the table, take a bag, and if it says '1', to put one thing in, [and so on].*
>
> *Nora was [working with a boy]. She held up one of his bags and asked what number it was. He correctly identified "one". "Can you put one item in?" and he dropped in one item. "How many are in here?" And he responded, "one". Then she showed him the "two" bag, but he identified the number as "three". She asked another child to help him, and she said it was "two". She then asked the boy to put two items into the bag. He did. Then she moved to the "three" bag. He couldn't identify the number, so she again got another child to help him. Then she asked him to put three items in. He picked up two blocks at once and dropped them in. Nora said, "two...", then stopped him as he went to drop in a whole handful of items.*
>
> *As she continued this same process with one more child, I realized something. Nora was having the children fill the bags, sure, and was counting the objects with them (or for them) as they dropped them in. But as soon as they had the right number of objects in the bag, she would immediately ask them her next question, or if they tried to put in another object, she would close the bag opening in her fist to prevent them, such that she was forcing them to get the correct number of objects in their bags.*

Clearly the teacher was eliciting and reinforcing correct responses. But she did not in any way attempt to consider the thinking underlying the child's response. She did not ask the child why he did what he did. She did not even let him play out his responses so that she could observe what he wanted to do. We think this is a big mistake; it limits teaching options. The teacher had no idea what the child understood or failed to understand and hence no idea about how to help him. Our claim is that the cognitive approach is superior: it suggests various teaching activities responsive to the child's cognitive needs. How can you teach effectively if you do not know what the child knows?

Here is an example.

> On Ms. Theresa's table there were four bowls – one with yarn pieces, one with short lengths of straws (some red, some purple), one with orange colored ziti, and one with green and purple colored penne. She told them that she had three bowls with different shapes and colors and identified them with the children. They named the straw pieces SHORTs, the ziti FATs, and the penne LONGs. She then showed them a pattern of the shapes she had taped to a piece of cardboard – SHORT, LONG, SHORT, LONG, SHORT, LONG. She told the children to take their strings and make this pattern.
>
> [Later] Ms. Theresa turned her attention to the two children who had not yet successfully completed the first pattern. By this point, the boy had finished stringing all of his pieces. Ms. Theresa said, "This is good. What's the pattern?" The boy started from the right and said LONG GREEN, LONG GREEN, LONG GREEN then SHORT RED, SHORT RED, SHORT RED. Ms. Theresa followed his lead. "So you made your own pattern. What would come next?" He said LONG GREEN, LONG GREEN, LONG GREEN. Ms. Theresa gave him three more greens and had him add them to his pattern.

So a second key aspect of teaching, at any level, is understanding the student's mind.

Use of materials

A third key element of teaching is the selection and use of materials or manipulatives in teaching mathematics. If used appropriately, manipulatives can improve students' achievement (Ball, 1992; Baroody, 1989). But as we will see, effective use of manipulatives is neither simple nor obvious and requires serious thought on the teacher's part.

The BMLK curriculum often states what *types* of materials are to be used for each activity, thus leaving room for teacher choice. But even when the list of materials is quite specific, teachers may choose substitutes because of their convenience or availability, or even because of personal preference. We found that some teachers have difficulty in choosing appropriate manipulatives. For example, the *Bag It* activity guide specifies the following regarding the items to be placed into the bags: objects for counting (such as counters, tiles, buttons, and plastic people, animals, and cars). We have seen teachers present their children with many different materials to be counted, from a selection of connecting cubes to a variety of different counters, and from an array of buttons to a box of toys. Each of these choices has ramifications, as different materials can represent the mathematics in different ways. For example, some plastic cubes can be connected with each other. When this is done, is the result two cubes or one combined cube? A child might legitimately assume that either is the case, with the result that confusion ensues.

One teacher presented her children with a bin of various counters and other math materials, including number cubes.

> *I observed one girl who found a cube with numerals on each side (a die with numbers). She turned it around and around until she saw the number "3". Then she put it in her 3 bag. She found another number die with a 2 on it and put it in her 2 bag. When the teacher came to correct, she said, "You only have one in each!"*

The teacher had not recognized in either her selection or her assessment how the material could represent a mathematical idea in a way she had not intended. The selection and use of materials is not easy. To do so effectively requires an analysis of the materials' properties, knowledge of the mathematics, and consideration of the fit between the materials and the mathematics. It also requires taking the child's perspective to anticipate potential difficulties and confusions.

For example, consider a teacher who was working with the pasta necklace activity that follows the reading of *The Table of Phinneas Fable*. She had given careful thought to the mathematical fit of her materials, their alignment with the mathematical content of the activity, and the child's possible interpretation of them.

> *Doris said that when she was looking for the materials this morning, she had found some colored macaroni, but didn't want to use the colored macaroni yet, as the color introduces another element to patterns, which she didn't feel most of the children were ready for yet. She also acknowledged that the whole pasta thing presented other problems. She's found that she can't use the actual names of the pastas because many children's experiences are that everything is "macaroni". That's why she calls them by their size. But she also talked about how the pasta pieces don't align with the shapes presented in the story. She said that*

next time she might have them use cookie cutters with play dough and have them cut shapes – as that would be more of a direct translation from the story.

Teachers need to think deeply about the materials they use if they are to help children learn the intended mathematical ideas. The selection and use of materials is another demonstration of our claim that early childhood teaching level is complex – more complex than usually assumed.

Evaluation

BMLK has undergone an evaluation study (Lewis-Presser, Clements, Ginsburg, & Ertle, 2015) to determine its efficacy for helping young children learn math. The study involved a two-year longitudinal cluster-randomized control trial involving two groups, *BMLK* and a Business-as-Usual group that for the most part used *Creative Curriculum* (Dodge et al., 2002). During the study we conducted many informal classroom observations, many of which were reported earlier.

The formal evaluation study focused on overall student achievement. The primary outcome measure for the study was the Early Childhood Longitudinal Study, Birth Cohort (ECLS-B) Direct Mathematics Assessment (National Center for Educational Statistics, 2000). This measure is not directly tied to the *BMLK* curriculum and thus allowed for a general evaluation of its success. The study also employed a short mathematics language measure that focused on vocabulary and verbal justification.

The results of the study showed that the BMLK group performed better than the comparison group, although the significant difference between the two groups did not emerge until the kindergarten year. The study also offered modest support for the proposition that BMLK children were more adept than the comparison children in employing both mathematical words and justifications.

With these results, it appears that even given contextual factors (like the chaos of the schools) and implementation challenges (like curriculum materials in closets, not classrooms), an ECME curriculum that introduces big ideas, structured teaching, and a developmental sequence can have an overall positive impact on children's learning of mathematics.

Although the results are generally supportive of BMLK, and although we recognize that evaluation is essential, our general conclusion is that the evaluation was largely a waste of time and effort. Here is why.

First, the evaluation measure, which our funder required us to use, yields very little insight into what the children learned. The ECLS-B measures the general "construct" of mathematics achievement and is "valid" in the very general sense that it correlates with other, similar measures. But this kind of validity is a circular process: none of the available global measures, including the TEMA (Ginsburg & Baroody, 2003), of which one of us is an author, provides useful information into the specifics of children's learning – for example, the kinds of strategies they use to solve problems. The traditional concept of concurrent validity merely assures that one global test receives its imprimatur through its correlation with another global test. The general measures do not provide the kind of information that a cognitive psychologist, teacher, or mathematics educator would find of interest: strategy, concepts, motivation, and the like.

Second, the overall evaluation results are of not any practical value for teachers. Although showing that, in general, BMLK "works," the results say nothing about classroom practices that might be effective or ineffective. Surely not everything in BMLK or any other program is perfect. Any extensive mathematics curriculum involves a host of educational practices and materials that vary in quality and effectiveness. Insight into what "works" at this level would be valuable for educators; but the general measures are mute on issues like these.

Third, evaluation is best conducted not with typical classrooms but with atypical ones: those with talented teachers in supportive environments who implement the program effectively. In one case, two experienced teachers provided a rich setting in which to evaluate a program (Gersten, 2005). Sometimes evaluation efforts attempt to control for this factor by employing measures of "fidelity of implementation." In fact, we used such measures. But we learned that they are not very effective: it is easy to see whether teachers implemented a particular lesson, but it is very hard to measure how well they did it. And, of course, it is impossible to know whether and how well teachers implement lessons on days when they are not observed. So not only are general measures of children's learning weak, but also there do not appear to be sound standard methods for measuring effective early mathematics teaching.

We believe that current "rigorous" approaches to evaluation have got everything backwards. The research should build from the bottom up. Gersten (2005) recommends use of small "design experiments" in which student interviews play a key role. Evaluation should begin with deep, qualitative analyses of teaching and learning in the all too rare classrooms run by talented teachers. The goal should be to gain insight into the teaching and learning of specific topics in specific lessons. The researcher, along with the teacher, should do a kind of "lesson study" (Mast & Ginsburg, 2009) uncovering what "works" and what does not. The process should aim at the iterative improvement of the activities and at the identification and measurement of both effective teaching and deep student learning. Work like this would take years to accomplish. But then the conventional evaluation studies could draw on the research insights to produce valuable information concerning student achievement.

We regret that we did not spend our evaluation time on the kinds of qualitative studies just described. Had we done so, we would know a lot more than that BMLK seems to "work." We would have some insight into what works and how. And we might even have gained knowledge that would allow us to develop better overall tests of teaching and learning that could be "valid" in a large scale evaluation study of curriculum use in typical conditions.

But we could never have been funded to do that kind of work. The conventional wisdom in the field does not consider the approach we describe to be sufficiently rigorous. We believe that strategies for evaluation need to be re-evaluated, and that the field could benefit more from cognitive insights and careful observation by both researchers and master teachers than from traditional psychometrics.

Conclusions

As we have seen, there is a long journey from psychological research that results in creation of a curriculum – the thing to be given away – to its successful implementation in a classroom. The research plays a vital role: it provides the intellectual foundation for the innovation. But many other factors are substantially more influential than is research in determining the success of the enterprise. In the United States at least (we cannot speak for other countries), political forces are largely responsible both for initiating the journey and for making it difficult to undertake. The federal government paid for creation of various early mathematics curricula. Many states have adopted a "common core" of math standards (National Governors Association Center for Best Practices & Council of Chief State School Officers, 2010). From our point of view, this is all to the good.

But these public authorities have at the same time largely failed to provide adequate funding or support for implementation of the mandated programs. Thus, school systems often fail to provide teachers with useful and intensive in-service workshops, coaching, and lesson study. The school systems often fail to involve talented and knowledgeable teachers in the implementation process, for example, to decide how the new curriculum can best be integrated with other classroom activities and curricula. How a reform is introduced may be almost as important as its content. Government authorities also fail to pay adequate teacher salaries and, therefore, cannot attract or retain the most talented individuals. The United States system of higher education is also complicit in the failure: courses in early childhood mathematics are rare in colleges and universities, which often see education as a low status topic of study (Hyson & Woods, 2014).

In short, within the United States, the body politic seems to appreciate the need for ECME but does not have the will or desire to support it adequately. Psychological research provided a framework for development of new mathematics curricula; but public policy and the values on which it is based play the lion's role in determining the success of their implementation.

The difficulties of improving education often lead to feelings of helplessness and despair. Maria Montessori, the famous early childhood educator who worked in the early 1900s with children in the slums of Rome, put it like this: "Ah, before such dense and willful disregard of the life which is growing within these children, we should hide our heads in shame and cover our guilty faces with our hands!" (Montessori, 1964). And the very rational philosopher Alfred North Whitehead, who with Bertrand Russell wrote one of the seminal books on the foundations of mathematics, said, "When one considers... the importance of this question of the education of a nation's young, the broken lives, the defeated hopes, the national failures, which result from the frivolous inertia with which it is treated, it is difficult to restrain within oneself a savage rage" (Whitehead, 1929).

What then can we as psychologists do? We can conduct research that will illuminate children's thinking, the strategies they use, their mathematical metacognition and language, and their conceptual models. This kind of knowledge can transform teachers' understanding of children's learning and their approaches to teaching. It may also be true that we have something to learn from talented teachers' insights into classroom learning! Our research can also contribute to a sensible approach to evaluation that is not based solely on the kind of global measures now considered "valid."

We can also contribute in a major way to the single most important problem in American education, and perhaps in education around the world, namely the professional development of teachers at all levels (Ginsburg, Hyson, & Woods, 2014).

We have seen that young children want to learn mathematics and that mathematics curricula are available for teachers to use. But teachers of young children often do not want to teach mathematics, do not understand it or their students, or do not know how to teach it. This needs to be changed. Psychologists can assist by involving themselves in the college or university education of prospective teachers and in the in-service education of practicing teachers. We can help them to understand the child's mind and the processes of teaching and learning. Doing so is another useful way in which we can give away psychology for the public good. And we can only hope that the political system and society as a whole will decide to value children's education.

References

Anderson, A. (1993). Wondering – One child's questions and mathematics learning. *Canadian Children, 18*(2), 26–30.

Arnold, D. H., & Doctoroff, G. L. (2003). The early education of socioeconomically disadvantaged children. *Annual Review of Psychology, 54*, 517–545.

Ball, D. L. (1992). Magical hopes: Manipulatives and the reform of math education. *American Educator, 16*(1), 14–18, 46–47.

Ball, D. L. (1993). With an eye on the mathematical horizon: Dilemmas of teaching elementary school mathematics. *The Elementary School Journal, 93*(4), 373–397.

Baroody, A. J. (1985). Mastery of basic number combinations: Internalization of relationships or facts? *Journal for Research in Mathematics Education, 16*, 83–98.

Baroody, A. J. (1989). Manipulatives don't come with guarantees. *The Arithmetic Teacher, 37*(2), 4–5.

Baroody, A. J. (1992). The development of preschoolers' counting skills and principles. In J. Bideaud, C. Meljac, & J. P. Fischer (Eds.), *Pathways to number: Children's developing numerical abilities* (pp. 99–126). Hillsdale, NJ: Lawrence Erlbaum Associates.

Baroody, A. J., Lai, M., & Mix, K. S. (2006). The development of young children"s early number and operation sense and its implications for early childhood education. In B. Spodek & O. Saracho (Eds.), *Handbook of research on the education of young children* (Vol. 2, pp. 187–221). Mahwah, NJ: Lawrence Erlbaum Associates.

Baroody, A. J., & Wilkins, J. L. M. (1999). The development of informal counting, number, and arithmetic skills and concepts. In J. V. Copley (Ed.), *Mathematics in the early years* (pp. 48–65). Reston, VA: National Council of Teachers of Mathematics.

Bloom, L. (1970). *Language development: Form and function in emerging grammars*. Research Monograph No. 59. Cambridge, MA: MIT Press.

Bowman, B. T., Donovan, M. S., & Burns, M. S. (Eds.). (2001). *Eager to learn: Educating our preschoolers*. Washington, DC: National Academy Press.

Bredekamp, S., & Copple, C. (Eds.). (1997). *Developmentally appropriate practice in early childhood programs* (Revised ed.). Washington, DC: National Association for the Education of Young Children.

Brosterman, N. (1997). *Inventing kindergarten*. New York: Harry N. Abrams, Inc.

Brush, L. R. (1978). Preschool children's knowledge of addition and subtraction. *Journal for Research in Mathematics Education, 9*, 44–54.

Case, R., & Okamoto, Y. (1996). The role of central conceptual structures in the development of children's thought. *Monographs of the Society for Research in Child Development, 61*(Serial No. 246, Nos. 1–2).

Clements, D. H. (1999). Geometric and spatial thinking in young children. In J. V. Copley (Ed.), *Mathematics in the early years* (pp. 66–79). Reston, VA: National Council of Teachers of Mathematics.

Clements, D. H. (2007). Curriculum research: Toward a framework for "research-based curricula". *Journal for Research in Mathematics Education, 38*(1), 35–70.

Clements, D. H., & Sarama, J. (2007). Early childhood mathematics learning. In F. K. Lester (Ed.), *Second handbook of research on mathematics teaching and learning* (pp. 461–555). Charlotte, NC: Information Age Publishing.

Clements, D. H., Sarama, J., & DiBiase, A.-M. (Eds.). (2004). *Engaging young children in mathematics: Standards for early childhood mathematics education*. Mahwah, NJ: Lawrence Erlbaum Associates.

Copley, J. V., Jones, C., & Dighe, J. (2007). *Mathematics: The creative curriculum approach*. Washington, DC: Teaching Strategies.

Court, S. R. A. (1920). Numbers, time, and space in the first five years of a child's life. *Pedagogical Seminary, 27*, 71–89.

Cross, C. T., Woods, T. A., & Schweingruber, H. (Eds.). (2009). *Mathematics learning in early childhood: Paths toward excellence and equity*. Washington, DC: National Academy Press.

Denton, K., & West, J. (2002). *Children's reading and mathematics achievement in kindergarten and first grade*. Washington, DC: National Center for Education Statistics.

Dewey, J. (1976). The child and the curriculum. In J. A. Boydston (Ed.), *John Dewey: The middle works, 1899–1924. Volume 2: 1902–1903* (pp. 273–291). Carbondale, IL: Southern Illinois University Press.

Dodge, D. T., Colker, L., & Heroman, C. (2002). *The creative curriculum for preschool* (4th ed.). Washington, DC: Teaching Strategies, Inc.

Durkin, K., Shire, B., Riem, R., Crowther, R. D., & Rutter, D. R. (1986). The social and linguistic context of early number word use. *British Journal of Developmental Psychology, 4*, 269–288.

Edwards, C., Gandini, L., & Forman, G. (Eds.). (1993). *The hundred languages of children: the Reggio Emilia approach to early childhood education*. Norwood, NJ: Ablex.

Gelman, R. (1980). What young children know about numbers. *Educational Psychologist, 15*, 54–68.

Gersten, R. (2005). Behind the scenes of an intervention research study. *Learning Disabilities Research & Practice, 20*(4), 200–212.

Ginsburg, H. P. (2006). Mathematical play and playful mathematics: A guide for early education. In D. Singer, R. M. Golinkoff, & K. Hirsh-Pasek (Eds.), *Play = Learning: How play motivates and enhances children's cognitive and social-emotional growth* (pp. 145–165). New York, NY: Oxford University Press.

Ginsburg, H. P. (2009). The challenge of formative assessment in mathematics education: Children's minds, teachers' minds. *Human Development, 52*, 109–128.

Ginsburg, H. P., & Amit, M. (2008). What is teaching mathematics to young children? A theoretical perspective and case study. *Journal of Applied Developmental Psychology, 29*(4), 274–285.

Ginsburg, H. P., & Baroody, A. J. (2003). *The test of early mathematics ability*, 3rd ed. Austin, TX: Pro Ed.

Ginsburg, H. P., Cannon, J., Eisenband, J. G., & Pappas, S. (2006). Mathematical thinking and learning. In K. McCartney & D. Phillips (Eds.), *Handbook of early child development* (pp. 208–229). Oxford, UK: Blackwell Publishing Ltd.

Ginsburg, H. P., Duch, H., Ertle, B., & Noble, K. G. (2012). How can parents help their children learn math? In B. W. Wasik (Ed.), *Handbook of family literacy* (pp. 51–65). New York: Routledge.

Ginsburg, H. P., Greenes, C., & Balfanz, R. (2003). *Big math for little kids*. Parsippany, NJ: Dale Seymour Publications.

Ginsburg, H. P., Hyson, M., & Woods, T. A. (Eds.). (2014). *Preparing early childhood educators to teach math: Professional development that works*. Baltimore, MD: Paul H. Brookes Publishing Co.

Ginsburg, H. P., Jamalian, A., & Creighan, S. (2013). Cognitive guidelines for the design and evaluation of early mathematics software: The example of MathemAntics. In L. D. English & J. T. Mulligan (Eds.), *Reconceptualizing early mathematics learning* (pp. 83–120). Dordrecht: Springer.

Ginsburg, H. P., & Pappas, S. (2004). SES, ethnic, and gender differences in young children's informal addition and subtraction: A clinical interview investigation. *Journal of Applied Developmental Psychology, 25*, 171–192.

Ginsburg, H. P., Pappas, S., & Seo, K.-H. (2001). Everyday mathematical knowledge: Asking young children what is developmentally appropriate. In S. L. Golbeck (Ed.), *Psychological perspectives on early childhood education: Reframing dilemmas in research and practice* (pp. 181–219). Mahwah, NJ: Lawrence Erlbaum Associates.

Ginsburg, H. P., & Russell, R. L. (1981). Social class and racial influences on early mathematical thinking. *Monographs of the Society for Research in Child Development, 46*(Serial No. 193, No. 6).

Groen, G., & Resnick, L. B. (1977). Can preschool children invent addition algorithms? *Journal of Educational Psychology, 69*, 645–652.

Helm, J. H., & Beneke, S. (2003). *The Power of Projects: Meeting Contemporary Challenges in Early Childhood Classrooms-Strategies and Solutions*. New York, NY: Teachers College Press.

Helm, J. H., & Katz, L. (2000). *Young investigators: The project approach in the early years*. New York, NY: Teachers College Press.

Hyson, M., & Woods, T. (2014). Practices, knowledge, and beliefs about professional development. In H. Ginsburg, M. Hyson, & T. Woods, T. (Eds.), *Preparing early childhood educators to teach math* (pp. 29–51). Baltimore, MD: Brookes Publishing.

Irwin, K., & Burgham, D. (1992). Big numbers and small children. *The New Zealand Mathematics Magazine, 29*(1), 9–19.

Jordan, N. C., Huttenlocher, L., & Levine, S. C. (1994). Assessing early arithmetic abilities: Effects of verbal and nonverbal response types on the calculation performance of middle- and low-income children. *Learning and Individual Differences, 6*, 413–432.

Jordan, N. C., Kaplan, D., Olah, L. N., & Locuniak, M. N. (2006). Number sense growth in Kindergarten: A longitudinal investigation of children at risk for mathematics difficulties. *Child Development, 77*(1), 153–175.

Kaartinen, S., & Kumpulainen, K. (2012). The emergence of mathematizing as a culture of participation in the early childhood classroom. *European Early Childhood Education Research Journal, 20*(2), 263–281.

262   *Herbert P. Ginsburg and Barbrina B. Ertle*

Klein, A., & Starkey, P. (1988). Universals in the development of early arithmetic cognition. In G. Saxe & M. Gearhart (Eds.), *Children's mathematics* (pp. 5–26). San Francisco, CA: Jossey-Bass.

Lee, V. E., & Burkham, D. T. (2002). *Inequality at the starting gate: Social background differences in achievement as children begin school.* Washington, DC: Economic Policy Institute.

Lewis-Presser, A., Clements, M., Ginsburg, H., & Ertle, B. (2015). Big Math for Little Kids: The effectiveness of a preschool and kindergarten mathematics curriculum. *Early Education and Development, 26,* 399–426.

Ma, L. (1999). *Knowing and teaching elementary mathematics.* Mahwah, NJ: Lawrence Erlbaum Associates.

Manfra, L., Dinehart, L. H., & Sembiante, S. F. (2014). Associations between counting ability in preschool and mathematic performance in First Grade among a sample of ethnically diverse, low-income children. *Journal of Research in Childhood Education, 28*(1), 101–114.

Mast, J. V., & Ginsburg, H. P. (2009). Child study/ lesson study: Developing minds to understand and teach children. In N. Lyons (Ed.), *Handbook of reflection and reflective inquiry: Mapping a way of knowing for professional reflective inquiry* (pp. 257–271). New York: Springer Publishing Co.

Montessori, M. (1964). *The Montessori method* (A. E. George, Trans.). New York: Schocken Books.

National Association for the Education of Young Children & National Council of Teachers of Mathematics (2002). Position statement. Early childhood mathematics: Promoting good beginnings. Retrieved on July 26, 2015 from https://www.naeyc.org/positionstatements/mathematics

National Center for Children in Poverty (1996). *One in four: America's youngest poor. Abridged Version.* New York: National Center for Children in Poverty.

National Center for Educational Statistics (2000). *America's kindergartners: Findings from the early childhood longitudinal study, kindergarten class of 1998–99, Fall 1998.* Washinton, DC: US Department of Education.

National Governors Association Center for Best Practices & Council of Chief State School Officers (2010). *Common Core State Standards for Mathematics.* Washington, DC: National Governors Association Center for Best Practices & Council of Chief State School Officers.

NCLB (2001) No Child Left Behind Act of 2001. P. L. 107–110, 20 U.S.C. Section 6301 et seq.

Nunes, T., Schliemann, A. D., & Carraher, D. W. (1993). *Street mathematics and school mathematics.* Cambridge, UK: Cambridge University Press.

Palmér, H., Henriksson, J., & Hussein, R. (2015). Integrating mathematical learning during caregiving routines: A study of toddlers in Swedish preschools. *Early Childhood Education Journal,* doi: 10.1007/s10643-014-0669-y

Pappas, S., Ginsburg, H. P., & Jiang, M. (2003). SES differences in young children's metacognition in the context of mathematical problem solving. *Cognitive Development, 18*(3), 431–450.

Petitto, A. L., & Ginsburg, H. P. (1982). Mental arithmetic in Africa and America: Strategies, principles, and explanations. *International Journal of Psychology, 17*, 81–102.

Piaget, J. (1952). *The child's conception of number* (C. Gattegno & F. M. Hodgson, Trans.). London: Routledge & Kegan Paul Ltd.

Purpura, D. J., Baroody, A. J., & Lonigan, C. J. (2013). The transition from informal to formal mathematical knowledge: Mediation by numeral knowledge. *Journal of Educational Psychology, 105*(2), 453–464.

Ramani, G. B., & Siegler, R. S. (2011). Reducing the gap in numerical knowledge between low-and middle-income preschoolers. *Journal of Applied Developmental Psychology, 32*(3), 146–159.

Saxe, G. B., Guberman, S. R., & Gearhart, M. (1987). Social processes in early number development. *Monographs of the Society for Research in Child Development, 52*(2, Serial No. 216).

Seo, K.-H., & Ginsburg, H. P. (2004). What is developmentally appropriate in early childhood mathematics education? Lessons from new research. In D. H. Clements, J. Sarama, & A.-M. DiBiase (Eds.), *Engaging young children in mathematics: Standards for early childhood mathematics education* (pp. 91–104). Hillsdale, NJ: Lawrence Erlbaum Associates.

Vygotsky, L. S. (1986). *Thought and language* (A. Kozulin, Trans.). Cambridge, MA: The MIT Press.

Wager, A. A. (2013). Practices that support mathematics learning in a play-based class-room. In L. English & J. Mulligan (Eds.), *Reconceptualizing early mathematics learning* (pp. 163–181). Dordrecht: Springer.

Walkerdine, V. (1988). *The mastery of reason: Cognitive development and the production of rationality*. London: Routledge.

Weisberg, D. S., Hirsh-Pasek, K., & Golinkoff, R. M. (2013). Guided play: Where curric-ular goals meet a playful pedagogy. *Mind, Brain, and Education, 7*(2), 104–112.

Whitehead, A. N. (1929). *The aims of education*. New York: Macmillan.

11

Toward a Truly Democratic Civics Education

Charles C. Helwig and Shaogang Yang

The tyranny of a prince in an oligarchy is not so dangerous to the public welfare as the apathy of a citizen in a democracy.

Charles de Secondat Montesquieu (1748/1990)

Politics ought to be the part-time profession of every citizen who would protect the rights and privileges of free people.

Dwight D. Eisenhower (1954)

The above quotes, separated by over two centuries and by continents, highlight some of the enduring challenges faced by contemporary civics education efforts. How do we assist children in developing the knowledge, skills, and attitudes that enable them to become involved, active citizens who contribute to social and political life? How can we foster the development of citizens who are willing to defend and protect not only their own rights but also those of their fellow citizens? And what, ideally, should be the role of the schools in this process?

Civics education operates from the belief that "democracies are most likely to function effectively when the population endorses the values and norms inherent in democratic regimes" (Finkel & Ernst, 2005, p. 334). This premise is noncontroversial and axiomatic to most school-based civics education programs. However, as we

The Wiley Handbook of Developmental Psychology in Practice: Implementation and Impact, First Edition.
Edited by Kevin Durkin and H. Rudolph Schaffer.
© 2016 John Wiley & Sons, Ltd. Published 2016 by John Wiley & Sons, Ltd.

shall see, civics education can be fraught with serious contradictions and problems that undermine its effectiveness if it is not implemented with due consideration given to what it means to be citizen in a modern democracy.

Accordingly, in this chapter, we will begin by outlining some of the central ideas and values that underlie democratic political systems and citizenship. Then, we will summarize research on the development of concepts of freedoms, rights, and democratic understandings in children and adolescents, as these concepts provide a foundation on which civics education efforts must rest. This is followed by a review and critical evaluation of civics education in practice, in order to elucidate some of the conditions under which such efforts have succeeded or failed. In particular, we will explore some of the contradictions and challenges encountered in attempts to implement a truly democratic civics education, as well as ways in which greater attention to developmental psychological theorizing and research findings may assist in this worthy goal. It will be argued that civics education efforts have frequently failed to engage students' moral reasoning because of the avoidance of political and moral conflicts that are at the heart of debates and deliberation in democratic society. Even worse, the process of civics education as commonly practiced in schools is often indoctrinatory and at variance with core democratic notions of respect for rational autonomy, open inquiry, and critical thinking. We will conclude by considering factors that have contributed to the failure of civics education as practiced to achieve its promise, and offer examples of some successful curricular innovations that point to ways these problems may be overcome.

Democracy as the Foundation of Civics Education

Civics education, as commonly understood in Western societies, is intimately related to conceptions of democracy (Blevins, LeCompte, & Wells, 2014; Levinson, 1999). Democracy itself is notoriously difficult to define, as it has taken many different forms throughout its 2500 year history (Held, 1996). Nevertheless, a central feature of all democratic systems is the notion of government by the people, achieved through a variety of procedural mechanisms, such as direct democracy (majority rule) or by the election of representatives who are selected by the people in fair and free elections to make decisions on their behalf. Modern democracies have incorporated the principal of *equality* and expanded political rights to include all adult members of a nation.

These structural or procedural aspects of democratic government further entail a series of substantive rights and responsibilities held by citizens, such as the right to vote, run for office, or otherwise influence political policy formation and decision making. Democracy is usually also seen to require the demarcation of a private sphere, in which individuals may exercise personal autonomy and individual choice, free from state interference (Levinson, 1999). This private sphere serves to enable persons to develop as free and autonomous individuals, contributing to the sense of agency necessary to sustain democratic involvement and participation. An additional set of specific rights are usually guaranteed within modern, liberal democracies, such as freedom of speech, freedom of conscience, and freedom of association. These rights protect personal autonomy and serve the political aim of ensuring that citizens in a modern democracy have the freedom of action necessary to participate in the public sphere, through the sharing of information and by associating with other like-minded citizens. Legal guarantee of these rights also is thought to provide a check on the exploitation of minorities by majority rule or by a democratically-elected government.

The democratic citizen

There are several core features of the ideal democratic citizen that democratic societies may be seen as having an interest in nurturing through civics education efforts (Torney-Purta, Lehmann, Oswald, & Shultz, 2001). First, to be effective politically, citizens must have a solid *understanding* of the structure and function of democratic institutions, along with knowledge of their rights and responsibilities as citizens. Second, citizens must also have an *evaluative commitment* to the principles of democratic government and its associated rights and responsibilities. If democracy is to have perceived legitimacy as a system of government, it must derive from people's moral conceptions of a just society, grounded on notions such as equality, freedoms, and rights. Without this, democracy would simply be a sterile and arbitrary set of administrative procedures and regulations. This dimension connects knowledge of democracy with moral reasoning and moral development.

Furthermore, democracy requires the development in citizens of *critical thinking* skills that permit them to understand the principled basis of democratic institutions and to anticipate the potential consequences of policy alternatives. Democratic citizenship also entails the ability to formulate a wider perspective (the public good) that may transcend individual preferences or private value judgments. Individuals may be required in some circumstances to accept decisions arrived at through a democratic process, even though they may personally disagree. Hence, they must be able to *tolerate* the expression of diverse viewpoints and possess a willingness to settle disputes through rational means (discussion), rather than by coercion.

In practice, then, democracy requires a certain degree of comfort with conflict, disagreement, and difference, exercised within a framework of mutual respect, procedural fairness, and a commitment to the common good. Democracy is thus sustained by citizens who are informed about public issues, who are willing to take the perspective of the larger good of society, who tolerate one another as citizens in equal possession of certain basic democratic rights, and who are motivated to engage with other citizens in democratic processes of deliberation in order to help formulate and debate important issues of public policy.

These requirements of course must be considered as ideals that may be approached in varying manner and to different degrees in any actual individual or population. However, the underlying premise of civics education is that children or adolescents are capable of comprehending and developing commitments to these basic features of democratic life. To be effective, then, civics education programs must provide a proper match between what is taught and students' level of political and moral competence at different ages. In the next section, we review findings of research on the development of key democratic concepts, such as majority rule, representation, freedoms, tolerance, and the public good. Most of the research to be reviewed has been conducted in societies with Western-style political systems; however, some studies (reviewed in Helwig, 2006, Helwig, Ruck, & Peterson-Badali, 2014; Turiel, 2015; Verkuyten & Slooter, 2008) indicate that children in other cultural settings, including Muslim communities and mainland China, also develop notions of basic freedoms and democratic understandings.

The Development of Political and Moral Understandings

Research on the development of political concepts has been conducted generally along two lines. One involves investigations of children's and adolescents' political knowledge, such as their understandings of the various functions of governmental institutions or of political processes and ideology. This research has generally found that children's understanding of the political sphere is quite limited. For example, children's political understandings have been characterized as concrete, fragmentary, and based on affect (Greenstein, 1965), or as personal, intuitive, and lacking in comprehension of abstract relations (Connell, 1971). Detailed political knowledge relating to the institutions of government or political ideology has been found to emerge mainly in early adolescence (see Berman, 1997, for a review).

A second general approach, more the focus of this chapter, has been to examine the development of moral understandings, including concepts such as rights and justice, that underlie more advanced political conceptions such as democracy (Melton, 1980; Tapp & Kohlberg, 1971). Initial research along these lines has characterized moral development as progressing through a series of stages moving from more concrete to more abstract moral conceptions (Piaget, 1932; Kohlberg, 1981).

In these approaches, moral understandings in childhood are characterized as concrete and oriented toward obedience to authority, existing social rules, and avoidance of punishment. Later on, typically in adolescence, morality begins to be defined in terms of abstract principles of justice and fairness that are differentiated from concerns with punishment and the necessity of obedience to authorities or existing social rules (Kohlberg, 1981).

However, more recent research on social and moral development has provided a contrasting view of children's moral reasoning and its development. A large body of research, conducted within a perspective termed "social domain theory," has shown that young children develop conceptions of morality that are not strictly determined by obedience to authority, avoidance of punishment, or an uncritical adherence to social rules or conventions (Turiel, 2015). Children's moral judgments, including even those of preschool-age children, are oriented toward issues of harm and fairness, at least when judging simple social situations. For example, children reject the authority of adults to issue commands that violate others' welfare or rights, such as to steal or to hurt others (Damon, 1977; Laupa & Turiel, 1986). By six years of age, children negatively evaluate hypothetical laws that discriminate against a class of people on the basis of physical characteristics or income, and they even believe that it would be acceptable for individuals to violate these unjust laws (Helwig & Jasiobedzka, 2001). Other research has shown that children apply basic notions of justice and rights to negatively evaluate social practices involving exclusion and prejudice occurring in schools, clubs, and the family (Killen, Sinno, & Margie, 2007; Killen, Mulvey, & Hitti, 2013). The capacity to evaluate rules, laws, and institutions from the moral perspective of justice or fairness underlies a variety of notions central to democracy, including majority rule and representation, political freedoms, tolerance, and the public good.

Majority rule and representation

Majority rule and representation are essential components of democratic political systems, because they provide a means for the people to have a voice in political decision making. Research on conceptions of majority rule has shown that children from six years of age on endorse majority rule as a fair procedure for making decisions in social groups (Helwig, Yang, Tan, Liu, & Shao, 2011; Kinoshita, 1989; Moessinger, 1981). As children develop, they understand and better distinguish the conditions under which majority rule is fair and appropriate. Adolescents are more likely than children to understand that majority rule as a general decision making procedure is fair only if the group is composed of shifting majorities, in which people are on different sides of different decisions over time, so that domination of the group by a fixed majority does not result (Moessinger, 1981).

Children extend basic democratic principles such as voice and majority rule into the political sphere in making judgments about the fairness of different forms of government. For example, elementary school children judge democratic governments, such as a direct democracy in which everyone votes on every important policy decision, or a representative democracy in which the people elect representatives to make decisions for them, as more fair than nondemocratic forms of government, such as an oligarchy, in which the most wealthy rule, or a meritocracy, in which the most knowledgeable govern (Helwig, 1998). Children appeal to basic democratic principles of voice (everyone has a say) or accountability in justifying why democratic systems of government are more fair.

However, children's understanding of the political concept of representation is limited in elementary school (Sinatra, Beck, & McKeown, 1992), as indeed are their opportunities to participate in democratic decision making (Thornberg & Elvstrand, 2012), leading them to prefer direct democracy (majority rule) to representative government. Children at this age do not fully appreciate some of the problems associated with direct democracy as a form of government. These include concerns over whether majority rule can adequately protect minority rights or whether it is the best way to arrive at informed decisions about complex issues of public policy. In contrast, adolescents (15–18 year olds) tend to judge representative democracy to be better, because this system fulfils both the democratic functions of voice and representation along with the pragmatic function of delegation of decision making to those who have the time to devote to formulating and debating public policy (Helwig, Arnold, Tan, & Boyd, 2007). In general, older children and adolescents make more distinctions between social contexts such as the peer group, family, or government, in judging which type of democratic decision making (e.g., consensus, majority rule, or representation) is most appropriate (Helwig & Kim, 1999).

Personal issues, rights, and civil liberties

Notions of personal freedom that place limits on interference by governments or other authorities in people's lives is a hallmark of modern, liberal conceptions of democracy (Levinson, 1999). Beginning very early in childhood, children begin to recognize a domain of "personal issues" (Nucci, 1981) over which they should be able to exercise their choices free from the interference of adults, such as parents or teachers. At younger ages, personal jurisdiction involves concrete issues such as choices over recreation or food preferences and basic notions of privacy, but the personal domain expands in adolescence to include many other areas of self-determination (Ruck, Abramovitch, & Keating, 1998).

Freedom of speech is one of the foundational rights of democratic political systems, as it sustains the exchange of information and perspectives necessary for full democratic participation. Research has found that children conceptualize freedom of speech and other civil liberties as universal, moral rights held by everyone that may not be arbitrarily taken away by governments (Helwig, 1995, 1997, 1998). In early childhood, freedom of speech is viewed as connected to basic psychological needs for personal choice and freedom. By middle childhood, however, children also begin to see freedom of speech as serving broader social and democratic functions, such as benefiting society by fostering communication and discovery, or as helping to address social injustices within a broader democratic political system.

The democratic function of freedom of speech is illustrated by findings from a dilemma posed in Helwig (1998), in which a democratically-elected government passes a law restricting the freedom of speech rights of a minority. When asked what could be done about it, six-year-olds tended to advocate obedience to the law or to simply state that people would have to live with it. Younger children seemed to have little sense of citizens' "political efficacy," or their ability to act to influence the political system. In contrast, 11-year-olds spontaneously mentioned a wide range of actions that those opposed to such a law could pursue, including political protests, boycotts, and petitions to the government. Children's perspective on civil liberties thus expands as they develop greater knowledge of the possibilities of political action afforded by democratic systems.

Tolerance

Freedom of speech is but one of many social and moral considerations that people apply to evaluate complex social situations. Research (Helwig, 1995; Verkuyten & Slooter, 2008) has found that adolescents and adults do not always endorse civil liberties but rather take into account a variety of issues, such as the potential for harm to ensue from exercising civil liberties (e.g., as in speech advocating violence or injustice) or upholding community traditions or law. One of the important issues faced by modern democracies concerns the nature and limits of tolerance. Liberal democratic government is predicated on granting citizens a wide range of freedom of thought and expression, although not necessarily freedom of action (Law, 2006).

In research exploring the limits of tolerance across a wide age range, Wainryb, Shaw, Langley, Cottam, and Lewis (2004) found that, starting at around five years of age and continuing through to adulthood, people are more tolerant of differences over personal matters of taste or factual opinion than over moral values pertaining to issues of justice or harm. Even regarding moral values, children draw greater distinctions as they grow older between dissenting beliefs, speech, and behavior (Wainryb, Shaw, & Maianu, 1998). For instance, although at no ages did participants in Wainryb et al. (1998) judge that it was OK for a father to discriminate against his daughters based on a belief that boys deserved greater rights and privileges, most participants 10 years of age and older judged that it was OK for him to hold such a belief, and a majority of these participants stated that it was even OK for him to express and advocate for this position at a public meeting. However, six-year-olds tended to be tolerant only of such beliefs, and not their expression.

The research of Wainryb and colleagues reveals that the crucial distinction between tolerance for such beliefs and their expression, but not necessarily tolerance for actions motivated from these beliefs, is well understood and applied by late childhood.

The public good

The notion of the public good plays an important role in most conceptions of democracy, and is emphasized within communitarian democratic perspectives (Althof & Berkowitz, 2006). Accordingly, the individual in a democratic political community is seen as ceding certain rights and freedoms to the state in order for the government to provide for the common good. However, in turn, the state must abide by certain limits to its authority over the citizen, as defined by civil liberties and basic freedoms (Gallatin & Adelson, 1970). Being able to formulate the notion of a public good that may transcend individual self-interest is thus an important feature of democratic policy deliberation.

Gallatin and Adelson (1970, 1971) explored the development of the notion of the public good, using a series of hypothetical conflicts between individual freedom and the public interest, such as whether individuals who do not have children should be exempt from an education tax. Children (11-year-olds) tended to take an individual perspective on this problem and to argue that people should not have to contribute to that which they do not use. In contrast, adolescents were more likely to argue that having an educated citizenry is a public good from which everyone benefits, and thus no one should be exempt from an education tax. However, other conflicts between individual rights and the public good were resolved differently, such as a law requiring men over a certain age to get yearly medical examinations. These laws were increasingly likely, with age, to be viewed as violations of individual rights. The variations in judgments across situations indicate that, in adolescence, the emerging notion of the public good is balanced and integrated with conceptions of individual freedom, with priority given to one or the other aspect, depending on the issue.

Summary

The review of the findings from developmental research on children's moral and political understandings reveals that children construct basic understandings such as concern for others and fairness at a very young age, and begin to comprehend ideas such as democratic government, majority rule, and civil liberties such as freedom of speech by the early elementary school years. Although much develops between childhood and adolescence, the presence throughout this age span of socio-cognitive capacities for reflection on the political sphere in the form of concerns with justice, basic democratic processes, and the rights and welfare of others, provides a solid foundation upon which civics education programs ought to be able to build.

Civics Education: A Mixed Record

Despite the promising findings from developmental psychological research, however, the success of most civics education efforts appears to be limited at best and generally disappointing. There have been numerous attempts to measure and document the political understandings of children and adolescents since the early decades of the 20th century. One line of work involves periodic large-scale surveys conducted since the 1930s by educators, sociologists, and political scientists. These surveys (mostly conducted in the United States) were designed to tap high school and junior high school students' knowledge of many of the basic political concepts taught in civics curricula. The surveys have consistently revealed serious deficiencies in students' understandings, although knowledge of these topics did tend to increase from early to late adolescence (see Niemi, Sanders, & Whittington, 2005, for a review). In commenting on the surveys, Anderson et al. (1990) state that "even by twelfth grade, students' civic achievement remained quite limited in many respects" and that "most students performed poorly on items that referred to technical vocabulary, detailed political process, or the historical and intellectual traditions of our government" (p. 67). More recently, Flanagan, Gallay, Gill, Gallay, and Nti (2005) found that only about 50% of American adolescents could give an adequate definition of democracy (that is, one that referred to one or more key features such as representation and majority rule, equality, or the protection of individual rights).

Even more unsettling is the poor or nonexistent relationship between adolescents' civic competence or political knowledge, and their evaluative commitment to the principles of democracy, as reflected in endorsements of democratic values and attitudes. As found in several large-scale studies, conducted in different societies, such as the United States, Israel, and South Africa, any gains in political knowledge associated with civics education programs do not tend to translate into greater endorsement of democratic attitudes and values, such as support for civil liberties, democratic participation, or tolerance (Finkel & Ernst, 2005; Niemi & Junn, 1998; Perlinger, Canetti-Nisim & Pedahzur, 2006). What might account for the disappointing level of civics knowledge in the population in general and, especially, its puzzling lack of association with democratic values and principles?

What is taught: The content of civics education

One explanation focuses on the content taught in civics and social studies courses. Many reviews of civics textbooks and curricula in the United States and Canada over several decades indicate that much of what is taught consists of dry, disembodied facts, definitions, or abstract, institutional mechanisms, such as the structure and workings of government (Berman, 1997). Students in civics courses learn much about how government works, but often the "why" is overlooked. More surprising is the observation that controversial issues and conflict tend to be downplayed or minimized in the curriculum, and the role of citizen participation is not stressed, except for voting (Carroll et al., 1989).

The failure to focus on real life problems, social issues, and conflicts, may mean that the civics curriculum rarely engages students' actual or potential moral reasoning. Accordingly, students may fail to see how concepts, laws, or procedures taught in the curricula are related to moral values and real life experiences. It is doubtful that such an approach is likely to help students to develop a deeper appreciation of the roots of democracy in processes of conflict and compromise. Instead, students may treat the civics curriculum as a set of meaningless facts and jargon ("technical vocabulary" or "detailed political process") to be memorized for tests and forgotten. It may not be surprising, then, that many adolescents are not able to "define" democracy. But as the findings from the developmental research reviewed earlier indicate, both children and adolescents do possess understandings of many of the components of democracy and apply these ideas when reasoning about situations that do engage their moral values.

Another reason for the poor record may simply be the failure to apply what we know about children's developing moral judgments in the political sphere when devising appropriate curricula for different ages. Students' own judgments about concepts such as rights, democratic government, and freedoms are rarely tapped or made use of in traditional civics pedagogy, and yet they may be crucial for successful learning. For example, one study examined Canadian students' understanding of the Canadian Charter of Rights and Freedoms (taught in schools) and found that knowledge about different rights contained within the Charter, including democratic rights and language rights, was highly correlated with whether or not students themselves supported these rights (Ungerleider, 1990). In other words, students were better able to assimilate information taught to them in the curricula if it was consistent with their own moral positions.

One potential "mismatch" between standard civics curricula and what we know from the developmental research on children's moral and political reasoning may be in the area of understandings of democratic government. Children in the United States and Canada are typically first taught about the structure of their representative system of government in the last years of elementary school (Masemann, 1989). However, as the developmental research has shown, elementary school age children poorly understand the justice implications of political representation (Sinatra et al., 1992), and they are more likely to view majority rule as a basic foundation of political fairness, leading them to prefer direct democracy to representative government (Helwig, 1998, Helwig et al., 2007). We do not know how children are assimilating the copious information they are receiving at these ages regarding the mechanics of representative government. One possibility is that they view much of the material presented in civics lessons as little more than technical or administrative details bearing no obvious connection to democratic principles of fairness and voice. Getting elementary school age children to appreciate these connections may require a more concrete approach that centers on issues that are relevant and meaningful to children and that engage their actual moral reasoning.

One example of such an approach comes from a field experiment conducted by Osborne and Seymour (1988), in which they compared upper-elementary school students who were taught using an experimental curriculum with those taught using the traditional civics curriculum. As part of the experimental curriculum, participants were presented with a series of story narratives in which students at a hypothetical elementary school faced issues or dilemmas of a political nature. For example, in one story, a teacher allows students to select, by vote of the class, what they will do with some extra class time they have earned. As it turns out, the votes are split, with the winning option receiving only a minority of votes, leading to conflict and charges of unfairness by some students. This story was meant to point up some of the problems with pluralities and majority rule. Another example dealt with a land use conflict involving a playground and a freeway development and a group of students who try, with their teacher's help, to influence city hall. This example was intended to stimulate students' thinking about the process of democratic decision making, their own political efficacy, and the conflicts of interest that lie behind many public issues. Throughout the experimental curriculum, students were encouraged to reflect on, discuss, and come up with potential solutions to the problems. In a posttest, it was found that students who were exposed to the experimental curriculum had a greater sense of political efficacy, were less cynical, and were more aware of and accepting of political conflict than those who were given only the standard curriculum.

The research of Osborne and Seymour illustrates how civics education can be effective in facilitating the development of democratic political attitudes when it is made relevant and interesting to children through the use of concrete, age appropriate issues and dilemmas. A second example of the effectiveness of civics curricula that take into account what we know about the development of children's political reasoning comes from a rights curriculum developed by Howe and Covell (2005). In their work, participants were presented with issues involving children's rights that were designed to be developmentally appropriate and of interest to students, with students themselves involved in the development of the curriculum. The researchers specifically drew on developmental research, such as that of Gallatin and Adelson (1970), in devising rights-related issues. Given that the ability to judge public policy from the standpoint of the broader community and the common good develops in mid-to-late adolescence, rights issues were presented to younger participants (11–12 year-olds) mainly in relation to the individual child. At these ages, children considered issues such as healthy living, personal safety, and basic freedom of speech and decision making. At older ages, students considered children's rights in relation to more public issues such as youth justice, employment and education, and global problems such as child labor and war-affected children. The curriculum included role playing and discussions of case studies and provided many opportunities for children to express their opinions and have them taken into account. The findings revealed that this curriculum was effective in generating a more sophisticated understanding of rights and a greater support for the rights of ethnic and sexual minorities among students who received this curriculum when compared with others who did not.

These examples of effective civics curricula indicate how important it is to consider the match between classroom work on specific civics-related concepts (e.g., majority rule, the public good) and what research has revealed about children's developing political reasoning capacities. These examples also point to the important role played by students' active reflection on political and moral issues within the civics curriculum. Civics is not just a content to be learned but is linked to processes of learning entailing rational reflection and discussion. It is to the role of these processes in civics education that we turn to next.

How it is taught: The process of civics education and the democratic ideal

One of the critical components of democratic citizenship is the notion of rational autonomy (Levinson, 2007). In the context of civics education, autonomy entails the ability to think critically and to develop one's own perspective on a public issue, as informed by individual reflection and deliberation with others. Autonomy in the political and civic sphere rests on the development of a host of rational thinking skills, such as the ability to read and to understand a variety of arguments, to reason effectively, and to think through the implications of different political positions. More broadly, it requires a general disposition to engage in formulating one's own position on issues in accordance with one's examined beliefs, convictions, and judgment, rather than simply deferring to a revered authority or an unexamined tradition (Moshman, 2009, 2011). In other words, it depends on citizens who take rationality seriously in their public and private life, and who are skilled and practiced both in listening critically to the views of others, in subjecting their own beliefs to rational scrutiny, and in communicating their own perspectives.

In educational and developmental psychology, the connection between rational autonomy and democratic social organization may be traced back to the theorizing of Piaget (1932) and Dewey (1916). Piaget contrasted autonomy and heteronomy in the context of describing differences in the presumed levels of moral development of young children versus adolescents (differences that have been called into question by some of the research discussed in earlier sections of this chapter, see also Helwig, 2008). Whereas heteronomy involves thought that is "under the authority of another" and constrained by received knowledge and tradition, autonomous thinking is regulated by the norms and laws of reason itself. Piaget believed that autonomous thinking tends to develop out of interactions among children who are relatively equal in status and power. In contrast, heteronomy is encouraged by unequal relationships in which individuals feel psychological pressure to align their thinking with that of superiors. Under circumstances of peer interaction in a climate of equality and mutual respect, children engage in reciprocal exchanges in which they begin to compare perspectives and take a critical stance on the products of their own and others' thinking. Out of these kinds of social experiences, children construct moral notions of justice, reciprocity, and equality. Similarly, Dewey (1916) believed that democracy was predicated on critical thinking ("reflective experience"), nurtured within a democratic school community in which children could put into practice democratic skills and behaviors that would carry over into adult community and political life.

Research in moral development has generally confirmed Piaget's claims about the importance of reflection, in the context of group or dyadic discussions, for stimulating moral development (see Enright, Lapsley, Harris, & Shawver, 1983 and Leming, 1981, for reviews). In the context of peer discussions, interactions in which one person "operates" on the thinking of another, for example, by expanding on or critiquing another person's assertion, are especially effective (Berkowitz & Gibbs, 1983). However, contrary to Piaget's contentions, studies of moral discussions in the family have shown that parent–child discussions can prove to be an important source of moral development, as long as parents in these discussions attempt to neutralize the status difference by using a more gentle "Socratic" approach that reflects and represents the child's reasoning back to the child, rather than through direct challenges or critiques (Walker, Hennig, & Krettenauer, 2000). In short, it is the style of interaction (democratic versus authoritarian) that seems to matter, more than who the participants are. Furthermore, discussions are most likely to be effective if they focus on actual dilemmas that engage the child's interest (Walker et al., 2000). There is some evidence linking these processes in the family to the promotion of greater civics understanding (Flanagan et al., 2005; Niemi & Junn, 1998). For example, Flanagan et al. (2005) found that adolescents who reported that their families frequently discussed current events and who had parents who encouraged their children to participate in these discussions were able to give more satisfactory definitions of democracy than those who reported fewer such discussions.

In the context of civics education, these issues have been examined most extensively through investigations of the role of class climate (democratic versus authoritarian) in promoting democratic values and attitudes. In a landmark study conducted in nine countries with over 30,000 adolescent students and teachers, Torney, Openheim, and Farnen (1975) examined the effect of the civics classroom climate on students' political knowledge, interest, and endorsement of democratic attitudes. Democratic attitudes in this study included measures of students' support for a variety of democratic notions discussed in earlier sections of this chapter, such as freedom of expression, the right to be represented, tolerance for diversity, and equality rights for all citizens. Across all nine countries examined, classroom environments in which students were encouraged to express their opinions and in which free discussions were held in class were associated with greater support for democratic attitudes, as well as increased political knowledge and interest. In contrast, antidemocratic or authoritarian attitudes were associated with classroom environments in which the pedagogy was dominated by the learning of facts, memorization, and the use of simple drills, and where participation in various patriotic rituals was emphasized. Subsequent studies, conducted in different nations (Hahn, 1999; Perlinger et al., 2006), have corroborated these patterns. For example, Perlinger et al. (2006) found that Israeli students who perceived their civics classroom as one in which controversial issues were discussed in an environment supportive of the expression of a wide spectrum of views were more likely to endorse democratic values, and expressed greater levels of political efficacy (one's perceived ability to influence the political system) than those who perceived their classroom environments as relatively lacking in these opportunities. Moreover, students from more democratic classrooms also reported greater levels of participation in actual political activities, such as writing letters to their representatives and newspapers, or involvement in school, community, or public affairs.

Research has explored the impact of other forms of democratic, participatory pedagogy, such as student role-playing and participation in political simulations (e.g., mock trials or legislatures), on various civic and democratic values (Finkel & Ernst, 2005). Finkel and Ernst's study, conducted in South Africa, found that active, participatory pedagogy such as role-playing and political simulations was strongly associated with a variety of positive civics outcomes. Students who experienced these forms of participatory pedagogy were more tolerant of the expression of divergent political views, more approving of various forms of political participation, such as voting, peaceful protests, or joining groups to solve problems in the community, and reported greater use of "civic skills", such as cooperation and leadership, in their lives in general, when compared with students who experienced little participatory pedagogy. An emerging literature on community service programs (e.g., volunteering to help out in a food shelter or an advocacy group for the disadvantaged) has found that students can develop greater civic commitment through these experiences, as long as the service addresses social issues and is combined with ample opportunities for reflection (Hart, Atkins, & Donnelly, 2006). Participation in democratically-structured voluntary organizations seems to be especially valuable in facilitating social trust and civic engagement, whereas participation in hierarchically-structured organizations where individuals have little opportunity to influence the group's decision making does not seem to provide these same benefits (Putnam, 1993).

In general, the research literature supports Dewey's (1916) contention that democracy is best fostered in a climate of intellectual reflection, exploration, and open exchange of perspectives, coupled with the provision of opportunities to practice and instantiate democratic rights and values in ways that students find directly meaningful. The findings are also consistent with Piaget's view that children construct moral understandings out of their social experiences, and that both poles of this interaction (judgments and experiences) need to be considered together in accounting for how democratic civic orientations are formed.

The process of civics education: The reality

Taking seriously the theorizing and research findings on civics education presented in the previous section should lead to a civics education pedagogy that encourages reflection, critical thinking, and the exchange of viewpoints among students, enhanced through class discussions, perspective taking, and other participatory opportunities. However, research on actual classroom practices in civics and other academic subjects, conducted over the last 50 years, reveals a starkly contrasting picture (Berman, 1997; Hess & Torney, 1967; Sirotnik, 1988; Torney-Purta et al.,

2001). Across both elementary and secondary levels, lectures followed by recitation or individual work comprise the dominant form of instruction, whereas group work, such as discussion, role play, and simulations are very rare (Berman, 1997). In a survey of 90,000 students in 28 countries, only 16% of students stated that their civics teachers sometimes allowed class discussions (Torney-Purta et al., 2001). In most classrooms, little time is spent on exercises that ask for higher-order thinking, in contrast to those that tap recall and comprehension skills (Sirotnik, 1988). Other forms of student participation, such as decision making inside and outside the classroom, are limited or nonexistent. For example, although mechanisms for student participation in decision making in the form of student councils exist in many schools, all too often their mandate is concerned with mundane or "safe" topics rather than real issues of concern to students (Howe & Covell, 2005).

One consequence of this state of affairs is that students have few opportunities to practice the skills of critical thinking and cooperation that are central to democracy. Another, perhaps more sinister result, is that the education process itself is directly at variance with what is being taught in the civics curriculum. As Sirotnik (1988, p. 62) wryly remarks, if the goal statements in the formal school curriculum were aligned with actual classroom life, they would read something like this: "to develop in students the abilities to think linearly, depend upon authority, speak when spoken to, work alone, become socially apathetic, learn passively and non-experientially, recall information, follow instructions….and so on." Rather than supporting a truly democratic civics education, this form of pedagogy is more consistent with indoctrination (Sears & Hughes, 2006).

These tensions between content and practice are not likely to be lost on students. Recent research has shown that children themselves are "curriculum theorists" who develop the capacity to evaluate different forms of curriculum and their appropriateness for different subject matter (Helwig, Ryerson, & Prencipe, 2008; Nicholls & Nelson, 1992). For example, by late elementary school, students reject the idea that teachers should teach a particular position on a controversial topic (e.g., whether more money should be spent on space exploration or health care), even when the teacher's position is consistent with their own (Nicholls & Nelson, 1992). Furthermore, students in late elementary school believe that active teaching methods, such as class discussions, are better than teacher-centered methods, such as simple memorization or lectures, for teaching value-laden or controversial issues, including moral values such as racial tolerance (Helwig et al., 2008). By around 10 years of age, students themselves explicitly criticize teacher-centered value education methods as failing to stimulate active thinking and as potentially indoctrinatory (Helwig et al., 2008). The prominence of teacher-centered methods in civics education may be likely to produce cynicism and disengagement in students, not only because these methods are ineffective, but more importantly because they are at variance with students' own developing pedagogical views and their judgments of the importance of freedom of expression and tolerance for divergent beliefs (Helwig, 1995; Wainryb et al., 1998).

Philosophical and practical barriers

The reasons for this paradoxical incompatibility between the content and process of civics education are probably varied and complex. One reason may be that civics education has sat uncomfortably alongside other forms of "moral" education in the schools, each with contrasting theoretical foundations. One current example is character education (Nucci, Krettenauer, & Narváez, 2008), which has emerged in recent decades as extremely popular and well-supported by governments. Both civics and character education frequently draw on the language of "citizenship," but this term has quite different senses within each approach. Traditionally, character education has been concerned with the question of how to instill in individuals the character traits deemed by society to be morally worthy, such as honesty, responsibility, loyalty, caring for others, a good work ethic, and so on. Character educators have largely "equated the good citizen with the good person, the man or woman who helps others, respects other people's rights, obeys the law, is suitably patriotic, and the like" (Osborne, 2004, p. 13). Correspondingly, character education is often tied to top-down pedagogical approaches that view the child as a passive recipient of fixed societal traditions and values ("right answers"), transmitted to children by adults and the educational system (Sears & Hughes, 2006).

In contrast, civics education is largely concerned with questions of public morality or virtue, such as justice, democratic processes, and the rights and duties of democratic citizenship. Within civics education, children are viewed as active constructors of their knowledge and values. Because of its public and deliberative focus, civics education is by nature "open to alternative views of the world" (Sears & Hughes, 2006). Although some character virtues may be indispensable for good citizenship (such as a sense of justice or fairness), others, such as loyalty or an excessive patriotism, may be less relevant or may even impair civic engagement in some circumstances (Torney et al., 1975). Some more recent forms of character education do attempt to incorporate active pedagogy (Berkowitz, Sherbloom, Bier, & Battisch, 2006). However, it is the more passive or indoctrinatory variants that seem to be much more prevalent in practice (Schaps, Shaeffer, & McDonnell, 2001). For example, methods commonly identified in character education programs in U.S. schools include: drills and memorization of values, stories with "pat" morals, classroom bulletin boards and banners that extol various virtues, upbeat public announcements and addresses, and public awards ceremonies for "good citizens" whose behavior is judged to represent target virtues (Schaps et al., 2001). Some commentators have drawn parallels between these practices in use in U.S. schools and those traditionally found in Communist China's moral education programs (To, Yang, & Helwig, 2014; Yu, 2004). As a result, the progressive democratic spirit of civics education may be in danger of being coopted by character education and its more passive and traditional view of the citizen's relationship to society.

Similar tensions between constructivist and traditional understandings of civics education are also found within non-Western societies. As noted by Osler and Starkey (2006), democratic civics education is seen as increasingly relevant not only to long-established, multicultural Western democracies but also to societies seeking to reestablish or strengthen democracy following war or conflict, or to authoritarian societies seeking to modernize. One example is the case of Lebanon. Following the 1975–1989 Civil War in Lebanon, the education curriculum was reformed in order to incorporate an emphasis on the principles of democracy, tolerance, and mutual respect as a way of unifying the nation and providing a peaceful means to resolve social conflicts. Surveys of teachers and students indicate the presence of broad support for these democratic ideas and principles (Akar, 2006). However, most students and some teachers expressed serious criticism of the curriculum itself for its emphasis on rote learning, memorization, and a passive model of citizenship in which students' active thinking and discussion and debate were deemphasized (Akar, 2006). Other teachers, however, endorsed top-down teaching methods and tended to report avoiding controversial topics in their teaching, in part because of concerns about conflicts with other cultural value systems, such as religious doctrines and traditional values held by students' parents and the society at large.

A second example comes from Mainland China. Recent developmental research has shown that Chinese adolescents endorse democratic concepts, such as freedom of speech and religion, political participation and voice, and students' active involvement in deciding matters of importance to them in the classroom, including greater control over the curriculum (Helwig, Arnold, Tan, & Boyd, 2003, 2007; Helwig et al., 2011; Lahat, Helwig, Yang, Tan, & Liu, 2009). However, as noted earlier, the traditional moral education curriculum in China has tended to stress top-down, passive learning, authority control, and the transmission of Marxist–Leninist political ideology (To et al., 2014; Yu, 2004). More recently, constructivist methods emphasizing greater student autonomy have been incorporated into the Chinese curriculum, mainly as a way of serving goals of economic modernization. As an extension of this process, however, some prominent Chinese educators have called for clearer distinctions between moral education and political (ideological) education, including the recommendation that moral education in China be formulated more along the lines of citizenship education (Li, Zhong, Lin, & Zhang, 2004). Accordingly, there would be greater focus in the curriculum on "how to deal with political and moral issues, rather than giving [students] preset answers to all problems" (Li et al., 2004, p. 459). This would mean acknowledging that "creative tensions exist between official positions and other political or moral alternatives" (Li et al., 2004, p. 461), that students should be permitted to explore alternatives and arrive at their own synthesis of personal perspectives and official ideology, and that "one-way indoctrination" should be replaced by more multilateral and reciprocal relations between students and educators (Li et al., 2004). The call for a more active citizenship education within China, and the general parameters of these debates, parallel the different positions encountered in Western educational discourse (To et al., 2014; Yu, 2004).

Attempts to implement a fully democratic civics education in societies such as China and Lebanon are inevitably constrained by other dominant cultural value systems and political ideologies. However, two points bear stressing. First, there is significant support for fundamental democratic principles, including among students, even within non-Western societies influenced by diverse cultural traditions and ideologies. Second, as in the West, there are controversies and debates within non-Western societies about how civics education should proceed, with some maintaining a traditional approach and others stressing more active pedagogy. The fundamental goals and challenges associated with civics education are therefore relevant to other societies besides those with Western-style cultural or political systems that have been the focus of this review.

Within Western societies, the resistance among teachers and administrators to democratic civics education has been traced to a variety of factors, both philosophical and practical (Berman, 1997). Many teachers and administrators themselves may hold a view of civics education that is philosophically more consistent with that of traditional character education. Some ethnographic studies (Leming, 1981) indicate that many teachers view the social studies curriculum as a means to promote socialization and to prepare students for conformity to existing social structures in the school and society at large, rather than as a way of instilling a critical, democratic consciousness. This view is not restricted to teachers or educational administrators but is held even at the highest levels of those who set educational policy. Indeed, in a number of decisions over the last several decades, the United States' Supreme Court has consistently ruled that the necessity of schools to maintain control over the curriculum takes priority over the Constitutional rights of students, including their rights to freedom of expression (Moshman, 2009). In contrast, democratic pedagogy means ceding some control of classroom activities to students, and many administrators and teachers may not believe in the benefits of such an approach or may fear the perceived consequences for maintaining classroom discipline and order. There is also the potential for retribution from parent organizations or other external influences should controversial issues be brought up in class and someone were to object.

Even when educators themselves are not opposed to democratic pedagogy, there may still be barriers. Teachers lack formal training in participatory methods and most will not even have experienced these methods in their own education (Berman, 1997). Teachers who wish to implement democratic pedagogy may not receive support from reluctant administrators. Other aspects of the overall educational climate, such as time pressures and a focus on standardized testing and "right answers," militate against use of student-centered methods (Yu, 2004). As Dewey (1916) pointed out long ago, however, democratic education requires a philosophical and practical commitment at all levels, from teachers and the school itself on up to those in charge of the whole educational system. Tensions and contradictions in theoretical outlook and practice between any of these levels can easily undermine the success of local initiatives meant to democratize student learning. The research findings indicate that educational theorists and developmental psychologists have a good understanding about what works and what needs to be done in order to implement an effective and truly democratic civics education. What is often missing is only the philosophical, political, and practical commitment to carry it out.

Conclusion: Overcoming the barriers

The problems and challenges discussed in the previous section present formidable obstacles to translating theory and research findings from psychology into good educational practice. This is not to say that they cannot be overcome. In the final section, we will consider some examples of how researchers have achieved important successes in helping to implement democratic civics education in schools within several jurisdictions. The examples come from the program of children's rights education of Howe and Covell (2005), discussed in an earlier section of this chapter. This program was initially developed and implemented in several schools in Nova Scotia, Canada, as part of an experimental curriculum. Its success subsequently led to aspects of this rights education program becoming a permanent part of the official curriculum throughout Nova Scotia. Subsequent interest in this initiative has spread to Great Britain, where an expanded version of the program was implemented within an entire school district (the county of Hampshire) and elsewhere (Howe & Covell, 2013).

A number of factors appear to have contributed to these successes. One is that the researchers themselves assessed and took seriously the concerns of teachers at the earliest stages of the implementation process. As part of the Canadian initiative (subsequently repeated in England), the researchers held discussion groups with teachers. In these sessions, teachers expressed many of the common reactions encountered when democratic civics education reforms are proposed (Howe & Covell, 2005). For example, teachers were concerned about accepting new teaching responsibilities and how the rights curriculum would fit with the present curriculum. Some even believed children's rights to be too sensitive a topic to discuss in school, or that teachers would inevitably lose authority if they let students know that they have rights. As a trainee teacher observed of similar proposals in Cassidy, Brunner and Webster (2014): "All Hell will break loose!"

Howe and Covell (2005) then took steps to address these concerns. Regarding teachers' worries about how the new curriculum fit in and the possibility of increased workload, the researchers responded by deliberately designing their children's rights curriculum to dovetail with the existing curricula wherever possible. For example, relevant material on children's rights (such as article 33 of the United Nations Convention on the Rights of the Child covering the right to protection from narcotics) was linked to the existing health curriculum on drug prevention. Additionally, the researchers held workshops with teachers in which the UN Convention on the Rights of the Child was discussed, along with the particular pedagogy to be used. Steps were taken to train teachers in the use of the pedagogy and to provide reassurance that it could be implemented without undermining the teacher's authority or other ill effects. In order to provide ongoing support, an Internet site was developed with resources on the topic for teachers and parents. These consultations and discussions and sharing of information helped to promote greater awareness of children's rights issues among teachers. Most importantly, since teachers were consulted and involved from the beginning of this process, their "ownership" of the new curriculum as partners to the researchers was thereby fostered.

The subsequent formal adoption of this curriculum within the province of Nova Scotia in Canada, however, must be considered but a partial success story. Although the content and some of the activities in the original curriculum were incorporated, the actual implementation is largely left up to individual teachers. Thus, some of the key aspects of the experimental curriculum, such as the use of class discussions and the overall democratization of the classroom environment, are not mandated.

This is in contrast to the version taken up and developed in Hampshire in England, in which the classroom and school environment overall is given much greater attention (Covell, Howe, & McNeil, 2008; Howe & Covell, 2013). For example, in the Hampshire initiative, the notion of respect for students' rights and dignity is instantiated in a variety of ways, including through rights-based classroom pedagogy, the use of democratic teaching practices, and through procedural mechanisms (e.g., student councils) that enable students to participate more fully in the formulation and implementation of school policies. These broader changes were possible in part because of the general interest in civics education generated by the recent nationwide curriculum reform in Great Britain, the perceived centrality of human rights education to this process, and the infusion of substantial resources for the development of educational initiatives (Osler & Starkey, 2006). The demonstrated success of this program in enhancing student engagement and reducing teacher burnout has led to its use in other districts in Great Britain, and to plans by educational authorities to implement a similar program throughout New Zealand (Katherine Covell, personal communication).

This example highlights how democratically-oriented reform of civics education must involve all levels of the educational system in order to achieve the possibility of lasting success. It is not enough for policymakers to formulate a curriculum whose content addresses democracy and rights and to assume that this curriculum will be effectively "taught" to students. Fundamental democratic principles of mutual respect and participation must govern every stage of this process, including researchers' relations with teachers as they attempt to transfer their knowledge to educational settings, student–teacher interactions within the classroom, and the broader school climate. Only then can Dewey's vision of democratic education, informed by the findings of social science research, stand a chance of becoming a reality.

Acknowledgment

Preparation of this chapter was supported by a grant to Charles C. Helwig from the Social Sciences and Humanities Research Council of Canada.

References

Akar, B. (2006). Teacher reflections on the challenges of teaching citizenship education in Lebanon: A qualitative pilot study. *Reflecting Education, 2*, 48–63.

Althof, W., & Berkowitz, M. W. (2006). Moral education and character education: Their relationship and roles in citizenship education. *Journal of Moral Education, 35*, 495–518.

Anderson, L., Jenkins, L. B., Leming, J., MacDonald, W. B., Mullis, I., Turner, M. J., & Wooster, J. S. (1990). *The civics report card*. Princeton, NJ: Educational Testing Service.

Berkowitz, M. W., & Gibbs, J. C. (1983). Measuring the developmental features of moral discussion. *Merrill-Palmer Quarterly, 29*, 399–410.

Berkowitz, M. W., Sherblom, S., Bier, M., & Battistich, V. (2006). Educating for positive youth development. In M. Killen & J. G. Smetana (Eds.), *Handbook of Moral Development* (pp. 683–701). Mahwah, NJ: Lawrence Erlbaum Associates.

Berman, S. (1997). *Children's social consciousness and the development of social responsibility*. Albany, NY: SUNY Press.

Blevins, B., LeCompte, K., & Wells, S. (2014). Citizenship education goes digital. *The Journal of Social Studies Research, 38*, 33–44.

Carroll, J. D., Broadnax, W., Contreras, G., Mann, T., Ornstein, N., & Stiehm, J. (1989). *We the people: A review of U.S. government and civics textbooks*. Washington, DC: People for the American Way.

Cassidy, C., Brunner, R., & Webster, E. (2014). Teaching human rights? 'All hell will break loose!'. *Education, Citizenship and Social Justice, 9*, 19–33.

Connell, R. W. (1971). *The child's construction of politics*. Melbourne, Australia: Melbourne University Press.

Covell, K., Howe, R. B., & McNeil, J. K. (2008). *"If there's a dead rat, don't leave it." Young children's understanding of their citizenship rights and responsibilities*. Unpublished manuscript.

Damon, W. (1977). *The social world of the child*. San Francisco, CA: Jossey-Bass.

Dewey, J. (1916). *Democracy and education*. New York: MacMillan.

Eisenhower, D. D. (1954). *Address recorded for the Republican Lincoln day dinners, January 28, 1954*. Washington, DC: Eisenhower Memorial Commission.

Enright, R. D., Lapsley, D. K., Harris, D. J., & Shawver, D. J. (1983). Moral development interventions in early adolescence. *Theory in Practice, 22*, 134–144.

Finkel, S. E., & Ernst, H. R. (2005). Civic education in post-Apartheid South Africa: Alternative paths to the development of political knowledge and democratic values. *Political Psychology, 26*, 333–364.

Flanagan, C., Gallay, L. S., Gill, S., Gallay, E., & Nti, N. (2005). What does democracy mean? Correlates of adolescents' views. *Journal of Adolescent Research, 20*, 193–218.

Gallatin, J., & Adelson, J. (1970). Individual rights and the public good: A cross-national study of adolescents. *Comparative Political Studies, 2*, 226–244.

Gallatin, J., & Adelson, J. (1971) Legal guarantees of individual freedom: A cross-national study of the development of political thought. *Journal of Social Issues, 27*, 93–108.

Greenstein, F. (1965). *Children and politics*. New Haven, CT: Yale University Press.

Hahn, C. L. (1999). Citizenship education: An empirical study of policy, practices and outcomes. *Oxford Review of Education, 25*, 231–250.

Hart, D., Atkins, R., & Donnelly, T. M. (2006). Community service and moral development. In M. Killen & J. G. Smetana (Eds.), *Handbook of Moral Development* (pp. 633–656). Mahwah, NJ: Lawrence Erlbaum Associates.

Held, D. (1996). *Models of democracy*. Cambridge, UK: Polity Press.

Helwig, C. C. (1995). Adolescents' and young adults' conceptions of civil liberties: Freedom of speech and religion. *Child Development, 66*, 152–166.

Helwig, C. C. (1997). The role of agent and social context in judgments of freedom of speech and religion. *Child Development, 68*, 484–495.

Helwig, C. C. (1998). Children's conceptions of fair government and freedom of speech. *Child Development, 69*, 518–531.

Helwig, C. C. (2006). The development of personal autonomy throughout cultures. *Cognitive Development, 21*, 458–473.

Helwig, C. C. (2008). The moral judgment of the child reevaluated: Heteronomy, early morality, and reasoning about social justice and inequalities. In C. Wainryb, J. G. Smetana, & E. Turiel (Eds.), *Social development, social inequalities, and social justice* (pp. 27–51). New York: Lawrence Erlbaum Associates.

Helwig, C. C., Arnold, M. L., Tan, D., & Boyd, D. (2003). Chinese adolescents' reasoning about democratic and authority-based decision making in peer, family, and school contexts. *Child Development, 74*, 783–800.

Helwig, C. C., Arnold, M. L., Tan, D., & Boyd, D. (2007). Mainland Chinese and Canadian adolescents' judgments and reasoning about the fairness of democratic and other forms of government. *Cognitive Development, 22*, 96–109.

Helwig, C. C., & Jasiobedzka, U. (2001). The relation between law and morality: Children's reasoning about socially beneficial and unjust laws. *Child Development, 72*, 1382–1393.

Helwig, C. C., & Kim, S. (1999). Children's evaluations of decision making procedures in peer, family, and school contexts. *Child Development, 70*, 502–517.

Helwig, C. C., Ruck, M. D., & Peterson-Badali, M. (2014). Rights, civil liberties, & democracy. In M. Killen & J. G. Smetana (Eds.) *Handbook of Moral Development*, 2nd ed. (pp. 46–69). New York: Psychology Press.

Helwig, C. C., Ryerson, R., & Prencipe, A. (2008). Children's, adolescents', and adults' judgments and reasoning about different methods of teaching values. *Cognitive Development, 23*, 119–135.

Helwig, C. C., Yang, S., Tan, D., Liu, C., & Shao, T. (2011). Urban and rural Chinese adolescents' judgments and reasoning about personal and group jurisdiction. *Child Development, 82*, 701–716.

Hess, R., & Torney, J., (1967). *The development of political attitudes in children*. Chicago, IL: Aldine.

Howe, R. B., & Covell, K. (2005). *Empowering children: Children's rights education as a pathway to citizenship*. Toronto, ON: University of Toronto Press.

Howe, R. B., & Covell, K. (2013). *Education in the best interests of the child: A Children's Rights perspective on closing the achievement gap*. Toronto, ON: University of Toronto Press.

Killen, M., Sinno, S., & Margie, N. G. (2007). Children's experiences and judgments about group exclusion and inclusion. *Advances in Child Development and Behavior, 35*, 173–218.

Killen, M., Mulvey, K. L., & Hitti, A. (2013). Social exclusion in childhood: A developmental intergroup perspective. *Child Development, 84*, 772–790.

Kinoshita, Y. (1989). Developmental changes in understanding the limitations of majority decisions. *British Journal of Developmental Psychology, 7*, 97–112.

Kohlberg, L. (1981). *Essays on moral development. Vol. 1: The philosophy of moral development*. San Francisco, CA: Harper & Row.

Lahat, A., Helwig, C. C., Yang, S., Tan, D., & Liu, C. (2009). Mainland Chinese adolescents' judgments and reasoning about self-determination and nurturance rights. *Social Development, 18*, 690–710.

Laupa, M., & Turiel, E. (1986). Children's conceptions of adult and peer authority. *Child Development, 57*, 405–412.

Law, S. (2006). *The war for children's minds*. New York: Routledge.

Leming, J. S. (1981). Curriculum effectiveness in moral/values education: A review of the research. *Journal of Moral Education, 10*, 147–164.

Levinson, M. (1999). Liberalism, pluralism, and political education: Paradox or paradigm? *Oxford Review of Education, 25*, 39–58.

Li., P., Zhong, M., Lin, B., & Zhang, H. (2004). *Deyu* as moral education in modern China: Ideological functions and transformations. *Journal of Moral Education, 33*, 449–469.

Masemann, V. (1989). The current status of teaching about citizenship in Canadian elementary and secondary schools. In K. McLeod (Ed.), *Canada and citizenship education* (pp. 27–52). Toronto, ON: Canadian Education Association.

Melton, G. B. (1980). Children's concepts of their rights. *Journal of Clinical Child Psychology, 9*, 186–190.

Moessinger, P. (1981). The development of the concept of majority decision: A pilot study. *Canadian Journal of Behavioral Science, 13*, 359–362.

Montesquieu, C. S. (1748/1990). *The spirit of the laws.* Cambridge, UK: Cambridge University Press.

Moshman, D. (2009). *Liberty and learning: Academic freedom for teachers and students.* Portsmouth, NH: Heinemann.

Moshman, D. (2011). *Adolescent rationality and development: Cognition, morality, and identity.* Mahwah, NJ: Lawrence Erlbaum Associates.

Nicholls, J. G., & Nelson, J. R. (1992). Students' conceptions of controversial knowledge. *Journal of Educational Psychology, 84*, 224–230.

Niemi, R. G., & Junn, J. (1998). *Civic education: What makes students learn?* New Haven, CT: Yale University Press.

Niemi, R. G., Sanders, M. S., & Whittington, D. (2005). Civic knowledge of elementary and secondary school students, 1933–1998. *Theory and Research in Social Education, 33*, 172–199.

Nucci, L. P. (1981). The development of personal concepts: A domain distinct from moral and societal concepts. *Child Development, 52*, 114–121.

Nucci, L. P., Krettenauer, T., & Narváez, D. (Eds.) (2008). *Handbook of moral and character education.* London: Routledge.

Osborne, K. (2004). Political and citizenship education: Teaching for civic engagement. *Education Canada, 45*, 13–16.

Osborne, K., & Seymour, J. (1988). Political education in upper elementary school. *International Journal of Social Education, 3*, 63–77.

Osler, A., & Starkey, H. (2006). Education for democratic citizenship: A review of research, policy, and practice 1995–2005. *Research Papers in Education, 21*, 433–466.

Perlinger, A., Canetti-Nisim, D., & Pedahzur, A. (2006). Democratic attitudes among high-school pupils: The role played by perceptions of class climate. *School Effectiveness and School Improvement, 17*, 119–140.

Piaget, J. (1932). *The moral judgment of the child.* London: Routledge & Kegan Paul.

Putnam, R. (1993). *Making democracy work: Civic traditions in modern Italy.* Princeton, NJ: Princeton University Press.

Ruck, M. D., Abramovitch, R., & Keating, D. P. (1998). Children's and adolescents' understanding of rights: Balancing nurturance and self-determination. *Child Development, 69*, 404–417.

Schaps, E., Shaeffer, E. F., & McDonnell, S. N. (2001). What's right and wrong in character education today. *Education Week, September 12, 40*, 44.

Sears, A., & Hughes, A. (2006). Citizenship: Education or Indoctrination? *Citizenship and Teacher Education, 2*, 3–17.

Sinatra, G. M., Beck, I. L., & McKeown, M.G. (1992). A longitudinal characterization of young students' knowledge of their country's government. *American Educational Research Journal, 29*, 633–661.

Sirotnik, K. A. (1988). What goes on in the classroom? Is this the way we want it? In L. E. Beyer and M. W. Apple (Eds.), *The curriculum: Problems, politics, and possibilities* (pp. 56–74). Albany, NY: State University of New York Press.

Tapp, J. L., & Kohlberg, L. (1971). Developing senses of law and legal justice. *Journal of Social Issues, 27*, 65–91.

Thornberg, R., & Elvstrand, H. (2012). Children's experiences of democracy, participation, and trust in school. *International Journal of Educational Research, 53*, 44–54.

To, S., Yang, S., & Helwig, C. C. (2014). Democratic moral education in China. In L. Nucci, D. Narvaez, & T. Krettenauer (Eds.), *Handbook of moral and character education*, 2nd ed. (pp. 401–419). New York: Routledge.

Torney, J., Oppenheim, A., & Farnen, R. (1975). *Civic education in ten countries: An empirical study*. New York: John Wiley & Sons, Inc.

Torney-Purta, J., Lehmann, R., Oswald, H., & Schultz, W. (2001). *Citizenship and education twenty-eight countries: Civic knowledge and engagement at age fourteen*. Amsterdam, The Netherlands: IEA.

Turiel, E. (2015). Moral development. In R. M. Lerner (Series Ed.) & W. F. Overton and P. C. M. Molenaar (Vol. Eds.), *Handbook of child psychology and developmental science. Vol. 3: Social, emotional, and personality development* (7th ed., pp. 484–522). Hoboken, NJ: John Wiley & Sons, Inc.

Ungerleider, C. S. (1990). Preparing for a more pluralistic future. *Multicultural Education Journal, 8*, 14–18.

Verkuyten, M., & Slooter, L. (2008). Muslim and non-Muslim adolescents' reasoning about freedom of speech and minority rights, *Child Development, 79*, 514–528.

Wainryb, C., Shaw, L., Langley, M., Cottam, K., & Lewis, R. (2004). Children's thinking about diversity of belief in the early school years: Judgments of relativism, tolerance, and disagreeing persons. *Child Development, 75*, 687–703.

Wainryb, C., Shaw, L., & Maianu, C. (1998). Tolerance and intolerance: Children's and adolescents' judgments of dissenting beliefs, speech, persons, and conduct. *Child Development, 69*, 1541–1555.

Walker, L. J., Hennig, K. H., & Krettenauer, T. (2000). Parent and peer contexts for children's moral reasoning development. *Child Development, 71*, 1033–1048.

Yu, T. (2004). *In the name of morality: Character education and political control*. New York: Peter Lang.

12

Research and Practice in the Study of School Bullying

Peter K. Smith

In this chapter I shall discuss research into school bullying and how research has inter-related with practice. In my view, this is in area where research has had a strong and generally positive impact. That is clearly not always the case and it has not always been the case when I look at my own research career. My earlier research was largely with preschool children and looked at the influence of preschool environments (Smith & Connolly, 1980), and later at the role of play in children's development (Smith, 1988, 1990, 1995). The findings were certainly relevant for some policy issues; but although the research was published in academic journals and in book chapters, I am not aware that it had any obvious impact on practice. Indeed, I recall being asked at a job interview in the mid-1990s as to the impact that my play research had had, and while I could point out the impact in academic terms, it was difficult to make a case beyond that. The same could largely be said for some research that I was involved in, on the role of grandparents with grandchildren in modern society (Smith, 2005a).

There are a variety of reasons for this often muted impact. I will review some later in the chapter, and indeed the raison d'être for this book is to consider this

The Wiley Handbook of Developmental Psychology in Practice: Implementation and Impact, First Edition.
Edited by Kevin Durkin and H. Rudolph Schaffer.
© 2016 John Wiley & Sons, Ltd. Published 2016 by John Wiley & Sons, Ltd.

set of issues. Equally, there are reasons why research sometimes does have a strong impact. The research on school bullying – my own, and that of many other colleagues – has had a strong and seemingly lasting impact, and that has been gratifying in personal and professional terms.

In the first half of this chapter I will review the research on school bullying and some of the societal impact it has had, through the decades from the 1980s. I will focus mainly on the United Kingdom context, and indeed mainly on England, as I can describe this knowledgeably and in detail. But similar research and often similar impact has been happening in other countries, for example in Europe (Olweus, 2004; Spiel, Salmivalli, & Smith, 2011), Australia (McGrath & Noble, 2006; Rigby, 1997) and North America (Espelage & Swearer, 2004). In the second half of the chapter I will discuss some factors that help research have an impact, as well as some that hinder this, reflecting on the school bullying domain.

Research on School Bullying

Bullying is usually taken to be a subset of aggressive (intentionally hurtful) behavior, characterized by repetition and an imbalance of power (Olweus, 1999, Figure 1.1; Smith, 2014). The behavior is repetitive, that is, a victim is targeted a number of times. Also, the victim cannot defend him/herself easily, for one or more reasons: he or she may be outnumbered, be smaller or less physically strong, or be less psychologically resilient, than the person(s) doing the bullying. The definition "a systematic abuse of power" (Smith & Sharp, 1994, p. 2) also captures these two features. Although these two criteria (repetition, and power imbalance) are not universally accepted, they are now widely used.

Bullying, by its nature, is likely to have particular characteristics. The imbalance of power both means that the victim is likely to need help, but also that s/he may be reluctant to do so or to tell anyone, for fear of reprisal. The relative defenselessness of the victim implies an obligation on others to intervene, if we take the democratic rights of the victim seriously. This, and the repetition in bullying, is also likely to lead to negative outcomes, such as development of low self-esteem, and depression, in the victim (Cook, Williams, Guerra, Kim, & Sadek, 2010). In addition, although short-term outcomes for bullying children may vary, unchecked bullying can set a life-course pattern of antisocial behavior which is clearly undesirable in social and often personal terms (Ttofi, Farrington, & Lösel, 2012).

Bullying can happen in many contexts – the workplace, the home, the armed forces, prisons, and so on. Indeed, topics such as workplace and prison bullying have been growing research areas from the 1990s onwards (Monks & Coyne, 2011). In school, too, we can think of teacher–teacher, teacher–pupil, pupil–teacher as well as pupil–pupil bullying. However, it is mainly pupil–pupil bullying that has been the focus of research up until now, and on which I will concentrate my chapter.

I have suggested (Smith, 2014) that we can consider a broad research program in school bullying developing in four phases. These are briefly outlined in the next sections.

Phase one: Origins

The first phase, origins, can be dated from the 1970s to 1988. The systematic study of school bullying can be said to have started in Scandinavia, with the publication of Olweus' first book, *Aggression in the schools: Bullies and whipping boys* (1978). This was followed by the development of the Olweus self-report questionnaire; a nationwide campaign against school bullying in Norway in 1983; and the development of the Olweus Bullying Prevention Program in Bergen. In 1988 a conference was organized in Stavanger by Roland, with an international audience including some attendees from the United Kingdom. These events form the backdrop for the development of interest and research in the United Kingdom.

School bullying remained a low-key issue in the whole of the United Kingdom well into the 1980s. Two early studies were by Lowenstein (1978a, 1978b), on characteristics of bullying and bullied children, relying mainly on teacher nominations. Arora and Thompson (1987) used a *Life in School* booklet to define the nature of bullying in a secondary school in the north of England (Arora, 1994a). However public and media attention became particularly focused on the issue in 1989–1990.

Phase two: Establishing a research program

From 1989 to the mid-1990s, a research program was established. The year 1989 was important for several reasons. The Stavanger conference disseminated wider knowledge of the Norwegian campaign and its effects. This impact was backed up by the publication of three books on school bullying in quick succession: Besag (1989), Roland and Munthe (1989) and Tattum and Lane (1989). In England, racist bullying had become recognized as a particularly worrying feature in some schools (Kelly & Cohn, 1988), with, in one well-known case, racist bullying resulting in a child's death (Burnage Report, 1989). Also, a Government report on discipline in schools appeared (the Elton Report) (Department of Education and Science, 1989); while primarily on teacher–pupil relations and discipline, this did mention that "recent studies of bullying in schools suggest that the problem is widespread and tends to be ignored by teachers ... Research suggests that bullying not only causes considerable suffering to individual pupils but also has a damaging effect on school atmosphere..." (Department of Education and Science, 1989, pp. 102–103). It recommended that schools should encourage pupils to tell staff of serious cases of bullying, deal firmly with bullying behavior, and take action based on clear rules and backed by appropriate sanctions and systems to protect and support victims.

No direct action on bullying was taken by the (renamed) Department for Education in London as an immediate result of the Elton Report. However, the Gulbenkian Foundation set up an advisory working group on "Bullying in schools" in 1989. This funded several initiatives. One was a 32-page booklet by Tattum and Herbert (1990). With the launch of this booklet it also supported a three-month extension of the Childline telephone service to a special Bullying Line, which received some 40–200 calls a day; an analysis of these was later published (LaFontaine, 1991). It also supported survey work at Sheffield University by myself and colleagues (Ahmad, Whitney, & Smith, 1991), adapting the Olweus question-naire, to get information on the nature and extent of school bullying; this was the first large-scale survey of school bullying, of nearly 7,000 pupils in 24 Sheffield schools. This and other survey results, reported between 1989 and 1991, revealed the widespread nature of school bullying in England. There were even newspaper headlines asking whether Britain was the "Bullying capital of Europe", following a press release for Roland and Munthe's book. (The bullying statistics for England did appear to be higher than those in Norway, but no higher than in many other European countries, or Japan, as subsequent research has shown).

By 1990 a number of ideas were being advocated for tackling bullying in England and Wales. These included the whole-school policy approach, and the Pikas Method of Shared Concern (Pikas, 1989), as well as assertiveness training, use of drama, and curriculum materials such as videos (Central Television, 1990). Slightly later, Maines and Robinson (1992; Robinson & Maines, 1997) advocated a "No Blame" (subsequently relabeled "Support Group") (Robinson & Maines, 2007) approach to bullying, similar in its nonpunitive, nondirect approach to the Pikas method. An early case study evaluation of an intervention in a secondary school was reported by Arora and colleagues (Arora, 1989; 1994b); apart from that, there had been little systematic evaluation of the claims made for these various methods.

Two edited collections on practical approaches to bullying, aimed for a general educational audience, were published by Elliott (1991) and Smith and Thompson (1991). At this time, the Gulbenkian Foundation funded the preparation of an annotated bibliography and resource guide on antibullying materials and strategies (Skinner, 1992; a second edition was published in 1996). Subsequently, it sup-ported the preparation of a package of materials for schools by Besag (1992), video materials by Tattum, Tattum and Herbert (1993), and a compilation of case studies by Tattum and Herbert (1993). The national charity Kidscape, with a long interest in child protection, produced materials and campaigned on the issue of school bullying. It also advocated bully courts (where children themselves elected a court to "sentence" those who bullied others), a more controversial initiative. These varied activities contributed to not only keeping bullying "on the agenda", but to providing sources of practical help for schools and teachers.

The survey findings and publicity referred to above led to the Department for Education funding the Sheffield AntiBullying Project (1991–1993), an intervention project inspired by that in Norway (Olweus, 1993), and based in 23 of the 24 schools in the earlier Sheffield survey. It was designed to evaluate just how useful particular interventions were. Interventions comprised a whole school policy, plus optional additional interventions. About eight of the primary schools and four of the secondary schools made good progress through all the stages of whole school policy development. In addition, all project schools tried out one or more of optional interventions that were offered, the most popular being training of lunchtime supervisors, drama work, assertiveness training, playground environment, video work, the Pikas approach, quality circles, literature, and peer counselling. Schools varied considerably in how much effort they put into these interventions.

The effects of the interventions were monitored over four school terms, using anonymous self-report questionnaires and other assessment measures. Significant reductions in bullying were obtained; these were larger in primary schools, and largest in those schools that had put most effort into interventions and consulted widely on policy development. In secondary schools, there were large increases in willingness to seek help when bullied. The findings are reported in Smith and Sharp (1994), with practical measures detailed in Sharp and Smith (1994); more details of whole school policy work are given in Thompson and Sharp (1994).

Two other projects were linked to the main Sheffield Project. Work on improving the playground environment was supported by a grant from the Gulbenkian Foundation, with intensive work with four primary schools on the design of the playground environment, using plans developed by each school (Higgins, 1994). For eight schools catering for special needs children, interviews with the children showed that children with special needs were at much greater risk of being bullied, than those without special needs (see also Conti-Ramsden & Durkin, Chapter 16, this volume). However, school policy development, as well as interventions such as assertiveness training, did bring about considerable reductions in this bullying (Whitney, Smith, & Thompson, 1994). Reflecting the responsiveness of the research process itself to topical concerns and debate in the broader society, the United Kingdom's premier social science funding body, the Economic and Social Research Council (ESRC), funded this work.

Another study was funded by the Police Research Group of the Home Office from 1991 to 1993; it was carried out in two deprived inner city areas, one in London and one in Liverpool. In each area, one primary school and one secondary school took part. The researchers set up a staff–student antibullying working party in each school to bring about, implement and monitor a policy and strategies to facilitate communication and prevent bullying. There were reductions in bullying in both primary schools and one of the secondary school (Pitts & Smith, 1995). An increase at the London secondary school was attributed to community factors, such as increased racial tensions at the time of the intervention.

This period also saw an expansion of media interest in the issue. Every year, several young people commit suicide, in part because of school bullying; and these now got more media attention. In 1992, the BBC TV "That's Life" program pursued the topic of school bullying vigorously, following the suicide of an adolescent girl due in part to bullying at school. Questions were asked in Parliament about what action the government was taking on bullying. At this point, the Sheffield Project was midway through; while stating that the report of this project was awaited, the Department for Education decided in the interim to circulate a "Scottish Pack" to all schools in England and Wales. This pack, *Action against bullying* (1992), by Johnstone, Munn and Edwards of the Scottish Council for Research in Education (SCRE), had been circulated to schools in Scotland some months previously.

Phase three: Internationalizing the research program

From around the mid-1990s to 2004, research into bullying became increasingly an international commitment. The research in the United Kingdom, including the Sheffield Project, took its place among other international initiatives, and had some influence elsewhere (Smith, Pepler, & Rigby, 2004). Nationally, in 1994 the Department for Education produced a Pack, *Don't Suffer in Silence*, based on the findings from the Sheffield project. This was offered free to state schools and was requested by 19,000 schools within the first three years.

A follow-up of some of the Sheffield project primary schools by Eslea and Smith (1998) pointed out the difficulties as well as opportunities facing schools in antibullying work. Of four schools followed up in detail beyond the second survey, two had reduced bullying further, in one there was little change, and in one it had got worse again. The continuing commitment of teaching staff and management to antibullying work was identified as an important factor in these outcomes.

Research in the early to mid-1990s increasingly pointed to certain at-risk groups for being bullied. It was documented that ethnic minority children can experience racist teasing and name-calling (Boulton, 1995; Moran, Smith, Thompson, &

Whitney, 1993). In secondary schools, children of different sexual orientation (gay, lesbian) were also likely to be bullied (Rivers, 1995). Several studies found that children with special educational needs were substantially more at risk of being involved in bully/victim situations (Dawkins, 1996; Mooney & Smith, 1995; Nabuzoka & Smith, 1993). Family factors were also implicated in the likelihood of a child becoming a bully or victim (Bowers, Smith, & Binney, 1994).

Boulton and Smith (1994) used peer nominations with middle school children; they reported moderate stability of both bully and victim status from one year to the next. On self-esteem measures, bullying children scored lower on behavioral items of the Harter scale (i.e., they accurately perceived their behavior to be less well accepted) but were not low in other respects; bullied children did score lower on several dimensions of self-esteem. Other research demonstrated the negative consequences of being bullied. Sharp (1995, 1996) studied correlates and consequences of bullying in secondary school aged pupils. Many pupils who reported having been bullied during the previous year said they would truant to avoid being bullied, found it difficult to concentrate on their school work, felt physically ill after being bullied and/or had experienced sleeping difficulties as a result of the bullying. A survey in East London by Williams, Chambers, Logan and Robinson (1996) of children aged 7–10 years showed that bullied children were significantly more likely to report not sleeping well, bed wetting, feeling sad, and experiencing more than occasional headaches and stomach aches. The implications of this for school health services were discussed by Dawkins (1995). Two large-scale studies reported on fear of being bullied at school (Balding, Regis, Wise, Bish, & Muirden, 1996; Francis & Jones, 1994). Salmon, James and Smith (1998) further demonstrated negative effects of bullying for anxiety, depression and low self-esteem.

Telephone help lines continued to be one source of support, and the ChildLine bullying line received further funding for seven months in 1994 as part of a BBC Social Action project. It received a total of 58,530 calls; the majority of callers were within the age range 11–14 years, predominantly girls. A detailed analysis of the calls, and of an associated survey on bullying, was given by McLeod and Morris (1996).

Interest in peer support and mediation approaches increased considerably. A survey of peer support schemes by Cowie (1998; Naylor & Cowie, 1999) found that there were benefits to the peer helpers in terms of confidence and responsibility, and to the school atmosphere generally; but there were also problems due to some degree of hostility to peer helpers from other pupils, and to issues of power sharing with staff, and ensuring sufficient time and resources for proper implementation (Cowie & Sharp, 1996).

By the late 1990s, successful legal actions (as well as some unsuccessful ones) had been taken by pupils or their parents against schools in which they were persistently bullied. In November 1996 a London school was sued by a 20-year-old former pupil who had suffered four years of victimization there; there was an out-of-court settlement of £30,000 (The Guardian, 1996). In November 1997, an 18-year-old schoolgirl lost an appeal against a three-month jail sentence; she had led a gang attack on a pupil who had later committed suicide (The Guardian, 1997). In February 1998, two 15-year-old boys received 9- and 12-month detention orders for bullying, including demanding money with menaces (The Guardian, 1998).

By the end of the century, the climate of knowledge and opinion on school bullying in England had changed radically from that prevailing 10 years earlier. It was now widely acknowledged that any school was likely to have some issues regarding bullying; it was no longer really plausible or acceptable to say "there is no bullying in this school". Rather, comparisons could be made of the effectiveness of antibullying policies and actions by different schools (Glover, Cartwright & Gleeson, 1998). In late 1999 it became a legal requirement for every state school to have some form of antibullying policy. The regular inspections of schools by the Office for Standards in education (OFSTED) now asked to what extent bullying was a problem in a school, and whether the school had taken measures to combat it, including having a policy. Much more material is now available to schools and teachers in the United Kingdom.

This and other developments led to a second edition of the antibullying pack *Don't Suffer in Silence*, published by the (renamed again) Department for Education and Employment in 2000; and with further small revisions by the (renamed yet again!) Department for Education and Skills (DfES) in 2002. This second edition omitted the details of the Sheffield project, and was generally shorter. It was only possible to retain reference to the No Blame approach by relabeling it the Support Group approach. There was much more material on peer support, following the development of this approach in the 1990s. This version of the Pack was also available on the government website. An OFSTED (2003) report described good practice in tackling bullying in secondary schools. The Children's Legal Centre produced a guide for parents and carers on what schools are required to do to prevent and deal with bullying effectively (Fiddy & Hamilton, 2004).

Over the last decade school bullying has continued to be a high profile topic in the United Kigdom and internationally, and the volume of research has increased quite dramatically (Olweus, 2013). Periodic research updates were provided by the National Children's Bureau for use by practitioners in their Highlight series (Smith, 2000, 2005b, 2010). In England a House of Commons Education and Skills Committee on Bullying (House of Commons, 2007a) made as series of recommendations to government. The response by the Government (House of Commons, 2007b) referred extensively to a new Safe to Learn guidance issued later in 2007 by the (renamed once more!) Department for Children, Schools and Families. This very extensive guidance was subsequently archived (http://webarchive.nationalarchives.gov.uk/20100413151441/http://teachernet.gov.uk/

wholeschool/behaviour/tacklingbullying/); the incoming Coalition government in 2010 has continued to support antibullying work, but with much shorter, web-based guidance (www.gov.uk/government/publications/preventing-and-tackling-bullying).

Phase four: The emergence of cyberbullying

There continues to be some consensus that bullying can take physical, verbal and relational (rumor spreading, social exclusion) forms. Those involved in both direct and relational bullying, or who are both bullies and victims, have been found to have the highest rate of behavioral problems (Wolke, Woods, Bloomfield, & Karstadt, 2000). However, the types of bullying expanded in the last decade; I have described the fourth phase of the school bullying research program as starting from around 2004, when cyberbullying became prominent (Smith, 2014). Cyberbullying has now become a major area of concern, in Europe and internationally (Bauman, 2011; Mora-Merchan & Jäger, 2010).

One lack has been longitudinal data on bullying in England on a national basis. This looked set to change, with the government-sponsored Tellus surveys (Tellus3 National Report, 2008; Tellus4 National Report, 2010), which produced annual nationwide figures on issues around child well-being, including bullying. While Tellus1 and Tellus2 were pilots and small-scale, Tellus3, carried out in 2008, provided data from nearly 149,000 pupils at years 6, 8 and 10 (approx. 11, 13 and 15 years). Tellus4, carried out in 2009, provided data from over 253,000 pupils in the same year groups. Unfortunately, Tellus surveys were discontinued from 2010 by the new Coalition Government. The comparison between Tellus3 and Tellus4, although not exact because of changes in question format and response options, did suggest some decline in rates of bullying, a trend also seen internationally (Rigby & Smith, 2011).

The effectiveness of particular interventions has continued to be reported on. Such studies include solution-based brief therapy as an intervention with individual pupils (Young & Holdorf, 2003), the operation of a bully court (Mahdavi & Smith, 2002), an evaluation of Checkpoints for Schools (Shaughnessy & Jennifer, 2004), and an evaluation of the CHIPS (ChildLine in Partnership with Schools) program (Smith & Watson, 2004). An evaluation of the second edition of the *Don't Suffer in Silence* pack (Smith & Samara, 2003) showed that schools generally felt that the problem of bullying had slightly decreased, since getting the Pack a year or so earlier. A government-sponsored project documented the range of interventions used in schools in England and their perceived success (Thompson & Smith, 2011). Meta-analyses of school-based interventions internationally suggest that many interventions have some success; Ttofi and Farrington (2011) analyzed 44 such intervention programs and found average reductions of around 20–23% in bullying rates and around 17–20% in victimization rates, with some individual programs (e.g., the Olweus Bullying Prevention Program in Norway, KiVa in Finland) producing reductions of around 40–50% (Spiel et al., 2011).

The Anti Bullying Alliance and Beatbullying

The Anti Bullying Alliance (ABA; http://www.antibullyingalliance.org.uk) was founded by NSPCC (National Society for the Prevention of Cruelty to Children) and NCB (National Children's Bureau) in 2002. ABA brings together over 50 national organizations from the voluntary and private sectors, local education authorities, professional associations and the research community into one network to work together to reduce bullying and create safer environments for children and young people to live, grow, play and learn. With funding from the DfES it has supported regional seminars, the development of a portfolio of resources, and regional support networks throughout England. An Anti-Bullying Week has been held at yearly intervals since 2004.

Another organization, Beatbullying, also campaigned nationally in the United Kingdom and introduced a cybermentors scheme in which young people themselves were trained as mentors and provided online advice and support. Similar schemes were introduced in six other European countries during 2013–2014, but unfortunately Beatbullying went into liquidation in November 2014 and this initiative is currently discontinued.

The International Picture

Internationally, school bullying has been written about and researched in most European countries, Canada, Australia (McGrath & Noble, 2006), New Zealand (Sullivan, Cleary & Sullivan, 2004), Japan (Tsuchiya, Smith, Soeda, & Oride, 2005), the USA (Espelage & Swearer, 2004), and elsewhere. Since 2000 at least one-half of European countries have some legal requirements on schools to tackle bullying (Ananiadou & Smith, 2002). The OECD held a conference in Stavanger in 2004 on school bullying and violence (Munthe, Solli, Ytre-Arne, & Roland, 2005). The Council of Europe prepared a Handbook on the topic (Gittins, 2006). An international *Handbook of Bullying in Schools* (Jimerson, Swearer, & Espelage, 2010) provides findings from many countries across the world. In 2011 the European Commission adopted an EU Agenda for the rights of the child, and the 8th European Forum held in 2013 included bullying and cyberbullying as one issue of particular concern where an integrated, multidisciplinary approach was needed. In fact, our knowledge and practice is now at a stage where coordination of activities at national and international levels will assist effective progress in reducing school bullying to lower levels.

Reflections on the Interaction Between Research and Practice

The above history has given quite a detailed account of how both research and practice have developed in the study of school bullying over the past nearly three decades; mainly emphasizing the experience in England. Having lived through this, this chapter now provides a good possibility to reflect on the relationship: on opportunities taken, and opportunities missed; on factors facilitating the relationship, and factors inhibiting it.

When does research have an impact?

(a) *Personal significance*. I think the first prerequisite for research to have an impact is that the topic is one that affects the lives and well-being of people. While this might be a small number of people in the case of some medical advances, in the case of school bullying it is the majority of people; we almost all went to school, and the majority of people become parents with children who will go to school. Being bullied is a significant concern for children, and their parents. Indeed pressure from parents, including legal actions brought by parents, have contributed to pressure for action, and thus indirectly for the need for research to inform such action. However, parent action only became evident on the wave of broader societal change.

(b) *Broader cultural and historical trends*. Schooling has been prevalent in European countries for well over a century, but research on bullying was sparse and had little impact until the 1980s–1990s. Why? There is little doubt that victims of bullying were suffering just as much in, say, the 1960s. Here the issue seems to be one of a broader cultural awareness, and moral attitudes. The twentieth century saw a vast increase in awareness of human rights generally, and of concern that rights should not be abused. Safety from bullying is a matter of individual rights (Greene, 2006), as well as impinging on areas of racial and sexual harassment, attitudes to sexual orientation, difference and disability. Whereas a predominant earlier view was that bullying was just "part of growing up", this became steadily less acceptable in the later decades of the last century. As noted above, schools themselves have changed radically in terms of their awareness of the problem and readiness to tackle it. Public opinion and parental pressure would require them to show they take the issue seriously if and when it occurs; and having an antibullying policy is now a legal requirement for English schools.

(c) *Research tools and findings.* Adequate research tools, and important findings using them, are another prerequisite. Here the work of Olweus was important in two respects. First, his Bully/Victim questionnaire provided a way in to studying the issue. Its wide-scale use revealed the extent of bullying. Secondly, the Bergen intervention program provided a practical way forward to put the concerns into practice and reduce bullying.

(d) *Synergy between research findings, the media, events, and research funding.* The media have a vital role in bringing research findings to the attention of the public, and thus (if the public are concerned) to politicians. Sometimes the research in itself may be news worthy, sometimes other events are necessary or provide greater impetus. In the case of school bullying, our initial survey reports led to the "Britain is the bullying capital of Europe" headlines. Although misleading if not quite wrong, these headlines did lead to questions in Parliament, and were an impetus to funding the Sheffield project. The tragic circumstance of children's suicides, due at least in part to school bullying, also focused attention in Britain; and was a vital component of national action in Norway in the 1980s (Olweus, 1999) and Japan in the 1990s (Morita, Soeda, Soeda, & Taki, 1999).

I describe this as a synergy, as the media need events and findings, but more detailed research can also then be given to a wider audience. Funding for further research, and for research-based intervention, is then more likely to be forthcoming.

(e) *A variety of funding sources.* The government in Britain was not seriously interested in the topic of school bullying, or supporting research into it, until the early 1990s. It was thus very fortunate that the Gulbenkian Foundation, a charitable organization with an interest in educational matters, was able to make the topic a priority area for funding as early as the late 1980s. Although the sums of money were relatively small, and for diverse causes, the results were very important for moving the area forward. Other funding bodies such as ESRC also supported research in this area, and since the 1990s the Department for Education has been consistently active in supporting antibullying initiatives, although less often supporting fundamental research.

(f) *Ensuring practical outcomes are available from the research.* One early practical outcome from the Gulbenkian funding was the booklet by Tattum and Herbert (1990) entitled *Bullying: A positive response.* This was widely available at low cost, suitable for parents as well as teachers, and was the first of a sequence of resources that as well as giving practical advice, did utilize research findings as a backdrop for the information given. Another practical outcome, feeding into research, was the launch of the special bullying line by the telephone helpline ChildLine, which received many calls (LaFontaine, 1991).

The Sheffield project itself led to the *Don't suffer in silence* pack. The advice was closely based on the research findings from the 23 participating schools; and the first edition included a section on how the research was done. This pack was free to any state school in England, and eventually went to most of them. This research, and subsequent research in the area, has fed into in-service training of teachers, subsequent manuals, and web-based advice.

(g) *Formalizing research–practice links.* Where some formal link can be made, this is likely to be productive. In England, the Anti Bullying Alliance has acted as one important focus for coordinating antibullying work in schools and for children and young people. Since 2005 it has produced digests of current research literature, contributed research briefings on selected topics (such as bullying and disability; homophobic bullying; cyberbullying), and generally helped to disseminate research findings and practice to people such as educational psychologists, teachers, social workers and other child professionals in the ABA. Other charities such as Beatbullying and Kidscape have also helped in this respect.

Factors that may inhibit research having an impact

Research does not always have the impact it should. Some reasons may simply be the obverse of factors discussed above. For example the topic may seem not so important for people's lives, it may not be "in vogue" at the time, clear research tools might be lacking, the media may not be interested or may have shifted attention to seemingly more exciting or still more alarming issues, adequate funding may not be available, it may be difficult formalizing links from the research, to the practitioner community. But there are other factors, too.

(a) *Incentives for university-based researchers.* First, some university-based researchers may have a lack of incentive for producing practical applications. Their immediate feedback from peers in the academic community, and prospects for promotion and salary increases, will depend on getting their researched published in high-quality refereed journals (or other respected academic outlets). This is and has been a primary indicator in the recurrent research assessment exercises in Great Britain; and also holds true rather widely internationally. The purely academic rewards for publishing accessible booklets for the general public, linking with practitioners, and so on, may be quite limited and might even be seen as detracting from pure research time. Of course, there can be other rewards (including financial ones if some finding was patented); but at present the institutional promotion procedures in universities and the national research assessment exercise (which strongly affects funding) give rather little reward or acknowledgement to such activities (although recently some credit has been given to the "impact" of research).

(b) *Lack of commitment to research from practitioners.* Equally, practitioners and government may not always be committed to research or receptive to research findings. For example, quite a number of schools have been reluctant to participate in research on school bullying, through surveys and interventions. They have felt that they are busy enough, and that this research might suggest that they have a problem. The latter attitude has decreased with the shift of public knowledge and attitudes on school bullying; but the general and continuing point is that practitioners have continuing immediate and practical concerns, and in the short-term "research" can seem a luxury that they are disinclined to be involved in or to make use of to change their practices.

(c) *Difficulties in implementation of research-led interventions.* Even when a school agrees to take part in a research-led intervention, there can be a range of difficulties encountered. First, not all teaching staff may be "on board" with a management-led decision to participate; teachers have their own tacit ideologies derived from educational theories and training, and their own practical experience. Second, there may be quite practical difficulties. Antibullying interventions require resources of time and sometimes space, which may conflict with other priorities; for example, it may prove difficult to provide a dedicated room for peer-counselling sessions. Third, interventions are often only partially implemented or are adapted in unexpected ways; for example, Smith, Howard and Thompson (2007) found that many English schools radically changed the way that the Support Group method was implemented. Such changes may be due to some difficulties in or lack of communication between researchers and practitioners, as well as the other factors just mentioned. Such issues make it very important to monitor program implementation and fidelity when carrying out evaluation studies.

(d) *Ideological rather than evidence-based assertions by politicians.* In addition, ideological rather than evidence-based positions may determine policy direction. This is probably more characteristic of the response of politicians and governments to research findings. Often, government is accused of deciding a position or policy direction on political grounds, and then cherry-picking research findings or choosing to interpret research findings in such a way as to support this. In the case of school bullying, attitudes to the use of punitive sanctions to deal with bullying has been a case in point.

There is a legitimate controversy about the relative efficacy of different kinds of sanctions for pupils who bully others. These range from nonpunitive stances, such as the No Blame (now Support Group) approach and Pikas Method, through Restorative Justice approaches, to quite direct and sometimes punitive sanctions (withdrawal of privileges, suspension, or ultimately exclusion from school). However, in recent years the United Kingdom government has taken a strong stance against nonpunitive approaches. This has been stated publicly by ministers, and echoed in parts of public government advice material. For example, the then Education Secretary vetoed mention of the No Blame approach in the second edition of the *Don't suffer in silence* pack (2002), although after representations some mention was allowed as the Support Group approach. This stance by the government was not evidence based. The limited research on nonpunitive methods shows that, in some circumstances at least, they can be successful; and they are well-liked by many teachers (Smith et al., 2007). The research evidence as yet does not allow strong statements on this, but some government statements, at least from politicians, reflect an ideological position that, in this particular case, can be basically inimical to either supporting objective research, or making use of such findings.

Summary

School bullying has become a major area of research and of practice in England, the United Kingdom generally, and many countries internationally. The climate of opinion on the topic has shifted noticeably; in England, especially during the 1990s. This chapter gives a brief history of the research and related practice regarding school bullying, especially in England. The main findings are reviewed, in chronological stages. Over the last 25–30 years there has been a very considerable body of research. There has also been a lot of practical impact, including government materials for schools, legislation on antibullying policies, a mushrooming of materials, advice packs and web sites, more legal actions brought by parents and young people, and a growth of initiatives such as peer-support schemes in schools. The Anti Bullying Alliance, and Beatbullying, are two organizations that are helping facilitate the continued use of research findings in practice.

In the second part of the chapter I reflect on some factors that have facilitated the practical application of research. These include: (a) the research having personal significance for people; (b) broader cultural and historical trends enhancing interest in or relevance of the research; (c) having appropriate research tools and findings to move the research agenda forward; (d) having a synergy between research findings, the media, events, and research funding; (e) having a variety of funding sources (and not just government and research councils); (f) ensuring practical outcomes are available from the research in accessible ways; and (g) formalising research-practice links.

In addition, some inhibiting factors are considered. Besides the obverse of those above, I consider (a) institutional and government factors that can negatively affect the likely motivation and reward structure for academic researchers to engage strongly in practical applications, (b) possible reluctance of practitioners to engage time in facilitating research or taking account of it in ways which may require a change in practice, (c) some difficulties in communication between researchers and practitioners, and in implementation of research-led interventions, and (d) how politicians and government may sometimes adopt ideological positions which do not favor the pursuit or use of objective research findings.

Overall, despite some difficulties, the link between research and practice in the area of school bullying has been a very positive one. It is satisfying to feel that the research work has had such positive outcomes and is contributing in important ways to making the life of children in schools safer.

References

Ahmad, Y., Whitney, I., & Smith, P. K. (1991). A survey service for schools on bully/victim problems. In P. K. Smith & D. A. Thompson (Eds.), *Practical approaches to bullying* (pp. 103–111). London: David Fulton.

Ananiadou, K., & Smith, P. K. (2002). Legal requirements and nationally circulated materials against school bullying in European countries. *Criminal Justice, 2*, 471–491.

Arora, C. M. J. (1989). Bullying – action and intervention. *Pastoral Care in Education, 7*, 44–47.

Arora, C. M. J. (1994a). Is there any point in trying to reduce bullying in secondary schools? *Educational Psychology in Practice, 10*, 155–162.

Arora, C. M. J., & Thompson, D. A. (1987). Defining bullying for a secondary school. *Education and Child Psychology, 14*, 110–120.

Arora, T. (1994b). Measuring bullying with the 'Life in School' checklist. *Pastoral Care in Education, 12*, 11–15.

Balding, J., Regis, D., Wise, A., Bish, D., & Muirden, J. (1996). *Bully off: Young people that fear going to school.* University of Exeter, UK: Schools Health Education Unit.

Bauman, S. (2011). *Cyberbullying: What counselors need to know.* Alexandria, VA: American Counseling Association.

Besag, V. (1989). *Bullies and victims in schools.* Milton Keynes, UK: Open University Press.

Besag, V. (1992). *We don't have bullies here!* 57 Manor House Road, Jesmond, Newcastle-upon-Tyne NE2 2LY.

Boulton, M. J. (1995). Patterns of bully/victim problems in mixed race groups of children. *Social Development, 4*, 277–293.

Boulton, M. J., & Smith, P. K. (1994). Bully/victim problems among middle school children: stability, self-perceived competence, and peer acceptance. *British Journal of Developmental Psychology, 12*, 315–329.

Bowers, L., Smith, P. K., & Binney, V. (1994). Perceived family relationships of bullies, victims and bully/victims in middle childhood. *Journal of Personal and Social Relationships, 11*, 215–232.

Burnage Report (1989). *Murder in the playground.* London: Longsight Press.

306 *Peter K. Smith*

Central Television (1990). *Sticks and stones*. Community Unit, Central Television, Birmingham, UK.

Cook, C. R., Williams, K. R., Guerra, N. G., Kim, T. E., & Sadek, S. (2010). Predictors of bullying and victimization in childhood and adolescence: A meta-analytic investigation. *School Psychology Quarterly, 25*, 65–83.

Cowie, H. (1998). Perspectives of teachers and pupils on the experience of peer support against bullying. *Educational Research and Evaluation, 4*, 108–125.

Cowie, H., & Sharp, S. (1996). *Peer counselling: A time to listen*. London: David Fulton.

Dawkins, J. L. (1995) Bullying in school: doctors' responsibilities. *British Medical Journal, 310*, 274–275.

Dawkins, J. L. (1996). Bullying, physical disability and the paediatric patient. *Developmental Medicine and Child Neurology, 38*, 603–612.

Department for Education (1994). *Bullying: Don't suffer in silence. An anti-bullying pack for schools*. London: HMSO. Second edition 2000, revised 2002.

Department of Education and Science (1989). *Discipline in schools: Report of the committee chaired by Lord Elton*. London: HMSO.

Elliott, M. (Ed.) (1991). *Bullying: A practical guide to coping for schools*. Harlow, UK: Longman.

Eslea, M., & Smith, P. K. (1998). The long-term effectiveness of anti-bullying work in primary schools. *Educational Research, 40*, 203–218.

Espelage, D. L., & Swearer, S. M. (Eds.) (2004). *Bullying in American schools: A socio-ecological perspective on prevention and intervention*. Mahwah, NJ and London: Lawrence Erlbaum Associates.

Fiddy, A., & Hamilton, C. (2004). *Bullying: A guide to the law*. Colchester, UK: Children's Legal Centre, University of Essex.

Francis, L. J., & Jones, S. H. (1994). The relationship between Eysenck's personality factors and fear of bullying among 13–15 year olds in England and Wales. *Evaluation and Research in Education, 8*, 111–118.

Gittins, C. (Ed.) (2006). *Violence reduction in schools – how to make a difference*. Strasbourg, France: Council of Europe.

Glover, D., Cartwright, N., & Gleeson, D. (1998). *Towards bully-free schools: Interventions in action*. Buckingham, UK: Open University Press.

Greene, M. B. (2006). Bullying in schools: A plea for a measure of human rights. *Journal of Social Issues, 62*, 63–79.

Higgins, C. (1994). Improving the school ground environment as an anti-bullying intervention. In P. K. Smith & S. Sharp (Eds.), *School bullying: Insights and perspectives* (pp. 160–192). London: Routledge.

House of Commons (2007a). *House of Commons Education and Skills Committee: Bullying. Third Report of Session 2006–07*. London: The Stationery Office.

House of Commons (2007b). *House of Commons Education and Skills Committee: Bullying: Response to the Committee's Third Report of Session 2006–07*. London: The Stationery Office.

Jimerson, S., Swearer, S., & Espelage, D. (Eds.) (2010). *Handbook of bullying in schools: An international perspective*. New York: Routledge.

Johnstone, M., Munn, P., & Edwards, L. (1992). *Action against bullying: A support pack for schools*. Edinburgh: SCRE.

Kelly, E., & Cohn, T. (1988). *Racism in schools: New research evidence*. Stoke-on-Trent, UK: Trentham Books.

LaFontaine, J. (1991). *Bullying: the child's view*. London: Calouste Gulbenkian Foundation.

Lowenstein, L. F. (1978a). Who is the bully? *Bulletin of the British Psychological Society, 31*, 147–149.

Lowenstein, L. F. (1978b). The bullied and non-bullied child. *Bulletin of the British Psychological Society, 31*, 316–318.

Mahdavi, J., & Smith, P. K. (2002). The operation of a bully court and perceptions of its success: A case study. *School Psychology International, 23*, 327–341.

Maines, G., & Robinson, B. (1992). *Michael's Story: The "No Blame" Approach*. Bristol, UK: Lame Duck Publishing.

McGrath, H., & Noble, T. (Eds.) (2006). *Bullying solutions: Evidence-based approaches to bullying in Australian schools* (pp. 189–201). NSW, Australia: Pearson.

McLeod, M., & Morris, S. (1996). *Why me? Children talking to ChildLine about bullying*. London: ChildLine.

Monks, C., & Coyne, I. (Eds.) (2011). *Bullying in different contexts*. Cambridge, UK: Cambridge University Press.

Mooney, S., & Smith, P. K. (1995). Bullying and the child who stammers. *British Journal of Special Education, 22*, 24–27.

Mora-Merchan, J., & Jäger, T. (Eds.). (2010). *Cyberbullying: A cross-national comparison*. Landau, Germany: Verlag Empirische Pädagogik.

Moran, S., Smith, P. K., Thompson, D., & Whitney, I. (1993). Ethnic differences in experiences of bullying: Asian and white children. *British Journal of Educational Psychology, 63*, 431–440.

Morita, Y., Soeda, H., Soeda, K., & Taki, M. (1999). Japan. In P. K. Smith, Y. Morita, J. Junger-Tas, D. Olweus, R. Catalano, & P. Slee (Eds.), *The nature of school bullying: A cross-national perspective* (pp. 309–323). London & New York: Routledge.

Munthe, E., Solli, E., Ytre-Arne, E., & Roland, E. (2005). *Taking fear out of schools*. Stavanger, Norway: Centre for Behavioural Research, University of Stavanger.

Nabuzoka, D., & Smith, P. K. (1993). Sociometric status and social behaviour of children with and without learning difficulties. *Journal of Child Psychology and Psychiatry, 34*, 1435–1448.

Naylor, P., & Cowie, H. (1999). The effectiveness of peer support systems in challenging bullying in schools: the perspectives and experiences of teachers and pupils. *Journal of Adolescence, 22*, 467–479.

OFSTED (2003). *Bullying: Effective action in secondary schools*. London: OFSTED.

Olweus, D. (1978). *Aggression in the schools: Bullies and whipping boys*. Washington, DC: Hemisphere.

Olweus, D. (1993). *Bullying at school: What we know and what we can do*. Oxford: Blackwell Publishing.

Olweus, D. (1999). Sweden. In P. K. Smith, Y. Morita, J. Junger-Tas, D. Olweus, R. Catalano, & P. Slee (Eds.) (1999). *The nature of school bullying: A cross-national perspective* (pp. 7–27). London & New York: Routledge.

Olweus, D. (2004). The Olweus Bullying Prevention Programme: design and implementation issues and a new national initiative in Norway. In P.K. Smith, D. Pepler, & K. Rigby (Eds.), *Bullying in schools: How successful can interventions be?* (pp. 13–36). Cambridge, UK: Cambridge University Press.

Olweus, D. (2013). School bullying: Development and some important challenges. *Annual Review of Clinical Psychology, 9,* 751–780.

Pikas, A. (1989). A pure concept of mobbing gives the best results for treatment. *School Psychology International, 10,* 95–104.

Pitts, J., & Smith, P. (1995). *Preventing school bullying.* London: Home Office Police Research Group.

Rigby, K. (1997). *Bullying in schools and what to do about it.* London: Jessica Kingsley.

Rigby, K., & Smith, P. K. (2011). Is school bullying really on the rise? *Social Psychology of Education, 14,* 441–455.

Rivers, I. (1995). Mental health issues among young lesbians and gay men bullied in school. *Health and Social Care in the Community, 3,* 380–383.

Robinson, G., & Maines, B. (1997). *Crying for help: the No Blame approach to bullying.* Bristol, UK: Lucky Duck Publishing.

Robinson, G., & Maines, B. (2007). *Bullying: A complete guide to the Support Group Method.* Bristol, UK: Lucky Duck Publishing.

Roland, E., & Munthe, E. (1989). *Bullying: An international perspective.* London: David Fulton.

Salmon, G., James, A., & Smith, D.M. (1998). Bullying in schools: self reported anxiety, depression, and self esteem in secondary school children. *British Medical Journal, 317,* 924–925.

Sharp, S. (1995). How much does bullying hurt? The effects of bullying on the personal well-being and educational progress of secondary aged students. *Educational and Child Psychology, 12,* 81–88.

Sharp, S. (1996). Self esteem, response style and victimisation: Possible ways of preventing victimisation through parenting and school based training programmes. *School Psychology International, 17,* 347–357.

Sharp, S., & Smith, P. K. (Eds.) (1994). *Tackling bullying in your school: A practical handbook for teachers.* London: Routledge.

Shaughnessy, J., & Jennifer, D. (2004). An evaluation of Checkpoints for Schools. UK Observatory web site (http://www.ukobservatory.com/downloadfiles/BLEA%20Exec%20Summary.pdf; last accessed August 11, 2015.

Skinner, A. (1992, 2nd ed. 1996). *Bullying: An annotated bibliography of literature and resources.* Leicester, UK: Youth Work Press.

Smith, P. K. (1988). Children's play and its role in early development: A reevaluation of the "play ethos". In A. D. Pellegrini (Ed.), *Psychological bases of early education* (pp. 207–226). Chichester, UK: John Wiley & Sons Ltd.

Smith, P. K. (1990). The role of play in the nursery and primary school curriculum. In P. Kutnick & C. Rogers (Eds.), *The social psychology of the primary school* (pp. 144–168). London: Routledge.

Smith, P. K. (1995). Play, ethology, and education: A personal account. In A. D. Pellegrini (Ed.), *The future of play theory* (pp. 3–21). New York: SUNY Press.

Smith, P. K. (2000). Bullying in schools. *Highlight*, no 174, London: National Children's Bureau.

Smith, P. K. (2005a). Grandparents & grandchildren. *The Psychologist, 18*, 684–687.

Smith, P. K. (2005b). Bullying in schools. *Highlight*, no 216. London: National Children's Bureau.

Smith, P. K. (2010). Bullying. *Highlight*, no 261, London: National Children's Bureau.

Smith, P. K. (2014). *Understanding school bullying: Its nature and prevention strategies*. London & Thousand Oaks, CA: Sage Publications.

Smith, P. K., & Connolly, K. J. (1980). *The ecology of preschool behaviour*. Cambridge, UK: Cambridge University Press.

Smith, P. K., Howard, S., & Thompson, F. (2007). Use of the Support Group Method to tackle bullying, and evaluation from schools and local authorities in England. *Pastoral Care in Education, 25*, 4–13.

Smith, P. K., Pepler, D., & Rigby, K. (Eds.) (2004). *Bullying in schools: How successful can interventions be?* Cambridge, UK: Cambridge University Press.

Smith, P. K., & Samara, M. (2003). *Evaluation of the DfES anti-bullying pack*. Research Brief No: RBX06-03. London: DfES.

Smith, P. K., & Sharp, S. (Eds.) (1994). *School bullying: Insights and perspectives*. London: Routledge.

Smith, P. K., & Thompson, D. A. (Eds) (1991). *Practical approaches to bullying*. London: David Fulton.

Smith, P. K., & Watson, D. (2004). *Evaluation of the CHIPS (ChildLine in Partnership with Schools) programme*. Research report RR570, London: DfES. Retrieved on July 15, 2015 from http://webarchive.nationalarchives.gov.uk/20130401151715/http://www.education. gov.uk/publications/eOrderingDownload/RR570.pdf.pdf

Spiel, C., Salmivalli, C., & Smith, P. K. (2011). Translational research: National strategies for violence prevention in school. *International Journal of Behavioral Development, 35*, 381–382.

Sullivan, K., Cleary, M., & Sullivan, G. (2004). *Bullying in secondary schools*. London: Paul Chapman.

Tattum, D. P., & Herbert, G. (1990). *Bullying – a positive response*. Cardiff: Faculty of Education, South Glamorgan Institute of Higher Education.

Tattum, D. P., & Herbert, G. (1993). *Countering bullying*. Stoke-on-Trent, UK: Trentham Books.

Tattum, D. P., & Lane, D. A. (1989). *Bullying in schools*. Stoke-on-Trent, UK: Trentham Books.

Tattum, D. P., Tattum, E., & Herbert, G. (1993). *Cycle of violence*. Cardiff: Drake Educational Associates.

Tellus 3 National Report (2008). Retrieved on July 15, 2015 from http://webarchive. nationalarchives.gov.uk/20141124154759/http://www.ofsted.gov.uk/resources/tellus3-national-report

Tellus 4 National Report (2010). Research Report DCSF-RR218. (https://www.nfer.ac.uk/ publications/TEL01/TEL01_home.cfm; last accessed August 11, 2015).

The Guardian (1996). School pays £30,000 to victim of bullying. November 16.

The Guardian (1997). School bully loses appeal. November 14.

The Guardian (1998). Judge orders detention for school bullies. February 24.

Thompson, D., & Sharp, S. (with Rose, D., & Ellis, M.) (1994). *Improving schools: Establishing and integrating whole school behaviour policies*. London: David Fulton.

Thompson, F., & Smith, P. K. (2011). *The use and effectiveness of anti-bullying strategies in schools*. Research Report DFE-RR098. London: DfE. Retrieved on July 15, 2015 from https://www.gov.uk/government/uploads/system/uploads/attachment_data/file/182421/DFE-RR098.pdf

Tsuchiya, M., Smith, P. K., Soeda, K., & Oride, K. (2005). *Ijime ni torikunda kuniguni [Responses to the issue of ijime/bullying]*. Kyoto, Japan: Minerva Publishing.

Ttofi, M. M., & Farrington, D. P. (2011). Effectiveness of school-based programs to reduce bullying: A systematic and meta-analytic review. *Journal of Experimental Criminology, 7*(1), 27–56.

Ttofi, M. M., Farrington, D. P., & Lösel, F. (2012). School bullying as a predictor of violence later in life: A systematic review and meta-analysis of prospective longitudinal studies. *Aggression and Violent Behavior, 17*, 405–418.

Whitney, I., Smith, P. K., & Thompson, D. (1994). Bullying and children with special educational needs. In P. K. Smith & S. Sharp (Eds), *School bullying: Insights and perspectives* (pp. 213–240). London: Routledge.

Williams, K., Chambers, M., Logan, S., & Robinson, D. (1996). Association of common health symptoms with bullying in primary school children. *British Medical Journal, 313*, 17–19.

Wolke, D., Woods, S., Bloomfield, L., & Karstadt, L. (2000). The association between direct and relational bullying and behaviour problems among primary school children. *Journal of Child Psychology and Psychiatry, 41*, 989–1002.

Young, S., & Holdorf, G. (2003). Using solution focused brief therapy in individual referrals for bullying. *Educational Psychology in Practice, 19*, 271–282.

13

Promoting Pedestrian Skill Development in Young Children: Implementation of a National Community-Centered Behavioral Training Scheme

James A. Thomson

It comes as a surprise to most people to learn that road traffic accidents are one of the ten leading causes of death and long-term disability in the modern world. Globally, they give rise to over a million deaths and up to 50 million injuries each year (Kopits & Cropper, 2005). They are the ninth leading cause of disability-adjusted life years (a measure of the global burden of disease, expressed as number of years lost due to ill health, disability or premature death) (Peden et al., 2008). In the hard light of economics, they cost governments, on average, between 1 and 2% of their gross national product each year (Jacobs, Aeron-Thomas, Astrop, 2000). The cost to grieving families is, of course, beyond estimation. Moreover, while there has been a significant improvement in accident rates in most high-income countries over the last 20 years, the opposite is the case in middle and low-income countries where motorization continues to expand (Zhang, Yau, & Zhang, 2014). Indeed, the World Health Organization predicts that road traffic accidents will rise from ninth to third position in the global burden of disease by 2020 (Peden et al., 2008).

The Wiley Handbook of Developmental Psychology in Practice: Implementation and Impact, First Edition.
Edited by Kevin Durkin and H. Rudolph Schaffer.
© 2016 John Wiley & Sons, Ltd. Published 2016 by John Wiley & Sons, Ltd.

Child pedestrians are among the most vulnerable of all road users, with an accident rate up to four times that of adults, even in highly developed countries where their exposure to traffic has been declining for several decades (DiGiuseppe, Roberts & Li, 1997; Hillman, Adams, & Whitelegg, 1990). The World Health Organization estimated that, in 2002 alone, over 180,000 child pedestrians were killed worldwide. This vulnerability follows, in part, from the severity of injuries that a child pedestrian is likely to sustain in the event of an accident. However, it also reflects the complexity of the traffic environment and the extent to which this taxes children's cognitive skills and experience. If child vulnerability is to be reduced, then we need to understand the skills and competences that pedestrians require in order to interact with traffic. We also need to investigate the extent to which these skills might be promoted in children through education or training. In addition, we might use our understanding of what road users find difficult in traffic to design environments that minimize these difficulties, making the environment intrinsically safer in the first place. However, this requires research on what these difficulties actually are.

It seems almost axiomatic that psychological theory and research should have a key role to play in this area. Historically, however, astonishingly little psychological research has addressed these problems and few interventions have been founded on clear psychological principles. In this chapter, we examine what more recent psychological research has to say about the skills and competences needed to interact safely with the urban traffic environment. We then look at the types of intervention that might realistically be expected to promote development of these skills in children and young people. Since it turns out that the most effective types of intervention are not altogether straightforward to implement, we also look at some of the barriers that might prevent adoption of effective interventions and consider one case study illustrating how, by working in partnership with government and other agencies, these have been overcome.

Traditional Approaches to Road Safety Education

At first sight, learning to cross the road does not seem especially complicated compared to other things that children need to learn and the reader may wonder what is so difficult about it. Perhaps, as adults, we have long since forgotten what acquiring these skills was like. Even researchers have sometimes come close to this view. For example, Rothengatter argued that "in contrast to other forms of traffic participation like driving, bicycling and flying, very few skills appear to be involved in participating in traffic as a pedestrian" (Rothengatter, 1981, p. 30). As we shall see, this fails to recognize the skills involved in pedestrian decision making but reflects traditional approaches to road safety education, which assume that what children require is general knowledge about how the traffic environment works, simple rules to guide their crossing behavior, and an emphasis on positive attitudes towards safety so that children would not choose to behave in a risky fashion.

Very little emphasis was placed on behavior within traditional educational approaches: the assumption was that improved knowledge and attitudes would automatically transfer to decision making at the roadside. Insofar as behavior was addressed at all, it was by means of verbal rules (such as the UK Green Cross Code or its equivalent in other countries). Such rules are typically formulated in a deliberately broad fashion so that they could, in principle, apply to a wide variety of situations. It was assumed that children would know intuitively how to implement such rules adaptively in the different traffic contexts they might encounter. The teaching was almost entirely verbal and classroom-based and the measure of performance was normally children's ability to recite the rules or respond verbally to questions posed by adults. Children thus learned by being *told* what to do rather than by actually *doing* anything. While the precepts of the Code were perfectly sensible in themselves, the approach was top-down, based on verbal learning in irrelevant contexts, and assumed a substantial capacity for transfer of learning in young children. From a developmental point of view, it is hard to identify any theoretical foundation that would justify this approach: indeed, it runs contrary to most of them (see Thomson, Tolmie, Foot & McLaren, 1996, Chapter 3, for a discussion). It does, however, conform to assumptions implicit in health promotion research that information transmission is paramount and that ensuring it reaches target audiences is the key challenge (Morrongiello & Matheis, 2004).

The main problem with these approaches is that interventions focusing on knowledge, attitudes or traffic rules typically make little, if any, impact on children's actual behavior in traffic. It is certainly true that children taught in this way give better answers to questions posed by adults. However, almost none of this seems to generalize to their behavior at the roadside (Rothengatter, 1981; Thomson, 1991; Zeedyk, Wallace, Carcary, Jones, & Larter, 2001). Likewise, the assumption that children would be able to deploy traffic rules effectively has proved optimistic. Children do generally "know" the rules they have been taught quite well. However, when attempting to put them into practice, they tend to do so in a rigid and somewhat stereotypical manner. Children show very little conceptual understanding of the purpose underlying rules taught as verbal drills, which presumably underpins the inappropriate way in which they often deploy them (Thomson et al., 1996; Tolmie, Thomson, & Foot, 2000).

The general inefficacy of traditional road safety education has raised in some authorities' minds the question as to whether anything worthwhile can be attained through education at all (Roberts, Mohan, & Abbassi, 2002). Such authors argue that a better approach might be to direct efforts exclusively towards creating an intrinsically safer environment where sophisticated traffic competences would not be required. Other critics have suggested that the failure of road safety education does not so much reflect shortcomings in educational practice as inherent limitations in what children can learn. This view can be traced to the early work of Sandels (1975) who, on the basis of her pioneering research in Sweden, concluded that "it is not possible to adapt fully young children (under 10 years) to the traffic environment [because] … they are biologically incapable of managing its many demands". She recommended that the principal aim of pedestrian safety should be to separate children from traffic altogether until such time as "childhood has matured out of them".

Skills and Behavioral Competences Required to Interact with Traffic

These arguments give rise to a very pessimistic outlook regarding the potential of traffic education. By the 1990s, the UK government was so concerned that it commissioned a major report aimed at clarifying the skills and competences needed to interact with traffic and assessing the realistic potential of interventions to improve these skills (Thomson et al., 1996). It also instigated a program of fundamental research in pursuit of these themes (Chapman, 1998).

A key aspect of these more recent analyses has been to recognize that pedestrian behavior is better characterized in terms of *skill* rather than *knowledge* and that solving traffic problems involves the deployment of a wide range of fundamental perceptual, motor and cognitive competences each of which has its own developmental history (see Thomson, 1991, for a review). Research has also started to focus on the meta-cognitive processes by which these psychological skills are deployed (Thomson et al., 2005; Whitebread & Neilson, 2000). According to this approach, the task for research is to define the skills and processes underlying pedestrian competence; show how these vary in road users with different levels of experience; and determine the extent to which they might be enhanced through training. Here, we review some of the more prominent skills that have been identified. Later, we consider whether these might be promoted through intervention and, if so, what form of intervention would most likely bring success.

Hazard Perception in Children

It stands to reason that if children are to take action to deal with hazards, they have to recognize them when they are encountered. However, studies show that the development of hazard perception is a protracted process. For example, Hill, Lewis and Dunbar (2000) presented children of different ages and adults with illustrations or video clips of a range of safe or dangerous situations that might arise around the home or at the roadside. Younger children were less likely than older children or adults to identify hazards even when cued to do so (for example, when told that one of four depicted situations was dangerous). They were also worse at identifying roadside hazards. In addition, children's performance was *much* worse if they were not primed to think about the scenes in terms of hazard. For example, when asked to sort pictures into groups using any criterion that seemed appropriate, the salience of danger was so great for adults that 90% of them spontaneously used it as the sorting criterion. By contrast, fewer than half of 9–10-year-olds used this criterion and far fewer of the younger children did so. Thus, even where children can demonstrate some limited ability to recognize hazards when heavily cued, hazard is not a salient dimension for them and they do not respond to it spontaneously. This is important because, as Sheehy, Chapman and David (1988) point out, it is not enough to be able to identify a hazard when prompted: unless the right features are attended to spontaneously as they arise, children cannot be expected to implement safety rules they have been taught because they will not see the need for them.

Interestingly, children's sensitivity to roadside hazards varied not only as a function of age but also as a function of their exposure to the traffic environment. Even among 5–7-year-olds, those who walked to school or played regularly in the street were significantly more sensitive to traffic dangers than those who did not. This suggests that children can learn to recognize traffic dangers if given opportunities to do so. We return to the implications of this for training below.

Ampofo-Boateng and Thomson (1991) undertook a series of studies focusing specifically on the perception of roadside hazards. The research was motivated by evidence that some types of roadside location are particularly prevalent in cases of child pedestrian injury. Examples include parked vehicles, sharp bends (especially if trees, hedges or other street "furniture" obstructs the view), positions beneath the brow of a hill, and intersections. The features that such sites have in common seems to be either that they restrict the child's view of traffic, or they involve complex traffic movements that tax the child's visual search and information-processing capacities. Such structures could also be expected to pose similar challenges to oncoming drivers.

In some experiments, the authors presented children with locations that were either very safe or manifestly dangerous and simply asked the children to say which was which. In others, children were asked in a more open-ended way to construct safe routes to destinations. Irrespective of testing method, the results revealed a clear and consistent pattern: five- and seven-year-old children exhibited almost no ability to distinguish safe from dangerous places to cross the road. Only from age nine did children begin to appreciate the risk posed by positions where the road cannot be seen properly and even 11-year-olds had not reached a ceiling with respect to such judgments.

The cues that younger children used in making their decisions were striking. If they could see a car anywhere in the vicinity, they judged the situation to be dangerous. On the other hand, if no vehicle was visible, they assumed that the situation was safe. They almost never realized that many roadside locations are dangerous precisely because cars cannot be seen. As a result, they would often prefer to cross at parked vehicles, at a bend, or below the brow of an obscuring hill. Even when cued by being told that one of two depicted situations was dangerous, unless a vehicle was present the children would insist that both scenes were safe. They appeared to be relying rigidly on a widely taught rule, namely "never cross if you can see cars". Only older children spotted the danger and suggested how it might be dealt with, for example by moving to a place nearby offering a better view of the road. These results have now been replicated in many studies (Ampofo-Boateng et al., 1993; Demetre & Gaffin, 1994; Tabibi & Pfeffer, 2003, 2007; Thomson & Whelan, 1997; Thomson et al., 1992; Tolmie et al., 2002).

These findings are consistent with arguments offered by Grieve and Williams (1985) and Hill et al. (2000) that children see danger as an intrinsic feature of objects. Matches, for example, are always dangerous but a toy is not. Because children lack the conceptual understanding to realize that danger is primarily contextual and that most objects move between being dangerous and benign depending on the situation, children often respond inappropriately to the presence or absence of objects deemed to be dangerous. In some cases, this leads to very cautious judgments, as when a child thinks a parked vehicle is dangerous because 'it might roll down the road and hit someone' (Underwood, Dillon, Farnsworth, & Twiner, 2007). On the other hand, the apparent absence of a danger object results in dangerous situations being judged safe.

Detecting the Presence of Traffic

Obviously, pedestrians have to look for traffic if they are to avoid it. However, looking (in the sense of pointing one's head in the right direction) does not guarantee that children or even adults will always "see" approaching traffic. This depends on the effectiveness of several underlying processes. The pedestrian requires an effective *visual search* strategy that, in turn, requires at least a basic representation of how cars move about the road environment. Without this, pedestrians would be unable to focus on locations where vehicles are most likely to come from and their visual search would be poorly structured and inefficient. The pedestrian also requires the attentional capacity to concentrate on cues that are relevant to the road crossing task while ignoring those that are irrelevant. Since irrelevant objects and events are frequently more interesting than relevant ones, there arises the problem of *distractibility* and how to counteract it.

There is considerable evidence that immature visual search and/or poor attentional control are implicated in children's vulnerability. For example, up to 70% of child pedestrian injuries have been attributed to "dart-outs" in which the child either did not look at all for traffic before stepping into the street or else used an inadequate search strategy, such as looking in some directions but not others (Kraus et al., 1996; Rivara, 1990; Zeedyk, Wallace & Spry, 2002). More significantly, several studies report that injuries commonly occur to children who did, in fact, look before crossing but somehow failed to "see" the approaching vehicle. In an extensive study of child victims across the United Kingdom, Grayson (1975a) estimated that 31% had looked but not seen the striking vehicle. Such "looked but failed to see" (LBFTS) errors are by no means limited to children. Brown (2002) estimated that 21% of accidents involving vehicles at junctions are of this type. Such LBFTS errors are generally considered to be forms of inattentional blindness, a phenomenon associated with resource-consuming tasks in a wide range of domains in both children and adults (Maples, DeRosier, Hoenes, Bendure & Moore, 2008; Richards, Hannon & Derakshan, 2010; Simons & Chabris, 1999).

Selective Attention and Visual Search

Consistent with the above findings, laboratory studies of children's visual search as they explore objects or scenes show their exploration to be inefficient and unstructured by comparison to adults or older children (Vurpillot, 1968; Zinchenko, van Chizti-tsi, & Tarakanov, 1965). According to Wright and Vliestra (1975), young children *explore* the environment in a spontaneous and playful manner, with their attention driven by the salience of surrounding stimuli rather than by logical features of the task at hand. As they mature, there is a shift towards increasingly organized and active *search*, in which attention becomes more intentional and goal-directed and, therefore, more governed by information relating to the demands of the task. The child thus concentrates more on relevant features, filtering out those that are irrelevant. However, children do not approach adult levels of control until 11–12 years of age (Barton, 2007; Tolmie, Thomson, Foot, McLaren, & Whelan, 1998).

In a specifically road crossing context, Dunbar, Hill, and Lewis (2001) developed tasks aimed at assessing two aspects of attentional performance: the capacity to *focus* attention and resist distractions; and the ability to *switch* attention when required. There were clear age trends on these tasks but what was more interesting was the relationship between performance and road crossing behavior. The latter was assessed by unobtrusively filming children and their parents as they approached the psychology department where testing took place. Across all age groups, children who were better at switching showed more awareness of traffic (e.g., they were more likely to disengage from talking to their parent and switch attention to the movement of traffic on the road). Correspondingly, children who were better at concentrating in the face of distractions crossed the road in a manner which the authors' judged less reckless. Dunbar et al. concluded that children's road crossing performance is directly related to the development of attentional skills.

Whitebread and Neilson (2000) investigated in more detail how children distribute their attention when deciding how to cross roads, which were presented by means of video monitors representing the view to left, right and straight ahead. They found older children and adults switched attention (i.e., looked in different directions) much more frequently than younger children. They also looked in each direction for a much shorter time. The authors interpreted this as showing that more experienced pedestrians know better what they are looking for and thus do not need to look in any one direction for very long. Older children were also much more likely to recheck what was happening in all directions immediately before deciding to cross. Younger children gazed at the screen in front of them, looking around much less frequently and in a haphazard fashion. The authors commented that these children appeared unsure of what they were expected to do when told to "look" for traffic.

The possibility that children might not understand what they should be looking for when making crossing decisions has been investigated by Tolmie et al. (1998), who constructed a series of dynamic, computer-generated traffic scenes containing both traffic-relevant and irrelevant features. Children and adults viewed the scenarios and, immediately afterwards, were asked to recall what they saw. In one condition, the task was presented as a memory game and participants were simply asked to report as much as they could remember. In another, the task was given a road-crossing focus by depicting a pedestrian at the roadside. Participants were asked to concentrate on features the pedestrian would need to attend to in order to cross safely and report what these were.

In the nontraffic condition, none of the groups showed a bias towards recalling traffic-relevant features, presumably because the task was not defined in this way. In the condition with a road-crossing focus, however, marked differences emerged between the age groups. Adults and 11-year-olds overwhelmingly stopped reporting irrelevant features. Their attention was clearly focused on features that were salient to the crossing task and their reporting was heavily biased towards these. Younger children, and especially five- and seven-year-olds, showed very little such attunement and continued to report a wide range of traffic- irrelevant features. This happened even though the tester regularly reminded participants of the purpose of the task throughout the experiment. Neither can the effect be due to younger children simply having poorer recall because, in the road focus condition, they actually reported more features in total than the older children. The authors concluded that younger children simply did not know what features were relevant when making road-crossing decisions and thus had much greater difficulty in suppressing those that should have been ignored.

These studies suggest that poor attention and visual search may underlie many of the difficulties that children face at the roadside. They also suggest that children have poor metacognitive understanding of the road crossing task and, therefore, have difficulty orienting their search to the informational demands of the task.

Strategic Planning at the Roadside

A number of studies investigating the "natural" road behavior of adults and children using unobtrusive observation (Grayson, 1975b; Howarth, Routledge, & Repetto-Wright, 1974; McLaren, 1993; Routledge, Howarth, & Repetto-Wright, 1976; van der Molen, 1983) have generated intriguing findings regarding how they approach the task from a strategic point of view. Although adults are many times less likely to be knocked down than children, this advantage does not arise as a result of greater willingness to adhere to road safety rules. In fact, adult behavior is simply nothing like that advocated by road safety education. Adults do not stop at the curb before crossing; do not wait for traffic to pass before stepping into the street; do not walk directly across the road; accept far tighter gaps in the traffic flow than any child would accept; and even use the crown of the road as a "half-way house", turning crossing into a two-stage process. Children, on the other hand, are much more likely than adults to stop at the curb; wait longer at the curb before attempting to cross; usually accept only large gaps in the traffic stream; are more likely to walk straight across the road; and do not use the crown of the road as a half-way house. In short, there is simply little correspondence between how adults behave and the road safety messages they were taught as children, yet adults are much safer in traffic. How can this discrepancy be explained?

The discrepancy seems to arise because adult road users adopt more sophisticated strategies than those taught by road safety education. Although contradicting road safety advice, most of these strategies are not really examples of "bad" behavior. For example, the reason adults do not stop and look for traffic at the roadside is that they assess the situation before arriving at the curb in the first place. This means there is no need to stop and they can cross without delay. The behavior does not reflect carelessness or incompetence: rather, it reflects anticipation and skill. Similarly, the tendency of adults to step into the street before a vehicle has passed is a strategy that maximizes the size of the gap into which they are stepping. This "tucking in" is possible because adults look ahead for suitable gaps in the traffic. As soon as the leading car has passed they are ready to step out smartly, thereby making the gap to the next car as big as possible. This also means they can accept somewhat smaller gaps than would otherwise be the case. This is obviously useful on busy roads where large gaps might not occur very often.

Children, on the other hand, show none of this anticipation. In fact, children do not look for gaps at all. Instead, they look for cars on an individual basis and focus on them in isolation. By examining cars one by one, children fail to see the relationships between them and fail to examine them far enough ahead. Because they tend not to consider whether a gap is big enough until the leading car has passed, gaps that were initially safe often become unsafe by the time the child gets round to evaluating them. Children miss many perfectly safe opportunities to cross in this way (Lee, Young, & McLaughlin, 1984).

Elementary road safety advice (such as waiting for the road to clear before crossing), then, provides no more than a "starter" strategy that children might use on very simple, quiet roads. It does not provide an adequate strategy for dealing with more complex or busier roads and *everyone* abandons it sooner or later. This suggests that a better approach might be to teach children explicitly how to cross roads of different types, adapting the strategies to suit the circumstances that different road situations impose.

Children's Perception of their Traffic Competence

A skill whose importance has been discussed by a number of authors is the ability to evaluate one's own skill level in relation to the demands of the task. For example, in deciding whether or not it is safe to cross through a gap in the traffic flow, the pedestrian must take into account not only the time *available* for crossing but also the time *required* to cross. The latter is not constant but varies as a function of such factors as the width of the road and the pedestrian's movement characteristics. Pedestrians need awareness of their movement capabilities and limitations, and must be able to calibrate this to visual information about road width in order to anticipate the time they will need to cross that particular road. As adults, we are not normally aware of this calibration unless it changes, as when one temporarily becomes lame. In the elderly, the calibration may gradually change as movement becomes more restricted. For children, of course, this will be an unfamiliar calibration that must be established, kept in tune and updated as the child grows.

Studies show that judging the fit between one's capabilities and the demands of the environment starts early and even infants adjust their actions in response to changing environmental demands. For example, infants quickly switch from walking to crawling when the surface of support changes from rigid to nonrigid (Gibson et al., 1987) or a flat surface becomes a slope (Adolph, Eppler & Gibson, 1993). In spite of this early sensitivity to affordances, children nevertheless tend to overestimate their abilities. For example, McKenzie, Skouteris, Day, Hartman, and Yonas (1993) found that children would stretch for objects that were well out of reach and would often have to be rescued from falling out of their seats as a result. The effect is not limited to very young children. McKenzie and Forbes (1992) found that 9- and 12-year-old boys consistently overestimated the height of steps they could climb. Heffernan and Thomson (1999) showed that this tendency is particularly marked during the growth spurt that, in boys, occurs around 12–13 year of age. Boys in this age group overestimated the distance they could reach, step or lean relative to both older *and* younger boys and regularly fell over as a result. Heffernan and Thomson argue that rapid growth produces a temporary imbalance in the perception of affordances and suggest that this may explain the clumsiness often reported in adolescents around this time.

The question arises as to whether this bias might be seen in children's traffic judgments. Thomson et al. (2005) reported that children in the age range 7–11 years underestimate the time required to cross a road in relation to the time actually required. This bias could be related to accident vulnerability because, if children think they need less time to cross than is the case, this would bias them towards accepting smaller traffic gaps. Moreover, Tolmie and Thomson (2003) reported that the tendency to overestimate one's traffic skills continues into adolescence. They presented 11–15-year-olds with computer-generated traffic problems and asked them to rate how difficult each problem would be to solve. They then asked the participants to actually solve the problem. Older adolescents overestimated their ability even more than younger ones and all performed less well than adults. Moreover, when subsequently given the opportunity to reevaluate the problem's difficulty in the light of their experience of trying to solve it, participants in many cases rated the problem as *easier* than they had done initially. In some cases, this happened even though the computer feedback showed participants that their decision would have resulted in a pedestrian being knocked down. Young adolescents appeared relatively insensitive to feedback on their performance, a result that may anticipate similar findings in the judgments of young drivers (Benda & Hoyos, 1983).

Promoting the Development of Pedestrian Skills in Children

It can be seen that interacting with traffic involves a wide range of psychological skills and capacities that research is now beginning to unravel. Perhaps it is not surprising that traditional educational approaches have proved relatively ineffective in changing children's behavior: just as it is not possible to learn to swim, ski or drive a car on the basis of purely verbal instruction, so the child pedestrian cannot be expected to acquire competence without corresponding practice in an appropriate environment. For pedestrian training, this must mean the roadside or something very like it, such as a simulation which adequately captures the salient characteristics of the roadside. Increasingly, interventions have adopted such a practical focus by evaluating children's competence and developing training programs either at the roadside or using virtual reality (VR) simulations. In this section, some of these studies are reviewed and their potential assessed to improve children's behavior.

Training Children to Recognize Dangerous Roadside Locations

We saw earlier why hazard detection is important in child pedestrian safety and in a number of studies we have examined whether these skills might be enhanced (Ampofo-Boateng et al., 1991, 1993; Thomson, 1997; Thomson & Whelan, 1997; Thomson et al., 1998). Using a method based on the principles of interactive learning, we developed a problem-solving approach in which children in the age range 5–6 years were taken to roadside locations where crossing would be dangerous and asked them to construct routes to destinations that would eliminate the danger. Training children in small groups, the trainer's task was to take a nondidactic approach, encouraging discussion among the children and intervening only to keep the discussion moving in productive directions. The aim was thus to get children to solve the problems through their own rather than the trainer's reasoning. The rationale was that this would improve children's conceptual understanding so that they would be better able to generalize their learning to new problems and avoid rote learning styles. Research on collaborative group learning in other domains, notably in scientific problem solving, shows this approach to be highly effective, at least in older children (see Tolmie et al., 2000, for the theory behind this approach).

When individually tested after training, the results showed that between four and six training sessions consistently produced substantial improvement in children's ability both to recognize dangerous roadside situations and devise routes through the environment that avoided them. They also showed much improved conceptual understanding of what renders roadside locations dangerous, as shown by their verbal reasoning when constructing routes. Moreover, the improvements were robust, with little or no decrease in performance when retested several months after the program ended. This suggests that practical training can produce substantial improvements even where the problems are conceptually challenging for children and cannot be solved simply by stringing together a set of rules.

Teaching Strategies for Crossing at Specific Road Structures

As we saw earlier, certain road structures pose particular difficulties for young children and, correspondingly, accidents are prevalent in the vicinity of these structures. Crossing at parked vehicles and at intersections poses particular difficulties for younger children (Demetre & Gaffin, 1994; Rothengatter, 1981). Even designated crossings, in spite of the intention that their use should be largely self-explanatory, turn out to have problematic features for children (Carsten, Sherborne, & Rothengatter, 1998; Tolmie et al., 2003), some of which are discussed here.

One response has been to devise strategies geared to the specific problems associated with such structures and teach them to children by means of guided practice. The first studies pioneering this approach were undertaken in the Netherlands, where strategies were developed for crossing at three roadside settings: roads offering a clear view of traffic; roads with parked vehicles; and junctions (Rothengatter, 1984). An instructional method based on social learning theory was devised in which adults modeled the correct behaviors and then assisted children to emulate them. Thomson and Whelan (1997) extended these strategies by introducing a stronger focus on the child's conceptual understanding of the principles underpinning the strategies, in line with the interactive learning approach described above. We have also applied this approach to teaching children how to use a range of designated crossings, in this case using VR (Tolmie et al., 2003). As in all the previous studies, the measure of improvement was children's ability to use the strategies adaptively at real roadside locations.

Prior to training, children's strategies were not uniformly poor but showed weaknesses in key areas and, in particular, their visual search strategy. At intersections, for example, children often did not look down all the streets and, when they did, their search pattern was haphazard in the manner described by Whitebread and Neilson (2000). At designated crossings, visual search was particularly weak: children appeared to assume that, because pedestrians have right of way at such structures, looking must be an optional activity. The attention children paid to approaching traffic lagged well behind that of adults, in spite of the fact that adults themselves were often not especially vigilant. At parked vehicles, younger children seldom checked to see whether either of the vehicles was occupied (and might therefore be about to move away); they frequently failed to stop at the line of sight (the outer edge of the line of vehicles, which is the first point where they would have a clear view of approaching traffic); and, when they did, they often failed to look appropriately.

Following training, these studies showed substantial improvements in all age groups. In some cases, the improvements were dramatic. For example, Tolmie et al. (2003) found, at posttest, the search behavior of six-year-olds to be indistinguishable from that of adults. The search behavior of 8- and 10-year-olds actually *surpassed* that of adults. Similarly, in Thomson and Whelan's (1997) study of crossing at parked vehicles, the frequency of some behaviors increased from 0 to over 80%. These improvements remained stable when children were retested two to three months later. It appears that strategic learning, when combined with an emphasis on conceptual grasp, can produce quite substantial improvements in the behavior of even very young children.

These studies suggest that practical methods focusing on clearly defined traffic skills offer by far the best opportunity to promote competence in children and bring about robust changes in their actual roadside behavior. Even complex skills appear to be amenable to training in children as young as five years. There is certainly no evidence to support the view that children cannot learn such skills before a certain developmental stage has been reached. The critical issue seems to be the methods that are adopted and the sort of experience they provide.

The key advantage of practical training is that it provides a meaningful context within which training takes place. Children are not required to "pretend" they are at the roadside when they are, in fact, sitting in the classroom. If they are (as with virtual reality training), well-designed simulations can provide enough context for meaningful, traffic-related interactions to take place. Neither are children asked to guess what would happen if they were to behave in such-and-such a way, because the training paradigms are designed to let them *see* what would happen. The importance of context is, of course, likely to be much greater in younger children whose conceptual model of traffic can be expected to be correspondingly rudimentary, making extrapolation from the child's immediate context especially difficult.

Problems in the Implementation of Practical Training Methods

Notwithstanding these advantages, most of the reported studies were experimental in nature, undertaken on a small scale, and normally engaged highly experienced staff as trainers. The question arises as to how realistic it would be to implement such training in the real world. Even though substantial improvements can be seen following as few as four 30-minute sessions at the roadside, this still represents a substantial input given the labor-intensive and time-consuming nature of the training. It is certainly hard to see how teachers or any of the professional groups involved in road safety education could be expected to devote the time necessary to such roadside exercises. In order to capitalize on the benefits of the practical approach, some means is needed to make it viable. This represented a potentially major barrier to the adoption of practical training schemes and a very considerable challenge for us at the time. It seems likely that many academics hoping to "give away" the fruits of their research will reach a similar point in the process. It is crucial that such barriers are identified and faced up to, otherwise there is every likelihood that the enterprise will grind to a halt and its promise remain unfulfilled.

One solution to the particular barrier identified in our case would be to engage parents to undertake the roadside training. Indeed, parents have long been advocated as a "resource" in road safety education and there is a widespread belief shared not only by professional groups but by parents themselves that the responsibility for road safety education rests in the first instance with parents (Sadler, 1972). Moreover, the use of parents in road safety education had been pioneered as long ago as the 1960s by the Scandinavian Traffic Clubs, which adopted a distance learning approach by sending parents materials illustrating activities they might undertake with their children. In the 1990s, a national traffic club was developed in the United Kingdom and this showed encouraging results (Bryan-Brown & Harland, 1999; West, Sammons, & West, 1993). However, this club focuses on elementary education for preschool children (such as holding a parent's hand), not on the complex skills envisaged here.

The traffic club idea is a good one, but two problems are associated with it. First, only a proportion of eligible parents typically enroll their children, with membership skewed towards higher socioeconomic groups. However, it is well known that accidents are markedly overrepresented among lower socioeconomic groups (Christie, 1995; Roberts & Power, 1996). This means that the children most in need of training may be the very ones least likely to get it. Second, whilst traffic clubs ensure that parents receive materials and are, therefore, better informed about what to do with their children, the clubs have no means of providing support or feedback as parents try to work their way through the program. This is likely to pose particular problems for parents who lack confidence in themselves as teachers.

An approach aimed at overcoming some of these problems was developed in the Netherlands by Rothengatter (1981) and van der Molen (1983). This group produced videos illustrating training procedures for teaching children how to deal with a range of traffic situations. These were shown to parents at evening meetings organized in local schools. In addition to demonstrating the methods, the meetings offered opportunities for parents to raise questions and, thus, represented an improvement over the approach taken by traditional traffic clubs because it offered tangible support, at least in the initial stages.

On the negative side, several problems persist. First, since not all parents attended the evening meetings it follows that only a proportion of the targeted children would receive training. The problem of "reach" thus persists. Second, the approach remains relatively passive because parents simply watched good teaching practice: they did not receive any guided experience of carrying out the training. Finally, it was difficult to determine how assiduously parents followed the program or to assess how robust the procedures were to variations in parental skill. Nevertheless, pre- and posttests showed that children's traffic competence improved relative to that of control children, and unobtrusive observation showed some generalization to children's unsupervised traffic behavior.

Developing a Community Approach to Road Safety Training: Kerbcraft and the Drumchapel Project

An opportunity to address some of these implementation issues arose when the author was approached by representatives of Strathclyde Regional Council, a large local authority in Scotland. They had become familiar with our arguments about practical training through presentations we had made to professional conferences, articles in professional journals, and some substantive coverage in the national press (Ampofo-Boateng & Thomson, 1990; Thomson, 1989a, 1989b, 1992). These communications turned out to be pivotal in the process of giving away our research and were instrumental in establishing a dialogue with road safety agencies at both local and national level.

The regional authorities were concerned about the high level of child pedestrian accidents in areas of social deprivation and, in particular, the Drumchapel area of Glasgow, a large peripheral housing estate with a child pedestrian accident rate several times the national average in spite of relatively low levels of car ownership. Initial consultations with the community suggested that these accidents were associated with blackspots close to schools, and traffic calming and other engineering measures had been implemented to address this. However, more detailed research on accident patterns using police data indicated that accidents were, in fact, very widely distributed across the area and not concentrated in the manner that had been expected. Because children appeared to be vulnerable almost everywhere, it was felt that an educational initiative aimed at improving children's ability to cope with the local traffic environment would be an important element of the accident reduction program.

For them, the key issue was to determine what kind of educational initiative would have most chance of success. They had, in fact, already attempted to increase educational provision in the area but, in line with a widespread malaise in the field as a whole, had become dissatisfied with existing materials and approaches. Our analysis appeared to offer a fresh perspective and, accordingly, they asked if I would be willing to construct a training program based on our research for piloting in the area. For us, this offered a unique opportunity to undertake studies on a much more substantive scale and, in particular, to address issues relating to the feasibility of implementing practical training methods widely. We had also been in discussion with colleagues at the Road Safety Division of the Department for Transport, which was aware that child pedestrian accidents in the United Kingdom were high in spite of a good road safety record overall and wanted to know more about the rationale behind the advocated approach and its potential role in road safety education.

Our approach was to develop *Kerbcraft,* a program with a number of distinctive features:

- The program was designed to teach 5–7-year-old children three clearly defined skills on the basis of their relationship to accident rates and their known lack of development in young children: learning to identify dangerous roadside locations and construct routes through the traffic environment that would avoid them; learning how to cross near parked cars where this is unavoidable; and learning how to cross at different kinds of intersection. The approach was progressive, with each skill being taught in a fixed order, allowing learning from previous skills to be incorporated sequentially. Each was taught by means of 4–6 roadside sessions at weekly intervals.
- In addition to teaching children procedures for solving these traffic problems, emphasis was placed on the child's conceptual understanding of the procedures, so that they would be better placed to adapt them to the varying circumstances they would encounter in the real world. We did this by means of the collaborative learning approach described above in which children, working in small groups, were presented with problems at the roadside and asked to solve them through joint discussion. The trainer's role was nondidactic, focusing instead on encouraging discussion between the children and keeping it moving in productive directions by asking questions or offering suggestions. Children were never told what they might do, except as a last resort. This collaborative approach lies at the heart of the Kerbcraft method.
- To address the issue of reaching all children in the community, we recruited volunteers who were asked to train *all* children in designated classes, not just their own children. This approach placed volunteers at the heart of the process. It was innovative but also represented the greatest risk to the success of the project. Would ordinary volunteers from a deprived community be able to teach children in the required manner? Would a sufficiently large number come forward who were able to make the commitment (several groups of children trained through at least one phase of the program over a period of 4–6 weeks)?

Based on earlier experimental research in which we had piloted the method (Thomson et al., 1998), we were confident that volunteers would be able to train children quite effectively but there was certainly a question mark over levels of volunteer recruitment, given that the project was to run concurrently in all 10 primary schools in the area. Perhaps unsurprisingly, the approach was greeted with a degree of skepticism by some colleagues in the local authority roads department. Nevertheless, the approach had features which both local and national authorities welcomed, notably the community nature of the approach in which local people would play an active role in addressing a community issue. The approach also promoted interagency cooperation between schools, police, local authority and other community agencies. Ultimately, it was the community-centered nature of the enterprise that underpinned the widespread adoption of the program at a later date, as described below.

• In line with the approach taken with children, volunteers themselves received roadside training and had the opportunity both to observe good practice and gain practical experience of working with children under the guidance of project staff. They also had the opportunity to discuss issues with each other and with staff after training sessions, when everyone would meet back at the school for tea. Thus, support and feedback were available on an ongoing basis, which turned out to be instrumental in maintaining volunteer commitment to the program.

Funding to set up the scheme was negotiated with Strathclyde Regional Council and the Drumchapel Initiative, a local community organization. In addition, the Department for Transport agreed to fund evaluation of the program (Thomson and Whelan, 1997). The scheme ran over a period of 30 months, during which 750 children were trained by over 100 volunteers. Contrary to our initial concerns, we found no ceiling on the number of volunteers who came forward: indeed, it became somewhat easier to recruit as the scheme developed and residents grew accustomed to seeing training groups on the streets. Evaluation showed substantial improvements in children's roadside behavior following training on all three skills, mirroring the effects earlier obtained in experimental studies. Volunteers' ability to promote learning showed no limitations relative to "expert" trainers: indeed, children trained by volunteers made marginally greater improvements, although not significantly so (Thomson & Whelan, 1997; Thomson et al., 1998).

The National Network of Child Pedestrian Training Schemes

Based on the success of the Drumchapel Project, the Department for Transport commissioned us to produce a manual and support materials detailing how similar schemes might be managed elsewhere (Thomson et al., 2008). They then secured dedicated funding from central and Scottish governments that was offered to local authorities across the United Kingdom wishing to implement Kerbcraft schemes. Funding was to enable authorities to run schemes of about the same size as Drumchapel in high risk areas, typically areas of social deprivation. Three tranches of funding were made available between 2002 and 2008 at a cost of approximately nine million pounds.

During this period, 138 Kerbcraft schemes were run across 98 local authorities in England, Scotland and Wales. By 2008, 1,418 schools were participating and 95,353 children were trained. The Department for Transport also financed a large scale independent evaluation focusing on behavioral outcomes; process issues relating to sustainability; additional benefits of the scheme for children, volunteers and the community; and an economic cost/benefit analysis (Powell, Towner, Whelan, & Errington, 2009; Whelan, Towner, Errington, & Powell, 2008a, 2008b).

The behavioral outcomes aligned well with the findings of the Drumchapel project but the national evaluation also focused on additional benefits, including support of broader educational targets that schools are required to meet. In addition to the targeted road safety behaviors, the scheme appeared to enhance other aspects of children's development, including observation and communication skills, attentional control, social interaction and group working skills, geographical and spatial understanding, as well as self-confidence and self-esteem. These findings reinforced the already high level of support from schools, who welcomed these broader additional benefits. Indeed, some schools included Kerbcraft as an example of good practice in their Ofsted reports.

The evaluation also focused on potential benefits for participating volunteers and the community more generally. Participation typically enhanced relations between schools, parents and residents, often leading to involvement in other school or community activities. Scheme coordinators reported that many volunteers requested references in relation to work or educational opportunities, with volunteers citing the confidence gained as a supporting factor. The scheme thus appeared to increase social capital in a number of ways, adding significant value beyond its primary aims.

From an economic point of view, the project was assessed in two ways: first, by expressing the cost of each scheme as a function of the number of children trained by it and, second, by expressing the cost as a function of demonstrated improvements in children's behavior. The cost of running the scheme averaged less than £40 per child and, when considered in relation to behavioral improvements, was significantly lower than this because children's scores continued to improve in the months after training ended when there were no longer any costs. Powell et al. concluded that "the dramatic fall in the cost per [unit of] change in safe behavior test scores suggests that investment in Kerbcraft would pay back benefits and value in terms of safe behaviors long after its implementation" (Powell et al., 2009, p. 213).

Since 2008, local authorities wishing to continue with Kerbcraft have been expected to mainline the scheme through their own funding and several reports have explored the extent to which this has happened. Hammond, Cherrett, and Waterson (2014) surveyed 101 local education authorities and found that 80% were either still offering the Kerbcraft program or programs closely modeled on Kerbcraft. In a report to the Welsh Government, Smith and Crow (2009) showed that, in the year after central funding was withdrawn, 23 Kerbcraft schemes were running across 377 schools in Wales and 10,635 children were trained in that year alone by 1,076 volunteers. The report concluded, "Now in its fifth year, MVA Consultancy's review of Kerbcraft shows a continuing expansion of the scheme throughout Wales. The scheme now involves more children and more schools than in any previous year".

Beyond the United Kingdom, Kerbcraft is currently being piloted in Bangladesh, which suffers one of the world's highest rates of road traffic injuries (Centre for Injury Prevention and Research, Bangladesh; http://www.ciprb.org/index.php?id=155). The Bangladesh Centre for Injury Prevention and Research has translated the Kerbcraft resources into Bengali and produced a training video adapted to local needs. If the pilot scheme is successful, the aim is to introduce the program nation-wide. In 2010, Kerbcraft was also introduced in Ethiopia, with 992 children receiving training that year (Salmon & Eckersley, 2010).

Impact on Road Safety Policy

At the level of policy, Kerbcraft features prominently within the UK government's child road safety policy. In the Strategic Framework for Road Safety (Department for Transport, 2011), it states that "the Kerbcraft scheme remains the basis for children's practical road safety training. It is a roadside pedestrian training scheme which has been proven to deliver a lasting improvement in road crossing skills. We encourage Local Authorities to adopt Kerbcraft or similar child pedestrian training schemes, rather than anything that is watered down or less effective and target it on high risk areas and groups" (p. 50). In a report on health strategy to the Department of Health, the Health Protection Agency also recommends "UK-wide implementation of successful interventions to include practical road safety programs, such as Kerbcraft" (Health Protection Agency, 2009, p. 23). Similarly, a report to the Northern Ireland Department of the Environment on child road safety (Wood et al., 2011) recommends that the Northern Ireland government should "enhance practical child pedestrian safety training in line with the 'Kerbcraft' scheme as operated in England, Scotland and Wales and to include parents in its delivery...

The Department for Transport's evaluation of this scheme found far reaching benefits within the community" (p. 30). Finally, the Welsh Government's draft Road Safety Delivery Plan (Welsh Government, 2012) reiterates its continuing support of Kerbcraft as part of its road safety strategy and commits itself to funding Kerbcraft as part of that strategy.

In the USA, the Child Pedestrian Safety Curriculum issued by the National Highway Traffic Safety Administration (US Department of Transport, 2011) also refers extensively to our research. The guidelines state that "Teachers should seek to engage students in teacher discussion and modeling by asking questions and prompting dialogue. Thus, children will incorporate these basic principles into their own behaviors. Teachers should also allow children to use social interactions with their peers to further promote positive behavior. The option of using older students as models for younger children is one such way to show significant increases in safe behaviors. Using older children as models and incorporating student–peer–adult discussion on a consistent basis are encouraged throughout the program" (p. 2). Several of our studies are cited in support of these recommendations. The impact of our research in the USA is further explored by Percer (2009).

In Australia, the Department of Education in Western Australia (Government of Western Australia, 2009) commissioned a study on the evidence base for road safety practice and issued 16 Principles for School Road Safety Education. Six of the principles reflect our research and these formed part of the Road Safety Education Plan for Western Australian Schools and Communities 2011–2013.

Similarly, a World Health Organization report (Peden et al., 2008) states "Current research on road safety education suggests that an approach that stresses behavior, focusing on the development of practical skills, is more likely to be effective for younger children. Children learn best through methods that develop problem solving and decision making skills". It goes on to cite Kerbcraft as an educational intervention that achieves these aims (p. 48). Kerbcraft also features as a case study in the European Child Safety Alliance's Child Safety Good Practice Guide (MacKay, Vincenten, Brussoni, & Towner, 2006). This document states that the roadside training undertaken in Kerbcraft "is an essential ingredient of pedestrian skills training".

Lessons in Giving Away Developmental Psychology

Overall, the research described above has had a substantial effect on both policy and practice in the United Kingdom, with practical roadside training now occupying a key role in road safety education. The research has also had significant impact internationally, with widespread recognition of the importance of practical training, collaborative learning methods, and placing the community at the heart of interventions. In this section, we consider some of the factors that facilitated acceptance of the Kerbcraft scheme as well as barriers that had to be overcome in gaining such acceptance.

The most significant factor by far in the government's eventual adoption of Kerbcraft was the strongly evidence-based nature of the intervention. Even during our earliest discussions with the Department for Transport and other agencies, we were able to present strong theoretical arguments and a substantial body of empirical data supporting our rationale. At early meetings, we were quizzed relentlessly on these topics. Had we approached them on the basis of an insubstantial evidence base, or evidence that such agencies perceived as containing weaknesses, it is unlikely that our proposals would have received the degree of consideration that they did. Colleagues cannot expect agencies to embark on significant reforms on the basis of a single finding or even a small number of confirming studies. The evidence will have to be compelling before they will consider this. On the whole, this is as it should be. Otherwise, practices would be liable to chop and change on the basis of whoever happens to be pressurizing government at the moment.

As noted earlier, a significant factor in our favor is that there was already concern about child pedestrian accident rates both locally and nationally and a corresponding disquiet over the effectiveness of existing educational measures. We thus enjoyed an element of luck by coming onto the scene at a time when receptivity to our ideas was likely to be high. Even so, the period of time over which we attempted to introduce our ideas beyond the academic community was fairly lengthy and involved many presentations to a wide range of agencies over a period of years. This included a number of presentations to professional (as opposed to academic) conferences and many invited talks to local authorities, the police, government departments and other agencies. In addition, we had written a number of articles explicitly aimed at practitioner and policymaking audiences (Ampofo-Boateng & Thomson, 1990; Thomson 1989a, 1989b). These forms of communication had also given rise to some substantive press coverage that had been widely read. These activities played a crucial role in bringing our work to the attention of practitioners and policymakers, paving the way for what followed.

So far as I can tell, the articles we published in the conventional psychological literature during this period made absolutely no impact on practitioner and policymaking audiences. Our experience was that academic and practitioner/policy audiences were quite distinct and different pathways were required to reach them. This problem will, of course, be less marked in areas where the distinction between academic and practitioner is more blurred. However, it seems likely that there are many areas where reaching the target audience will require a dedicated approach and this may well take academics out of their comfort zone. Academic colleagues must also be realistic about both the time and effort needed to translate research findings into action. At the very least, there will be a significant period of consultation and reflection on the implications of the proposals before any action is likely to be taken.

We were not aware of significant opposition to our recommendations on the basis of vested interests in the status quo and the main thrust of our arguments about practical training generally received a sympathetic hearing. A more significant problem, especially among practitioners, is that we were often perceived to be arguing that current practice was a waste of time. This was a very black and white interpretation but there is no denying we were critical of traditional road safety education. As it hardly helped our cause to alienate the very people we were trying to influence, considerable sensitivity was required in making our case. In retrospect, we were not always as successful in this as we could have been during the early days, when fighting to get our point across seemed the main objective. Researchers would be well advised to approach such matters thoughtfully and with tact. They should certainly not emulate one distinguished academic colleague who, as a prelude to his presentation to a national practitioners' conference, began by telling delegates that they were "doing it all wrong"!

The main challenge to our arguments centered on the feasibility of mounting roadside training schemes and discussion focused heavily on this theme. A common view was that roadside training schemes were a "Rolls Royce model" that would be too difficult or expensive to implement in the real world. There was a particular concern over who could be expected to undertake the roadside training and, if it were to be volunteers, how easily they could be recruited and how much support they would require. In addressing such concerns, the Drumchapel project played a pivotal role because it demonstrated what was, in fact, possible in communities of just the sort that local authorities would wish to target. It seems likely that a "demonstration project" will often have a key role to play in paving the way for larger scale implementation and colleagues might aim for this as a desirable intermediate stage. In addition, a demonstration project provides the opportunity for refinements, the need for which might not otherwise have been identified.

A feature of Kerbcraft that turned out to be pivotal in terms of its acceptance was the community-centered nature of the approach. The Department for Transport's Road Safety Good Practice Guide (TRL, 1993) had already highlighted the need for road safety education to be developed with key partners, including parents and members of the wider community, stressing that impact was greatest when a range of agencies were involved. They also argued that road safety professionals should maximize their time in support and advisory roles, rather than through direct intervention, and that capacity building was an important objective for them. Kerbcraft, with its emphasis on interagency collaboration, the situating of road safety in the wider community and not just an isolated school context, and the active involvement of parents and volunteers, was clearly consistent with this model. Because Kerbcraft was in this way consistent with accepted principles of good practice there was a much increased likelihood of its being adopted, even though it advocated a radical shift in the nature of road safety provision. Academics need to be aware of other people's perspectives and agendas when trying to gain influence and, as far as possible, work with rather than against them.

Recommendations for Giving Away Developmental Psychology

In summary, several key pieces of advice emerge from our experience of working with policymakers, road safety practitioners and educators that we hope will be of value to colleagues considering how best to "give away" the practical implications of their research in developmental psychology:

- A key aim should be to influence relevant agencies through appropriate, well-targeted dissemination. It should not be assumed that practitioners or policymakers will see or benefit from articles or presentations targeted in the first instance at academic audiences. A substantive effort should be made to reach nonacademic audiences directly.
- It is important to understand the agenda of target agencies and be able to show the opportunities your proposal provides. Be in a position to emphasize the extent to which the proposal works with, not against, their objectives. Stress features they are likely to see as positive. Be aware of potential barriers and be able to show how these might be overcome.
- Do not make proposals that the target agency will see as unworkable. It is easy to approach agencies with a certain evangelical zeal, which is understandable when the need for substantive change seems clear. However, making draconian proposals that fall outside the range of what is politically or practically possible will get you nowhere. Your proposals will have to be realistic from the point of view of whoever you are trying to influence and need to be tailored accordingly.
- Try to influence agencies which themselves have influence with whatever authorities you are primarily trying to influence. Get others on board and develop a groundswell of opinion. Change is more likely to come when there is widespread acknowledgement that change is needed.
- Aim for partial implementation as a first step, perhaps through a "demonstration project" in a localized area or setting if this is possible. A step-by-step approach is more likely to achieve support than immediate implementation of large scale, radical changes.

- Be prepared for a relatively long endeavor. In our experience, most agencies show an open and genuine interest in what academics have to offer. But the process of change is intrinsically lengthy and Rome really was not built in a day.

Conclusions

This chapter reports the evolution of a research program leading from basic research on the psychological factors influencing children's pedestrian decision making and behavior, through strategic research investigating the types of intervention that might promote pedestrian skill development, to the creation of a large-scale applied training scheme that has now been successfully implemented on a national scale. Drawing both on psychological theory and an analysis of the skills and competences involved in pedestrian behavior, we established a strong rationale for the emerging evidence that practical training in an appropriate context is by far the most effective way of promoting learning, particularly in younger children. We also showed that a form of collaborative learning, in which children solve problems jointly with the support of an adult facilitator, works well as a means of promoting relatively robust behavioral improvements and transfer of learning. This had the welcome corollary that children do not need to be trained individually which, from a practical point of view, is a significant bonus. Finally, I have explored the journey from research to application, reflecting on those factors that seemed to work in our favor and those that had to be overcome as we tried to translate knowledge for key stakeholders. I hope that the processes involved in doing this may be sufficiently generic that colleagues seeking to translate their own research into action may derive some benefit from the Kerbcraft story.

References

Adolph, K. E., Eppler, M. A., & Gibson, E. J. (1993). Crawling versus walking infants' perception of affordances for locomotion over sloping surfaces. *Child Development, 64,* 1158–1174.

Ampofo-Boateng, K., & Thomson, J. A. (1990). Child pedestrian accidents: A case for preventative medicine. *Health Education Research: Theory and Practice, 5,* 265–274.

Ampofo-Boateng, K., & Thomson, J. A. (1991). Children's perception of safety and danger on the road. *British Journal of Psychology, 82,* 487–505.

Ampofo-Boateng, K., Thomson, J. A., Grieve, R., Pitcairn, T., Lee, D. N., & Demetre, J. D. (1991). A developmental and training study of children's ability to find safe routes to cross the road. *British Journal of Developmental Psychology, 11,* 31–45.

Ampofo-Boateng K., Thomson J. A., Grieve R., Pitcairn T. K., Lee D. N., & Demetre J. D. (1993). A developmental and training study of children's ability to find safe routes to cross the road. *British Journal of Developmental Psychology, 11*, 31–45.

Barton B. (2007). Integrating selective attention into developmental pedestrian safety research. *Canadian Psychology, 47*, 203–210.

Benda, H. V., & Hoyos, C. G. (1983). Estimating hazards in traffic situations. *Accident Analysis & Prevention, 15*, 1–9.

Brown, I. D. (2002). A review of the 'look but failed to see' accident causation factor. In *Behavioural Research in Road Safety XI*. London: Department for Transport.

Bryan-Brown, K., & Harland, G. (1999). *The children's traffic club in Scotland*. Scottish Executive Central Research Unit: Edinburgh.

Carsten, O. M. J., Sherborne, D. J., & Rothengatter, J. A. (1998). Intelligent traffic signals for pedestrians: Evaluation of trials in three countries. *Transportation Research Part C, 6*, 213–229.

Chapman, A. J. (1998). *Road safety and child development research: A summary analysis*. Road Safety Research Report No. 5. London: Department for Transport.

Christie, N. (1995). *The high risk child pedestrian: Socio-economic and environmental factors in their accidents*. Crowthorn, UK: Transport Research Laboratory.

Demetre, J. D., & Gaffin, S. (1994). The salience of occluding vehicles to child pedestrians. *British Journal of Educational Psychology, 64*, 243–251.

Department for Transport (2011). *Strategic framework for road safety*. London: Department for Transport.

DiGuiseppi, C., Roberts, I., & and Li, L. (1997). Influence of changing travel patterns on child death rates from injury: trend analysis. *British Medical Journal, 314*, 710–713.

Dunbar, G., Hill, R., & Lewis, V. (2001). Children's attentional behavior and road behavior. *Journal of Experimental Psychology: Applied, 7*, 227–234.

Gibson, E. J., Ricchio, G., Schmuckler, M. A., Stoffregan, T. A., Rosenberg, D., & Taormina, J. (1987). Detection of the traversability of surfaces by crawling and walking infants. *Journal of Experimental Psychology: Human Perception and Performance, 13*, 533–544.

Government of Western Australia (2009). *Principles for school road safety education: A research summary*. East Perth, WA: School Drug Education and Road Aware. Retrieved July 17, 2015 from http://www.det.wa.edu.au/sdera/detcms/navigation/road-safety/principles-for-school-road-safety-education/

Grayson, G. B. (1975a). *The Hampshire child pedestrian accident study*. UK Department of the Environment Report 670. Crowthorne, UK: Transport and Road Research Laboratory.

Grayson, G. B. (1975b). *Observations of pedestrians at four sites*. UK Department of the Environment Report 671. Crowthorne, UK: Transport and Road Research Laboratory.

Grieve, R., & Williams, W. (1985). Young children's perception of danger. *British Journal of Developmental Psychology, 3*, 385–392.

Hammond, J., Cherrett, T., & Waterson, B. (2014). The development of child pedestrian training in the United Kingdom 2002–2011: a national survey of local authorities. *Journal of Transportation Safety and Security, 6*(2), 117–129.

Health Protection Agency (2009). *A Children's Environment and Health Strategy for the UK*. London: Health Protection Agency.

Heffernan, D. D., & Thomson, J. A. (1999). Gone fishin': perceiving what is reachable with rods during a period of rapid growth. In M. Grealy & J.A. Thomson (Eds.), *Studies in perception and action V*. Hillsdale, NJ: Lawrence Erlbaum Associates.

Hill, R., Lewis, V., & Dunbar, G. (2000). Young children's concepts of danger. *British Journal of Developmental Psychology, 18*, 103–120.

Hillman, M., Adams, J., & Whitelegg, J. (1990). *One false move; a study of children's independent mobility*. London: Policy Studies Institute.

Howarth, C. I., Routledge, D. A., & Repetto-Wright, R. (1974). An analysis of road accidents involving young children. *Ergonomics, 17*, 319–330.

Jacobs, G., Aeron-Thomas, A., & Astrop, A. (2000). *Estimating global road fatalities*. Crowthorne, UK: Transport Research Laboratory.

Kraus, J. F., Hooten, E. G., Brown, K. A., Peek-Asa, C., Heye, C., & McArthur, D. L. (1996). Child pedestrian and bicycling injuries: Results of community surveillance and a case-control study. *Injury Prevention, 2*, 212–218.

Kopits E., & Cropper, M. (2005). Traffic fatalities and economic growth. *Accident Analysis and Prevention, 37*, 169–178.

Lee, D. N., Young, D. S., & McLaughlin, C. M. (1984). A roadside simulation of road crossing for young children. *Ergonomics, 17*, 319–330.

MacKay, M., Vincenten, J., Brussoni, M., & Towner, E. L. M. (2006). *Child safety good practice guide: Good investments in unintentional child injury prevention and safety promotion*. Amsterdam: European Child Safety Alliance, Eurosafe.

Maples, W. C., DeRosier, W., Hoenes, R., Bendure, R., & Moore S. (2008). The effects of cell phone use on peripheral vision. *Optometry – Journal of the American Optometric Association, 79*, 36–42.

McKenzie, B. E., & Forbes, C. (1992). Does vision guide stair climbing? A developmental study. *Australian Journal of Psychology, 44*, 177–183.

McKenzie, B. E., Skouteris, H., Day, R. H., Hartman, B., & Yonas, A. (1993). Effective action by infants to contact objects by reaching and leaning. *Child Development, 64*, 415–429.

McLaren, B. D. (1993). *An observational study of behavioral sex differences in adult road crossing skill*. Unpublished Master's Dissertation, University of Strathclyde.

Morrongiello, B. A., & Matheis, S. (2004). Determinants of children's risk-taking in different social-situational contexts: The role of cognitions and emotions in predicting children's decisions. *Applied Developmental Psychology, 25*, 303–326.

Peden, M., Oyegbite, K., Ozanne-Smith, J., Hyder, A. A., Branche, C., Fazlur Rahman, A. K. M., et al. (2008). *World report on child injury prevention*. Geneva: World Health Organization.

Percer, J. (2009). *Child pedestrian safety education: Applying learning and developmental theories to develop safe street-crossing behaviors*. Washington DC: U.S. Department of Transportation, National Highway Traffic Safety Administration.

Powell, J., Towner, E., Whelan, K., & Errington, G. (2009). An economic evaluation of the Kerbcraft child pedestrian training pilot project. In *Behavioural research in road safety: Seventeenth seminar*. London: Department for Transport.

Richards, A., Hannon, E. M., & Derakshan, N. (2010). Predicting and manipulating the incidence of inattentional blindness. *Psychological Research, 74*, 513–523.

Rivara, F. P. (1990). Child pedestrian injuries in the United States: Current status of the problem, potential interventions, and future research needs. *American Journal of Diseases of Children, 144*, 692–696.

Roberts, I., & Power, C. (1996). Does the decline in child injury mortality vary by social class? A comparison of class specific mortality in 1981 and 1991. *British Medical Journal, 313*, 784–786.

Roberts I., Mohan D., & Abbassi, K.(2002). War on the roads. *British Medical Journal, 324*, 1107–1108.

Rothengatter, J. A. (1981). *Traffic safety education for young children*. Lisse: Swets and Reitlinger.

Rothengatter, J. A. (1984). A behavioral approach to improving traffic behavior of young children. *Ergonomics, 2*, 147–160.

Routledge, D. A., Howarth C. I., & Repetto-Wright, R. (1976). The development of road crossing skill by child pedestrians. In A. S. Hakkert (Ed.) *Proceedings of the international conference on road safety, Vol 1*. Haifa, Israel: Michlol Technion.

Sadler, J. (1972). *Children and road safety: A survey amongst mothers*. Report No SS 450. London: HMSO.

Salmon, R., & Eckersley, W. (2010). Where there's no green man: child road safety education in Ethiopia. *Development in Practice, 20*, 726–733.

Sandels, S. (1975). *Children in traffic*. London: Elek.

Sheehy, N. P., Chapman, A. J., & David, S. (1988). Children's expectations and recollections of potentially hazardous events. In M. M. Gruneberg, P. E. Morris, & R. N. Sykes (Eds.) *Practical aspects of memory: Current research and issues: Vol. 1. Memory in everyday life*. Chichester, UK: John Wiley & Sons Ltd.

Simons, D. J., & Chabris, C. F. (1999). Gorillas in our midst: Sustained inattentional blindness for dynamic events. *Perception, 28*, 1059–1074.

Smith, E. W., & Crow, H. (2009). *Teaching safe behaviour: Kerbcraft in Wales progress report for the Welsh Assembly government*. Woking, UK: MVA Consultancy.

Tabibi, Z., & Pfeffer, K. (2003). Choosing a safe place to cross the road: the relationship between attention and identification of safe and dangerous road crossing sites. *Child: Care, Health and Development, 29*(4), 237–244.

Tabibi, Z., & Pfeffer, K. (2007). Finding a safe place to cross the road: the effect of distractors and the role of attention in children's identification of safe and dangerous road-crossing sites. *Infant and Child Development, 16*, 193–206.

Thomson, J. A. (1989a). Road safety education: how do we make our children streetwise? *Safety Education, 3*, 13–16.

Thomson, J. A. (1989b). Safe to school: improving road safety education. *Scottish Council for Research in Education Newsletter, 44*, 4–5.

Thomson, J. A. (1991). *The facts about child pedestrian accidents*. London: Cassell.

Thomson, J. A. (1992) Road safety education and the school: which way forward? *TOPIC: Journal of the National Foundation for Educational Research, 7*, 1–6.

Thomson, J. A. (1997). Developing safe route planning strategies in young child pedestrians. *Journal of Applied Developmental Psychology, 18*, 271–281.

Thomson J. A., Ampofo-Boateng K., Grieve R., Pitcairn T. K., Lee D. N., & Demetre J. D. (1998). The effectiveness of parents in promoting the development of road crossing skills in young children. *British Journal of Educational Psychology, 68*, 475–491.

Thomson, J. A., Ampofo-Boateng, K., Pitcairn, T., Grieve, R., Lee D. N., & Demetre, J. D. (1992). Behavioral group training of children to find safe routes to cross the road. *British Journal of Educational Psychology, 62*, 173–183.

Thomson, J. A., Tolmie, A. K., Foot, H. C., & McLaren, B. (1996). *Child development and the aims of road safety education: A review and analysis.* London: HMSO.

Thomson J. A., Tolmie A. K., Foot, H. C., Sarvary P., Whelan K. M., & Morrison S. (2005). Influence of virtual reality training on the roadside crossing judgments of child pedestrians. *Journal of Experimental Psychology: Applied, 11*, 175–186.

Thomson, J. A., & Whelan, K. M. (1997). *A community approach to road safety education using practical training methods: The Drumchapel project.* Road Safety Research Report No. 3. London: Department of the Environment, Transport & the Regions.

Thomson, J. A., Whelan, K., Stephenson, C., Dickson, M., McBrearty, L., MacLean, S., et al. (2008). *Kerbcraft: A handbook for road safety professionals.* London: Department for Transport.

Tolmie, A. K., & Thomson, J. A. (2003). Attitudes, social norms and perceived behavioral control in adolescent pedestrian decision making. In *Behavioral research in road safety.* London: Department for Transport.

Tolmie, A. K., Thomson, J. A., & Foot, H. C. (2000). The role of adult guidance and peer collaboration in child pedestrian training. In R. W. Joiner, & D. Faulkener (Eds.), *Rethinking collaborative learning.* London: Free Association Press.

Tolmie, A. K., Thomson, J. A., Foot, H. C., Burkes, M., Wu, C, Towner, E. L. M., et al. (2003). *Training children in the safe use of designated crossings.* Road Safety Research Report No. 34. London: Department for Transport.

Tolmie, A. K., Thomson, J. A., Foot, H. C., McLaren, B., & Whelan, K. M. (1998). *Problems of attention and visual search in the context of child pedestrian behavior.* Road Safety Research Report No. 8. London: Department of the Environment, Transport & the Regions.

Tolmie, A. K., Thomson, J. A., Foot, H. C., Whelan, K. M., McLaren, B., & Morrison, S. (2005). The effects of adult guidance and peer discussion on the development of children's representations. *British Journal of Psychology, 96*, 181–204.

Tolmie, A. K., Thomson, J. A., Foot, H. C., Whelan, K. M., Sarvary, P., & Morrison, S. (2002). *Development and evaluation of a computer-based pedestrian training resource for children aged 5 to 12 years.* Road Safety Research Report No. 27. London: Department of the Environment, Transport & the Regions.

TRL (Transport Research Laboratory) (1993). *Road safety good practice guide.* London: Department for Transport.

Underwood, J., Dillon, G., Farnsworth, B., & Twiner, A. (2007). Reading the road: The influence of age and sex on child pedestrians' perceptions of road risk. *British Journal of Psychology, 93*, 98–110.

U.S. Department for Transportation (2011). *Child Pedestrian Safety Curriculum: Teachers Guide*. National Highway Traffic Safety Administration. Retrieved on July 18, 2015 from http://www.nhtsa.gov/ChildPedestrianSafetyCurriculum

van der Molen, H. H. (1983). *Pedestrian ethology*. Doctoral dissertation, University of Groningen, The Netherlands.

Vurpillot, E. (1968). The development of scanning strategies and their relation to visual differentiation. *Journal of Experimental Child Psychology, 6*, 632–650.

Welsh Government (2012). *Draft road safety delivery plan*. Consultation Document No. 16555. Retrieved on July 18, 2015 from http://wales.gov.uk/docs/det/consultation/120919roadsafetydelplanen.pdf

West, R., Sammons, P., & West, A. (1993). Effects of a Traffic Club on road safety knowledge and self-reported behaviour of young children and their carers. *Accident Analysis and Prevention, 25*, 609–618.

Whelan, K. M., Towner, E. L. M., Errington, G., & Powell, J. (2008a). *Evaluation of the national network of child pedestrian training pilot projects*. Road Safety Research Report No. 82. London: Department for Transport.

Whelan, K. M., Towner, E. L. M., Errington, G., & Powell, J. (2008b). *Evaluation of the national network of child pedestrian training pilot projects in Scotland*. Edinburgh: Scottish Government Social Research.

Whitebread, D., & Neilson, K. (2000). The contribution of visual search strategies to the development of pedestrian skills by 4–11 year-old children. *British Journal of Educational Psychology, 70*, 539–557.

Wood, S., Stephenson, C., Christie, N., Towner, E., Colgan, J., & Burroughs, H. (2011). *Child road safety and poverty research project*. Report for the Department of the Environment Northern Ireland. London: MVA Consultancy. Retrieved on July 18, 2015 from http://www.doeni.gov.uk/roadsafety/final_report__no_appendices_final.pdf

Wright, J. C., & Vlietstra, A. G. (1975). The development of selective attention: from perceptual exploration to logical search. In H. W. Reese (Ed.), *Advances in Child Development and Behavior, Vol. 10*. New York: Academic Press.

Zeedyk, M. S., Wallace, L., Carcary, B., Jones, K., & Larter, K. (2001). Children and road safety: Increasing knowledge does not improve behavior. *British Journal of Educational Psychology, 71*, 573–594.

Zeedyk, M. S., Wallace, L., & Spry, L. (2002). Stop, look, listen and think? What young children really do when crossing the road. *Accident Analysis and Prevention, 34*, 43–50.

Zhang, G., Yau, K. K., & Zhang, X. (2014). Analyzing fault and severity in pedestrian–motor vehicle accidents in China. *Accident Analysis and Prevention, 73*, 141–150.

Zinchenko, V. P., van Chzhi-tsin, & Tarakanov, V. V. (1965). The formation and development of perceptual activity. *Soviet Psychology and Psychiatry, 2*, 3–12.

14

Researcher–Practitioner Partnerships in the Development of Intervention to Reduce Prejudice Among Children

Lindsey Cameron and Adam Rutland

[with contributions from research partners WEDG (Charlotte Tagart) and Rights & Equality Sandwell (Belinda Blake)]

Unfavorable attitudes towards stigmatized groups are relatively common amongst children in early and middle childhood (Aboud, 1988; see Quintana & McKown, 2008; Brown, 2010). There is evidence that children's attitudes towards stigmatized out-groups can be improved through school-based interventions (for review: Aboud et al., 2012; Beelmann & Heinemann, 2014; Pfeifer, Brown, & Juvonen, 2007; for example: Cameron, Rutland, Brown, & Douch, 2006; Pahlke, Bigler, & Martin, 2014, Vezzali, Stathi, Giovannini, Capozza, & Trifiletti, 2015). However, the field is marred by a lack of collaboration between the two major exponents of work in this area: social developmental psychologists and practitioners (including nonacademic organizations such as charities and campaign groups) working in the field (Aboud & Levy, 2000; Abrams & Killen, 2014; Cameron & Rutland, 2008; Oskamp, 2000).

The Wiley Handbook of Developmental Psychology in Practice: Implementation and Impact, First Edition.
Edited by Kevin Durkin and H. Rudolph Schaffer.
© 2016 John Wiley & Sons, Ltd. Published 2016 by John Wiley & Sons, Ltd.

Social developmental psychologists have concentrated their efforts on developing and testing theories that account for the development of prejudice in children. In contrast, practitioners have focused on designing and implementing interventions to reduce prejudice, often with the larger goal of enhancing community cohesion and creating harmonious communities through the reduction of childhood prejudice. These interventions are often highly practical and well-suited to the school context but are based on practitioners' gut instincts rather than psychological theory, any empirical foundation and often lack rigorous evaluation. To date, efforts to systematically tackle prejudice and discrimination amongst children and adolescents have been hindered by a lack of collaboration between practitioners and researchers, where theory informs practice and vice versa.

In this chapter, we argue that in order to develop effective prejudice-reduction interventions in schools, it is essential that practitioners and researchers collaborate to create interventions that are both theoretically driven and practical, and are subject to thorough and systematic evaluation. Such collaborations can gauge the impact of interventions, the conditions under which they are most effective and with whom they have the biggest impact. In this way both practitioners and academics benefit, as the findings will have theoretical implications but can also shape future interventions.

We also outline the many benefits and challenges facing academic–practitioner collaborations and discuss the crucial role "giving psychology away" plays in this process. Finally, we present a working model for how to initiate, develop and manage effective researcher–practitioner partnerships to create prejudice-reduction interventions with positive impact.

Interventions to Encourage Positive Out-group Orientation: The Researcher's Contribution

According to Oskamp, "few [researchers] have concentrated their research energies on the key questions of how to reduce prejudice and create a society where equality and social justice are the norm instead of exception." (Oskamp, 2000, p. 7). This call for academics to develop and test prejudice-reduction interventions in the field has propelled a number of social developmental psychologists to conduct research that directly addresses this question. Importantly, the research has been published not only in academic journals but also outlets that reach practitioners and policymakers (Aboud et al., 2012; Killen, Rutland, & Ruck, 2012; Pfeifer et al., 2007; Rutland & Killen, 2015). In this section we illustrate, using contemporary research, the knowledge and expertise that researchers have to offer practitioners in developing prejudice-reduction interventions. We consider how psychological theory and findings can shape the content of intervention, and how expertise in research methods can inform the design and evaluation of interventions.

Within the field of developmental social psychology, research has shown intergroup bias towards stigmatized groups is relatively common amongst children in early and middle childhood (Killen & Rutland, 2011; Raabe & Beelmann, 2011) and has been shown in several domains, including ethnicity, gender, nationality, disability and size (Levy & Killen, 2008 for review). Psychological research has also illustrated the myriad of ways in which young people's attitudes and interactions are biased towards their own group, including attitudes and expectations, stereotypes, resources allocation, friendships, and peer exclusion and inclusion (Killen, Lee-Kim, McGlothlin, & Stangor, 2002; Killen, Mulvey, & Hitti, 2014; Monteiro, de Franca, & Rodrigues, 2009; Mulvey, Hitti, Rutland, Abrams, & Killen, 2014; Rutland, Cameron, Bennett, & Ferrell, 2005). These findings not only highlight the importance of tackling children's out-group orientation but also emphasize the need for interventions to tackle a variety of attitudes and behaviors.

Two main theoretical approaches to prejudice development that are potentially useful for practitioners, and have direct implications for prejudice-reduction interventions, are sociocognitive developmental theory (Aboud, 1988) and the intergroup contact hypothesis (Allport, 1954).

Sociocognitive theory (SCT)

According to sociocognitive developmental theorists, such as Aboud (1988; also see Aboud, 2008), children's intergroup attitudes are affected by their cognitive abilities. These cognitive abilities determine the way in which children think about and construct their social world. According to SCT, children aged approximately 6–7 years enter an ethnocentric stage of cognitive development where they are focused on how groups differ from each other, and how people within groups are similar to each other. At this stage, ethnic prejudice and stereotyping are expected to be high.

There are a number of other social cognitive abilities that may be related to the development of prejudice in children, for instance social moral reasoning (Abrams & Killen, 2014) and empathy and perspective taking (Aboud & Levy, 2000). One social cognitive ability that has been linked to reduced prejudice is the ability to classify people along multiple dimensions simultaneously (Aboud, 1988; Bigler, 1995; Bigler, Jones, & Lobliner, 1997; Bigler & Liben, 1992). Up to around the age of three, children are able to sort objects along one dimension only; as they get older their classification skills become more advanced (Piaget, 1965). Eventually, in middle childhood, children develop the ability to classify objects and people along multiple dimensions, or social categories, simultaneously. Sometimes these groups will be incongruent or surprising, as they do not match traditional stereotypes, for example, a woman who is also an engineer (Bigler & Liben, 1992).

Multiple classification *interventions* attempts to accelerate children's ability to engage in multiple classification (Bigler & Liben, 1992; see Pfeifer et al., 2007, for review) and involves, for instance, training children to classify stimuli along more than one dimension. Bigler and Liben (1992) found that following a multiple classification interventions, in which 5–10-year-old children were trained to classify objects and people along multiple cross-cutting dimensions (i.e., classify men and women according to gender and occupation), children were less likely to stereotype, or generalize across, the out-group. The effect of multiple classification training on stereotypes has been replicated in a number of studies (Bigler, 1995; Bigler et al., 1997). However, some research suggests the impact of such training on intergroup attitudes may be more limited (Beelmann & Heinemann, 2014; Cameron, Rutland, & Brown, 2007).

Prejudice-reduction interventions based on social moral reasoning have received comparatively little empirical attention by researchers or practitioners. However, empathy and perspective taking have been linked with prejudice (Beelmann & Heinemann, 2014) and interventions that focus on these abilities appear to be beneficial for promoting positive intergroup attitudes (Beelmann & Heinemann, 2014; Levy et al., 2005; Sierksma, Thijs, & Verkuyten, 2015).

Implications of sociocognitive developmental theory for future interventions   The idea that prejudice levels are tied to children's cognitive development has a number of general implications for prejudice-reduction interventions. First, this approach highlights the importance of designing prejudice-reduction interventions that are tailored to suit children's social cognitive abilities, since children will be unable to process information that is beyond their cognitive abilities (Bigler, 1999). For instance, children aged 6–7 will be unable to process individuating information because at that age they will be focused on groups and exaggerate between group differences and within group similarities; therefore, any interventions that require this ability will be ineffective with that age group (Aboud & Fenwick, 1999). In order to create effective prejudice-reduction interventions for young children, the developmental constraints on their cognitive abilities should be taken into consideration.

However, SCT also implies that training children in certain cognitive abilities (e.g. multiple classification ability) or building on their ability or propensity to use other abilities, such as empathy and perspective taking, should be associated with more positive intergroup attitudes. Sociocognitive interventions that enhance empathy and perspective taking have a lot of potential for use in the classroom, since these techniques are practical, adaptable, and have been shown to be effective (see Beelmann & Heinemann, 2014, for meta-analysis). The impact of training in categorization and multiple classification is less certain, and to date research has focused on the impact on stereotypes. More research is needed that examines the impact of such training on a range of indicators of out-group orientation. Therefore, it is advisable that multiple classification training should be used in conjunction with other social cognitive techniques.

Intergroup contact hypothesis

One of the most influential social psychological theories of prejudice and inter-group relations that is directly relevant to practitioners developing interventions is Allport's intergroup contact hypothesis (Allport, 1954). According to this theory, under a given set of conditions, contact between members of different groups reduces existing prejudices. These conditions are equal status between the groups, common goals, support for the intergroup contact from authority figures and no competition between groups (Allport, 1954). In the last 60 years, research has generally supported Allport's predictions and suggests that intergroup contact can lead to a reduction in negative intergroup bias in children and adults, especially when Allport's conditions are met (Pettigrew & Tropp, 2006).

Intergroup contact interventions for children have taken many forms, from cooperative learning groups (Cummings, Williams, & Ellis, 2002; Maras & Brown, 1996, 2000) and bilingual education and racially integrated schooling (McGlothlin & Killen, 2005; Wright & Tropp, 2005) to "vicarious" contact through TV and fictional stories (Cameron et al., 2006; Cole, Labin, & del Rocio Galarza, 2008; Durkin, Nesdale, Dempsey, & McLean, 2012; Vezzali et al., 2015) and even, most recently, *imagined* contact (Stathi, Cameron, Hartley, & Bradford, 2014).

Cooperative learning interventions are among the most researched intergroup contact interventions. These interventions have been found to improve inter-group attitudes in majority group children (Maras & Brown, 1996). One of the most popular cooperative learning interventions is the Jigsaw Classroom technique (Bratt, 2008). For instance, Maras and Brown (1996) evaluated a cooperative learning intervention that involved mainstream children taking part in regular activities with disabled children. These activities were carefully structured so that children had to collaborate in order to complete the tasks, one of Allport's optimal conditions. Maras and Brown (1996) found that the majority group, nondisabled children who took part in the program, expressed greater liking for the out-group (the disabled) compared to a control condition where children received no intervention.

Research on integrated schooling has also shown the positive effects of attending schools with ethnically diverse intakes (Schofield & Eurich-Fulcer, 2001). Children in diverse schools tend to be more inclusive in their friendships and show less in-group bias (McGlothlin & Killen, 2005; Rutland et al., 2005).

While intergroup contact is important, intergroup friendships appear to have a particular role in mitigating intergroup bias (Davies, Tropp, Aron, Pettigrew, & Wright, 2011; Turner, Hewstone, Voci, Paolini, & Christ, 2007). Children in very ethnically diverse settings, where cross-ethnic friendships are more likely, are less prone to exhibit in-group bias (Feddes, Noack, & Rutland, 2009; Rutland et al., 2005), more likely to nominate out-group peers as close friends (Bellmore, Nishina, Witkow, Graham, & Juvoven, 2007; Jackson, Barth, Powell, & Lochman, 2006) more likely to interpret out-group members behavior positively and to believe that intergroup friendships are likely (McGlothlin & Killen, 2006).

Cross-group *friendships*, as opposed to mere *opportunity* for contact, appears to be particularly important for tackling prejudice (Aboud, Mendelson, & Purdy, 2003; Jackson et al., 2006; Turner, Hewstone, & Voci, 2007). This is particularly problematic when one considers that cross-group friendships have significantly less longevity than same-race friendships and there is a decline in cross-group friendships with age (Aboud et al., 2003). This suggests there are specific hurdles facing cross-group friendship even in diverse communities (Davies et al., 2011).

How does intergroup contact work?   Research suggests that intergroup contact, and especially friendships, improve intergroup attitudes by reducing anxiety about interacting with out-group members (Paolini, Hewstone, Cairns, & Voci, 2004; Turner, Hewstone, & Voci, 2007) and fostering contexts in which children are less likely to perceive normative barriers to intergroup friendship (de Tezanos-Pinto, Bratt & Brown, 2010; Turner, Hewstone, Voci, Paolini, & Christ, 2007). Children are highly sensitive to prevailing norms for intergroup relations, such as those of their peer group (Nesdale, Maass, Durkin, & Griffiths, 2005; Nesdale, Griffiths, Durkin, & Maass, 2007) and those of their classroom (Thijs, Verkuyten, & Grundel, 2014). In fact, perceived group norms for intergroup friendship may be one of the barriers to forming intergroup friendships. Aboud and Sankar (2007) found that, when considering intergroup friendships, children were concerned about what their in-group peers would think about an out-group friend, and whether they would get along with them. Research has also shown that self-disclosure (sharing intimate and personal details with another person) and intergroup trust are also important drivers of the contact–attitude relationship (Turner, Hewstone, & Voci, 2007). This might be why cross-group *friendships*, in particular, are so important for changing intergroup attitudes: mere contact between groups, just attending ethnically mixed schools or youth clubs, may not provide the opportunity for those children involved to form close friendships and develop empathy and intergroup trust, or engage in self-disclosure (Miller, 2002; Turner, Hewstone, & Voci, 2007).

Indirect contact   More recently, researchers have been exploring the utility of indirect contact as a prejudice reduction intervention. This is the experience of contact with an out-group member without face-to-face, direct interaction. This may be particularly useful in contexts in which direct contact is not possible (Crisp & Turner, 2009). A number of forms of indirect contact have been examined, including extended contact, where individuals are merely aware of a cross-group friendships between a member of one's own group and another group (Wright, Aron, McLaughlin-Volpe, & Ropp, 1997), vicarious contact, where children observe fictional cross-group friendships (Cameron et al., 2006; Cole et al., 2008), and imagined contact, which involves merely imagining interaction with an out-group member (Stathi et al., 2014). There is evidence that indirect contact interventions can encourage positive out-group attitudes among children in multiple contexts and across a range of outgroups (Cameron et al., 2006; Miles & Crisp, 2014; Turner, Hewstone, & Voci, 2007).

For instance, in a series of studies, Cameron and colleagues developed vicarious extended contact interventions for children as young as five years (Cameron & Rutland, 2008). These interventions exposed children to intergroup friendships through reading, together with a researcher, illustrated stories that portrayed friendships between in-group and out-group members (e.g., English children and refugee children). In each of the intervention programs, children took part in approximately six extended contact sessions, where they would read and discuss the stories.

Overall, Cameron and colleagues found that their extended contact intervention was effective in improving majority group children's attitudes towards out-groups across the age range tested and across a number of different stigmatized out-groups, including the disabled, refugees and Asian people (Cameron & Rutland, 2006; Cameron et al., 2006, 2007). Psychological research has also identified a number of mechanisms driving the indirect contact effect, which appear to be similar to that of direct contact, including social norms, anxiety and social identity (Cameron & Turner, 2010; Miles & Crisp, 2014).

Furthermore, researchers have identified conditions under which indirect contact may have the biggest impact on attitudes. It appears that indirect contact effects may be limited to contexts in which opportunity for direct contact is low. That is, those individuals with high (positive) direct contact are unlikely to benefit from indirect contact as their out-group attitudes are already likely to be more positive as a result of the direct contact they have experienced (Cameron, Rutland, Hossain, & Petley, 2011). This finding is consistent with the original conceptualization of imagined contact. As Crisp and Turner (2009) initially contended, indirect contact interventions such as imagined contact should not be considered as a replacement for direct contact, but rather as a complementary intervention that can be used *alongside* direct contact, or prior to direct contact, in order to ensure the direct contact experience goes more smoothly (Crisp, Husnu, Meleady,

Stathi, & Turner, 2011). This is because the indirect contact could reduce anxiety, and increase positivity about future contact experiences, making subsequent contact more successful. Importantly, however, the impact of imagined contact on subsequent direct contact has not yet to be tested and the capacity for this technique to impact *negative* attitudes and out-group behavior has been questioned (Bigler & Hughes, 2010).

Implications for intergroup contact interventions   Research suggests that in order to maximize impact, direct contact interventions should involve carefully controlled cooperative activities, where young people work towards a common goal, as in the Jigsaw Classroom. Research has shown that intergroup *friendship* is particularly important for fostering positive intergroup attitudes. However, there are barriers to the formation and maintenance of such friendships even in diverse settings. Aboud and Sankar (2007), examining the qualities of cross-ethnic friendships, found that children's opportunity to play with out-group peers and their style of play differed from that of within-group friendships. They found that most children spent less time playing alone with out-group friends, and when they did spend time with them play tended to occur in the school playground. Thus, children did not have an opportunity to form close, high-quality and personalized friendships, involving multiple activities in a number of settings, which are so important in order for friendships to flourish.

Further research is needed to investigate the barriers to cross-group friendship. But the findings to date suggest that direct contact interventions should provide an opportunity for cross-group friendships to form and create conditions in schools that support cross-group friendship formation and maintenance; for example, by creating inclusive social norms around the acceptability of cross-group friendship (Jugert, Noack, & Rutland, 2011; Tropp, O'Brien, & Migacheva, 2014). In order to form high-quality friendships, and personalized contact, contact intervention should provide children with the opportunity to engage in multiple activities with out-group peers, and this should take place in school and in settings outside of school, for example sports clubs, or at home. This may involve meeting repeatedly, in multiple contexts, and over extended periods of time (Davies et al., 2011).

Direct and indirect contact research highlights the role of intergroup anxiety as an important driver of the effect of intergroup contact: direct and indirect contact appears to reduce anxiety about interacting with out-group members, and this then leads to more positive out-group orientation. The reasons for this anxiety are still unclear, but may lie in unfamiliarity, expectations of rejection and/or concerns about "saying the wrong thing". This suggests contact interventions should provide opportunities for these anxieties to be addressed, perhaps through discussion prior to contact, and during intergroup contact itself. But beyond contact interventions, other interventions designed to tackle prejudice could also focus on identifying and addressing deep seated anxieties about interacting with "the other".

Sociocognitive developmental theorists would argue that children's attitudes are, in part, a result of their social cognitive stage and ability, and also that intervention must be tailored to suit differing levels of cognitive development and ability. The general finding that direct and indirect contact impacts positively on children's attitudes across a wide age range suggests that contact has a positive impact regardless of age and cognitive ability, and underlines the suitability of such interventions across a broad age range. It is possible that contact pulls on the more emotional aspects of intergroup attitudes and behaviors, and the impact of this occurs regardless of cognitive skills and categorization, although this has yet to be investigated.

The findings in the intergroup contact literature also highlight the importance of choosing the contact intervention that is best suited to the child's context. For instance, indirect contact may be a valuable tool in a low diversity, ethnically homogeneous setting. Meanwhile, in more diverse settings where children have a greater *opportunity* to connect with out-group members, other interventions that increase the likelihood that children will form and maintain high-quality friendships with their diverse classmates, could be more useful.

Researchers' Contribution to the Design, Implementation and Evaluation of Interventions

So far in this chapter, the contribution psychological researchers could and have made to the *content* of interventions has been examined, focusing on two robust lines of research: intergroup contact and social cognitive interventions. Researchers can also contribute to the development of effective interventions through their expertise in conducting rigorous evaluations of the impact of prejudice-reduction interventions (Paluck & Green, 2009).

Evaluating interventions

Very few prejudice-reduction interventions are systematically evaluated (Bigler, 1999; Paluck, 2006). In those cases where interventions have been assessed, they have sometimes produced disappointing results (Beelmann & Heinemann, 2014). Collaborating with researchers allows practitioners to capitalize on the formers' empirical expertise in order to determine whether the intervention is having the desired effect on children's attitudes. This process allows one to reliably test more nuanced effects of the intervention, such as whether the impact on attitudes is the same across the target age range, or whether one particular format of delivery is more effective than another.

In the past 60 years, developmental researchers have become very sophisticated in measuring children's intergroup attitudes, and have at their disposal an array of measures that tap into different aspects of children's out-group orientation, including measures of explicit attitudes, intended behavior, peer nominations, and, more recently, measures of implicit bias. Children's intergroup orientation is multifaceted, and manifests itself in, for instance, their emotions, implicit attitudes, stereotypes, interaction styles, resource allocation and prosocial behaviors. Interventions should be evaluated using a range of indicators in order to capture more completely the impact of the intervention (Beelmann & Heinemann, 2014). But also, interventions can be designed that focus in on particular outcomes. For instance, researchers have recently turned their attention to the design of prejudice-reduction interventions that aim to change the nature and quality of intergroup interactions and increase prosocial behaviors (Abbott & Cameron, 2014; Aboud & Joong, 2008; Paluck, 2011).

In order to reliably evaluate an intervention, there are a number of specific requirements in the design and content of the intervention that must be present. Paluck (2006) recommends the use of randomized controlled experimental designs when evaluating interventions. This requires random assignment of participants to either intervention or control conditions, with participants receiving no intervention training in the control condition. This allows for more reliable conclusions to be drawn from intervention evaluations using this experimental design. This may lead to "tension" as, in the field, it is often difficult to meet these requirements.

Combining interventions

Research suggests that children's out-group orientation is multifaceted and some interventions may be more suitable for tackling some aspects of explicit intergroup attitudes than others (Pfeifer et al., 2007). For instance, multiple classification interventions may be better suited at tackling stereotypes than general attitudes (Cameron et al., 2007). Therefore, it is advisable that, in order to tackle a number of aspects of out-group orientation, a number of intervention techniques should be employed. For instance, if the aim is to tackle stereotypes and intergroup attitudes in general, multiple classification training should be used in conjunction with another technique, such as intergroup or extended contact.

There may also be some advantage to applying different techniques in succession to increase the success of later, potentially more stressful, intervention stages. For instance, initial expectations and stereotypes of the out-group are important in determining the outcome of direct intergroup contact (Brown, Vivian, & Hewstone, 1999). Therefore, inducing a more positive affect towards an out-group prior to direct contact, through an extended contact intervention or multiple classification skills training, could lead to more positive outcomes of actual contact between groups. In other words, boosting positive attitudes towards the out-group prior to actual intergroup contact could improve the chances that the interaction will be successful, that intergroup acquaintances (and perhaps also friendships) may develop and lead to more positive effects of intergroup contact.

Notably, while combining intervention techniques is useful, in order to identify the individual impact of each component, it is important that the individual techniques of an intervention programme are isolated initially, and tested separately.

Duration

Most of the interventions discussed in this chapter have consisted of short-term programs, over a series of weeks (Cameron et al., 2006, 2007). A number of researchers have suggested that long-term interventions are required to produce any real, long-lasting change in out-group attitudes and behaviors (Duckitt, 1992; see Bigler, 1999). One way in which more long-term interventions can be introduced is through incorporating interventions into the curriculum, rather than holding one-off events. This "transformative" approach to prejudice reduction (Banks, 1995) involves extensive changes to the curriculum (Bigler, 1999) and the introduction of a whole program of activities designed to combat prejudice, of which direct and extended intergroup contact would play a large part.

Summary

Academic researchers have expertise that can be drawn on to inform the content, design and evaluation of prejudice-reduction interventions. Their input in the design stage could allow rigorous evaluation providing insights into the best form of the intervention, or the age groups with whom it is most effective. This is important for maximizing the impact of the intervention. However, in order to capitalize on this expertise, it preferable that researchers should be involved from the design stage of the intervention in order to ensure that controls are in place to allow adequate evaluation (e.g., there is a large enough sample and adequate control groups). Researchers have a lot of to offer, and practitioners have a lot to gain from researcher–practitioner collaborations. At the same time, as elaborated below, practitioners also have much of their own expertise to offer in researcher–practitioner collaborations.

Practitioners' Contributions to the Researcher–Practitioner Partnership

So far, we have argued that academic–practitioner collaborations are crucial for the successful development of interventions with impact, but have focused on the contribution academics make in such endeavors. We now turn to the significant expertise and experience that practitioners bring to such collaborative projects. Based on our own experiences working with external organizations, the distinctive and essential role practitioners play in the successful development of prejudice-reduction interventions are outlined.

The authors have developed research collaborations with two organizations: WEDG (World Education Development Group), which is based in Canterbury, England, and Rights and Equality Sandwell (RES), which is based in Sandwell, near Birmingham in England. Together with these partner organizations, the first author has developed, implemented and evaluated prejudice reduction interventions in school settings, and also conducted research with children in order to answer critical research questions that are pertinent to the objectives of these organization, for example, examining the particular challenges facing Dual Heritage adolescents (Rights & Equality Sandwell). Collaborating with WEDG, RES and other practitioners has made us aware of a number of ways in which researchers can benefit from practitioner–researcher collaborations.

Firstly, practitioners and "nonacademic" organizations are well positioned to disseminate research beyond the typical academic outlets for publication. They are embedded in national and international networks of organizations, and often have direct links with policymakers in strategic positions to implement change, such as introducing new education guidelines or changes in policy and practice, on a national level. These links are essential in order to ensure research findings, and interventions, reach the right audience in order to influence policy and practice. Crucially, organizations like RES and WEDG are experienced in dealing with policymakers, and are not only familiar with the latest jargon or "buzz words" but can also help to translate research findings or theories into a language that is accessible for audiences from a nonpsychology background.

Furthermore, collaborating with nonacademic organizations, like RES and WEDG, opens up new funding streams, but also ensures research remains current, addressing topical issues of the day. Organizations such as WEDG and RES have an excellent grasp of the social issues that are currently being tackled by policymakers and the kind of issues facing young people in society that government *should* be dealing with. To provide an example, since we began our research in 2001, the demographics of the country have changed and, consequently, the burning issues that government, policymakers and race equality organizations believe should be dealt with have also changed. In 2001, as a result of changes in government legislation in the United Kingdom, there was heightened concern about the integration of disabled children into classrooms, and our initial research sprang from these concerns. In the following six or seven years, in response to the changing public concerns and patterns of immigration, we developed interventions that address majority group children's attitudes towards refugees and Asians. Our collaborators are quick to inform us that presently the national or ethnic group of greatest concern is Eastern European immigrants, and sexism and misogyny, and the need to protect LGBTQ (Lesbian, Gay, Bisexual, Trans, and Queer) adults and children from discrimination, are high on the agenda. Practitioners provide an insight into the main issues of the day, what the main concerns of politicians and policymakers are, in the classroom, on the street or in the playground. They are a vital source of information in order to keep research current and responsive to changes in society.

Finally, practitioners are experienced in working in the field and can provide an insight into the types of interventions that are practical for educational professionals to deliver, and engaging for children. This can lead to competing pressures within a collaboration to create interventions that are true to the theoretical bases and core premises identified by psychological research but are also engaging and practical interventions. Likewise, practical concerns regarding intervention delivery (e.g., need for control groups) does not always fit with practical necessities of delivering the intervention in schools. It is recommended that interventions should retain the theoretical basis and core premises of the theory upon which the new technique is based, and incorporate the requirement of rigorous evaluation of interventions wherever possible.

How can we Initiate, Develop and Manage Effective Researcher–Practitioner Partnerships?

Considering the benefits described thus far in practitioner–researcher partnerships, it seems pertinent now to consider how these partnerships can be established and maintained, and how they can be organized in such a way that they are mutually beneficial.

Finding practitioner partners

The first step in collaborations is to find a collaborator to work with. This ostensibly obvious step is not necessarily achieved easily. In our experience, the best way to do this is through disseminating findings to as wide an audience as possible, through reports to government, reports to schools and other education professionals, and also through the media. And, in fact, it was through the media publicity (e.g., BBC radio or newspaper reports) that contact with RES and WEDG were initiated.

Developing the partnership

If a researcher–practitioner partnership is to be mutually beneficial it is important that each of the parties is upfront about their goals from the beginning. Presumably, one goal is to create an effective prejudice-reduction intervention, but there may be additional goals related to career progression, for example, publications in academic journals, reports or guidelines for educators, publication of text books. These might be obvious and highly motivating considerations to one party but opaque or secondary to another; it is crucial that collaborators – especially collaborators from different professional backgrounds – be frank with each other about goals and obligations that influence how they work. Second, both parties need to consider whether they have the relevant expertise in the area and can help meet those goals.

When we began our research, we designed our own interventions and administered and evaluated these ourselves. We had a number of reasons for this: it gave us an element of control, allowing us to test specific psychological principles and hypotheses, as well as ensuring the intervention was delivered regularly and in a uniform manner. This is essential if the intervention is to be evaluated reliably.

There are some limitations to this method. Namely, prejudice-reduction interventions resulting from the above approach can lead to interventions that are true to the theoretical bases on from which they are derived, but are impractical and not sustainable for use in the classroom. This is particularly the case if the intervention is designed with little input from the end users, the teachers. One of the most important lessons researchers have learned concerning interventions is that they should not be one-off events but should be durable and incorporated into the school curriculum over a sustained period. Unfortunately, the above approach, where researchers develop, implement and test prejudice-reduction interventions in the classroom, does not appear to be well suited to creating sustainable interventions that can be embedded in the curriculum, as they are often impractical.

There are a number of alternatives to the above approach that may perhaps overcome these problems and create sustainable interventions that are both practical and theoretically sound, and will hopefully continue even after the research project is finished. One approach is to evaluate an intervention that is already being implemented; for example, the first author is currently evaluating an intervention designed and implemented by WEDG, that uses Persona Dolls to provide preschool children with contact with different cultures. While WEDG is responsible for intervention delivery, the first author's role is mainly in evaluation. The evaluation will provide valuable evidence regarding the effect of the dolls on children, and will also inform WEDG on how the dolls are being used and how best practitioners can be supported in using the dolls. Although this approach does not provide as reliable an evaluation of the intervention, or answer precise research questions, the project will hopefully result in an intervention that is practical and sustainable beyond the lifetime of this project.

A second approach, which we recommend, is the close collaboration between practitioners and researchers from the beginning stages of the intervention design, through to evaluation and dissemination of the findings. The advantage of this approach is that, as the intervention has been designed in consultation with the practitioners, it is more likely to be practical and useable. But also, the involvement of academics from the outset should ensure necessary conditions are in place to allow a reliable evaluation of the impact of the intervention.

So far we have considered the benefits and drawbacks of practitioner–academic collaborations and how these should be managed, from our own perspectives as academic researchers. In the interests of providing a more balanced view of such collaborations, we also asked two of our nonacademic partners, WEDG and RES, for their thoughts on the benefits and drawbacks of collaborating with researchers to develop and implement prejudice-reduction interventions (Box 14.1).

A Model of Designing and Implementing Prejudice-Reduction Interventions

In this chapter we have highlighted the important role researchers and practitioners play in the development of prejudice-reduction interventions. Academic–practitioner collaborations can lead to theoretically-based interventions that have been systematically evaluated, and are practical. Based on our experiences, a series of stages is suggested in order to achieve successful and productive academic–practitioner collaborations, which begin and end with "giving psychology away":

Box 14.1   Practitioners' perspectives on sharing the applications of developmental psychology

WEDG – a Development Education Centre

It has been an enormous benefit to collaborate over the project with a professional in a closely related field who also has the time to discuss and jointly reflect on the project. Here are a few observations from our collaborative research with Dr Cameron:

Goals of the collaboration partners should be made clear from the outset. There is overlap in the goals of academic and nonacademic organizations when engaging in a collaborative project of this kind: both want to create an effective prejudice-reduction intervention. However, while academics are concerned with rigorous evaluation and academic publications, nonacademic partners' are relatively more concerned with creating practical guides for using the intervention, disseminating the findings to user groups and policymakers. Although in recent times academics' interest in "impact" has increased. From the outset, partners should be clear about their goals and what they hope to achieve by completing the project, and recognize the outputs required by each partner.

Different audiences, different styles. The rigorous analysis provided by academic researchers is useful for validating the prejudice-reduction interventions we develop. However, the level of detail and breadth of analyses required for academic audiences does not always match that required for general dissemination of findings. We write for very different audiences and, potentially, this is where the two worlds of academic and nonacademic could diverge, but keeping honest and open lines of communication, and acknowledging these differences will maintain confidence in the collaboration.

Access to networks and participant pools. By working collaboratively with a local organization like WEDG, developmental psychologists who work in a predominantly academic environment can access schools that have already been identified as open to working with outside agencies and where positive relationships with key personnel have been established.

Embed scientific rigor in our practice. One of the clear benefits of collaborating with academic partners is the perceived increased credibility of our organization with other partners and sponsors. To be able to mention that a long-established university is working alongside and conducting the research element of our projects creates an instant positive impression with recipients, other partners, and funders and will no doubt reap benefits for the organization in the future.

Involve each other in your organizations. Dr Cameron has joined our Steering Group and has been Chair of this committee, which has provided her with an insight into the workings of our organization, and created more general impact on how we operate. Likewise, Dr Cameron has invited us to attend relevant events, and indeed to hold our own events, at the University. This has broadened the reach and perspective of both parties.

Rights and Equality Sandwell (RES)

Some of the above points are echoed in the reflections of another organization with whom the authors have collaborated, Rights and Equality Sandwell (RES). RES believes that through partnership working both the researcher and practitioner can help the other by providing a completely different set of "lenses" with which to look at the subject matter. Both can become blinkered by their own fields and vision. Practitioners and researchers need to be willing to cross over into the others arena, so that valuable and practical research can be embarked on and then suitably implemented. Its suggestions for successful academic-practitioner collaborations are outlined here.

The need for academics to publicize findings more widely. RES first became aware of Dr Cameron and Professor Rutland's research through the BBC TV program "Child of Our Time". This program featured their research on the development of ethnic stereotypes in early childhood. Interestingly, WEDG also became aware of the authors research through a BBC Radio 4 program. This highlighted the need for academics to continue to engage with the media in order to make contacts, and to capitalize on connections that result for media appearances. But it also highlights a need for a more strategic approach to identifying organizations with similar goals, sharing findings with them, and building collaborative networks. Academic research should be disseminated in multiple outlets and formats in order to reach practitioners.

Practitioners need to know that academics want to work with them. When I initially approached the authors, I had no idea that academic researchers would be willing or able to work with us. Indeed, it came as a surprise to learn that academics are being encouraged to work with community groups and ensure their research has "impact", and collaborations with practitioners can help them to achieve this. Academics need to be more forthcoming in initiating such collaborations.

Start small. We initially worked together on two small-scale projects; this allowed us to develop a good working relationship. Academics and practitioners work in different ways, in terms of jargon, aims, approach, priorities, perspectives, expectations to name a few. Small projects allow you to find common ground and ways of working together that benefit both parties. It allows you to develop an effective working relationship and understanding, as well as appreciation for each other and each other's perspectives. The track record of successfully completing smaller grants builds a compelling reputation on which to build future large-scale grant applications.

Academics and practitioners have different but complementary strengths. These should be recognized and appreciated. Academics have an excellent grasp of theories, while practitioners have a good understanding of what can be achieved "out there", and the practical aspects of delivering a project. Both parties should recognize these distinctive and complementary strengths.

Practitioners should be involved in the research. It is helpful if practitioners are actively involved in undertaking the research in terms of design, practice and analysis. This helps to embed research skills within the nonacademic organizations. It also maintains ownership of the research element and keeps the research in line with the overall aims of the project.

Research is useful. Research findings are useful in terms of guiding practice, highlighting the needs within communities or areas for work. In terms of attracting funding for implementation projects, research findings are essential for providing evidence of need.

Stage 1: Publicizing the research

First, it is essential that academic researchers publicize their research to a wide audience, using accessible language. Academics must be proactive in reaching out to practitioners, policymakers and organizations who are likely to have an interest in their research findings. In the case of prejudice reduction, this includes educators, policymakers, global education charities and equality organizations. In addition to our own findings, we can also share well-established psychological theories and concepts, making them accessible to a range of audiences. This can be done through engaging with the media, including electronic media, building links with local and national organizations and writing reports of varying levels of detail and distributing these widely. Another approach is to hold large-scale, themed "dissemination" events, to which multiple charities, policymakers and funders are invited. Such events provide an opportunity to create connections, collaborations, and, potentially, research impact. An example of an event organized by the first author is the "Researching Social Exclusion: Relevance for Public Policy and Practice" one-day workshop (http://www.kent.ac.uk/psychology/socialexclusion2014/). This event was attended by nearly 100 academics, funders, policymakers, charities and campaign groups, and attracted high profile speakers (academics and representatives of charities and funding bodies). It was an opportunity to create connections between academic and nonacademic partners, with complementary goals.

Stage 2: Developing an intervention

Having identified a potential partner, it is necessary to hold a series of meetings, presentations and discussions to identify overlap in interests, and to investigate potential funding streams. Develop a relatively small scale prejudice-reduction intervention project as starting point, and build the collaboration from there with larger scale projects. In each case, it is essential that both partners' motivations, goals and responsibilities are identified from the outset. Have open channels of communication. Both parties should be involved in each stage of the development and testing of the intervention. However, the complementary expertise of both parties should be drawn on: practitioners' expertise on the practicalities of designing and delivering the intervention must be considered, and the academics knowledge of theory and rigorous evaluation should be drawn on. Tensions between the two perspectives are likely, and compromises are likely to be required. For instance, the evaluation may not be as rigorous as one would find in a psychological laboratory experiment, but should as far as possible meet the standards outlined by Paluck and Green (2009).

Stage 3: Implementation and evaluation of the impact of the intervention

The intervention should be designed such that it can be delivered by practitioners in the field, or in an educational setting. This ensures that the intervention is sustainable beyond the length of the project. However, a brand new intervention may benefit from being delivered by research assistants in the first instance, in order to tweak the technique, ensure it is being delivered as intended, or to compare different forms of the intervention. It is important, however, that the end product is fit for purpose and can be embedded in a school setting without requiring additional staff members to deliver it. Responsibility for the evaluation of the intervention impact will usually lie with the academic researcher partner, but it is beneficial to include the practitioners and nonacademic organization in this stage, so that they can appreciate the importance of the evaluation element, and have a sense of ownership of the project.

Stage 4: Dissemination of findings

Again, "giving psychology away" is critical at this stage. Academics expertise can be applied to the rigorous evaluation of the intervention impact, and conducting and presenting detailed analyses. However, it is essential that the level of detail, style of presentation and range of findings presented are tailored to suit the audience. The practitioner and nonacademic partner are essential for providing advice to ensure this is achieved. The network and contacts of practitioner and nonacademic partners are essential for the widespread dissemination of findings. This dissemination would, we hope, provide both partners with further exposure and lead to further future collaborations with other partners.

Conclusions

Over the last couple of decades, researchers have amassed a rich body of work on the development of prejudice in children. This is underpinned by major theoretical frameworks, addressing fundamental themes of social cognitive development and intergroup contact. More recently, researchers have also begun to intensify their efforts towards answering the compelling, "giving away", question: "How can we apply our theories, evidence and methods to help to reduce prejudice in children?" Again, the research base on interventions is now growing. As this activity moves from the laboratory to real world interventions, cooperation with practitioner colleagues is not only desirable to meet logistical challenges but also enormously beneficial in terms of keeping the research attuned to the environments, circumstances and events in which children encounter, formulate and share prejudice – and sometimes reduce it.

References

Abbott, N., & Cameron, L. (2014). From bystanders to 'upstanders': Evaluating the effectiveness of a role-play anti-bullying intervention for promoting assertive bystander intentions and actual bystander behaviour. Presentation at the British Psychological Society Developmental Section, Amsterdam, September, 2014.

Aboud, F. E. (1988). *Children and prejudice*. Oxford: Blackwell Publishing.

Aboud, F. E. (2008). A social-cognitive developmental theory of prejudice. In S. M. Quintana & C. McKown (Eds.), *Handbook of RACCE, racism and the developing child* (pp. 55–72). USA: John Wiley & Sons Inc.

Aboud, F. E., & Fenwick, V. (1999). Exploring and evaluating school-based interventions to reduce prejudice. *Journal of Social Issues, 55*, 767–785.

Aboud, F. E., & Joong, A. (2008). Intergroup name-calling and conditions for creating assertive bystanders. In S. R. Levy & M. Killen (Eds.), *Intergroup attitudes and relations in childhood through adulthood* (pp. 249–260). Oxford: Oxford University Press.

Aboud, F. E., & Levy, S. R. (2000). Interventions to reduce prejudice and discrimination in children and adolescents. In S. Oskamp, (Ed.), *Reducing prejudice and discrimination* (pp. 269–293). NJ, USA: Lawrence Erlbaum Associates Publishers.

Aboud, F. E., & Sankar, J. (2007). Friendship and identity in a language-integrated school. *International Journal of Behavioral Development, 31*, 445–453.

Aboud, F. E., Mendelson, M. J., & Purdy, K. T. (2003). Cross-race peer relations and friendship quality. *International Journal of Behavioral Development, 27*, 165–173.

Aboud, F. E., Tredoux, C., Tropp, L. R., Brown, C. S., Niens, U., & Noor, N. M. (2012). Interventions to reduce prejudice and enhance inclusion and respect for ethnic differences in early childhood: A systematic review. *Developmental Review, 32*(4), 307–336. doi: 10.1016/j.dr.2012.05.001

Abrams, D., & Killen, M. (2014). Social exclusion in childhood: A developmental intergroup perspective. *Child Development, 84*(3), 772–790. doi: 10.1111/cdev.12012

Allport, G. W. (1954). *The nature of prejudice.* New York: Doubleday Anchor Books.

Banks, J.A. (1995). Multicultural education: Its effects on students' racial and gender role attitudes. In J. A. Banks & C. A. M. Banks (Eds.), *Handbook of research on multicultural education* (pp. 617–627). New York: Macmillan.

Beelmann, A., & Heinemann, K. S. (2014). Preventing prejudice and improving inter-group attitudes: A meta-analysis of child and adolescent training programs. *Journal of Applied Developmental Psychology, 35*, 10–14.

Bellmore, A. D., Nishina, A., Witkow, M. R., Graham, S., & Juvonen, J. (2007). The influence of classroom ethnic composition on same- and other-ethnicity peer nominations in middle school. *Social Development, 16*, 720–740.

Bigler, R. S. (1995). The role of classification skill in moderating environmental influences on children's gender stereotyping: A study of the functional use of gender in the classroom. *Child Development, 66*, 1072–1087.

Bigler, R. S. (1999). The use of multicultural curricula and materials to counter racism in children. *Journal of Social Issues, 55*, 687–705.

Bigler, R. S., & Hughes, J. M. (2010). Reasons for scepticism about the efficacy of simulated social contact interventions. *American Psychologist, 65*(2), 132–133.

Bigler, R. S., & Liben, L. S. (1992). Cognitive mechanisms in children's gender stereo-typing: Theoretical and educational implications of a cognitive-based intervention. *Child Development, 63*, 1351–1363.

Bigler, R. S., Jones, L. C., & Lobliner, D. B. (1997). Social categorisation and the formation of intergroup attitudes in children. *Child Development, 68*, 530–543.

Bratt, C. (2008). The jigsaw classroom under test: No effect on intergroup relations evident. *Journal of Community and Applied Social Psychology, 18*, 403–419.

Brown, R. J. (2010). *Prejudice: Its social psychology.* Oxford: Blackwell Publishing.

Brown, R. J., Vivian, J., & Hewstone, M. (1999). Changing attitudes through intergroup contact: The effects of group membership salience. *European Journal of Social Psychology, 29*, 741–764.

Cameron, L., & Rutland, A. (2006). Extended contact through story reading in school: Reducing children's prejudice towards the disabled. *Journal of Social Issues, 62*, 469–488.

Cameron, L., & Rutland, A. (2008). An integrative approach to changing children's intergroup attitudes. In S. Levy & M. Killen (Eds.), *Intergroup relations: Attitudes and relationship in childhood through adulthood* (pp. 191–203). New York, NY: Oxford University Press.

Cameron, L., Rutland, A., & Brown, R. (2007). Promoting children's positive intergroup attitudes towards stigmatized groups: Extended contact and multiple classification skills training. *International Journal of Behavioral Development, 31*, 454–466.

Cameron, L., Rutland, A., Brown, R. J., & Douch, R. (2006). Changing children's intergroup attitudes towards refugees: Testing different models of extended contact. *Child Development, 77*, 1208–1219.

Cameron, L., Rutland, A., Hossain, R., & Petley, R. (2011). When and why does extended contact work? The role of high quality direct contact and group norms in the development of positive ethnic intergroup attitudes amongst children. *Group Processes & Intergroup Relations, 14*, 193–206.

Cameron, L., & Turner, R. N. (2010). The applications of diversity-based interventions to reduce prejudice. In R. J. Crisp (Ed.), *The psychology of social and cultural diversity* (pp. 322–352). Malden, MA: Blackwell Publishing.

Cole, C. F., Labin, D. B., & del Rocio Galarza, M. (2008). Begin with the children: What research on Sesame Street's international coproductions reveals about using media to promote a new more peaceful world. *International Journal of Behavioral Development, 32*, 359–365.

Crisp. R., Husnu, S., Meleady, R., & Stathi, S. (2011). From imagery to intention: A dual route model of imagined contact effects. *European Review of Social Psychology, 21*(1), 188–236.

Crisp, R., & Turner, R. (2009). Can imagined interactions produce positive perceptions? Reducing prejudice through simulated contact. *American Psychologist, 64*, 231–240.

Cummings, S. M., Williams, M. M., & Ellis, R. A. (2002). Impact of an intergenerational programme on 4th Graders' attitudes toward elders and school behaviors. *Journal of Human Behavior, 6*(3), 91–107. doi: 10.1300/J137v06n03_06

Davies, K., Tropp, L. R., Aron, A., Pettigrew, T., & Wright, S. C. (2011). Cross-group friendships and intergroup attitudes: A meta-analytic review. *Personality and Social Psychology Review, 15*, 332–351.

de Tezanos-Pinto, P., Bratt, C., & Brown, R. (2010). What will others think? In-group norms as a mediator of the effects of intergroup contact. *British Journal of Social Psychology, 49*, 507–523. doi: 10.1348/014466609X471020

Duckitt, J. (1992). *The social psychology of prejudice*. New York: Praeger.

Durkin, K., Nesdale, D., Dempsey, G., & McLean, A. (2012). Young children's responses to media representations of intergroup threat and ethnicity. *British Journal of Developmental Psychology, 30*(3), 459–476.

Feddes, A. R., Noack, P., & Rutland, A. (2009). Direct and extended friendship effects on minority and majority children's interethnic attitudes: A longitudinal study. *Child Development, 80*, 377–390. doi: 10.1111/j.1467-8624.2009.01266.x

Jackson, M. F., Barth, J. M., Powell, N., & Lochman, J. E. (2006). Classroom contextual effects of race on children's peer nominations. *Child Development, 77*, 1325–1337.

Jugert, P., Noack, P., & Rutland, A. (2011). Friendship preferences among German and Turkish preadolescents. *Child Development, 82*, 812–829.

Killen, M., Lee-Kim, J. McGlothlin, H., & Stangor, C. (2002). How children and adolescents evaluate gender and racial exclusion. *Monographs of the Society for Research in Child Development, 67*.

Killen, M., Mulvey, K. L., & Hitti, A. (2014). Social exclusion in childhood: A developmental intergroup perspective. *Child Development, 84*, 3, 772–790. doi: 10.1111/cdev.12012

Killen, M., & Rutland, A. (2011). *Children and social exclusion: Morality, prejudice, and group identity.* John Wiley & Sons Ltd.

Killen, M., Rutland, A., & Ruck, M. (2012). Promoting equity and justice in childhood: Policy implications. *Social Policy Report, 25*(4), 1–25.

Levy, S. R., & Killen, M. (2008). *Intergroup attitudes and relations in childhood through adulthood.* Oxford University Press.

Levy, S. R., West, T. L., Bigler, R. S., Karafantis, D. M., Ramirez, L., & Velilla, E. (2005). Messages about the uniqueness and similarities of people: Impact on U.S. Black and Latino youth. *Journal of Applied Developmental Psychology, 26*, 714–733.

Maras, P., & Brown, R. (1996). Effects of contact on children's attitudes towards disability: A longitudinal study. *Journal of Applied Social Psychology, 26*, 2113–2134.

Maras, P., & Brown, R. (2000). Effects of different forms of school contact on children's attitudes toward disabled and non-disabled peers. *British Journal of Educational Psychology, 70*, 337–351.

McGlothlin, H., & Killen, M. (2005). Children's perceptions of intergroup and intragroup similarity and the role of social experience. *Applied Developmental Psychology, 26*, 680–698.

McGlothlin, H., & Killen, M. (2006). Intergroup attitudes of European American children attending ethnically homogeneous schools. *Child Development, 77*, 1375–1386.

Miles, E., & Crisp, R. J. (2014). A meta-analytic test of the imagined contact hypothesis. *Group Processes and Intergroup Relations, 17*, 3–26.

Miller, N. (2002). Personalization and the promise of contact theory. *Journal of Social Issues, 58*, 387–410.

Monteiro, M. B. Franca, D. X., & Rodrigues, R. (2009).The development of intergroup bias in childhood: How social norms can shape children's racial behaviours. *International Journal of Psychology, 44*(1), 29–39. doi: 10.1080/00207590802057910

Mulvey, K. L., Hitti, A., Rutland, A., Abrams, D., & Killen, M. (2014). When do children dislike ingroup members? Resource allocation from individual and group perspectives. *Journal of Social Issues, 70*(1), 29–46. doi: 10.1111/josi.12045

Nesdale, D., Maass, A., Durkin, K., & Griffiths, J. (2005). Group norms, threat and children's racial prejudice. *Child Development, 76*, 652–663.

Nesdale, D., Griffiths, J. A., Durkin, K., & Maass, A. (2007). Effects of group membership, intergroup competition and out-group ethnicity on children's ratings of in-group and out-group similarity and positivity. *British Journal of Developmental Psychology, 25*, 359–373.

Oskamp, S. (2000). *Reducing prejudice and discrimination.* NJ, US: Lawrence Erlbaum Associates Publishers.

Pahlke, E., Bigler, R. S., & Martin, C. L. (2014). Can fostering children's ability to challenge sexism improve critical analysis, internalization, and enactment of inclusive, egalitarian peer relationships? *Journal of Social Issues, 70*(1), 115–133.

Paluck, E. L. (2006). Diversity training and intergroup contact: A call to action research. *Journal of Social Issues, 62*, 439–451.

Paluck, E. L. (2011). Peer pressure against prejudice: A high school field experiment examining social network change. *Journal of Experimental Social Psychology, 47*, 350–358.

Paluck, E. L., & Green, D. P. (2009). Prejudice reduction: What works? A critical look at evidence from the field and the laboratory. *Annual Review of Psychology, 60*, 339–367.

Paolini, S., Hewstone, M., Cairns, E., & Voci, A. (2004). Effect of direct and indirect cross-group friendships on judgements of Catholics and Protestants in Northern Ireland: The mediating role of an anxiety-reduction mechanism. *Personality and Social Psychology Bulletin, 30*, 770–786.

Pettigrew, T. F., & Tropp, L. R. (2006). A meta-analytic test of intergroup contact theory. *Journal of Personality and Social Psychology, 90*, 751–783.

Pfeifer, J. H., Brown, C. S., & Juvonen, J. (2007). Teaching tolerance in schools: Lessons learned since Brown vs Board of Education about the development and reduction of children's prejudice. *Social Policy Report: Giving Child and Youth Development Knowledge Away*, Volume *XXI* (II).

Piaget, J. (1965). *The moral judgment of the child*. New York: Free Press.

Quintana, S. M., & McKown, C. (2008). *Handbook of race, racism, and the developing child*. Hoboken, NJ: John Wiley & Sons, Inc.

Raabe, T., & Beelmann, A. (2011). Development of ethnic, racial and national prejudice in childhood and adolescence. *Child Development, 82*, 1715–1737. doi: 10.1111/j.1467-8624.2011.01668.x

Rutland, A., Cameron, L., Bennett, L., & Ferrell, J. (2005). Interracial contact and racial constancy: A multi-site study of racial intergroup bias in 3-5 year old Anglo-British children. *Journal of Applied Developmental Psychology, 26*, 699–713.

Rutland, A., & Killen, M. (2015). A developmental science approach to reducing prejudice and social exclusion: Intergroup processes, social-cognitive development, and moral reasoning. *Social Issues and Policy Review, 9*(1), 121–154.

Schofield, J. W., & Eurich-Fulcer, R. (2001). When and how school desegregation improves intergroup relations. In R. Brown & S. Gaertner (Eds.), *Intergroup processes*, Oxford: Blackwell Publishing.

Sierksma, J., Thijs, J., & Verkuyten, M. (2015). In-group bias in children's intention to help can be overpowered by inducing empathy. *British Journal of Developmental Psychology 33*(1), 45–56. doi: 10.1111/bjdp.12065

Stathi, S., Cameron, L., Hartley, B., & Bradford, S. (2014). Imagined contact as a prejudice-reduction intervention in schools: The underlying role of similarity and attitudes. *Journal of Applied Social Psychology, 44*(8), 523–578. doi: 10.1111/jasp.12245

Thijs, J., Verkuyten, M., & Grundel, M. (2014). Ethnic classroom composition and peer victimization: The moderating role of classroom attitudes. *Journal of Social Issues, 70*(1), 134–150.

Tropp, L. R., O'Brien, T. C., & Migacheva, K. (2014). How peer norms of inclusion and exclusion predict children's interest in cross-ethnic friendships. *Journal of Social Issues, 70*, 151–166.

Turner, R. N., Hewstone, M., Voci, A., Paolini, S., & Christ, O. (2007a). Reducing prejudice via direct and extended cross-group friendship. *European Review of Social Psychology, 18*, 212–255.

Turner, R. N., Hewstone, M., & Voci, A. (2007b). Reducing explicit and implicit prejudice via direct and extended contact: The mediating role of self-disclosure and intergroup anxiety. *Journal of Personality and Social Psychology, 93*, 369–388.

Vezzali, L., Stathi, S., Giovannini, D., Capozza, D., & Trifiletti, E. (2015). The greatest magic of Harry Potter: Reducing prejudice. *Journal of Applied Social Psychology, 45*(2), 105–121. doi: 10.1111/jasp.12279

Wright, S. C., Aron, A., McLaughlin-Volpe, T., & Ropp, S. A. (1997). The extended contact effect: Knowledge of cross-group friendships and prejudice. *Journal of Personality and Social Psychology, 73*, 73–90.

Wright, S. C., & Tropp, L. R. (2005). Language and intergroup contact: Investigating the impact of bilingual instruction on children's intergroup attitudes. *Group Processes and Intergroup Relations, 8*, 309–328.

PART III

Clinical Aspects

15

What Do We Know and Why Does It Matter? The Dissemination of Evidence-Based Interventions for Child Maltreatment

Dante Cicchetti, Sheree L. Toth, Wendy J. Nilsen, and Jody Todd Manly

Research on child maltreatment has an urgency characteristic of all problems of great social concern. The costs to society are enormous (Fang, Brown, Florence, & Mercy, 2012; Meadows, Tunstill, George, Dhudwar, & Kurtz, 2011); in the United States, for example, the financial repercussions are estimated at over 120 billion dollars annually (Fang et al., 2012; and see Sethi et al., 2013, for comparable figures for several European nations). The costs to individuals and families, in terms of psychological damage, reduced quality of life, impaired productivity and lifespan prospects, are beyond financial accounting. In light of the alarming epidemiological rates of maltreatment (Cicchetti & Toth, 2003, 2005; Sedlak et al., 1997; Sethi et al., 2013), which likely underestimate the prevalence of child abuse and neglect (Barnett, Manly, & Cicchetti, 1993; Meadows et al., 2011; Prinz, Sanders, Shapiro, Whitaker, & Lutzker, 2009), it is essential that scientists who conduct research investigations on the developmental pathways to maladaptation, psychopathology, and resilience in abused and neglected children rapidly translate their findings into

The Wiley Handbook of Developmental Psychology in Practice: Implementation and Impact, First Edition.
Edited by Kevin Durkin and H. Rudolph Schaffer.
© 2016 John Wiley & Sons, Ltd. Published 2016 by John Wiley & Sons, Ltd.

the practice arena. Such translational efforts could inform the development of prevention and intervention initiatives to divert affected children from developing trauma-related maladaptive functioning and psychopathology, contribute toward reducing the burden of mental illness in traumatized children, and promote the development of resilient functioning in children experiencing significant adversity (Cicchetti, 2013a; Cicchetti & Toth, 2005; Luthar & Cicchetti, 2000; Toth & Cicchetti, 1999).

Some three decades ago, Aber and Cicchetti (1984) emphasized the criticality of conducting studies on the developmental sequelae of maltreatment and asserted that such investigations could serve to enhance the quality of clinical, legal, and policymaking decisions for abused and neglected children. Aber and Cicchetti (1984) further stated that child welfare issues, such as the effect of removing a child coercively from the home, the development of specific services to meet the psychological needs of maltreated children, and the evaluation of these services, would benefit from a more solid and sophisticated data base on the developmental consequences of child abuse and neglect. They cautioned that "without rigor in design and method ... myth will be put forward in place of knowledge as a guide to social action" (Aber & Cicchetti, 1984, pp. 196–197).

In times of fiscal austerity, human services have come under the scrutiny of budget-conscious government administrators and legislators. Increasingly, providers are expected to document the beneficial impact of their prevention and intervention efforts. Now that research on the psychological development of maltreated children has advanced over the past several decades, basic scientific investigations in the area of child abuse and neglect are in a strong position to contribute to the kind of evaluation research required to justify service dollars. Likewise, these empirical findings can be utilized to modify existing ineffective intervention programs or policies so that the needs of maltreated children and their families can be better served.

In order for scientific findings to be brought to the clinical arena and to exert a positive impact on the development of social policies that emanate from empirical evidence, researchers must become increasingly cognizant of the types of data that clinicians and policymakers need for effective decision making, including how to use such data to make sound decisions. Reciprocally, clinical, legal, and policy decision makers must become more aware of the natural limits of any policy-relevant developmental research. Closer collaborations among researchers, clinicians, and policymakers will, ultimately, promote improved research that can be directed toward the development of services on behalf of maltreated children and families.

Goals of the Chapter

In this chapter, we first summarize what we know about the impact of child maltreatment, with an emphasis on its deleterious effects on attachment and self-development in young children. Throughout the chapter, child maltreatment is used to refer to the occurrence of single or multiple experiences involving physical abuse, sexual abuse, neglect, and emotional maltreatment. It is important to highlight that there is a high amount of comorbidity among maltreatment subtypes and that many maltreated children experience more than one form of maltreatment. Therefore, we use maltreatment more globally and provide information on subtypes when it is pertinent to our discussion. We then describe Mt. Hope Family Center (MHFC) as an example of an effective university–community partnership that contributed to the design and implementation of randomized control trials (RCTs) for maltreating families. The overarching goal of this chapter is to describe this collaborative process so as to convey how the outcomes from RCTs can be exported into the broader community. In particular, we emphasize that policy change is possible when university, government, and community entities achieve mutual understanding and a shared commitment to improving the delivery of services to vulnerable children and families.

The Impact of Maltreatment on Children's Psychological Development

At the level of individual psychological development, the negotiation of the stage-salient tasks of each developmental period organizes a child's developmental trajectory toward subsequent competence or incompetence (Cicchetti & Lynch, 1995; Cicchetti & Toth, 1995, 2005). An organizational perspective views child development as a progressive sequence of age- and stage-appropriate issues in which successful resolution of tasks at each developmental period must be coordinated and integrated with the environment, as well as with subsequently emerging issues across the life course (Cicchetti & Lynch, 1993, 1995).

From infancy through childhood, these tasks include the development of emotion regulation, the formation of secure attachment relationships, the development of an autonomous self, the formation of effective peer relationships, and the successful adaptation to school. Thus, stage-salient tasks are hierarchically organized as each new task builds upon, and is influenced by, the resolution of previous developmental tasks (Cicchetti & Schneider-Rosen, 1986; Waters & Sroufe, 1983). Poor resolution of stage-salient issues may contribute to maladaptation over time as genetic endowment and prior experiential history influence the selection, engagement, and interpretation of subsequent experience; however, the current developmental context is in constant transaction with environmental supports and stressors (Cicchetti, 2013a, 2013b; Cicchetti & Lynch, 1993; Sroufe, 1983; Sroufe & Rutter, 1984). Accordingly, individual development is an ongoing dynamic process, and, consistent with Gottlieb's (1991, 1992; Gottlieb & Halpern, 2002) notions of probabilistic epigenesis, individuals are continually affected by new biological and psychological developments, experiences, and transitions, leaving developmental pathways susceptible to modifications throughout the life span (Cicchetti & Lynch, 1995; Cicchetti & Tucker, 1994).

In keeping with the dynamic systems concepts of equifinality and multifinality (Cicchetti, 2013a; Cicchetti & Rogosch, 1996), multiple pathways to adaptation and maladaptation, as well as varied developmental outcomes are possible for maltreated children. The ecological conditions associated with maltreatment represent a severe deviation from the average expectable environment. Without adequate environmental supports, the probabilistic path of ontogenesis for maltreated children is characterized by an increased risk for unsuccessful resolution of the stage-salient developmental issues. Failure at any stage-salient task increases the risk of unsuccessful resolution of subsequent developmental challenges.

Maltreated children are likely to exhibit atypical physiological responsiveness, difficulties in affect differentiation and regulation, dysfunctional attachment relationships, anomalies in self-system processes, deficits in representational development, problematic peer relationships, and trouble adapting to school (for reviews see Cicchetti, 1989, 2013a; Cicchetti & Lynch, 1995; Cicchetti & Toth, 1995, 2005; Cicchetti & Valentino, 2006). These repeated developmental disruptions create a profile of relatively enduring vulnerability factors that place maltreated children at heightened risk for future maladaptive functioning, behavior problems, and psychopathology (Banny, Cicchetti, Rogosch, Oshri, & Crick, 2013; Cicchetti & Manly, 2001; Cicchetti & Toth, 2005; Dodge, Pettit, & Bates, 1997; Egeland, 2007; Hecht, Cicchetti, Rogosch, & Crick, 2014; Jaffee, Caspi, Moffitt, & Taylor, 2004; Johnson, Cohen, Brown, Smailes, & Bernstein, 1999; Kim & Cicchetti, 2003, 2004; Masten & Cicchetti, 2010; Rogosch & Cicchetti, 2005; Toth, Cicchetti, & Kim, 2002). Although not all maltreated children who have difficulty resolving stage-salient issues will develop psychopathology, later disturbances in functioning are more likely to occur.

Relatively little work has been conducted investigating the pathways to resilient outcomes in maltreated children, though attention to this crucial question for applied developmentalists has been growing (Cicchetti & Rogosch, 2012; Kim-Cohen, & Turkewitz, 2012; Masten, 2014; Obradović, 2012; Rutter, 2012).

The achievement of competent functioning in a subset of maltreated children constitutes but one example of how some individuals who have endured deleterious experiences nonetheless manage to develop adaptively. Resilience is a dynamic developmental process that has been operationalized as an individual's attainment of positive adaptation and competent functioning despite having experienced chronic stress or detrimental circumstances, or following exposure to prolonged or severe trauma (Cicchetti, 2013a; Egeland, Carlson, & Sroufe, 1993; Luthar, Cicchetti, & Becker, 2000; Rutter, 2012). Resilience is multidimensional in nature, exemplified by findings that high-risk individuals may manifest competence in some domains and contexts, whereas they may exhibit problems in others (Luthar et al., 2000; Rutter, 2012; Sapienza & Masten, 2011).

Despite the paucity of research on the determinants of resilient functioning in maltreated children, findings are beginning to coalesce that self-system process (e.g., self-determination, positive self-esteem, and self-efficacy) and personality factors (e.g., ego resiliency and ego-overcontrol) play prominent roles in pathways to resilient functioning in maltreated children (Cicchetti & Rogosch, 1997; Flores, Cicchetti, & Rogosch, 2005). Consistent with the broader resilience literature in which the vast majority of research has examined the psychosocial correlates and contributors to resilience, researchers investigating the pathways to resilient adaptation in maltreated children largely have eschewed the inclusion of genetic and biological measures. Recently, several groups of scientists have embarked upon a more multilevel approach to the examination of resilience, including assessments of neuroendocrine regulation, hemispheric activation electroencephalogram (EEG) asymmetries, and the interaction of genetic polymorphisms and well-defined candidate environmental pathogens, into their psychosocial measurement batteries (Cicchetti, 2013a, 2013b; Cicchetti & Curtis, 2006, 2007; Cicchetti & Rogosch, 2012; Cicchetti, Rogosch, & Oshri, 2011; Curtis & Cicchetti, 2003; Feder, Nestler, & Charney, 2009; Karatsoreos & McEwan, 2012). This multiple level of analysis approach to resilience has broadened the understanding of pathways to resilient adaptation in maltreated children. For example, Cicchetti and Rogosch (2007) found that different levels of analysis contributed to resilient functioning in maltreated children – personality features, the interaction between cortisol regulation and maltreatment, and diurnal variation of dehydroepiandrosterone (DHA) each demonstrated independent effects in explaining variation in resilient functioning in abused, neglected, and nonmaltreated children. In addition, Curtis and Cicchetti (2007) reported that emotion regulation abilities and greater left hemispheric EEG activation distinguished between resilient and nonresilient children. An observational measure of emotion regulation significantly contributed to the prediction of resilience in the maltreated and nonmaltreated children; however, EEG asymmetry in central cortical regions predicted resilience only in the maltreated group.

Mt. Hope Family Center

Although Mt. Hope Family Center (MHFC) is located within the Department of Clinical and Social Sciences in Psychology at the University of Rochester, from its inception MHFC sought to forge a strong partnership with the community. However, the formation of a successful partnership was not without its challenges. When a renowned researcher in Developmental and Clinical psychology assumed the directorship of MHFC in 1985, the community initially feared that an exclusive focus on research would become the driving mission of the Center and that it would minimize efforts to provide services to maltreated children. Therefore, efforts needed to be directed toward reducing this perception in order to truly bridge research and practice. During its early years, MHFC staff psychologists were expected to devote equal energies to conducting research and to providing clinical services to children who were referred from the County's Department of Human Services (DHS) for concerns related to child maltreatment. Such close involvement in clinical endeavors not only informed future research questions, but also communicated a strong commitment to patient care to frontline practitioners and to funding bodies. Rather than being viewed as ivory tower researchers, MHFC became recognized as an educational resource for the community. Training sessions were offered annually to new caseworkers in the DHS and long before evidence-based treatments became a popular buzz-word, we emphasized that basic research was necessary in order to inform the delivery of effective treatment.

All clinical staff members hired at MHFC were also selected based on an interest in, and an openness to, both basic and evaluation research. Thus, a culture in which research and practice were accorded equal respect was developed and fostered. In turn, this perspective contributed to receptivity within the child welfare and clinical communities regarding the importance of theoretically-informed and empirically-supported treatments. Because the community recognized the need for treatment evaluations, barriers to participant recruitment for basic research and, subsequently, for conducting RCTs were minimized. For example, the administration of the local DHS worked with MHFC research staff to develop a system of identifying eligible participants for research projects. The cooperation of the DHS enabled us to enroll representative and random samples of maltreating parents and their children into our research investigations. Moreover, when data on efficacious interventions were obtained, DHS administrators were committed to providing funding to sustain the provision of services independent of the costs associated with research evaluation. To highlight the journey from research to practice, the basic research we conducted that served as the foundation for developing the RCTs for maltreated infants and preschoolers is described next.

Basic Research on the Development of Attachment and Mental Representations in Maltreated Children

In our early research at Mt. Hope Family Center, we investigated the development of attachment relationships in maltreated infants and young children. In a later section of this chapter, we illustrate how the conduct of this research on the quality of attachment and relationships in maltreated children served as the foundation for translating this work into attachment-theory informed RCTs for abused and neglected children.

Attachment

Although we found that maltreated children formed attachments, the main issue concerned the quality of these attachments and the internal representational models of attachment figures, the self, and the self in relation to others. Children form such representational models based on their relationship history with their primary caregiver (Bowlby, 1969/1982). Through these mental models, children's affects, cognitions, and expectations about future interactions are organized and carried forward into subsequent relationships (Bretherton, 1991; Sroufe & Fleeson, 1986; Zeanah, Berlin, & Boris, 2011). According to the predictions of attachment theorists (Bowlby, 1969/1982; Sroufe & Fleeson, 1986, 1988), the poor quality representational models of attachment figures that accompany these insecure disorganized attachments, with their complementary mental models of self in relation to other, may generalize to new relationships, thereby leading to negative expectations of how others will behave and how successful the self will be in relation to others. It has been theorized that the disorganized attachments found in maltreated infants are the result of frightened and/or frightening parental behavior (Hesse & Main, 2006; Main & Hesse, 1990). If maltreated infants' mental representations are reflective of fear of their caregivers, then the result may be maladaptive patterns of interaction with other relationship partners (e.g., peers, teachers – cf. Lynch & Cicchetti, 1991, 1992). Thus, the presence of insecure attachments during the early years of life may set in motion a cascade of subsequent difficulties with future teachers, peers, and romantic partners.

Several early investigations examining the sequelae of child maltreatment revealed that the attachments maltreated children form with their caregivers were more likely to be insecure than were those of nonmaltreated children (Schneider-Rosen, Braunwald, Carlson, & Cicchetti, 1985; Schneider-Rosen & Cicchetti, 1984). In a contribution to normal attachment theory and research made through observations of maltreated youngsters, a number of investigators found that the observed patterns of attachment behavior of many maltreated infants and toddlers observed in a standardized mother-child interaction paradigm referred to as the "strange situation" (Ainsworth, Blehar, Waters, & Wall, 1978) did not fit smoothly into the original Ainsworth et al. (1978) classification system. Unlike infants and toddlers with more typical [i.e., secure (Type B), insecure-avoidant (Type A), and insecure-resistant (Type C)] patterns of attachment, it was discovered that maltreated infants and toddlers often lacked organized strategies for dealing with separations from and reunions with their caregiver. Main and Solomon (1986, 1990) described this pattern of attachment as "disorganized/disoriented" (Type D). In addition, infants and toddlers with disorganized attachments display other bizarre symptoms in the presence of their caregiver, including interrupted movements, over-bright affect expressions, dazing, freezing, and stilling behaviors, and apprehension.

Within a revised attachment classification scheme that includes these atypical patterns of attachment, maltreated infants and toddlers have been shown to demonstrate a preponderance of disorganized attachments (Carlson, Cicchetti, Barnett, & Braunwald, 1989; Crittenden, 1988; Lyons-Ruth, Connell, Zoll, & Stahl, 1987). In the studies conducted to date, the rate of disorganized attachment in maltreated infants and toddlers has been as high as 90% (Barnett, Ganiban, & Cicchetti, 1999; Carlson et al., 1989; Cicchetti, Rogosch, & Toth, 2006; Lyons-Ruth et al., 1987; Lyons-Ruth et al., 1990; van IZjendoorn, Schuengel, & Bakermans-Kranenburg, 1999). Furthermore, these disorganized patterns of attachment have been found to exhibit substantial stability from infancy to toddlerhood (Barnett et al., 1999; Lyons-Ruth et al., 1990).

Disorganized attachment has been shown to exert an extremely deleterious effect on later development. In particular, children with disorganized attachments to their primary caregiver have been shown to be significantly more likely to develop along maladaptive pathways and to be at high risk for increased aggression, depression and other forms of psychopathology (Cicchetti & Toth, 1998; Fearon, Bakermans-Kranenburg, van IJzendoorn, Lapsley, & Roisman, 2010; Groh, van IJzendoorn, Bakermans-Kranenburg, & Fearon, 2012; Lyons-Ruth & Easterbrooks, 1995; Lyons-Ruth, Easterbrooks, & Cibelli, 1997). In order to prevent the negative developmental cascade from disorganized attachment to maladaptive functioning and psychopathology in maltreated children, the design and implementation of attachment theory-informed interventions with these youngsters holds great promise for reducing the burden of later maladaptation and mental illness in abused and neglected children.

Representational processes

At MHFC we also conducted a number of studies examining the development of self-system processes and of representational models of self and other in maltreated toddlers and preschoolers (see Cicchetti, 1991, and Cicchetti & Toth, 2005, for reviews). Herein we focus on research utilizing story-stem narratives to investigate representational processes of self and other, particularly the mother. As we detail later in this chapter, our basic research on representational models of self and self in relation to mother in maltreated youngsters enabled us to translate the findings of this work into a theory-informed preventive intervention with abused and neglected children.

We have conducted several studies on maltreated children's representations of their caregivers, of themselves, and of themselves in relation to others. These investigations have utilized the MacArthur Story Stem Battery (MSSB) (Bretherton, Oppenheim, Buchsbaum, Emde, & the MacArthur Narrative Group, 1990). The MSSB contains story beginnings that describe a range of emotionally laden interactions among family members. Each story stem involves a combination of family dolls, including a mother, a father, and two same-sex children. The gender and race of the dolls are matched to those of the child. For each narrative, the child is instructed to listen to the beginning of a story told by the experimenter and then to finish it using the characters and simple toy props. Interestingly, this basic paradigm has roots in play therapy and its utility for clinical practice is being increasingly explored (Robinson, 2007). Narratives are videotaped and coded according to the MacArthur Narrative Coding Manual (Robinson, Mantz-Simmons, & Macfie, 1992), with a system that involves a presence–absence method of rating content, representation, and child performance. Among the dependent variables that have been reliably coded across a number of investigations with normal and high-risk children are positive and negative maternal representations, positive and negative self-representations, controllingness, and relationship with the examiner (Emde, Wolf, & Oppenheim, 2003).

Toth, Cicchetti, Macfie, and Emde (1997) utilized the MSSB to examine maternal and self-representations in neglected, physically abused, sexually abused, and nonmaltreated preschool children. The narratives of the maltreated youngsters contained more negative maternal representations and more negative self-representations than did the narratives of nonmaltreated children. Maltreated preschool children also were more controlling with, and less responsive to, the examiner. In our investigations of the differential impact of maltreatment subtype, on maternal and self-representations, physically abused children evidenced the most negative maternal representations; moreover, they also had more negative self-representations than did nonmaltreated children. Sexually abused youngsters manifested more positive self-representations than did the neglected children. Despite the differences exhibited in the nature of their maternal and self-representations, physically and sexually abused preschool children were both found to be more controlling and less responsive to the examiner than were the neglected and nonmaltreated children. The examination of the different patterns evidenced by physically abused, sexually abused, and neglected children on the self-representation variables suggests interesting interpretations for the representational models of these respective groups. The finding that the sexually abused children had a high level of positive self-representations raises the possibility that these representations are not genuine but are more consistent with the "false self" that has been described in the literature (Calverley, Fischer, & Ayoub, 1994; Crittenden & DiLalla, 1988; Koenig, Cicchetti, & Rogosch, 2000; Westen, Betan, & DeFife, 2011).

Whereas physically abused children have high levels of negative self-representations, it was the neglected children who had low levels of positive self-representation. Thus, these two groups of maltreated children differ in the positive versus negative valence of their self-views. The fact that neglected children have restricted positive self-representations is consistent with the reality of these children's lives, in which they most likely receive minimal attention to their basic needs. Conversely, physically abused children, although also confronted with parenting dysfunction, may experience periods during which they are responded to, possibly even positively, by their physically abusive parents. Thus, it may well be that physically abused children are more likely to develop some sense of self as positive, whereas neglected children have far fewer opportunities to do so. Additionally, the tendency for neglect to be a more ongoing, chronic condition involving parental acts of omission, whereas physical abuse may involve intermittent acts of commission, also may be influencing the differences evidenced between these groups of children. The fact that physically abused children also seem to accurately perceive the negativity of their caregiving environments, as evidenced by their elevated negative maternal representations, attests to a possible strength that they possess. It may be more realistic to help children move beyond a history of maltreatment if they are in touch with its negativity than if they are prone to deny the realities that confront them.

Toth, Cicchetti, Macfie, Maughan, and VanMeenan (2000) conducted a one-year longitudinal investigation of the narrative representations of parents and of self, as well as of child behavior using the MSSB assessment, in maltreated and nonmaltreated comparison youngsters. Interestingly, at the first measurement period, when children were approximately four years old, the only significant difference obtained was that the maltreated preschool children evidenced fewer positive representations of parents and of self. However, one year later, maltreated children were found to exhibit more negative representations of parent and of self as well as more negative behavior with the examiner. Consequently, during the preschool period, a time noted for developmental transformations in the self, the representational models of maltreated children appear to become increasingly more negative.

Translating Maltreatment Research Into Practice: The Implementation of Randomized Control Trials to Improve Attachment Insecurity and Negative Representational Models of Self and Other in Maltreated Youngsters

These findings suggest that it may be critical to intervene with maltreated children early in the preschool period, when their representational models may be more easily modified by relational experiences that challenge earlier negative experiences with caregivers. Because maltreated children are likely to generalize such negative representational models of attachment figures to future relationship partners (Howes & Segal, 1993; Lynch & Cicchetti, 1991), this underscores the need for intervening before mental representations of relationships become more refractory to change. Therefore, the initiation of intervention prior to the consolidation of negative representational models of self and other may be much more effective than would intervention that is begun subsequent to the crystallization of negative representational models.

Before directing our attention to the RCTs that emanated from research on the sequelae of child maltreatment, it is important to discuss the "evidence" that emerges from RCTs and to describe how results from RCTs might be exported to the child welfare community. This process requires clarification of "efficacy" versus "effectiveness" research.

Efficacy versus effectiveness

When examining issues associated with determining the support for various treatment approaches, discussions frequently turn to queries regarding what extent of evidence qualifies a treatment as empirically-supported. Clinical efficacy investigations typically involve RCTs and manuals, as well as clear sample inclusion and exclusion criteria, significant training and supervision of therapists, and monitoring of the delivery of the intervention in accord with the study pro-tocol. Given these well-controlled parameters, it is not surprising that efficacious treatments may not be as effective in less-controlled clinical settings. In clinic populations, problems are likely to be more severe and multifaceted. Effectiveness research involves the conduct of treatment evaluations in naturalistic settings that do not exert as high a level of control as that associated with efficacy trials. Although effectiveness designs are more generalizable to the broader population than are efficacy investigations, this advantage may be countered by threats to internal validity.

Increasingly, a consensus exists that in order to be evidence-based, treatments must be manualized, evaluated via well-controlled experiments (the gold standard being randomized control trials), and be replicated at a site other than where the treatment was developed (Kazdin & Weisz, 2003). Although the value of efficacy studies in contributing to the evidence-base of psychological treatments is apparent, it cannot be the final step if the goal is improving the availability and utilization of empirically-supported treatments. Rather, when efficacy studies are designed, the ultimate population that might benefit needs to be considered. In some instances, minimizing exclusion criteria might ultimately result in a greater likelihood of an efficacious treatment being effective in real world clinical contexts. In addition, a commitment to establishing effectiveness in less controlled settings is critical. Although the RCTs that we next describe were designed within the parameters of efficacy investigations, knowledge regarding the "real world" problems associated with providing services to maltreating families was incorporated into their design. Thus, we hoped that ultimately the findings from these RCTs could be exported into the clinical community more broadly.

Guided by an organizational perspective on development, which emphasizes the hierarchical nature of development within and across various biological and psychological systems, as well as by empirical research documenting that maltreated youngsters manifest impairments in attachment organization, self-development, and representational models of self and other (Cicchetti & Toth, 1995, 2005; Toth et al., 1997, 2000), we have implemented two randomized control trial interventions (RCTs) early in the life course of children who have experienced child maltreatment. These RCTs are discussed in the next section.

Preventive Intervention for Maltreated Infants

An overarching goal of the field of prevention science is to intervene in the course of development to ameliorate or eliminate the emergence of maladaptation and psychopathology (Ialongo et al., 2006). The discipline of developmental psychopathology, with its focus on the dialectic between the study of normality and psychopathology, provides an important theoretical foundation for prevention science (Bryck & Fisher, 2012; Cicchetti & Hinshaw, 2002; Cicchetti & Toth, 1992; Institute of Medicine, 1994).

Because maltreated infants predominantly develop insecure disorganized attachments, there is a high probability that these babies will unsuccessfully resolve subsequent developmental issues (Cicchetti & Toth, 2005) and proceed along maladaptive developmental pathways Accordingly, we reasoned that preventive interventions to promote the attainment of secure attachment organization in maltreated infants were essential in order to redirect their course of development onto a more adaptive pathway.

Sharing the common goal of improving attachment insecurity and increasing the occurrence of positive developmental outcomes in maltreated infants, we implemented two intervention models that differed in their strategies for attaining this goal. The first intervention model, child–parent psychotherapy (CPP), consisted of dyadic infant–mother therapy sessions designed to improve infant–mother attachment relationships by altering the influence of negative maternal representational models of attachment on mother–infant relations. The second intervention model, psychoeducational parenting intervention (PPI), focused on providing mothers with didactic training in child development, parenting skills, coping strategies for managing stresses in the immediate environment, and assistance in developing social support networks.

Design and recruitment

The baseline (pre-) and postintervention attachment relationships of mothers and infants in both CPP and PPI interventions were compared with the functioning of mothers and their maltreated infants who received services typically available when a child had been maltreated – the community standard (CS) group. A fourth non-maltreated comparison (NC) group, comprised of infants and mothers who were demographically comparable to the three maltreatment groups, was also included. The NC group was recruited in order to compare normative developmental changes over time in a group of babies who had not experienced maltreatment, but who had similar environmental stressors (e.g., poverty, lack of access to quality child care, community violence, etc.) with those who had been identified by the DHS for child abuse and/or neglect. All maltreated infants and their mothers were randomly assigned to either the CPP, PPI, or the CS group.

In order to facilitate enrollment of maltreated infants and their mothers into our program, the DHS agreed to allow us to hire a staff member who could work for us, but who, based on responsibilities unrelated to our project needs, also functioned as an employee of the DHS. This individual served as the liaison who was able to recruit families to participate in our RCT. Because of constraints imposed by confidentiality, only a DHS staff member could have knowledge of families with reports of child maltreatment. Thus, the initial gatekeeper for approaching families had to be a staff member employed by the DHS. The DHS liaison was instructed to approach all families who met study inclusion criteria and ask if they were willing to be contacted by our project staff. A family's name was released to our project's staff only after a consent form was signed by the caregiver. By working closely with a DHS liaison, timely recruitment and maintenance of family confidentiality were assured. Finally, our project staff, not the DHS, was solely responsible for randomization of families to the active treatment conditions or to the treatment as usual (CS) condition.

Using this model to recruit young infants and their mothers in maltreating families, a DHS recruitment liaison was able to access the DHS Child Protective Services (CPS) and preventive services records to identify all infants who were living in maltreating families with their biological mothers. Infants who had been placed in foster care were not targeted for inclusion because of the limited ongoing contact with their mothers. Families were not excluded from study participation because of ethnic or racial considerations, and the racial/ethnic backgrounds of the participants were reflective of the local demographics of victims of child maltreatment. To be included in the preventive intervention, mothers and infants could not have any significant cognitive or physical limitations that would hamper their ability to understand and/or participate in the research or the clinical interventions. Despite these exclusionary considerations, the population was not further restricted based on issues such as the presence of domestic violence, parental substance use, or parental psychiatric illness. Therefore, we believed that ultimately the results of the RCT could be more easily assimilated by frontline professionals in clinic settings.

In order to avoid any possible perceptions of coercion, the voluntary nature of the program was stressed and mothers were assured that their refusal to participate would have no adverse effects on their status with the DHS. Rather, the benefits of participation through the potential provision of supplemental interventions for the mother and her infant were emphasized.

All families, maltreating and nonmaltreating alike, were informed that, as mandated reporters, our project staff was obliged to report any suspected cases of child maltreatment to the DHS. Based on our experience conducting research with maltreating and nonmaltreating families from low-socioeconomic backgrounds, we have found that families are generally accepting of these reports if they are conducted in an open, sensitive fashion and framed as efforts to get the family the support it needs.

It is important to clarify that because we also examined the CS group, referral to our project did not necessarily result in assignment to one of our intervention models. Rather, referral indicated a willingness to participate in our research project and the possibility of receiving enhanced services. It is also important to note that even though a family was assigned to the CS condition and not to a treatment group, they still received referrals, linkage to resources and support that would have been more difficult for families to access outside of the research. Thus, to potential families and DHS staff, even those who were in the CS condition could receive additional resources and benefit from participation in the research.

Nonmaltreating (NC) families were chosen randomly by the liaison from the County's list of recipients of Temporary Assistance to Needy Families (TANF). Because prior experience has revealed that the majority of maltreating families referred to the DHS are socioeconomically disadvantaged, utilization of TANF lists provided us with access to a demographically similar population. Although all families were asked whether they had ever received child protective services, we have learned that families are not always forthcoming with this information. Therefore, during our initial contact, consent was obtained to verify nonmaltreatment status by accessing the DHS central registry data.

Reviews of the CPS registry were utilized to confirm that children in the non-maltreated comparison group did not have histories of maltreatment. The registry is a database of all CPS referrals in the state. Any reports or observations indicative of maltreatment during the course of the study, such as disclosures of maltreatment by the families themselves or observations by project staff of parenting failures severe enough to warrant a CPS report, excluded families from the comparison group. Additionally, we administered the Maternal Maltreatment Classification Interview (MMCI) (Cicchetti, Toth, & Manly, 2003) to *all* mothers as an independent verification of maltreatment status. If a family refused to consent to this procedure, then they were not enrolled in the investigation. Only those families who had never received services through the DHS child protective or preventive units were included in the NC group.

A number of lessons emerged from the conduct of these RCTs that possess relevance for professionals who are providing intervention to this vulnerable population. First, it became clear that mothers valued the opportunity to meet with consistent staff members who were invested in hearing about their experiences of parenting. Although an actual therapeutic experience was not provided during the conduct of the research visits, women became quite attached to the research team. Even mothers who did not receive the active interventions reported feeling positive about their involvement because they felt that they benefited from quality time with their child during assessments and that they also learned more about child development as a function of their participation in the observational paradigms. It also was clear that engagement with mothers was facilitated by assisting them in gaining access to basic resources, such as food and clothing. Women also described feeling "good" about being able to take part in an important research project. This enabled them to feel that they were giving rather than being the recipients of assistance, a very different and empowering experience for individuals who had spent years being buffeted about by the welfare and court systems.

Description of the Interventions

As previously noted, two theoretically informed models of intervention were evaluated in the investigation. Manuals were developed and implemented for each of the two interventions. Because the DHS becomes active via case monitoring, management, or referral when reports of child maltreatment are received, this served as a constant across all conditions. Therefore, all families in which maltreatment had been identified received some services, even if they were not randomized to our theoretically guided intervention conditions.

The provision of intervention to multiproblem populations, such as those with whom we intervened, requires flexibility and responsivity to the frequent crises and challenges that confront these families. Although we strove to evaluate the potential efficacy of two theoretically different models of treatment, from an ethical practice standpoint, issues such as domestic violence, inadequate housing, and substance abuse needed to be addressed as they arose. Our models of treatment were focused on the improvement of parenting and the elimination of maltreatment and its sequelae, but we also had to be responsive to myriad related issues that we encountered during our clinical contacts with this population. To this end, therapists in both intervention models not only received extensive training on the respective models of treatment that they were providing, but also on the importance of cultural sensitivity and on how to deal with the extensive needs of these families. In our view, neither treatment model could be effective in the absence of responsivity to the multiple challenges present in maltreating families. The ability to respond to such issues also increases the portability of the models into the community clinic settings. Because the interventions were home-based, comfort and skill in navigating inner-city neighborhoods where drug use and violence were normative were necessary.

Child–parent psychotherapy (CPP) model

This model of intervention is derived from the work of Fraiberg, Adelson, and Shapiro (1975) and has been shown to be efficacious in fostering secure attachment in high risk, low income, immigrant families (Lieberman, 1991, 1992; Lieberman & Pawl, 1988). A guiding assumption of CPP is that difficulties in the parent–infant relationship do not result from deficits in parenting knowledge and skill alone. Rather, the problems that maltreating mothers have in relating sensitively and responsively to their infants stem from insecure internal representational models that evolved in response to the mother's own experiences in childhood. The infant evokes affects and memories associated with the mother's childhood relationship experiences and, in the process, a mother's unresolved and conflictual feelings can be projected onto the infant, resulting in distorted perceptions of the infant, a lack of attunement, and insensitive care.

In CPP, the patient is not the mother or the infant, but rather it is the relationship between the mother and her baby. Masters level therapists met weekly with mothers and their 12-month-old infants during sessions conducted in the home over the course of one year. The approach is supportive, nondirective, and nondidactic, and includes developmental guidance based on the mother's concerns. During the sessions, the therapist and the mother engage in joint observation of the infant. The therapist's empathic responsiveness to the mother and the baby allows for expansion of parental understanding and exploration of maternal misperceptions of the infant. Therapists strive to link distorted emotional reactions and perceptions of the infant as they are enacted during mother–infant interaction with associated memories and affect from the mother's prior childhood experiences. Through respect, empathic concern, and unfailing positive regard, the therapeutic relationship provides the mother with a corrective emotional experience, through which she is able to differentiate current from past relationships and to form positive internal representations of herself and of herself in relationship to others, particularly her infant. As a result of this process, mothers are able to expand their responsiveness, sensitivity, and attunement to the infant, fostering security in the mother–child relationship and promoting emerging autonomy in the child.

The following goals were addressed in the CPP intervention:

- The therapist expanded the mother's empathic responsiveness, sensitivity, and attunement to her infant.
- The therapist promoted maternal fostering of infant autonomy and positive negotiation of maternal and child goals.
- Distorted perceptions and reactions to the infant stemming from maternal representational models were altered and more positive representations of the infant were developed.

Psychoeducational parenting intervention (PPI) model

In addition to services typically made available to maltreating parents (CS), weekly home visitation was provided via the PPI model. This intervention approach has been shown to be an effective model for preventing damage to vulnerable children (Shirk, Talmi, & Olds, 2000). In fact, the U.S. Advisory Board on Child Abuse and Neglect (1990) indentified home visitation services as the best documented strategy for preventing child maltreatment. Prevention data on the effectiveness of home visitation have emerged (Olds et al., 1997, 1998); yet to be conducted are studies on the effectiveness of home visitation services for families where maltreatment has already occurred, as well as assessments of whether home visitation services can alter the future life course development in infants who have been maltreated.

The PPI model utilized in this investigation was provided by therapists on a weekly basis in one-hour home-based sessions, with a focus on two primary goals: the provision of parent education regarding infant development and developmentally appropriate parenting skills and the development of adequate maternal self-care skills, including assisting mothers with personal needs, fostering adaptive functioning, and improving social supports.

Therapists were trained in the provision of an ecologically informed model of influences on mother and child. This model strives to address how factors at different levels of proximity to the mother and child interact to form a system of influences on functioning. Practically, this results in the simultaneous examination of maternal personal resources, social support, and stresses in the home, family, and community that can affect maternal caregiving. We employed as interveners master's-level therapists who were adept at attending to the needs of multiproblem families, were knowledgeable regarding accessing community resources, and had expertise in addressing community violence. Weekly 60-minute home visits were conducted over a period of 12 months.

The PPI model was a psychoeducationally-based model grounded in the present that strives to educate, improve parenting, decrease maternal stress, and increase life satisfaction. The approach is didactic in nature, providing mothers with specific information, facts, procedures, and practices. Within a core agenda of topics on parenting and improved social skills to be addressed, flexibility and latitude in the amount of time spent on various topics was stressed in order to respond to the individual needs of each mother. This flexibility is consistent with that utilized by other home-based interveners working with disadvantaged populations. An initial assessment of client needs within the domains of parenting and maternal self-care was conducted to delineate specific areas most in need of intervention. Thus, although there was a consistent range of issues to be addressed with each mother, the model allows for special emphasis on areas particularly germane to individual mothers.

Both the CPP and PPI interventions were manualized, with central components and core principles of each approach specified. Therapists participated in individual and group supervision on a weekly basis, and checks on the fidelity of the intervention implementation for each approach were conducted throughout the course of intervention. Extensive outreach was typically necessary to engage mothers in the interventions. The planned length of the intervention was one year. Although intervention sessions in the home were scheduled weekly, fewer sessions were conducted as a result of cancellations and missed appointments. On average, 22 sessions were held in the CPP group and 25 sessions in the PPI group.

Community standard (CS)

In the CS condition, the DHS managed cases in accord with their standard approach. Although variability existed, with service provision ranging from no service to referral to existing community clinics, this condition represents the community standard with which the PPI and CPP models were compared. The use of a CS comparison group enabled us to determine the effects of standard practices on child and family functioning, as compared with theoretically informed delivery of services. The approaches that the DHS used with families who have been reported for maltreatment and are participating in the proposed investigation were systematically recorded via a standardized services questionnaire.

Intervention outcome

Assessments of the quality of attachment, utilizing the Strange Situation (Ainsworth et al., 1978), were conducted at baseline (infant age of 13 months) and at the conclusion of the intervention (infant age of 26 months) in order to evaluate the efficacy of the interventions. Videotapes of the strange situations were coded independently by individuals who were unaware of maltreatment status or intervention treatment conditions.

At baseline, there were no differences among the three maltreatment groups (CPP, PPI, and CS) in the percentage of infants who were securely attached to their mothers. These results attest to the success of our randomization procedure. Notably, 3.6% of the infants in the CPP and 0% of the babies in the PPI and CS groups were securely attached. These findings are consistent with the broader attachment literature that includes the coding of Type D attachments, which reveals that a very small percentage of maltreated babies develop secure attachments with their primary caregiver (Cicchetti & Toth, 2005).

Although a significantly greater percentage of infants in the nonmaltreated group were securely attached than were infants in any of the three maltreatment groups, the rate of security among the comparisons (33%) underscores that the NC comparisons are a very high-risk group. Recall that the youngsters in the nonmaltreatment group were very closely matched to the maltreated infants on a variety of sociodemographic indices. The lower than average rate of attachment security found in the NC group (33% versus the typical rate of 50–60% in nonrisk samples) is but one illustration of the developmental context of these nonmaltreated babies reared in lower socioeconomic status conditions.

In addition, at baseline, the three groups of maltreated infants each displayed extremely high rates of attachment disorganization (86% CPP; 82% PPI; 91%

CS). These percentages of disorganized attachment did not significantly differ among the three maltreatment groups. In contrast, the rate of Type D attachment in the NC group was 20%.

Postintervention attachment findings revealed compelling results. The maltreated infants in the CS group had a 1.9% attachment security rate, a nonsignificant improvement over their 0% baseline rate of security. The maltreated infants in each of the two interventions exhibited large increases in attachment security from baseline to postintervention (CPP: 3.6 to 60.7%; PPI: 0 to 54.5%). Importantly, both the CPP and PPI interventions were equally successful in modifying attachment insecurity. The percentage of attachment security remained at 39% in the infants in the NC group.

Furthermore, assessments conducted at the conclusion of the intervention revealed that the percentage of Type D attachment had declined from 86% to 32% for the CPP group and from 82% to 46% for the PPI group. Conversely, the infants in the CS group continued to exhibit high rates of disorganization (78%); the percentages of Type D attachment in the NC group at baseline and postintervention were virtually identical (20% and 19%).

The results of this RCT demonstrate that an intervention informed by attachment theory (CPP) and an intervention that focuses on improving parenting skills, increasing maternal knowledge of child development, and enhancing the coping and social support skills of maltreating mothers (PPI), were both successful in altering the predominantly insecure and disorganized attachment organizations of maltreated infants. A follow-up investigation conducted 12 months subsequent to the intervention showed that children who had received CPP continued to show higher rates of secure attachment (56%) and fewer children in this group manifested disorganized attachment (26%); the improvements in the children who had received PPI, however, were less enduring (Pickreign Stronach, Toth, Rogosch, & Cicchetti, 2013).

Given the initial success of both interventions, it becomes important to consider why only CPP was effective in altering attachment security over time. A number of components of these interventions may have contributed to their initial success and it is important to consider them when analyzing the feasibility of exporting these interventions into real world clinical contexts. First, all therapists received extensive training before implementing the interventions, and they were familiar not only with the intervention modality but also with the theory from which the interventions was derived. All therapists also had considerable prior experience working with low-income maltreating families. Both models were manualized, weekly individual and group supervision was provided, and therapists' adherence to their respective model was monitored for each case throughout the provision of the intervention. Caseloads were maintained at levels considerably lower than is typical of outpatient mental health settings; therapists were therefore able to devote considerable time to engaging mothers and to conceptualizing treatment plans. The positive outcome of this investigation supports the importance of investing in more costly interventions, including allowing therapists sufficient time for training and supervision. The qualified success of the PPI intervention leads us to suspect that this approach, while furnishing important skills, may not have prepared mothers adequately to help them respond to the changing attachment-related needs of their children (Pickreign Stronach et al., 2013). Attachment is a dynamic process that can be modified but then requires ongoing support in order to sustain increased security as children and parents navigate future developmental challenges.

Clearly, as predicted by the organizational perspective, the early insecure, generally disorganized attachments displayed by maltreated infants do not doom these youngsters to have poor-quality relationship expectations and negative self-representations throughout development. The success of the interventions, informed by basic research knowledge on the etiology and developmental sequelae of child maltreatment, suggests that attachment organization is modifiable, even if a high percentage of Type D attachment is initially characteristic of the sample. Following the organizational perspective on development, it is expected that these maltreated youngsters, now that they are traversing a more positive trajectory, will be more likely to continue on an adaptive pathway and successfully resolve future salient developmental tasks (cf. Sroufe, Carlson, Levy, & Egeland, 1999). The preventive interventions have demonstrated that behavioral plasticity is possible, at least in the early years of life. Importantly, the sustained efficacy of CPP highlights the possibility of maintaining early gains as development progresses.

Preventive Interventions for Maltreated Preschoolers

The preschool years are an especially important time for symbolic and representational development; it is during this period that representational models of self and of self in relation to others evolving from the attachment relationship become increasingly structured and organized. Although developing children are likely to maintain specific models of individual relationships, these models become increasingly integrated into more generalized models of relationships over time (Crittenden, 1990), thereby affecting children's future relationship expectations. Because maltreated children internalize relational features of their caregiving experiences, they are likely to generalize negative representations of self and the self in relation to others to novel situations and relationship partners (Howes & Segal, 1993; Lynch & Cicchetti, 1991, 1992; Toth & Cicchetti, 1996).

As discussed in our literature review earlier in this chapter, research investigations have documented the deleterious effects of maltreatment on the representational development of abused and neglected children. The cross-sectional and longitudinal studies reported provide a solid foundation on which to conclude that maltreatment does exert negative effects on representational development, that these effects become more entrenched as development proceeds, and that the representational themes enacted in children's narratives are reflective of their maltreatment experiences and are related to child behavior problems (Toth et al., 2000). Based on our empirical work, we concluded that the provision of interventions designed to modify maladaptive representational development in maltreated preschoolers were necessary.

Early Intervention Development Initiative for Maltreated Preschoolers

In this second RCT, participants were again recruited through the DHS. We employed recruitment strategies, determination of child maltreatment, verification of nonmaltreatment status, and videotaped measure coding procedures that were consistent with those utilized in our preventive interventions with maltreated infants described earlier in this chapter (Toth, Maughan, Manly, Spagnola, & Cicchetti, 2002). Maltreating mothers and their preschoolers were randomly assigned to one of three intervention groups: Child–Parent Psychotherapy (CPP), Psychoeducational Parenting Intervention (PPI), and Community Standard (CS). The CPP and PPI interventions were manualized and were very similar to those employed in our interventions with maltreated babies delineated in an earlier section of this chapter. The only modifications made to these interventions were those necessary to accommodate the more sophisticated developmental competencies (e.g., language; symbolic and representational abilities) possessed by preschoolers in comparison to infants (Toth & Cicchetti, 1999).

Intervention outcome

At baseline and at postintervention, 10 narrative story-stems, selected from the MSSB (Bretherton et al., 1990) described previously, were individually administered to child participants. The narratives utilized depicted moral dilemmas and emotionally charged events in the context of parent–child and family relationships. Narrative story-stems included vignettes designed to elicit children's perceptions of the parent–child relationship, of self, and of maternal behavior in response to child transgressions, intrafamilial conflicts, and child accidents.

Maternal representations were coded from the children's narratives. These included: *positive mother* (the maternal figure is described or portrayed in the narrative as protective, affectionate, providing care, warm, or helpful); *negative mother* (the maternal figure is described or portrayed in the narrative as punitive, harsh, ineffectual, or rejecting); *controlling mother* (the maternal figure is described or portrayed in the narrative as controlling the child's behavior, independent of disciplining actions); *incongruent mother* (the maternal figure is described or portrayed in the narrative as dealing with child-related situations in an opposite or inconsistent manner); and *disciplining mother* (the maternal figure is described or portrayed in the narrative as an authority figure who disciplines the child; inappropriate and harsh forms of punishment were not scored here, but rather were coded as negative mother). A presence/absence method of coding was used to score children's maternal representations.

Self-representation scores were also coded from the children's narratives and were derived from coding any behaviors or references that were made in relation to any child character or when the child participant appeared to be experiencing relevant feelings in response to narrative content. Representational codes of self included: *positive self* (a child figure is described or portrayed in the narrative as empathic or helpful, proud, or feeling good about self in any domain); *negative self* (a child figure is described or portrayed in the narrative as aggressive toward self or other, experiencing feelings of shame or self-blame, or feeling bad about self in any domain); and *false self* (a child figure is described or portrayed in the narrative as overly compliant or reports inappropriate positive feelings, for example, in an anger- or fear-producing situation). Consistent with maternal representation coding procedures, a presence/absence method of scoring was used to assess children's self-representations.

In addition to maternal and self-representation codes, a modified version of Bickham and Friese's (1999) global relationship expectation scale was utilized to capture children's expectations of the mother–child relationship. For the current investigation, the scale was modified to assess children's global expectations of the mother–child relationship as portrayed in the children's 11 narratives. In accord with Bickham and Friese's coding procedures, children's expectations of the mother–child relationship were determined by the overall degree of predictability and trustworthiness portrayed between mother and child characters across all 10 narrative administrations. Specifically, the following five relationship dimensions were used to aid in coding children's overall expectation of the mother–child relationship: predictable versus unpredictable, disappointing versus fulfilling, supportive or protective versus threatening, warm or close versus cold or distant, and genuine or trustworthy versus artificial or deceptive. Global mother–child relationship expectation ratings were based on a five-point scale, ranging from very low (participant's narratives describe or portray the mother–child relationship as dissatisfying, unpredictable, and/or dangerous) to very high (participant's narratives describe or portray the mother–child relationship as fulfilling, safe, rewarding, and reliable).

Following the provision of the interventions, preschool-age children in the CPP intervention evidenced a greater decline in maladaptive maternal representations over time than did preschoolers in the PPI and CS interventions. In addition, children who took part in the CPP intervention displayed a greater decrease in negative self-representations than did children in the PPI, CS, and NC groups.

Additionally, the mother–child relationship expectations of CPP children became more positive over the course of the intervention as compared with children in the PPI, CS, and NC groups. These results suggest that a model of intervention informed by attachment theory (CPP) is more efficacious at improving representations of self and of caregivers than is a didactic model of intervention (PPI) directed at parenting skills. Because the intervention focused on changing representational models utilizing a narrative story-stem measure, outcomes that might be expected to improve more dramatically in the PPI model (e.g., parenting skills, knowledge of child development) could not be addressed. Consistent with the approach described in our discussion of factors contributing to the success of the mother–infant interventions, we believe that the utilization of skilled and well-trained therapists, adherence to manualized treatment models, and monitoring of the fidelity of the provision of the interventions contributed to the efficacious findings. Moreover, given prior research that has found that the type of maternal attachment insecurity that is present may affect maternal responsivity to various intervention strategies (Bakermans-Kranenburg, Juffer, & van IJzendoorn, 1998), it will be important to assess baseline attachment organization of mothers in relation to intervention outcome.

These intervention results point to the potential malleability of these representations of self and of self in relation to others when an intervention derived from attachment theory is provided. Rather than assuming that "sensitive" periods exist during infancy and that the attachment relationship becomes less amenable to change over the course of development, our findings suggest that, at least during the preschool years, the internalized mother–child relationship continues to evolve and remains open to reorganizations (and see Bernard et al., 2012; Joseph, O'Connor, Briskman, Maughan, & Scott, 2014; Moss et al., 2011, for other evidence, including positive changes and healthier attachment formations later in childhood).

Given that prior research has discovered that self-determination, positive self-esteem, and other self-system processes are predictors of resilient functioning in maltreated children, the improvements in self representations found in the children in the CPP intervention are a positive sign that resilient self-strivings may have been initiated in these youngsters (cf. Cicchetti & Rogosch, 1997, 2007). If so, then the developments that occurred in self-system processes may prove to serve a beneficial protective function in future years. Moreover, the positive changes in the maltreated preschoolers who received the CPP intervention may also bode well for these children's future relationships with peers and other relationship partners.

From Research to Practice

The translation of basic research knowledge on the developmental sequelae of child maltreatment into the conduct of RCTs at MHFC underscores the importance of broadening such efforts in the future. The finding that developmental plasticity is possible during infancy and that attachment insecurity, including its most disorganized form, and negative representations of self and other, are modifiable in extremely dysfunctional mother–child dyads, offers significant hope for thousands of maltreated children and their families. Through fostering these positive developments in both attachment organization and representational models of the self and of attachment figures, costlier interventions such as foster care placement, special education services, residential treatment, and incarceration can be averted.

Despite the optimism engendered by the results of our interventions, our findings also highlight the harsh reality of the ineffectiveness of services presently being provided in many communities across the nation. It is essential that clinicians, government officials, social policy advocates, and mental health insurers recognize the criticality of investing in the delivery of theoretically informed, evidence-based interventions. Although the implementation of such evidence-based interventions into clinical practice holds great potential for enhancing positive developmental outcomes, preventing the dissolution of families, and decreasing the individual and societal burden of mental illness, it has proven to be extremely difficult to gain broad support from government officials for exporting such empirically supported treatments into the community.

In his commentary on a national evaluation of Sure Start Local Programmes for youngsters under four and their families from deprived communities in England, Sir Michael Rutter (2007) enunciated a point of view that is consistent with our assertion that, in general, government agencies have not been overly responsive to utilizing the results of translational research (i.e., basic to applied research) to modify their extant policies. Although Rutter (2007) expressed his hope that government agencies could profitably utilize information gleaned from empirical research to modify their policies, he concluded that he had serious doubt that government officials would show even the slightest interest in research evidence when examining its own policies.

This view highlights the challenges associated with exporting evidence-based practices into the broader community, particularly with respect to barriers that preclude government administrators from embracing evidence-based strategies. In our experience, however, policy change is possible. In fact, the partnership that was forged between Mt. Hope Family Center (MHFC), a university-based entity, and local county officials in the Department of Human Services (DHS), a county government, demonstrates that progress can occur when a message is delivered consistently and when trust exists among researchers, clinicians, and policymakers. In Monroe County, New York, county officials, the United Way of Greater Rochester, and private foundations have become increasingly invested in the provision of evidence-based services to at risk children and families. We believe that this commitment stems, in part, from the close working relationship and educational exchanges that have occurred between Mt. Hope Family Center and the county over a period of two decades. We want to stress the reciprocal nature of these communications. We believe that attempting to advocate for the importance of evidence-based services without thoroughly understanding the realities that confront front-line clinicians and appreciating the myriad challenges that are associated with funding decisions in the child welfare system would doom efforts to effect policy change to failure. Because, from its inception, MHFC provided services as well as conducted research that possessed implications for intervention development and delivery, county officials were receptive to discussions regarding the need to ensure that dollars were directed toward services that had an empirical base to support their probability of resulting in positive outcomes.

Community initiatives

A number of initiatives have been undertaken by the county that clearly reflect a commitment to providing evidence-based treatments. The growth in the development and accessibility of evidence-based programs has provided opportunities for dissemination, to the extent that community interest and commitment exists, to support such approaches. One example of community dedication to implementing evidence-based interventions began with recognition on the part of the County DHS and the United Way of Greater Rochester that insufficient efforts were being directed toward the prevention of child maltreatment. Thanks in part to the wisdom and leadership of the Department of Human Services and the United Way at the time, a group of community leaders was convened to examine the issue and to identify solutions

Building Healthy Children

In 2007 Monroe County, in conjunction with the United Way of Greater Rochester, issued a Request for Proposals (RFP) to develop and to evaluate a preventive intervention for mothers who had their first child prior to the age of 21 and who were impoverished. Central components of the RFP called for the provision of evidence-based services, two of which were being provided at MHFC, and for the evaluation of the continued effectiveness of the services following their exportation into the broader community. This innovative RFP highlights the possibility of government entities recognizing and promoting the provision of evidence-based intervention. Particularly noteworthy was the agreement that, in order to evaluate the services being provided, funding bodies needed to support the importance of randomly assigning mothers and their offspring to this preventive model or to receiving services routinely available. A decade ago, the mere mention of randomization would cause considerable angst among service providers and funding bodies. The fact that a sea change has occurred attests to the possibility of progressive thinking. Because we view the issuance and subsequent receipt of the RFP by MHFC to be an example of how research can inform practice and ultimately can be translated to the broader community, we next discuss this collaborative initiative, referred to as Building Healthy Children, in more detail.

Although MHFC possessed the capability of providing all of the services requested in the RFP, we believed that the development of a collaborative partnership with other community service providers could best capitalize on community expertise and foster the ultimate exportation of evidence-based treatments into the broader community. Therefore, MHFC initially partnered with the Society for the Protection and Care of Children (SPCC) and the Social Work Division at the University of Rochester Medical Center (URMC). SPCC has an extensive history of providing services to teen parents and URMC has consistently provided culturally-sensitive outreach services to impoverished mothers and their young children. Because the RFP requested that referrals be obtained from a pediatric practice, URMC's close ties with the medical center's pediatric department also was considered to be a strength that would facilitate the referral process. The five-year grant, with an annual budget of approximately one million dollars, was awarded to the organizations in this partnership consistent with our mission; MHFC's role was to provide two evidence-based forms of intervention, including CPP and Interpersonal Psychotherapy for depression (Weissman, Markowitz, & Klerman, 2000) and to oversee the process of program evaluation.

The vision demonstrated by the funding bodies and community partners around the launching of the Building Healthy Children project is noteworthy and demonstrates the power of a collaborative initiative. The Building Healthy Children program reflects a culmination of over two decades of discussions and the building of trust among MHFC, a university-based organization, and government and private funding sources. It is clear that such effective partnerships are possible, but that commitment across systems and the ability to recognize and build on the strengths of diverse organizations are integral to success.

Local funding was leveraged to secure federal funding, and with support from the U.S. Administration on Children and Families, the Building Healthy Children program became one of 17 national evidence-based home visitation demonstration projects. Once the federal grant ended, local funders continued to support sustainability of the project. Funding has been continued beyond the initial five-year grant and some changes with respect to service consolidation have occurred to reduce administrative costs and to allow more dollars to be directed into expanding program capacity. The program has expanded to partner with multiple pediatric and family medical practices, and the services have been integrated into the children's medical homes, including documentation of progress in children's electronic medical records. The evaluation component of the program has yielded promising outcomes with respect to increases in attendance at well-child visits (Paradis, Sandler, Manly, & Valentine, 2013). Preliminary data are also revealing positive outcomes for mothers, including decreases in depressive symptoms and increases in perceptions of their efficacy as mothers.

The collaborations formed at MHFC have continued to grow and affect policy, although increasingly the shift toward national policy change has appeared. This is evident in yet another project, Fostering Recovery, which combined decades of research at MHFC on attachment-based interventions for young children with a strategic focus on system's change. Fostering Recovery, funded by the Administration for Children and Families, targeted the well-being of infants exposed to parental substance abuse in the child welfare system, but also provided multiple elements designed to shift knowledge and practice at both DHS and the courts. This program extended our DHS recruitment liaison program to also employ a certified substance and alcohol counselor who worked half-time at the DHS to institute evidenced-based substance abuse screening and develop a rapid referral program for those identified as needing treatment, with the goal of improving outcomes for all families suffering from chemical dependency who enter the CPS system. This program included contributions from the County, the court system, and the University, thus, effectively making child welfare services a responsibility of the entire community. Fostering Recovery also included an evaluation component even though the funding was designated for service projects. This program was not just a focus of the Monroe County area but also across the nation, as the initial RFP was proposed as a method of nationally identifying best practices in addressing the cooccurrence of substance abuse in the child welfare population and improving the well-being of its youngest consumers.

Although concern remains that human services continue to be inconsistent, often ineffective, and sometimes harmful (Institute of Medicine, 2001; President's New Freedom Commission on Mental Health, 2003; USDHHS, 1999, 2001), we believe that the approaches to incorporating evidence-based parenting practices into the community that we highlight increase the probability of implementing and sustaining evidence-based practices in community settings. Moreover, we maintain that such initiatives will ultimately serve to bridge the schism between research and practice and exert a sustained impact on improving the quality and accessibility of human services.

Conclusion

This chapter highlights the potential for developmental and clinical researchers to export theory and research to the broader community, especially those families involved with child welfare. Work such as that done at MHFC bridges the boundaries between efficacy and effectiveness and moves "ivory tower" research into the community. Relationships such as those that we have developed with the DHS may realize Rutter's (2007) hope that government agencies can profitably utilize information gleaned from empirical research to modify their policies. These relationships also ensure that developmental theory informs prevention and intervention and that, ultimately, empirically-supported treatments will be more easily accessible to human services and community practitioners and not relegated to the annals of scientific journals.

To facilitate the move from research to evidenced-based practice, we have highlighted lessons that we and our colleagues have learned in over nearly three decades of advocating for the importance of providing developmentally-informed and empirically-supported treatments to children and families in the child welfare system. Our work demonstrates that rigorous science can take place within the community, if the time and effort are made in developing mutually supportive partnerships between researchers, community agencies, and funders. Mutuality is perhaps the most important ingredient in giving away our developmental knowledge, in that RCTs and data collection in the child welfare community cannot occur without a process that benefits all parties. Researchers require publications and funding to survive, but human services and court officials require evidence to justify and support their budgetary decisions. The chasm that we now face in regards to implementing what we have defined through careful research can be bridged by ensuring that scientific knowledge is developed and collected in this community forum. If these investigations take place in the real world and the community is an active partner in this process, then both needs can be met. The ultimate goal of science is to benefit from the generation of a knowledge base. By developing relationships between policymakers and researchers, social policy initiatives also can build upon empirical evidence. In this way, our research can reach those for whom it would be most beneficial.

Acknowledgments

The work described in this chapter was supported by grants from the National Institute of Mental Health (MH54643) and the Spunk Fund, Inc. We would like to extend our thanks to the leadership of Monroe County Department of Human Services and to the United Way of Greater Rochester for their visionary thinking.

References

Aber, J. L., & Cicchetti, D. (1984). Socioemotional development in maltreated children: An empirical and theoretical analysis. In H. E. Fitzgerald, B. Lester, & M. Yogman (Eds.), *Theory and research in behavioral pediatrics* (Vol. 2, pp. 147–205). New York: Plenum Press.

Ainsworth, M. D. S., Blehar, M. C., Waters, E., & Wall, S. (1978). *Patterns of attachment: A psychological study of the Strange Situation.* Hillsdale, NJ: Lawrence Erlbaum Associates.

Bakermans-Kranenburg, M. J., Juffer, F., & van IJzendoorn, M. H. (1998). Interventions with video feedback and attachment discussions: Does type of maternal insecurity make a difference? *Infant Mental Health Journal, 19*, 202–219.

Banny, A. M., Cicchetti, D., Rogosch, F. A., Oshri, A., & Crick, N. R. (2013). Vulnerability to depression: A moderated mediation model of the roles of child maltreatment, peer victimization, and serotonin transporter linked polymorphic region genetic variation among children from low socioeconomic status backgrounds. *Development and Psychopathology, 25*(3), 599–614.

Barnett, D., Ganiban, J., & Cicchetti, D. (1999). Maltreatment, negative expressivity, and the development of Type D attachments from 12- to 24-months of age. *Society for Research in Child Development Monograph, 64*, 97–118.

Barnett, D., Manly, J. T., & Cicchetti, D. (1993). Defining child maltreatment: The interface between policy and research. In D. Cicchetti & S. L. Toth (Eds.), *Child abuse, child development, and social policy* (pp. 7–73). Norwood, NJ: Ablex.

Bernard, K., Dozier, M., Bick, J., Lewis-Morrarty, E., Lindhiem, O., & Carlson, E. (2012). Enhancing attachment organization among maltreated children: Results of a randomized clinical trial. *Child Development, 83*(2), 623–636.

Bickham, N., & Friese, B. (1999). *Child narrative coding system.* Syracuse, NY: Syracuse University.

Bowlby, J. (1969/1982). *Attachment*. New York: Basic Books.

Bretherton, I. (1991). Pouring new wine into old bottles: The social self as internal working model. In M. Gunnar & L. A. Sroufe (Eds.), *Minnesota symposia on child psychology: Self processes and development* (Vol. 2, pp. 1–41). Hillsdale, NJ: Lawrence Erlbaum Associates.

Bretherton, I., Oppenheim, D., Buchsbaum, H., Emde, R. N., & the MacArthur Narrative Group (1990). *MacArthur Story-Stem Battery*. Unpublished manuscript.

Bryck, R. L., & Fisher, P. A. (2012). Training the brain: practical applications of neural plasticity from the intersection of cognitive neuroscience, developmental psychology, and prevention science. *American Psychologist, 67*(2), 87–100.

Calverley, R. M., Fischer, K. W., & Ayoub, C. (1994). Complex splitting of self representations in sexually abused adolescent girls. *Development and Psychopathology, 6*, 195–213.

Carlson, V., Cicchetti, D., Barnett, D., & Braunwald, K. (1989). Finding order in disorganization: Lessons from research on maltreated infant's attachments to their caregivers. In D. Cicchetti & V. Carlson (Eds.), *Child maltreatment: Theory and research on the causes and consequences of child abuse and neglect* (pp. 494–528). New York: Cambridge University Press.

Cicchetti, D. (1989). How research on child maltreatment has informed the study of child development: Perspectives from developmental psychopathology. In D. Cicchetti & V. Carlson (Eds.), *Child maltreatment: Theory and research on the causes and consequences of child abuse and neglect* (pp. 377–431). New York: Cambridge University Press.

Cicchetti, D. (1991). Fractures in the crystal: Developmental psychopathology and the emergence of the self. *Developmental Review, 11*, 271–287.

Cicchetti, D. (2013a). Annual research review: Resilient functioning in maltreated children–past, present, and future perspectives. *Journal of Child Psychology and Psychiatry, 54*(4), 402–422.

Cicchetti, D. (2013b). Developmental psychopathology. In P. Zelazo (Ed.), *Oxford handbook of developmental psychology* (Vol. 2, pp. 455–480). New York: Oxford University Press.

Cicchetti, D., & Curtis, W. J. (2006). The developing brain and neural plasticity: Implications for normality, psychopathology, and resilience. In D. Cicchetti & D. Cohen (Eds.), *Developmental Psychopathology (2nd ed.), Vol. 2: Developmental Neuroscience* (pp. 1–64). Hoboken, NJ: John Wiley & Sons, Inc.

Cicchetti, D., & Curtis, W. J. (Eds.). (2007). A multi-level approach to resilience [Special Issue]. *Development and Psychopathology, 19*(3), 627–955.

Cicchetti, D., & Hinshaw, S. P. (Eds.) (2002). Prevention and intervention science: Contributions to developmental theory [Special Issue]. *Development and Psychopathology, 14*(4), 667–981.

Cicchetti, D., & Lynch, M. (1993). Toward an ecological/transactional model of community violence and child maltreatment: Consequences for children's development. *Psychiatry, 56*, 96–118.

Cicchetti, D., & Lynch, M. (1995). Failures in the expectable environment and their impact on individual development: The case of child maltreatment. In D. Cicchetti & D. J. Cohen (Eds.), *Developmental psychopathology: Risk, disorder, and adaptation* (Vol. 2, pp. 32–71). New York: John Wiley & Sons, Inc.

Cicchetti, D., & Manly, J. T. (Eds.) (2001). Operationalizing child maltreatment: Developmental processes and outcomes [Special Issue]. *Development and Psychopathology,* *13*(4), 755–1048.

Cicchetti, D., & Rogosch, F. A. (1996). Equifinality and multifinality in developmental psychopathology. *Development and Psychopathology, 8,* 597–600.

Cicchetti, D., & Rogosch, F. A. (1997). The role of self-organization in the promotion of resilience in maltreated children. *Development and Psychopathology, 9,* 799–817.

Cicchetti, D., & Rogosch, F. A. (2007). Personality, adrenal steroid hormones, and resilience in maltreated children: A multi-level perspective. *Development and Psychopathology,* *19*(3), 787–809.

Cicchetti, D., & Rogosch, F. A. (2102). Gene× Environment interaction and resilience: Effects of child maltreatment and serotonin, corticotropin releasing hormone, dopamine, and oxytocin genes. *Development and Psychopathology, 24,* (2), 411–427.

Cicchetti, D., Rogosch, F. A., & Oshri, A. (2011). Interactive effects of corticotropin releasing hormone receptor 1, serotonin transporter linked polymorphic region, and child maltreatment on diurnal cortisol regulation and internalizing symptomatology. *Development and Psychopathology, 23,* 1125–1138.

Cicchetti, D., Rogosch, F. A., & Toth, S. L. (2006). Fostering secure attachment in infants in maltreating families through preventive interventions. *Development and Psychopathology,* *18*(3), 623–649.

Cicchetti, D., & Schneider-Rosen, K. (1986). An organizational approach to childhood depression. In M. Rutter, C. Izard, & P. Read (Eds.), *Depression in young people, clinical and developmental perspectives* (pp. 71–134). New York: Guilford Press.

Cicchetti, D., & Toth, S. L. (Eds.) (1992). Developmental approaches to prevention and intervention [Special Issue]. *Development and Psychopathology,* *4*(4), 489–728.

Cicchetti, D., & Toth, S. L. (1995). A developmental psychopathology perspective on child abuse and neglect. *Journal of the American Academy of Child and Adolescent Psychiatry, 34,* 541–565.

Cicchetti, D., & Toth, S. L. (1998). Perspectives on research and practice in developmental psychopathology. In W. Damon (Ed.), *Handbook of child psychology* (5th ed., Vol. 4, pp. 479–583). New York: John Wiley & Sons, Inc.

Cicchetti, D., & Toth, S. L. (2003). Child maltreatment: Past, present, and future perspectives. In R. P. Weissberg, L. H. Weiss, O. Reyes, & H. J. Walberg (Eds.), *Trends in the well-being of children and youth* (Vol. 2, pp. 181–206). Washington, DC: CWLA Press.

Cicchetti, D., & Toth, S. L. (2005). Child maltreatment. *Annual Review of Clinical Psychology, 1,* 409–438.

Cicchetti, D., Toth, S. L., & Manly, J. T. (2003). *Maternal Maltreatment Interview.* Unpublished manuscript, Rochester, NY.

Cicchetti, D., & Tucker, D. (1994). Development and self-regulatory structures of the mind. *Development and Psychopathology, 6,* 533–549.

Cicchetti, D., & Valentino, K. (2006). An ecological transactional perspective on child maltreatment: Failure of the average expectable environment and its influence upon child development. In D. Cicchetti & D. J. Cohen (Eds.), *Developmental psychopathology (2nd ed.), Vol. 3: Risk, disorder, and adaptation* (pp. 129–201). New York: John Wiley & Sons, Inc.

Crittenden, P. M. (1988). Relationships at risk. In J. Belsky & T. Nezworski (Eds.), *Clinical implications of attachment theory* (pp. 136–174). Hillsdale, NJ: Lawrence Erlbaum Associates.

Crittenden, P. M. (1990). Internal representational models of attachment relationships. *Infant Mental Health Journal, 11*, 259–277.

Crittenden, P. M., & DiLalla, D. (1988). Compulsive compliance: The development of an inhibitory coping strategy in infancy. *Journal of Abnormal Child Psychology, 16*, 585–599.

Curtis, W. J., & Cicchetti, D. (2003). Moving research on resilience into the 21st century: Theoretical and methodological considerations in examining the biological contributors to resilience. *Development and Psychopathology, 15*, 773–810.

Curtis, W. J., & Cicchetti, D. (2007). Emotion and resilience: A multi-level investigation of hemispheric electroencephalogram asymmetry and emotion regulation in maltreated and non-maltreated children. *Development and Psychopathology, 19*(3), 811–840.

Dodge, K. A., Pettit, G. S., & Bates, J. E. (1997). How the experience of early physical abuse leads children to become chronically aggressive. In D. Cicchetti & S. L. Toth (Eds.), *Rochester symposium on developmental psychopathology: Trauma: Perspectives on theory, research, and intervention* (Vol. 8, pp. 263–288). Rochester, NY: University of Rochester Press.

Egeland, B. (2007). Understanding developmental processes of resilience and psychology: Implications for policy and practice. In A. Masten (Ed.) *Minnesota symposia on child psychology* (Vol. 34, pp. 83–117). Mahwah, New Jersey: Lawrence Erlbaum Associates.

Egeland, B., Carlson, E. A., & Sroufe, L. A. (1993). Resilience as process. *Development and Psychopathology, 5*, 517–528.

Emde, R. N., Wolf, D. P., & Oppenheim, D. (Eds.). (2003). *Revealing the inner worlds of young children*. Oxford, NY: Oxford University Press.

Fang, X., Brown, D. S., Florence, C. S., & Mercy, J. A. (2012). The economic burden of child maltreatment in the United States and implications for prevention. *Child Abuse & Neglect, 36*(2), 156–165.

Fearon, R. P., Bakermans-Kranenburg, M. J., van IJzendoorn, M. H., Lapsley, A. M., & Roisman, G. I. (2010). The significance of insecure attachment and disorganization in the development of children's externalizing behavior: A meta-analytic study. *Child Development, 81*(2), 435–456.

Feder, A., Nestler, E. J., & Charney, D. S. (2009). Psychobiology and molecular genetics of resilience. *Nature, 10*, 446–457.

Flores, E., Cicchetti, D., & Rogosch, F. A. (2005). Predictors of resilience in maltreated and nonmaltreated Latino children. *Developmental Psychology, 41*(2), 338–351.

Fraiberg, S., Adelson, E., & Shapiro, V. (1975). Ghosts in the nursery: A psychoanalytic approach to impaired infant-mother relationships. *Journal of the American Academy of Child Psychiatry, 14*, 387–421.

Gottlieb, G. (1991). Experiential canalization of behavioral development: Theory. *Developmental Psychology, 27*, 4–13.

Gottlieb, G. (1992). *Individual development and evolution: The genesis of novel behavior*. New York: Oxford University Press.

Gottlieb, G., & Halpern, C. T. (2002). A relational view of causality in normal and abnormal development. *Development and Psychopathology, 14*(3), 421–436.

Groh, A. M., Roisman, G. I., van IJzendoorn, M. H., Bakermans-Kranenburg, M. J., & Fearon, R. (2012). The significance of insecure and disorganized attachment for children's internalizing symptoms: A meta-analytic study. *Child Development, 83*(2), 591–610.

Hecht, K. F., Cicchetti, D., Rogosch, F. A., & Crick, N. R. (2014). Borderline personality features in childhood: The role of subtype, developmental timing, and chronicity of child maltreatment. *Development and Psychopathology, 26*(3), 805–815.

Hesse, E., & Main, M. (2006). Frightened, threatening, and dissociative parental behavior in low-risk samples: Description, discussion, and interpretations. *Development and Psychopathology, 18*, 309–343.

Howes, C., & Segal, J. (1993). Children's relationships with alternative caregivers: The special case of maltreated children removed from their homes. *Journal of Applied Developmental Psychology, 14*, 71–81.

Ialongo, N., Rogosch, F. A., Cicchetti, D., Toth, S. L., Buckley, J., Petras, H., & Neiderhiser, J. (2006). A developmental psychopathology approach to the prevention of mental health disorders. In D. Cicchetti & D. Cohen (Eds.), *Developmental psychopathology (2nd ed.), Vol. 1: Theory and Method* (pp. 968–1018). New York: John Wiley & Sons, Inc.

Institute of Medicine (1994). *Reducing risks for mental disorders: Frontiers for preventive intervention research*. Washington, DC: National Academy Press.

Institute of Medicine (Committee on Quality Health Care in America) (2001). *Crossing the quality chasm: A new health system for the 21ˢᵗ century*. Washington, DC: National Academy Press.

Jaffee, S. R., Caspi, A., Moffitt, T. E., & Taylor, A. (2004). Physical maltreatment victim to antisocial child: Evidence of an environmentally mediated process. *Journal of Abnormal Psychology, 113*(1), 44–55.

Johnson, J. G., Cohen, P., Brown, J., Smailes, E. M., & Bernstein, D. P. (1999). Childhood maltreatment increases risk for personality disorders during early adulthood. *Archives of General Psychiatry, 56*, 600–606.

Joseph, M. A., O'Connor, T. G., Briskman, J. A., Maughan, B., & Scott, S. (2014). The formation of secure new attachments by children who were maltreated: An observational study of adolescents in foster care. *Development and Psychopathology, 26*(1), 67–80.

Karatsoreos, I. N., & McEwen, B. S. (2012). Psychobiological allostasis: Resistance, resilience and vulnerability. *Trends in Cognitive Sciences, 15*, 576–584.

Kazdin, A. E., & Weisz, J. (2003). *Evidence-based psychotherapies for children and adolescents*. New York: Guildford Press.

Kim, J. E., & Cicchetti, D. (2003). Social self-efficacy and behavior problems in maltreated and nonmaltreated children. *Journal of Clinical Child and Adolescent Psychology, 32*, 106–117.

Kim, J. E., & Cicchetti, D. (2004). A process model of mother-child relatedness and psychological adjustment among maltreated and nonmaltreated children: The role of self-esteem and social competence. *Journal of Abnormal Child Psychology, 32*, 341–354.

Kim-Cohen, J., & Turkewitz, R. (2012). Resilience and measured gene–environment inter-actions. *Development and Psychopathology, 24*(4), 1297–1306.

Koenig, A. L., Cicchetti, D., & Rogosch, F. A. (2000). Child compliance/noncompliance and maternal contributors to internalization in maltreating and nonmaltreating dyads. *Child Development, 71,* 1018–1032.

Lieberman, A. F. (1991). Attachment theory and infant-parent psychotherapy: Some conceptual, clinical, and research considerations. In D. Cicchetti & S. L. Toth (Eds.), *Rochester symposium on developmental psychopathology: Models and integrations* (Vol. 3, pp. 261–287). Rochester, NY: University of Rochester Press.

Lieberman, A. F. (1992). Infant-parent psychotherapy with toddlers. *Development and Psychopathology, 4,* 559–574.

Lieberman, A. F., & Pawl, J. H. (1988). Clinical applications of attachment theory. In J. Belsky & T. Nezworski (Eds.), *Clinical implications of attachment* (pp. 325–351). Hillsdale, NJ: Lawrence Erlbaum Associates.

Luthar, S. S., & Cicchetti, D. (2000). The construct of resilience: Implications for interven-tion and social policy. *Development and Psychopathology, 12,* 857–885.

Luthar, S. S., Cicchetti, D., & Becker, B. (2000). The construct of resilience: A critical evaluation and guidelines for future work. *Child Development, 71,* 543–562.

Lynch, M., & Cicchetti, D. (1991). Patterns of relatedness in maltreated and nonmal-treated children: Connections among multiple representational models. *Development and Psychopathology, 3,* 207–226.

Lynch, M., & Cicchetti, D. (1992). Maltreated children's reports of relatedness to their teachers. *New Directions for Child Development, 57,* 81–107.

Lyons-Ruth, K., Connell, D., Grunebaum, H., & Botein, D. (1990). Infants at social risk: Maternal depression and family support services as mediators of infant development and security of attachment. *Child Development, 61,* 85–98. [Abstracted in *Pediatrics Digest* (1990) *8,* 26–27.]

Lyons-Ruth, K., Connell, D., Zoll, D., & Stahl, J. (1987). Infants at social risk: Relationships among infant maltreatment, maternal behavior, and infant attachment behavior. *Developmental Psychology, 23,* 223–232.

Lyons-Ruth, K., & Easterbrooks, A. (1995). Attachment relationships among children with aggressive behavior problems: The role of disorganized/controlling early attachment strategies. *Journal of Consulting and Clinical Psychology, 64,* 64–73.

Lyons-Ruth, K., Easterbrooks, A., & Cibelli, C. (1997). Infant attachment strategies, infant mental lag, and maternal depressive symptoms: Predictors of internalizing and external-izing problems at age 7. *Developmental Psychology, 33,* 681–692.

Main, M., & Hesse, P. (1990). Parents' unresolved traumatic experiences are related to infant disorganized attachment status: Is frightened and/or frightening parent behavior the linking mechanism? In M. Greenberg, D. Cicchetti, & E. M. Cummings (Eds.), *Attachment in the preschool years* (pp. 161–182). Chicago, IL: University of Chicago Press.

Main, M., & Solomon, J. (1986). Discovery of a disorganized/disoriented attachment pattern. In T. B. Brazelton & M. W. Yogman (Eds.), *Affective development in infancy* (pp. 95–124). Norwood, NJ: Ablex.

Main, M., & Solomon, J. (1990). Procedures for identifying infants as disorganized/disoriented during the Ainsworth Strange Situation. In M. Greenberg, D. Cicchetti, & E. M. Cummings (Eds.), *Attachment in the preschool years* (pp. 121–160). Chicago, IL: University of Chicago Press.

Masten, A. S. (2014). Global perspectives on resilience in children and youth. *Child Development, 85*(1), 6–20.

Masten, A. S., & Cicchetti, D. (2010). Developmental cascades. *Development and Psychopathology, 22*, 491–495.

Meadows, P., Tunstill, J., George, A., Dhudwar, A., & Kurtz, Z. (2011). *The costs and consequences of child maltreatment*. London: NSPCC.

Moss, E., Dubois-Comtois, K., Cyr, C., Tarabulsy, G. M., St-Laurent, D., & Bernier, A. (2011). Efficacy of a home-visiting intervention aimed at improving maternal sensitivity, child attachment, and behavioral outcomes for maltreated children: A randomized control trial. *Development and Psychopathology, 23*(1), 195–210.

New Freedom Commission on Mental Health. (2003). *Achieving the promise: Transforming mental health care in America*. Final Report. [DHHS Pub. No. SMA-03-3832]. Rochville, MD: New Freedom Commission on Mental Health.

Obradović, J. (2012). How can the study of physiological reactivity contribute to our understanding of adversity and resilience processes in development? *Development and Psychopathology, 24*(2), 371–387.

Olds, D., Eckenrode, J., Henderson, C., Kitzman, H., Powers, J., Cole, R., et al. (1997). Long-term effects of home visitation on maternal life course and child abuse and neglect: Fifteen-year follow-up of a randomized trial. *Journal of the American Medical Association, 278*, 637–643.

Olds, D., Henderson, C., Kitzman, H., Eckenrode, J., Cole, R., & Tatelbaum, R. (1998). The promise of home visitation: Results of two randomized trials. *Journal of Community Psychology, 26*, 5–21.

Paradis, H. A., Sandler, M., Manly, J. T., & Valentine, L. (2013). Building Healthy Children: Evidence-based home visitation integrated with pediatric medical homes. *Pediatrics, 132*: S174–179.

Pickreign Stronach, E., Toth, S. L., Rogosch, F. A., & Cicchetti, D. (2013). Preventive interventions and sustained attachment security in maltreated children. *Development and Psychopathology, 26*, 919–930.

Prinz, R. J., Sanders, M. R., Shapiro, C. J., Whitaker, D. J., & Lutzker, J. R. (2009). Population-based prevention of child maltreatment: The U.S. Triple P system population trial. *Prevention Science, 10*, 1–12.

Robinson, J. (2007). Story stem narratives with young children: Moving to clinical research and practice. *Attachment & Human Development, 9*, 179–185.

Robinson, J., Mantz-Simmons, L., Macfie, J., & the MacArthur Narrative Group (1992). *Narrative coding manual*. Unpublished manuscript.

Rogosch, F. A., & Cicchetti, D. (2005). Child maltreatment, attention networks, and potential precursors to borderline personality disorder. *Development and Psychopathology, 17*(4), 1071–1089.

Rutter, M. (2007). Sure Start Local Programmes: An outsider's perspective. In J. Belsky, J. Barnes, & E. Melhuish (Eds.), *The national evaluation of Sure Start: Does area-based early intervention work?* (pp. 197–210). Bristol, UK: The Policy Press.

Rutter, M. (2012). Resilience as a dynamic concept. *Development and Psychopathology*, *24*(2), 335–344.

Sapienza, J. K., & Masten, A. S. (2011). Understanding and promoting resilience in children and youth. *Current Opinion in Psychiatry*, *24*, 267–273.

Schneider-Rosen, K., Braunwald, K., Carlson, V., & Cicchetti, D. (1985). Current perspectives in attachment theory: Illustrations from the study of maltreated infants. *Monographs of the Society for Research in Child Development*, *50*, 194–210.

Schneider-Rosen, K., & Cicchetti, D. (1984). The relationship between affect and cognition in maltreated infants: Quality of attachment and the development of visual self-recognition. *Child Development*, *55*, 648–658.

Sedlak, A. J., Broadhurst, D., Shapiro, G., Kalton, G., Gosksel, H., Burke, J., & Brown, J. (1997). *Third national incidence study of child abuse and neglect: Analysis report* (Prepared under contract to the National Center on Child Abuse and Neglect, US Department of Health and Human Services). Rockville, MD: Westat.

Sethi, D., Bellis, M. A., Hughes, K., Gilbert, R., Mitis, F., & Galea, G. (2013). *European report on preventing child maltreatment.* Copenhagen, Denmark: World Health Organization.

Shirk, S. R., Talmi, A., & Olds, D. (2000). A developmental psychopathology perspective on child and adolescent treatment policy. *Development and Psychopathology*, *12*, 835–855.

Sroufe, L. A. (1983). Infant-caregiver attachment and patterns of adaptation in preschool: The roots of maladaptation and competence. In M. Perlmutter (Ed.), *Minnesota symposium in child psychology* (Vol. 16, pp. 41–83). Hillsdale, NJ: Lawrence Erlbaum Associates.

Sroufe, L. A., Carlson, E. A., Levy, A. K., & Egeland, B. (1999). Implications of attachment theory for developmental psychopathology. *Development and Psychopathology*, *11*, 1–13.

Sroufe, L. A., & Fleeson, J. (1986). Attachment and the construction of relationships. In W. Hartup & Z. Rubin (Eds.), *Relationships and development* (pp. 51–76). Hillsdale, NJ: Lawrence Erlbaum Associates.

Sroufe, L. A., & Fleeson, J. (1988). The coherence of family relationships. In R. A. Hinde & J. Stevenson-Hinde (Eds.), *Relationships within families: Mutual influences* (pp. 27–47). Oxford, UK: Oxford University Press.

Sroufe, L. A., & Rutter, M. (1984). The domain of developmental psychopathology. *Child Development*, *55*, 17–29.

Toth, S. L., & Cicchetti, D. (1996). Patterns of relatedness and depressive symptomatology in maltreated children. *Journal of Consulting and Clinical Psychology*, *64*, 32–41.

Toth, S. L., & Cicchetti, D. (1999). Developmental psychopathology and child psychotherapy. In S. Russ & T. Ollendick (Eds.), *Handbook of psychotherapies with children and families* (pp. 15–44). New York: Plenum Press.

Toth, S. L., Cicchetti, D., & Kim, J. E. (2002). Relations among children's perceptions of maternal behavior, attributional styles, and behavioral symptomatology in maltreated children. *Journal of Abnormal Child Psychology*, *30*, 487–501.

Toth, S. L., Cicchetti, D., Macfie, J., & Emde, R. N. (1997). Representations of self and other in the narratives of neglected, physically abused, and sexually abused preschoolers. *Development and Psychopathology, 9,* 781–796.

Toth, S. L., Cicchetti, D., Macfie, J., Maughan, A., & VanMeenan, K. (2000). Narrative representations of caregivers and self in maltreated preschoolers. *Attachment and Human Development, 2,* 271–305.

Toth, S. L., Maughan, A., Manly, J. T., Spagnola, M., & Cicchetti, D. (2002). The relative efficacy of two interventions in altering maltreated preschool children's representational models: Implications for attachment theory. *Development and Psychopathology, 14,* 877–908.

US Advisory Board on Child Abuse and Neglect. (1990). *Child abuse and neglect: Critical first steps in response to a national emergency.* Washington, DC: Department of Health and Human Services.

USDHSS (US Department of Health and Human Services) (1999). *Mental health: A report of the Surgeon General.* Rockville, MD: Substance Abuse and Mental Health Services Administration.

USDHSS (US Department of Health and Human Services) (2001). *Mental health: Culture, race, and ethnicity: A supplement to mental health: A report of the Surgeon General.* Rockville, MD: U.S. Department of Health and Human Services, Substance Abuse and Mental Health Services Administration, Center for Mental Health Services.

van IJzendoorn, M. H., Schuengel, C., & Bakersman-Kranenburg, M. J. (1999). Disorganized attachment in early childhood: Meta-analyses of precursors concomitants, and sequelae. *Development and Psychopathology, 11,* 225–249.

Waters, E., & Sroufe, L. A. (1983). Competence as a developmental construct. *Developmental Review, 3,* 79–97.

Weissman, M. M., Markowitz, J. C., & Klerman, G. L. (2000). *Comprehensive guide to interpersonal psychotherapy.* New York, NY: Basic Books.

Westen, D., Betan, E., & DeFife, J. A. (2011). Identity disturbance in adolescence: Associations with borderline personality disorder. *Development and Psychopathology, 23*(1), 305–313.

Zeanah, C. H., Berlin, L. J., & Boris, N. W. (2011). Practitioner review: Clinical applications of attachment theory and research for infants and young children. *Journal of Child Psychology and Psychiatry, 52*(8), 819–833.

16

Language Impairment and Adolescent Outcomes

Gina Conti-Ramsden and Kevin Durkin

One of the landmarks that parents look forward to is their baby's first words. Although a great deal of social-communicative development has occurred prior to this stage (Miller & Lossia, 2013; Olson & Masur, 2013; Wu & Gros-Louis, 2014), the onset of use of the baby's home language signals an important advance in that child's development. There is variation in the developmental timing of babies' first words (Labrell et al., 2014; Wehberg et al., 2007), but most parents will begin to worry about their child if she or he has not produced single words by two years of age.

There are many reasons why a child may not produce first words as expected. Of particular interest is that there are children who have difficulties with language, that is, producing words to communicate and/or understanding what is said to them, whilst "everything else" appears to be normal. That everything else has traditionally been defined to include adequate input from the senses: normal hearing and normal/corrected vision. It also includes an adequate biological basis to develop language (they have no obvious signs of brain damage) and an adequate basis for learning, that is, their nonverbal abilities as measured by IQ are similar to those of their peers of the same age (at least in childhood) (Conti-Ramsden, St. Clair,

The Wiley Handbook of Developmental Psychology in Practice: Implementation and Impact, First Edition.
Edited by Kevin Durkin and H. Rudolph Schaffer.
© 2016 John Wiley & Sons, Ltd. Published 2016 by John Wiley & Sons, Ltd.

Pickles, & Durkin, 2012). A desire to engage socially is also important: such children seek to interact socially with adults and peers and as such are not like children with autism who are not as socially engaged. These children are usually referred to as children with language impairment (LI).

LI is often considered a condition of early to middle childhood. As we will discuss in greater detail below, having a history of LI, for many children, predicts continuing language and associated problems into later childhood, adolescence and adulthood. What are the implications for these young people's entry into society? In this chapter we will examine the developmental outcomes for children with LI in adolescence in four areas of functioning: educational progress and occupational entry, mental health, friendships and independence. It will become evident that although LI has been conceptualized as a relatively "pure" disorder of language, the condition is quite heterogeneous, with wide-ranging sequelae, and the language impairment may not be as clearly distinguishable from everything else as the standard definition presupposes. Current research suggests the picture is more complex and the traditional definition needs to be revisited (Bishop, 2014; Reilly et al., 2014). We will discuss the implication of these findings for practice and importantly the issues surrounding the sharing of this information with relevant user groups.

LI: From Childhood to Adolescence

What are children with LI like?

Infants who are likely to later have LI are, in the first instance, late talkers in the nontechnical sense. That is, the appearance of their first words is usually delayed compared to what is expected of most young children (Everitt, Hannaford & Conti-Ramsden, 2013; but also see Ukoumunne et al., 2012). When children with LI eventually produce their first words these may not be that easy for the listener to understand. Speech difficulties involving pronunciation may accompany LI, but are not considered to be a hallmark of the disorder. As they get older, the delay in language use is still evident. Word combinations such as "want juice", "bye-bye teddy" also appear at a later age than would be expected. Thus, children with LI have a hard time using language to communicate with others (Bishop, 2013; Conti-Ramsden & Durkin, 2012a).

Children with LI can also have difficulties in understanding what is said to them. For example, following instructions such as "bring me the big ball" (from amongst an array of balls) they may follow the gist of the sentence (and retrieve a ball) but miss qualifying details (and fail to select the big ball). Some researchers have identified subtypes of LI based on how impaired their comprehension abilities may be (Conti-Ramsden & Botting, 1999; Rapin, 1996). Children with expressive LI have more difficulty with talking (producing words, also referred to as expressive language) than with understanding what is said to them (comprehending language, also referred to as receptive language). Although difficulties with talking attract the most attention and can occur in isolation, many children present with difficulties in both talking and understanding (Bishop, 2013; Leonard, 2014). These children are referred to as having expressive–receptive LI or mixed LI. It is much rarer to see children who have problems understanding what is said to them but can talk relatively normally (except in the case of children with autism). However, there are some children with LI who appear to have difficulties with social understanding but do not present with the cluster of deficits related to autism. These children are referred to in the Diagnostic and Statistical Manual of Mental Disorders (APA, 2013) as having social communication difficulties (Bishop, 1998; Bishop & Norbury, 2002; Botting & Conti-Ramsden, 2003; Mok, Pickles, Durkin, & Conti-Ramsden, 2014; Norbury, 2014).

Thus, many children with LI can appear "normal", with no outward signs of their difficulty. People may think of them as quiet or shy and nothing more. LI is a hidden difficulty. This lack of visibility of the impairment has at least partly influenced the lack of public awareness of this disorder.

Interestingly, LI is much more prevalent than other difficulties that have received more public attention, for example, autism (Bishop, 2010). LI is a common disorder: current research suggests that approximately 7% of children experience LI (Tomblin et al., 1997) compared to 1% for autism (Baird et al., 2006). In this sense, LI forms one of the largest groups of young people with special needs that professionals are likely to encounter.

As mentioned above, until recently, LI was thought to be a disorder of childhood. Follow-up studies into later childhood and adolescence have revealed that although some appear to "grow out of it", for a significant proportion of children this disorder is persistent (approximately 3% of adolescents experience LI) (Mckinley & Larson, 1989). Adolescents with LI continue to show significant problems with areas of language such as processing morphology and syntax (Nippold, Mansfield, Billow, & Tomblin, 2009; Stuart & van der Lely, 2015), extent and depth of vocabulary knowledge (McGregor, Oleson, Bahnsen, & Duff, 2013) and their spontaneous utterances often show an avoidance of complex structures (Tuller, Henry, Sizaret, & Barthez, 2012). Those children who appear to grow out of it tend to have good comprehension abilities, but even this group of "resolved" children can experience language-related difficulties in later childhood (Nippold & Schwartz, 2002; Rescorla, 2005; Simkin & Conti-Ramsden, 2006; Stothard, Snowling, Bishop, Chipchase & Kaplan, 1998).

Longitudinal studies have indicated that persistent LI is associated with poorer reading and school progress (Snowling, Adams, Bishop & Stothard, 2001), a decline in nonverbal functioning (Botting, 2005; Conti-Ramsden, St. Clair, Pickles, & Durkin, 2012), and social and psychiatric difficulties (Beitchman et al., 2001; Conti-Ramsden & Botting, 2004; Conti-Ramsden, Mok, Pickles, & Durkin, 2013; Yew & O'Kearney, 2013). However, the assumption that the primary difficulty with language is the defining characteristic of LI, and that, if persistent, it remains with them as they grow into adolescence and young adulthood, is still very much part of current thinking. We do not see in textbooks or manuals a change in the definition of LI from childhood to adolescence, for example. Textbooks and manuals are likely to acknowledge that LI is a developmental condition, that it can be persistent and stay with children as they grow up, and that it can be heterogeneous (i.e., that variation is observed and you can have different types of language deficits in LI). Yet, the current definition of LI most commonly used is in a way static and does not explicitly tell us about what to expect as children with LI grow up.

Educational progress and occupational entry

Language is central to many areas of educational activity and language impairment presents a considerable barrier to classroom work. Almost everything children are learning about in their early school years is mediated by talk, and they soon face increasing literacy demands. Both reading and writing are areas of difficulty for these children (Bishop & Snowling, 2004; Dockrell, Lindsay, Connelly, & Mackie, 2007). Not surprisingly, children with language impairments in the elementary years show, on average, poorer educational attainment than their peers without a history of language difficulties (Cowan, Donlan, Newton, & Lloyd, 2005; Dockrell & Lindsay, 1998; Durkin, Mok, & Conti-Ramsden, 2013, 2015). These problems continue into adolescence and beyond, such that individuals with LI score lower on standard curriculum tests, and are sometimes less likely to be put forward to take the tests (Conti-Ramsden, Durkin, Simkin, & Knox, 2009; Dockrell, Palikara, Lyndsay, & Cullen, 2007; Hall & Tomblin, 1978; Johnson, Beitchman, & Brownlie, 2010; Snowling et al., 2001).

As they approach the workforce and are guided into short-term work placements (this is an official part of the curriculum in many UK high schools), students with LI are more likely to be placed in lower skilled, elementary jobs (e.g., shelf stacker), while their peers without a history of language problems are more likely to be placed in employment that was considered personal service with greater potential for skills development (e.g., child carer, classroom assistant) (Durkin, Fraser, & Conti-Ramsden, 2012).

In terms of access to part-time or casual employment alongside schooling, Durkin et al. found that the percentage of adolescents with LI reporting never having had a job (other than preparatory work experience placements) was almost twice as high as the percentage of young people without a history of language difficulties (62% versus 32%). Although the proportion of adolescents with LI remaining in post-compulsory education is comparable to the proportion of non-LI students doing so (Dockrell, Palikara, et al., 2007; Durkin, Simkin, Knox, & Conti-Ramsden, 2009), those with LI continue, on average, to move into lower educational courses or to find themselves out of work (Conti-Ramsden & Durkin, 2012b). This is consistent with the findings of Howlin, Mawhood, and Rutter (2000) who reported that participants with language disorders tended to have jobs requiring limited education or training, such as street cleaning, store work, security guard, drain maintenance, factory work. Johnson et al. (2010) found that, in young adulthood, their participants with LI held jobs that were classifiable as lower in socioeconomic status than did those young people without a history of language difficulties. The investigators report, for example, that while participants from both their language impaired and nonimpaired samples found jobs within the food industry, only 10% of those from the LI group had managerial positions and 90% were food servers. In contrast, in the comparison group 43% were managers and 56% were servers.

Educational and life prospects, then, are circumscribed by LI. It is important to keep in mind (as stressed above) that disadvantageous comparisons with peers without a history of language problems hold *on average*. There are exceptions, and some young people with LI do progress well in education and in posteducational careers (Dockrell, Palikara, et al., 2007; Durkin et al., 2009; Johnson et al., 2010). Two factors appear to be particularly influential, namely the severity of the impairment and the quality of support received (both professionally, from therapists and teachers, and personally, from family and friends) (Carroll & Dockrell, 2012; Clegg, Ansorge, Stackhouse, & Donlan, 2012; Conti-Ramsden et al., 2009; Dockrell, Palikara, et al., 2007; Durkin et al., 2009; Snowling & Hulme, 2012). The positive impact of support, in particular, underscores the potential for researchers and practitioners in applied developmental psychology, speech and language therapy, and cognate specialisms to contribute towards improving outcomes for young people with this challenging but not insuperable condition.

Mental health in adolescents with LI

There have been some studies examining quality of life and psychiatric outcomes in adolescents with LI (Beitchman et al., 2001; Clegg, Hollis, Mawhood, & Rutter, 2005). Beitchman and colleagues followed up a group of children with LI from five years through adolescence and into their early 30s and throughout this period they assessed them for the presence of possible psychiatric difficulties. They found that children with LI were at greater risk of having attention deficit hyperactivity disorders (Beitchman et al., 1996a) and later had higher rates of anxiety disorders (Beitchman et al., 2001), aggressive behavior (Brownlie et al., 2004) and increased substance abuse (Beitchman et al., 2001). At age 31, there were no significant differences in mental health outcomes between those with LI and their peers without a history of language difficulties (Beitchman, Brownlie, & Bao, 2014), though the authors point out that the higher rate of attrition in the former group limits the inferences that can be made about continuity of psychiatric difficulties. In a nationwide longitudinal cohort study in the United Kingdom, Schoon, Parsons, Rush, and Law (2010) found that early receptive language problems predicted mental health problems at age 34. Clegg, Hollis, Mawhood, and Rutter (2005) followed a cohort of children from four years to mid-adulthood and found an increased risk of psychiatric impairment (compared to both peers and siblings), particularly concerning depression, social anxiety and schizoform/personality disorders. Psychiatric problems, then, are more likely in adolescents with LI (though by no means experienced in all) and in some cases will continue into young adulthood.

Other studies have examined language in populations referred primarily for behavioral, offending and/or psychiatric difficulties. Although selected for nonlinguistic reasons, these samples often show significantly higher levels of language and communication problems than would be expected in the general population (Gregory & Bryan, 2011; Helland, Lundervold, Heimann, & Posserud, 2014; Snow & Sanger, 2011). Cohen and colleagues (1998, 2013), for example, found higher than expected rates of undiagnosed language impairment (40–45%) in clinic samples.

Conti-Ramsden and Botting (2008) found that 16-year-old adolescents with LI had higher scores than their peers without a history of language difficulties for both anxiety and depression. In addition, the proportion of adolescents scoring above the clinical threshold was larger in the LI group as compared to their peers for both anxiety (12% versus 2%) and depression (39% versus 14%). We also examined predictors of increased anxiety and depression. The results suggest that there were virtually no associations between language ability and the development of anxiety and depression. Examination of earlier language ability once again showed remarkably few associations. Thus, language was not a predictor of mental health in adolescents with LI. This finding held when the same participants were followed up at age 17 (Wadman, Botting, Durkin, & Conti-Ramsden, 2011). At 17, the adolescents with LI continued to show significantly more anxiety symptoms than in their peers without a history of language problems, but the two groups did not differ significantly in depressive symptoms.

Interestingly, a concurrent study on the bullying experiences of the same 16-year-old adolescents with LI revealed a significant correlation between being bullied at 16 years and anxiety and depression symptoms (Knox & Conti-Ramsden, 2007). Such a relationship was not evident for a group of comparison peers. This longitudinal study used two general questions regarding being teased or bullied now or when they were younger. The questions did not draw the adolescents' attention to particular types of bullying (e.g., nonverbal bullying, cyber bullying), thus the results of the study are likely to be only indicative and may underestimate the bullying experiences of young people. Results revealed that there was a decrease in the bullying experiences of young people over time (as has been found by other studies, e.g., Pepler et al., 2006; Sumter, Baumgartner, Valkenburg, & Peter, 2012; Smith, Chapter 12, this volume). 44% of adolescents with LI recall being teased or bullied when they were younger whilst 17% report current bullying. A similar pattern was found for the comparison group of peers, with 22% of adolescents recalling being teased or bullied but only 2.4% experiencing bullying at 16 years of age. However, the positive notion that bullying incidence decreases with increasing maturity is overshadowed by the finding that 13% of young people with LI have experienced bullying that persists over time. These findings, combined with the significant correlation of bullying with anxiety and depression in the LI group, emphasize the vulnerability of young people with LI to mental health problems and their changing needs in adolescence.

The results of the above investigations raise a number of key issues that relate to our understanding of LI in adolescence. Our data show that adolescents with LI are at greater risk than their peers of experiencing anxiety symptoms and, at least during some phases, of depressive symptoms. This finding replicates other studies that have shown raised prevalence of psychiatric difficulties in those with communication impairments (Clegg et al., 2005) and increased language impairment in children referred psychiatrically (Cohen et al., 1998, 2013) and reviews affirming the association (Toppelberg & Shapiro, 2000; Yew & O'Kearney, 2013). As mentioned already, Beitchman and colleagues (2001), in particular, found increased anxiety in a similar cohort with LI at 19 years of age. The association has often been assumed to be causal in that either long-term language impairment may lead to (or exacerbate) wider difficulties, or that psychiatric impairment may constrain communication skill.

However, apart from the fact that those with LI have increased symptoms, surprisingly few clear associations exist between language and the development of emotional health symptoms. This is similar to the findings of Clegg et al. (2005) and Lindsay and Dockrell (2012), who also failed to find a clear relationship between the two. The lack of association with language scores thus makes it more difficult to interpret the relationship between having poor language and mental health difficulties as a directly developmentally causal one: that is, having ongoing poor communicative experiences do not appear to "make you" increasingly depressed or anxious *per se*. Rather, the association appears to be with LI itself, with the disorder. Thus, other factors are likely to play a role in making some individuals more vulnerable, but there is a dearth of research in this area. From our own work, we suggest these can range from family history of anxiety and depression (Conti-Ramsden & Botting, 2008) to environmental factors, such as being bullied (Knox & Conti-Ramsden, 2007). Once again, evidence indicates that guidance and support make an important contribution to the emotional and mental well-being of young people with LI (Durkin & Conti-Ramsden, 2010). However, further research is needed to better understand the range of factors that may be contributing to adolescents' emotional health. For example, Joffe and Black (2012) report that adolescents with low language abilities self-report higher levels of emotional symptoms than are indicated in teacher reports (using the same instrument); while various explanations could be suggested, the possibility that language impaired individuals are less able than other children to express their emotional problems verbally (making them harder for teachers to detect) warrants investigation.

Friendship quality in adolescents with LI

Friendships are a vital dimension of an individual's development. They are key markers of the selectivity of interpersonal relations, providing social and cognitive scaffolding (Hartup, 1996), serving variously as sources of support and information as well as buffers against many of life's problems, with enduring implications for self-esteem and well-being (Hartup & Stevens, 1999; Shulman, 1993). Children and adolescents without friends, or with poor friendship quality, are at risk of loneliness, stress and poorer health (Bagwell & Schmidt, 2013; Kingery, Erdley, & Marshall, 2011; Ladd, Kochenderfer, & Coleman, 1996; Mundt, & Zakletskaia, 2014).

Friendship relations are complex and this reflects in part the ways in which they interweave with other developmental processes, such as developing interpersonal and communicative skills, increasing social cognitive competence and changing personal needs. For example, very young children form friendships largely on the basis of proximity and shared activities; during middle childhood friendships involve greater levels of interchange and awareness of individual attributes; and in adolescence many people seek via friendships to satisfy psychological needs for intimacy, shared outlooks and identity formulation (Buhrmester, 1990, 1996; Dishion & Tipsord, 2011; Parker & Gottman, 1989; Steinberg & Morris, 2001).

Durkin and Conti-Ramsden (2007) examined friendship quality in the same sample of 16-year-old adolescents with LI and their peers without a history of language difficulties as reported in the studies above. We asked them a series of questions regarding friends and acquaintances. For example: How easy do you find to get on with other people? If you were at a party or social gathering, would you try to talk to people you had not met before? Overall as a group, adolescents with LI were at risk of poorer quality of friendships.

We then examined predictors of friendships. Our results suggest that spoken language abilities (expression and understanding of language) as well as literacy skills (reading) were associated with friendship quality. But language was *not* the strongest predictor. These were difficult behavior and prosocial behavior. We found that, in the sample as a whole, language and literacy measures accounted for an additional 7% of variance. Thus, language ability is predictive of adolescents' friendship quality when other behavioral characteristics known to be influential in peer relations (problem behavior, prosocial behavior) are controlled for, but its overall influence is small. There was also a small influence of nonverbal IQ. Thus, the predictor variables were, in order, difficult behavior, prosocial behavior, language and literacy, and nonverbal IQ.

There was also evidence of variability in friendship quality, that is, heterogeneity within our sample of adolescents with LI. A large proportion of adolescents with LI appear to have good quality of friendships. Factors that potentially distinguish between those with good quality of friendships (60%) and those with poor quality of friendships (40%) were examined. Briefly, the findings suggest a marked developmental consistency in the pattern of poor language for the poor friendships group across a nine-year span, from 7 to 16 years of age.

Thus, language impairment itself appears to be a risk factor for poorer friendship development. It is known to be associated with social problems in childhood and adolescence, and it is reasonable to assume that these bear on peer relations and friendship development (Fujiki, Brinton, Hart, & Fitzgerald, 1999; Mok et al., 2014; St. Clair, Pickles, Durkin & Conti-Ramsden, 2011; Wadman, Durkin, & Conti-Ramsden, 2011). At the same time, there are individual differences in the nature and severity of problems experienced. Although we found that the group of participants with LI as a whole scored less favorably on our measure of friendship quality, they also showed considerable within-group heterogeneity, and many had good scores with about 40% having poor quality of friendships. These data taken together suggest that poor quality of friendships in LI, although related to poor language, may not be simply a consequence of the severity of the language problem experienced but is an additional difficulty present in LI, particularly evident during adolescence. Interestingly, poor quality of friendships does not appear to be strongly associated with mental health difficulties. We found that in this sample, only 7% of adolescents showed difficulties in both friendships and mental health; 32% showed difficulties with friendships in the context of adequate mental health and 4% had the reverse pattern. 57% of the sample did not show difficulties in either area.

Independence in adolescents with LI

The achievement of personal autonomy has long been recognized as a fundamental task of adolescent development (Erikson, 1968; Freud, 1958; Steinberg & Silverberg, 1986; Zimmer-Gembeck & Collins, 2003). Most contemporary researchers agree that autonomy is multidimensional, entailing behavioral, cognitive and affective components (Zimmer-Gembeck & Collins, 2003; Van Petegem, Beyers, Vansteenkiste, & Soenens, 2012). Our concern here is with aspects of behavioral autonomy: the capacity for self-regulation, self-governance, the formulation and pursuit of goals and the successful execution of personal decisions (Feldman & Rosenthal, 1991; Noom, Deković, & Meeus, 2001). These skills underpin the practical aspects of entry into the adult world and are crucial in establishing independence, in due course facilitating occupational paths and independent living arrangements (Arnett, 2000).

Behavioral autonomy as it relates to independence thus covers a number of different skills. These skills are likely to be affected by a young person's language ability. For example, young people need to be able to define their own goals, their personal aims prior to executing these goals (Noom et al., 2001). Language is likely to be involved in both the formulation of goals and their successful execution. Interestingly though, but perhaps because language is transparent (integral to most human activity) its role in the achievement of behavioral autonomy has been neglected. This is despite extensive research illuminating the importance of social interactions and interpersonal relations to the development of autonomy (Zimmer-Gembeck & Collins, 2003).

How do adolescents with LI fare with regards to independence? We studied independent functioning in domains relevant to everyday living in the same cohort of 16-year-old adolescents and their peers (Conti-Ramsden & Durkin, 2008). Domains examined included self-care activities, travelling and meeting people, managing finances, among others. Autonomy in these kinds of task is foremost in young people's subjective sense of reaching adulthood: accepting responsibility for one's self, making independent decisions, and financial independence are consistently ranked among the top criteria (Arnett, 2000). By the end of compulsory schooling (i.e., 16 years of age) most adolescents appeared competent in the areas of independence examined. As would be expected, they were developing competence in the basic skills associated with self-sufficiency. In contrast, adolescents with LI fared significantly less well in both parental and self reports on independence.

Although adolescents with LI were less independent than their peers overall, there was greater heterogeneity in this group. Some young people were performing very much like their peers without a history of language impairment while others were having difficulties in a number of areas related to independent functioning. This is in line with previous studies, where outcomes for individuals with a history of LI have been found to be variable and sometimes difficult to predict (Beitchman, Wilson, Brownlie, Walters & Lancee, 1996b; Beitchman et al., 1996c; Howlin et al., 2000; Johnson et al., 2010). The sample size in Conti-Ramsden and Durkin (2008) allows for confidence in estimating the proportion of adolescents with LI who do manifest problems in respect of independence, and our data indicate that approximately 36% fall into this category.

Regression analyses involving the adolescents with LI revealed language and literacy to be key associates of independent functioning. When examining concurrent variables, reading with understanding was found to be the one significant factor related to independence in adolescents with LI. However, the reading measure was significantly correlated with both expressive and receptive language in adolescents with LI. The longitudinal nature of this investigation also afforded the examination of early predictors of adolescent independence in LI. Expressive language ability at seven years of age was found to be significantly related to independence at 16 years in young people with LI. Furthermore, examination the psycholinguistic profiles of young people with low versus adequate independence groups revealed that adolescents with low independence exhibited more severe language difficulties in childhood. It is important to note that in persistent LI, expressive and receptive skills are usually found to be correlated. Thus, the early predictor identified reflects not only level of expressive language but its association with depressed receptive skills. The group categorized as low independence in adolescence continued to exhibit language difficulties but in addition presented with problems in reading with understanding.

The results briefly presented above indicate that adolescents with poor language and literacy skills are at increased risk for low independence. In the specific case of adolescents with LI, the risk of poorer scores on independence is magnified, with approximately one-third of the sample not being able to fully look after themselves without help at 16 years of age and evidence of discrepancies between adolescents with LI and their peers in areas that do not appear to be directly related to language *per se*, for example, remembering a doctor's appointment, managing money. These findings suggest that LI is a developmental condition with associated problems in a number of areas, including independence, which are particularly evident in adolescence. In addition, an investigation involving parents of the 16-year-old participants of the above studies revealed that lack of independence was the key concern of parents who were worried about their offspring with LI (Conti-Ramsden, Botting, & Durkin, 2008). Interestingly, in a qualitative study with adolescents with LI who were attending a specialist leisure center designed to facilitate peer interactions in a supportive context, Myers, Davies-Jones, Chiat, Joffe, and Botting (2011) found that one of the principal attractions identified by the participants was the scope to "be me", that is, to express their autonomy and individuality.

Outcomes in adolescence: Revisiting the definition of LI

The findings presented briefly above point to the heterogeneity in outcomes in adolescents with LI. This heterogeneity is evident both within LI, that is, across individuals (different adolescents have different types of difficulties of different severity), as well as within an individual (there appears to be variation over time in the constellation of difficulties an adolescent may experience and in the severity of these difficulties). In a large sample, such as the Manchester Language Study, we see a wide variation in outcomes: from those managing to be independent to those who can not fully look after themselves; from those enjoying good quality of friendships to those with difficulties developing such relationships; from those experiencing anxiety and/or depressive symptoms or bullying to those having adequate emotional health (Beitchman, & Brownlie, 2013; Dockrell et al., 2007).

Conti-Ramsden (2008) points out that parents and practitioners will interpret this "variability" or "heterogeneity" as things being "messy" in LI. They are. Heterogeneity translates to issues being more complex in practice. It is hard to predict from the individual's language problem other likely associated difficulties. Yet, very importantly, the risk of poor outcomes in all the domains discussed above is strongly associated with LI itself. In contrast, language abilities may be important for some outcomes but not for others, and are sometimes a predictor of some outcomes but not at other times in relation to other outcomes.

Awareness that LI is not a pure disorder of language is not a new idea (Leonard, 1987, 1991, 2014). What is perhaps debated but less well established is the suggestion that at least some of the associated difficulties present in LI are *not* directly related to the language difficulties present in LI. We want to argue that the heterogeneity observed in the outcomes of adolescents with LI, both within and across individuals, is a reflection of LI being more than a language problem. The evidence points to a need to redefine LI and this concern is occasioning much debate among specialists as we strive for a fuller understanding and, arguably, more adequate diagnostic criteria and terminology for the disorder (Bishop, 2014; Reilly et al., 2014).

First, LI is a developmental disorder for which language is a primary manifestation in early childhood. It is the case that there are a number of children of preschool age who present with primary language problems with other areas of development apparently intact. The issue is that this profile of LI does not remain this way for long for a large proportion of children as they grow up. Other areas of functioning show deficits, including areas that can not be related directly to language *per se*. LI has associated difficulties that become more evident with development, only some of which are related to the severity and type of language problem experienced.

Second, in LI, the primary difficulty with language is assumed to hold the key to the explanation as to why these children have these difficulties with language and other areas. The evidence presented in this chapter in terms of outcomes at age 16 years suggests that factors other than difficulties with language may well be crucial in understanding the range of deficits that individuals with LI experience throughout their childhood and adolescence.

Finally, in LI the primary difficulty with language is assumed to be a defining characteristic that is persistent, stays with children as they grow into adolescence and young adulthood. This may well be the case for some individuals. The key issue raised by the findings reported above is that other areas of functioning may well be at least as problematic as the language deficit in adolescence. Thus, for adolescents with LI, language may no longer be a primary deficit, nor the most important target variable for realizing optimal outcome.

The Potential Contribution of Findings to Practice

Language impairment is a common difficulty but, until recently, it has been relatively neglected by researchers and practitioners (Bishop, 2010). There is an urgent need to ensure that research findings are made available and accessible. In this way, the fruits of research can form the basis for evidence-based practice and informed policy. Research findings can also open the door to understanding and options for young people and their families. Furthermore, the process of sharing research findings can be (and in a way, should be) a truly bidirectional process and, as such, can provide an opportunity for users to influence not only the research endeavor itself but directions for future research.

An essential step in sharing research results with others, that is, knowledge exchange, is to translate key research findings into clear messages that are relevant to specific user groups. This can then be followed by activities that aim to implement the research knowledge into practice. This process is discussed here for four user groups: professionals–practitioners, policymakers, parents, and young people with LI themselves. The section ends with some reflections about some of the issues relating to knowledge exchange which apply to most user groups.

Professional–practitioners

Many professionals are likely to become involved with adolescents with LI. Some, such as Speech and Language Therapists (SLTs) and Educational Psychologists (EPs), will typically be very familiar with the disability, though their training may lead them to focus on particular dimensions and, in our experience, leave them feeling low-skilled in respect of others. For example, SLTs are well-informed on language-related issues but may not have training in how to help children and families deal with emotional or behavioral problems; EPs may be the reverse. The obvious potential for complementary teamwork is not always realized in practice because of disciplinary boundaries and organizational structures. Some teachers will have received training in language development and language disorders – but many will not (McCartney & Ellis, 2013). Similar variability exists among legal professionals, who may work with young people as witnesses, victims and offenders (Snow, Powell, & Sanger, 2012). Of course, all of these professionals have much to offer to young people with special needs, but only some will be sensitive to and prepared for the particular constellations of needs that come with LI.

Encouragingly, recent evidence suggests that professionals not previously trained in language disorders can profit from specialist guidance on how to modify their own language to support adolescents with language impairment. Starling, Munro, Toger and Arcuili (2012) trained teachers in a variety of techniques to help them simplify, clarify, repeat and rephrase utterances, to engage students in discussion, and to illustrate instructional vocabulary effectively. The teachers showed gains in these skills and their students with LI showed improvements in written expression and listening comprehension; there were no changes in a comparison group of teachers or their students with LI.

Some of the messages drawn from the research findings described above that we propose are relevant to professional practice involving young people with LI are shown in Box 16.1.

A crucial element in the knowledge exchange process is bidirectionality. Highlighting the messages for professionals–practitioners emphasizes an important component of the knowledge exchange process but at the same time *may* de-emphasize the other. Researchers do not just impart information but also have the opportunity to listen, learn and be responsive to the views of users of the research.

When discussing the messages shown in Box 16.1 with colleagues involved in practice, it became clear to us that the user group "professionals–practitioners" was too imprecise a grouping to be working with. Are we talking about teachers, speech and language therapists, educational psychologists, health workers, others? In other words, who were we trying to reach? As researchers, we learned from practitioners that our target audience needed to be defined more precisely in order to examine the implications of these messages to practice. After discussion of the research team with colleagues involved in practice, we decided to have two target groups: Workers in education (in particular teachers in secondary education and special needs teachers/coordinators) and workers in health (we wanted to target point of contact mental health services, which in the United Kingdom means workers in Children

Box 16.1   Messages for practitioners

1. Recognition (Be alert):
   - The main manifestation of LI at school entry age (4–5 years) is not the same as it is in adolescence (secondary school age).
   - Development matters: things can change in adolescence.
   - LI has other areas of difficulty besides language.
   - LI is heterogeneous, i.e., it is variable.
   - Problems that adolescents develop, e.g., mental health, are likely to have their roots earlier in development.
2. What other areas of difficulty can be expected?
   - Educational
     (i) The language, and often closely associated literacy, difficulties of LI will most likely impact on educational progress, from the elementary years onwards. Educators need to be alert to the possibility that a child falling behind in his or her schoolwork may have language difficulties that affect understanding and participation.
     (ii) Some children with LI will have a diagnosis as such, others may be included under more general categorization as having "special educational needs", and the language problems of some may not be detected at all. Whether or not the child receives specialized provision will be influenced substantially by the diagnostic label he or she receives.
     (iii) Children with LI are disadvantaged but not incapable of attainment; some achieve very positive educational outcomes. Research and policy are needed to find and extend ways of providing the support needed to reach optimal outcomes.
     (iv) LI is easily overlooked. Individuals with LI are at risk of being bypassed when important educational routes are chosen: for example, they may not be entered into some assessments, or they may not be encouraged to take up more challenging work placements.
   - Mental health: anxiety, depression, bullying
     (i) Adolescents with LI have an increased risk of anxiety and depression.
     (ii) Bullying is not as common in later secondary school (14-16 years) as it is in earlier school life. But, adolescents with LI are still at an increased risk for bullying.
     (iii) Adolescents with LI who are bullied are more likely to have associated anxiety and depression.
   - Friendships and independence
     (i) More adolescents with LI have difficulties developing social relationships, i.e., developing friendships.
     (ii) More adolescents with LI have difficulties developing skills that lead to independence.

(iii) Early language difficulties, particularly the presence of problems with both language expression and language understanding are associated with poorer quality of friendships in adolescence.

(iv) Early language difficulties and later literacy difficulties are associated with poorer level of independence.

and Adolescent Mental Health [CAMH] Teams). A draft of the potential implications for practice for these two target groups is presented in Box 16.2.

Our experience had not prepared us for the scale of the above endeavor. In the United Kingdom there are tens of thousands of secondary schools and within each secondary school, a number of staff. How could we reach this audience? Were our messages presented in the right format? Were they clear enough? Would they be useful? We started by looking at what material currently exists for secondary school teachers. What do they consult or use in their everyday practice? Besides researching this issue we also consulted with practitioners themselves. What would they find most useful? It became evident that a flexible resource was needed as well as a number of activities to disseminate it. It also became clear that the same resource would not be suitable for education workers and for workers in health. Thus, we had to reduce the scale of our knowledge exchange and once again, make our target audience more specific. We decided to concentrate on workers in education, in particular teachers and special needs teachers/coordinators in secondary schools. Further discussions with the relevant professionals led to agreement that an online resource (i.e., web site) would be the most flexible. The resources available would all be downloadable and include, among others: basic fact sheets about the research findings and recommendations for practice; PowerPoint presentations of the research findings and recommendations for practice, with greater visual impact; toolkits with suggestions of how to mix and match resources to encourage workshops, training and discussion forums in schools or with professional groups, its own dedicated query facility, and hyperlinks with key organizations (e.g., in the United Kingdom, the Department for Children, Schools and Families, a government department). We felt strongly that the content of the resource needed to be accessible and relevant. It also became clear to us that this could only be achieved by jointly developing it with relevant practitioners as an interactive two-way process. Researchers could not do this job alone.

Further down the line, there would be a need to promote the resource. A number of activities would be carried out, including promotional e-mails to key e-mailing groups (in the United Kingdom an example would be TeacherNet, http://www.teachernetuk.org.uk/), mailshots of promotional

---

Box 16.2   Implications for practice

Professionals in education

1. The recognition that problems have their roots early does not mean that the early years should be the only period targeted for services.
2. There is a need to re-think the breadth and level of support adolescents with LI may need in secondary school.
   - Mental health
     - (i) Role of education workers to include picking up the adolescents with mental health problems
     - (ii) Provision of or referral to counselling and support for mental health issues, i.e., anxiety, depression, bullying
     - (iii) Education workers are likely to require a closer relationship with mental health workers
   - Friendships and independence
     - (i) School support for facilitating social relationships
     - (ii) School support for developing independence

Professionals in health

- The recognition that problems have their roots early does not mean that the early years should be the only period targeted for services.
- There is a need for access and provision of mental health services for adolescents with LI.
- Point-of-contact mental health services need to include language in their assessments of adolescents.
- Difficulties with language – especially language comprehension – should be regarded as a red flag, signaling the risk of a range of associated problems.
- Closer liaison is needed between health workers and education workers.
- There is a need for the development of effective interventions and support models for adolescents who have problems with language.
- Communication itself and the language used by professionals are likely to be a challenge with these adolescents in health-related assessments and in intervention.

---

flyers to selected establishments, press releases in key professional association bulletin/newsletters as well as in the national press (in the United Kingdom some national newspapers, e.g., *The Guardian*, have dedicated space for issues related to education, usually once a week, http://education.guardian.co.uk/), and seminars/workshops for members of the target user group.

With the development of this plan came the realization that its implementation required a budget. Although academics who are involved in research usually have at their disposal some resources for dissemination activities related to their research, we found that the plans outlined above well exceeded any such support. Thus, we faced the next challenge in the knowledge exchange process: obtaining funding for the implementation above and beyond the funding for the project(s) that provided the knowledge to be exchanged in the first place. In the United Kingdom, traditionally, dissemination of research findings and knowledge exchange was most commonly limited to one's peer group. The researcher would present findings to other researchers interested in the area via conferences, workshops, seminars. There were notable exceptions, particularly in clinical areas such as LI, where conferences or such meetings were usually open to practitioners as well as academics. However, it would be accurate to describe knowledge exchange as generally having been quite limited. Then there was a change in UK policy and user engagement, impact and public understanding of science became a more important dimension in the research evaluation and research process. Applications for funding started to have specific sections that needed to be filled out, for example, a section entitled "user engagement", where plans involving nonacademic users had to be specified as well as specific documents identifying stakeholders and potential beneficiaries, for example, a document entitled "Pathways to Impact". Activities in this area have grown in the United Kingdom and stand-alone implementation projects like the one described above are more likely to attract funding from awarding bodies today than they did ten years ago.

Policymakers

For policy makers, implementing research knowledge into practice means influencing changes in policy. There are many challenges in influencing policy regarding the need for the provision of a range of support services for adolescents with LI and their families. The first obstacle has to do with timescale. Unless the research project is directly related to policy or practice implications, when one is proposing to carry out a research project it is not always clear how the findings may be relevant to policy. This is much better understood once research findings in an area are accumulated, evaluated and together they make for a clear message that requires the notice of policymakers. In a way, developmental psychology research that influences policy has to do more with a critical mass of knowledge pointing in a particular direction than one-off discoveries. Thus, anticipating who the key policymakers that need to be influenced may be is not always straightforward when one is involved in a stand-alone research project.

The second obstacle is getting policymakers' attention. As several contributions to this Handbook have shown, this is a general issue in knowledge exchange, how to get a hold of your user, and policymakers are perhaps one of the hardest users to get a hold of. Our experience is that policymakers will agree to be part of the research, attend an advisory group to the project, for example, but they usually are represented by someone who is interested in the area and has responsibility at some level within the organization, but is not the policymaker himself/herself. In other words, after initial contact, they typically delegate. Perhaps this is a good strategy, as the representative will pass on information that is likely to be of concern to current policy. For our studies on outcomes of young people with LI in adolescence we have an advisory group, which includes a representative from the UK government department responsible for education, including education for children and young people with special needs. This representative has become quite familiar with our study. We have shared with this representative details of specific results (drafts of our academic articles) as well as provide summaries and general conclusions for discussion and feedback. With hindsight, it would have been useful to also have in our advisory group a representative from the UK government department responsible for health, and mental health in particular. But, at the time of the application this was not as evident to us as it is now. In our follow-up into early adulthood we have been able to achieve this aim and secured such a representative.

Another obstacle is competing priorities. Policymakers have priorities and areas they are working on. If the research findings feed into current priorities it is much more likely that policymakers will take notice. One of the jobs that a researcher needs to get done is to study and thoroughly understand the priorities of the policymaking body she or he is attempting to influence. Researchers have to do some learning themselves. The next step is to find ways for policymakers to listen, capture their imagination, present the findings within the context of their priorities and, if one is dealing with representatives, encourage them to disseminate that information further within the policymaking body. This, in turn, provides the researcher with further opportunities to listen and to learn from policymakers themselves. Brainstorming and discussions about research findings can lead to major changes in policy, priorities and courses of action (see, for example, Chapter 12 in this volume by Smith on bullying). However, our experience working with young people with LI and their families suggests that this may be a long and complex process that requires energy and attention from researchers interested in this area.

There is no doubt that, once senior policymakers are engaged, substantial advances become viable. In the United Kingdom, for example, the Bercow Report (Bercow, 2008) involved academics and policymakers in a review of the services provided for young people with language, speech and other communication needs. Detailed recommendations were made to, and accepted by, the then government,

This gave a major impetus to awareness of language impairment, including a National Year of Speech, Language and Communication in 2011, and the appointment of a national Communication Champion for Children whose brief was to promote change and improvement in the ways children with the poorest communication skills were supported. These developments led to increased recognition of the need for improved services, prompted the inclusion of communication skills in the official mechanisms for inspecting schools, and inspired a range of local government initiatives and campaigns. Much of this work was evidence-based and data were collected on the effectiveness of new developments (see Gross, 2011, for a fuller account). The government's continued commitment to addressing communication issues was followed up with further funding for research and the establishment of the Better Communication Research Programme (BCRP), which has generated numerous invaluable reports on the development, evaluation, and economics of assessment and services (Dockrell, Lindsay, Law, & Roulstone, 2014; Lindsay & Dockrell, 2014) and continues to influence policy development.

Parents

When considering parents, one aspect of knowledge exchange has to do with making relevant information available to individuals who are involved in the care of children and young people with LI and the implications of such knowledge to their everyday lives and their parenting practices. In our experience, this process also provides an opportunity to engage with the thoughts and concerns parents may have regarding the issues raised by the research findings and, wherever possible, to address those concerns as part of the knowledge exchange process. This implies the involvement of parents in any plans for knowledge exchange. Importantly, Gross (2011) reports that the greater awareness brought about by the post-Bercow developments described above led to considerably increased demand from parents for information, advice and services. The greater involvement and empowerment of these key stakeholders is a very desirable process that can, in turn, inform researchers. In the knowledge exchange process with parents, we have usually presented our research findings as a mixture of specific results (e.g., adolescents with LI are more likely to become anxious) along with general conclusions (e.g., LI can be very variable). Some of the messages gathered from the research evidence that we believe are relevant to parents of adolescents with LI are shown in Box 16.3.

The implications for parenting practice are offered here (Box 16.4) along with some issues relating to recurring parental concerns (Box 16.5).

How do we reach parents? In the United Kingdom there is an association (Afasic, www.afasic.org.uk) to help children and young people with LI, their families and

---

Box 16.3   Messages for parents of adolescents with LI

Your growing child: Issues in adolescence
- The main manifestation of LI at school entry age (4–5 years) is not the same as it is in adolescence (secondary school age).
- Development matters: things can change in adolescence.
- LI is heterogeneous, i.e., it is variable. Your adolescent's profile is likely to have commonalities with the profile of other individuals with LI but it will also be unique.
- LI can be associated with other areas of difficulty besides language.
- Your adolescent *may* show one or more of the following: difficulties with literacy and educational attainment, the transition from education to employment, anxiety, depression, still be very dependent on you and/or be socially isolated (have few or no friends).

Box 16.4   Implications for parenting practice

- In adolescence, some young people with LI may find academic work challenging and the transition to the world of employment difficult. Your adolescent may need your support with school work and making choices regarding further education, vocational training and/or employment postschool.
- In adolescence, some young people with LI may become more anxious and depressed. Watch for signs that this may be the case for your adolescent. Your adolescent may need your support in helping him/her to access counselling to help them through.
- In adolescence, young people need to develop their skills for independence. It is sometimes hard to let your youngster do activities outside the home on their own, for fear of something going wrong. Young people with LI need the experience to develop skills, such as taking public transport, organizing a meal for themselves, etc. You can support your adolescent to experience independence: starting with small steps helps with the transition to a more independent lifestyle.
- In adolescence, some young people with LI do not have many friends. Your adolescent may need your support in developing social relationships and engage in social activities like joining a club where other young people go.

---

the professionals working with them. Many parents belong to this association and they make use of the association helpline. Afasic workers who answer the helpline have access to information that form the basis for their advice to those calling. Our implementation plans involve developing, in consultation with parents and Afasic

---

Box 16.5   Parental concerns

1. Is it my fault?
   • Problems that adolescents develop are likely to have their roots earlier in development.
2. I am more worried now that he is an adolescent than I was when s/he was a child.
   • A number of parents are worried about the transition to adulthood for their children.
   • A number of parents are worried about their children's future independence: How will he/she manage when I am not there?

   This is natural.

   You are not alone

---

workers, an information sheet containing the messages, implications for parenting and parental concerns presented above that will form part of Afasic's portfolio.

In 2011, a group of researchers and practitioners established RALLI (Raising Awareness of Language Learning Impairments), a web-based information network (Bishop, Clark, Conti-Ramsden, Norbury, & Snowling, 2012; Conti-Ramsden, Bishop, Clark, Norbury, & Snowling, 2014). Aiming to place accessible materials on the Internet in a form that would attract attention from the general public, in 2012 the group launched a YouTube channel (www.youtube.com/rallicampaign) targeted at three principal audiences: families of children who may have LI, professionals working with children – particularly in education – and young people with LI themselves. The site presents information, illustration and advice, all presented via short video clips with many of the video clips having links to further information that is shared in www.slideshare.net. Most of the materials are in English but, in response to global interest in the theme and the site, additional clips from a range of other languages are now available and more are encouraged.

Young people with LI

When considering adolescents with LI, knowledge exchange involves making sure the young people themselves have access to the information provided by the research in an accessible manner. There is also the opportunity for researchers to hear the voice of the young people themselves and listen to their views.

Our experience of dissemination focuses on those young people who have participated in our national longitudinal study (The Manchester Language Study) for

---

Box 16.6   Key messages for young people with LI

Now that you are growing up:
- A lot of things can change in adolescence.
- In adolescence, some young people become more anxious and depressed. If you are feeling quite low for a period of time, talk to someone about it: a teacher, your parents or your doctor can help.

---

the past 20 years. With this in mind, for the duration of the project we developed a web site for our participants with the help of a company mindful of the types of communication problems our target user group may have. We found the web site received a substantial number of hits per month. We promoted the web site with a number of activities, including sending our participants a free mouse mat with the web site address on it. In this way, they would have easy access to the web site address and also it may be noticed by other people visiting the families participating in the study. The web site provided participants in the study a forum for contact with the research team and a place where they can find out the team's activities, any news, and information about current research projects. Importantly, they could also tell us about themselves and share their views. The web site was also designed to be informative to visitors who have not participated in the study. Prior to the establishment of the web site, we used to send a Christmas newsletter out with information on our latest research findings and any news. We also used the web site to include some of the key messages for young people based on our research findings (Box 16.6).

Unlike the other target user groups, participants in one's study are a readily accessible audience and user group; they represent a clear opportunity. They are individuals who have agreed to be part of the investigation and, in a sense, one already has captured their interest. Extending such information to other young people with similar difficulties who have not participated in the study presents more of a challenge, but in our experience making sure the resource is open to others is one way towards ensuring there is potential access to anyone who may be interested. Another challenge is servicing the web site: updating the information, responding to contact, developing materials all takes time and resources. How long should a web site such as ours be around for? For the duration of a project? A specified number of years after the end of the project? If so, how many? The longitudinal nature of our research meant we did not have to address this question for our web site until recently. At the end of the 20 years of the project, after discussions and consultations, we decided to develop a short, accessible web page that clearly summarized information on the Manchester Language Study and provided key links to information and dissemination of the study findings. This web page link is accessible from the principal investigator's webpage, http://www.psych-sci.manchester.ac.uk/staff/ginaconti-ramsden/.

Some Reflections on Knowledge Exchange in the Field of LI

If you are a reader with little experience of knowledge exchange, you may be asking yourself some fundamental questions: How does one get started? How does one find and make contact with potential user groups/organizations in the field of LI? The Economic and Social Research Council (ESRC) in the United Kingdom defines knowledge exchange as "starting a conversation". As in all good conversations, it is a two-way process. It is about spending time, learning from others as well as sharing experiences and ideas. By establishing more of a dialogue between researchers interested in LI and users of the research, research findings in this field and their implications are more likely to be implemented into practice. The experiences we have discussed suggests that we need to be clear about what is it that we are going to talk about (the message or messages) and who we are going to talk with (the users). To ensure we have a two-way process it is very important and helpful to have potential research users involved from the beginning, preferably as one is developing one's ideas for a project. This allows researchers to get to know the users and vice versa. This fosters a shared vocabulary, an understanding of each others' backgrounds, ideas and concerns. It allows for the development of a relationship, a partnership.

In the field of LI, researchers who are not directly involved in clinical practice or are starting to work in a new area in LI, may find it difficult at first to identify the most appropriate professional group they should be working with or the most appropriate policymaking organization(s) they should be approaching. There will be involvement of users and knowledge exchange activities that will be more successful than others. Evaluation is a key aspect of the process; through evaluation lessons can be learned for the next time. The important thing in the field of LI is to consider engaging with knowledge exchange and developing one's experience. In a relatively young field such as LI this is particularly crucial. Much of the research in LI involves relatively small groups and fact finding, and we are only beginning to develop a critical mass of research findings in certain areas. Disseminating available information is, therefore, very important. At present, public awareness of the disorder is quite limited and it is likely that the process of knowledge exchange will take some time. However, from little acorns big oak trees may grow. Knowledge exchange can make a difference to society and to the lives of children and young people for whom communicating their needs may itself be a challenge.

Summary

Language impairment (LI) is a developmental disorder in which language learning is challenging and protracted without identifiable cause, such as low general intelligence, neurological damage, hearing impairment or autism. Whilst LI used to be thought of as a largely early years disorder, there is now mounting evidence that the language difficulties can persist into adolescence and even adulthood. For about half the children with language difficulties at five years of age, persisting impairment appears to be a reality, and, furthermore, as these individuals develop, the challenges widen to include areas of difficulty that are not directly concerned with language skills. Despite being a relatively common disorder affecting 7% of the population, its status as a childhood disorder means that, unlike acquired adult disorders of language, LI has been under-investigated in terms of outcomes beyond the early years.

In this chapter we have examined a range of outcomes for young people with LI in adolescence. Educational and life prospects for adolescents with LI can be circumscribed. On average, young people with LI have poorer educational attainment than their peers and less opportunities for employment, and when they have such experiences they tend to be in elementary, lower skilled jobs. We present evidence that suggests that although 60% of adolescents with LI experience good quality of friendships, the remainder do not. In the same vein, we have found that a number of adolescents have difficulties developing independence at 16 years and that level of independence is associated with poor early language and poor later literacy skills. Level of independence was also found to influence how concerned parents were about their offspring at this stage of their development. In addition, our findings reveal that although there is a decrease in the experience of bullying during secondary schooling, 13% of young people with LI experience persisting bullying during this period and that bullying experiences are associated with anxiety and depression in adolescence in LI. Overall, adolescents with LI are more likely to have emotional health symptoms, with 40% reporting experiencing anxiety and/or depression in adolescence. Results of this body of work reveal remarkable heterogeneity in the outcomes of young people with LI at 16 years, with some adolescents performing very much like their peers without a history of language difficulties but others exhibiting considerable impairments in one or more of the areas examined. It is important to note, then, that considerable variability is observed in all the areas of functioning discussed here. Negative sequelae are not inevitable and a number of individuals achieve positive outcomes. More research is needed to determine the pathways that lead to these varied outcomes.

Some of the opportunities and challenges we have experienced when engaging with four user groups (professionals–practitioners, policymakers, parents, and the young people with LI themselves) have been presented as well as specific activities that we have carried out. The issues involved in "giving away" research-based knowledge in this area to those involved in practice were also considered. At present, public awareness of LI is quite limited, not least because of the lack of visibility of the disorder: LI is a hidden disability. Children and young people with LI usually appear quite normal, with no outward signs of their difficulty. Furthermore, the study of LI is a relatively young field, thus making the dissemination of available information and engagement with knowledge exchange of particular importance.

Acknowledgments

Writing of this chapter was made possible by the support of the Economic and Social Research Council (grant RES-062-23-2745). The authors also gratefully acknowledge the support of the Nuffield Foundation (grants AT 251 [OD], DIR/28 and EDU 8366) and the Wellcome Trust (grant 060774) which supported the studies reported. Thanks also to the Research Assistants who were involved with data collection and the schools and families who gave their time so generously.

References

APA (2013). *Diagnostic and Statistical Manual of Mental Disorders (DSM-5)*. Arlington, VA: American Psychiatric Association.

Arnett, J. J. (2000). Emerging adulthood. A theory of development from the late teens through the twenties. *American Psychologist, 55*, 469–480.

Bagwell, C. L., & Schmidt, M. E. (2013). *Friendships in childhood and adolescence*. New York, NY: Guilford Press.

Baird, G., Simonoff, E., Pickles, A., Chandler, S., Loucas, T., Meldrum, D., & Charman, T. (2006). Prevalence of disorders of the autism spectrum in a population cohort of children in South Thames: the Special Needs and Autism Project (SNAP). *The Lancet, 368*(9531), 210–215.

Beitchman, J., & Brownlie, E. B. (2013). *Language disorders in children* (Vol. 28). Oxford: Hogrefe Verlag.

Beitchman, E. B., Brownlie, E. B., Inglis, A., Ferguson, B., Schachter, D., Lancee, et al. (1996a). Seven-year follow-up of speech/language impaired and control children: Psychiatric outcome. *Journal of Child Psychology and Psychiatry, 37*, 961–970.

Beitchman, J. H., Brownlie, E. B., & Bao, L. (2014). Age 31 mental health outcomes of childhood language and speech disorders. *Journal of the American Academy of Child & Adolescent Psychiatry, 53*, 1102–1110.

Beitchman, J. H., Wilson, B., Brownlie, E. B., Walters, H., Inglis, A., & Lancee, W. (1996b). Long-term consistency in speech/language profiles: II. Behavioral, emotional and social outcomes. *Journal of the American Academy of Child and Adolescent Psychiatry,* 35, 815–825.

Beitchman, J. H., Wilson, B., Brownlie, E. B., Walters, H., & Lancee, W. (1996c). Long-term consistency in speech/language profiles: Developmental and academic outcomes. *Journal of the American Academy of Child and Adolescent Psychiatry,* 35, 804–814.

Beitchman, J. H., Wilson, B., Johnson, C. J., Atkinson, L., Young, A., Adlaf, E., et al. (2001). Fourteen year follow-up of speech/language impaired and control children: psychiatric outcome. *Journal of the American Academy of Child and Adolescent Psychiatry,* 40, 75–82.

Bercow J. (2008). *The Bercow report: A review of services for children and young people (0–19) with speech, language and communication needs.* Nottingham: DCSF Publications. Retrieved on July 26, 2015 from *http://www.dcsf.gov.uk/slcnaction/downloads/7771-DCSF-BERCOW.PDF*

Bishop, D. V. M. (1998). Development of the Children's Communication Checklist (CCC): A method for assessing qualitative aspects of communicative impairment in children. *Journal of Child Psychology and Psychiatry,* 39, 879–893.

Bishop, D. V. M. (2010). Which neurodevelopmental disorders get researched and why. *PLoS One,* 5(11), e15112.

Bishop, D. V. M. (2013). *Uncommon understanding: Development and disorders of language comprehension in children.* Hove, UK: Psychology Press.

Bishop, D. V. M. (2014). Ten questions about terminology for children with unexplained language problems. *International Journal of Language & Communication Disorders,* 49, 381–415.

Bishop, D. V. M., Clark, B., Conti-Ramsden, G., Norbury, C. F., & Snowling, M. J. (2012). RALLI: An internet campaign for raising awareness of language learning impairments. *Child Language Teaching and Therapy,* 28, 259–262.

Bishop, D. V. M., & Norbury, C. F. (2002). Exploring the borderlands of autistic disorder and specific language impairment: A study using standardised diagnostic instruments. *Journal of Child Psychology and Psychiatry,* 43, 917–930.

Bishop, D. V. M., & Snowling, M. J. (2004). Developmental dyslexia and specific language impairment: Same or different? *Psychological Bulletin,* 130, 858–886.

Botting, N. (2005). Non-verbal cognitive development and language impairment. *Journal of Child Psychology and Psychiatry,* 46, 317–327.

Botting, N., & Conti-Ramsden, G. (2003). Autism, primary pragmatic difficulties and specific language impairment: Can we distinguish them using Psycholinguistic markers? *Developmental Medicine and Child Neurology,* 45, 515–524.

Brownlie, E. B., Beitchman, J. H., Escobar, M., Young, A., Atkinson, L., Johnson, C., et al. (2004). Early language impairment and young adult delinquent and aggressive behavior. *Journal of Child Psychology and Psychiatry,* 32, 453–467.

Buhrmester, D. (1990). Intimacy of friendship, interpersonal competence, and adjustment during preadolescence and adolescence. *Child Development,* 61, 1101–1111.

Buhrmester, D. (1996). Need fulfillment, interpersonal competence and the developmental contexts of early adolescent friendship. In W. M. Bukowski, A. F. Newcomb, & W. W. Hartup (Eds.), *The company they keep: Friendship in childhood and adolescence* (pp. 158–185). New York: Cambridge University Press.

Carroll, C., & Dockrell, J. (2012). Enablers and challenges of post-16 education and employment outcomes: the perspectives of young adults with a history of LI. *International Journal of Language & Communication Disorders, 47*, 567–577.

Clegg, J., Ansorge, L., Stackhouse, J., & Donlan, C. (2012). Developmental communication impairments in adults: Outcomes and life experiences of adults and their parents. *Language, Speech, and Hearing Services in Schools, 43*, 521–535.

Clegg, J., Hollis, C., Mawhood, L., & Rutter, M. (2005). Developmental language disorders – a follow-up in later adult life: Cognitive, language and psychosocial outcomes. *Journal of Child Psychology and Psychiatry, 46*, 128–149.

Cohen, N. J., Barwick, M., Horodezky, N., Vallance, D. D., & Im, N. (1998). Language, achievement, and cognitive processing in psychiatrically disturbed children with previously identified and unsuspected language impairments. *Journal of Child Psychology and Psychiatry, 36*, 865–878.

Cohen, N. J., Farnia, F., & Im-Bolter, N. (2013). Higher order language competence and adolescent mental health. *Journal of Child Psychology and Psychiatry, 54*, 733–744.

Conti-Ramsden, G. (2008). Heterogeneity of specific language impairment (SLI): Outcomes in adolescence. In C. Norbury, B. Tomblin, & D. V. M. Bishop (Eds.), *Understanding developmental language disorders in children: From theory to practice* (pp. 115–129). Hove, UK: Psychology Press.

Conti-Ramsden, G., Bishop, D. V., Clark, B., Norbury, C. F., & Snowling, M. J. (2014). Specific language impairment (SLI): The internet RALLI campaign to raise awareness of LI. *Psychology of Language and Communication, 18*, 143–148.

Conti-Ramsden, G., & Botting, N. (1999). Classification of children with specific language impairment: Longitudinal considerations. *Journal of Speech, Language and Hearing Research, 42*, 1195–1204.

Conti-Ramsden, G., & Botting, N. (2004). Social difficulties and victimization in children with LI at 11 years of age. *Journal of Speech, Language and Hearing Research, 47*, 145–161.

Conti-Ramsden, G., & Botting, N. (2008). Emotional health in adolescents with and without a history of specific language impairment (SLI). *Journal of Child Psychology and Psychiatry, 49*, 516–525.

Conti-Ramsden, G., Botting, N., & Durkin, K. (2008). Parental perspectives during the transition to adulthood in adolescents with a history of specific language impairment (SLI). *Journal of Speech, Language and Hearing Research, 51*, 84–96.

Conti-Ramsden, G., & Durkin, K. (2008). Language and independence in adolescents with and without a history of specific language impairment (SLI). *Journal of Speech, Language and Hearing Research, 51*, 70–83.

Conti-Ramsden, G., & Durkin, K. (2012a). Language development and assessment in the preschool period. *Neuropsychology Review, 22*, 384–401.

Conti-Ramsden, G., & Durkin, K. (2012b). Postschool educational and employment experiences of young people with specific language impairment. *Language, Speech, and Hearing Services in Schools, 43*, 507–520.

Conti-Ramsden, G., Durkin, K., Simkin, Z., & Knox, E. (2009). Specific language impairment and school outcomes. I: Identifying and explaining variability at the end of compulsory education. *International Journal of Language & Communication Disorders, 44*, 15–35.

Conti-Ramsden, G., Mok, P. L., Pickles, A., & Durkin, K. (2013). Adolescents with a history of specific language impairment (SLI): Strengths and difficulties in social, emotional and behavioral functioning. *Research in Developmental Disabilities, 34,* 4161–4169.

Conti-Ramsden, G., St. Clair, M. C., Pickles, A., & Durkin, K. (2012). Developmental trajectories of verbal and nonverbal skills in individuals with a history of specific language impairment: from childhood to adolescence. *Journal of Speech, Language, and Hearing Research,* 55, 1716–1735.

Cowan, R., Donlan, C., Newton, E. J., & Llyod, D. (2005). Number skills and knowledge in children with Specific Language Impairment. *Journal of Educational Psychology,* 97, 732–744.

Dishion, T. J., & Tipsord, J. M. (2011). Peer contagion in child and adolescent social and emotional development. *Annual Review of Psychology,* 62, 189–214.

Dockrell, J., & Lindsay, G. (1998). The ways in which speech and language difficulties impact on children's access to the curriculum. *Child Language Teaching and Therapy,* 14, 117–133.

Dockrell, J., Lindsay, G., Connelly, V., & Mackie, C. (2007a). Constraints in the production of written text in children with specific language impairments. *Exceptional Children,* 73, 147–164.

Dockrell, J., Lindsay, G., Law, J., & Roulstone, S. (2014). Supporting children with speech language and communication needs: an overview of the results of the Better Communication Research Programme. *International Journal of Language and Communication Disorders,* 49(5), 543–557.

Dockrell, J., Palikara, O., Lyndsay, G., & Cullen, M. A. (2007b). *Raising the achievements of children and young people with specific speech and language difficulties and other special educational needs through school to work and college.* London, UK: Department for Education and Skills.

Durkin, K., & Conti-Ramsden, G. (2007). Language, social behaviour, and the quality of friendships in adolescents with and without a history of specific language impairment. *Child Development,* 78, 1441–1457.

Durkin, K., & Conti-Ramsden, G. (2010). Young people with specific language impairment: A review of social and emotional functioning in adolescence. *Child Language Teaching and Therapy,* 26, 105–121.

Durkin, K., Fraser, J., & Conti-Ramsden, G. (2012). School-age prework experiences of young people with a history of specific language impairment. *The Journal of Special Education.* 45, 242–255.

Durkin, K., Mok, P. L., & Conti-Ramsden, G. (2013). Severity of specific language impairment predicts delayed development in number skills. *Frontiers in Psychology,* 4, 581.

Durkin, K., Mok, P. L., & Conti-Ramsden, G. (2015). Core subjects at the end of primary school: Identifying and explaining relative strengths of children with specific language impairment (SLI). *International Journal of Language & Communication Disorders,* 50(2), 226–240.

Durkin, K., Simkin, Z., Knox, E., & Conti-Ramsden, G. (2009). Specific language impairment and school outcomes. II: Educational context, student satisfaction, and post-compulsory progress. *International Journal of Language & Communication Disorders,* 44, 36–55.

Erikson, E. H. (1968). *Identity: Youth and crisis.* New York: Norton.

Everitt, A., Hannaford, P., & Conti-Ramsden, G. (2013). Markers for persistent specific expressive language delay in 3–4-year-olds. *International Journal of Language & Communication Disorders, 48,* 534–553.

Feldman, S. S., & Rosenthal, D. A. (1991). Age expectations of behavioral autonomy in Hong Kong, Australian and American youths: The influence of family variables and adolescent values. *International Journal Psychology, 26,* 1–23

Freud, A. (1958). Adolescence. *Psychoanalytic Study of the Child, 13,* 255–278.

Fujiki, M., Brinton, B., Hart, C. H., & Fitzgerald, A. H. (1999). Peer acceptance and friendship in children with specific language impairment. *Topics in Language Disorders, 19,* 34–48.

Gregory, J., & Bryan, K. (2011). Speech and language therapy intervention with a group of persistent and prolific young offenders in a non-custodial setting with previously undiagnosed speech, language and communication difficulties. *International Journal of Language & Communication Disorders, 46,* 202–215.

Gross, J. (2011). Two years on: Final report of the Communication Champion for children. Retrieved on July 26, 2015 from https://www.thecommunicationtrust.org.uk/media/9683/nwm_final_jean_gross_two_years_on_report.pdf

Hall, P. K., & Tomblin, J. B. (1978). A follow-up study of children with articulation and language disorders. *Journal of Speech and Hearing Disorders, 43,* 227–241.

Hartup, W. W. (1996). The company they keep: Friendships and their developmental significance. *Child Development, 67,* 1–13.

Hartup, W. W., & Stevens, N. (1999). Friendships and adaptation across the lifespan. *Current Directions in Psychological Science, 8,* 76–79.

Helland, W. A., Lundervold, A. J., Heimann, M., & Posserud, M. B. (2014). Stable associations between behavioral problems and language impairments across childhood – The importance of pragmatic language problems. *Research in Developmental Disabilities, 35,* 943–951.

Howlin, P., Mawhood, L., & Rutter, M. (2000). Autism and developmental receptive language disorders – A follow-up comparison in early adult life. II. Social, behavioral and psychiatric outcomes. *Journal of Child Psychology and Psychiatry, 41,* 561–578.

Joffe, V. L., & Black, E. (2012). Social, emotional, and behavioral functioning of secondary school students with low academic and language performance: Perspectives from students, teachers, and parents. *Language, Speech, and Hearing Services in Schools, 43,* 461–473.

Johnson, C. J., Beitchman, J. H., & Brownlie, E. B. (2010). Twenty-year follow-up of children with and without speech-language impairments: Family, educational, occupational, and quality of life outcomes. *American Journal of Speech-Language Pathology, 19,* 51–65.

Kingery, J. N., Erdley, C. A., & Marshall, K. C. (2011). Peer acceptance and friendship as predictors of early adolescents' adjustment across the middle school transition. *Merrill-Palmer Quarterly, 57,* 215–243.

Knox, E., & Conti-Ramsden, G. (2007). Bullying in young people with a history of specific language impairment (SLI). *Educational and Child Psychology, 24,* 130–141.

Labrell, F., van Geert, P., Declercq, C., Baltazart, V., Caillies, S., Olivier, M., & Le Sourn-Bissaoui, S. (2014). Speaking volumes: A longitudinal study of lexical and grammatical growth between 17 and 42 months. *First Language, 34,* 97–124.

Ladd, G. W., Kochenderfer, B. J., & Coleman, C. C. (1996). Friendship quality as a predictor of young children's early school adjustment. *Child Development, 67,* 1103–1118.

Leonard, L. B. (1987). Is specific language impairment a useful construct? In S. Rosenberg (Ed.), *Advances in applied psycholinguistics, 1, Disorders of first-language development* (pp. 1–39). New York: Cambridge University Press.

Leonard, L. B. (1991). Specific language impairment as a clinical category. *Language, Speech, and Hearing Services in Schools, 22,* 66–68.

Leonard, L. B. (2014). *Children with specific language impairment.* Cambridge, Massachusetts: The MIT Press.

Lindsay, G., & Dockrell, J. E. (2012). Longitudinal patterns of behavioral, emotional, and social difficulties and self-concepts in adolescents with a history of specific language impairment. *Language, Speech, and Hearing Services in Schools, 43*(4), 445–460.

Lindsay, G., & Dockrell, J. (2014). Evidence based policy and practice: The Better Communication Research Programme. *Journal of Research in Special Educational Needs, 14,* 210–214.

McCartney, E., & Ellis, S. (2013). The linguistically aware teacher and the teacher-aware linguist. *Clinical Linguistics & Phonetics, 27*(6–7), 419–427.

McGregor, K. K., Oleson, J., Bahnsen, A., & Duff, D. (2013). Children with developmental language impairment have vocabulary deficits characterized by limited breadth and depth. *International Journal of Language & Communication Disorders, 48,* 307–319.

McKinley, N., & Larson, V. L. (1989). Students who can't communicate: Speech-language service at the secondary level. *Curriculum Report, 19,* 1–8.

Miller, J. L., & Lossia, A. K. (2013). Prelinguistic infants' communicative system: Role of caregiver social feedback. *First Language, 33,* 524–544.

Mok, P. L., Pickles, A., Durkin, K., & Conti-Ramsden, G. (2014). Longitudinal trajectories of peer relations in children with specific language impairment. *Journal of Child Psychology and Psychiatry, 55,* 516–527.

Mundt, M. P., & Zakletskaia, L. I. (2014). That's what friends are for: Adolescent peer social status, health-related quality of life and healthcare costs. *Applied Health Economics and Health Policy, 12,* 191–201.

Myers, L., Davies-Jones, C., Chiat, S., Joffe, V., & Botting, N. (2011). 'A place where I can be me': A role for social and leisure provision to support young people with language impairment. *International Journal of Language & Communication Disorders, 46,* 739–750.

Nippold, M. A., Mansfield, T. C., Billow, J. L., & Tomblin, J. B. (2009). Syntactic development in adolescents with a history of language impairments: A follow-up investigation. *American Journal of Speech-Language Pathology, 18,* 241–251.

Nippold, M. A., & Schwarz, I. E. (2002). Do children recover from specific language impairment? *International Journal of Speech-Language Pathology, 4,* 41–49.

Noom, M. J., Deković, M., & Meeus, W. (2001). Conceptual analysis and measurement of adolescent autonomy. *Journal of Youth and Adolescence, 30,* 577–595.

Norbury, C. F. (2014). Practitioner review: Social (pragmatic) communication disorder conceptualization, evidence and clinical implications. *Journal of Child Psychology and Psychiatry,* 55, 204–216.

Olson, J., & Masur, E. F. (2013). Mothers respond differently to infants' gestural versus nongestural communicative bids. *First Language,* 33, 372–387.

Parker, J. G., & Gottman, J. M. (1989). Social and emotional development in a relational context: Friendship interaction from early childhood to adolescence. In T. J. Berndt & G. W. Ladd (Eds.), *Peer relationships in child development* (pp. 95–131). New York: John Wiley & Sons, Inc.

Pepler, D. J., Craig, W. M., Connolly, J. A., Yuile, A., McMaster, L., & Jiang, D. (2006). A developmental perspective on bullying. *Aggressive Behaviour,* 32, 376–384.

Rapin, I. (1996). Developmental language disorders: A clinical update. *Journal of Child Psychology and Psychiatry,* 37, 643–656.

Reilly, S., Tomblin, B., Law, J., McKean, C., Mensah, F. K., Morgan, A., et al. (2014). Specific language impairment: a convenient label for whom? *International Journal of Language & Communication Disorders,* 49, 416–451.

Rescorla, L. (2005). Age 13 language and reading outcomes in late-talking toddlers. *Journal of Speech, Language, and Hearing Research,* 48, 459–472.

Schoon, I., Parsons, S., Rush, R., & Law, J. (2010). Children's language ability and psycho-social development: a 29-year follow-up study. *Pediatrics,* 126(1), e73–e80.

Shulman, S. (1993). Close relationships and coping behavior in adolescence. *Journal of Adolescence,* 16, 267–283.

Simkin, Z., & Conti-Ramsden, G. (2006). Evidence of reading difficulties in Subgroups of children with specific language impairment. *Child Language Teaching and Therapy,* 22, 315–331.

Snow, P. C., Powell, M. B., & Sanger, D. D. (2012). Oral language competence, young speakers, and the law. *Language, Speech, and Hearing Services in Schools,* 43(4), 496–506.

Snow, P. C., & Sanger, D. D. (2011). Restorative justice conferencing and the youth offender: Exploring the role of oral language competence. *International Journal of Language & Communication Disorders,* 46, 324–333.

Snowling, M. J., Adams, J. W., Bishop, D. V. M., & Stothard, S. E., (2001). Educational attainments of school leavers with a preschool history of speech-language impairments. *International Journal of Language and Communication Disorders,* 36, 173–183.

Snowling, M. J., & Hulme, C. (2012). Interventions for children's language and literacy difficulties. *International Journal of Language & Communication Disorders,* 47, 27–34.

St. Clair, M. C., Pickles, A., Durkin, K., & Conti-Ramsden, G. (2011). A longitudinal study of behavioral, emotional and social difficulties in individuals with a history of specific language impairment (SLI). *Journal of Communication Disorders,* 44, 186–199.

Starling, J., Munro, N., Togher, L., & Arciuli, J. (2012). Training secondary school teachers in instructional language modification techniques to support adolescents with language impairment: A randomized controlled trial. *Language, Speech, and Hearing Services in Schools,* 43, 474–495.

Steinberg, L., & Morris, A. S. (2001). Adolescent development. *Annual Review of Psychology,* 52, 83–110.

Steinberg, L., & Silverberg, S. B. (1986). The vicissitudes of autonomy in early adolescence. *Child Development,* 57, 841–851.

Stothard, S. E., Snowling, M. J., Bishop, D. V. M., Chipchase, B. B., & Kaplan, C. (1998). Language impaired preschoolers: A follow-up into adolescence. *Journal of Speech and Hearing Research,* 41, 407–418.

Stuart, N. J., & van der Lely, H. (2015). Role of aspect in understanding tense: An investigation with adolescents with LI. *International Journal of Language & Communication Disorders,* 50(2), 187–201.

Sumter, S. R., Baumgartner, S. E., Valkenburg, P. M., & Peter, J. (2012). Developmental trajectories of peer victimization: Off-line and online experiences during adolescence. *Journal of Adolescent Health,* 50, 607–613.

Tomblin, J. B., Records, N. L., Buckwalter, P., Zhang, X., Smith, E., & O'Brien, M. (1997). Prevalence of specific language impairment in kindergarten children. *Journal of Speech, Language and Hearing Research,* 40, 1245–1260.

Toppelberg, C. O., & Shapiro, T. (2000). Language disorders: A 10-year research update review. *Journal of the American Academy of Child and Adolescent Psychiatry,* 39, 143–152.

Tuller, L., Henry, C., Sizaret, E., & Barthez, M. A. (2012). Specific language impairment at adolescence: Avoiding complexity. *Applied Psycholinguistics,* 33, 161–184.

Ukoumunne, O. C., Wake, M., Carlin, J., Bavin, E. L., Lum, J., Skeat, J., et al. (2012). Profiles of language development in pre-school children: a longitudinal latent class analysis of data from the Early Language in Victoria Study. *Child: Care, Health and Development,* 38, 341–349.

Van Petegem, S., Beyers, W., Vansteenkiste, M., & Soenens, B. (2012). On the association between adolescent autonomy and psychosocial functioning: Examining decisional independence from a self-determination theory perspective. *Developmental Psychology,* 48, 76–88.

Wadman, R., Botting, N., Durkin, K., & Conti-Ramsden, G. (2011a). Changes in emotional health symptoms in adolescents with specific language impairment. *International Journal of Language & Communication Disorders,* 46, 641–656.

Wadman, R., Durkin, K., & Conti-Ramsden, G. (2011b). Close relationships in adolescents with and without a history of specific language impairment. *Language, Speech, and Hearing Services in Schools,* 42, 41–51.

Wehberg, S., Vach, W., Bleses, D., Thomsen, P., Madsen, T. O., & Basbøll, H. (2007). Danish children's first words: Analysing longitudinal data based on monthly CDI parental reports. *First Language,* 27, 361–383.

Wu, Z., & Gros-Louis, J. (2014). Infants' prelinguistic communicative acts and maternal responses: Relations to linguistic development. *First Language,* 34, 72–90.

Yew, S. G. K., & O'Kearney, R. (2013). Emotional and behavioural outcomes later in childhood and adolescence for children with specific language impairments: meta-analyses of controlled prospective studies. *Journal of Child Psychology and Psychiatry,* 54, 516–524.

Zimmer-Gembeck, M. J., & Collins, W. A. (2003). Autonomy development during adolescence. In G. R. Adams & M. Berzonsky (Eds.), *Blackwell Handbook of Adolescence,* (pp. 175–204). Oxford: Blackwell Publishers.

17

Translating Models of Adolescent Problem Behavior into Effective Intervention: Trials, Tribulations and Future Directions

Thomas J. Dishion and Miwa Yasui

Explaining and Preventing Antisocial Behavior: Historical Perspective

In this chapter we provide a historical overview of a program of research designed, first, to test empirically developmental models of antisocial behavior and, second, to use these models to design and test innovative prevention strategies. The central assumption underlying this "model building" approach is that this research strategy is optimal for translating developmental science to achieve improved intervention strategies for children and families that improve mental health and social adjustment. There is one critical condition, however, that promotes the success of the model building strategy that is deceptively simple: That empirical models systematically and consistently acknowledge and respond to scientific findings, both successes and failures (Dishion & Patterson, 1999).

The program of research described in this chapter was initiated by Jerry Patterson, the founder of the Oregon Social Learning Center (OSLC), and continues on

The Wiley Handbook of Developmental Psychology in Practice: Implementation and Impact, First Edition.
Edited by Kevin Durkin and H. Rudolph Schaffer.
© 2016 John Wiley & Sons, Ltd. Published 2016 by John Wiley & Sons, Ltd.

today in the venue of differentiated research programs of several psychologists who were trained at OSLC and are working in applied psychology (Bank, Capaldi, Chamberlain, Dishion, Eddy, Fisher, Forgatch, Reid, Snyder, Stoolmiller). Original research on the operant underpinnings of aggressive behavior (Patterson, 1973; Patterson, Littman, & Bricker, 1967; Patterson & Reid, 1970) is now translated into empirically supported prevention programs for antisocial behavior, drug use, treatment foster care, and empirically supported treatment programs for national healthcare systems.

There are several concepts required to appreciate the model building approach to applied psychology. The first is the concept of a "construct", which is the translation of a psychological concept into a quantitative measurement with known scientific properties of validity and reliability (Cronbach & Meehl, 1955). The second is the concept of a model, which is a quantitative statement of a network of hypotheses regarding the direct and indirect causal linkages among constructs in the explanation of a behavior of interest, for example, problem behavior. Third is the concept of model fit, which refers to the extent that a complex, multivariate model "fits" the observed pattern of covariation among constructs within a collected data set. Given that modeling building is approached pragmatically, one end game outcome from which one can judge a multivariate model is the extent the model informs the design of interventions that are effective, efficient, less expensive and ethical.

As shown in Figure 17.1, we see building translational models as an iterative dynamic process, where successes and failures in measurement and modeling testing refine the next stage in the model building effort. Note that the end goal of the

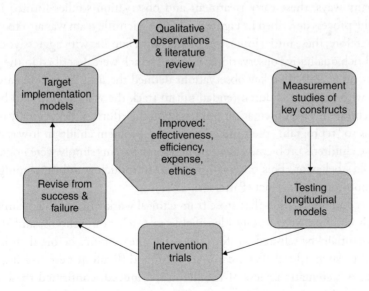

Figure 17.1   A model building strategy for translational research for children and families.

model building process is the design of empirically supported interventions that this program of research improve real-world effectiveness (can be delivered in the real world), improve efficiency, and reduce expense. It is also crucial that any interventions are conducted ethically and with full sensitivity to the needs and responsivity of children and families. We will discuss each of these issues as they apply to our program of research on adolescent problem behavior.

In the 1970s, the senior author joined a group of investigators at the Oregon Social Learning Center interested in modifying the behavior of aggressive children by virtue of the analysis of social interaction between parents and children, and by systematically altering those action reaction patterns in behavior modification interventions. The analysis of social interaction patterns revealed a process of coercion, which is predicated on escape conditioning: children's escalation in problem behavior "turns off" parents efforts to socialize, and, therefore, the parent "learns" to give up and the child learns to escalate (Patterson, 1973, 1974a, 1976, 1977; Patterson & Cobb, 1971, 1973; Patterson & Dawes, 1975; Patterson & Reid, 1970). These "functional" analyses of clinically referred children were consonant with a simultaneous trend for interventions that increased parent positive reinforcement and improved limit setting skills to reduce aggressive behavior in children (Forgatch & Toobert, 1979; Patterson, 1974b; Patterson & Fleischman, 1979; Patterson & Reid, 1973; Patterson, Reid, Jones, & Conger, 1975). The findings of this substantial body of research confirmed that the promise of linking etiological research with the design of treatment programs was successful. However, a larger question emerged in the group, and that was: To what extent could problem behavior in children and adolescents be prevented?

In many ways, these early treatment and observation studies formed the first step in the process described in Figure 17.1. The scientific team was also the clinical team; therefore, these initial intensive contacts with families with aggressive children afforded rich qualitative observations, many of which were described in the volume by Patterson (1982). Two key observations defined the next stage of research: that families with problem children tended not to track the whereabouts and behavior of their children. This observation was based on the efforts of behaviorally oriented clinicians to "reprogram" their interactions with problem children. It was difficult to change children's problem behavior when some parents simply were not aware of their child's behavior. This observation led to introducing and developing of the parent monitoring construct (Patterson, 1982).

The second observation that arose from clinical work with troubled families was that such children were readily identifiable to teachers in schools, and therefore could potentially be selected out for preventive interventions before their behavior escalated to such a level that treatment became difficult at best and impossible at worse. A systematic review of the literature, indeed, confirmed these clinical observations, in that one of the best predictors of adolescent delinquency was poor parenting in general and the lack of supervision in particular. The literature had also established that problem behavior in the primary school years was the second best predictor of adolescent delinquency (Loeber & Dishion, 1983).

At this point, we set out to develop measurement protocols and to test them to determine the validity of the measures on a sample of 4th, 7th and 10th grade boys. This pilot study resulted in the validation of the parent monitoring construct (Dishion & Loeber, 1985; Patterson & Stouthamer-Loeber, 1984) as well as the validity of parenting constructs for identifying problem behavior in males (Loeber & Dishion, 1984; Patterson & Dishion, 1985; Patterson, Dishion, & Bank, 1984; Snyder, Dishion, & Patterson, 1986). During the pilot study, we happened upon another key construct that had been underexamined in the treatment studies, the importance of the deviant peer group (Dishion & Loeber, 1985; Patterson & Dishion, 1985). Finally, we tested a version of a multiple gating strategy for identifying youth most at risk to become delinquent. In essence, this applied multistage assessment protocols to define teacher ratings, parent report and family assessment as the first, second and third stage screens for identifying youth most likely to become delinquent (Dishion & Patterson, 1993; Loeber & Dishion, 1987; Loeber, Dishion, & Patterson, 1984).

The success of the pilot study led to the formulation of a longitudinal study of 206 boys residing in high risk Oregon neighborhoods, referred to as the Oregon Youth Study (OYS) (Capaldi & Patterson, 1987; Patterson, Reid & Dishion, 1992). From these studies we tested a variety of longitudinal models revealing that a construct of family management, which included parental monitoring, accounted for unique variance in child and adolescent problem behavior (Capaldi, 1992; Capaldi & Patterson, 1987; Dishion, Capaldi, Spracklen, & Li, 1995; Patterson, 1986; Patterson, Reid, & Dishion, 1992). The central idea of the emerging model of antisocial behavior was that family management in general, and parent monitoring in particular, mediated the relation between the child's ecology and the child's behavior, as shown in Figure 17.2. Although deviant peer involvement was considered a proximal predictor of problem behavior, it was thought of as largely an outcome of poor parental monitoring.

It is important to point out that advances in multivariate statistics influenced our thinking about model building. The timely publication of a book on structural equation modeling help bring this hitherto esoteric technique to the forefront for applied developmental researchers who shared interests in measurement, longitudinal data analysis and intervention trials (Dwyer, 1983). This basic statistics text articulated an approach that permitted the testing of competing measurement models, structural longitudinal models, and proposed that interventions could be incorporated into model testing. Finally, the link between the assessment of measurement validity using multiple indicators (Campbell & Fiske, 1959) and model testing was finally made clear and practical tests were provided for this purpose.

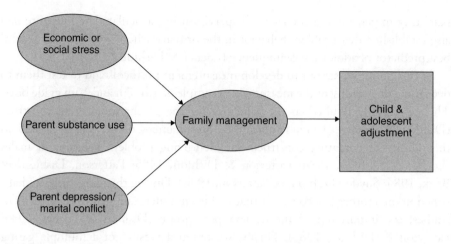

Figure 17.2   Family management as a mediator of contextual influences.

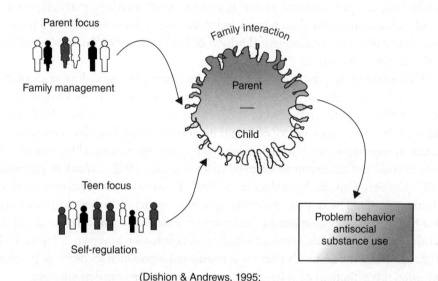

(Dishion & Andrews, 1995;
Dishion, McCord, & Poulin, 1999; Poulin et al,, 2001)

Figure 17.3   The Adolescent Transitions Program pilot study.

In the late 1980s we embarked on our first effort to apply the model for the development of adolescent problem behavior to prevent the emergence of substance use among high-risk adolescents (Dishion, Reid, & Patterson, 1988). This NIDA-funded study tested two model-driven intervention paradigms to formulate the core components of what has been called the Adolescent Transitions Program. As shown in Figure 17.3, the basic idea was simple. We would randomly assign high-risk youth to a combination of two interventions: one emphasizing family management skills and the second emphasizing the support of adolescent self-regulation, which is defined as the ability to control attention, initiate and inhibit behavior according to the environmental context (Rothbart & Rueda, 2005). In making the shift from treatment to prevention, we improved the efficiency of the intervention program by delivering both intervention components in groups. Thus, we randomly assigned 120 youth to: (i) family management only; (ii) self-regulation only; (iii) both, and; (iv) self-directed change (receiving intervention materials only). Later, we added a group of 39 youth as quasi-experimental controls that received no intervention but were assessed at equivalent points. Adolescents and families were selected as high risk based on parent report. We followed the young people from age 12 to 15 to evaluate whether we were successful in preventing the emergence of drug use and other problem behavior.

We experienced success and failure in this initial field experiment. The success was that the family management component clearly led to reductions in problem behavior at home and school, reduced early onset of substance use and improved family interaction (Dishion & Andrews, 1995; Dishion, Andrews, Soberman, & Kavanagh, 1996). Moreover, for the first time, we were able to document that changes in observed parent–adolescent conflict mediated reductions in antisocial behavior at school (Dishion, Patterson, & Kavanagh, 1992).

Unfortunately, the failures were more salient. Much to our chagrin, we found quite early in our follow-up assessments, that adolescents assigned randomly to the self-regulation groups *increased* smoking (Dishion & Andrews, 1995). Unfortunately, this trend only worsened over time, in that smoking and school reports of delinquent behavior increased up to three years following the intervention! Our small working group was quite alarmed by these initial findings, but began to converge on an explanation. We hypothesized that it was the problem of aggregating high-risk peers to the intervention that was responsible for the increase. Collaboration with Dr Joan McCord, and the reanalysis of the Cambridge Somerville youth study provided even more compelling evidence that aggregating youth may, indeed, be iatrogenic (Dishion, McCord, & Poulin, 1999; Poulin, Dishion, & Burraston, 2001). Videotaping our intervention groups turned out to be critical for linking the implementation of the model to the negative outcomes, confirming that "deviancy training" interactions with peers in the group led to increases in problem behavior (Dishion, Poulin, & Burraston, 2001; Dishion & Tipsord, 2011). Although the finding of iatrogenic effects for aggregation of high-risk youth was troubling, reporting these findings led to a series of studies that were both confirmatory (Feldman, Stiffman, Evans, & Orme, 1982; Palinkas, Atkins, Miller, & Fereira, 1996) as well as validating that deviant peer influences need to be taken quite seriously in the design of universal, selected and indicated interventions (Dishion & Dodge, 2005; Dodge, Dishion, & Lansford, 2006).

There was one other annoying outcome of the first prevention trial of our model of problem behavior. We found that indicators for the parent-monitoring construct (self, parent and staff impressions) did not change in the same direction. Where some indicators now showed change, others revealed opposite trends that were statistically unreliable. These findings led us to formulate a concept that has since proved quite useful; that we needed to develop measurements that were sensitive to change (Eddy, Dishion, & Stoolmiller, 1998).

Building on the successes of the first component analysis of the Adolescent Transitions Program (ATP), we dropped the self-regulation intervention component as delivered in groups and focused on the parenting intervention. Our next step was to take the intervention from a community center and implement it into schools. To do this, we needed to make several revisions in our implementation model. First, we needed to create a context for the parent intervention in the public school organizational environment that, traditionally, did not intervene with parents, at least not systematically. Second, we needed to make our parent intervention more efficient, so that parent groups were not the only format in which we delivered family management material. Third, we needed a strategy to proactively identify youth "selected" for a family intervention. Fourth, we wanted to create an adaptive and tailored approach to family intervention in the school context, to render the intervention more efficient, providing the level and kind of intervention optimal for each family (Dishion, Kavanagh, & Kiesner, 1998). These three considerations led to the formulation of the ATP in its current form, which is described in detail below. We now refer to our intervention strategy as an ecological approach to family intervention and treatment, or EcoFIT.

It is noteworthy that we relabeled our intervention approach after stepping back and observing where our research had led us: through success and failure, we found that for prevention to be effective, it was critical to design interventions that are integrated into the children's and families' ecology, and are mindful of important contextual factors such as aggregating high risk peers. Thus, we deemed the EcoFIT model would render our intervention model as more effective, efficient and less expensive in the effort to both prevent and treat problem behavior in children and adolescents (Dishion & Stormshak, 2007).

EcoFIT Model

To implement family-centered interventions in the public school setting, it is necessary to embed intervention activities within the host environment. Leaders in public schools can take a variety of steps to facilitate home–school collaboration.

The first and most pragmatic steps are to create a physical space that is appropriate for meetings with families and parents. The second is to agree to use the parent consultant as an ally when responding to problem behavior and emotional difficulties of individual students, so that parents can be recruited early to effectively remediate the problem. Third, a less tangible but nonetheless important step is for the principal and vice-principal to acknowledge daily that collaborating with and supporting families is central to the education of students. Our investigations led us to the conclusion that it is important for staff at every school to ask themselves: What are three changes we could make to increase involvement of parents?

The Family Resource Center

The first step for establishing family-based services in a school setting is to create a family resource center (FRC). FRC goals are to (i) establish an infrastructure for collaboration between school staff and parents, (ii) promote norms and strategies for empirically validated family management practices, and (iii) provide a vehicle through which a program of specific family-centered interventions can be implemented and coordinated with educational services in the school. Some examples are the family check-up (FCU; discussed later), parent management training, and follow-up academic monitoring services to parents.

It is critical for the FRC to have a parent consultant who is trained and knowledgeable in working therapeutically with parents. The parent consultant will have a central role in the process of "giving away" the fruits of theoretically-driven research and clinical experience, as well as monitoring obstacles and feeding back his or her experiences of the practicalities of implementation. It is critical that school staff (teachers, administrators, supportive staff) view this person as an ally when they are responding to problem behavior and emotional difficulties of individual students, so that parents can be recruited early to effectively remediate the problem. Changing one's parenting practices can be a difficult and emotional journey that requires the skillful intervention of professionals who know how to use effective interventions as well as work with resistance to change (Patterson & Forgatch, 1985). A variety of strategies can be used to engage caregivers at various stages in the continuum of risk, all of which serve to establish rapport and collaboration in the best interest of the student (Henggeler, Schoenwald, Borduin, Rowland, & Cunningham, 1998; Szapocznik & Kurtines, 1989). The key strategies are discussed below.

Home visits. If you want to work effectively with parents, you must visit them in their own home (Szapocznik & Kurtines, 1989). We have repeatedly found that initial engagement of parents into either parent groups or the FCU requires that the parent first meets the parent consultant. We found that about 20% of the parents who initially agreed to participate in groups actually attended the group meeting. Among a new group of parents, however, a brief home visit pushed the attendance rate to more than 75%. Similarly, when we initially offered the FCU in a public school environment, we had relatively low engagement. However, conducting a brief home visit at the end of the summer, before the school year began, substantially increased the use of the FRC and the FCU.

An important component to consider when implementing school interventions is how to effectively identify the families needing support. Thus, we designed a cost-effective screening strategy for proactively identifying students most in need of additional support in the public school environment. The approach is called the *multiple gating strategy* (Dishion & Patterson, 1993; Loeber & Dishion, 1987; Loeber, Dishion, & Patterson, 1984). The key concept is that decisions regarding children's level of risk are largely based on systematically collected data and less on day-to-day reactions of school staff to students' behavior. This approach has been adopted and found to be quite feasible in public schools (Feil, Walker, & Severson, 1995).

In general, we found that comprehensive teacher ratings of behavioral risk can be an inexpensive way to identify families who need interventions and who are likely to engage. Paradoxically, when analyzing the long-term results of our intervention program, we found that the families at highest risk were the most likely to engage in the intervention, and also the most likely to benefit. That is, six years later, compared with their randomly assigned controls, families with children at high risk who were proactively identified and who engaged in the intervention were least likely to increase drug use or be arrested by the police (Connell, Dishion, Yasui, & Kavanagh, 2007).

The family check-up. Selected interventions are designed for those youth who are identified as at high risk for an emergent health problem. The family check-up (FCU) is a selected intervention offering family assessment, professional support, and motivation to change. As described by Dishion and Kavanagh (2003), the FCU's in-depth method supports parents' accurate appraisal of their child's risk status and leads to a range of empirically supported interventions. This brief family intervention has been effective for reducing risk factors and promoting adjustment, and is feasible to implement in a public school setting. An overview of the EcoFIT model linking the FCU with a set of interventions is summarized in Figure 17.4.

The FCU, which is based on motivational interviewing (Miller & Rollnick, 2002), is a three-session intervention that consists of (i) an initial interview, (ii) a comprehensive multiagent, multimethod assessment, and (iii) a family feedback session. The treatment uses motivational techniques to encourage maintenance of current positive practices and change of disruptive practices.

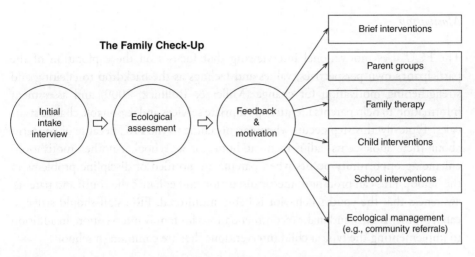

The Family Check-Up

Initial intake interview ⇨ Ecological assessment ⇨ Feedback & motivation

- Brief interventions
- Parent groups
- Family therapy
- Child interventions
- School interventions
- Ecological management (e.g., community referrals)

Figure 17.4   An overview of the EcoFIT Strategy (Dishion & Stormshak, 2007).

The strength of EcoFIT in general, and the FCU in particular, is the formal integration of diverse perspectives in developing motivation to change. Often, outpatient clinics use unstructured interviews and questionnaires and rely almost exclusively on parent report to guide their judgment about diagnosis and treatment. In contrast, we integrate multiple perspectives and assessment strategies. Specifically, we obtain structured reports from parents, teachers, and the child and then compare the reports using normative standards. In addition, we directly observe family interactions. These diverse data sources provide the parent consultant with a "family-centered perspective"; that is, one that is inclusive but not overly reliant on any one reporting agent.

Feedback

Data are a critical feature of motivational interviewing and change. Not only are data useful for helping parents reconsider "issues" (e.g., aggressiveness) as serious problems that need attention and change, but data also guide the tailoring of the intervention to fit the school setting and individual family. Thus, a fundamental step of the feedback journey is sharing data with the parent; especially useful are data that come from other sources, such as teachers and direct observation. Over the years, innovative family intervention researchers have suggested that providing feedback to parents from the findings of psychological assessments is conducive to change (Sanders & Lawton, 1993; Sanders & Calam, Chapter 5, this volume). The critical feature of such feedback is that it be presented in a supportive and motivating manner.

Motivation

The FCU uses motivational interviewing that focuses on the exploration of the participant's own perspectives, values and feelings as the backdrop to eliciting and strengthening motivation for change (Miller & Rollnick, 2009) and assessment information to help parents identify appropriate services and reasonable change strategies. Typically, this step occurs when parents come to the FRC because of concerns about their adolescents' adjustment at home or at school. Another motivation-enhancing opportunity occurs when parents are notified of discipline problems in the school. This can prompt domestic discussion and enhance the youth and parents' awareness that the youth's behavior is being monitored. FRC staff should strive to catch problems early and make recommendations for family intervention, in addition to implementing the typical child interventions that are common in schools.

Intervention menu

The EcoFIT approach is a tailored, adaptive intervention strategy (Collins, Murphy, & Bierman, 2004) in that the interventions that follow the FCU are tailored to the assessed and expressed needs of the family. Unlike most parenting programs that have a set agenda (albeit a flexible delivery format), our approach allows a focus on only one aspect of parenting. For example, a parent who is aware of his/her student's performance and knows only to criticize failures would benefit tremendously from a tailored intervention about positive reinforcement. The FCU would have identified this need, as well as parenting strengths, and the motivational interviewing would be targeted to encourage the caregiver in the process of providing positive reinforcement.

The presumption underlying the menu of family intervention services is that a variety of family-centered interventions can be equally effective for reducing problem behavior (Webster-Stratton, 1984; Webster-Stratton, Kolpacoff, & Hollingsworth, 1988). The indicated intervention menu typically includes three levels of intervention sessions (Dishion & Stormshak, 2007). The first level provides motivation, support, and problem solving of relatively minor problems and adjustment issues. Following the FCU, many parents request only follow-up telephone calls from the parent consultant often referred to as *check-ins*. We use the hierarchy of strategies shown in Figure 17.5 for managing these brief intervention sessions.

A recent but atypical drop in grades, a discipline problem at school, or recent problem behavior that is relatively isolated would most likely be handled using this brief intervention. On the basis of the strengths and weaknesses profile, a parent consultant may strategically collaborate with parents about how best to handle

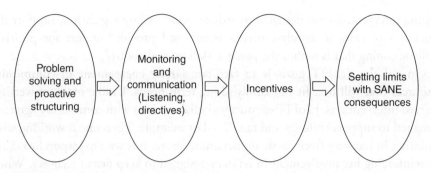

Figure 17.5 The hierarchy of strategies for brief family intervention.

these difficulties. For example, in a recently divorced family the adolescent daughter's grades have dropped. She reports normal class attendance, but a recent report card reveals many absences. The parent consultant may establish an e-mail connection with the parents regarding attendance, so that one of the parents can monitor attendance on a daily basis and compare the daughter's report with that of the teachers. The monitoring system may itself alleviate the problem. It may also reveal more serious concerns, such as drug use, lying, and problems with peers, that require more intensive interventions, including limit setting and more pervasive monitoring in and out of school.

The second type of indicated intervention is what we refer to as *skill-building interventions.* They involve actively working with parents to improve their family management skills and closely follow the principles of parental management training (Forgatch, Patterson, & DeGarmo, 2005). The skills include positive reinforcement, setting limits, monitoring, problem solving, and communication. We conduct these sessions either individually with parents, such as in behavioral family therapy, or we may work with parents in groups. In either venue, the Family Management Curriculum, derived from more than 30 years of research at the Oregon Social Learning Center, serves as the manual for these interventions (Dishion, Kavanagh, et al., 2003).

Families at high risk are often contending with severe stressors that disrupt parents' emotional regulation and attention (Dishion et al., 2008). On occasion, these stressors may be chronic and nascent and do not emerge until a parent consultant has established rapport and a working relationship with a family. For example, sexual abuse, an ongoing affair, or domestic violence may be kept quiet by a parent until he/she feels a connection to a professional with whom such an issue can be shared and addressed. Thus, the family goes into crisis as a function of engagement, not as a cause.

Working with multiproblem families is often challenging with respect to addressing severe life stressors, potential abuse, and family disruption, such as divorce and remarriage, which can create a volatile, emotionally dysregulated atmosphere that is not conducive to caregiver positive behavior support. Family adaptation and coping interventions are designed to reduce emotional dysregulation, support the parents' attention on family-centered issues, and provide support for positive, realistic coping that is within the parents' skill set and control.

One of the EcoFIT goals is to facilitate family engagement in community resources that will best fit the family's long-term needs. Unlike many university-derived interventions, EcoFIT encourages collaborations with community agencies designed to support children and families. For example, when one is working with a mother in recovery from methamphetamine abuse, it is wise to respond to crises by reinforcing her involvement in services designed to keep her in recovery. When a breech in services occurs, the parent consultant can support the caregiver in taking steps to reengage in services.

There are a variety of barriers to effective parenting; some are historical (e.g., past abuse and trauma), some are contextual (poverty, low resources in communities), and others are chronic individual difficulties (e.g., long-term disabilities, health problems). In these circumstances, a key role of the parent consultant is to support caregivers in the course of coping, problem solving, and making efforts to reduce harm to the youth. At times, this requires guiding the caregiver into services that are more appropriate for recovery or safety. Thus, one key function of the parent consultant during the FCU and beyond is to provide a parent with the insight and motivation to seek realistic levels of support to make family changes and to adapt to the stressor.

Outcomes

Specific tests of the EcoFIT approach to engaging parents within the context of school are relatively rare. During the past 10 years, we have been engaged in a randomized prevention trial in which half of the sixth-grade population of metropolitan middle schools was randomly assigned at the individual level to the FRC versus public middle school as usual. Parent consultants were each assigned to a school where they attempted to engage parents of youth who were identified as at risk by teachers. Services were provided primarily in the seventh and eighth grades of middle school.

Engagement   We actively engaged 25% of the families in the FCU during the two years of service, across the three schools. We had contact with an additional 25% of the families, but did not conduct an FCU with them. By and large, we found that the families at highest risk were the most likely to participate in the FCU. Connell, Dishion, and Deater-Deckard (2006) found that single-parent families, those with students involved in a deviant peer group, and those rated by teachers as at high risk were the most likely to engage in the FCU.

During the course of the two years, there was an average of six hours of parent consultant contact among the families at highest risk. As one would expect, the contact time decreased as a function of the student's risk level. Students at moderate risk engaged in approximately 3.5 hours of contact. The families at low risk had on average less than one hour of contact. Contact included telephone calls as well as personal contact and was recorded by the parent consultants by the minute (Dishion, Kavanagh, Schneiger, Nelson, & Kaufman, 2002).

We conducted an effectiveness trial of the EcoFIT model in another set of four public middle schools. In this study we also carefully counted the minutes of contact with parents of students. Parent consultants were creative in engaging parents. In one middle school, the parent consultant established a coffee cart for parents and would meet parents as they dropped off their middle school child and picked up coffee. In this study, we found that simply the number of parent contacts in Grades 6, 7, and 8 was associated with reductions in growth in teacher ratings of risk (Stormshak, Dishion, Light, & Yasui, 2005).

Several reports have been published about intervention effects on substance use. The first revealed that randomization to the FRC in sixth grade was associated with reductions in substance use (Dishion, Kavangh, et al., 2002) as well as in deviant peer involvement (Dishion, Bullock, & Granic, 2002). We found that for the youth at highest risk, reductions in drug use were mediated by changes in observed parent monitoring practices (Dishion, Nelson, & Kavanagh, 2003).

Our recent analyses concur with these findings, suggesting that the most dramatic effects of EcoFIT are with sixth-grade students who are most severely problematic and whose families are most in need of services (Connell et al., 2007). We have recently used prevention trial statistical methods to incorporate the level of parents' engagement in the FCU in the evaluation of long-term outcomes. Using an intention-to-treat design (i.e., including all participants initially involved in the intervention, irrespective of whether they went on to complete all stages), outcomes to age 17 were modest. However, if one considers the level at which a family was engaged in the intervention, compared with that of control participants who would also have likely engaged in the FCU intervention, the effects are quite dramatic. The approach to the analysis of engagement with an intervention is referred to as complier average causal effect (CACE) analysis (Jo, 2002). The challenge for many randomized prevention trials is that many of the participants do not actually engage in the intervention, especially when it is offered on a voluntary basis. For example, when we tested the EcoFIT intervention in public middle schools, 25% of the families in the randomized intervention group engaged in a FCU when it was offered to all. Using CACE analyses, one can use the information collected prior to the intervention about those participants who engaged, and estimate an "engager" control group resembling those who eventually

Table 17.1   Summary of outcomes applying EcoFIT to public middle schools.

11th-Grade outcomes	Engagers (Intervention)	Engagers (Control)	Declined (All)
Percentage arrested at least once	15	100	5
Frequency of marijuana use last month	1	5	0.3
Days absent from school	13	32	12

participated in the FCU. Similarly, those who are in the intervention group and declined the FCU can be used to identify those who would most likely decline in the control group. In doing this we found that single-parent families whose sixth-grade student reported deviant peer involvement and family conflict were the most likely to engage in the intervention condition.

Two outcome studies on these findings, which are summarized in Table 17.1, reveal the outcomes for the four groups described earlier, but with control and intervention participants who were classified as having declined aggregated into one group, because the findings were nearly identical. In our analysis of problem behavior, we found that there was a marked reduction in the percentage of youth arrested in the "engager" group (15%) who actually received the FCU compared to the control (100%). Thus, sixth-grade students at high risk whose parents were in need of support were six times more likely to be arrested within the next five years if they were not offered the FCU. Similarly, they used marijuana five times more frequently during a one-month period than did the intervention group. These findings were extended to marijuana and tobacco dependence by age 18 as well. These analyses revealed that random assignment to the EcoFIT intervention reliably reduced substance use, antisocial behavior, and the probability of arrest (Connell et al., 2006).

Table 17.1 also reveals that random assignment to the intervention resulted in a 50% reduction in days absent from high school from 6th through the 11th grade. Control engagers missed an average of 32 days during the school year, and intervention youth missed only 13. These results were also statistically reliable for days absent from school (Stormshak, Connell, & Dishion, 2009).

Another trend is particularly important to consider when inspecting Table 17.1. Although it is often said that only families that are at low or no risk will receive family-based services offered in the school, we did not find this to be the case. Our proactive approach to offering the FCU suggested that, in fact, the families who declined participation were those who were at the lowest risk of all. In other words, these parents accurately assessed their young adolescents' risk status and did not feel the need to receive information or support on behavior management strategies. This is an optimistic finding indeed, because it suggests that if we have the appropriate outreach and engagement strategies in place for caregivers of the highest risk students, we are likely to reduce their long-term risk by supporting their use of positive behavior support strategies and coordinating with school staff in supporting student success.

Interventions with Ethnic Minority Families: Ethical and Intercultural Problems and Solutions

A cornerstone of the EcoFIT approach is proactive identification (i.e., multiple gating) of youth at risk in contexts such as public schools and to provide intervention support to reduce their risk status. One potential ethical problem is the possibility that we are intervening in a system that is biased and unfair towards children, such as on the basis of racial, ethnic or class background. If true, the identification of risk process could simply serve to further marginalize youth and families from the public school system *vis a vis* invalid predictions that are inherently negative. Despite evidence supporting the predictive validity and cost effectiveness of teacher ratings, some studies have nevertheless reported possible bias in teachers' assessment of problem behavior. Several studies have revealed that teachers generally tend to not only rate ethnic minority students negatively on measures of personality, behavior, motivation to learn, and classroom performance (Reid, Casat, Norton, Anastopoulos, & Temple, 2001), but they also report lower academic expectations for them and treat minority students less favorably than they treat European American students (Cooper, Baron, & Lowe, 1975; Murray, 1996; Plewis, 1997). Differential treatment of ethnic minority students has been evident in institutional practices and referral rates to special education programs (Contreras & Lee, 1990; McFadden, Marsh, Price, & Hwang, 1992; Saft & Pianta, 2001; Serwatka, Deering, & Grant, 1995; Shaw & Braden, 1990). Similarly, minority children tend to be rated higher on undercontrolled and other problem behaviors compared with their European American counterparts (Epstein, March, Conners, & Jackson, 1998; Kelly, Bullock, & Dykes, 1977; Reid et al., 1998).

Numerous other studies have revealed the reality of teacher bias and the impact it has on minority students. In their exploration of African American and Latino adolescents' reports of teacher discrimination, Rosenbloom and Way (2004) found that teachers showed preference for Asian American students on the basis of their "model minority" bias. Wayman (2002) found that from among a sample of 2,409 Mexican American and non-Latino white adolescents, Mexican American adolescents reported the highest levels of differential treatment by teachers because of their ethnicity. The study concluded that teacher ethnic bias has a negative impact on teacher–student relationships and results in student alienation and increased rates of school drop out. In his study of African American and Caucasian middle school students, Casteel (1998) found that Caucasian students received more positive interactions, such as increased positive feedback, more praise, and more frequent clues from their teachers, than did African American students. African American students, particularly boys, tended to receive more negative feedback and less personal contact, and were less called on by name to answer questions. Similarly, in Marcus, Gross, and Seefeldt's (1991) study, African American boys reported having received significantly different treatment from teachers than had other groups (i.e., White boys and girls, African American girls). African American boys indicated that their teachers expected less from them academically, called on them less often, and gave them fewer choices compared with White students or African American girls. Finally, Reid and colleagues (1998) also reported parallel findings for the interaction effect for gender and ethnicity by which African American boys were rated as having the highest symptoms of ADHD and Caucasian girls as the lowest.

We examined the possibility that teachers were biased in their ratings of students of color in a sample of diverse youth who were involved in a middle school prevention trial described above. Results of our analyses found that teacher ratings of child behavior served as a viable predictor of adolescent problem behavior measured by adolescent antisocial behavior, deviant peer association, arrest and substance use particularly for European American youth. In contrast, teacher ratings of risk did not predict well either positive or problematic behavior in African American students, regardless of the reporting agent – mother, youth and court records (Yasui & Dishion, under review). A possible explanation for these findings is that teachers tend to see African American youth as "more problematic", either because of biases or because of a lack of understanding for cultural differences in youths' responding to the school environment and academic engagement. In fact, we have found that the predictive validity of our brief teacher rating screening measure improves when we standardize scores within teachers, suggesting that a significant proportion of the variance in the ratings of risk can be attributed more to the shared variance in teachers' perceptions and less to the students' actual behavior.

A review of our findings regarding possible teacher bias due to student ethnicity prompted several suggestive steps to eliminate such biases in the identification of youth behavior. First, one approach in improving the predictive validity of a teacher rating first gate in the multiple gating procedure is to train teachers in rating student behavior, so that they are more objective in their perceptions as well as deeper in their understanding of how particular reaction or behaviors of students may be culturally based rather than a negative behavioral response. An agreed-upon definition of positive student behavior and problematic student behavior that encompasses culturally-based behavior is a fundamental component of positive behavior support. A second strategy for improving systematic screening is to include multiple sources of assessment. Aggregating measures from different agents, such as teachers, parents and youth, as well as direct observations of the child's behavior may allow for the detection of rater bias that can be identified by discrepancy among informants. Moreover, including multiple sources provides an overall reflection of the child's behavior across various contexts. A third strategy is to measure numerous student behaviors repeatedly across time. For example, assessment of teacher ratings, school grades, attendance, and engagement in extracurricular activities repeatedly is useful to know whether the student is behavior is improving, declining, or staying the same during the course of the school year. Such information is useful in evaluating the student's responsiveness to an intervention or to suggest that an intervention is needed soon to prevent further deterioration. We are currently revising our process of identifying high-risk students in the school context to eliminate the problem of bias and invalid predictions, and, therefore, improve the ethics of systematic screening.

A second critical feature of the EcoFIT approach is to use assessments to tailor and adapt interventions to the needs of youth and families who are clearly at risk. However, what if our key measure, behavior observation of family interaction, is biased towards European American families and, by virtue of this feature, provides estimates of parenting that are culturally insensitive and potentially stigmatizing? For example, giving feedback to a parent that their monitoring practices are poor, and disregarding their cultural practice of having extended families participate in the child rearing and monitoring practice. Such could be the case when working with American Indian families, for example (Boyd-Ball & Dishion, 2006; see also Robinson, Tyler, Jones, Silburn, & Zubrick, 2012, for a discussion of similar considerations in interventions with Australian Aboriginal families).

The cultural sensitivity of assessment measures is a growing area of concern within the domain of developmental psychology (see also Moreland & Dumas, Chapter 4, this volume). More often than not, psychological research has been conducted on research questions developed from the perspectives of researchers, which differ from the questions that the community and individuals perceive as important. Especially when studying multiethnic populations, many researchers tend to use the "one model fits all" assumption, thus minimizing the presence of cultural differences. It is critical for researchers to examine the generalizability of current measures, in particular, that measures are equivalent in meaning for children and families across various ethnic groups.

Our own examination of the cultural validity of assessment measures included a study that examined the influence of coder ethnicity on the validity and reliability of direct observations of family management (Yasui & Dishion, 2008). Eight coders, four European American and four African American, were randomly assigned to conduct behavior ratings of videotaped family interactions of European American and African American families. Results suggested that when using behavior ratings of family interactions of culturally diverse families, preconceptions secondary to the perceptions of the observer might undermine the validity of the ratings. We found that European American coders tended to rate African American families as having fewer problem-solving skills and poorer mother–child relationships compared with European American families. In contrast, African American coders' ratings of family interactions were relatively similar across European American and African American families, suggesting that African American coders did not perceive significant differences in family interactions across European American and African American families. The results of this study highlight the difficulty of eliminating the influence our cultural filters may have on how we interpret and understand how families interact. This study not only examined differences in coder perceptions of family interactions, but suggested that coder training systems developed by European American researchers and tested on European American samples may not be comparably effective or unbiased when used to examine families of diverse cultural backgrounds.

Our findings are just one example of the implications of possible systematic cultural bias within current instruments widely used with diverse populations, highlighting the importance of integrating adaptive methods for obtaining culturally reliable and valid data. Several researchers have implemented culturally sensitive ways to achieve this goal of equivalence across groups; for example, Hughes and DuMont (1993) have used focus group interviews to tap into cultural constructs and further define their meanings. Fisher and Ball (2002) integrated members of the community as research staff who examined whether the assessments and intervention components addressed the concerns of the community. Fisher and Ball (2002) have also incorporated the use of storytelling of Native American legends into their behavior observation task because it serves as a vessel for Native American youth and families to connect with the task, and also provides a culturally sanctioned method to discuss problematic topics with youth. Recommendations for future research thus include the use of multi-method multiagent approaches to assessment, application of a mixed methods approach (e.g., use of ethnographic assessment procedures with quantitative measures), piloting of assessments and assessment procedures in the community of interest, including stakeholders from the culture or community into the research process, as well as increasing ethnic diversity among the research team that would create a climate of cultural awareness and promote cultural competence and adaptability of the research.

Summary

Over the course of 20 years, our developmental and intervention trial research has evolved in an iterative fashion, as suggested by Figure 17.1. The original ATP model has evolved into a general approach to family intervention that is applicable to children and families across the developmental spectrum. We found that random assignment to the family check-up, for example, improved parenting and reduced problem behavior in early childhood (Dishion et al., 2008; Gardner, Shaw, Dishion, Burton, & Supplee, 2007; Shaw, Dishion, Supplee, Gardner, & Arnds, 2006). By way of summary, the intervention model has improved by virtue of a data driven, iterative approach:

- *Effectiveness*: We improved the effectiveness of the intervention approach by eliminating the peer aggregation component of the original model and designing the FCU. We now see significant intervention effects four years after the intervention, and seven years after the intervention using statistical analysis strategies that incorporate intervention engagement.
- *Efficiency*: The current version of the intervention program requires approximately six hours of intervention time for the highest risk families, while maintaining and even enhancing intervention effects.
- *Expense*: Because high-risk families tend to select themselves into the intervention, and because of the reduced number of sessions for even high-risk families, the intervention is now affordable to be delivered in a public school context.
- *Ethics*: Given the growing number of ethnically diverse children in the United States, it is untenable that teacher ratings or family assessments would be biased for minority youth and families. It is also unethical to provide family interventions with a monocultural bias. We are currently developing measurement and intervention protocols that are unbiased and that are experienced as respectful for a wider range of families.

In general, we see progress in translational developmental science as emerging necessarily over the course of a program of research that adheres to the following three principles. The first is iteration: to make progress in rendering developmental research as more useful for the design of empirically effective intervention services, it is necessary to repeat the process described in Figure 17.1 repeatedly. Thus, it is advisable to persevere within a program of research, as well as to work within a research group with a variety of investigations within one domain. The second principle is to be problem focused: it is important to attempt to solve a human problem amenable to the integration of developmental and intervention research. For example, Patterson set out to develop an effective intervention for aggressive children, as, at that time, all interventions were found to be ineffective (Patterson, Dishion, & Chamberlain, 1993). As the field progresses, some basic issues will evolve, such as measurement, conceptualization and definition. However, keeping an eye on the long-term goal is helpful to make progress. Third, is integrity: it is critical that we look for the weaknesses and inaccuracies in our model, and not simply confirm the successes. It is relatively rare for scientific research to publish failures in translations from developmental models to effective interventions. This is unfortunate, as it is almost assured that other investigators will repeat the mistakes and progress will be undermined. In this sense, success in applied research requires some comfort in failure. It is when we embrace learning from our setbacks, that we can propel forward our scientific research in accurately addressing complex multifaceted problems that challenge our children and families.

References

Boyd-Ball, A. J., & Dishion, T. J. (2006). Family-centered treatment for American Indian adolescent substance abuse: Toward a culturally and historically informed strategy. In H. Liddle & C. Rowe (Eds.), *Treating adolescent substance abuse: State of the science* (pp. 423–428). New York, NY: Cambridge University Press.

Campbell, D. T., & Fiske, D. W. (1959). Convergent and discriminant validation by the multitrait and multimethod matrix. *Psychological Bulletin, 56*(2), 81–105.

Capaldi, D. M. (1992). Co-occurrence of conduct problems and depressive symptoms in early adolescent boys: II. A 2-year follow-up at Grade 8. *Development and Psychopathology, 4*, 125–144.

Capaldi, D. M., & Patterson, G. R. (1987). An approach to the problem of recruitment and retention rates for longitudinal research. *Behavioral Assessment, 9*, 169–177.

Casteel, C. A. (1998). Teacher-student interactions and race in integrated classrooms. *Journal of Educational Research, 92*(2), 115–120.

Collins, L., Murphy, S., & Bierman, K. (2004). A conceptual framework for adaptive preventive interventions. *Prevention Science, 5*, 185–196.

Connell, A. M., Dishion, T. J., & Deater-Deckard, K. (2006). Variable- and person-centered approaches to the analysis of early adolescent substance use: Linking peer, family, and intervention effects with developmental trajectories. [Special Issue]. *Merrill-Palmer Quarterly, 52*(3), 421–448.

Connell, A., Dishion, T., Yasui, M., & Kavanagh, K. (2007). An adaptive approach to family intervention: Linking engagement in family-centered intervention to reductions in adolescent problem behavior. *Journal of Consulting and Clinical Psychology, 75*, 568–579.

Contreras, A., & Lee, O. (1990). Differential treatment of students by middle school science teachers: Unintended cultural bias. *Science Education, 74*(4), 433–444.

Cooper, H. M., Baron, R. M., & Lowe, C. A. (1975). The importance of race and social class information in the formation of expectancies about academic performance. *Journal of Educational Psychology, 67*(2), 312–319.

Cronbach, L. J., & Meehl, P. E. (1955). Construct validity in psychological tests. *Psychological Bulletin, 52*, 281–302.

Dishion, T. J., & Andrews, D. (1995). Preventing escalations in problem behaviors with high-risk young adolescents: Immediate and 1-year outcomes. *Journal of Consulting and Clinical Psychology, 63*, 538–548.

Dishion, T. J., Andrews, D. W., Kavanagh, K., & Soberman, L. H. (1996). Preventive interventions for high-risk youth: The Adolescent Transitions Program. In B. McMahon & R. D. Peters (Eds.), *Conduct disorders, substance abuse and delinquency: Prevention and early intervention approaches* (pp. 184–214). Newbury Park, CA: Sage.

Dishion, T.J., Bullock, B. M., & Granic, I. (2002a). Pragmatism in modeling peer influence: Dynamics, outcomes, and change processes. *Development and Psychopathology, 14*, 969–981.

Dishion, T. J., Capaldi, D., Spracklen, K. M., & Li, F. (1995). Peer ecology of male adolescent drug use. *Development and Psychopathology, 7*, 803–824.

Dishion, T. J., & Dodge, K. A. (2005). Peer contagion in interventions for children and adolescents: Moving toward an understanding of the ecology and dynamics of change. *Journal of Abnormal Child Psychology, 33*(3), 395–400.

Dishion, T. J., & Kavanagh, K. (2003). *Intervening in adolescent problem behavior: A family-centered approach*. New York: Guilford Press.

Dishion, T. J., Kavanagh, K., & Kiesner, J. (1998). Prevention of early adolescent substance use among high-risk youth: A multiple gating approach to parent intervention. Drug abuse prevention through family interventions. In R. S. Ashery, E. B. Robertson, & K. L. Kumpfer (Eds.), *NIDA Research Monograph, 177*. Washington, DC: National Institute on Drug Abuse.

Dishion, T. J., Kavanagh, K., Schneiger, A., Nelson, S. E., & Kaufman, N. (2002b). Preventing early adolescent substance use: A family-centered strategy for the public middle-school ecology. In R. L. Spoth, K. Kavanagh, & T. J. Dishion (Eds.), Universal family-centered prevention strategies: Current findings and critical issues for public health impact [Special Issue]. *Prevention Science, 3*, 191–201.

Dishion, T. J., Kavanagh, K., Veltman, M., McCartney, T., Soberman, L., & Stormshak, E. A. (2003). *Family Management Curriculum V.2.0: Leader's guide*. Eugene, OR: Child and Family Center Publications (http://cfc.uoregon.edu).

Dishion, T. J., & Loeber, R. (1985). Adolescent marijuana and alcohol use: The role of parents and peers revisited. *American Journal of Drug and Alcohol Abuse, 11*, 11–25.

Dishion, T. J., McCord, J., & Poulin, F. (1999). When interventions harm: Peer groups and problem behavior. *American Psychologist, 54*(9), 755–764.

Dishion, T. J., Nelson, S. E., & Kavanagh, K. (2003b). The Family Check-Up for high-risk adolescents: Preventing early-onset substance use by parent monitoring. In J. E. Lochman & R. Salekin (Eds.), Behavior-oriented interventions for children with aggressive behavior and/or conduct problems [Special Issue]. *Behavior Therapy, 34*(5), 553–571.

Dishion, T. J., & Patterson, G. R. (1993). Childhood screening for early adolescent problem behavior: A multiple gating strategy. In M. Singer, L. Singer, & T. M. Anglin (Eds.), *Handbook for screening adolescents at psychosocial risk* (pp. 375–399). New York: Lexington Books.

Dishion, T. J., & Patterson, G. R. (1999). Model-building in developmental psychopathology: A pragmatic approach to understanding and intervention. *Journal of Clinical Child Psychology, 28*(4), 502–512.

Dishion, T. J., Patterson, G. R., & Kavanagh, K. (1992). An experimental test of the coercion model: Linking theory, measurement, and intervention. In J. McCord & R. Trembley (Eds.), *The interaction of theory and practice: Experimental studies of interventions* (pp. 253–282). New York: Guilford Press.

Dishion, T. J., Poulin, F., & Burraston, B. (2001). Peer group dynamics associated with iatrogenic effects in group interventions with high-risk young adolescents. In D. W. Nangle & C. A. Erdley (Eds.), *The role of friendship in psychological adjustment* (pp. 79–92). San Francisco, CA: Jossey-Bass.

Dishion, T. J., Reid, J. B., & Patterson, G. R. (1988). Empirical guidelines for the development of a treatment for early adolescent substance use. In R. E. Coombs (Ed.), *The family context of adolescent drug use* (pp. 189–224). New York: Haworth.

Dishion, T. J., Shaw, D. S., Connell, A., Wilson, M. N., Gardner, F., & Weaver, C. M. (2008). The Family Check-Up with high-risk indigent families: Outcomes on positive parenting and problem behavior from ages 2 through 4 years. *Child Development, 79*(5), 1395–1414.

Dishion, T. J., & Stormshak, E. (2007). *Intervening in children's lives: An ecological, family-centered approach to mental health care.* Washington, DC: APA Books.

Dishion, T. J., & Tipsord, J. M. (2011). Peer contagion in child and adolescent social and emotional development. *Annual Review of Psychology, 62*, 189–214.

Dodge, K. A., Dishion, T. J., & Lansford, J. E. (Eds.). (2006). *Deviant peer influences in programs for youth: Problems and solutions.* New York: Guilford Press.

Dwyer, J. H. (1983). *Statistical models for the social and behavioral sciences.* New York: Oxford University Press.

Eddy, J. M., Dishion, T. J., & Stoolmiller, M. (1998). The analysis of intervention change in children and families: Methodological and conceptual issues embedded in intervention studies. *Journal of Abnormal Child Psychology, 26*, 53–69.

Epstein, J. N., March, J. S., Conners, C. K., & Jackson, D. L. (1998). Racial differences on the Conners Teacher Rating Scale. *Journal of Abnormal Child Psychology, 26*, 109–118.

Feil, E. G., Walker, H. M., & Severson, H. H. (1995). The Early Screening Project for young children with behavior problems. *Journal of Emotional and Behavioral Disorders, 3*(4), 194–202.

Feldman, R. A., Stiffman, A. R., Evans, D. A., & Orme, J. G. (1982). Prevention research, social work, and mental illness. *Social Work Research & Abstracts, 18*(3), 4–13.

Fisher, P. A., & Ball, T. J. (2002). The Indian Wellness Project: An application of the tribal participatory research model. *Prevention Science, 3*, 235–40.

Forgatch, M. S., Patterson, G. R., & DeGarmo, D. S. (2005). Evaluating fidelity: Predictive validity for a measure of competent adherence to the Oregon Model of Parent Management Training. *Behavior Therapy, 36*, 3–13.

Forgatch, M., & Toobert, D. J. (1979). A cost-effective parent training program for use with normal preschool children. *Journal of Pediatric Psychology, 4*(2), 129–145.

Gardner, F., Shaw, D., Dishion, T. J., Burton, J., & Supplee, L. (2007). Randomized prevention trial for early conduct problems: Effects on proactive parenting and links to toddler disruptive behavior. *Journal of Family Psychology, 21*(3), 398–406.

Henggeler, S. W., Schoenwald, S. K., Borduin, C. M., Rowland, M. D., & Cunningham, P. B. (1998). *Multisystemic treatment of antisocial behavior in children and adolescents.* New York: Guilford.

Hughes, D., & Dumont, K. (1993). Using focus groups to facilitate culturally-anchored research. *American Journal of Community Psychology, 21*(4), 775–806.

Jo, B. (2002). Model misspecification sensitivity analysis in estimating causal effects of interventions with noncompliance. *Statistics in Medicine, 21*, 3161–3181.

Kelly, J., Bullock, L. M., & Dykes, M. K., (1977). Behavioral disorders: Teachers' perceptions. *Exceptional Children, 43*, 316–318.

Loeber, R., & Dishion, T. (1983). Early predictors of male delinquency: A review. *Psychological Bulletin, 94*(1), 68–99.

Loeber, R., & Dishion, T. J. (1984). Boys who fight at home and school: Family conditions influencing cross-setting consistency. *Journal of Consulting and Clinical Psychology, 52*, 759–768.

Loeber, R., & Dishion, T. J. (1987). Antisocial and delinquent youth: Methods for their early identification. In J. D. Burchard & S. N. Burchard (Eds.), *Prevention of delinquent behavior* (Vol. 10, pp. 75–89). Newbury Park, CA: Sage.

Loeber, R., Dishion, T. J., & Patterson, G. R. (1984). Multiple-gating: A multistage assessment procedure for identifying youths at-risk for delinquency. *Journal of Research in Crime and Delinquency, 21*, 7–32.

Marcus, G., Gross, S., & Seefeldt, C. (1991). Black and White students' perceptions of teacher treatment. *Journal of Educational Research, 84*(6), 363–367.

McFadden, A. C., Marsh, G. E., Price, B. J., & Hwang, Y. (1992). A study of race and gender bias in the punishment of handicapped school children. *Urban Review, 24*(4), 239–251.

Miller, W. R., & Rollnick, S. (2002). *Motivational interviewing: Preparing people for change* (2nd ed.). New York: Guilford Press.

Miller, W. R., & Rollnick, S. (2009). Ten things that Motivational Interviewing is not. *Behavioural and Cognitive Psychotherapy, 37*, 129–140.

Murray, C. B. (1996). Estimating performance: A confirmation bias. *Journal of Black Psychology, 22*, 67–85.

Palinkas, L. A., Atkins, C. J., Miller, C., & Fereira, D. (1996). Social skills training for drug prevention in high-risk female adolescents. *Preventive Medicine, 25*, 692–701.

Patterson, G. R. (1973). Changes in status of family members as controlling stimuli: A basis for describing treatment process. In L. A. Hamerlynck, L. C. Handy, & E. J. Mash (Eds.), *Behavior change: Methodology, concepts, and practices* (pp. 169–191). Champaign, IL: Research Press.

Patterson, G. R. (1974a). A basis for identifying stimuli which control behaviors in natural settings. *Child Development, 45*, 900–911.

Patterson, G. R. (1974b). Interventions for boys with conduct problems: Multiple settings, treatments, and criteria. *Journal of Consulting and Clinical Psychology, 42*, 471–481.

Patterson, G. R. (1976). The aggressive child: Victim and architect of a coercive system. In E. J. Mash, L. A. Hamerlynck, & L. C. Handy (Eds.), *Behavior modification and families* (pp. 267–316). New York: Brunner/Mazel.

Patterson, G. R. (1977). A three-stage functional analysis for children's coercive behaviors: A tactic for developing a performance theory. In D. Baer, B. C. Etzel, & J. M. L. Blanc (Eds.), *New developments in behavioral research: Theory, methods, and applications* (pp. 59–79). *In honor of Sidney W. Bijou*. Hillsdale, NJ: Lawrence Erlbaum Associates.

Patterson, G. R. (1982). *A social learning approach: III. Coercive family process*. Eugene, OR: Castalia.

Patterson, G. R. (1986). Maternal rejection: Determinant or product for deviant child behavior? In W. Hartup & Z. Rubin (Eds.), *Relationships and development* (pp. 73–94). Hillsdale, NJ: Lawrence Erlbaum Associates.

Patterson, G. R., & Cobb, J. A. (1971). A dyadic analysis of 'aggressive' behaviors. In J. P. Hill (Ed.), *Minnesota symposia on child psychology* (pp. 72–129). Minneapolis: University of Minnesota Press.

Patterson, G. R., & J. A. Cobb (1973). Stimulus control for classes of noxious behaviors. In J. F. Knutson (Ed.), *The control of aggression: Implications from basic research* (pp. 144–199). Chicago, IL: Aldine.

Patterson, G. R., & Dawes, R. M. (1975). A Guttman scale of children's coercive behaviors. *Journal of Clinical and Consulting Psychology, 43*(4), 594.

Patterson, G. R., & Dishion, T. J. (1985). Contributions of families and peers to delinquency. *Criminology, 23*, 63–79.

Patterson, G. R., Dishion, T. J., & Bank, L. (1984). Family interaction: A process model of deviancy training. *Aggressive Behavior, 10*(3), 253–267.

Patterson, G. R., Dishion, T. J., & Chamberlain, P. (1993). Outcomes and methodological issues relating to treatment of antisocial children. In T. R. Giles (Ed.), *Effective psychotherapy: A handbook of comparative research* (pp. 43–88). New York: Plenum.

Patterson, G. R., & Fleischman, M. J. (1979). Maintenance of treatment effects: Some considerations concerning family systems and follow-up data. *Behavior Therapy, 10*, 168–195.

Patterson, G. R., & Forgatch, M. S. (1985). Therapist behavior as a determinant for client resistance: A paradox for the behavior modifier. *Journal of Consulting and Clinical Psychology, 53*(6), 846–851.

Patterson, G. R., Littman, R. A., & Bricker, W. (1967). Assertive behavior in children: A step toward a theory of aggression. *Monographs of the Society for Research in Child Development, 32*(5, Serial No. 113), 1–43.

Patterson, G. R., & Reid, J. R. (1970). Reciprocity and coercion: Two facets of social systems. In C. Neuringer and J. L. Michael (Eds.), *Behavior modification in clinical psychology* (pp. 133–177). New York: Appleton-Century-Crofts.

Patterson, G. R., & Reid, J. B. (1973). Intervention for families of aggressive boys: A replication study. *Behavior Research and Therapy, 11*, 383–394.

Patterson, G. R., Reid, J. B., & Dishion, T. J. (1992). *Antisocial boys*. Eugene, OR: Castalia.

Patterson, G. R., Reid, J. B., Jones, R. R., & Conger, R. E. (1975). *A social learning approach to family intervention: Families with aggressive children*. Eugene, OR: Castalia.

Patterson, G. R., & Stouthamer-Loeber, M. (1984). The correlation of family management practices and delinquency. *Child Development, 55*, 1299–1307.

Plewis, I. (1997). Inferences about teacher expectations from national assessment at Key Stage One. *British Journal of Educational Psychology, 67*(2), 235–247.

Poulin, F., Dishion, T. J., & Burraston, B. (2001). 3-Year iatrogenic effects associated with aggregating high-risk adolescents in cognitive–behavioral preventive interventions. *Applied Developmental Science, 5*(4), 214–224.

Reid, R., Casat, C. D., Norton, H. J., Anastropoulos, A. D., & Temple, E. P. (2001). Using behavior rating scales for ADHD across ethnic groups: The IOWA Conners. *Journal of Emotional and Behavioral Disorders, 9*, 210–218.

Reid, R., DuPaul, G. J., Power, T. J., Anastopoulos, A. D., Roger-Adkinson, D., Noll, M. B., et al. (1998). Assessing culturally different students for attention deficit hyperactivity disorder using behavior rating scales. *Journal of Abnormal Child Psychology, 26*(3), 187–198.

Robinson, G., Tyler, W., Jones, Y., Silburn, S., & Zubrick, S. (2012). Context, diversity and engagement: early intervention with Australian Aboriginal families in urban and remote contexts. *Children & Society, 26*, 343–355.

Rosenbloom, S. R., & Way, N. (2004). Experiences of discrimination among African American, Asian American, and Latino Adolescents in an urban high school. *Youth & Society, 35*, 420–451.

Rothbart, M. K., & Rueda, M. R. (2005). The development of effortful control. In U. Mayr, E. Awh, & S. W. Keele (Eds.), *Developing individuality in the human brain: A tribute to Michael I. Posner* (pp. 167–188). Washington, DC: APA.

Saft. E. W., & Pianta, R. C. (2001). Teacher's perceptions of their relationships with students: Effects of child age, gender and ethnicity of teachers and children. *School Psychology Quarterly, 16*, 125–141.

Sanders, M. R., & Lawton, J. M. (1993). Discussing assessment findings with families: A guided participation model of information transfer. *Child and Family Behavior Therapy, 15*, 5–33.

Serwatka, T. S., Deering, S., & Grant, P. (1995). Disproportionate representation of African Americans in emotionally handicapped classes. *Journal of Black Studies, 25*(4), 492–506.

Shaw, S. R., & Braden, J. P. (1990). Race and gender bias in the administration of corporal punishment. *School Psychology Review, 19*, 378–383.

Shaw, D. S., Dishion, T. J., Supplee, L., Gardner, F., & Arnds, K. (2006). Randomized trial of a family-centered approach to the prevention of early conduct problems: Two-year effects of the Family Check-Up in early childhood. *Journal of Consulting and Clinical Psychology, 74*(1), 1–9.

Snyder, J., Dishion, T. J., & Patterson, G. R. (1986). Determinants and consequences of associating with deviant peers during preadolescence and adolescence. *Journal of Early Adolescence, 6*, 29–43.

Stormshak, E. A., Connell, A., & Dishion, T. J. (2009). An adaptive approach to family-centered intervention in schools: Linking intervention engagement to academic outcomes in middle and high school. *Prevention Science, 10*(3), 221–235.

Stormshak, E. A., Dishion, T. J., Light, J., & Yasui, M. (2005). Implementing family-centered interventions within the public middle school: Linking service delivery change to change in problem behavior. *Journal of Abnormal Child Psychology, 33*(6), 723–733.

Szapocznik, J., & Kurtines, W. M. (1989). *Breakthroughs in family therapy with drug-abusing and problem youth.* New York: Springer.

Wayman, J. C. (2002). Student perceptions of teacher ethnic bias: A comparison of Mexican American and non-Latino White dropouts and students. *The High School Journal, 85*(3), 27–37.

Webster-Stratton, C. (1984). Randomized trial of two parent-training programs for families with conduct-disordered children. *Journal of Consulting and Clinical Psychology, 52*(4), 666–678.

Webster-Stratton, C., Kolpacoff, M., & Hollingsworth, T. (1988). Self-administered videotape therapy for families with conduct-problem children: Comparison with two cost-effective treatments and a control group. *Journal of Consulting and Clinical Psychology, 56*, 558–566.

Yasui, M., & Dishion, T. J. (2008). Direct observation of adolescent family management: Validity and reliability as a function of coder ethnicity and training. *Behavior Therapy, 39*(4), 336–347.

Yasui, M., & Dishion, T. J. (under review). *Teacher ratings and screening for high-risk youth: Differential predictive validity as a function of student ethnicity.* Unpublished manuscript, University of Chicago.

18

Giving Knowledge about Children's Mental Health Away: Challenges and Opportunities

Janice Cooper and Jane Knitzer

This chapter examines the complex challenges of "giving knowledge away" for the purpose of improving the public policies to support good practice for children (including young children, school-aged children, adolescents and older youth) with, or at risk of, mental health problems. The analysis is based on the experiences of the two authors, who collectively have been involved in efforts to improve children's mental health policies and practices for over 30 years. Knitzer has conducted major policy studies of children's mental health (Knitzer, 1982; Knitzer, Steinberg, & Fleish, 1990), actively advocated for improvements, and, most recently, focused both her research and policy analysis on the importance of addressing too-often-ignored early childhood mental health issues through a family lens (Knitzer & Perry, 2011). Cooper brings particular expertise in fiscal analysis, as well as direct experience in managing a state children's mental health system. She was also the director of Unclaimed Children Revisited, a 50 state policy study based on the 1982 study, whose findings are discussed throughout this chapter.

The chapter focuses on a very challenging, indeed, vexing question. Why is it so difficult to embed new knowledge about how to prevent or reduce the emergence

The Wiley Handbook of Developmental Psychology in Practice: Implementation and Impact, First Edition.
Edited by Kevin Durkin and H. Rudolph Schaffer.
© 2016 John Wiley & Sons, Ltd. Published 2016 by John Wiley & Sons, Ltd.

of children's mental health problems, and to intervene with appropriate early intervention and treatment when problems are identified? To examine this question, the chapter first highlights the state-of-the-art in our understanding of children's mental health, comparing what was known in 1982, when Knitzer authored the first major policy study of children's mental health, and today (Knitzer, 1982). Then it paints a brief portrait of the nature of the emerging knowledge about children's mental health that has the potential to significantly improve outcomes for children and their families who struggle with, or who are at risk of, the kinds of the negative consequences that come with mental health problems. These include poor school performance, problematic relationships, the risk of involvement with child welfare and juvenile justice, and the likelihood in adulthood of problematic employment and potentially spill-over into the next generation. The third section maps the capacity in the United States to implement lessons from the knowledge base given the current set of policies and fiscal practices that shape what kinds of mental health services and supports can be paid for. The last section examines the challenges and opportunities to recraft policy frameworks to be more responsive to emerging knowledge both within states and nationally.

Setting the Context: The Status of Children's Mental Health in the United States

What makes the exploration of the challenges and opportunities to give knowledge away so critical is that overall, children with, or at risk of, mental health problems are not doing very well, either in accessing services or in improving their functioning, a reality that has lasted for many years.

Unclaimed children: Defining an issue

Attention to children's mental health as a policy matter first surfaced in the United States in 1969, with the release of a Congressionally-mandated report entitled "Crisis in Children's Mental Health" that highlighted the lack of attention to children who needed mental health services (Joint Commission on the Mental Health of Children, 1970). More than a decade later, in 1982, a 50 state policy study documented the continuing crisis, this time, calling attention to the fragile commitment to children's mental health across the states (Knitzer, 1999). The report, based on surveys of state mental health agencies, residential treatment programs and state mental health associations (state and local mental health advocacy organizations), as well as interviews with families, found that:

- Too many children were unserved or underserved: only 20% of children in need of services got them, with the most seriously troubled least likely to access services.
- Families struggled greatly to find help for children with serious problems. They faced stigma, disrespect from professionals, frequent evaluations without follow-up services, loss of jobs because of absences related to trying to meet their children's needs, financial hardship, and, sometimes, having to relinquish custody in order to get services.
- In general, the only services that were available were either outpatient weekly therapy or residential placement, although there was no research to support the efficacy of residential placement and some research indicated that what mattered was what kind of aftercare children received when they reentered the community.
- There was no recognition of the need for respite care for families struggling to keep their children home, in contrast to families whose children had other disabilities, and while examples of intensive community-based services existed (and were described in the report) these were very limited.
- Although children were typically involved with multiple systems (e.g., schools, child welfare, and juvenile justice) there was no coordination of services or cross-system planning, leaving parents as the de facto case managers without authority.
- As a policy matter, children's mental health was a low priority within state mental health systems: fewer than half had a children's mental health budget or even had one dedicated staff person for children's mental health.
- Children with the most serious problems were more likely to be the responsibility of special education agencies, child welfare agencies and juvenile justice agencies, rather than mental health agencies, and many moved from one system to another.

Pointing the way toward new directions, "Unclaimed Children" identified what were then seen as effective community-based practices across the age spectrum, starting in early childhood and continuing through the schools. It also highlighted data showing that although parents first reported serious problems in early childhood, most children did not get any help until at least the fourth grade. Above all, it underscored the need for the development of a new kind of service delivery system: one that offered intensive services in the community to replace the overreliance on high-cost residential placements, and, on behalf of these children and youth, one that emphasized the importance of taking a cross-system perspective, given the reality that many were, in fact, from a systems perspective, "exchangeable children". "Unclaimed Children" also called for giving families a clear voice in treatment planning and decisions for their own children, and for helping to reshape the overall system. Although the landmark 1974 special education law began the process of giving voice to parents of children with disabilities, in fact, largely because of the stigma associated with mental illness, it was not until 1988 that isolated parents of children with mental health problems came together to form a stand-alone national advocacy group, the Federation of Families for Children's Mental Health (Huff, 1998; Rehabilitation Act of 1973, 1973).

Tracing the impacts

"Unclaimed Children" was a helpful catalyst for stakeholders to come together to improve children's mental health (Lourie & Hernandez, 2003). For example, it spurred new attention to the needs of the most troubled children and particularly new approaches to delivering services on behalf of children whose needs had been largely ignored. Second, it led to the promulgation of a widely accepted set of values and principles, embedded in the concept of a "system of care" first called for by Knitzer, but refined and developed in a seminal document that has guided policy and practice over the last two decades by Stroul and Friedman (Stroul & Friedman, 1986, 1996). These included: care in the least restrictive, most normal setting, building partnerships with families, responding to cultural and ethnic diversity in competent ways; and, tailoring services to individual needs. In turn, these principles and values served as a catalyst for policy and practice-level efforts to make sure families were part of the treatment processes, and at decision making tables. The system of care principles also spurred efforts to focus, both conceptually and in research, on strategies to define, deliver and measure culturally and linguistically competent services (Cablas, 1998; Cross, Bazron, Dennis, & Isaacs, 1989; Lourie & Hernandez, 2003).

The emphasis on system-of-care service delivery principles also legitimized and fostered "on-the-ground" service delivery innovations, particularly through strategies to make operational the philosophy of "wrap-around", which emerged in part from efforts to provide alternative services to youth (Lourie & Hernandez, 2003). Wrap-around care represents a family-focused care management approach that has built-in flexibility to adjust clinical and nonclinical interventions in response to the needs of individual children and family, using, as the core mechanisms, child/youth and family team meetings (Vanderberg & Grealish, 1996). The system of care framework also legitimized the concept of "whatever it takes", aiming to build flexibility not just into treatment plans but into packaging resources in new ways responsive to specific family need (Dennis & Lourie, 2006). So, for example, it might mean using mental health funds to purchase behavioral aides as individual coaches, so children ostracized from their peers could participate in normalizing experiences, or reengaging disconnected relatives on behalf of youth to create an informal support system.

The system-of-care concepts have also spread to, and been adapted by, systems other than mental health, including child welfare, juvenile justice and early childhood mental health (Knitzer & Cooper, 2006). For example, early childhood systems-of-care are defined as a support to the broader early childhood community, and explicitly include prevention, early intervention and treatment (Kaufmann & Hepburn, 2007; Kaufman, Perry, Hepburn, & Duran, 2012).

In 1984, the federal government, through the Child and Adolescent Services System Program (CASSP), provided funds to states to develop systems of care and promote family voices in the delivery of children's mental health services. Eight years later, in 1992, Congress, drawing on the systems-of-care principles and CASSP, enacted the Comprehensive Community Mental Health Services for Children and Families Act, which provided funds for demonstration grants to communities to develop systems of care (Lourie & Hernandez, 2003). The legislation differed from CASSP in that it had no focus on engaging states in the development of the community demonstration grants. But like CASSP, the population of focus was the most troubled children and youth whose needs had so clearly been ignored, requiring that to be part of a "system of care" the children and youth had to have been seriously disturbed for at least one year. Evaluation results of the demonstration sites funded show a pattern of mixed results (Holden & Santiago, 2003; Stephens, Holden, & Hernandez, 2004). Critics of this approach as implemented charge that it failed to attend sufficiently to the quality and efficacy of actual clinical and treatment practices (Bickman, Noser, & Summerfelt, 1999; Cook & Kilmer, 2004). It has also been criticized for excluding children and youth *at risk of* developing serious emotional and behavioral disorders, and thus precluding either selective prevention or early intervention on their behalf (Knitzer, 2005).

Children's mental health today

Notwithstanding reform efforts, the big picture with respect to children's mental health status three decades after "Unclaimed Children" is dismayingly similar. Overall, estimates are still that only 20–25% of children with identified needs get mental health services, with evidence of widespread racial and ethnic disparities (Aratani & Cooper, 2012a; Kataoka, Zhang, & Wells, 2002). Approximately one-third of

White children access needed care, compared to 12% for children of color (Kataoka et al., 2002). Perhaps most troubling, parents are still forced to give up custody of their children as a condition of getting services. A Congressional report estimated that in one year alone this impacted at least 12,000 families (and many believe this is a serious undercount) (USHR, 2004).

Access problems are especially acute for young children, and youth aging out of the public systems. For example, with respect to young children, despite evidence that serious mental health disorders start as early as five, and one study based in pediatric practices finds overall prevalence rates of diagnosable disorders at 17%, which is not too different from that for older children, only 1% of children seen by community mental health centers are under six (Costello, Compton, Keeler, & Angold, 2003; Kessler, Beglund, Demler, Jin, & Walters, 2005; Pottick et al., 2002). Data on young children at risk of developing diagnosable disorders are even more startling. A national study has found that young children, including in some instances, infants and toddlers, are actually expelled from child care and early learning settings, largely for what have been called "challenging behaviors" at three times the rates of students expelled in K-12 (Gilliam, 2005). For young children of color the expulsion rates range from two to five times that of their white peers (Gilliam, 2005). Early aggressive behavior is not only predictive of later conduct disorders, but also a marker for academic and other negative markers. Yet only half of all the states reported statewide early childhood initiatives (Cooper et al., 2008).

At the other end of the age spectrum there are also special problems, particularly for youth aging out of the foster care system or leaving juvenile justice facilities, clearly one of the most vulnerable groups of youth in society. State system leaders admit that in many instances there is no system to address the needs of youth with mental health problems transitioning into adulthood. Nearly half of all state adult mental health directors and a quarter of all child mental health directors report that there are no services in place for this age group (Davis, Geller, & Hunt, 2006). Where services exist they are very limited and lack the scale to meet the needs of the young people who should be receiving them.

Data on outcomes even for the most troubled children, although spotty, also paint a portrait not too dissimilar from what Knitzer found in 1982. For example, of children and adolescents with identified disabilities, children and adolescents with serious behavioral and emotional disorders are *still* the most likely to be expelled from or fail school (Marder, Wagner, & Sumi, 2003; Wagner, 2003). This is so even though there is progress in keeping all children with disabilities in school, including those with serious emotional and behavioral disorders. For them, the proportion staying in school has significantly increased; in 1982, about 60% dropped out, that is now about 44%. Compared to their peers, children and youth with mental health problems face poorer postsecondary school outcomes.

They experienced the highest rates of negative consequences (for example disciplinary actions, being fired from their job, or being arrested) associated with their behaviors and inferior employment opportunities and experiences (Wagner, 2005). And, of great concern, families still struggle mightily. The financial burden with respect to out-of-pocket costs has been reduced, but the search for help is still a lonely, stigmatizing journey, with a still-too-long lag time between the time families (or others) identify problems and treatment, and the costs for siblings and parental employment are high (Busch & Barry, 2007).

At the same time, within this larger picture there have been important changes. One major change is the greater involvement of primary health providers, particularly pediatricians, in diagnosing and sometimes treating mental health problems in children. From 1979 to 1996, the proportion of primary care visits (to community pediatricians or family practitioners) of children and youth with identified psychosocial problems almost doubled (Kelleher, McInerny, Gardner, Childs, & Wasserman, 2000). Primary care providers, however, have a less than stellar record in identifying, appropriately assessing and treating children and youth with mental health problems (Leaf et al., 2004). Barriers include insufficient referral sources, inadequate capacity among mental health referral sources, and lack of time within an already abbreviated primary care visit (Horowitz et al., 2007). Limited research on efforts to train primary healthcare providers about child behavioral health was associated with increased identification, better management of psychosocial problems in pediatric settings (Leaf et al., 2004). However, their role in the healthcare infrastructure as gatekeepers in many managed care networks, combined with the obvious nonstigmatizing entry points they provide, and the need and renewed impetus for integrated care all point to reasons why they need to be part of a larger systematic strategy to "give knowledge away".

The Knowledge Explosion

Against this picture of a field "muddling through" to respond to children's mental health needs is the explosion of knowledge over the past several decades about the causes and consequences of children's mental health problems on resilience, about effective (and ineffective) treatment strategies, the risk factors that portend difficulty, and effective prevention strategies. Collectively, this knowledge opens up new possibilities for improving outcomes to children with or at risk of serious emotional and behavioral problems and their families. To set the stage for the discussion of what it will take to truly embed this knowledge into ongoing policies and practices, first consider some of the key take-home messages from several clusters of research.

Knowledge related to evidence-based treatment,
prevention and early intervention

The first area in which knowledge has grown exponentially is about clinical treatment strategies, particularly for the most troubled children and youth. Unlike 1982, there is now an array of evidence-based practices that have been rigorously tested in at least two or more randomized control trials that show positive impacts ("Blueprints for Violence Prevention"; Hoagwood, Burns, Kiser, Ringelsen, & Schoenwald, 2001; SAMHSA, 2007). Examples of evidence-based practices include: Multisystemic Therapy (MST), which appears to be particularly effective with conduct disordered youth involved with juvenile justice systems, Multidimensional Therapeutic Foster Care (MDTFC), Functional Family Therapy (FFT) and Parent–Child Interaction Therapy (PCIT), which appear to be especially helpful for children and families involved with child welfare agencies (Gruttadaro, Burns, Duckworth, & Crudo, 2007). Cognitive behavior therapy (CBT) and treatments for attention deficit/hyperactivity disorder (ADHD) based on the Multimodal Treatment study are available for children and youth with mental health disorders (Goldman, Genel, Bezman, Slanetz, & Council on Scientific Affairs American Medical Association, 1998). From a prevention, early intervention perspective there is research showing the efficacy of community-based strategies and empirically tested parent training strategies, such as the Incredible Years, Parent Management Training Oregon Model (PMTO) and the Triple P programs (Gruttadaro et al., 2007; Sanders & Calam, Chapter 5, this volume; Spoth, Clair, & Greenberg, 2007).

Also important is the growing evidence base about what kinds of intervention strategies are ineffective and may even be harmful, such as various versions of "boot camp" type models and poorly designed and implemented strategies that isolate or retraumatize children and youth (Cooper, Masi, Dababnah, Aratani, & Knitzer, 2007). Also compelling is research showing that, for specific conditions, the usual and customary treatment is largely ineffective. Comparing the use of manualized interventions with routine interventions related to anxiety disorders, ADHD and depression, Weisz and his colleagues found that usual and customary therapy yield effect sizes of zero: in other words, they had no positive impacts (Weisz, Sandler, Durlak, & Anton, 2005). Other data suggest that only an estimated one-third of clinicians use evidence-based practices with consistency or fidelity (Walrath, Sheehan, Holden, Hernandez, & Blau, 2006) and lack of knowledge about evidence-based practices tends to be associated with negative attitudes towards them (Nakamura, Higa-McMillan, Okamura, & Shimabukuro, 2011).

The body of knowledge just highlighted largely reflects a clinical focus on treatment interventions. Also important is a growing body of research about the nature and importance of nonclinical factors in shaping outcomes. In particular, this research emphasizes the importance of such factors as family perspectives, cultural and linguistic competence and service coordination. For example, one body of research focuses on how to engage and retain families in treatment, especially low-income family members, so they will benefit from the evidence-based practice (Dababnah & Cooper, 2006; McKay et al., 2004). Still others have focused on the kinds of adaptations necessary to be successful with culturally diverse populations; for example, translating the underlying principles of Parent–Child Interaction Therapy or Trauma-Focus Therapy into language and concepts meaningful to Native American and Latino populations ("Culturally Modified Trauma-Focused Therapy"; Indian Country Child Trauma Center, 2006; McCabe, Yeh, Garland, Lau, & Chavez, 2005). In addition, research in child welfare suggests that some of the disparities in access based on race/ethnicity can be ameliorated with the coordination and collaboration (Hurlburt et al., 2004). The literature carries an important message: most evidence-based practices have not been tested on children and youth from diverse cultural, racial/ethnic or linguistic communities. However, if appropriately adapted, some evidence-based practices work can be effective with populations not typically involved in the initial research on efficacy. Certainly there is much more to be learned about evidence-based practices, including when the evidence is robust enough to consider large scale adoption, but it is also clear that there is much more knowledge about specific treatments than is actually being used.

Thus it is not surprising that a new body of research, often called implementation science, is emerging that examines the factors that determine uptake of innovative practices (Fixsen, Naoom, Blase, Friedman, & Wallace, 2005; Stirman et al., 2012). For example, it explores how to train the workforce to use evidence-based practices, including how to get buy-in, monitor fidelity in a cost-effective way, and measure outcomes (Hemmelgarn, Glisson, & James, 2006). In particular, recognizing the "chasm" between the actual knowledge base and everyday practice by clinicians has propelled researchers to study various approaches to changing the behaviors of mental health professionals (Institute of Medicine, 2005). In addition, they have identified components that are predictive of success, such as paying attention to organizational context, fidelity and process (Hemmelgarn et al., 2006). Some researchers are also exploring different strategies to embed evidence-based practices in systems, trying to identify when a system is ready, and how best to phase in the intervention (Patti Chamberlain, Personal Communication, October 30, 2007). One early message from this research, as well as research in other fields such as early education, is that for adult behavior to change, the usual and customary approach of didactic or even limited experiential short workshops is not effective. Whether the target population is clinicians, paraprofessionals or teachers, it appears that there must be very explicit, individually tailored feedback loops, along with organizational or fiscal incentives to have the changes "take" (Pianta, 2005).

Taken together, this body of knowledge about how to improve the take up of both evidence-based prevention and treatment success rates seems to offer ready-made opportunities to both practitioners and policymakers to intentionally address the very disturbing reality highlighted above – the overall lack of progress in improving access to effective mental health services for children who need them.

Knowledge related to risk and protective factors and the roots of mental illness

Another major area in which there has been an explosion of knowledge is in the understanding of how child, familial and environmental risk and protective factors impact developmental outcomes, and promote or undermine resilience, defined as the ability to adapt positively to challenging circumstance. Much of this information comes from developmental psychology and psychopathology, although increasingly new understandings from neuroscience are reinforcing the findings from this body of research, shedding light on brain development, particularly in the earliest years and in adolescence (Shonkoff, Phillips, & Council, 2000; Spoth et al., 2007). Put most simply, there are three take-home messages from this body of research. First, the quality of a child's relationships with significant people, particularly parents, matters greatly, especially in the earliest years. Developmental researchers teach us that parents are the most important protective factors in the child's world and that when parent–child relationships are seriously problematic, with harsh, indifferent or inconsistent parenting, children suffer the kinds of consequences, including poor self-regulation and impulse control that result in their involvement with children's mental health systems (Luthar, 2006; Schaffer, 1998; Cummings, Faircloth, Mitchell, McCoy, & Schermerhorn, Chapter 3, this volume; Dishion & Yasui, Chapter 17, this volume). Neuroscientists are adding to these understandings, showing that in the face of extreme exposure to abuse and violence, the resulting toxic stress can even impede brain development (National Scientific Council on the Developing Child, 2005; Cicchetti, Toth, Nilsen, & Todd Manly, Chapter 15, this volume). Similarly, it is well established that mental health problems in the parent(s) increase the risk of both internalizing and externalizing difficulties in the child (Turney, 2012). The first take-home message is that how parents interact with their children, the issues they bring to parenting (e.g., their own exposure to violence and trauma, their own mental health) and the supports they have as parents all feed into their children's healthy development and mental health, or the converse.

The second take-home message from this body of research is that, in general, the more risk factors children experience, together with absent countervailing protective factors (such as at least one consistent, caring relationship, a positive temperament, or a supportive nonfamily environment), the more likely they are to experience poor outcomes. Researchers have long focused on older children to show this pattern of multiple risks yielding greater problems (Masten & Wright, 1998). Most recently, researchers have shown that for young children, the more risk factors parents experience, the worse the cognitive and behavioral outcomes in young children (Watamura, Phillips, Morrissey, McCartney, & Bub; 2011; Whitaker, Orzol, & Kahn, 2006; Yoshikawa, Aber, & Beardslee, 2012).

The third take-home message from this body of literature that has implications for children's mental health is that, although the family is the most important influence, other settings (such as schools, community environments) and those in settings (i.e., teachers and childcare providers) can have important negative or positive impacts on children's mental health (Bronfenbrenner, 1979; Jones et al., 2010; Silberg, Maes, & Eaves, 2010;. Tolan & Dodge, 2005). For adolescents, paying attention to peer interactions, acceptance in peer groups and peer group attributes appear to be important and are associated with protective factors (Masten & Powell, 2003; Seidman & Pedersen, 2003). An ecological view of child development has led to the development of interventions that not only engage families and peers, but also engage early childhood programs and schools in giving children and youth skills and opportunities to override negative influences likely to result in mental health challenges. A growing number of these reflect evidence-based prevention science practices (Tolan & Dodge, 2005). In the aggregate, this body of literature has implications for efforts to use knowledge about children's mental health to inform the delivery of services and policies, particularly for preventive and early intervention efforts. It suggests very directly that parents and parenting should be legitimate targets for intervention approaches to improving children's mental health both for treatment and prevention. But it also provides evidence that enhancing the capacity of others in the child's world, besides parents – that is teachers, coaches, and pediatricians – to promote children's mental health should be designed, tested and taken to full scale. It is, in fact, this body of knowledge that has informed the preventive and early intervention strategies highlighted above.

Knowledge related to the intergenerational nature of mental illness

As understanding of parental risk factors, gene environment interaction and how these affect children's mental health deepen, it is becoming clear that for children exposed to multiple familial and environmental risk factors, addressing parental mental health issues such as depression, can prevent or reduce well-documented cognitive and behavioral problems for young children, and for older children, reduce the risk of their own mental health disorders (Goodman et al., 2011;

Weissman et al., 2006; Whitaker et al., 2006). Research suggests that between 20 and 45% of children of adults with mental illness are increased risk for developing mental health disorders (Hammen, 2003; Hammen, Hazel, Brennan, & Najman, 2012). These data, in effect, suggest a blurring of the lines between prevention and intervention: treatment for one generation is prevention for the next, particularly if the intervention also includes attention to the child and parent relationships.

Knowledge related to trauma

Cutting across the understandings of both effective treatment and prevention and early intervention strategies is a growing recognition of how trauma exposure for parents, or children, or both impacts children's mental health. Since 1982, we have many more data on the prevalence of trauma, linked not just to natural disasters, or even to man-made disasters, such as the Oklahoma bombings or to 9/11, or war-linked family trauma, but through the everyday of occurrence of abuse and violence as well. Overall, it is estimated that one in four Americans is exposed to significant trauma, but for subpopulations the rates are much higher (Cooper et al., 2007). The problem is particularly acute in low-income communities where it is not uncommon for over 80% of children and youth to have been exposed to one or more traumatic events (Gorman-Smith, Henry, & Tolan, 2004). Youth who are homeless and who have a cooccurring substance use disorder face increased vulnerability for trauma (Cooper et al., 2007), and are at risk of school dropout (Aratani & Cooper, 2012b). In Massachusetts, in recognition of how widespread exposure to trauma is among school-age students, through staunch advocacy efforts the state has funded 34 school districts to establish trauma-informed environments in schools; these are focused on infrastructure, training, service linkages and support (Massachusetts Advocates for Children, 2007).

Through the National Child Trauma Stress Network the federal government has also sought to generate new knowledge about effective intervention strategies to help children and families cope with trauma, recognizing both how pervasive trauma is and how destructive. Related and very powerful research on adults further reinforces this core finding. Felitti and his colleagues, analyzing survey data from over 17,000 respondents enrolled in the Kaiser Permanente Health Plans, found, through what they call the Adverse Childhood Experiences (ACE) Study, that the more adverse experiences a child experienced (including loss of a parent, substance abuse, homelessness, poverty, etc.) the greater the likelihood of serious, high-cost health consequences (cardiac problems, obesity, issues related to smoking), continued mental health costs and even premature morbidity (Felitti et al., 1998). As with the other bodies of knowledge just highlighted, increasing the skills and capacity to address trauma in communities across the United States should be a core part of the children's mental health agenda.

The Role of Public Policy

In the United States, as in many other societies, who gets access to health and mental health services, and for what is largely shaped by public policies. Therefore, the extent to which public policies allow for, and indeed provide incentives for, taking into account the rich knowledge base just highlighted is a crucial part of the picture of what it takes to give children's mental health knowledge away. Right now, there is a huge disconnect between that knowledge base and what the public policy framework actually supports. Therefore, to set the stage for a discussion of what can improve the use of children's mental health knowledge, we first highlight the current policy framework that guides how dollars are allocated.

Children's mental health policy at a glance

Unlike many other aspects of children's policy (food, education, health care) there has never been comprehensive legislation to provide a national legislative framework for children's mental health. Essentially, there have been two types of targeted legislation; one enacted in the 1970s and repealed by the 1980s and one enacted in 1992, reflecting markedly different, but ultimately, limited approaches. In the early 1970s in response to the Congressionally-mandated report entitled "Crisis in Children's Mental Health" highlighted above, Congress enacted legislation to require that community mental health centers, which had been created in the 1960s to address adult deinstitutionalization, provide a range of services to children. The legislation was successful in dramatically increasing attention to children in mental health centers, as well as in some free-standing child guidance centers (Lourie & Hernandez, 2003). Predictably, outpatient therapy was a required service, but so, too, was consultation to early childhood programs and schools. But changing administrations in the United States mean changing approaches and the specific requirements for children's mental health disappeared, as a block grant approach to funding mental health was put in place in 1981. Through the federal community mental health block grant, in return for flexibility, states accepted decreased dollars. That block grant is still in effect today. Initially, the block grant was silent on the mental health needs of children. In 1984, two years after "Unclaimed Children" was released, States were asked to set aside a portion of the block grant monies for children (at least 10%) (USGAO, 1987). This amount it should be noted, was in no way proportional and, in most states, the bulk of the block grant (and rather limited) resources went to, and continues to go to, adults, although it is also true that some states do spend a much more significant proportion of their block grant funds on children (Cooper, 2008).

In 1992, Congress enacted the Comprehensive Community Mental Health Services for Children and Families Act. But the title is, in fact, misleading, since the legislation, as noted above, allowed resources to be used only for children and youth who met the restrictive eligibility criteria for serious emotional and behavioral disorders. Public policy is a blunt tool. In an effort to correct the inattention to a highly vulnerable and often desperate group of children and families, Congress enacted legislation that has precluded the development of a more balanced, public health oriented approach to children's mental health. It has failed to also encompass children in danger of experiencing serious emotional and behavioral disorders by virtue of combinations of familial, community or other risk factors (Knitzer, 1996). There is also another important aspect of the federal legislative framework for children and youth with respect to mental health issues. Under the public health insurance program known as Medicaid, every eligible low-income child is required to have periodic screening for health and developmental delays. In theory, this provision, known as Early Periodic Screening, Diagnosis and Treatment (EPSDT) is a potentially powerful lever to recognize and intervene with behavioral and emotional problems early. Unfortunately, despite decades of lawsuits, this aspect of health policy for children has been very poorly implemented, resulting in limited state capacity for early screening and intervention.

The legislative framework reflects one layer of the policy framework. But it is also important to "follow the money" – that is to examine administratively determined fiscal policies and practices that shape the real policy infrastructure for children's mental health. During the 1980s, states bore the primary responsibility for designing and paying for children's mental health services. Today, the lion's share of funding is paid for through health insurance, either through private managed care entities or through Medicaid and SCHIP (State Children's Health Insurance Program), America's health insurance programs for low-income children. In 41 states, for example, public health insurance covers children and youth at or above 200% of the poverty level. Thirty-nine percent of children in U.S. families are in families with incomes at 200% of the poverty level or less (Chau, 2009; Chau & Douglas-Hall, 2007).

Overall, data indicate that America spends a total of around $14 billion on children's mental health services out of a national behavioral health expenditure report of an estimated $104 billion (Cooper, 2008; Mark, Coffey, Vandivort-Warren, Harwood, & King, 2005). And yet, despite this investment, a large proportion of the children and youth who need services and support do not get any services, and others do not get the kind of services most likely to be effective. Prevention and early intervention services are not widespread. Most troubling is the continuing level of investment in residential treatment with no evidence of positive outcomes. In 2002 alone, states and the federal government spent about $4.2 billion on residential treatment for children and youth (Atay & Survey and Analysis Branch, 2005). Further, the financing streams are fraught with restrictions that often put fiscal policies out of sync with research-informed policies and practices designed to improve services for youth, and/or they do not provide the incentives, flexibility or the mechanisms to support quality improvement and "giving knowledge away" to clinicians, program administrators and families.

Beyond this "big picture" perspective there are also some very important challenges that are specific to Medicaid, which is the single most important funding stream for children's mental health (Cooper, 2008; Howell, 2004). Right now, Medicaid is narrowly constructed using a medical model that does not fully support the use of evidence-based practice, does not recognize or endorse the psychosocial nature of mental health problems, and does not take into account both the shorter and longer term potential pay-off for more strategic investment in targeted prevention and early intervention (Felitti et al., 1998). Some examples of the ways in which Medicaid fiscal practices undermine the use of emerging knowledge to guide the allocation of public policy resources are:

- *Medicaid policy makes it difficult to implement evidence-based practices.* The essence of evidence-based treatment is a holistic approach to carrying out all aspects of a particular treatment approach. These often combine clinical and nonclinical components that are delivered by nonmedical providers, and that target parents and teachers. But rather than reimburse for all the components of an evidence-based practice, Medicaid fragments the process, often into billable 15-minute segments.
- *Medicaid policy in general is not responsive to developmentally appropriate practice, particularly for young children and for children aging out of either the mental health system, the child welfare system or the juvenile justice system.* There are three core problems with respect to young children. First, Medicaid only reimburses for children with diagnoses, thus excluding young children showing risk factors that are predictive of problems. Concretely, this means that no state can pay for mental health consultation through Medicaid to early childhood programs unless it involves a child with a diagnosis, rather than a child showing signs of problems. Second, in many states, Medicaid does not require the use of standardized screening and assessment tools for young children (Rosenthal & Kaye, 2005). Third, in many states, it does not allow reimbursement for nonphysician providers, even if they have specialty knowledge about early childhood and the

physicians do not (Rosenthal & Kaye, 2005). Youth transitioning to adulthood with mental health problems also face significant challenges accessing services. Many do not have the level of severity to meet the criteria for adult mental services, and when they do these services are often not appropriate to meet the needs of young adults. For former foster care youth transitioning to adulthood, despite federal efforts to increase access to services through health insurance after their 18th birthday only 17 states currently take advantage of this option through Medicaid (Jaudes et al., 2012; Patel & Roherty, 2007).

• *Medicaid policy is not supportive of interventions that target parents, because of the requirement that the child be the "indicated" client.* Increasingly, research suggests that the best way to help children is to teach parents new ways of responding to their child's problematic behaviors. Parent training strategies have been effective across the developmental age span. But Medicaid typically requires that all interventions be focused on the child, who is the "indicated" client. This is counterproductive. In some states, the focus on the indicated client even precludes the use of family therapy for infants and toddlers. It also promotes a mismatch between services and need. For example, a recent study of school-based mental health practices found that the major need was for family-focused short-term interventions, but funding could be used only for child-focused interventions (Foster et al., 2005).

• *Medicaid policies make it hard to deliver consultation and treatment in interventions in nonmedical, nonspecialty settings like early childhood programs and schools.* In some states, community mental health based providers can be reimbursed for services if delivered in office-based practices or health centers, but not if they are delivered in schools (Cooper, 2008). Paying for preventive school-based mental health interventions, such as Positive Behavioral Supports, which focuses on creating a climate to facilitate learning and reduce violence, and also allows for enhanced interventions for high-risk youth, is also problematic. Similarly, consultation to primary care settings, particularly early childhood and health settings, is also difficult to fund (Johnson & Knitzer, 2005).

• *Medicaid policy ignores the intergenerational nature of mental illness.* Only a handful of state Medicaid programs permit Medicaid reimbursement for pediatric providers who screen for maternal depression, and in most states if treatment is needed, unless parents qualify for Medicaid themselves, they cannot get it (Rosenthal & Kaye, 2005). Most parents do not, even very poor parents (Stebbins & Knitzer, 2007). Basically, under current policy, we have a children's mental health system that cannot provide treatment to adults and an adult mental health system that rarely considers whether adults are parents, and what kinds of parenting issues they face because of their illness (Nicholson, Biebel, Katz-Levy, & Williams, 2004). There is almost no capacity to deliver family-focused mental health services.

Preliminary data from "Unclaimed Children Revisited" make it clear that many states are struggling to surmount these barriers, particularly with respect to paying for evidence-based treatment. While 46 states reported that they have instituted specific strategies to support the appropriate use of evidence-based practices, less than half provided funds for implementation or supported an infrastructure for dissemination with state-wide capacity. Moreover, only ten states provided fiscal incentives to support uptake of evidence-based practices. A number of states have also found ways to pay for some of the nonclinical components of effective treatment highlighted above. But all of this is being done in a piecemeal way, with success limited in both scale and scope, without any outside review of how current fiscal practices undermine or facilitate the delivery of the most appropriate mental health services. Instead, the assumption that mental health treatment means treating *only* the child gets in the way of crafting research-informed policies that recognize that often the best way to help children is to help those who are closest to them, both through treatment and early intervention and prevention strategies. This means that how to get Medicaid and other mental health funding in sync with the knowledge base is, therefore, the most central knowledge transfer-to-policy challenge that the United States faces with respect to children's mental health policy.

Toward the Future

This, then, is the picture in the United States with respect to children's mental health. Readers from other nations may see similarities and differences in relation to their own systems. Put most succinctly, the growing knowledge base is not well-integrated into the ongoing policy framework, particularly with respect to fiscal policies. We suspect this will be the case in many other countries, too (see Bradshaw, Keung, Rees, & Goswami, 2011, for a discussion of global trends). This section explores some challenges to bridging the knowledge-to-policy divide and concludes with some recommendations to move the agenda forward.

Understanding the barriers

In our collective experience, there seem to be three sets of challenges that make it difficult to create policy mechanisms that are flexible enough, accountable enough and responsive enough to integrate emerging knowledge about how to improve outcomes for children with mental health problems: the broad resistance in the United States to family-focused, proactive, preventive policies; the entrenched nature of a medical model paradigm that does not comfortably fit with emerging knowledge; and the lack of knowledge about how to craft mechanisms to retrain a work force in more effective clinical practices. Each of these is considered briefly.

The family versus the state responsibility challenge

The United States' default position in crafting public policies for children is to invest significant dollars in trying to remedy problems, often for youth in "deep end systems", that is, mental health, juvenile justice and child welfare, largely because of the belief that raising children is a private, family responsibility. There are certainly, and increasingly, exceptions to this rule, but overall it remains very difficult to build a proactive set of policies to support healthy development for children and youth. For example, most other developed countries have understood the importance of a coherent set of public policies to support access to quality child care and early learning, a range of youth development strategies and to provide universal health insurance. The United States is still undecided, making piecemeal, half-hearted attempts to provide universal supports.

Beneath this reality is a fundamental tension about whether the state has any responsibility for children's well-being, except for children who are unsafe or otherwise threatened. The roots of this are deep. Policy is rarely seen as a way to partner with families to promote the well-being of the next generation to benefit both families and society. Rather, most typically, it is seen as a tool to intrude on families (Grubb & Lazerson, 1982). Even publicly supported child care is suspect, and the notion of universal screening brings out widespread opposition and backlash (Lenzer, 2004). No wonder that for children's mental health, and particularly for low-income children, the prevailing policy framework represents a patch work of funding streams that largely support the most traditional mental health approaches.

The children's mental health paradigm challenge

The second major challenge to translating children's mental health knowledge into policy is the need to replace the medical model with one that represents a better fit with the research – a more ecologically focused paradigm (Tolan & Dodge, 2005). Right now, there are, in effect, two conflicting paradigms, or world views about how to understand and think about children's mental health. One, the most traditional and deeply embedded one that, as was just described, largely governs fiscal practice is known as the "medical model". To simplify, in this model, the child is "ill" and needs to be "fixed" by giving him or her the correct dosage to solve the problem. Thus, to access services, there must be a medical diagnosis based on a psychiatric classification system, with the child as the "indicated client". The medical model reflects a child-centric view; engaging parents or teachers is described as a "collateral activity" and, as noted above, is very difficult to pay for. It also focuses exclusively on the most troubled children. The medical model has been translated from the physical healthcare model, but in the physical healthcare system there is growing attention to wellness and prevention (Berwick, 2002).

In contrast to this medical model is the ecologically-grounded paradigm highlighted above. In this view, neither treatment nor prevention focuses exclusively on the child or youth, but rather, uses the ecology of the child/youth's world to support a child/youth and family's strengths and help them better cope. In an effort to integrate this broader understanding of how children develop into mentally healthy adults, there are increasing calls for shifting the fundamental paradigm that now governs children's mental health policies to a more balanced one that integrates research-informed promotion, prevention, early intervention and treatment. This, in fact, was called for in a recent Presidential Commission on Mental Health, although it was not supported by any real implementation proposals or resources (New Freedom Commission on Mental Health, 2003). Replacing the current medical model paradigm with a public health approach will require reaching a tipping point, where this new paradigm has enough credibility and support among mental health policymakers, advocates, clinicians and others to reshape current policies, particularly at the federal level. It will also have to deal with the realistic concerns of families of the most troubled children that they will lose out. However, this more balanced approach, with a more accountable system also holds out the promise of better outcomes for these children as well.

Stepping up to the challenge to promote effective practice

Policy support for efforts to reach the right children and youth with the right interventions requires a focus on some on-the-ground realities. First, it means building workforce capacity. Significant and projected shortages in workforce capacity cut across every system working with children with mental health needs and contribute to the difficulty of adopting empirically supported practices. In addition, many new providers enter the workforce with no training in evidence-based practices. Second, it means increasing community capacity to embed evidence-based interventions in the ongoing daily work of the systems that have responsibility for children across the age span. There is a need to develop tools and strategies to reallocate or find new monies to pay for continuing education and quality assurance processes. This is further complicated by the proprietary nature of many evidence-based practices that require states and communities to pay licensing fees and, in some cases, consultation costs. For some systems, some evidence-based practices are simply financially out of reach for public agencies and their community-based partners (Roberto Avina, Chief Executive Officer, La Familia Guidance Center, St. Paul, MN, Personal Communication, October 8, 2007). Replicating efficacious and effective interventions also requires that communities measure outcomes. But agreeing upon outcomes, processes for measuring these and accountability mechanisms for achieving them takes more than funding, it also takes leadership and political will.

Some states and communities are rising to the challenges and investing in mechanisms to disseminate evidence-based practices. Examples of these initiatives include the California Institute for Mental Health's Values-Driven Evidence-based Practices initiative, the Evidence-Based Dissemination Center of New York State, and Ohio's Department of Mental Health's Center for Innovative Practice (California Institute for Mental Health, 2005; Hoagwood, 2007; Hoagwood et al., 2014; Ohio Department of Mental Health, 2007). In addition, some communities are redirecting resources previously devoted to out-of-home placements to implementation of evidence-based practices. For example, in Ramsey and Dakota counties in Minnesota, the results of previously primarily grant-funded initiatives of functional family therapy, an evidence-based intervention, with juvenile justice involved families and youth provided the proof local officials needed to divert dollars to support the initiatives (Chris Bray, Minnesota Department of Corrections, Personal communication, October 8, 2007). Michigan's nearly decade long focus on both on creating local acceptance of evidence-based practice and on measuring outcomes through its Level of Functioning Project, is paying off. Now in 62 of the state's 83 counties, the initiative requires the systematic use of validated assessment tools and collection, analysis and use of data for continuous quality improvement (Jim Wotring, Michigan Department of Community Mental Health, Personal communication, October 18, 2007). Finally, nine states reported in the "Unclaimed Children Revisited Survey" that they had some form of legislative mandate to implement evidence-based practices.

Toward a Responsive Policy Framework

While these examples of innovative state policy mark important developments, they still reach only a relatively small proportion of children and youth in need, and do not fully address the core fiscal and paradigm challenges highlighted above, particularly with respect to broadening the paradigm to include attention to prevention and early intervention. As this analysis makes clear, it is relatively easy to "give knowledge away". Over the years, a number of strategies have emerged to target easily digestible information about emerging knowledge to policymakers and program administrators, and in the U.S. policy briefs that link knowledge with policy implications on virtually every aspect of psychological knowledge exist. The real challenge is getting the principles and the findings from that knowledge embedded into the infrastructure, policy frameworks and the resource allocation matrices to actually align decisions by policymakers, practices by clinicians, and, most importantly, the appropriation of public resources.

So given this, what does it take to build a responsive policy framework that can facilitate and enable improved practice? Experiences to date suggest that it will take:

• Mechanisms to engage the "end users" in owning the new intervention or in understanding the underlying theory. Essentially, this requires making the connections between their own world view and the theory to provide support and mentoring in the use of new practices, and to provide incentives in policy, fiscal or otherwise. On the surface this may appear fairly straight-forward – target the end users, including communities, service providers, system administrators and policymakers, and, especially, families and youth. Engaging families and youth is particularly important because right now there is little evidence that families and youth understand the available empirically-based treatment choices (United Advocates for Children of California, 2006). Indeed, there is research to suggest much skepticism on the part of family members about the net benefit to them of evidence-based treatments. Similarly among communities, especially those of color that urge caution in the application of some evidence-based interventions not tested among children and youth of color. To target service providers, an intentional strategy to disseminate the knowledge demands engagement not only with higher educational institutions but also with professional organizations and directly with providers.

• Ongoing support to refine the knowledge base and expand what we know from research not only about what knowledge should be given away, but *how* best to give it away. We need, in other words to deepen the implementation science research to include studies of policy frameworks that support the use of evidence-based practices. Several lessons from the research on implementation suggest that child mental health must attend to considerations that range from infrastructure to politics and economics and to research itself. Consider infrastructural requirements, how does the workforce change to accommodate an evidence-based culture or what variation in practice context is acceptable? For example, how is service design altered in rural areas, underserved areas, communities of color or special practice settings and what level of tension between fidelity to the model and adaptations to fit specific populations is tolerable? Politically, how do leaders manage inevitable fallout associated with promotion of an evidence-based culture? If an evidence-based culture threatens the survival of local clinical practices there are also implications for the economic base of communities. From an economic perspective, how do policymakers and administrators line up financing to make implementation of practice more effective? How do communities recognize and redirect funding to support organizations as they attempt to transform practice?

- Accountability measures that include tracking the outcomes to make sure that the promised findings are, in fact, realized. For example, all kinds of practical considerations can get in the way. These may include: implementation with a lack of fidelity to the intervention, lack of support for front-line workers by supervisors and administrators, or failure to get consensus on measures and measurement tools. Consider that many children and youth engage many systems; they are all at different levels in their ability to track their own outcomes let alone across systems. They also all have their own mechanisms and tools for tracking outcomes. Many of these systems lack transparency and developing the ability for interoperability among systems serving children may prove extremely challenging.

- Resources dedicated to making the knowledge transfer happen. Scarce resources demand that policymakers, administrators and communities choose strategies carefully. This is the "be careful what you wish for" lesson, one of which is taking efforts to scale prematurely. Indeed, there are examples of efforts to promote what were promising but insufficiently documented practices by pushing take up, only to find that more research yielded different results (Jensen et al., 2007). For example, recent data on effective treatments for ADHD portend changes for generally accepted guideline level care with implications for healthcare financing in general and more specifically refining health insurance benefits (Jensen et al., 2007).

- Research to refine the knowledge base, as well as to design and test mechanisms to promote quality improvement and increased workforce capacity. Current research has defined a level of practice effectiveness. How do communities establish implementation success? What is good enough? What criteria should be agreed upon? What should it reflect? How salient is this set of criteria for the end users? The push-back on emerging knowledge suggests the need to continue to develop the knowledge-base to reflect the diversity of population and practice settings in mental health.

Conclusion

This is an exciting time to be involved in children's mental health. There are many new possibilities for bringing hope and help to children and their families who experience, or who are at risk of experiencing, poor outcomes related to mental health issues. But to take these new possibilities to full scale we need a new approach to creating a policy framework that tracks knowledge as well as dollars. The children and families, and the taxpayers, deserve no less.

References

Aratani, Y., & Cooper, J. L. (2012a). Racial and ethnic disparities in the continuation of community-based children's mental health services. *Journal of Behavioral Health Services and Research, 39*, 116–129.

Aratani, Y., & Cooper, J. L. (2012b). The effects of runaway-homeless episodes on high school dropout. *Youth & Society.* doi: 10.1177/0044118X12456406.

Atay, J., & Survey and Analysis Branch (2005). 2002 State Tables. Table 15. Expenditures (in Thousands of Dollars) By Owner According to Organization Type: 2002 IMHO. Rockville, MD: Center for Mental Health Services, Substance Abuse and Mental Health Services Administration.

Berwick, D. M. (2002). A User's manual for the IOM's 'Quality Chasm' report. *Health Affairs, 21*(3), 80–90.

Bickman, L., Noser, K., & Summerfelt, W. T. (1999). Long-term effects of a system of care on children and adolescents. *Journal of Behavioral Health Services Research, 26*(2), 185–202.

"Blueprints for Violence Prevention". Boulder, CO: Center for the Study and Prevention of Violence (CSPV), Institute of Behavioral Science (IBS). Retrieved on October 28, 2007 from http://www.colorado.edu/cspv/blueprints/

Bradshaw, J., Keung, A., Rees, G., & Goswami, H. (2011). Children's subjective well-being: International comparative perspectives. *Children and Youth Services Review, 33*, 548–556.

Bronfenbrenner, U. (1979). *The ecology of human development: experiments by nature and design.* Cambridge, MA: Harvard University Press.

Busch, S., & Barry, C. (2007). Mental health disorders in childhood: Assessing the burden on families. *Health Affairs, 26*(4), 1088–1095.

Cablas, A. (1998). Culturally competent methods based on evaluation and research. How to use research results in systems of care. In M. Hernandez & M. R. Isaacs (Eds.), *Promoting cultural competence in children's mental health services.* Baltimore, MD: Paul H. Brookes Publishing Co.

California Institute for Mental Health (2005). A Snapshot of values-driven evidence-based practices (VEP) implementation in California. *CIMH Bulletin*(1).

Chau, M. M. (2009). *Low-income children in the United States: National and state trend data, 1998–2008,* Columbia University Academic Commons, http://hdl.handle.net/10022/AC:P:8871.

Chau, M., & Douglas-Hall, A. (2007). *Low-income children in the United States: National and state trend data 1996–2006.* New York, NY: National Center for Children in Poverty, Mailman School of Public Health, Columbia University. Retrieved on October 30, 2007 from http://www.nccp.org/publications/pdf/text_761.pdf

Cole, S. F., Eisner, A., Gregory, M., & Ristuccia, J. (2013). *Helping traumatized children learn 2: Creating and advocating for trauma sensitive schools.* Massachusetts Advocates for Children. Retrieved on August 14, 2015 from http://traumasensitiveschools.org/tlpi-publications/

Cook, J. R., & Kilmer, R. P. (2004). Evaluating systems of care: Missing links in children's mental health research. *Journal of Community Psychology, 32*(6), 655–674.

Cooper, J. L. (2008). *Towards better behavioral health for children, youth and their families: Financing that supports knowledge.* New York, NY: National Center for Children in Poverty, Mailman School of Public Health, Columbia University.

Cooper, J. L., Aratani, Y., Knitzer, J., Douglas-Hall, A., Masi, R., Banghart, P., et al. (2008). *Unclaimed Children Revisited: The status of children's mental health policy in the United States.* New York, NY: National Center for Children in Poverty, Mailman School of Public Health, Columbia University.

Cooper, J., Masi, R., Dababnah, S., Aratani, Y., & Knitzer, J. (2007). *Strengthening policies to support children, youth and families who experience trauma.* New York, NY: National Center for Children in Poverty, Mailman School of Public Health, Columbia University.

Costello, E. J., Compton, S. N., Keeler, G., & Angold, A. (2003). Relationships between poverty and psychopathology a natural experiment. *JAMA, 290*(15), 2023–2029.

Cross, T. L., Bazron, B. J., Dennis, K. W., & Isaacs, M. R. (1989). *Towards a culturally competent system of care: A monograph on effective services for minority children who are severely emotionally disturbed: Vol. I.* Washington, DC: Georgetown University Child Development Center.

"Culturally Modified Trauma-Focused Therapy". National Child Traumatic Stress Network. Retrieved on October 28, 2007 from http://www.nctsnet.org/nctsn_assets/pdfs/promising_practices/CM-TFT_fact_sheet_3-21-07.pdf

Dababnah, S., & Cooper, J. (2006). *Challenges and opportunities in children's mental health: A view from families and youth.* New York, NY: National Center for Children in Poverty, Mailman School of Public Health, Columbia University.

Davis, M., Geller, J. L., & Hunt, B. (2006). Within-State availability of transition-to-adulthood services for youths with serious mental health conditions. *Psychiatric Services 57*(11), 1594–1599.

Dennis, K., & Lourie, I. (2006). *Everything is normal until proven otherwise: A book about wraparound services.* Washington, DC: Child Welfare League of America Inc. Press.

Felitti, V., Anda, R., Nordenberg, D., Williamson, D. F., Spitz, A., Edwards, V., et al. (1998). Relationship of childhood abuse and household dysfunction to many of the leading causes of death in adults the adverse childhood experiences (ACE) study. *American Journal of Preventive Medicine, 14*(4), 245–258.

Fixsen, D. L., Naoom, S. F., Blase, K., Friedman, R. M., & Wallace, F. (2005). *Implementation research: A synthesis of the literature.* Tampa, FL: University of South Florida, Louis de la Parte Florida Mental Health Institute, The National Implementation Research Network.

Foster, S., Rollefson, M., Doksum, T., Noonan, D., Robinson, G., & Teich, J. (2005). *School mental health services in the United States 2002–2003.* DHHS Publication No. SMA 05-4068. Rockville, MD: Center for Mental Health Services, Substance Abuse and Mental Health Services Administration.

Gilliam, W. S. (2005). Prekindergarteners left behind: Expulsion rates in state prekindergarten systems. New York, NY: Foundation for Child Development. Retrieved on July 24, 2015 from http://fcd-us.org/resources/prekindergartners-left-behind-expulsion-rates-state-prekindergarten-programs

Goldman, L. S., Genel, M., Bezman, R. J., Slanetz, P. J., & Council on Scientific Affairs American Medical Association (1998). Diagnosis and treatment of attention-deficit/hyperactivity disorder. *JAMA, 279*(14), 1100–1107.

Goodman, S. H., Rouse, M. H., Connell, A. M., Broth, M. R., Hall, C. M., & Heyward, D. (2011). Maternal depression and child psychopathology: A meta-analytic review. *Clinical child and Family Psychology Review, 14*, 1–27.

Gorman-Smith, D., Henry, D. B., & Tolan, P. H. (2004). Exposure to community violence and violence perpetration: The protective effects of family functioning. *Journal of Clinical Child and Adolescent Psychology, 33*(3), 439–449.

Grubb, W. N., & Lazerson, M. (1982). *Broken promises: How Americans fail their children.* New York, NY: Basic Books.

Gruttadaro, D., Burns, B., Duckworth, K., & Crudo, D. (2007). *Choosing the right treatment: What families need to know about evidence-based treatment.* Alexandria, VA: NAMI.

Hammen, C. (2003). Risk and protective factors for children of depressed parents. In S. S. Luthar (Ed.), *Resilience and vulnerability: Adaptation in the context of childhood adversities.* New York, NY: Cambridge University Press.

Hammen, C., Hazel, N. A., Brennan, P. A., & Najman, J. (2012). Intergenerational transmission and continuity of stress and depression: depressed women and their offspring in 20 years of follow-up. *Psychological Medicine, 42*, 931–942.

Hemmelgarn, A. L., Glisson, C., & James, C. R. (2006). Organizational culture and climate: Implications for services and intervention research. *Clinical Psychology: Science and Practice, 13*(1), 73–89.

Hoagwood, K. (2007). Evidence-based Treatment Dissemination Center (EBTDC): A training and consultation initiative for children in New York State's Office of Mental Health. New York, NY: Columbia University.

Hoagwood, K., Burns, B. J., Kiser, L., Ringelsen, H., & Schoenwald, S. K. (2001). Evidence-based practice in child and adolescent mental health services. *Psychiatric Services, 52*(9), 1179–1189.

Hoagwood, K. E., Olin, S. S., Horwitz, S., McKay, M., Cleek, A., Gleacher, A., … & Hogan, M. (2014). Scaling up evidence-based practices for children and families in New York State: Toward evidence-based policies on implementation for state mental health systems. *Journal of Clinical Child & Adolescent Psychology, 43*, 145–157.

Holden, W., & Santiago, R. (2003). Findings on the implementation of systems of care at nine CMHS grant communities. *System-of-Care Evaluation Brief, 5*(2), 1–4.

Horowitz, S. M., Kelleher, K. J., Stein, R. K., Storfer-Isser, A., Youngstrum, E. A., Park, E. R., et al. (2007). Barriers to the identification and management of psychosocial problems in children and maternal depression. *Pediatrics, 119*, e208–e219.

Howell, E. (2004). *Access to children's mental health services under Medicaid and SCHIP.* Washington, DC: Urban Institute.

Huff, B. (1998). Federation celebrates 10-year anniversary. *Claiming Children* (pp. 1–3). Alexandria, VA: Federation of Families for Children's Mental Health.

Hurlburt, M. S., Leslie, L. K., Landsverk, J., Barth, R., Burns, B., Gibbons, R. D., et al. (2004). Contextual predictors of mental health service use among children open to child welfare. *Archives of General Psychiatry, 61*, 1217–1224.

Indian Country Child Trauma Center (2006). Honoring children, making relatives. Retrieved on August 14, 2015 from http://www.icctc.org/Honoring%20Children%20 Making%20Relatives%2006-21-2011Final%20Submission.pdf

Institute of Medicine of the National Academies (2005). *Improving the quality of health care for mental and substance use conditions.* Washington, DC: National Academy of Sciences.

Jaudes, P. K., Szilagyi, M. A., Fierson, W., Harmon, D. A., High, P., Jones, V. F., ... & Rubin, D. (2012). Health care of youth aging out of foster care. *Pediatrics, 130*(6), 1170–1173.

Jensen, P., Arnold, E., Swanson, J. M., Vitiello, B., Abikoff, H. B., Greenhill, L. L., et al. (2007). 3-Year follow-up of the NIMH MTA study. *Journal of the American Academy of Child and Adolescent Psychiatry, 46*(8), 989–1002.

Johnson, K., & Knitzer, J. (2005). *Spending smarter: A funding guide for policymakers and advocates to promote social and emotional health and school readiness.* New York, NY: National Center for Children in Poverty, Mailman School of Public Health, Columbia University.

Joint Commission on the Mental Health of Children (1970). *Crisis in children's mental health: Challenge for the 1970s.* New York, NY: Harper & Row.

Jones, D., Godwin, J., Dodge, K. A., Bierman, K. L., Coie, J. D., Greenberg, M. T., et al. (2010). Impact of the Fast Track prevention program on health services use by conduct-problem youth. *Pediatrics, 125*(1), e130–e136.

Kataoka, S., Zhang, L., & Wells, K. (2002). Unmet need for mental health care among U.S. children: Variation by ethnicity and insurance status. *American Journal of Psychiatry, 159*(9), 1548–1555.

Kaufmann, R. K., & Hepburn, K. S. (2007). Early childhood mental health services and supports through a systems approach. In D. F. Perry, R. Kaufmann, & J. Knitzer (Eds.), *Social and emotional health in early childhood: Building bridges between services and systems* (pp. 63–96). Baltimore, MD: Brookes.

Kaufmann, R. K., Perry, D. F., Hepburn, K., & Duran, F. (2012). Assessing fidelity for early childhood mental health consultation: Lessons from the field and next steps. *Infant Mental Health Journal, 33*, 274–282.

Kelleher, K. J., McInerny, T. K., Gardner, W. P., Childs, G. E., & Wasserman, R. C. (2000). Increasing identification of psychosocial problems: 1979–1996. *Pediatrics, 105*(6), 1313–1321.

Kessler, R. C., Beglund, P., Demler, O., Jin, R., & Walters, E. E. (2005). Life-time prevalence and the age of onset distribution of DSM-IV disorders in the national co-morbidity survey replication. *Archives of General Psychiatry, 62*, 593–602.

Knitzer, J. (1982). *Unclaimed Children: The failure of public responsibility to children in need of mental health services.* Washington, DC Children's Defense Fund.

Knitzer, J. (1996). Children's mental health: Changing paradigms and policies. In E. F. Zigler, S. L. Kagan, & N. W. Hall (Eds.), *Children, families and government: Preparing for the twenty-first century* (pp. 207–232). New York: Cambridge University Press.

Knitzer, J. (1999). Early childhood mental health services: A policy and systems development perspective. In J. P. Schonkoff & S. J. Meisels (Eds.), *Handbook of early childhood intervention* (pp. 907–956). New York, NY: Cambridge University Press.

Knitzer, J. (2005). Advocacy for children's mental health: A personal journey. *Journal of Clinical Child and Adolescent Psychology, 34*(4), 612–618.

Knitzer, J., & Cooper, J. (2006). Beyond integration: Challenges For children's mental health. *Health Affairs, 25*(3), 670–679.

Knitzer, J., & Perry, D. F. (2011). Poverty and infant and toddler development. *Handbook of Infant Mental Health,* 135–151

Knitzer, J., Steinberg, Z., & Fleish, B. (1990). *At the schoolhouse door: An examination of programs and policies for children with emotional and behavioral problems.* New York, NY: Bank Street College of Education.

Leaf, P., Owens, P., Leventhal, J. M., Forsyth, B. W. C., Vaden-Kiernan, M., Epstein, L. D., et al. (2004). Pediatricians' training and identification and management of psychosocial problems. *Clinical Pediatrics, 43*(4), 355–365.

Lenzer, J. (2004). Bush plans to screen whole US population for mental illness. *BMJ, 328,* 1458.

Lourie, I., & Hernandez, M. (2003). A historical perspective on national child mental health policy. *Journal of Emotional and Behavioral Disorders, 11,* 5–9.

Luthar, S. S. (2006). Resilience in development: A synthesis of research across five decades. In D. Cicchetti & D. J. Cohen (Eds.), *Developmental psychopathology: risk, disorder and adaptation.* Hoboken, NJ: John Wiley & Sons, Inc.

Marder, C., Wagner, M., & Sumi, C. (2003). The social adjustment of youth with disabilities. In M. Wagner, C. Marder, J. Blackorby, R. Cameto, L. Newman, P. Levine, et al. *The achievements of youth with disabilities during secondary school* (pp. 5.1–5.18). Menlo Park, CA: SRI International.

Mark, T. L., Coffey, R. M., Vandivort-Warren, R., Harwood, J., & King, E. C. (2005). U.S. spending for mental health and substance abuse treatment, 1991–2001, *Health Affairs,* W5-133-W135-142. Published Online March 29, 2005. doi 10.1377/hlthaff. W5.133.

Masten, A. S., & Powell, J. L. (2003). A resilience framework for research, policy and practice. In S. S. Luthar (Ed.), *Resilience and vulnerability: Adaptation in the context of childhood adversities.* New York, NY: Cambridge University Press.

Masten, A. S., & Wright, M. O. D. (1998). Cumulative risks and protective models in child maltreatment. In B. R. R. Rossman & M. S. Rosenberg (Eds.), *Multiple victimization of children: Conceptual, developmental, research and treatment issues* (pp. 7–30). Binghamton, NY: Haworth.

McCabe, K., Yeh, M., Garland, A., Lau, A., & Chavez, G. (2005). The GANA program: A tailoring approach to adapting parent child interaction therapy for Mexican Americans. *Education and Treatment of Children, 28*(2), 111–129.

McKay, M. M., Hibbert, R., Hoagwood, K., Rodriguez, J., Murray, L., Legerski, J., et al. (2004). Integrating evidence-based engagement interventions into "real world" child mental health settings. *Brief Treatment and Crisis Intervention, 4*(2), 177–186.

Nakamura, B. J., Higa-McMillan, C. K., Okamura, K. H., & Shimabukuro, S. (2011). Knowledge of and attitudes towards evidence-based practices in community child mental health practitioners. *Administration and Policy in Mental Health and Mental Health Services Research, 38*(4), 287–300.

National Scientific Council on the Developing Child (2005). *Excessive stress disrupts the architecture of the brain.* Working Paper # 3. Retrieved on July 24, 2015 from http://developingchild.harvard.edu/resources/reports_and_working_papers/working_papers/wp3/

New Freedom Commission on Mental Health (2003). Achieving the promise: transforming mental health care in America. Final report. Retrieved on August 14, 2015 from http://govinfo.library.unt.edu/mentalhealthcommission/reports/FinalReport/downloads/downloads.html

Nicholson, J., Biebel, K., Katz-Levy, K., & Williams, V. F. (2004). The prevalence of parenthood in adults with mental illness: Implications for State and Federal policymakers, programs and providers. In R. Manderscheid & M. Henderson (Eds.), *Mental Health, United States, 2002.* Rockville, MD: Substance Abuse and Mental Health Services Administration.

Ohio Department of Mental Health (2007) Center for Innovative Practices: CIP Overview. Retrieved on August 14, 2015 from http://begun.case.edu/cip/practices/integrated treatment

Patel, S., & Roherty, M. A. (2007). *Medicaid access for youth aging out of foster care.* Washington, DC: American Public Human Services Association.

Pianta, R. (2005). Standardized observation and professional development: A focus on individualized implementation and practices. In M. Zaslow & I. Martinez-Beck (Eds.), *Critical issue in early childhood professional development* (pp. 231–254). Baltimore, MD: Brookes Publishing.

Pottick, K. J., Warner, L. A., Isaacs, M., Henderson, M., Milazzo Sayre, B. A., & Manderscheid, R. (2002). *Children and adolescents admitted to specialty mental health care programs in the United States, 1986 and 1997.* DHHS Publication No. SMA 04-3938. Washington, DC: Center for Mental Health Services, Substance Abuse and Mental Health Services Administration.

Rehabilitation Act of 1973, P.L. 93-112, 87 Stat. 394 (1973).

Rosenthal, J., & Kaye, N. (2005). *State approaches to promoting young children's healthy development: A survey of Medicaid, and maternal and child health, and mental health agencies.* Portland, ME: National Academy for State Health Policy.

SAMHSA (2007) National registry of evidence-based programs and practices. Retrieved ON October 28, 2007 from http://www.nrepp.samhsa.gov/

Schaffer, H. R. (1998). *Making decisions about children: Psychological questions and answers.* Oxford: Blackwell Publishing.

Seidman, E., & Pedersen, S. (2003). Holistic contextual perspectives on risk, protection, and competence among low-income urban adolescents. In S. S. Luthar (Ed.), *Resilience and Vulnerability: Adaptation in the context of childhood adversity.* New York, NY: Cambridge University Press.

Shonkoff, J., Phillips, D. A., & Council, N. R. (Eds.) (2000). *From neurons to neighborhoods: The science of early childhood development.* Washington, DC: National Academy Press.

Silberg, J. L., Maes, H., & Eaves, L. J. (2010). Genetic and environmental influences on the transmission of parental depression to children's depression and conduct disturbance: An extended children of twins study. *Journal of Child Psychology and Psychiatry, 51*(6), 734–744.

Spoth, R., Clair, S., & Greenberg, M. (2007). Toward dissemination of evidence-based family interventions: maintenance of community-based partnership recruitment results and associated factors. *Journal of Family Psychology, 21*(2), 137–148.

Stebbins, H., & Knitzer, J. (2007). *United States health and nutrition: State choices to promote quality. Improving the Odds: State Early Childhood Profiles.* New York, NY: National Center for Children in Poverty, Mailman School of Public Health, Columbia University. Retrieved on September 25, 2007 from http://www.nccp.org/profiles/state_profile.php?state=US&id=18

Stephens, R. L., Holden, E. W., & Hernandez, M. (2004). System-of-care practice review scores as predictors of behavioral symptomatology and functional impairment. *Journal of Child and Family Studies, 13*(2), 179–191.

Stirman, S. W., Kimberly, J., Cook, N., Calloway, A., Castro, F., & Charns, M. (2012). The sustainability of new programs and innovations: a review of the empirical literature and recommendations for future research. *Implementation Science, 7*, 1–19.

Stroul, B. A., & Friedman, R. (1986). *A system of care for children and youth with emotional disturbances.* Washington, DC: Technical Assistance Center for Children's Mental Health, Georgetown University Child Development Center.

Stroul, B. A., & Friedman, R. M. (1996). The system of care concept and philosophy. In B. A. Stroul (Ed.), *Children's mental health creating systems of care in a changing society.* Baltimore, MD: Paul H. Brookes Publishing Co.

Tolan, P., & Dodge, K. (2005). Children's mental health as a primary care and concern: A system for comprehensive support and service. *American Psychologist, 60*(6), 601–614.

Turney, K. (2012). Pathways of disadvantage: explaining the relationship between maternal depression and children's problem behaviors. *Social Science Research, 41*, 1546–1564.

United Advocates for Children of California (2006). *The roles of family organizations in the evidence-based practices movement.* Sacramento, CA: United Advocates for Children of California.

USGAO (United States Government Accounting Office) (1987). *Block grants: Federal set-asides for substance abuse and mental health services.* Publication No. GAO/HED-88-17. Washington, DC: United States Government Accounting Office.

USHR (United States House of Representatives) (2004). *Incarceration of youth who are waiting for community mental health services in the United States.* Retrieved on August 14, 2015 from https://www.ncjrs.gov/App/publications/abstract.aspx?ID=206991

Vandenberg, J., & Grealish, M. (1996). Individualized services and supports through the wraparound process: Philosophy and procedures. *Journal of Child and Family Studies, 5*, 7–21.

Wagner, M. (2003). Assessing the achievements of youth with disabilities during secondary school. In M. Wagner, C. Marder, J. Blackorby, R. Cameto, L. Newman, P. Levine, et al. *The achievements of youth with disabilities during secondary school* (pp. 1.1–1.9). Menlo Park: SRI International.

Wagner, M. (2005). Youth with disabilities leaving secondary school. In *Changes over time in the early post school outcomes of youth with disabilities: A report of findings from the National Longitudinal Transition Study (NTLS) and the National Longitudinal Transition Study-2 (NTLS2)* (pp. 2.1–2.6). Menlo Park, CA: SRI International.

Walrath, C. M., Sheehan, A., Holden, E. W., Hernandez, M., & Blau, G. (2006). Evidence-based treatments in the field: A brief report on provider knowledge, implementation, and practice. *The Journal of Behavioral Health Services & Research, 33*(2), 244–253.

Watamura, S. E., Phillips, D. A., Morrissey, T. W., McCartney, K., & Bub, K. (2011). Double jeopardy: Poorer social-emotional outcomes for children in the NICHD SECCYD experiencing home and child-care environments that confer risk. *Child Development, 82*, 48–65.

Weissman, M. M., Pilowsky, D. J., Wickramaratne, P. J., Talati, A., Wisniewski, S. R., Fava, M., et al. (2006). Remissions in maternal depression and child psychopathology: A STAR*D-Child report. *JAMA, 295*(12), 1389–1398.

Weisz, J. R., Sandler, I. N., Durlak, J. A., & Anton, B. S. (2005). Promoting and protecting youth mental health through evidence-based prevention and treatment. *American Psychologist, 60*(6), 628–648.

Whitaker, R. C., Orzol, S. M., & Kahn, R. S. (2006). Maternal mental health, substance use and domestic violence in the year after delivery and subsequent behavior problems in children at age 3 years. *Archives of General Psychiatry, 63*, 551–560.

Yoshikawa, H., Aber, J. L., & Beardslee, W. R. (2012). The effects of poverty on the mental, emotional, and behavioral health of children and youth: implications for prevention. *American Psychologist, 67*, 272–284.

Author Index

Mora-Merchan, J., 298
Moran, G., 183
Moran, S., 295
Moreland, A., 3, 4, 14, 15, 79–96
Morgan, J.R., 61
Morgan, P.S., 176
Morita, Y., 300
Morningstar, E., 172
Morris, A.S., 414
Morrison, F.J., 10
Morris, S., 296
Morrissey, K.E., 59
Morrissey, T.W., 477
Morrongiello, B.A., 313
Mosher, W.D., 171
Moshman, D., 276, 282
Moss, E., 392
Mott, L., 173
Moyer, A.M., 123
Muenchow, S.153
Muirden, J., 296
Mülberger, A., 21
Mullis, I.V.S., 206
Mulvey, K.L., 268, 343
Mundt, M.P., 414
Munn, P., 295
Munro, N., 420
Munthe, E., 292, 293, 299
Murkoff, H, E., 42
Murphy, S., 450
Murray, C.B., 455
Myers, L. (Leann), 174
Myers, L. (Lucy), 417

Nabuzoka, D., 296
Najman, J., 478
Namerow, P.B., 176
Narváez, D., 280
Nation, M., 59, 62, 87, 88
Naylor, P., 296
Neilson, K., 314, 318, 323
Nelson, J.R., 279
Nelson, M.M., 80

Nelson, S.E., 453
Nesdale, D., 345, 346
Nestler, E.J., 373
Neuman, G., 172
Newcombe, N.S., 149
Newton, E.J., 410
Nicholls, J.G., 279
Nicholson, J., 482
Niemi, R.G., 272, 273, 276
Nilsen, W.J., 369–406
Nippold, M.A., 409
Nishina, A., 346
Nitz, K., 174, 175, 184
Noack, P., 346, 348
Noble, K.G., 224
Noble, T., 291, 299
Nolen-Hoeksema, S., 172
Noom, M.J., 416
Norbury, C.F., 409, 429
Nordstrom, A., 88
Norris, D., 156
Norton, H.J., 455
Nti, N., 290
Nu'Man, S.J., 61
Nucci, L.P., 269, 280
Nunes, S., 217
Nunes, T., 226

O'Brien, T.C., 348
O'Hare, E., 172
O'Kearney, R., 410, 413
O'Neill, S., 15
O'Rourke, K.M., 178
Obama, B. (President), 153
Oberlander, S.E., 174
Obradović, J., 372
O'Brien, M., 156
O'Connor, T.G., 392
Oh, W., 173
Okamoto, Y., 228
Olah, L.N., 228
Olds, D., 385
Olds, D.L., 176, 180

Subject Index

socioeconomic status, 45, 46, 88, 124,
    145, 172, 173, 207, 325, 382f., 411
    see also poverty; low income families
sociocognitive theory, 343f.
South Africa, 124, 126, 272, 278
South Carolina, 178
Spain, 124, 126
special needs/special education, 150, 208,
    239, 296, 393, 421, 422, 425, 455,
    469, 470
spelling, 203–219
'spoiled' children, 24, 33
staff, 14, 15, 62, 85f.
    of child care centers/schools, 46, 145f.,
    241, 243, 293, 295f., 303, 324, 359,
    422, 446–448, 455
    of prevention/intervention programs,
    62–65, 85f., 91f., 109f., 180f., 328,
    359, 374, 381–383, 450, 458, 469
    turnover of 64, 89, 146f., 154, 155
stigma, 102, 104, 107, 115, 341–364,
    457, 469, 470, 473 *see also* prejudice
Strange Situation, 387 *see also* attachment
structural equation modeling, 443
subitizing, 234
substance use/abuse, 81, 175, 179, 182,
    382, 384, 396, 412, 444, 445,
    451–454, 456, 478
Supernanny, 39, 100, 103, 106, 116
Sure Start Local Programmes, 393
surrogate parenting, 122–123
swaddling, 26
Sweden, 124, 126, 150, 152, 314
syntax, 408
synthetic, phonics, 18, 203ff.

tantrums, 34, 107
TAPP *see* Teen Alliance for Prepared
    Parenting
taxpayers, 3, 171, 271
teachable moment, the, 230f.
teachers, 7, 14, 16, 45, 49, 83, 86, 134,
    144–148, 153, 154, 156, 157, 204,

207–209, 211, 212, 219, 223–258,
269, 274, 277, 279, 281–285,
292–294, 297, 301–304, 324, 325,
331, 354, 375, 411, 414, 420, 422,
429, 442, 443, 447–449, 451–453,
455–457, 459, 475, 477, 481, 485
    see also schools; staff
    teacher bias, 455f.
teenage pregnancy, 150, 171–190
teenage sexuality, 171–180
Teen Alliance for Prepared Parenting, 180
Tennessee, 158
Texas, 238
time out, 40
Times Educational Supplement, 212
toilet training, 34, 36, 41
tolerance, 270f.
toy preferences, 129
tracking participants, 91–92 *see also*
    attrition; recruiting participants
traditional parenting, 27, 35
transgender, 124
translational research, 16, 17, 54f., 64,
    68ff., 333, 370, 379f., 393f., 419f.,
    440–466 *see also* knowledge
    exchange
    definition of, 54
treatment efficacy, 65, 69
treatment fidelity, 63, 92–93, 256, 386
Triple P Program, 17, 102ff., 474
truancy, 296 *see also* school dropout

Uruguay, 124, 126

validity, 54, 58, 66–68, 89, 93, 256, 379,
    441, 443, 455–458 *see also* fidelity
verbal reasoning, 322
Vermont, 160
Virgina, 125
virtual reality, 322, 324
visual search, 315f.
volunteers, 15, 40, 278, 299f., 327f., 334,
    382f., 453